A Dictionary of Scottish History

A Dictionary of Scottish History

GORDON DONALDSON
ROBERT S. MORPETH

JOHN DONALD PUBLISHERS LTD
EDINBURGH

John Donald Publishers Ltd., Unit 8 Canongate Venture, 5 New Street, Edinburgh EH8 8BH

ISBN 0 85976 018 9

Reprinted 1988
Reprinted 1992
Reprinted 1994
Reprinted 1997
Reprinted 1999

Printed in Great Britain by
J. W. Arrowsmith Ltd., Bristol

PREFACE

Scottish historians are not ill equipped with substantial and reliable works of reference. It is hardly an exaggeration to say that Dunbar's *Scottish Kings* consists of Scottish history arranged chronologically, the *Ordnance Gazetteer* consists of Scottish history (and much else besides) arranged topographically and the *Scots Peerage* consists of Scottish history arranged biographically and dynastically. Those often over-worked epithets, 'invaluable' and 'indispensable' are most fittingly applied to such older books, as well as to more recent works like Dr I.B. Cowan's *Parishes of Medieval Scotland* and his revision of Dr D.E. Easson's *Religious Houses: Scotland*, Professor Duncan's revision of Professor Pryde's list of *The Burghs of Scotland* (though it does not include the many parliamentary and police burghs created in the nineteenth century) and G.F. Black's *The Surnames of Scotland*. Other works deal with the clergy and the holders of various offices. Besides, much information about Scottish history is to be found in the *Dictionary of National Biography*, various Encyclopaedias and the great Dictionaries, especially the *Dictionary of the Older Scottish Tongue* and the *Scottish National Dictionary*. But, while those books are the everyday working tools of the professional historian, and of the amateur who has the time and opportunity to use a good library, many of them are at once too bulky and too costly (if obtainable at all) to be in the homes of many people who want ready access to essential facts.

This volume is an attempt to compress into modest compass the information which we believe to be most frequently sought. We have tried to be comprehensive with events, with institutions (both civil and ecclesiastical) and with titles and offices. But beyond that, selection was necessary. To cover even all the Scottish castles and towers (numbering probably some 2000) and the old parish churches (numbering about 1000) would have taken far too much space and would have made the book look like a gazetteer. So far as biographical notices are concerned, there would be hardly any limits at all. It was also impossible to do justice to all the commercial and industrial undertakings. The reasons for the selection we have made may not always be at once apparent, for no doubt every individual has his own views as to the questions to which enquirers are most likely to want answers.

Italics have been used to indicate names or terms which are more fully explained in another entry and are in effect the equivalent of '(q.v.)'. The sign x between dates indicates 'not earlier than . . . and not later than . . .', e.g. 1153 x 1165 indicates 'not earlier than 1153 and not later than 1165'.

Non-Scottish readers should perhaps be reminded that references to 'King', 'Parliament', 'Privy Council' and so forth are to the Scottish institutions of those names and that sums of money, unless otherwise stated, are in Scots currency.

Gordon Donaldson.
Robert S. Morpeth.

A

Abbey Craig (Stirling). From this height *William Wallace* is assumed to have attacked the English at *Stirling Bridge*; Wallace monument completed 1869. See Rochead, John Thomas.
'Abbey Lairds'. Debtors who took refuge in the sanctuary at *Holyrood.*
Abbey St Bathans Nunnery (*Cistercian*) (Berwickshire). Founded probably in 13th century; erected into *temporal lordship* for David Lindsay 1622; portion incorporated in present parish church.
Abbot of Unreason (or **Abbot of Narent**). Presiding figure at Mayday festivities in *Edinburgh* and some other towns before *Reformation.*
Abbotsford (Roxburghshire). Property formerly called Cartley Hole, acquired in 1811 by *Sir Walter Scott,* who built a house there.
Abbotsford Club. Founded in *Edinburgh* 1833, issued over 30 volumes of historical source material and 'reached its termination' 1866.
Abell, Adam. See Bell.
Aberbrothock. Old name of *Arbroath.*
Abercorn (West Lothian). Site of monastery where *Trumwin* was bishop 681; present church, restored 1838, incorporates some 12th century work. Lands belonged to Avenel family before passing by marriage to a Graham in mid-13th century, then went to Reginald Mure by marriage in early 14th and by c. 1400 to *Douglases.* Of the castle, captured by the crown in 1455 (on fall of Douglases), only a green mound marks site. *Burgh of barony* (sometimes called Newton of A.) created for Lord Abercorn 1603.
Abercorn, Lordship, Earldom, Marquisate and Dukedom. Lordship created 1587 for *Lord Claud Hamilton;* earldom created for James, his eldest son, 1606; marquisate 1790; dukedom 1868.
Abercrombie, Lordship. Created for Sir James Sandilands 1647; extinct with death of his son 1681.
Abercromby, Sir Ralph (1734-1801). Born *Menstrie;* served in Seven Years' War; M.P. for Clackmannanshire 1774-5; commanded in West Indies, Ireland, Scotland and Mediterranean 1795-1801; died of wounds at Alexandria.
Aberdeen. *Royal burgh* under *David I;* castle existed in 12th and 13th centuries but evidently was not restored after *War of Independence.*
Aberdeen and Banff Railway. Authorised 1855 to join Aberdeen to *Turriff, Banff* and *Macduff;* merged in *Great North of Scotland Railway.*
Aberdeen Banking Company. (1) In business 1749-53; first Scottish bank based outside *Edinburgh* and first private company in Scotland to issue notes. (2) Established 1767; merged with *Union Bank* 1849.
Aberdeen, Bishopric. Probably bishops at *Mortlach* before 'Nechtan, Bishop of Aberdeen', appeared 1131-2; his successor, Edward, the first Norman bishop, was in office by 1150.
Aberdeen Breviary. Compiled by *William Elphinstone* and printed 1510 by *Walter Chepman* and *Andrew Millar,* it contained legends of Scottish saints and was ordained by *James IV* to supersede the Sarum Breviary. Reprinted 1854.
Aberdeen Cathedral (dedicated to St. Mary and *St. Machar*). Built of granite, mainly in 15th century; lead of roof removed 1568; much damaged by *Covenanters* 1640; central tower fell 1688; nave still in use, with heraldic ceiling of early 16th century.
Aberdeen, Christ College. A divinity hall of the *Free Church*; erected 1850; merged in *University* after union of 1929. See Church of Scotland.
Aberdeen, Church of St Nicholas. Referred to as *collegiate* before 1500, but collegiate constitution not completed until 1540.
Aberdeen Doctors. Group of divines eminent for scholarship who opposed *National Covenant* 1638: *John Forbes,* Robert Baron and William Leslie, professors in the *University,* and James Sibbald, Alexander Scroggie and Alexander Ross, *ministers* in the city.
Aberdeen, Earldom. Created 1682 for Sir George Gordon of Haddo (1637-1720), *Chancellor* 1682-4. George Hamilton Gordon, 4th Earl (1784-1860) was Prime Minister 1852-5; John Campbell Gordon, 7th Earl (1847-1934), successively Lord Lieutenant of Ireland and Governor General of Canada, was created Marquis of Aberdeen and Temair 1915.
Aberdeen Ecclesiological Society. Founded 1888 for study of 'the principles of Christian worship and of church architecture with its allied arts'. Merged in *Scottish Ecclesiological Society* 1903.
Aberdeen Friary (*Carmelite*). Founded c. 1273; lands granted to *burgh* 1583.
Aberdeen Friary (*Dominican*). Founded 1230x1249; possessions granted 1587 to

George, Earl Marischal, who gave them to *Marischal College.*

Aberdeen Friary (Observant *Franciscan*). Founded 1469; property resigned by friars to town 1559 and confirmed to town 1567, for conversion into hospital; but some buildings went to *George, Earl Marischal,* who bestowed them on *Marischal College.*

Aberdeen Friary (*Trinitarian*). Founded by 1274; property conveyed to Gilbert Menzies of Cowlie 1561.

Aberdeen Grammar School. Foundation attributed to 1156 and a 'ruler of the schools of Aberdeen' mentioned 1262, but first clear record of *Grammar School* 1418 and complete list of rectors from 1479.

Aberdeen Hospitals. (1) St Anne's, for poor ladies, existed by 1519. (2) St Mary's almshouse, founded near cathedral by *Bishop Gavin Dunbar* 1532, existed until 18th century. (3) St. Peter's, founded by Bishop Matthew (1172-9), in operation 1541. (4) St Thomas the Martyr's, founded by John Clat 1459, still in use after 1660. (5) Leper hospital, existed 1333 and continued until late 16th century.

Aberdeen, King's College and Marischal College. See Aberdeen, Universities.

Aberdeen, Old. See Old Aberdeen.

'Aberdeen Press and Journal'. 'Aberdeen Journal', founded 1747, was the earliest newspaper north of Forth; amalgamated with 'Aberdeen Free Press' 1922 and became 'Aberdeen Press and Journal'; title now 'Press and Journal' (since 1939).

Aberdeen, Provost Ross's House. Built c. 1594 for Alexander Farquhar; property of John Ross 1702; acquired by *National Trust* and restored 1954.

Aberdeen, Provost Skene's House. Property dates from 16th century; much altered in 17th; belonged to Sir George Skene (1619-1707), *provost* 1676-85; acquired by city 1926 and restored as museum.

Aberdeen Railway. Opened 1850, from Aberdeen to junction at Friockheim; merged in *Caledonian Railway.*

Aberdeen, Robert Gordon's College. See Robert Gordon's College.

Aberdeen Town and County Banking Company. Established 1825; merged with *North of Scotland Bank* 1908.

Aberdeen, Universities. King's College, founded 1495 by papal bull on petition of *James IV,* elaborated by *William Elphinstone* 1505; Marischal College founded 1593 by *George, Earl Marischal*; the two united as University of Aberdeen 1860.

Aberdeen-Angus Cattle. First shown 1829. Breed's Society dates from 1879.

Aberdeenshire Canal. From Aberdeen Harbour to Port Elphinstone near *Inverurie* (18 miles), completed 1807.

Aberdeenshire Highland Regiment (81st). Raised by William Gordon, brother of *Earl of Aberdeen,* 1778; disbanded in *Edinburgh* 1783.

Aberdour (Aberdeenshire). That there was a Celtic monastery is not substantiated.

Aberdour (Fife). Lands and *barony* held from mid-14th century by *Douglases,* later promoted to *Earldom of Morton;* the castle, of which there are substantial remains, is partly 14th century, but was extended in 16th and 17th and accidentally burned in early 18th. The parish church of St. *Fillan,* after standing roofless since 1796, was restored in 1926 and is substantially 12th century. Aberdour was a *burgh of barony* under Abbot of *Inchcolm* 1501 and a *burgh of regality* for Earl of Morton 1638.

Aberdour Nunnery (Fife). Founded 1486 by 1st *Earl of Morton* and absorbed endowments of Hospital of St Martha which he had founded in 1474; property leased to 4th Earl of Morton 1560.

Aberfeldy (Perthshire). *Police burgh* 1887. *Wade* Bridge dates from 1733 and a monument commemorates the raising of the *Black Watch.*

Abergeldie Castle (Aberdeenshire). Lands acquired by son of 1st *Earl of Huntly* 1482 and original castle probably built by his son; acquired by Prince Consort 1848 and castle much enlarged.

Aberlour (or Charleston of Aberlour) (Banffshire). *Burgh of barony* for Grant of Wester Elchies 1814. Orphanage established by *Episcopal Church* 1875.

Abernethy (Perthshire). A seat of *Pictish* kings, who established an episcopal see here for a time, probably in early 8th century. Round tower, 73 feet high, probably 9th century. *Culdees* continued until 13th century, then superseded c. 1272 by *Augustinian* canons, who were in turn replaced by *collegiate church* by 1345. A 'ruler of the schools of Abernethy' (part of Celtic establishment) is mentioned c. 1100. The lands belonged to the *Earls of Angus,* of various families, and a *burgh of barony* was erected for the Earl in 1459.

Abernethy (Strathspey). *Iron* works operated 1730-9.

Abernethy, William. See Drummond, William Abernethy.
Aberuchill Castle (Perthshire). The area was contested by MacGregors and *Campbells,* and Colin, son of Campbell of Lawers, was authorised to build a castle in 1602; it was enlarged and altered in 19th century.
Aboyne (Aberdeenshire). Lands and castle (originally a *motte-and-bailey* structure of 12th century) passed from William Bisset to the *Templars,* the *Frasers* of Cowie, Sir William Keith, *Marischal* of Scotland (c. 1355), and, early in 15th century, the *Gordons.* A castle of 1671 was built by 1st Earl of Aboyne and a later mansion dates from 1801. A *burgh of barony,* sometimes called Charlestown of Aboyne, was erected for Earl of Aboyne 1676.
Aboyne, Earldom. Created 1660 for Charles *Gordon* (d. 1681), son of 2nd *Marquis of Huntly*; absorbed into marquisate of Huntly 1836.
Abraham. A Jew in Edinburgh, recorded in 1171 as having lent £80 to *Robert de Quincy.*
Academies. Established from later 18th century for teaching English, mathematics and other subjects not included in the classical curriculum of the *grammar schools. Perth* (1760) seems to have been the first.
Accession Oath. See Coronation Oath.
Accountants, Scottish Institute of Chartered. Formed 1854 by A.W. Robertson and fourteen other practising accountants in *Edinburgh.*
Achadun Castle *(Lismore).* 13th century castle, residence of bishops of *Argyll*; decayed after early 16th century.
Achaius. A dubious 'King of *Scots*' assigned to 787 or 796 to 826 and credited with originating the '*Auld Alliance*' by a treaty with Charlemagne and with founding the *Order of the Thistle.* There were kings called '*Eochaid*', but 'Achaius' cannot be fitted into the ascertained chronology.
Achallader Castle *(Argyll).* Home of a Fletcher family; scene of a conference in 1691 between the *1st Earl of Breadalbane* and some Highland chiefs who had been in arms for *James VII* and who agreed to an armistice.
Acheson House (*Canongate, Edinburgh*). Built 1633 by Sir Archibald Acheson, *Lord of Session;* bought by Marquis of *Bute* 1935 and restored; now a craft centre.
Acre. The old Scots acre was 6150 square yards.
Act of Classes, 23 January 1649. Designed to exclude from office all but the most rigid *Covenanters*; it specified four classes, ranging from the prominent supporters of *Montrose* and of the *Engagement* down to those guilty of neglect of family worship, with periods of exclusion varying from life to one year.
Act Rescissory, 1661. Rescinded acts of *Parliament* since 1633.
Acts of Sederunt. See Sederunt.
Ada (d. 1178). Daughter of Guillaume de Varenne and wife of *Henry,* son of *David I.*
Adair, John (c. 1718). Commissioned by *Privy Council* to map the shires, 1681; prepared over forty county maps and coastal charts, most of them not printed.
Adam of Dryburgh (c.1140-1212). Abbot of *Dryburgh* 1184; entered *Carthusian* order 1188; his 'Works' (published Paris 1518) include over 80 sermons.
Adam, Alexander (1741-1809). Son of a farmer at Lauriston in *Moray;* Rector of *High School, Edinburgh,* from 1768 and had *Sir Walter Scott* as a pupil; author of a Latin Grammar (1762) and other textbooks.
Adam, Robert (1728-92). Son of *William Adam*; born *Kirkcaldy;* with his brothers James (1731-94) and John (1721-92) he led an architectural fashion based on the classical models they studied; architect to George III; M.P. for Kinross-shire 1768; among his works were the *Register House, Old College* and *Charlotte Square* in *Edinburgh, Culzean Castle* and *Mellerstain House.*
Adam, William (d. 1748). Architect for part of *Hopetoun House,* which his sons completed.
Adamnan (or Adomnan) (c. 625-704). Abbot of *Iona* 679; author of a 'Life' of *Columba* and a work on the holy places.
Adamson, Patrick (?1537-92). *Minister* of *Ceres* 1562; studied in France 1564-72; Archbishop of *St Andrews* 1575; leader of *episcopal* party and chief opponent of *Andrew Melville.*
Admirable Crichton. See Crichton, James.
Admiral of Scotland. Office held by Earls of Bothwell from 1488 to forfeiture of *4th Earl* in 1567 and restored to *Earl Francis Stewart* 1581.
Admiralty Court. Evidently operated in 15th century, and its jurisdiction first directly referred to in 1493. The Admirals Depute or Judge Admirals held courts in various centres with authority in all maritime causes, civil and criminal, but crime seems usually to have fallen to the *Justiciary Court.* In 1825 prize jurisdiction was transferred from the Scottish Admiralty Court (which had retained judicial functions after 1707) to the British Court of Admiralty, and in 1830 the remaining func-

tions were transferred to the *Court of Session* and *Sheriff Courts.*

Adrian, St (d. c. 870). Said to have come from Hungary, but possibly from Ireland; settled in east of Fife with St *Monan;* the latter was killed by invading Scandinavians and Adrian took refuge in the *May Island* and met the same fate, possibly in 870 or 875.

Advocate. Various terms—procurator, prelocutor, forespeaker—were for a time applied to the person appearing in court to plead on behalf of a party, but in the 16th century 'advocate' became standard usage at least in the central courts. 'Advocate' is used also in the inferior courts in *Aberdeen,* whereas in *Glasgow* the term is 'procurator'.

Advocate for the Poor. In 1424 and 1535 it was provided that the representatives of poor litigants should be reimbursed for their labours, and such provision was ratified in 1587. An *Act of Sederunt* of 1819 arranged that a number of advocates and solicitors should be available to serve as agents for persons on the *Poor's Roll.* The Legal Aid Act of 1949 superseded previous arrangements.

Advocates, Faculty of. The *Court of Session* made provision in 1532 for ten (eight named) 'general procurators of the council', from whom the Faculty traces its origin.

Advocates' Library. Founded in *Edinburgh* 1680 by *Sir George Mackenzie* as dean; became a copyright library, entitled to a copy of every book published in Britain, in 1709; made over by Faculty to become *National Library of Scotland* 1925.

Aed (or **Aodh,** i.e. Hugh). The name of several early kings: a son of Eochaid, King in *Dalriada,* d. 777; King in Dalriada, d. 839; and a son of *Kenneth mac Alpin,* King of *Picts* or of *Scotia,* d. 879.

Aemonia (or **Emonia**). Ancient name of *Inchcolm.*

Aeneas Sylvius Piccolomini. Afterwards Pope Pius II (1458-64); visited Scotland in 1435 and wrote a description of the country.

Affleck Castle *(Angus).* 15th century tower house, built by Auchinlecks who held land in 1471; passed by early 18th century to Reids; in very good condition.

African Lakes Company. Founded 1878 by *Glasgow* commercial magnates 'to advance the kingdom of God by honest trade'; succeeded 1893 by African Lakes Corporation, with greater emphasis on business.

'Age, The'. *Edinburgh* newspaper published on Saturdays, 1850-60.

Agnes, Black. See Black Agnes.

Agnew Family. Believed to be of Norman origin (Agneaux, a barony in Normandy); settled in *Galloway* by 1363, when they became hereditary *sheriffs*; held the office until 1747.

Agricola, Gnaeus Julius (37-93). Roman governor of Britain, 77 or 78 to 85; defeated *Caledonians* at *Mons Graupius;* father-in-law of historian Tacitus, who wrote his 'Life'. See Inchtuthill.

Aidan (d. 606). Inaugurated by *Columba* as King of *Dalriada* c. 574; defeated by Angles at *Degsastan* 603.

Aidan, St (d. 651). Monk of *Iona,* evangelised Northumbria from Lindisfarne, where, as Abbot, he was Bishop of the Angles.

Aikenhead, Thomas (?1678-97). Son of *Edinburgh* apothecary; as a student he jested about the doctrine of the Trinity and was hanged for violating a statute against blasphemy.

Aikman, William (1682-1732). Son of laird of Cairney, *Angus*; studied under *Sir John Medina* and then in Italy; returned to *Edinburgh* 1712 and succeeded Medina as portrait-painter; went to London 1723.

Ailsa, Marquisate. See Cassillis, Earldom.

Airdrie (Fife). Lands and *barony* belonged to Lumsdens from c. 1450 and later passed to Prestons, Anstruthers and Erskines; castle built by a Lumsden 1588; additions made later.

Airdrie (Lanarkshire). *Burgh of barony* for Aitchison of Rochsolloch 1821; *parliamentary burgh* 1833.

Airds (or **Airs) Moss** (Ayrshire), **Battle of,** 22 July 1680. *Cameronians* defeated by government forces.

Airlie Castle *(Angus).* Stronghold of *Ogilvies* from c. 1430; burned by *Argyll* and *Covenanters* 1640; largely superseded by mansion of 1793.

Airlie, Earldom. Created 1639 for James, Lord Ogilvie (c. 1593-1646), who joined *Montrose* 1644. James, 2nd Earl (1615-1703), also fought with Montrose, was captured at *Philiphaugh* but escaped. David, Lord Ogilvy (1725-1813), son of 4th Earl, fought with *Jacobites* in 1745 and subsequently joined French army; he was pardoned in 1778 but the title was not restored until 1826.

Airth (Stirlingshire). Earlier castle superseded by 15th century tower, later enlarged. In 15th century the heiress of the Airths of that *ilk* married a Bruce, and later a Bruce heiress carried the property to Elphinstones, from whom it was acquired by Grahams in 1717. Airth was a *royal burgh* between 1195 and

1203, but was made a *burgh of barony* for John Bruce 1597.

Airth, Earldom. Created 1633 for *William Graham, 7th Earl of Menteith;* dormant 1694.

Alan, Lord of Galloway (d. 1234). *Constable of Scotland;* married Margaret, eldest daughter of *David, Earl of Huntingdon,* and was father of *Devorguilla.*

Alba. The kingdom of the *Picts* and *Scots* north of Forth and *Clyde,* c. 844-1018.

Albannaich. *Gaelic* term for the inhabitants of Scotland.

Albany. Derives from *'Alba',* by which *Gaelic* speakers meant Scotland. 'Albani' is said to have been the warcry of Highlanders at the battle of the *Standard.*

Albany, Alexander Stewart, Duke of (?1454-85). Brother of *James III;* imprisoned in *Edinburgh Castle* 1479 but escaped and became an agent of England; finally went to France, where he died.

Albany, Dukedom. Created 1398; for nearly 300 years held intermittently by princes, usually a king's second son. *Charles Edward* used title Count of Albany in his later years and created his illegitimate daughter Duchess of Albany. In Hanoverian times brothers of George I and George IV received the title (along with York) and Victoria conferred it on her youngest son, whose son (also Duke of Saxe-Coburg) was the last holder.

Albany Herald. First mentioned 1401.

Albany, John Stewart, Duke of (c. 1484-1536). Son of *Alexander;* born in France; *Governor* of Scotland 1515-24; returned to France and died there childless.

Albany, Murdoch Stewart, Duke of (c. 1362-1425). Son of *Robert, Duke of Albany*; prisoner in England from *Homildon* until 1415; succeeded father as *Governor,* but lacked capacity; after return of *James I* was executed.

Albany, Robert, Duke of (1339-1420). Third son of *Robert II; Earl of Fife* and *Menteith* by marriage and inheritance; *Chamberlain* 1382-1408; *Governor* of Scotland on behalf of his aged father 1388; dominant during reign of *Robert III* and suspected of causing death of the heir, *David, Duke of Rothesay;* Governor during captivity of *James I,* from 1406.

Albert Institute, Dundee. Erected 1865-8 as memorial to Prince Consort; acquired by town 1879 as museum, gallery and lecture-rooms.

Alclut (or **Ail Cluade).** 'The Rock of Clyde', now *Dumbarton Rock,* capital of British kingdom of *Strathclyde.*

Aldie Castle (Fife). Built in early 16th century by Mercer family; recently restored.

Alexander I, King of Scots (c. 1077-1124). Fifth son of *Malcolm III* and *Margaret,* succeeded 1107; his brother, afterwards *David I,* ruled southern Scotland as 'Earl'; founded *Augustinian* houses at *Scone* and *Inchcolm;* refused to allow *bishops of St. Andrews* to acknowledge English supremacy; said to have become known as 'the Fierce' from his suppression of a northern rising; married Sybilla, an illegitimate daughter of Henry I of England; had no legitimate children.

Alexander II, King of Scots (1198-1249). Son of *William I*; succeeded 1214; suppressed insurrections and disorder in *Moray, Argyll, Caithness* and *Galloway*; accepted English estates in return for renouncing claims to three northern English counties, 1237; began operations against Scandinavian rule in western isles, and died at Kerrera; married (1) Joan, daughter of King John of England and (2) Marie de Coucy, daughter of a Picard lord, by whom he had his only son.

Alexander III, King of Scots (1241-1286). Son of *Alexander II;* succeeded 1249; King Haakon of Norway attempted to reassert his authority in the west, but withdrew after the battle of *Largs* and the *Hebrides* were ceded by the *Treaty of Perth*; close ties with England continued, but Alexander resisted English demands for homage for his kingdom; married (1) *Margaret,* daughter of Henry III, and (2) *Yolande,* daughter of the Comte de Dreux; accidentally killed near *Kinghorn;* his children—*Alexander,* David and *Margaret*—predeceased him.

Alexander Family. The name appears also as 'Alshounder' and is a truncated patronymic, from 'Alexanderson', which was common in Lowland Scotland in 15th century. The Alexanders of *Menstrie,* however, claimed relationship with MacAlastairs in Kintyre.

Alexander, Prince of Scotland (1264-84). Elder son of *Alexander III;* married Margaret of Flanders but had no issue.

Alexander, Sir William, Earl of Stirling (?1567-1640). Born *Menstrie Castle*; his poetry brought him to the notice of *James VI* and as a courtier he received many favours, including the gift of *Nova Scotia* (1621) and the office of *Secretary of State* (1626); among his works were 'Aurora' (1604), 'Monarchick Tragedies' (1607), 'Doomsday' (1614) and—collected works—'Recreations with the Muses' (1637); his association with unpopular royal policies caused him to be regarded with disfavour.

Alford (Aberdeenshire). *Burgh of barony* for Lord *Forbes* 1595.
Alford, Battle of, 2 July 1645. Victory of *Montrose* over *Baillie.*
Alford, Earldom. 'Peerage' conferred by *'James VIII'* in 1760 on John Graeme his secretary, son and heir of James Graeme of Newton, who had been *Solicitor General* in 1688; Graeme died 1773.
Alien Act, 1705. After the Scottish *Parliament* had passed the Act of *Security* (1704), the English Parliament retorted with an act which declared that Scots should be treated as aliens in England and that certain exports from Scotland should cease, until Scotland had appointed commissioners to treat for *union* or had accepted the Hanoverian succession.
Alison, Sir Archibald (1792-1867). Born Shropshire, son of an *Edinburgh minister;* a lawyer who held various official appointments; best known for his 'Modern History of Europe'.
Allan, David (1744-1796). Born *Alloa*; studied for many years in Rome; painted scenes of everyday Scottish life; illustrated *Allan Ramsay's* 'Gentle Shepherd' and some of *Robert Burns'* 'Poems'.
Allan Glen's School, Glasgow. Founded by bequest of Allan Glen (1772-1850), a wright and *burgess* of *Glasgow,* for the education of fifty boys; opened 1853; by the Education Act of 1872 and an Act of 1876 the Trustees were empowered to enlarge the school and to charge fees, but free education and clothes were still provided for the foundationers; the school later passed to Glasgow Corporation.
Allan's Hospital, Stirling. Founded 1724 by James Allan, writer, for education of sons of tradesmen.
Alloa (Clackmannanshire). Lands conferred by *David II* on Sir Robert *Erskine, Chamberlain,* 1360, and have remained with his descendants, who became *Earls of Mar,* ever since. The tower probably mainly 15th century, though on site of earlier castle. *Burgh of regality* for *Lord Erskine* by 1497 and for *Earl of Mar* 1620; *police burgh* 1863.
Alness (or Obstule) (Ross). *Burgh of barony* for Mackintosh of Torcastle 1690.
Alpin. A somewhat dubious 'King of *Scots*', possibly inserted into list of kings of *Dalriada* to provide a royal father for *Kenneth mac Alpin,* who became king c. 840. An earlier Alpin was King of Dalriada c. 736.
Altimarlach (or Allt-na-marlach) *(Caithness),* **Battle of,** 1680. *Sir John Campbell of Glenorchy,* who claimed *earldom of Caithness,* defeated the rightful claimant who, however, later obtained the earldom.
Alva (Clackmannanshire). *Police burgh* 1876.
Alyth (Perthshire). *Burgh of barony* for *Earl of Airlie* 1488; *police burgh* 1875.
Am Fasgadh ('The Shelter'). Highland folk museum, founded at *Iona* in 1935 by Dr. I.F. Grant; moved to Laggan and then *Kingussie,* where responsibility was assumed by Scottish universities.
Amercement. A fine levied by a court, usually at a fixed rate, often for failure to *compear.*
American Declaration of Independence. See Wilson, James; Witherspoon, John.
Amisfield (Dumfriesshire). Belonged to *Charteris family* from 13th century; *burgh of barony* for Charteris of Amisfield 1613; fine square tower dates from c. 1600.
An Comunn Gaidhealach ('The Gaelic, or Highland, Association'). Founded in *Oban* 1891; held first *Mod* 1892.
'Ancaria'. Unidentified *Cistercian* house mentioned 1530.
Anchor Line. Shipping Company founded in *Glasgow* 1856.
Ancram, Earldom. Created 1633 for Sir Robert Ker of Ancram (1578-1654), grandson of Andrew Ker of Ferniehirst; his 2nd son succeeded to this earldom, his eldest son married the heiress to the *Earldom of Lothian,* and the son of that marriage became 3rd Earl.
Ancrum Moor, Battle of, 27 February 1545. English under Sir Ralph Eure and Sir Brian Layton defeated by *Earl of Angus.*
Ancrum, Nether (Roxburghshire). *Burgh of barony* for *Earl of Roxburgh* 1639.
Anderson, Alexander (1845-1909). Railwayman at Kirkconnel who wrote verses under name 'Surfaceman'.
Anderson, James (1662-1728). Born *Edinburgh*; *Writer to the Signet* whose antiquarian interests and participation in controversies preceding *Union* of 1707 led him to prepare the collection of facsimiles of documents, coins and seals known as 'Anderson's Diplomata', published 1739 (by *Thomas Ruddiman*); also compiled 'Collections on *Mary,* Queen of Scots' (1727).
Anderson, Sir John, Viscount Waverley (1882-1958). Educated *George Watson's College* and *Edinburgh University*; civil servant 1905; Governor of Bengal 1932; Lord Privy Seal 1938; Home Secretary 1939; created viscount 1952.
Anderson, Sir Robert Rowand (1835-1920).

Born *Edinburgh;* architect for various Edinburgh Board Schools, Edinburgh University New Medical Buildings, MacEwan Hall, *National Museum of Antiquities* and a number of churches; started systematic recording of Scottish buildings.

Anderson's University or College or Institute. John Anderson (1726-96), professor of *natural philosophy* at *Glasgow,* left endowment for education of the 'unacademical classes'; absorbed partly into *Glasgow and West of Scotland Technical College* 1886 and partly into *Glasgow University* 1947.

Anderston (Glasgow). *Burgh of barony* for *burgesses* 1824; annexed to *Glasgow* 1846; foundry established by *Henry Houldsworth* 1836.

Andrew, St. According to tradition, Andrew evangelised Scythia and was martyred at Patras, whence his remains were taken to Constantinople and later to Amalfi. Legends associated with *King Angus* and St *Regulus* sought to explain why he became Scotland's patron saint and how his relics came to be at *St Andrews.* The cult evidently reached St Andrews in the 8th century and St Andrew's cross appeared on the seal of the *Guardians* in 1286. St Andrew's Day is November 30th.

Angel (or **Angel Noble).** English coin first struck in 1465 and often referred to in Scotland; equated with £1, 4s. Scots c. 1490, with £2, 12s. in the 1530s and with £6, 13. 4d. in 1600.

Angus. Evidently a province of the *Pictish* kingdom; *mormaer* mentioned 939.

Angus (d. 761). Son of Fergus; King of *Picts;* led campaigns against the *Scots,* Britons and Angles and legend related that at *Athelstaneford* he won a victory by the intervention of St *Andrew,* to whom he dedicated a church at *St Andrews.* Some accounts assign the foundation of the church at St Andrews to a later King Angus (d. 854).

Angus (d. 1130). Son of a daughter of *Lulach; mormaer* of *Moray;* rebelled against *David I,* was deposed and killed.

Angus, Archibald Douglas, 5th Earl of (c. 1449-1513). Succeeded 1463; gained nickname of 'Bell the Cat' 1482 when at *Lauder* he undertook to lead attack on *James III's* favourites; evidently pursued an unreliable and devious course, which led to his occasional disgrace and imprisonment under *James IV.*

Angus, Archibald Douglas, 6th Earl of (c. 1489-1557). Succeeded *5th Earl,* his grandfather; in 1514 married *Margaret Tudor,* played an erratic part for many years, and from late 1525 controlled the person of *James V* and dominated the country; when the King escaped, in 1528, Angus fled to England, where he remained until 1543; then for a time he acted as an English agent, but led the Scots to victory at *Ancrum Moor* and shared the command in the defeat at *Pinkie.*

Angus, Archibald Douglas, 8th Earl of (1555-88). Son of 7th Earl (d. 1557); ward of *James, 4th Earl of Morton,* and on latter's fall was forfeited and fled to England; returned after *Ruthven Raid* but banished 1584; after returning at end of 1585 he remained a patron of the ultra-Protestant and *Presbyterian* party.

Angus, Earldom. Passed by marriage from native line to the *De Umfravilles,* who lost it through supporting the English against *Robert I.* Conferred in 1328 on Sir John Stewart of Boncle, whose grand-daughter was mother of George, 1st Douglas Earl of Angus (d. 1403). The 4th Douglas Earl, George (d. 1462) profited by the fall of the *Black Douglases* after commanding the royal forces against them at *Arkinholm.* Raised to marquisate of Douglas 1633; 3rd Marquis became *Duke of Douglas* 1703; title now held by *Duke of Hamilton.*

Angus Og. See John, 4th Lord of the Isles.

Annabella, Queen. See Drummond.

Annan (Dumfriesshire). Burgh held by *Bruces* in 13th century, but *royal burgh* 1539. Hospital mentioned c. 1258 and 1446. Castle mentioned c. 1124, presumably then a *motte-and-bailey* structure; as a Bruce stronghold it played a part in the *War of Independence* and figured in operations so late as 1570, but nothing now remains of it.

Annan, Battle of, 17 December 1332. *Edward Balliol* routed by Scots.

Annandale, Earldom and Marquisate. Earldom created 1624 for *John Murray* and anew for James Johnstone 1661; raised to marquisate 1701; dormant 1792.

Annandale, Lordship. Conferred by *David I* on Robert de Brus c. 1124; *Robert I* transferred it to *Thomas Randolph;* it passed by marriage to the Dunbars, *Earls of March,* and then to the *Douglases* until their forfeiture in 1455.

Anne of Denmark (1574-1619). Daughter of Frederick II; married *James VI* in Oslo 24 November 1589.

Annexation, Acts of. Passed from time to time to recover and conserve resources of the crown; the best known are one in 1455, after the fall of the *Black Douglases,* and one in 1587 which annexed the *temporalities* of ecclesiastical benefices.

Annexed Estates. See Forfeited Estates.

Annual of Norway. See Perth, Treaty of.

Anointing. Earlier attempts to procure papal sanction for the anointing of Scottish kings had been blocked by England, but in 1329 *Robert I* secured permission for the rite; *David II* first king to be anointed.

Anstruther Easter (Fife). *Royal burgh* 1583.

Anstruther Wester (Fife). Non-royal burgh dependent on *Pittenweem Priory;* but received charter as *royal burgh* 1587.

Anti-Burghers. See Burghers.

Antiquaries, Society of. Instituted 1780 on initiative of *11th Earl of Buchan*; built up collection which was made over to form *National Museum of Antiquities;* published 5 volumes of 'Archaeologia Scotica' and since 1851 its 'Proceedings'.

Antonine Wall. Erected by Lollius Urbicus in reign of Antoninus Pius (139-161) from Carriden on the Forth to Old Kilpatrick on the *Clyde;* abandoned c. 185.

Anwoth (Kirkcudbrightshire). See Cardoness.

Apologetical Declaration, 1684. Composed by *James Renwick;* threatened death to all engaged in proceedings against *Cameronians.*

Appin *(Argyll). Gaelic* 'Apuinn', Middle Irish 'Apdaine', meaning 'abbey land', in this case the patrimony of the early monastery on *Lismore,* extending from Loch Creran to Loch Leven. The home of several Stewart families, it was known as 'Apuinn nan Stiubhartach'.

Appin (Perthshire). Cf. preceding. In this case the monastery was that of *Dull.* Known as 'Apuinn nam Mèinnearach' or 'Appin of the Menzieses'.

Appin Banner. Carried by Appin Regiment at *Culloden*; conveyed from the field wrapped round a man's body and now in *Edinburgh Castle.*

Appin Murder, 14 May 1752. *Colin Campbell of Glenure* ('the Red Fox'), on his way to evict tenants of *Jacobite* chiefs, was murdered in the Wood of Lettermore, between Ballachulish Ferry and Kentallen. *James Stewart of the Glens* was hanged for the crime, but local tradition attributed it to a Stewart of Ballachulish.

Appropriation. Process whereby a proportion of the *teinds* of a parish was appropriated to the use of a religious house or other institution.

Aquhorthies (Aberdeenshire). Site of Roman Catholic College from 1799 to 1829, when it was transferred to *Blairs.*

Arbroath. Burgh under abbey of Arbroath from 1178x1182; *royal burgh* 1599. A hospital of St John Baptist appears 1352; there was also an almshouse, mentioned in 15th and 16th centuries.

Arbroath Abbey (*Tironensian*) *(Angus).* Founded by *William I* 1178, dedicated to St Thomas Becket; erected into lordship for *Marquis of Hamilton* 1606.

Arbroath Banking Company. Established 1825; merged with *Commercial Bank* 1844.

Arbroath, Battle of, 23 January 1446. The son of 2nd *Earl of Crawford* defeated the *Ogilvies* and Sir Alexander *Seton.*

Arbroath, Declaration of, 6 April 1320. Letter of Scottish barons to Pope John XXII, affirming their determination to maintain Scottish independence and support *Robert I* unless he showed signs of yielding.

Arbuthnott (Kincardineshire). *Burgh of barony* for Barclay of Mathers 1543.

Arbuthnot(t), Alexander (1538-83). First post-*Reformation* principal of *King's College, Aberdeen,* appointed 1569.

Arbuthnott, Viscountcy. Created 1641 for Sir Robert Arbuthnott, whose family had held the lands since 12th century.

'Archaeologia Scotica'. See Antiquaries, Society of.

Archdeacon. Dignitary who exercised supervision, under the bishop, of the whole or part of a diocese. *St Andrews, Glasgow* and *Orkney* each had two archdeaconries, and the Archdeacon of the *Isles* was a relic of the days when the diocese of the Isles, in its undivided state, had one archdeacon in *Man* and one in the *Hebrides.*

Archdean. Term frequently used erroneously for *Archdeacon.*

Archers, Royal Company of (H.M. Bodyguard for Scotland). Founded 1676, received charter from Queen Anne 1707. See also King's Guard.

Ardblair Castle (Perthshire). Lands granted by *David II* to Thomas Blair, son of B. of Balthayock, and remained with Blairs until they passed by marriage to *Oliphants* of Gask 1792. The building, on the L-plan, is little altered externally from its original state of c. 1600.

Ardchattan Priory (*Valliscaulian*) (*Argyll*). Founded 1230 by Duncan *MacDougal*; property fell into hands of *Campbells,* and its annexation to bishopric of the *Isles* 1615 was ineffective. A modern mansion incorporates part of the medieval buildings.

Ardchonnel Castle. See Innis Chonnel.

Ardeer (Ayrshire). Works set up by British Dynamite Company 1871.

Arderydd (?Arthuret in Liddesdale), **Battle of,** 573 or 575. Apparently a victory of *Aidan,* King of *Dalriada,* and *Rhydderich Hael,* King of *Strathclyde,* over other Britons.

Ardgay (Ross). See Bonarness.

Ardgour *(Argyll).* District between Loch Linnhe, Morvern, Loch Sunart and Loch Shiel, dominated by *MacLeans.*

Ardgowan (Renfrewshire). *Burgh of barony* for Stewart of Blackhall 1634.

Ardmaddy Castle *(Argyll).* A modern mansion incorporates the lower levels of a 14th century structure; originally *MacDougal* property, it passed to *Campbells* and became a residence of the *Earls of Breadalbane.*

Ardmillan Castle (Ayrshire). Originally a small 16th century tower, altered and modernised, it belonged to Kennedys of Bargany and passed by marriage to James Crawford of Baidland in later 17th century; a member of the Crawford family was a *Lord of Session* as Lord Ardmillan 1855.

Ardoch Roman Camp (Perthshire). Originally established by *Agricola*; used again so late as time of *Septimius Severus.*

Ardross Castle (Fife). Ruins of a stronghold supposed to have been built c. 1370 by William Dishington, whose family long held the lands. There was a hospital nearby at the terminus of a ferry across the Firth of Forth.

Ardrossan (Ayrshire). The lands belonged to one Fergus in the reign of *Robert I* and later there was a barony held by the Lords *Montgomery.* A castle, in ruins, dates probably from late 13th century and figured in the exploits of *William Wallace*; it was destroyed by Cromwell. The place became a *burgh of barony* for £5 householders 1846.

Ardtornish Castle. On the mainland side of the Sound of Mull, a seat of the *Lords of the Isles;* only fragments remain. See Westminster-Ardtornish.

Ardvreck Castle (*Sutherland*). Built c. 1591 by MacLeod of Assynt; *Montrose* brought there after his capture; only ruins remain.

Argathelians. The political party or faction which followed the *2nd* and *3rd Dukes of Argyll.*

Argyll (Earra-Ghàidheal = the coastland of the Gael). Originally North Argyll extended from Loch Broom to about Arisaig, and South Argyll was roughly coextensive with the later county; the term is sometimes used to denote mid-Argyll, the area round Loch Awe.

Argyll and Sutherland Highlanders. Formed 1881, when Argyll Highlanders became 1st Battalion and 93rd Sutherland Highlanders became 2nd Battalion; reduced to one battalion 1948; called 'Rory's'.

Argyll, Archibald Campbell, 8th Earl and **1st Marquis of** (1607-61). 'Gillespie Gruamach' or cross-eyed Archibald; succeeded 1638; led more radical *Covenanters* against *Charles I* but came to terms with *Charles II,* whom he crowned 1651; his compliance with the *Cromwellian administration* led to his execution when Charles II was restored.

Argyll, Archibald Campbell, 9th Earl of (1629-85). Son of preceding; active royalist 1650-1 and under *Cromwellian administration;* in favour after *Restoration,* but refused *Test Act* 1681; condemned to death for treason, but escaped; raised rebellion on accession of *James VII* but was captured and executed.

Argyll, Archibald Campbell, 3rd Duke of (1682-1761). Brother of 2nd Duke; Earl of Islay 1706; shared his brother's political power.

Argyll, Bishopric. Separated from bishopric of *Dunkeld* c. 1190; see also Lismore.

Argyll, Earldom, Marquisate and Dukedom. Earldom created for Colin Campbell 1457; 8th Earl created Marquis 1641, but marquisate did not descend to his son, 9th Earl; 10th Earl created Duke 1701.

Argyll Highlanders. (1) 74th Highlanders, raised 1778 by Col. John Campbell of Barbreck; served in America; disbanded 1783. (2) Raised as 98th Regiment 1794 by 5th Duke of Argyll; 91st Regiment of Foot 1798; 91st (Princess Louise's) Argyllshire Highlanders 1871.

Argyll, John Campbell, 2nd Duke of (1678-1743). Succeeded 1703; made Earl (later Duke) of Greenwich for his support of the *Union;* served in War of Spanish Succession; commanded government forces against *Jacobites* 1715; dominated Scottish politics in his later years.

Argyll's Lodging. Built in Castle Wynd, *Stirling,* in 1630, by *Sir William Alexander, Earl of Stirling;* passed to *Marquis of Argyll* 1640; bought by government for use as hospital 1799.

Argyll's Rebellion, 1685. The *9th Earl of Argyll* intended a rebellion to coincide with that of the Duke of Monmouth in England; comprised minor operations in Firth of *Clyde* area.

Argyllshire Highlanders. Raised by *Earl of*

Argyll 1689; served in Highlands and in Flanders; disbanded 1697.

Arkinholm (Dumfriesshire), **Battle of,** 1 May 1455. The three brothers of *9th Earl of Douglas* were defeated on the Esk, near *Langholm,* by an army composed of leading Border families; marks downfall of *Black Douglases.*

Arles. Nominal payment, often of a penny, in token of a bargain or as earnest for payment of more substantial sum.

Armadale (West Lothian). *Police burgh;* developed rapidly with shale mining in late 19th century.

Armadale Castle (Skye). Built for Lord MacDonald by *Gillespie Graham,* 1815.

Armorial Bearings. Earliest known achievement of family arms, with supporters and crest, is on seal of *Earl of March* 1334.

Armorial de Gelre. Earliest roll of Scottish coats of arms, containing forty-two, emblazoned between 1370 and 1388; MS in Bibliothèque Royale, Brussels.

Armour, Jean (1767-1834). Wife of *Robert Burns.*

Arms, Public Register of All. Authorised by statute of 1592, which forbade use of arms not approved by *Lyon King of Arms*; extant from 1672.

Armstrongs. A family, or rather group of families, in the southwest, particularly Liddesdale, which by 1500 had become notorious for its unruliness. The subject of the famous ballad, 'Johnnie Armstrong', was either John Armstrong of Gilknockie, whose hasty execution at Carlanrigg, on the road to *Langholm,* is assigned to 1529, or John Armstrong (otherwise 'Black Jock'), brother of Thomas A. of Mangerton, who was sentenced to death on 1 April 1530. William A. (fl. 1596) was the 'Kinmont Willie' who was imprisoned in Carlisle Castle, whence he was rescued by *Scott of Buccleuch.*

Arnage Castle (Aberdeenshire). 16th century tower on Z-plan, built by *Cheynes,* who had held lands since 14th century, and sold by them to John Sibbald 1643; bought in 1702 by *Provost* John Ross of *Aberdeen;* his granddaughter married Alexander Leith of Freefield, whose descendants took name of Leith-Ross.

Arniston House (Midlothian). Designed by *William Adam* for the *Dundas* family, who had held lands since 1571.

Arnot, Hugo (1749-86). *Advocate;* published 'History of *Edinburgh*' (1779) and 'Criminal Trials' (1785).

Aros Castle *(Argyll).* On south shore of Sound of Mull, a stronghold of Lords of the *Isles*; in 1608 Lord Ochiltree entertained some chiefs on his ship there and arrested them.

Arran, Earldom. Created for *Thomas Boyd* 1467; lapsed on his forfeiture; created anew for *James, Lord Hamilton,* 1503, and remained with Hamiltons except when held by *James Stewart* 1581-5.

Arran, James Hamilton, 2nd Earl of (c. 1516-75). Succeeded father 1529; as heir presumptive he was *Governor* in Queen *Mary's* minority until 1554; figurehead of revolution of 1559-60; rebelled against Mary on her marriage to *Darnley,* 1566, and in exile until 1569; a leader of *Queen's Party* until 1573.

Arran, James Hamilton, 3rd Earl of (1537/8-1609). Hostage for his father with *Cardinal Beaton,* then with the captors of *St Andrews Castle* 1547 and then in France; candidate for hand of Elizabeth 1560 and for that of *Mary* 1561; attempted to seize Mary 1562; declared insane and confined until his death.

Arran, James Stewart, Earl of (c. 1545-96). 2nd son of Lord Ochiltree; soldier on continent; returned 1577-8 and rose to prominence; Earl of Arran 1581, on ground of insanity of *3rd Hamilton Earl* and his own wife's descent from 1st Hamilton Earl; *Chancellor* and head of administration 1584-5; overthrown November 1585; murdered 1596.

Arran, Thomas Boyd, Earl of (d. 1473). Son of *Robert, 1st Lord Boyd;* shared in his family's brief ascendancy and married Mary, sister of *James III,* who later married *Lord Hamilton,* whose son became Earl of Arran.

Arrat *(Angus).* Hospital mentioned in 15th century.

Arrestment. Seizure of goods of person against whom legal proceedings had been successfully taken, usually at instance of a creditor.

Arrol, Sir William (1839-1913). Born *Houston,* Renfrewshire; began work in thread factory at age of nine; apprenticed to blacksmith; became boiler-maker and went into *iron* working on large scale; engineer for second *Tay Bridge* and *Forth Railway Bridge.*

Arthur's Oven or **Arthur's O'on.** Structure near *Falkirk,* probably a Roman temple, but claimed as the burial place of King Arthur; demolished 1743.

Articles, Lords of the. A committee of *Parliament,* in existence from at least 1467, consisting of members drawn from all *estates,* plus the officers of state, which prepared business for the full house. Owing to the crown's control over the method of appointment and its tendency to reduce parliament to 'a registrar of decisions made elsewhere' it became unpopular. Abolished 1641, restored 1660 and abolished 1690.

Ascog Castle (Bute). Lamont stronghold, destroyed by *Campbells* 1646 and now a ruin.

Ashestiel (Selkirkshire). *Sir Walter Scott's* home 1804-12.

Assembly Hall and **Rooms.** A social organisation called 'The Assembly' existed in *Edinburgh* in 1710 and the first Assembly Room was in the West Bow, followed by one in Old Assembly Close; the Assembly Rooms in George Street date from 1787. The Assembly Hall on the *Mound* was built 1858-9 as the meeting place of the General Assembly of the *Free Church* and since 1929 has housed the *General Assembly* of the *Church of Scotland.*

Assumption of Thirds. See Thirds of Benefices.

Asswanley House (Aberdeenshire). The property belonged to Calders from 1440 until 1768 and the laird's house was built 1792.

Athelstaneford, Battle of, 735 (?). Later tradition related that *Angus mac Fergus,* king of the *Picts,* won a battle against 'Athelstane', a king of the Northumbrians, with the aid of St *Andrew,* whose cross appeared in the blue sky. The tale is commemorated by a *saltire* flag flying on the site.

Atholl. Presumably a *Pictish* province; although no *mormaer* is recorded, there was a *'comes'* in the reign of *David I.*

Atholl Brose. Various recipes exist, the most staple ingredients being honey, whisky and oatmeal. Associated with an Earl of Atholl who was said to have captured the Lord of the *Isles* in 1476 by doctoring a well with the mixture.

Atholl, Earldom, Marquisate and Dukedom. Native line of earls ended with Henry (d.c. 1210 and the earldom then passed, through a series of heiresses, to various families, finally that of Strathbogie, descended from *Earls of Fife.* They lost it for their adherence to England against *Robert I*; held briefly by a *Campbell,* a *Douglas* and by royal Stewarts, finally *Walter;* John Stewart (d. 1440-1512), son of *Joan,* widow of *James I,* by her second husband, was created Earl c. 1455; this line died out 1595 and, after tenure by a collateral until 1626, the title went to John Murray of *Tullibardine* 1629. Marquisate created 1676 and dukedom 1703.

Atholl Highlanders. Raised by Duke of Atholl as 77th Highland Regiment 1778; served in Ireland; ordered to East Indies in breach of terms of enlistment, and refused to embark; government acknowledged mistake but regiment disbanded 1783. The title is now used by the Duke of Atholl's own regiment at *Blair Atholl.*

Atholl, John Murray, Earl of (c. 1635-1703). *Justice-General* 1670-8; succeeded to earldom of *Tullibardine* 1670; created Marquis of A. 1676.

Atholl, John Murray, Marquis of (1659-1724). *Secretary of State* 1696-8; Duke of A. 1703; opposed *Union* but supported George I in 1715.

Atholl, John Stewart, Earl of (d. 1579). Opposed reformers in 1560; fought for *Mary* at *Corrichie;* joined *Confederate Lords* 1567; opposed *Regent Morton; Chancellor* 1578.

Atholl, Katharine, Duchess of (1874-1960). Daughter of Sir James Ramsay of Bamff, married 1899 Marquis of *Tullibardine,* who became 8th Duke of Atholl 1917; Unionist M.P. for Kinross and West Perth 1923-38; wrote 'Women in Politics' (1931), 'Searchlight on Spain' (1938) and 'The Tragedy of Warsaw' (1945).

Atholl, Walter Stewart, Earl of (d. 1437). Youngest son of *Robert II;* created *Earl of Caithness* c. 1401, Earl of Atholl 1404 and *Earl of Strathearn* 1427; the murderers of *James I,* including his grandson, Sir Robert Stewart, intended to make him King; executed after the murder.

Auchindoun (Banffshire). Castle said to date originally from 12th century and to have been rebuilt by *Robert Cochrane;* lands held of old by *Ogilvies,* but acquired by Gordons c. 1535. See Gordon, Adam, of Auchindoun.

Auchindrain Museum. 5 miles south of *Inveraray,* preserves township with houses, implements, etc. of last three centuries.

Auchinleck (Ayrshire). Lands originally belonged to Auchinlecks of that *ilk* but in 1504 were granted to Thomas Boswell, who had married the Auchinleck heiress, and a *burgh of barony* was created for Boswell in 1507. See Boswell, Alexander and James.

Auchterarder (Perthshire). Royal estate and castle traditionally from 11th century, authentically from 1227; *royal burgh* by 1246; *barony* granted by *Robert I* to Sir William Montfichet and it passed through an heiress to Drummonds. There are only slight remains of the castle. The well of St *Kessog* was reputed to have curative powers.

Auchterarder Case, 1838-42. Majority of parishioners objected to patron's nominee to parish; *Court of Session* upheld patron's rights; one of the crises in the *Ten Years' Conflict.*
Auchtergaven (Perthshire). *Burgh of barony* for *Lord Nairn* 1681.
Auchterhouse *(Angus). Burgh of barony* for *Earl of Buchan* 1497.
Auchtermuchty (Fife). *Royal burgh* by charter 1517.
Auchtertool, Milton of (Fife). *Burgh of barony* for Forbes of Mayne or *Craigievar* 1617.
Augustinian Order. Canons regular; see Abernethy, Blantyre, Cambuskenneth, Canonbie, Holyrood, Inchaffray, Inchcolm, Inchmahome, Jedburgh, Lochleven, May, Monymusk, Oronsay, Pittenweem, Restennet, St Andrews, St Mary's Isle, Scone, Strathfillan.
Auld Alliance. See Franco-Scottish alliance.
Auld Reekie. Nickname for *Edinburgh,* which looked 'reekie' or smoky with so many houses concentrated in the Old Town; used by *Scott* in 'Heart of Midlothian' (1818) and 'The Abbot' (1820).
Auld Sang. 'There's an end to an auld sang' is said to have been the remark of the 1st *Earl of Seafield* at the dissolution of the last Scottish *Parliament* on 28 April 1707.
Auldearn (Nairnshire). *Royal burgh* by 1179x1182; *burgh of barony* for Dunbar of *Cumnock* 1511.
Auldearn, Battle of, 9 May 1645. *Montrose* defeated *Covenanters* under *Hurry.*
Aungervyle Society. Founded *Edinburgh* 1881 for reprinting rare pamphlets; ceased operations 1888.
Avignon Popes. See Papal Schism.
Avoch Castle (Ross). Near village of Avoch in the Black Isle, it was the property of the *Moray* family to which *Wallace's* companion and the *Guardian* of the 1330s belonged; later passed to *Earls of Ross* and then to the crown; only site is known.
Avondale (Lanarkshire). Belonged to Bairds, *Sinclairs* and *Douglases,* on whose fall in 1455 it was given to *Andrew Stewart,* created Lord Avondale; acquired by *Sir James Hamilton of Finnart.*
Ayala, Pedro de. Spanish envoy to court of *James IV;* his account of Scotland has been preserved.
Ayr. The charter of *William I* creating Ayr a *royal burgh* (1203x1206) is the earliest such charter extant. William referred to his 'new castle upon the River Ayr'; Ayr castle was captured by English 1306 and by *Robert I* 1314 but thereafter disappears from history; the *Cromwellian* government built a Citadel, erected into a *burgh of barony* for *Earl of Eglinton* 1663. There was a bridge at Ayr by 1236, but the present 'Auld Brig' seems to date from between 1470 and 1525; it was restored 1907. Hospital of St Leonard mentioned 1408x1420 and 1506; also leper-house, 15th-16th centuries.
Ayr Bank (Douglas, Heron & Co.). Established 1769; suspended payment 1772, causing widespread distress.
Ayr, Barns of. Supposed to have been barracks of English troops, attacked and burned by *William Wallace* in May 1297.
Ayr, Friaries. (1) *Dominican,* founded by 1242; (2) Observant *Franciscan,* founded 1488x1497; properties both made over to burgh 1567.
Ayr Manuscript. Collection of old laws and legal styles, dating probably from late 13th and early 14th centuries. Apparently once the property of the *burgh* of Ayr, it was purchased at a book-stall there in 1824 and is now in the *Register House.*
Ayr, Schools. A 'master of the schools' mentioned 1233 and it is believed that there was a school connected with St John's Church; by 1502 the *burgh* had assumed responsibility. *Academy* founded 1794 but soon united with the *grammar school* as the High School.
Ayre (Latin 'iter', English 'eyre'). Circuit of *Justices* for criminal cases and of *Chamberlain* to review affairs of *royal burghs.*
Ayrshire and Galloway Archaeological Association. Founded 1887 as Ayrshire and Wigtonshire Archaeological Association; changed name 1885; dissolved 1897.
Ayrshire Banking Company. Established 1830; absorbed in *Western Bank* 1845.
Ayrshire Cattle. Developed in first half of 19th century, but no decisive date at which the breed was established.
Ayrshire Yeomanry. Raised c. 1798 by *Earl of Cassillis;* used in 1820 to suppress radicals in *Paisley and Glasgow;* in Boer War formed part of 17th Company of Imperial Yeomanry; in World War II divided into 151st and 152nd Regiments; armoured regiment 1947; in later reorganisation became two companies as infantrymen in Territorial and Army Reserve.
Ayton, Sir Robert (1570-1638). A Latin panegyric on *James VI* brought him royal favour;

became secretary to Queen *Anne* and Henrietta Maria; his poems, sometimes in English, sometimes in Latin, are of such merit that he has been called 'the Father of the Cavalier lyric'.

Aytoun, William Edmonstoun (1813-65). Born *Edinburgh; advocate,* then Professor of Belles-lettres in Edinburgh; involved in stirrings of nationalism in 1850s; author of 'Bon Gaultier Ballads' and 'Lays of the Scottish Cavaliers'.

B

Badenoch, Lordship. (*Gaelic* 'Bàideanach', 'the drowned land'.) Held by *Comyns* from reign of *Alexander II* to that of *Robert I,* who gave it to *Randolph, Earl of Moray;* granted by *Robert II* to his son, *Alexander Stewart,* 1377; passed to *Earls of Huntly* by 1452; associated with Clan Chattan and especially Macphersons.

Badenoch, Wolf of. See Stewart, Alexander.

Bagimond's Roll. Valuation of the benefices of the Scottish Church, made by Baiamund de Vicci, papal collector, 1276; basis of taxation until after 1660.

Bagpipes. Formerly used in many countries, not least in central and eastern Europe; first depicted in Scotland in stone carvings at *Melrose Abbey* (14th century) and *Roslin Chapel* (15th century).

Bailie. (1) Officer administering an estate. (2) Magistrate in *burgh.* (3) Person whom a granter of land authorised to give *sasine* (bailie 'in hac parte').

Baillie, Grizel (1665-1746). Daughter of *Sir Patrick Hume,* whom she fed when he was hiding in the family vault; retired to Holland with him and came back at *Revolution*; wrote poems published posthumously; married George Baillie of Jerviswoode 1692.

Baillie, Robert (1602-62). Born *Glasgow; minister* of *Kilwinning* 1631; reluctantly accepted anti-episcopal policy of *Covenanters* 1638; wrote works against *Charles I's* policy; professor at Glasgow 1642; at *Westminster Assembly; Resolutioner;* principal of Glasgow 1660; his 'Letters and Journals' an important source.

Baillie, Robert, of Jerviswoode (c. 1634-84). Opposed government of *Charles II* and plotted with English Whigs who were involved in Rye House Plot to shoot the King; fined and executed.

Baillie, William, of Letham (fl. 1640s). Natural son of Sir William B. of *Lamington;* served under Gustavus Adolphus and under *Earl of Leven* in England; defeated by *Montrose* at *Alford* and *Kilsyth;* took part in *Preston* campaign and surrendered.

Baird, Sir David (1757-1829). Born Newbyth. Fought in India against Tippoo Sahib and won battle of Seringapatam.

Baird, John Logie (1886-1946). Born *Helensburgh;* invented first practicable television system 1929, but it was superseded 1936.

Baird Lectures. Endowed 1873 by James Baird of Auchmedden; given by a *Presbyterian minister* on a subject bearing on the Church and its work.

Baithene, St (536-600). Cousin of *Columba* and his successor as Abbot of *Iona.*

Bajan. See Bejan(t).

Balantrodoch (Midlothian). (*Gaelic* 'Baile nan Trodach', 'place or stead of the warriors'.) See Temple.

Balbithan House or **Castle** (Aberdeenshire). Built on L-plan c. 1667 by William Chalmers, whose family had held lands from c. 1490; passed by marriage to James Balfour by 1696 and then through various hands; recently restored.

Balcanquhal, Walter (1548-1616). *Minister* of *St Giles', Edinburgh,* 1574; refugee in England for his opposition to episcopacy 1584-5; minister of *Trinity College Church, Edinburgh* 1598.

Balcanquhal, Walter (?1586-1645). Son of preceding; educated *Edinburgh* and Oxford; chaplain to *James VI;* attended Synod of *Dort*; personal friend of *George Heriot* and negotiator for his educational bequest; dean of Durham 1639; author of 'A Large Declaration' defending *Charles I's* policy.

Balcarres, Earldom. Estate of B. purchased 1587 by *John Lindsay* (1552-98); his 2nd son, David (1586-1641) became Lord L. of B. 1633 and his son, Alexander, was created Earl 1651; Colin, 3rd Earl (c. 1654-1723), plotted on behalf of *James VII* and fled to Holland 1690, returned to support the *Union* but joined *Jacobites* in 1715; Alexander, 6th Earl, became Earl of *Crawford* 1808.

Balcomie Castle (Fife). Built in 16th century by Learmonth family; Sir James Learmonth welcomed *Mary of Guise* there in 1538 on her arrival from France; portions survive.

Baldernock (Stirlingshire). Lands held by Galbraiths from 13th century; passed to a Hamilton; a ruined castle is on Baldowie Loch.

Baldred, St (d. ?608). Possibly disciple of *Kentigern;* had hermitage on *Bass Rock;* also associated with *Tyninghame.*
Balfour, Arthur James (1848-1930). *Secretary for Scotland* 1886; Prime Minister 1902-5; Foreign Secretary 1916-9; Earl of Balfour 1922.
Balfour House (Fife). Lands originally Balfour property, passed by 16th century to Beatons, who built house.
Balfour, Sir James, of Pittendreich (c. 1525-83). Involved in murder of *Cardinal Beaton;* a *commissary* of *Edinburgh* 1564; *Clerk Register* 1566; President of *Court of Session* 1567; probably involved in murder of *Darnley;* compiled 'Practicks', a collection of court decisions (published 1754).
Balfour, Sir James, of Denmilne and Kinnaird (c. 1598-1657). Antiquary who collected charters, especially of religious houses; knighted and appointed *Lord Lyon* 1630; officiated at coronations of *Charles I* and *Charles II;* compiled 'Annales'; his collections now in *National Library.*
Balfour, John, of Kinloch (fl. 1679). 'Called Captain Burleigh'; one of the murderers of *Archbishop Sharp;* forfeited 1683.
Balfour of Burleigh, Lordship. Created 1607 for Sir Michael Balfour; 5th Lord attainted after *'Fifteen;* attainder reversed 1868 in favour of Alexander Hugh Bruce, 6th Lord (1849-1921), who was *Secretary for Scotland* 1895-1903. See Burleigh Castle.
Balgonie Castle (Fife). Early 15th century tower built by Sir John Sibbald; passed to Sir Robert Lundie and then to *Alexander Leslie, Earl of Leven,* who reconstructed tower; sold by Earl of Leven to Balfour family 1824; later additions decayed but the old tower remained and is being restored.
Balgownie (Aberdeenshire). Brig of, across Don, built 1320 by Bishop Henry *Cheyne.*
Balgownie (*Angus*). *Burgh of barony* for Lord *Gray* 1707; hospital mentioned 15th-17th centuries.
Balhousie Castle (*Perth*). Home of Eviot family until sold to Mercers 1478, but Eviots re-acquired it and it later passed to *Hays,* ancestors of *Earls of Kinnoull;* largely superseded by 19th century house; regimental headquarters and museum of *Black Watch,* 1962.
Ballantrae (Ayrshire). *Burgh of barony* for Kennedy of Bargany 1541.
Ballantyne, James (1772-1833). At school in *Kelso* with *Sir Walter Scott;* solicitor in Kelso; printed local newspaper; printed Scott's works from 1802 and with his brother John (1774-1821) set up business in *Edinburgh;* ruined by bankruptcy of *Constable* and Co., 1826.
Ballantyne, Robert Michael (1825-94). Clerk with Hudson Bay Co; in firm of *Thomas Constable, Edinburgh,* 1848-55; wrote stories for boys.
Ballater (Aberdeenshire). Founded c. 1770 for visitors to mineral wells; *police burgh.*
Ballencrieff (East Lothian). Site of hospital called 'Red Spittal' from 13th century to 15th.
Ballengeich. N.E. of *Stirling Castle; James V* took name 'Gudeman of Ballengeich' when he wandered in disguise.
Balliol College (Oxford). Provision was made for some scholars by John de Balliol, father of *King John,* and his widow, *Devorguilla,* issued a charter constituting the college in 1282. See also Snell, John.
Balliol, Edward (?1283-1364). Elder son of *King John;* shared father's exile in France, but in 1324 England began to cultivate him as a threat to *Robert I*; in 1332, with a party of *'Disinherited',* he defeated Scots at *Dupplin* and was crowned; maintained his position for some years, with vicissitudes, and surrendered southern counties to Edward III; made last appearance in Scotland 1346.
Balliol Family. Originated at Bailleul, Normandy. Bernard appeared in Scotland under *David I,* and Henry was *Chamberlain* under *Alexander II.* John (d. 1269) married *Devorguilla* and their son became *King John.*
Balliol, John. See John, King of Scots.
Balliol's Castle. Originally on an island in Loch Doon, *Galloway;* when water-level was raised to create a reservoir for electricity production, ruins were dismantled and re-erected on the shore.
Balloch Castle. See Taymouth.
Balmanno Castle (Perthshire). Built in 16th century by George Auchinleck, who had acquired estate from Balmannos of that *ilk;* restored by *Sir Robert Lorimer* 1916-21.
Balmerino Abbey (*Cistercian*) (Fife). Founded by Ermengarde, widow of *William I,* and *Alexander II,* c. 1227; erected into *temporal lordship* for Sir James Elphinstone 1603.
Balmerino, Arthur Elphinstone, 6th Lord (1688-1746). On *Jacobite* side in 'Fifteen; escaped to continent; pardoned 1733; joined Jacobites again 1745; captured at *Culloden* and executed in London.
Balmerino, James Elphinstone, 1st Lord (c. 1553-1612). An *Octavian; Secretary of State*

1598; lost office because of alleged correspondence with the Pope.

Balmerino, John Elphinstone, 2nd Lord (d. 1649). Tried for treason 1634 because he had handled a supplication complaining of *Charles I's* arbitrary proceedings.

Balmoral Castle (Aberdeenshire). Estate acquired by Queen Victoria from *Earl of Fife*; castle built by William Smith of *Aberdeen* 1853-5 in Scottish baronial style.

Balmyle, Nicholas de (d. 1320). Held offices under *King John*; '*official*' of *St Andrews* 1297; *Chancellor* 1301; Bishop of *Dunblane* 1307; strong supporter of *Robert I*.

Balnaves, Henry (d. 1579). Educated *St Andrews* and Cologne; in touch with Swiss and German reformers; *Lord of Session* 1538; associated with murderers of *Cardinal Beaton;* prisoner in French galleys and at Rouen, where he wrote a treatise on 'Justification by Faith'.

Baltersan Castle (Ayrshire). Built in late 16th century by David Kennedy on lands acquired from nearby *Crossraguel Abbey;* now ruinous.

Balvaird Castle (Fife). 15th century building on L-plan, now in ruins; lands passed from Barclays through an heiress who married a son of Murray of *Tullibardine*.

Balvaird, Lordship. Created 1641 for Andrew Murray (d. 1644); his eldest son succeeded as 2nd Lord and also inherited titles of *Viscount Stormont* and *Lord Scone*. See Mansfield, Earldom.

Balvenie Castle (Banffshire). Perhaps originally a *Comyn* castle of 13th century, but much altered in 14th and 15th centuries, when it belonged to *Douglases;* with the fall of the *Black Douglases* in 1455 the property went to the Stewart *Earls of Atholl*, one of whom rebuilt the north part of the castle in late 16th century; the estate passed later to the Duff family who became *Earls of Fife*, and the castle was unroofed in 1724.

Balwearie Castle (Fife). William Scott licensed to build a tower 1463; now in ruins.

Bamff Castle (Perthshire). Lands held by Ramsays from early 13th century; castle incorporates 16th century tower and later additions.

Banff. Mentioned as *royal burgh* 1189x1198. Castle visited by 12th century kings; *Earls of Buchan*, as constables, acquired proprietorship, and in 1636 sold it to Robert Sharp; it was in ruins by 1746 and a later castle was built by 6th *Earl of Seafield*. A chapel was bestowed on the *Carmelite* friary by *Robert I* 1321; the friars' property was granted to *King's College, Aberdeen*, 1574. Banff had a leper-house, extinct by 1590.

Banffshire Field Club. Founded 1880 for study of 'natural sciences, archaeology etc.'

Bank of Scotland. Act for erection passed 17 July 1695, with monopoly for 21 years; first office in Mylne Square, off High Street, *Edinburgh;* absorbed Central Bank of Scotland, *Caledonian Bank* (1907), *Union Bank* (1954) and *National Commercial Bank* (1969).

Bankers, Institute of. Formed in *Edinburgh* 1875, the first such institute in the world; its aims were to improve the qualifications of banking employees and raise their status and influence.

Bannatyne Club. Founded 1823 for publication of materials relating to history and literature of Scotland; *Sir Walter Scott* first president; *David Laing* secretary from beginning until dissolution in 1861. See Thomson, Thomas.

Bannatyne Manuscript. A folio volume of almost 800 pages, constituting a unique source of a large body of Middle *Scots* poetry, including works of *Dunbar* and *Henryson;* compiled by George Bannatyne (1545-1608), an *Edinburgh* merchant who took up the collection of verse when in the country to avoid the plague in 1568; in *National Library of Scotland*.

Bannerman, John MacDonald (1901-69). As a rugby player capped for Scotland 37 times; Scottish nationalist and *Gaelic* enthusiast; stood as Liberal candidate, without success; created Lord Bannerman of Kildonan 1967.

Bannockburn, Battle of, 23-24 June 1314. Scots under *Robert I* defeated English under Edward II.

Banquho. Mythically the companion of *Macbeth;* his supposed son, Fleance, identified with Flaald, ancestor of the *Stewart* kings.

Bara (East Lothian). Hospital mentioned c. 1340.

Barbour, John (?1320-95). Archdeacon of *Aberdeen* by 1357; thrice licensed to visit Oxford and once to visit France; held financial offices in royal household; author of 'The Brus' (c. 1375), in which he drew on recollections of older men who had been associated with *Robert I*; his verses regarded as useful historical source, though his aim at a romantic quasi-epic conflicted with strict accuracy.

Barcaldine Castle *(Argyll)*. Built by *Duncan Campbell of Glenorchy* c. 1600; roofless in 19th century, but restored after 1896.

Barclay, David, of Urie (1610-86). Served under Gustavus Adolphus and returned to join

Covenanters; an *'Engager'*, but came to terms with Cromwell and sat in his parliaments; in prison briefly after *Restoration;* converted to *Quakerism.*

Barclay, John. See Bereans.

Barclay, Robert (1648-90). Son of David B; followed father into *Quakerism* 1667; wrote several books on his faith, engaged in debates and more than once imprisoned, but latterly treated with respect; a party to a scheme for a colony in New Jersey 1682.

Barclay, William (c. 1546-1608). Studied at *Aberdeen,* Paris and Bourges; professor of civil law at Port-a-Mousson; in England 1603-4; professor of civil law at Angers 1605; his most important work 'De Regno et Regali Potestate' (1600).

Barclay, William (c. 1570-1630). M.A. and M.D., Louvain; professor of humanity at Paris; practised medicine in Scotland, but returned to France and settled at Nantes; wrote 'Nepenthes, or the Vertues of Tobacco' (1614).

Bard of Brechin. See Laing, Alexander.

'Barleycorn, John'. The malt-liquor used in the making of whisky; name of poem by *Robert Burns.*

Barnbougle Castle (West Lothian). Lands held by Moubrays from 12th century until sold to *1st Earl of Haddington* 1615; bought from *Earl of Haddington* by *Sir Archibald Primrose* 1662; tower restored 1880 by *Earl of Rosebery.*

Barnweil Monument (Tarbolton, Ayrshire). Commemorates burning of the *Barns of Ayr* by *William Wallace.*

Baron Bailie. Appointed by baron to preside over his court and generally administer the *barony.*

Barons of Exchequer. Judges of *Exchequer Court* set up after *Union.*

Barony. From 12th century, lands granted by crown to a tenant-in-chief might be incorporated or erected into a barony, carrying jurisdiction and forming an economic and social unit.

Barony, Courts of. Courts for tenants of a *barony,* presided over by baron or his *bailie;* with power to settle civil disputes and to fine, imprison and execute for criminal offences, they played a useful part within the old agricultural system, when disputes were frequent between neighbours; though not abolished with other *heritable jurisdictions,* they gradually fell into desuetude.

Barr Castle (Ayrshire). 15th century tower, erected by Lockhart family and sold to Campbell of Cessnock 1670; *John Knox* preached there 1556; now used as masonic lodge.

Barra Castle (Aberdeenshire). Lands passed from family of King to Setons of Meldrum, Reids and Ramsays and finally Irvines of Drum; castle built in 17th century on earlier nucleus.

Barra Castle *(Hebrides).* See Kisimul.

Barra Hill (Aberdeenshire), **Battle of,** 24 December 1307. *Robert I* defeated John *Comyn, Earl of Buchan.*

Barrie, James Matthew (1860-1937). Son of a *Kirriemuir* weaver; became a journalist in the English midlands and then in London; although his greatest successes, which brought him fame, fortune and a baronetcy (1913), had little or no connection with Scotland, other works reflected facets of Scottish life—'Auld Licht Idylls', 'A Window in Thrums [Kirriemuir]' and 'The Little Minister'—and the whimsical 'Mary Rose' is set in the Celtic Twilight.

Barrier Act, 1697. By this act, any measure approved by the *General Assembly* of the *Church of Scotland* must be remitted to *presbyteries* and only if approved by a majority of them can it be finally passed by the Assembly

Bartholomew, John George (1860-1920). Managed his father's firm, *Edinburgh* Geographical Institute, founded 1826; his 'Times Survey Atlas of the World' completed 1921.

Barton, Andrew (d. 1511). Son of John B., a *Leith* seaman who had commanded one of *James III's* ships, Andrew was engaged with his brothers in privateering as well as peaceful commerce in the 1490s; he was so destructive of English shipping in 1511 that Henry VIII sent Sir Edward Howard against him, and in the engagement which followed Andrew lost both his ships and was fatally wounded.

Barton, Robert (c. 1470-1540). Brother of preceding; from privateering and commerce he went on to lending money to nobles and others, with the result that he acquired extensive estates, especially Over Barnton; commander in expedition to help King Hans of Denmark 1502 and in western isles 1504 and 1505; served in French navy 1512; favourable to French alliance and to *John, Duke of Albany;* who made him *Comptroller* 1516; *Treasurer* 1529.

'Basilikon Doron'. Written by *James VI* for the instruction of his son *Henry,* it outlines his ideas of kingcraft; first printed, privately, 1599; revised edition published 1603.

Basket-Hilted Broadsword. Introduced in 17th century, when armour had gone out of use and the steel gauntlet had disappeared; retained as official sword of officers in Scottish regiments.

Bassandyne, Thomas (d. 1577). Studied printing in Leyden and by 1567 was printer and bookseller in *Edinburgh;* in 1576, with Alexander Arbuthnot, licensed by *Privy Council* to print Bible; New Testament appeared 1576; completed 1579.

Bass Rock. Basaltic rock, 320 feet high, at entrance to Firth of Forth, always famed as breeding-place of gannets; had hermitage of St *Baldred* and later a chapel; *James I* waited on the Bass for the ship which was to take him to France; belonged for centuries to *Lauder family;* used as prison for *Covenanters;* four *Jacobites,* imprisoned here in 1691, overpowered their guard and held the rock for King James VII until 1694.

Bathgate (West Lothian). Lands granted by *Robert I* to *Walter Stewart,* his son-in-law; seat of constabulary or *sheriff*dom in later middle ages; *burgh of barony* for Hamilton of Bathgate 1663, reconstituted 1824 and *police burgh* 1865.

Bathgate Academy. John Newlands, a native of *Bathgate,* was a carpenter who emigrated to Jamaica, where he became a successful and wealthy planter; on his death in 1799 he left the bulk of his fortune to erect a free school in the parish; reorganised 1869 and superseded by comprehensive school 1967.

Battle of the Shirts. See Shirts, Battle of.

Baugé, Battle of, 22 March 1421. Scots and French under *John Stewart, Earl of Buchan,* defeated English.

Bavelaw Castle (Midlothian). Lands granted 1628 to Laurence Scott of Harperrig on resignation of Walter *Dundas*; 17th century structure, restored.

Bawbee. A halfpenny; originally a coin worth 3 Scots pence and perhaps named from Alexander Orrok of Sillebawbe, *mint*-master 1538.

'Bawbee'. Daily morning newspaper which ran for a few issues in *Edinburgh* in 1857, sold for a halfpenny.

'Beacon'. Published in *Edinburgh* January-September 1821; virulently pro-*Tory.*

Bean. Alleged first bishop of *Mortlach,* 11th century.

Bean, Sawney. Said to have been a native of East Lothian who settled in a cave at Bennane Head, near Ballantrae, in the reign of *James I* (or perhaps *James VI)* and lived by robbery, murder and cannibalism.

Beardmore, William (1856-1936). Born Greenwich, of *Glasgow* father; apprenticed at Parkhead Forge, founded by *David Napier* and acquired by his father; his firm of William B. and Co., besides building many naval ships and liners, built the R 34, first airship to make double crossing of Atlantic; yard closed 1930; Beardmore created Lord Invernairn 1921.

Beaton, David (?1494-1546). Nephew of *James B.* (I); *Commendator* of *Arbroath* 1524; ambassador to France 1519, 1533, 1538; Bishop of Mirepoix in France 1537; Cardinal 1538; Archbishop of *St Andrews* 1539; leader of French and papal party; *Chancellor* 1543; his anti-English policy led to retaliation in the shape of the *Rough Wooing,* and his prosecutions of *heretics* added to his unpopularity; his murder (29 May 1546) was partly an act of vengeance for the execution of *George Wishart.*

Beaton, James (I) (c. 1480-1539). *Commendator* of *Dunfermline* 1504; *Treasurer* 1505-9; Archbishop of Glasgow 1509; *Chancellor* 1513-26; Archbishop of *St Andrews* 1522; a supporter of the French connection and an element of stability in the minority of *James V,* but not in much favour with that King after he began to rule in person.

Beaton, James (II) (c. 1523-1603). Nephew of *Cardinal David Beaton,* whom he succeeded as *Commendator* of *Arbroath* 1543; Archbishop of *Glasgow* 1551; attached to French cause and on the success of the reformers in 1560 went off to France, taking with him the records of his see and depriving the conservatives of a leader; acted as agent for Queen *Mary* in France and also similarly served successive administrations under *James VI;* forfeited 1567 but restored partially 1587 and wholly 1598.

Beaton, Mary (c. 1543-c. 1597). One of the 'Queen's *Maries';* daughter of Robert B. of Creich and niece of *Cardinal B;* married Alexander Ogilvy of Boyne 1566.

Beaton's Tower. In grounds of *Melville House,* Fife; remains of residence built by Archbishops *James Beaton* and *David Beaton.*

Beattie, James (1735-1803). Schoolmaster of *Fordoun* 1753-8; professor of moral philosophy, *Marischal College, Aberdeen,* 1760; wrote 'Essay on Truth' and 'Elements of Moral Sciences', but gained more fame by his poetry, especially 'The Minstrel' (1773-4).

Beaufort, Joan. See Joan.

Beauly (or Fraserdale or Lovat). *Burgh of regality* for Mackenzie of Prestonhall 1704.

Beauly Priory (*Valliscaulian,* later *Cistercian*) (Inverness-shire). Probably founded c. 1230;

Valliscaulian order finally superseded by Cistercian 1510 and house thereafter closely associated with *Kinloss;* granted to bishopric of *Ross* 1634, but passed to Lord *Lovat* later; roofless church remains.

Bedesman. Originally a man endowed to pray for others; later a licensed beggar. See also King's Bedesmen.

Beehive Huts. Primitive dwellings, roofed by bringing in successive courses of stones until they completed a dome; best-known examples on *Eileach an Naoimh.*

Begg, James (1808-83). Born New Monkland; *minister* of *Paisley* and Liberton and, after *Disruption,* in *Free Church* at Newington, *Edinburgh;* investigated housing conditions in Edinburgh and *Glasgow* and urged improvements; also advocated temperance, better education and devolution for Scotland.

Beggars' Benison. 18th century clubs with professedly erotic interests issued diplomas of highly indecent character.

'Beggar's mantle'. Term said to have been applied by *James VI* to Fife, which, with its flourishing chain of coastal *burghs,* was like a beggar's mantle with a fringe of pearls.

Beggars' Summons. Posted on doors of friaries 1 January 1559 or earlier, ordering friars to quit in favour of the poor at *Whitsunday* term following.

Bejan, Bejant. A first-year student at *St Andrews* and *Aberdeen.*

Belhaven, John Hamilton, 2nd Lord (1656-1708). In 1681 his opposition to the prospective accession of *James VII* led to a term of imprisonment; active on behalf of *William of Orange* 1689; subscribed £1000 to the *Company of Scotland*; associated with *Jacobites* and strenuously opposed *Union;* an early agrarian *'Improver'.*

Belhaven, Lordship. Created 1647 for Sir John Hamilton of Broomhouse.

Bell (or Abell), Adam (16th century). A canon of *Inchaffray* who transferred to the Observantine Friars at *Jedburgh*; wrote chronicle called 'The Wheel of Time' which contains useful material on reign of *James V.*

Bell, Alexander Graham (1847-1922). Born *Edinburgh;* professor of vocal physiology at Boston, U.S.A., 1873; invented telephone 1876.

Bell, Andrew (1753-1832). Born *St Andrews;* developed a pupil-teacher system of education while a chaplain at Madras; his methods widely adopted; left bequests for schools (including *Madras College,* St Andrews) and for chairs of education in *Edinburgh* and St Andrews.

Bell, Sir Charles (1774-1842). Born *Edinburgh;* surgeon, *Edinburgh Royal Infirmary;* professor of anatomical surgery, Royal College of Surgeons, London, 1824; principal of medical school, University College, London, 1828; professor of surgery, Edinburgh, 1836; pioneered work on nervous system.

Bell, Henry (1767-1830). Designed the '*Comet*', the first vessel to be propelled by steam on a navigable river in Europe, built at *Port Glasgow* 1812.

Bell, Patrick (1799-1869). Born *Auchterhouse; minister* of Carmylie, *Arbroath;* invented reaping machine.

Bell Rock. Tidal rock 12 miles S.E. of *Arbroath* and a prime danger to shipping. Legend, immortalised by Southey in 'The Inchcape Rock', related that an abbot of Arbroath fixed a bell as a warning signal and that it was cut away by a pirate who himself perished on the rock. Lighthouse erected 1808-11. See Stevenson, Robert.

'Bell-the-Cat'. See Angus, Archibald Douglas, 5th Earl of.

Bellenden, John (c. 1490-c. 1550). D.D. of Paris; *archdeacon* of *Moray* 1533; held office under *James V,* on whose commission he translated *Boece's* 'History' (1536); also translated part of Livy.

Bellenden, Sir John, of Auchnoule (d. 1577). Son of *Thomas B.,* whom he succeeded as *Justice-Clerk* 1547; joined *Confederate Lords* 1567 and helped to frame *Pacification of Perth* 1573.

Bellenden, Sir Lewis, of Auchnoule (d. 1591). Son of preceding, whom he succeeded as *Justice-Clerk; Lord of Session* 1584; in Denmark with *James VI,* 1589-90.

Bellenden, Robert (fl. 1500). As Abbot of *Holyrood* founded hospital of St Leonard and chapel of St *Ninian* in North *Leith;* built bridge to join North and South Leith; made repairs to his abbey; in 1500, despairing of the *Augustinian* order, he became a *Carthusian.*

Bellenden, Thomas, of Auchnoule (d. 1547). Son of Patrick Bellenden, parish clerk of *Holyrood; Lord of Session* 1535; *Justice-Clerk* 1539.

Belliehill (*Moray*). *Burgh of barony* for *Earl of Huntly* 1500.

Belsh and Company. Banking firm in *Stirling,* founded 1804; failed 1806.

Beltane *(Gaelic* 'Bealltuinn' = 'mouth of the beacon fire'). Festival marking beginning of summer, still observed especially at *Peebles,* with a 'Beltane Queen' and riding of the marches.

Belted Plaid. See Breacan-an-fhéilidh.

Bemersyde (Berwickshire). On Tweed near *Dryburgh;* lands held by *Haigs* in 12th century; 16th century tower forms part of later mansion, as altered and enlarged in 1691, 1761 and 1796; alienated from Haigs in 19th century, but presented by nation to *Field Marshal Earl Haig.*

Ben Line Shipping Company. Alexander and William Thomson, sons of James Thomson, an *Edinburgh* builder, acquired first ship 1839; firm became William Thomson and Co. 1847; the first 'Ben' was the 'Bencleuch' of 1853, but the practice of naming ships after mountains did not become general until 1890s; have maintained Far Eastern Trade.

Ben Nevis Observatory. Built by Scottish Meteorological Society 1881. See Wilson, Charles Thomson Rees.

Benedictine Order. See Coldingham, Dunfermline, Eynhallow, Iona, May, Pluscarden, Rhynd, Urquhart.

Benholm's Tower. In Nethergate, *Aberdeen;* built by Sir Robert Keith of Benholm, brother of *5th Earl Marischal,* c. 1610, on Z-plan; acquired by Town Council 1918.

Benrig, Battle of, 1382. Scots under George, Earl of *Dunbar* and *March,* defeated English under Baron of Greystoke when he was on his way to occupy *Roxburgh* Castle.

Bereans. Sect founded by John Barclay (1734-98), assistant *minister* of *Fettercairn,* who was suspected of heresy and had to obtain ordination in England. He then returned to *Edinburgh* and founded a new church, known as Bereans (from Acts xvii, 10 ff.), which stressed the supernatural and mystical in Calvinism. After his death the body dwindled and was largely absorbed in *Congregationalism.*

Beregonium. Ptolemy's geography notes a Rerigonium, apparently in *Galloway*; the name, mis-read, was erroneously placed in *Lochaber* and later attached to a hill-fort in Benderloch, properly Dun-mac-Uisneach.

Bernard de Linton (d. 1331). *Parson* of Mordington 1296; *Chancellor* of *Robert I* c. 1308-28; Abbot of *Arbroath* 1311; credited with drafting *Declaration of Arbroath* and other state papers; Bishop of *Isles* 1328.

Berne Manuscript. Volume containing old laws and legal styles, dating from c. 1300, recovered in 1814 from Public Library at Berne and now in *Register House.*

Bernera Barracks. At Glenelg; built after *Glenshiel* to accommodate 200 soldiers; after '*Forty-Five* garrison gradually reduced; building abandoned c. 1790.

Bernham, David de (d. 1253). Bishop of *St Andrews* 1239-53; his Pontifical, recording his consecration of many churches, has been preserved.

Berowald. See Innes.

Bertha. Roman camp on site of later town of *Perth.*

Bervie. See Inverbervie.

Berwick. *Burgh* in existence by c. 1120; taken by English 1296 and then changed hands many times down to 1482, when it finally fell to England; medieval castle survived to be destroyed when railway was built, but 16th century walls of town survive.

Berwick, Duke of. See James.

Berwick Friaries. (1) *Augustinian,* in existence by 1299. (2) *Carmelite,* allegedly founded 1270. (3) *Dominican,* founded by *Alexander II* before 1141. (4) Conventual *Franciscan,* founded c. 1231. (5) Of the Sack, founded by 1267. See Friars of the Sack. (6) *Trinitarian,* founded before c. 1240.

Berwick Hospitals. (1) St. Edward's, in existence by 1234; passed to *Trinitarian* friars. (2) St Leonard's, in existence 1297. (3) St Mary Magdalene's, in existence 1296; later only a chapel, to which *Segden* was annexed. (4) Leper house, in existence 1240. (5) Maison Dieu, founded in reign of *Alexander III.*

Berwick Nunnery (*Cistercian*). Described as foundation of *David I.*

Berwick, Pacification of. See Bishops' Wars.

Berwick, Treaties of. (1) 3 October 1357. *David II* to be released for ransom of 100,000 merks. (2) 27 February 1560. Queen Elizabeth of England agreed to support *Lords of the Congregation* against French forces of *Mary of Guise.*

Berwickshire Naturalists' Club. Founded 1831 for study of natural history and antiquities of county and adjacent districts.

Bethoc. Daughter of *Malcolm II;* married *Crinan, Abbot of Dunkeld,* and was mother of *Duncan I.*

Bethoc. Daughter of *Donald Bane*; her daughter by Huctred of Tynedale married Richard *Comyn,* and their descendant, John Comyn, was a *Competitor* in 1291.

'Betty Burke'. Name assumed by *Charles Edward* when he was disguised as a maidservant.

Bible. An Act of 1543 permitted use of scriptures in vernacular. No version in Scots was ever printed, though a Scottish version of an English translation has survived in MS. from early 16th century. Tyndale's New Testament arrived in Scotland c. 1527 and was succeeded by Coverdale's version and the 'Geneva' version, the first to be printed in Scotland (1579). King James's version (1611) was never formally authorised in Scotland, but made rapid headway. Kirke's Irish version was in use in Highlands from 1690. *Gaelic* edition of New Testament published 1767, of Old Testament 1783-1801.

Bier-Rite Trial. In a search for a murderer, suspects were called to approach body of victim; if fresh blood appeared, the person present was held to be guilty; used so late as 1688.

Biggar (Lanarkshire). *Burgh of barony* for Fleming of Biggar 1451; *collegiate church* founded by Malcolm, Lord Fleming, 1546; St Leonard's hospital is mentioned 1446 and an almshouse may later have been attached, in its place, to the collegiate church; *Grammar School* began in connection with collegiate church and was taken over by Town Council.

Biggar, Battle of, 1297. Victory of Scots under *William Wallace* over English.

Biggar Jug. Archery trophy competed for by *Royal Company of Archers* at Biggar; money prize instituted 1852, silver jug substituted c. 1870.

Billings, Robert William (1813-74). Born London; architect who worked on restoration of buildings in England and Scotland and illustrated architectural works; published 'Baronial and Ecclesiastical Antiquities of Scotland' (1845-52).

Binning, Lordship. Created 1613 for *Thomas Hamilton,* later 1st *Earl of Haddington.*

Binns (West Lothian). Part of house dates from 1478 and some plaster ceilings from 1612-30, but it is mainly c. 1800; property of *Sir Thomas Dalyell*; presented to *National Trust* 1944.

'Bird Catchers'. See Royal Scots Greys.

Birgham, Treaty of, 18 July 1290. Between Scotland and England for marriage of *Margaret, Maid of Norway,* to Edward, son of Edward I; safeguarded rights of Scotland, though with some ambiguity.

Birlaymen. See Burlaw Courts.

Birnie (Moray). For a time the seat of bishops of *Moray* in 12th century; part of parish church dates from that period. See Ronnel Bell.

Birrel, Robert (fl. c. 1567-1605). *Edinburgh burgess* whose Diary refers to events of 1532-1605 without partisan comment.

Birrens (Dumfriesshire). Roman fort and camp used intermittently from late 1st century to early 3rd, sometimes as outpost of frontier further south.

Birsay (Orkney). The Brough of B., a tidal island, has early remains including probably those of the residence of *Earl Thorfinn* and the 'minster' or cathedral he built c. 1060; on the Mainland are the remains of a palace built by *Robert Stewart, Earl of Orkney.*

Birth Brieves. Letters patent providing pedigrees, kept by *Lyon* in his Public Register of all Genealogies and Birthbrieves, and also in the archives of certain local authorities, notably the *burgh* of *Aberdeen*; used generally by Scots going overseas.

Births, Marriages and Deaths, Registration of. Parochial registers had previously recorded baptisms, marriages and burials; compulsory registration in civil registers began in 1855, under supervision of *Registrar General.*

'Bishop of the Scots'. Title of bishops of *St Andrews* until 13th century, indicating their early pre-eminence among Scottish bishops.

Bishoprics. See Abercorn, Aberdeen, Abernethy, Argyll, Brechin, Caithness, Dunblane, Dunkeld, Edinburgh, Galloway, Glasgow, Isles, Moray, Orkney, Ross, St Andrews.

Bishops' Wars. (1) May-June 1639. *Charles I's* forces reached Border to find *Covenanters* encamped on Duns Law; negotiations led to Pacification of Berwick. (2) August-September 1640. Scots crossed Border and occupied Newcastle; little fighting, but peace not concluded until Treaty of Ripon, June 1641.

Bisset, Baldred (fl. 1300). '*Official*' of *St Andrews* and *parson* of *Kinghorn* in 1280s; delegate to papal court to present Scottish case against England 1301.

'Black Acts', May 1584. Reaffirmed episcopal government and asserted supremacy of King, *Parliament* and *Council* over all *estates,* spiritual and temporal.

Black, Adam (1784-1874). Publisher of '*Encyclopaedia Britannica*'; Lord *Provost* of *Edinburgh*; Liberal M.P. for city 1856-65.

'Black Agnes'. Daughter of *Thomas Randolph, Earl of Moray*; defended *Dunbar Castle* against Earls of Salisbury and Arundel 1338.

Black and Red Books of Clanranald. *Gaelic* MSS compiled mainly in 17th century by the MacMhuirich family, bards to Clanranald, containing much genealogical matter and an account of the *Montrose* wars.

'Black Beard'. Patrick, 8th *Earl of Dunbar* (or *March*), a *Competitor* in 1291.

'Black Bitches'. Inhabitants of *Linlithgow*; a black bitch (said to have been a hound of *James IV*) figures on the *burgh* coat of arms.

Black Book. Contains account of parliamentary proceedings 1357-1402.

Black Book of Taymouth. History of the Campbells of Glenorchy 1432-1648; important source for social and economic history of Highlands.

Black Castle. (1) Near Moulin, Perthshire, said to have been begun by Sir John Campbell of Lochawe, to whom *Robert I* granted the lands. (2) *Barcaldine Castle*, Benderloch, *Argyll*.

Black Cattle. Usual term for native Highland cattle in 18th and early 19th centuries; there is no reason to believe that they were literally black; they were more likely dark red. See Drove Roads, Trysts.

Black Chanter of Cluny. A pipe *chanter* preserved at Cluny Castle, said to have fallen from heaven to replace one lost at the *Clan Fight at Perth*.

'Black Colonel'. See Farquharson, John, of Inverey.

'Black Comyn' (d. ? 1300). See Comyn, John, Lord of Badenoch.

Black Death. Struck England in August 1348 and reached Scotland 1349-50; further attacks of plague followed in 1362, 1379, 1417 and many later years down to the mid-17th century.

'Black Dinner', 28 November 1440. William, 6th *Earl of Douglas*, and his brother, were invited by *Sir William Crichton* to a meal with the young *James II* in *Edinburgh Castle*; at the end of the meal, a black bull's head was placed on the table, whereupon the Douglases were seized and beheaded.

Black Douglases. 'The Black Douglas' was *Sir James Douglas*. The term was applied to the senior branch of the family, which ended with the *9th Earl of Douglas*, to distinguish them from the Red Douglases or *Earls of Angus*.

'Black Duncan of the Cowl'. See Campbell, Duncan, of Glenorchy.

Black Dwarf. David Ritchie, born c. 1735 in parish of *Stobo*; only 3½ feet tall and known as 'Bowed Davie', he was strong and misanthropic; lived in a cottage at Manor, near *Peebles*, with a special 'Dwarf's Door'; died 1811.

Black Friars. See Dominicans.

Black Friday, 6 December 1745. *Charles Edward* and his army retired from Derby.

Black, Joseph (1728-99). Born Bordeaux, son of Ulster Scot; student and assistant of *Cullen* at *Glasgow*; professor of medicine, first in Glasgow, then in *Edinburgh*; his investigations of latent heat and specific heat contributed to development of steam engine.

Black Knight of Lorne. See Stewart, Sir James.

Black Parliament, August 1320. William de *Soules* and a dozen more persons tried for conspiracy against *Robert I*.

Black Rood of Scotland. Reliquary containing piece of True Cross, brought to Scotland by *Queen Margaret* and presented to *Holyrood* Abbey by *David I*. Seized by Edward I, it is said to have been restored in 1328 and lost again at *Neville's Cross*. It was long preserved at Durham, but lost at *Reformation*.

Black Saturday. (1) 30 July 1547. Surrender to the French of *St Andrews Castle*, held by murderers of *Cardinal Beaton*. (2) 10 September 1547. *Battle of Pinkie*.

Black Stone. Stone on which students sat while being examined at *St Andrews*, first mentioned 1524.

'Black Turnpike'. At head of Kennedy's Close, on S. side of High Street of *Edinburgh* between *Tron* and *Mercat Cross*; erroneously supposed to have been town house of *Sir Simon Preston*, actually town house of bishops of *Dunkeld*, dating from 15th century; *George Buchanan* died there; demolished 1788.

Black Watch Regiment (43rd, later 42nd). Formed 1739 from six independent companies of Highlanders enlisted in 1725 by *General Wade* to police the Highlands. First British Regiment to wear Highland uniform, and named 'The Black Watch' from the contrast between their dark tartan and the 'Redcoats'. See Balhousie Castle.

Blackadder, Adam (d. 1696). Son of *John B., elder*; apprenticed to merchant in *Stirling*; frequently imprisoned as a *Covenanter*; wrote account of his father.

Blackadder, John, elder (1615-86). *Minister* of Troqueer; deprived 1662; preached in *conventicles*; outlawed 1674 and fled to Rotterdam; returned 1679; imprisoned on *Bass Rock* 1681 and died there.

Blackadder, John, younger (1664-1729). Son of preceding; served in *Cameronian regiment* 1689; promoted to command 1709.

Blackadder, Robert (c. 1445-1508). Canon of *Glasgow* and *parson* of *Lasswade*; elected Bishop of *Aberdeen* 1480, but not consecrated; provided to bishopric of Glasgow 1483; Archbishop 1492; several times an envoy to France, Spain and England; died on pilgrimage to Holy Land.

Blackford (Perthshire). *Burgh of barony* for Graham of Fintray 1706.

Blackhall, Gilbert (fl. 1637-66). Roman Catholic missionary in N.E. c. 1637-43; wrote 'Breiffe Narrative of the services done to three noble ladyes' [members of families of Errol and Aboyne].

Blackie, John Stuart (1809-95). Born *Glasgow*; professor of *humanity, Aberdeen,* 1841, and of Greek, *Edinburgh,* 1852; his sentimental attachment to Celtic culture led to foundation of chair of Celtic at Edinburgh 1882 and also involved him in political agitation on behalf of Highlanders.

Blackness (West Lothian). Formerly the port of *Linlithgow*; a medieval castle was the scene of a meeting when *James III* and his rebellious nobles effected a temporary pacification (1488); used as royal prison; maintenance of fortress guaranteed 1707; transformed into armaments depot in 1870s.

Blacksmith's Dues. Payment at harvest time of local blacksmith for his year's work, by, e.g., a load of sheaves of corn, every seventh stook, the head of every *mart,* or sheepskins.

Blackwood, Adam (1539-1613). Trained at Paris and Toulouse as lawyer and philosopher and wrote on political theory in opposition to the ideas of resistance advocated by *George Buchanan*; published account of sufferings of *Mary,* Queen of Scots.

Blackwood, William (1776-1834). Antiquarian bookseller in *Edinburgh;* entered publishing and in 1817 started his famous '*Magazine*', with a *Tory* tone in opposition to the *'Edinburgh Review'* and with contributors including *John Wilson, James Hogg, J.G. Lockhart* and *David Macbeth Moir.*

'Blackwood's Magazine'. Founded by *William Blackwood*; successive editors were his eldest son, Alexander (d. 1845), Alexander's brother, John (d. 1879), John's nephew, William (d. 1912), William's nephew, George William (d. 1942), George William's brother, James (retired 1948) and James's son, Douglas, with whose retiral in 1976 the succession ended.

Blaeu's Atlas. See Gordon, Robert, and Pont, Timothy.

Blair Castle (Ayrshire). 15th century tower with 17th century additions, belonging to family of Blair.

Blair Castle (or **Blair Atholl**) (Perthshire). Part supposed to have been built by *John Comyn, Lord of Badenoch,* 1269; later work by successive families who held *Earldom of Atholl*; garrisoned 1689 by *Viscount Dundee,* whose body was brought to it after *Killiecrankie*; occupied 1745 by government troops and besieged by *Lord George Murray*; restored and extended in 19th century.

Blair, Hugh (1718-1800). Born *Edinburgh, minister* of Collessie, *Canongate* (1743), Lady Yester's (1754) and *St Giles'* (1758); professor of rhetoric and belles lettres, Edinburgh, 1762-83; associated with notable writers of the day and published lectures and sermons.

Blair, James (1656-1743). Probably born in *Edinburgh; minister* of *Cranston;* emigrated to Virginia 1685 and became commissary of the Bishop of London in the colonies; founded William and Mary College 1693; Governor of Virginia 1740-1.

Blair, Robert (1699-1746). *Minister* of Athelstaneford 1731; wrote successful poem, 'The Grave'.

Blairadam Club. Founded by William Adam (1731-1839), a judge, with *Sir Walter Scott* and others, to meet at weekends at his home, Blairadam, Kinross, 1816.

Blairgowrie (Perthshire). *Burgh of barony* for Drummond of Blair 1634; *police burgh* 1862.

Blairs College. On Dee, 6 miles S.W. of *Aberdeen*; estate given to Roman Catholic Church in 1829 to house a seminary; seminaries had previously existed at Loch Morar (1714), Scalan (1717-99), Guidale (1737-46), Buorblach, *Aquhorthies* and *Lismore* (from 1801); the two last-named were united in 1829 to become St Mary's College at Blairs; the college has many historic treasures, but the archives formerly there are now in Columba House, *Edinburgh.* See Menzies, John.

Blane, St. Said to have been born in Bute c. 565 and trained by his uncle St Catan in the monastery of Kingarth there; credited with missions in southern Scotland and northern England and with foundation of church at *Dunblane* c. 602.

Blane, Sir Gilbert (1749-1843). M.D. *Glasgow;*

physician in navy from 1779; did much for sanitary conditions on ships and for health of seamen; baronet 1812; physician to George IV.

Blantyre (Lanarkshire). *Burgh of barony* for Lord Blantyre 1599; developed as centre of *cotton* industry from 1785.

Blantyre Priory (*Augustinian*). Founded by Patrick, *Earl of Dunbar*, 1239x1248; dependency of *Jedburgh Abbey*; erected into *temporal lordship* 1599 for *Walter Stewart*, who became Lord Blantyre 1606.

Blew Stane. Huge boulder formerly below gates of *Edinburgh Castle*, under present esplanade; site of executions.

Blind Harry. See Harry the Minstrel.

Bloody Banner. A covenanting banner inscribed, 'No quarter for the active enemies of the *Covenant*', preserved in the Museum of the *Cameronian Regiment* at *Lanark*.

'Bloody Vespers'. Fight between followers of William Innes and those of Alexander Dunbar in *Elgin Cathedral* 1 January 1555.

Blue Blanket. Flag of the *craftsmen* of *Edinburgh*, under which they marched to battle and rose to defend their privileges; said to have been presented by *James III;* now in *Trades Maiden Hospital.*

Blue Gowns. See King's Bedesmen.

Blue Hackle. Granted to *Queen's Own Cameron Highlanders* in 1940, when the kilt ceased to be the dress for active service; now worn by *Queen's Own Highlanders*, who incorporate *Seaforths*.

'Bluidy Clavers'. See Graham, John, of Claverhouse.

'Bluidy Mackenzie'. See Mackenzie, Sir George, of Rosehaugh.

Board of Agriculture. Set up in 1911 to take over functions of older Boards of Agriculture and Fisheries and *Congested Districts Board.*

Board of Commissioners in Lunacy. Appointed 1857; title changed in 1913 to General Board of Control for Scotland.

Board of Supervision. Erected 1845 to administer *Poor Law*; superseded in 1894 by Local Government Board and in 1919 by Board of Health.

Board of Trustees for Manufactures. Set up 1727 to administer revenues available in terms of Treaty of *Union* of 1707 in favour of *linen* and fishing industries. Wound up 1844 and residual funds devoted to *National Gallery.*

Boar's Chase (or Cursus Apri). A tract of land in and around *St Andrews*, named from a great wild boar which terrorised the district, forming part of the ancient endowment of the church of St Andrews and re-granted to it by *Alexander I.*

Boath Dovecot. A 17th century dovecot at *Auldearn*, on site of ancient castle; presented to *National Trust* 1947.

'Bobbing John'. See Mar, John Erskine, 11th Earl of.

Bodle. A 17th century copper coin worth 2 pence.

Boece, Hector (c. 1465-1536). Professor at Montaigu (1492-8) and principal of *King's College, Aberdeen*; wrote 'Lives of the Bishops of Aberdeen' (1522) and 'History of Scotland' (1527), the latter under royal patronage but marked by extreme credulity and much invention.

Boethius. Latin version of *Boece.*

Boharm (Banffshire). Hospital 'beside the bridge of Spey' founded by Muriel de Polloc before 1235.

Boisil, St (d. 664). Abbot of Old *Melrose;* his name preserved in St Boswell's.

Boll. Measure of capacity, containing 4 firlots; equated with 6 bushels.

Bolton (East Lothian). Belonged to St Hilaries and Viponts before passing to *Lord Haliburton* c. 1450, then the *Earls of Bothwell* and the Maitlands; the *Earl of Lauderdale* was Lord Bolton (1624).

Bolton Hearse. Dates from 1785; used for members of family of *Robert Burns;* used until 1844; transferred to *Royal Scottish Museum* 1932.

Bombie (Kirkcudbright). Belonged from 15th century to Maclellans, who became *Lords Kirkcudbright.*

Bonaly Friday Club. Founded 1842 by sons of members of *Friday Club*, to meet at Bonaly, Lord *Cockburn's* house near Colinton.

Bonar, Horatius (1808-89). *Minister* of *Kelso*; joined *Free Church*; minister of Chalmers Memorial Church, *Edinburgh*, 1866; edited periodicals and wrote hymns.

Bonarness (or **Ardgay**) (Ross). *Burgh of barony* for Ross of Balnagowan 1686.

Bonawe *(Argyll)*. Ironworks founded 1753 and operated, with some intermission, until c. 1870.

Bonds of Manrent, Maintenance and Alliance. By a Bond of Manrent a man of lesser rank undertook to assist a more powerful one, who reciprocated by a Bond of Maintenance promising him protection. A Bond of Alliance, between families of similar status, was aimed at contributing to peace and stability, but could also foster feuds.

Bone, Sir Muirhead (1876-1953). Born *Glasgow;* studied art there; moved to London 1901; famed for his etchings, drypoints and portraits; an official artist in both World Wars.

Bo'ness (or Borrowstounness) (West Lothian). *Burgh of regality* for *Duchess of Hamilton* 1668; *police burgh* 1880.

Boniface, St. Associated with *Rosemarkie,* he has been identified with Curitan, who in early 8th century was active in the organisation of the church in *Pict*land.

Bonnet Laird. Properly a farmer owning his farm, or the proprietor of a small estate, but sometimes used of a farmer who had a long lease for a small duty.

Bonnet Piece. Gold *ducat* of *James V.*

Bonnie Dundee. See Graham, John, of Claverhouse.

Bonnie Earl o' Moray. See Moray, James Stewart, Earl of.

Bonnymuir Skirmish, April 1820. A body of radical weavers from *Glasgow* was routed near *Falkirk* by detachment of hussars and yeomanry.

Bonnyrigg (Midlothian). *Police burgh* 1862.

Book of Canons. See Code of Canons.

Book of Common Order. Service book of congregation of English exiles at Geneva; introduced into Scotland from 1560, it largely superseded English Prayer Book. Known later as '*Knox's* Liturgy', it was prescribed by the *General Assembly* in 1562 and 1564 and remained the official service-book for eighty years. A similar book was not officially authorised again until 1928, followed by another in 1940.

Book of the Dean of Lismore. Anthology of *Gaelic* verse (poems by Scottish authors, poems by Irish authors, and Ossianic ballads), compiled by *James MacGregor,* dean of *Lismore,* and his brother Duncan, 1512-26. Now in *National Library of Scotland.*

Books of Council and Session. Register of Deeds of *Court of Session,* beginning 1554.

Books of Discipline. See Discipline.

Boorlaw Court, Boorlaw Men. See Burlaw.

Border Commission. Set up by *James VI,* 1605, consisting of five Scottish and five English justices, to put down disorder. It had at its disposal a body of 25 mounted police under Sir William Cranston.

Border Counties Railway. From Riccarton Junction to the Border, where it joined the Carlisle-Newcastle line. Amalgamated with *North British* 1860.

Borestone. Stone with a hole in which a standard was set. There are fragments of the alleged borestone of *Robert I* at *Bannockburn,* and one is pointed out at *Sheriffmuir.* A stone built into the wall of Morningside Church, *Edinburgh,* was said, quite without foundation, to have been used for a muster before *Flodden.*

Boroughmuir. See Burgh Muir.

Borrowstounness. See Bo'ness.

Borthwick (Midlothian). Castle, built probably by 1st Lord B. c. 1430, is a massive structure, vaulted throughout and still inhabited; Queen *Mary* and *Bothwell* were besieged there by *Confederate Lords* 1567; suffered damage in Cromwellian attack; during Second World War it housed treasures from *National Galleries* and records from *Registrar General's* Department.

Borthwick, Sir John (fl. 1540-60). Fled to England to avoid punishment for heresy, but condemned in absence and burned in effigy, 1540; served Henry VIII on various missions; returned to Scotland and had his sentence revoked 1561.

Borthwick, Lordship. Created for Sir William Borthwick c. 1430. From death of 10th Lord (1674-5) title was dormant until 1762; again dormant 1772-1870 and from 1910.

Boston, Thomas (1677-1732). Son of covenanting *minister* who was imprisoned; minister of Simprim, *Ettrick* and *Closeburn;* influenced by *Cameronian* tradition and conservative theology, which he enunciated in his 'Fourfold State of Man' (1720); prepared way for *First Secession.*

Boswell, Alexander (1706-82). Graduated Leyden 1727; *advocate* 1729; *Lord of Session* (Auchinleck), 1754.

Boswell, Sir Alexander (1775-1822). Son of *James B;* famous for his library and printing press; killed in duel.

Boswell Family. Originated with a Norman in *William I's* reign; their first lands were in Berwickshire, but by marriage they acquired Auchterderran and Balmuto (Fife) in 14th century; received *Auchinleck* (Ayrshire) from *James IV.*

Boswell, James (1740-95). Son of *Alexander B;* entered London society 1760; studied law, but more interested in society of litterateurs; met Samuel Johnson 1763 and brought him to Scotland 1773; visited Corsica (1765) and Ireland (1769); called to English bar 1786; 'Life of Johnson' published 1791.

Botanic Gardens (*Edinburgh*). Originated in *Physic Gardens* which appeared in Edinburgh from 1656 onwards, and particularly one established at *Holyrood* 1670; moved to site of present Haddington Place 1763 and to Inverleith 1820.

Bothans (or *Yester*) **Collegiate Church** (East Lothian). Founded 1421 on petition of Lords of *Yester*; choir, transepts and crossing still entire in grounds of Yester House.

Bothwell (Lanarkshire). *Burgh of barony* for *Earl of Angus 1602.*

Bothwell, Adam (c. 1530-1593). Son of Francis B., *Provost* of *Edinburgh* and *Lord of Session*; *Parson* of Ashkirk; Bishop of *Orkney* 1559; joined reformers and reformed his diocese; Lord of Session 1564; married *Queen Mary* to *Earl of Bothwell* and anointed *James VI* at his coronation; surrendered bishopric in exchange for abbey of *Holyrood* 1568.

Bothwell Brig, Battle of, 22 June 1679. Defeat of *Covenanters* by Duke of Monmouth.

Bothwell Castle. Magnificent ruin, including a huge circular donjon probably of mid-13th century date and an enclosure of curtain walls and round towers, with highly sophisticated work, of slightly later period; built by *Lords of Bothwell* and held by *Douglases* 1362 to 1859, when it passed to *Lord Home.*

Bothwell Collegiate Church. Petition of *Archibald, Earl of Douglas,* for promotion of parish church to *collegiate* status granted by Pope 1398; erection enlarged 1478.

Bothwell, Francis Stewart, 5th Earl of (1563-1612). Son of *John Stewart,* illegitimate son of *James V,* and Jean, sister of *4th Earl of B*; *Commendator* of *Kelso,* 1567; Earl of Bothwell 1581; accused of dealing with witches for destruction of King; several times attacked royal residences and terrorised James; mainly associated with ultra-Protestants but sometimes connected with *Earl of Huntly*; forfeited 1595; died in Naples.

Bothwell, James Hepburn, 4th Earl of (c. 1535-1578). Succeeded 1556; attached to *Reformation* but hostile to England and loyal to *Mary of Guise*; out of favour while *Queen Mary* pursued a policy of rapprochement with England, but in favour from 1565; after *Darnley's* murder, in which he certainly had a hand, he was created *Duke of Orkney* and married Mary (15 May 1567); after encounter at *Carberry* fled to his dukedom and thence to Norway; died in prison in Danish castle of Dragsholm.

Bothwell, Lordship and Earldom. Lordship created for John Ramsay by *James III;* 1st Earl was Patrick Hepburn, Lord Hailes (17 October 1488); *James, 4th Earl,* husband of *Queen Mary,* was forfeited, and *James VI* bestowed title on *Francis Stewart.*

Bovate (or Oxgang). An eighth of a *ploughgate*

Bow. Arched gateway, as Netherbow and West Bow in *Edinburgh.*

Bowden (Roxburghshire). A *barony* under abbey of *Kelso,* the 'Rental' of which gives much information about its agriculture from late 13th century; its military liabilities—four *husbandmen* and 30 archers under a man equipped with armour—are defined 1327.

Bower, Walter (c. 1385-1449). Abbot of *Inchcolm* 1418; amplified work of *John of Fordun* and continued it to 1437 as the *Scotichronicon,* printed 1759.

Bowes, Elizabeth (c. 1502-1568). Born Elizabeth Aske and married to Richard Bowes, captain of Norham Castle, she became a disciple of *John Knox,* who married her daughter Marjory.

Bowes-Lyon. See Lyon Family.

Boyd, Lordship. The Boyd family was well established in Ayrshire before the reign of *Robert I*; lordship created for *Robert Boyd* 1454; William, 10th Lord, was made *Earl of Kilmarnock* 1661.

Boyd, Robert, 1st Lord (d. 1481). Son of Sir Thomas B. of *Kilmarnock* (d. 1439); created Lord Boyd 1454; with his brother, Sir Alexander, in effect kidnapped *James III* 1466 and established an ascendancy which lasted until 1469; sentenced to death and fled to England.

Boyd, Robert, of Trochrig (1578-1627). Professor at Saumur 1606, principal of *Glasgow University* 1615 and of *Edinburgh* 1622.

Boyd, Sir Thomas. See Arran, Earl of.

Boyd, William. See Kilmarnock, Earl of.

Boyd, Zachary (c. 1585-1653). In France c. 1607-21 and *regent* at Saumur; *minister* of Barony Church, *Glasgow,* 1623, and vice-chancellor of university of Glasgow; took little part in *Covenanting* movement, but concentrated on theological and devotional work and metrical paraphrases of scripture in 'Zion's Flowers', known as 'Boyd's Bible'.

Boyd-Orr, John (1880-1971). Born *Kilmaurs;* professor of agriculture, *Aberdeen;* M.P. for Scottish Universities 1945; director-general, United Nations Food and Agricultural Organisation; won Nobel Prize 1949 and created a baron.

Boys' Brigade. Founded in *Glasgow* by *Sir William Smith* 1883.
Braco (Perthshire). For Roman camp, see Ardoch. Braco Castle probably dates originally from 16th century; in 17th it was the seat of a Graham family, cadets of *Earls of Montrose;* William G., second son of 3rd Earl, created baronet of Braco 1625; castle garrisoned by *Jacobites* 1715; estate passed from Grahams at end of 18th century.
Braemar Castle (Aberdeenshire). Built 1628 by 7th Earl of Mar; held for government by the Earl in 1689, but on his death captured by *Jacobites* under *Farquharson of Inverey;* in 1715 *8th Earl of Mar* raised standard of King James nearby; on Mar's forfeiture passed in 1732 to Farquharsons; garrisoned by government 1745 to 1797; restored by 12th Laird of Invercauld, who entertained Queen Victoria there.
Braes, Battle of. In April 1882 some crofter-fishermen in Skye defied their landlord's factor when he attempted to abrogate certain grazing rights.
Brahan Seer. See Mackenzie, Kenneth.
Braidfute, Marion. Traditionally wife of *Sir William Wallace.*
Bran. Traditionally the dog of *Fingal.*
Brander, Pass of. Valley in which Loch Awe is drained by the River Awe, *Argyll;* scene of battle, probably in mid-August 1308, in which *Robert I* defeated *MacDougal* of *Lorne.*
Brandon, St. See Brendan.
Branks. Metal collar hinged to enclose the neck, with a short chain behind and a prong in front, projecting inwards for insertion in mouth; used to punish witches and scolds.
Branxholm Tower (Roxburghshire). Lands belonged to Scotts from reign of *James I;* tower burned 1532 in an English invasion and blown up by Surrey 1570, but rebuilt 1571-4.
Braw Lads' Gathering. Annual festival at *Galashiels,* when a Braw Lad and a Braw Lass, with a mounted entourage, ride the *marches* of the town; at one point red and white roses are mixed to commemorate the marriage of *James IV* and *Margaret Tudor.*
Braxfield, Robert MacQueen, Lord (1722-99). Born in Lanarkshire; *advocate* 1744; as an expert on land law was employed by crown in connection with forfeiture of *Jacobites; Lord of Session* 1776; *Justice Clerk* 1788; presided at trials of *Thomas Muir* and other radicals in 1793 and gained a reputation as a 'hanging judge' from his hectoring and brutal attitude.
Breacan-an-Fhèilidh. The belted plaid, consisting of 12 ells of cloth; the lower portion, pleated and fastened round the waist with a belt, formed a kilt, the upper half, thrown over the shoulder, formed the plaid.
Breachachadh Castle (Coll). A *MacLean* stronghold dating from 15th century; seized by Duart MacLeans in 1578 and 1593; Donald MacLean of Coll garrisoned it against *9th Earl of Argyll* 1679; Hector MacLean, 13th of Coll, built a new house nearby which was visited by Johnson and *Boswell* 1773; old castle bought 1965 and made habitable again.
Breadalbane (Bràghaid-Alban = the upland of *Alba*). Valley of upper Tay, including the lands on both sides of *Loch Tay.*
Breadalbane, Earldom and Marquisate. Earldom created 1681 and still continues; U.K. marquisate conferred on 4th Earl 1831, became extinct with death of 2nd Marquis 1862; second U.K. marquisate conferred on 7th Earl 1885, died with him 1922.
Breadalbane, John Campbell, 1st Earl of (1635-1717). Son of Sir John Campbell of Glenorchy; married daughter of 1st Earl of Holland, 1657; created *Earl of Caithness* 1677, but rightful heir was subsequently restored to the title and Campbell became Earl of Breadalbane and Holland, 1681; regarded as cunning and slippery, he took a non-committal attitude at the *Revolution* but *William of Orange* entrusted him with money to bring *Jacobite* chiefs to terms, which he did; his understanding with them led to the *massacre of Glencoe,* for which he was blamed; imprisoned 1695 for Jacobite dealings; did not vote for *Union* in 1706, but sat as a representative peer 1713-5; repeated his habitual double-dealing in the 'Fifteen.
Brecbannoch. The banner of St *Columba,* in the custody of the abbey of *Arbroath.* See Monymusk Reliquary.
Brechin. The *burgh* was originally dependent on the bishop, but its achievement of the status of a *royal burgh* was ratified by *parliament* 1641. Grammar School or High School originated in the pre-Reformation *song* and *grammar schools* and a rector is mentioned 1485; it was administered by Town Council from *Reformation* until 1872. The Maison-Dieu was founded before 1267 by William de Brechin; *bedesmen* continued until after Reformation and the mastership was conjoined with that of the grammar school. The Riding of the Muir is a joint exercise by a *bailie* and the

citizens, at Trinity and *Lammas* Fairs.

Brechin, Battle of, 18 May 1452. Royal army under Alexander Seton, 1st *Earl of Huntly,* defeated *Alexander Lindsay, 4th Earl of Crawford.*

Brechin, Bishopric and Cathedral. Brechin was 'given to the Lord' c. 990 and its round tower may date from about that point; an early abbey was secularised by the 12th century, but *Culdees* continued to form the original *chapter* of the diocesan bishops who were recorded from c. 1150. The cathedral, dedicated to Holy Trinity, is mainly 13th century, with tower of 14th; radically altered in 19th century restoration.

Brendan, St (484-577). Irish priest whose journeyings to western and northern islands formed basis of 'Navigation of St Brendan'; commemorated in place-names Kilbrandon and Kilbrannan.

Brewster, Sir David (1781-1868). Born *Jedburgh;* proceeded from *Edinburgh University* to ordination in *Church of Scotland;* edited '*Encyclopaedia Britannica*' for 22 years from 1807; wrote on optics, polarisation of light and astronomical subjects; a founder of British Association 1831; principal of universities of *St Andrews* 1838 and Edinburgh 1848.

Brice (d. 1222). Bishop of *Moray* from 1203; in 1208, on his petition relating that previous bishops had used the churches of *Birnie, Spynie* and Kinneddar as their seats, the Pope agreed that Spynie should in future be the fixed seat and cathedral; Brice drew up a constitution accordingly, but the abandonment of Spynie was authorised 1224 and the see transferred to *Elgin.*

Bride, St. A pagan goddess in Celtic mythology, associated with spring, was identified with the Christian St. Bride of Kildare (c. 452-525), whose festival (the 'day of Bride') was on 1 February and was linked with the revival of vegetation and the resumption of outdoor farming work.

Bridge of Allan (Perth and Stirling shires). *Police burgh* 1870.

Bridge of Weir. See Quarrier, William.

Bridgeness (West Lothian). *Burgh of barony* for Sir William Belchier 1750.

'Bridie, James' (1888-1951). Osborne Henry Mavor, a physician who held the chair of medicine at *Anderson's College,* Glasgow, was the author, under the name of James Bridie, of several plays—'The Anatomist', 'Jonah and the Whale' and 'Storm in a Teacup' among others.

Brieve. Document conveying instruction, usually from central government to one of its officers, e.g. a *sheriff.*

Brisbane House (Ayrshire). Dates from 1636 and was acquired from the Kelso family by James Brisbane of Bishopton 1671.

Brisbane, Sir Thomas (1773-1860). Born Brisbane House; served as soldier but spent much time on astronomy; Governor of New South Wales 1821-5; built observatories at *Makerstoun,* Scotland, and near Sydney; K.C.B. 1814, baronet 1836.

British and Irish Grand Junction Railway. See Portpatrick Railway.

British Fisheries Society. Founded in London 1786, with 5th *Duke of Argyll* as governor; established fishing stations at Lochbay in N.W. Skye, Ullapool and *Tobermory,* with varying results; most successful effort at Pulteneytown, *Wick.*

British Linen Bank. Founded as British Linen Company 1746; soon took up banking, pioneered establishment of branches and took over *Paisley Bank* 1836, but not chartered as bank until 1849 and not named British Linen Bank until 1906; united with *Bank of Scotland* 1969.

Britons. The Celtic inhabitants of most of Britain in Roman times, gradually driven to the west with the Anglo-Saxon invasions. In Scotland they were ousted from the south-east but remained in the south-western kingdom of *Strathclyde.*

Broadsword, Basket-Hilted. See Basket-hilted broadsword.

Brochs. Cavity-walled circular towers of dry masonry, still standing to heights up to about 45 feet, mainly in *Orkney and Shetland, Caithness* and *Sutherland,* but also down west coast and islands, to the number in all of over 400; assigned to 1st century A.D.

Brockie, Marianus (1687-1755). Monk in Scottish abbeys at *Ratisbon* and *Erfurt*; missionary in Scotland 1727-39; compiled 'Monasticon Scoticon', an account of religious houses, in which invention played a large part. Cf. Schottenklöster.

Brodick Castle (Arran). The so-called 'Bruce Tower' is not authentic; oldest existing building dates from c. 1558; additions c. 1650 and in 19th century; passed from *Duke of Hamilton* to *Duke of Montrose* by marriage; given to *National Trust* 1958.

Brodie, William (d. 1788). *Edinburgh* cabinetmaker, *deacon* of the *Incorporation* of Wrights and Masons and a town councillor;

formed a gang of burglars who carried out several robberies in 1787; after breaking into the Excise Office in Chessel's Court he fled to Holland but, as one of his accomplices turned King's Evidence, he was traced and was hanged; his double life is said to have inspired *R.L. Stevenson's* 'Dr Jekyll and Mr Hyde'.

Brooch of Lorne. In an engagement with *MacDougals* of Lorne, kinsmen of the *Red Comyn,* at *Dalrigh,* near Tyndrum, *Robert I* escaped only by leaving his cloak and brooch in the hands of an assailant. A brooch now in the possession of the MacDougal family of Dunollie is claimed as Bruce's brooch, but has been pronounced to be of later date.

Brougham and Vaux, Henry, Lord (1778-1868). Born and educated in *Edinburgh; advocate* 1800; admitted to English bar 1808; M.P. 1810; Lord Chancellor 1830-34; contributor to '*Edinburgh Review*'.

Broughton, Barony of (*Edinburgh*). Part of the property of abbey of *Holyrood,* including large areas on north side of Edinburgh and with its centre in a site commemorated by Broughton Street; granted in 1587 to *Sir John Bellenden,* who became Lord Bellenden of Broughton; *barony* passed in 1627 to *Earl of Roxburghe* and later to *Heriot's* Trust; *tolbooth* demolished 1829.

Broughty *(Angus).* A castle of the Lords *Gray,* built from c. 1500; held by English 1547-50; bought by government 1850 and restored as fortification. There was a 'hospital' in late 12th century, but it had only a short life and may have been no more than an inn.

Brown, George Douglas (1869-1902). Son of Ayrshire farmer, educated *Glasgow* and Oxford, turned to authorship, and in reaction against the sentimental tone of most writing about Scottish life, produced the starkly realistic 'House with the Green Shutters' (1900).

Brown, Gilbert (d. 1612). Abbot of *Sweetheart*; did much to maintain Roman Catholicism in the area and was finally banished, to die at Paris.

Brown, James (1862-1939). Ayrshire miner; M.P; appointed *Lord High Commissioner* to the *General Assembly* of the Church of Scotland by the first Labour Government 1924 and again 1930 and 1931.

Brown, John (c. 1637-85). Known as 'the Christian carrier', lived at Priestfield or Priesthill, Ayrshire, and associated with the more radical *Covenanters* in their rebellious attitude; shot by *John Graham of Claverhouse* after arms had been found in his house.

Brown, John (1722-87). As a herd-boy taught himself Latin, Greek and Hebrew; *minister* to *Burgher* congregation at *Haddington,* 1750-87, and professor of divinity for Burgher students from 1768; his 'Self-interpreting Bible' (1778), a popular commentary, circulated widely.

Brown, John (1735-88). Attacked the traditional teaching of the *Edinburgh* professors of medicine, *Monro* and *Cullen*; went to London to practise; published his views in 'Elementa Medicinae' (1780).

Brown, John (1810-82). Great-grandson of John Brown (1722-87) and grandson and son of other *Burgher* or *Relief ministers;* practised medicine in *Edinburgh*; author of 'Horae Subsecivae' and 'Rab and his Friends' (1859).

Brown, John (1826-83). Personal servant to Queen Victoria, in whose Journal he is first mentioned in 1849.

Bruce. See Robert I.

'Bruce (or**Brus**)**, The'.** See Barbour, John.

Bruce, Alexander Hugh. See Balfour of Burleigh.

Bruce, Edward (c. 1276-1318). Younger brother of *Robert I*; aided his brother in his campaigns, and his agreement with the governor of *Stirling Castle* led to the battle of *Bannockburn,* where he commanded a division; raided England 1314; went to Ireland 1315 and crowned King there 1316 but killed at Dundalk 14 October 1318; created *Lord of Galloway* 1308, *Earl of Carrick* probably 1313 and styled *Lord of Annandale* and *Man*; declared heir presumptive 1315.

Bruce, Edward (c. 1549-1611). *Commissary* of *Edinburgh*; *Commendator* of *Kinloss* 1583; ambassador to England 1594 and 1601; *Lord of Session* 1597; Lord Bruce of Kinloss 1603; Master of the Rolls.

Bruce Family. From Brix in the Cotentin, Normandy. The first Robert de Brus to appear in Scotland evidently came north with *David I* and received the lands of *Annandale* c. 1124. A descendant married Isabella, daughter of *David, Earl of Huntingdon,* and their son was *Robert* (1210-95).

Bruce, Sir George, of Carnock (d. 1625). As proprietor of estates on north side of Firth of Forth he improved agriculture, but his main achievement was the development of *coal*-mining and *salt* manufacture at *Culross,* where he constructed a mine under the sea, with an entrance from an artificial island, and built the 'Palace'.

Bruce, Isabella (fl. 1293). Sister of *Robert I*;

married in 1293 Erik, King of Norway, whose first wife had been a daughter of *Alexander III.*

Bruce, James (1730-94). Son of David Bruce of Kinnaird, he became consul in Algiers 1763 and, after exploring North Africa, set out in 1768 up the Nile and reached Abyssinia; on returning to Britain 1774 he wrote an account of his travels (published in 5 vols., 1790) which was thought so incredible that he was accused of writing fiction.

Bruce, James (1811-63). See Elgin, Earl of.

Bruce, Marjory (d. 1316). Daughter of *Robert I,* married *Walter the Steward* and was mother of *Robert II.*

Bruce, Michael (1746-67). Born Kinnesswood, Kinross-shire; of a poor family, educated at *Edinburgh University* and became a schoolmaster; died of consumption; his poems published posthumously 1770.

Bruce, Robert (1210-95). *Lord of Annandale,* son of Isabella, second daughter of *David, Earl of Huntingdon*; took active part in affairs in England, where he had extensive estates, and went on crusade with youngest son of Henry III; claimed throne on death of *Alexander III* and was a *Competitor* 1291, on the ground that he had been declared heir presumptive in 1238, before birth of Alexander III; his son married the heiress of *Carrick* and his grandson became *Robert I.* See also Turnberry Bond.

Bruce, Robert, King of Scots. See Robert I.

Bruce, Robert (c. 1554-1631). Son of laird of *Airth,* who gave him the estate of *Kinnaird; minister* in *Edinburgh* 1587; anointed Queen Anne at her coronation 1590; his ordination (without imposition of hands) disputed 1598; his association with unyielding *presbyterians* against *James VI*'s policies led to his banishment to *Inverness* 1605; wrote 'Sermons on the Sacraments'.

Bruce, Thomas (1766-1841). See Elgin, Earl of.

Bruce, Sir William, of Kinross (1630-1710). Son of Robert Bruce of Blairhall; baronet 1668; King's Surveyor and *Master of Works* 1671; architect for restoration and extension of palace of *Holyrood* (1671-8); acquired lands of *Kinross* and built Kinross House (1685-92); designed central part of *Hopetoun House.*

Bruce's Heart. When *Robert I* died, his embalmed heart was taken by *Sir James Douglas* to fight against the infidels, in fulfilment of the King's intention to go on a crusade; when Douglas was killed in action in Spain, the heart was brought back by *Sir William Keith* for burial in *Melrose,* which seems to have been the King's original wish.

Bruce's Stone. (1) In Glen Trool, Kirkcudbrightshire, commemorating victory of *Robert I* over English in March or April 1307. (2) Near Kildonan, Kintyre, where Bruce is said to have rested with Sir Neil Campbell of Lochawe, his future brother-in-law, when fleeing from the *MacDougals.*

Bruce's Well. At *Kingcase,* near *Prestwick*; a legend to explain the existence of a hospital or leper-house, said to have been founded by *Robert I* there, relates that he was miraculously refreshed by water which welled up when he thrust his spear into the sand.

Brude, son of Maelchon (d. 584). King of *Picts* in time of *Columba.*

Brude, son of Bile (d. 693). King of *Picts* from c. 671; victorious against Irish of *Dalriada* 683; overthrew Angles at *Nechtansmere* 685.

Brude, son of Derile (d. 706). King of *Picts,* probably grandson of preceding.

Brude, son of Feredach (d. 843). Last king of separate *Pictish* realm.

Brunanburgh, Battle of, 937. Defeat of *Constantine II* of *Alba* and his allies by Athelstan, King of England; has been identified with Burnswark or Birrenswark, Dumfriesshire.

Brunstane (Midlothian). The lands, also called Gilbertoun, were held from 1410 by *Crichtons,* who went to Ulster c. 1600 and sold Brunstane to widow of *John Maitland of Thirlestane;* her son, 1st *Earl of Lauderdale,* built a house in 1639 on site of older one; passed in 18th century to *Duke of Argyll* and then 3rd *Earl of Abercorn,* whose descendant sold it in 1878 to the Benhar Coal Co.

Bruntsfield House (*Edinburgh*). Probably originated in 15th century, but enlarged or rebuilt c. 1605, which date it bears; belonged to Fairlies, but bought 1695 by George Warrender, who became Lord *Provost* of Edinburgh 1713, and remained with his family until acquired by Town Council in 1930s.

Bryce, David (1803-76). Partner of *William Burn*; architect at over a hundred country houses, notably *Kinnaird Castle*; designed *Fettes College* (1865-70); credited with almost the invention of 'Scottish baronial' style, but was also a master of Italian Palazzo style.

'Bubbly Jocks'. See Royal Scots Greys.

Buccleuch, Lordship, Earldom and Dukedom. Lordship created 1606 for *Sir Walter Scott of Buccleuch*; 2nd Lord created Earl 1612; dukedom created 1663 for James, Duke of Monmouth, on his marriage to Anna, Countess of Buccleuch (see Monmouth); 2nd Duke married heiress of 2nd Duke of *Queensberry.*

Buccleuch, Walter Francis, 5th Duke of (1806-84). Lord Privy Seal 1842-6; Lord President of Council 1846; built harbour at *Granton.*

Buchan, Alexander (1829-1907). Born Kinross-shire; secretary of Scottish Meteorological Society and librarian of *Royal Society of Edinburgh*; examination of data obtained from the observatory on *Ben Nevis* enabled him to produce a scheme of cold and warm periods each year.

Buchan, Anna (d. 1948). Sister of *John Buchan*; wrote novels under name 'O. Douglas'.

Buchan, David Stewart Erskine, 11th Earl of (1742-1829). Founder of *Society of Antiquaries of Scotland* 1780; carried out restoration at *Dryburgh* and *Inchcolm* Abbeys; freed elections of Scottish peers from government interference.

Buchan, Earldom. The district, extending from the Don to the Deveron, was evidently a province of the *Pictish* kingdom, under a *mormaer*; earldom emerged in 12th-13th centuries and passed to the *Comyn* family by marriage; held briefly by a number of members of the royal family from c. 1382, it passed from a half-brother of *James II,* earl in 1470, through his descendants to Christian, who married Robert Douglas 1574; his granddaughter married c. 1616 James *Erskine,* from whom Erskine earls descended.

Buchan, Elizabeth (1738-91). Born Banffshire; persuaded *minister* of *Relief Church* in *Irvine* that she was divinely inspired, and founded sect of Buchanites; expelled from Irvine, she settled at *Closeburn,* Dumfriesshire.

Buchan Field Club. Founded 1887 for study of natural science, archaeology, folklore, history and literature of Buchan.

Buchan, Isabella, Countess of. Sister of Duncan, *Earl of Fife* (c. 1285-c. 1353), and wife of John *Comyn,* Earl of Buchan; said to have crowned *Robert I* at Scone 1306; imprisoned by Edward I in cage at *Berwick* Castle.

Buchan, John (1875-1940). Educated *Glasgow* and Oxford, where he started writing; private secretary to Lord Milner in South Africa 1901-3; correspondent in France in World War I; M.P. for Scottish Universities 1927-35; *Lord High Commissioner* to *General Assembly,* 1933-4, and Governor General of Canada 1935-40; created Baron Tweedsmuir 1935; author of successful adventure novels and of historical works, including 'Montrose'.

Buchan, John Stewart, Earl of (c. 1380-1424). Son of *Robert, Duke of Albany*; *Chamberlain* Scotland 1407-24; led some 7000 Scots to France 1420; defeated English at *Baugé*; appointed Constable of France; killed at *Verneuil.*

Buchanan, David (c. 1595-c. 1652). Writer of history who published, and possibly wrote, Book V of *John Knox's* 'History of the Reformation'.

Buchanan, George (1506-82). Born Killearn, Stirlingshire; studied at Paris and *St Andrews*; prosecuted as a heretic and escaped to England; went to France and Portugal, where he was imprisoned by the Inquisition for a year and a half; in Paris 1551-61; principal of *St Leonard's College,* St Andrews, 1566; preceptor to *James VI;* famed for his Latin poems and dramas, as a pamphleteer against Queen *Mary* and as author of a 'History of Scotland' which was influential but a vehicle for his propaganda.

Buchanites. See Buchan, Elizabeth.

Buchan's Cold Spells. See Buchan, Alexander.

Buchlyvie (Stirlingshire). *Burgh of barony* for Graham of Buchlyvie 1672.

Buckhaven and Methil (Fife). *Burgh of barony* for *Earl of Wemyss* 1662.

Buckie (Banffshire). *Police burgh* 1888; harbour constructed by *Gordon* of Cluny 1874-80.

Buckstone. *March* stone at Braid Hills, *Edinburgh;* said to have marked place where King's hounds were released when he was hunting; now in a wall niche 250 yards from original site.

Buick, David Dunbar (1854-1929). Born *Arbroath*; emigrated to Detroit; invented glazing process for baths and founded company to make motor cars 1902, but died a poor man.

Buittle (Kirkcudbrightshire). Lands conferred on *Sir James Douglas* 1325 'cum libertate burgi', but no *burgh* seems to have existed.

Bull Stone. At *Leslie,* Fife, formerly used to tether a bull used in bull-baiting.

Bunkle (Berwickshire). Passed by marriage of heiress from family of De Bonkyl to Sir John Stewart 1288; he was followed by Stewart *Earls of Angus* and Douglas Earls of Angus; finally passed to *Earls of Home.*

Burgess. Originally any inhabitant of a *burgh* who held a piece of land there from the crown or other *superior*; later restricted to merchants and *craftsmen,* especially the former, who carried the chief sway in burgh affairs. See Merchant Guilds.

Burgh Courts. Presided over by *bailies,* they retained jurisdiction in petty offences and small debts until abolished in 1975 and their functions transferred to district courts.

Burgh Muir (*Edinburgh*). An open common south of the town, where *John Randolph, Earl of Moray,* and the *Earl of Dunbar* defeated English 1335; cleared of trees 1504; was sometimes a place of execution. See also St Roche.

Burgh Reform Act, 1833. Instituted an elective system for appointment of town councils to replace the system whereby they had been largely self-perpetuating or had appointed members by co-option.

Burghead (*Moray*). Takes name from a 'borg', probably built by Scandinavians, who called the place Torfnes; a *police burgh*; harbour constructed 1807-10 and breakwater extended 1832.

Burghers and Anti-Burghers. The *First Secession* split in 1745-7 over an oath whereby certain *burgesses* had to acknowledge 'the true religion presently professed within this realm', which, the precise contended, implied an acknowledgment of the established Church. Each section split again at the end of the century into 'Old Light' and 'New Light' groups, over the power to be assigned to the state in matters of religion and especially in the enforcement of church discipline.

Burghs. First mentioned early in 12th century. Crown charters usually conferred rights and privileges on them in varying degrees, and distinctions developed between royal and non-royal burghs. From early 14th century representatives of burghs attended *parliament.* The Local Government Act of 1929 divided burghs into three categories—4 cities, 19 large burghs and 178 small burghs. All burghs passed out of existence with the reorganisation of local government in 1975. See Wheatley Report.

Burghs, Court of Four. Existed in 13th century, with delegates from *Berwick, Edinburgh, Roxburgh* and *Stirling,* presided over by *Chamberlain,* to hear disputes between *burghs* and 'appeals' from *burgh courts.* In 1369 *Lanark* and *Linlithgow* replaced *Roxburgh* and Berwick, which were in English hands. See also Convention of Royal Burghs.

Burghs of Barony. Term first used c. 1400. But from 12th century the King had authorised landholders to have *burghs* on their lands. They proliferated from 15th century, usually with powers to hold markets and fairs for local trade but not to infringe the *royal burghs'* monopoly of foreign trade.

Burghs of Regality. Not a distinct category of *burgh,* but simply a burgh which had as its *superior* a secular lord or an ecclesiastical corporation whose property constituted a *regality.*

Burghs, Royal. As burghs were differentiated, the royal burghs, which originally were distinct from others simply in that they were on royal lands, acquired a monopoly of foreign trade, and it was in the main (though not entirely) the royal burghs, ultimately numbering 66, which sent commissioners to *parliament* and paid the burghal share of a taxation.

Burke, William (1792-1829). William Hare and he enticed people to their house in *Edinburgh* and murdered them for disposal to surgeons. Burke was hanged, Hare turned King's Evidence and was released. See Knox, Robert.

Burlaw Court, Burlaw Men. System of local jurisprudence to settle disputes among neighbours by arbitration.

Burleigh Castle (Kinross-shire). Property acquired by *Balfours* 1446, and part of castle goes back to about that time; though roofless, it is fairly complete.

Burleigh, Lordship. See Balfour of Burleigh.

Burn, William (1789-1870). Son of Robert Burn, an architect, he practised in London and *Edinburgh* as an architect; designed St John's Episcopal Church, the *Academy, John Watson's Hospital* and the Music Hall, all in Edinburgh, *Tyninghame* House and, as consulting architect to the government, the Custom House in *Greenock.*

Burne, Nicol (fl. 1581). A professor at *St Andrews University* who turned Roman Catholic; banished 1581 and at Paris produced a virulent attack on the reformers.

Burnet, Alexander (1614-84). Bishop of *Aberdeen* 1663, Archbishop of *Glasgow* 1664 and of *St Andrews* 1679; his intransigence did nothing to conciliate the dissidents of the south-west.

Burnet, Gilbert (1643-1715). Born *Edinburgh; minister* of *Saltoun* 1665; professor of divinity at *Glasgow* 1669; went to London and associated with *Whig* opposition; on accession of *James VII* went to Holland, whence he returned with *William of Orange,* who made him Bishop of Salisbury; wrote 'Memoirs of Dukes of *Hamilton*', 'History of *Reformation*' and 'History of his Own Times'.

Burnet, James (1788-1816). Brother of *John B*; born *Musselburgh*; successful painter, especially from nature; worked in London from 1810; died of consumption.

Burnet, John (1784-1868). Brother of preceding; born *Musselburgh;* fellow-student of *David Wilkie* at *Trustees' Academy*; went to

London 1806 and started engraving for Wilkie, then executed many engravings of old masters; his own paintings were much in the Wilkie tradition.

Burnett, James. See Monboddo, Lord.

Burns, George (1795-1890). With his brother James (1789-1871) pioneered steam navigation from *Glasgow* and in 1839, with Samuel Cunard, *Robert Napier* and others, formed Cunard Shipping Company.

Burns, Robert (1759-96). Born Alloway, Ayrshire, son of small farmer, and farmed at Mossgiel; in 1786 published at *Kilmarnock* 'Poems, chiefly in the Scottish Dialect', with a view to raising money to emigrate, but the volume's success brought him popularity and fame; he failed to make a success of farming (at Ellisland, Dumfriesshire) or of a position in the Excise. See Armour, Jean.

Burnt Candlemas, 1356. Devastating invasion of Scotland by Edward III.

Burntisland (Fife). Erected as *royal burgh* 1541 and, after dispute with abbey of *Dunfermline,* ratified 1586. See also Granton.

Burntisland, Lordship. Created for Sir James Wemyss of Caskieberry 1672 for his lifetime; he died 1682.

Burrell, Sir William (1861-1958). *Glasgow* shipowner who bought many paintings, especially by contemporaries, which he presented to Glasgow.

Burry Man. At the annual fair at South *Queensferry* a man dressed in a costume covered with prickly burrs perambulates the streets.

Burton, John Hill (1809-81). *Advocate* and secretary of *Prison Commission*; wrote an 8-volume History of Scotland (1852-70); H.M. Historiographer for Scotland 1867.

'Butcher'. See William, Duke of *Cumberland.*

Bute, Earldom. Created for James Stewart 1703; marquisate created 1796 for 4th Earl, whose son married heiress of *Earl of Dumfries* 1792; 5th Earl succeeded to that title 1803.

Bute House. In Charlotte Square, *Edinburgh*; presented by 5th *Marquis of Bute* as residence for *Secretary of State* for Scotland.

Bute, John Patrick Crichton Stuart, 3rd Marquis of (1847-1900). A convert to Roman Catholicism 1868; wrote many works on historical and antiquarian subjects.

Bute, John Stuart, 3rd Earl of (1713-92). Prime minister 1761-3.

Bute Pursuivant. First mentioned 1488. See Pursuivants.

Butts. Ground in or near a *burgh* set apart for archery practice.

Butts, Battle of, 1544. Victory of *Regent Arran* over *Earl of Glencairn* at the *Butts* in *Glasgow.*

Byland, Battle of, 14 October 1322. Victory of *Robert I* against Edward II near Byland Abbey, Yorkshire.

Byre Theatre. Founded in *St Andrews* 1933.

Byron, George Gordon, 6th Lord (1788-1824). Son of Catherine Gordon of Gight and brought up largely in *Aberdeen*; succeeded to title 1798 and then sent to Harrow and Cambridge; his career as poet, traveller, and fighter for Greek independence had little to do with Scotland.

C

Cadell, Francis Campbell Boileau (1883-1937). Painter, born *Edinburgh*; studied Paris and Munich; settled in Edinburgh 1909; associated with *Peploe, Hunter* and *Fergusson* and founded Society of Eight 1912.

Cadzow (Lanarkshire). The castle, of which little remains, was from the reign of *Robert I* the seat of the *Hamilton* family, who gave their name to the adjoining town.

Caerlaverock Castle (Dumfriesshire). Assigned to late 13th century, and in 1300 the scene of a famous siege; besides the fine round towers and curtain walls of the original structure, it contains a decorative seventeenth-century range; belonged mainly to *Lords Maxwell.*

Cain. An ancient due, mentioned in 12th century; paid to the king or other *superior*; later equated with certain rents paid in kind.

Caiplie Caves (Fife). Near *Crail,* carved crosses suggest early Christian use and a possible association with St *Adrian.*

Cairnburghmore Castle (Treshnish Isles, north-west of Mull). Mentioned in document of 1354 and included in list of eleven castles in the west compiled by *Fordun.*

Cairnpapple. Prehistoric monument in Torphichen parish, West Lothian, comprising, within a setting of boulders and a rampart, a mound containing cremations and graves.

Caithness. Derived from 'cat', a tribal name, and Norse 'ness', a peninsula; part of Norse *earldom of Orkney* until c. 1200, and thereafter held by Earls of Orkney under Scottish crown. See Caithness, Earldom.

Caithness Banking Company. Formed at *Wick* 1814; taken over by *Commercial Bank* 1826.

Caithness, Bishopric. Probably founded by *David I*; included modern *Sutherland* and Caithness; original seat probably at *Halkirk*. See Dornoch.

Caithness, Earldom. The first earl not associated with the *Orkney* line was David, 5th son of *Robert II* (created 1375-7); his daughter resigned it to her uncle Walter (*Earl of Atholl*), whose two sons held it until 1437; fresh creation for George Crichton 1452, but he died 1454; held from 1455 by various branches of the *Sinclair* family, except 1677-81, when it was held by John Campbell, later *Earl of Breadalbane*.

Caithness, George Sinclair, 4th Earl of (d. 1582). Inclined to conservative side at *Reformation;* foreman of the jury at trial of *James Hepburn, Earl of Bothwell*; joined *Queen's Party* 1568.

Caithness, George Sinclair, 5th Earl of (c. 1566-1643). A troublesome subject, engaged in feuds with *Earl of Sutherland*; led force which suppressed rebellion in *Orkney* 1615; again the subject of '*Letters of Fire and Sword*' 1623.

Caithness, James Sinclair, 14th Earl of (1821-81). Invented steamcarriage and other devices; wrote 'Lectures on Popular and Scientific Subjects'.

Calder (Midlothian) or **Mid Calder.** Property of Sandilands family from 15th century; Calder House has work probably of 15th century date; *John Knox* celebrated Communion there; there is an unusually fine late medieval parish church.

Calder (Nairnshire). See Cawdor.

Calderwood, David (1575-1651). *Minister* of Crailing, Roxburghshire, 1604; refused to cooperate in episcopal administration revived by *James VI* and in 1619 was banished to Holland, where he wrote a massive defence of *presbyterianism,* 'Altare Damascenum' (1619); returned to Scotland after 1625 and collected material which formed his 'History of the *Church of Scotland*', published 1678; influential in *Glasgow Assembly* 1638; minister of *Pencaitland.*

Caledonia. The Caledonii are referred to by Tacitus as the inhabitants of northern Scotland c. 80 A.D; name preserved in *Dunkeld* and Schiehallion.

Caledonian and Dunbartonshire Railway. From Bowling to Balloch to link *Clyde* steamers with those of Loch Lomond.

Caledonian Ball. Held annually in London since 1849 to aid Scottish charities there.

Caledonian Bank. Founded at *Inverness* 1838; amalgamated with *Bank of Scotland* 1907.

Caledonian Canal. From *Inverness* to Corpach, near *Fort William,* with length of 60 miles, 37 of which are composed of Lochs Ness, Oich and Lochy; begun 1803, opened to traffic 1822 but not completed until 1847.

Caledonian Curling Club. Formed 1838.

'Caledonian Mercury'. Newspaper founded 1720 and twice-weekly journal; from 1726 a five-times-weekly paper and in 1866 an evening paper; bought by '*Scotsman*' 1867.

Caledonian Railway. Linked *Edinburgh* and *Glasgow* with Carlisle via *Carstairs* 1848; direct line between Edinburgh and Glasgow 1866; extended north to *Aberdeen* and took over lines to *Oban, Portpatrick* and *Peebles.*

Calendar. Although 1 January became *New Year's Day* in 1600, Scotland did not adopt the Gregorian Calendar (at the cost of 'losing eleven days') until England did so in 1752.

Calgacus (fl. c. 84). Mentioned by Tacitus as leader of the Caledonii at *Mons Graupius*; name possibly connected with 'calgach' or swordsman.

Calico Printing. Developed by Crum of Thornliebank, *Glasgow,* in early 19th century; Calico Printers Association formed 1899.

Callander (Perthshire). *Police burgh* 1866.

Callander and Oban Railway. Completed 1880; absorbed in *Caledonian.*

Callander, Earldom. Created 1641 for James Livingston (d. 1674), 3rd son of Alexander, 1st *Earl of Linlithgow,* and a supporter of *Charles I,* whom he tried to rescue; 4th Earl *forfeited* for *Jacobitism* 1716.

Callendar (Stirlingshire). Property of Livingston family from time of *Robert I*; Callendar House has 15th century tower embedded in an ornate mansion of later date; gives its name to earldom, though that is spelled differently.

Callernish (or **Callanish) Standing Stones.** Group of standing stones, apparently connected with sun-worship, in island of *Lewis.*

Calton (*Edinburgh*). *Burgh of barony* for Lord *Balmerino* 1669; absorbed in Edinburgh 1856.

Calton (*Glasgow*). *Burgh of barony* 1817; absorbed in Glasgow 1846.

Camanachd. See Shinty.

Cambuskenneth Abbey (*Augustinian*) (Stirlingshire). Founded by *David I* c. 1140, but there were already canons in *Stirling,* by which name the house was at first known; *James III* and his Queen buried there; fell into hands of *Erskines* and in 1604 erected as a lordship, with *Dryburgh* and *Inchmahome,* for *John, Earl of Mar*; a free-standing tower remains.

Cambuslang (Lanarkshire). Hospital of St Leonard founded by 1455, but nothing is known of later history.

Cameron, Sir Alan, of Erracht (1753-1828). Son and grandson of active *Jacobites*; as an emigrant in America joined Royal Highland Emigrant Corps; returned to Scotland 1785; formed 79th Highlanders 1793 and served in Holland, Egypt and the Peninsula.

Cameron, Archibald (1707-53). Younger brother of *Donald C. of Lochiel*; a physician; executed for part in *Jacobite* plot.

Cameron, David Young (1865-1945). Born *Glasgow*; at first noted for his etchings, based on continental travels, but from 1898 lived at Kippen and concentrated on scenes among the Highland hills, of which he conveyed the atmosphere; knighted 1924; King's Painter and Limner in Scotland 1933.

Cameron, Donald, of Lochiel (c. 1695-1748), 'the gentle Lochiel'. His father John was attainted after the '*Fifteen*; he had no hope that the '*Forty-Five* would succeed, but Prince *Charles Edward's* appeals made him join, with 800 of his clan; severely wounded at *Culloden,* but escaped to France, where he died.

Cameron Highlanders. See Queen's Own Cameron Highlanders.

Cameron, John (d. 1446). *Provost* of *Lincluden*; keeper of *privy seal* 1425; Bishop of *Glasgow* and *Chancellor* 1426; attended Council of Basel.

Cameron, Richard (1648-80), the 'Lion of the *Covenant*'. Schoolmaster at *Falkland,* but joined covenanting field preachers; his severe attitude to *ministers* who accepted the *Indulgences* cut him off from majority of *Presbyterians,* and he went to Holland, where he was ordained; returned 1680 to head extremists who were known by his name; publicly renounced King's authority in the *Sanquhar Declaration*; killed at *Aird's Moss.*

Cameronian Regiment. Raised from *Cameronians* at *Revolution*; became 26th Regiment, amalgamated 1881 with 90th Perthshire Light Infantry; retained customs based on practice of *Conventicles,* e.g. carrying arms to church, posting sentries during services; disbanded 1968.

Cameronians. Followers of *Richard Cameron*; rejected *Revolution* settlement of Church and retained their identity to become the Reformed Presbyterian Church, the majority of whose members joined the *Free Church,* 1876, leaving a continuing remnant.

Campbell, Alexander (1788-1866). Born Antrim; studied at *Glasgow;* followed his father, a *Secession minister,* to United States 1809 and was ordained in his father's sect; associated with Baptists but left them 1826 to found 'The Church of the Disciples', called Campbellites.

Campbell, Archibald, Earls and Dukes of Argyll. See Argyll.

Campbell Castle (Clackmannanshire). Originally Castle Gloume, it was acquired by *Earl of Argyll* in late 15th century; part of a 14th century tower and additions of 16th and 17th centuries remain.

Campbell, Colin (fl. 1315). Son of *Neil C;* received lands of Lochawe from *Robert I* 1315.

Campbell, Colin (d. 1729). Architect of Rolls House, Chancery Lane, London, and *Drumlanrig Castle;* published 'Vitruvius Britannicus' (1717-25).

Campbell, Colin, of Glenure (d. 1752). See Appin Murder.

Campbell, Sir Colin, Lord Clyde (1792-1863). Son of *Glasgow* carpenter named Macliver, but took mother's surname; commanded Highland Brigade at Alma and Balaclava and commanded in India during Mutiny; promoted Field Marshal 1862.

Campbell, Donald, of Shawfield (c. 1671-1753). *Glasgow* merchant whose house was burned 1725 by mob protesting against *Malt Tax*; bought property in Islay 1727.

Campbell, Duncan, of Glenorchy (c. 1553-1631). 'Black Duncan of the Cowl' and 'Black Duncan of the Castles'; built or improved castles of *Balloch* (Taymouth), *Kilchurn, Finlarig,* Lochdochart and *Barcaldine*; greatly extended family estates; great-grandfather of *1st Earl of Breadalbane.*

Campbell Family. Authentic pedigree extends to Gillespie (fl. 1263), father of Colin Campbell of Lochaw (d. c. 1296), from whom successive chiefs were named MacCailean Mhor. In 1445 Sir Duncan Campbell became Lord C. See Argyll.

Campbell, Lord Frederick (1729-1816). Son of 4th *Duke of Argyll*; Lord *Clerk Register* 1768-1816.

Campbell, Ilay (1734-1823). *Lord Advocate* 1784; *Lord President* (Lord Succoth) 1799; as an *advocate* was engaged in *Douglas Cause.*

Campbell, John, Earl of Breadalbane. See Breadalbane.

Campbell, John, Duke of Argyll. See Argyll.

Campbell, John, Earl of Loudoun. See Loudoun.

Campbell, John McLeod (1800-72). *Minister* of Rhu, Dunbartonshire, 1825; preached with 'almost apostolic zeal' and taught the universality of the Atonement, contrary to views officially held; deposed by *General Assembly* 1831, but although he continued to preach he refused to join or found a sect; wrote 'The Nature of the Atonement'.

Campbell, Neil (d. c. 1316). Supported *Robert I,* whose sister he married.

Campbell, Thomas (1777-1844). Born *Glasgow* and educated *Glasgow University,* but in his poetry largely identified himself with England—'Ye mariners of England', 'The Battle of the Baltic' and so forth.

Campbell, Willielma. See Glenorchy, Lady.

Campbell-Bannerman, Sir Henry (1836-1908). Son of Sir James Campbell, a *Glasgow* draper who became Lord *Provost;* took name Bannerman in terms of the will of an uncle who left him a fortune; M.P. for *Stirling* burghs from 1868; held many offices, was knighted 1895 and as leader of the Liberal party became Prime Minister 1905.

Campbellites. See Campbell, Alexander.

Campbell's Highlanders. Raised 1759 as 88th Regiment by Major John Campbell of *Dunoon,* at *Stirling;* served on continent; disbanded 1763.

Campbeltown (*Argyll*). Authorised as *burgh of barony* for Campbell of *Cawdor* 1623; established as burgh of barony for *Earl of Argyll* 1667; *royal burgh* 1700. See also Kilkerran.

Camperdown, Viscount of. See Duncan, Adam.

Campvere. Now Veere, on island of Walcheren, Holland. For long periods it was the site of the Scottish *Staple* with its *Conservator.*

Canada Company. See Galt, John.

Candida Casa. See Whithorn.

Candlemas. Feast of the Purification of the Blessed Virgin, 2 February, in use as a *term-day.*

Canmore. See Malcolm III.

Canonbie Priory (*Augustinian*) (Dumfriesshire). Dependent on *Jedburgh Abbey,* to which it was confirmed 1165x1171; erected into lordship for Alexander, *Lord Home,* 1606; no remains.

Canongate. *Burgh* which abbey of *Holyrood* was authorised by *David I* to institute; *burgh of regality* for Bellenden of Auchnoule 1587; dependent on city of *Edinburgh* 1639; amalgamated with Edinburgh 1856. *Grammar School* presumably existed under monastic auspices in middle ages and is authenticated 1529; closed 1822. Parish church erected 1688 to design by *James Smith* when the nave of Holyrood Abbey, previously used for parochial worship, was converted into a chapel for the Order of the *Thistle.*

Canons. See Code of Canons.

Cant, Andrew (c. 1590-1664). *Minister* of Pitsligo; accepted *National Covenant* 1638; minister of *Newbattle* 1638; returned to *Aberdeen* 1641; attached himself to more extreme *Covenanters* and opposed invasion of England on behalf of *Charles II* 1651; resigned charge 1660.

Canter of Coltbrig, 16 September 1745. *Jacobites* routed dragoons on outskirts of *Edinburgh.*

Canterbury, Quitclaim of, 5 December 1189. Richard I of England surrendered to *William I,* for 10,000 merks, the feudal subjection into which William had been forced by the *Treaty of Falaise.*

Capacity, Measures of. 1 chalder = 16 bolls; 1 boll = 4 firlots; 1 firlot = 4 pecks (1 peck = 2 gallons or ¼ bushel).

Cape Club. Formed in *Edinburgh* 1762 for convivial purposes, with members wearing capes; among the members was Deacon *Brodie;* wound up 1841.

Cape Wrath. Lighthouse erected 1828.

Caption. A form of *diligence* involving personal arrest.

Carberry Hill, 15 June 1567. *Queen Mary* surrendered to rebel lords.

Carbisdale, Battle of, 27 April 1650. *Montrose* defeated by *Strachan.*

Cardinals. See Beaton, David; Erskine, Charles; Heard, William Theodore; and Wardlaw, Walter. Gordon Gray (b. 1910), Archbishop of *St Andrews* and *Edinburgh* 1951, became a Cardinal 1969.

Cardoness (or **Clachan of Anwoth**) (Kirkcudbrightshire). *Burgh of barony* for Maxwell of Cardoness 1702.

Cardross (Dunbartonshire). On Castlehill stood the castle in which *Robert I* died; St. Peter's Roman Catholic College restored the medieval chapel of St Mahew 1955.

Cardross (*Menteith,* Perthshire). The tower-house of the *Erskine* family gave its name to lordship created from abbeys of *Cambuskenneth* and *Dryburgh* and priory of *Inchmahome.*

Cargill, Donald (1619-81). Born Rattray, Perthshire; *minister* of Barony Church, *Glasgow,* 1650; dispossessed at *Restoration;* joined extreme *Covenanters* and bitterly condemned *Indulgences;* wounded at *Bothwell Brig;* fled to Holland but returned to associate with *Richard Cameron*; arrested 1681 and executed.

Carham, Battle of, ? 1018. *Malcolm II* of Scotland and Owen, King of *Strathclyde,* defeated Northumbrian army on the Tweed.

Carluke (Lanarkshire). *Burgh of barony* for Lockhart of *Lee* 1662.

Carlyle, Alexander (1722-1805). 'Jupiter'; born Prestonpans; *minister* of *Inveresk* 1746; a leader of the *Moderates* in the Church and prominent in cultivated society; his 'Autobiography' published 1860.

Carlyle, Jane Baillie Welsh. See Welsh.

Carlyle, Lordship. Created 1473-4 for Sir John C. of Torthorwald; became extinct, or lapsed, in early 17th century.

Carlyle, Thomas (1795-1881). Born Ecclefechan, Annandale, where his birthplace is in the keeping of the *National Trust*; taught at *Annan* and *Kirkcaldy*; removed to Craigenputtock, Dumfriesshire, after his marriage (1826) and to London 1834; publications began with 'Sartor Resartus' (1831) and included 'The French Revolution', 'Oliver Cromwell' and 'Frederick the Great'.

Carmelite Friaries. See Aberdeen, Banff, Berwick, Edinburgh, Inverbervie, Irvine, Kingussie, Linlithgow, Luffness, Queensferry, Tullilum.

Carmichael, Alexander (1832-1912). Born *Lismore*; as an excise officer in the west Highlands and islands he collected folk-lore which he incorporated in 'Carmina Gadelica'.

Carmichael, Lordship. Created 1647 for Sir James C; 2nd Lord became *Earl of Hyndford.*

Carnasserie Castle *(Argyll).* A late 16th century castle, of which the walls are almost complete, which was the home of *John Carswell* and passed to *Campbells* of Auchinbreck.

Carnegie, Andrew (1835-1919). Son of *Dunfermline linen* weaver; emigrated to Pittsburgh 1848; worked his way up in railroad industry and moved on to iron and steel production; became one of the richest men of the time and in his lifetime gave away over 350,000,000 dollars, most of it to Dunfermline, libraries and universities; bought Skibo Castle, *Sutherland,* 1898.

Carnegie, David, of Colluthie (c. 1535-98). Son of Sir Robert C. of *Kinnaird*; member of commission on the laws 1578; *privy councillor* 1588; an *Octavian*; his eldest son was 1st *Earl of Southesk* and his next son *Earl of Northesk.*

Carnwath (Lanarkshire). *Burgh of barony* for *Lord Somerville* 1451. *Collegiate Church* supposed to have been founded by Thomas Somerville c. 1424, and there was a hospital, evidently not connected with collegiate church. Lands passed from Somervilles to *Lockharts* in 17th century.

Carnwath, Earldom. Created 1639 for Sir Robert Dalyell.

Carrick *(Orkney). Burgh of barony* for *Earl of Carrick* 1632.

Caroline Park. See Granton.

Carrick Castle (Loch Goil, *Argyll*). Originally belonged to *Lamonts,* but passed to *Campbells*; dates from 13th century.

Carrick, Earldom. Carrick, the southernmost division of Ayrshire, was once part of *Galloway;* first Earl recorded was Duncan, 1189-96; earldom passed to *Bruces* through marriage of Marjory, the Countess, to Robert, father of *Robert I;* held by *Edward Bruce,* by Alexander, his illegitimate son, and by William Cunningham (1362-8), but from 1368 by the heir apparent except for its tenure by Robert, 3rd son of *James VI* (1602). A second earldom of C., associated with C. in Orkney, was created for John, second son of *Robert, Earl of Orkney,* in 1628 and lapsed with his death c. 1644.

Carrick Pursuivant. First mentioned 1364. See Pursuivants.

Carrington (Midlothian). *Burgh of barony* for Lord *Ramsay* 1664; *burgh of regality* for Viscount Primrose 1706.

Carrodie Club. See Corrodie.

Carron Company. Founded 1759, with *iron*works near *Falkirk;* gave name to 'carronade', a gun made there.

Carsphairn, Kirkton of (Kirkcudbrightshire). *Burgh of barony* for Gierson of Lag 1635.

Carstairs (Lanarkshire). Lands belonged to *bishopric of Glasgow* and were erected into *barony* in 14th century; granted by *James VI* to Sir William Stewart; later passed to *Lockharts.*

Carstares, William (1649-1715). Born Cathcart, son of *Presbyterian minister* deprived in 1662; joined father in Holland 1669 and entered service of William, Prince of Orange, for whom he acted as an agent with the disaffected in England and Scotland; arrested and examined under torture 1683; released and returned to Holland 1684; at *Revolution* used his influence with William in favour of presbyterianism and mediated between King and *General Assembly*; principal of *Edinburgh University* 1703.

Carswell, John (c. 1525-72). *Parson* of Kilmartin 1551 and *Chancellor* of *chapel royal*; *superintendent* of *Argyll* c. 1562; *Bishop of Isles* 1567; translated *Book of Common Order* into *Gaelic*. See also Carnasserie.

Carthusian Order. See Perth Priory.

Cartland (Lanarkshire). *Burgh of barony* for Lockhart of *Lee* 1607.

Cartsdyke (Renfrewshire). *Burgh of barony* for Thomas Crawford 1669.

Carver. The office of hereditary carver belonged to the Anstruther family, baronets since 1694.

Casket Letters. Claimed to have been discovered in *Edinburgh Castle* in 1567 in a silver casket, identified with one preserved at *Lennoxlove*; produced as evidence to incriminate Queen *Mary* in conspiring with *Bothwell* for the murder of *Darnley*; as originals are not extant, it is impossible to pronounce on their authenticity, but opinion is that they represent a concoction of genuine letters, some of them written to Bothwell but not by Mary, with interpolated material.

Cassillis, Earldom. Created for David, 3rd Lord Kennedy, 1509; Gilbert, 3rd Earl (1517-1558, succeeded 1527) was captured at *Solway Moss,* was active in the English interest and was *Treasurer* from 1554 until his death at Dieppe, when he was a commissioner for the marriage of *Mary* to the Dauphin Francis; Gilbert, 4th Earl (1541-76), fought for Queen Mary at *Langside* and is notorious for his treatment of *Allan Stewart, Commendator of Crossraguel*; John, 6th Earl (c. 1595-1668, succeeded 1615), was *Justice General* 1649 and supported *Presbyterian* cause at *Restoration*; John, 7th Earl (c. 1646-1701), opposed the administration of *Lauderdale* and later supported *William of Orange*; 12th Earl created Marquis of Ailsa 1831.

Castellum (or Castrum) Puellarum. Medieval name for *Edinburgh Castle,* explained by a tale that *Pictish* kings kept their daughters there or that there was a nunnery; but the term 'Maiden Castle' is applied to various ancient fortresses, and no theory to explain it has gained general acceptance.

Castilians. (1) The rebels who held *St Andrews Castle* after murdering *Cardinal David Beaton* 1546; (2) the supporters of *Queen Mary* who held *Edinburgh Castle* until 1573.

Castlecary (Stirlingshire). Site of one of the forts on the *Antonine Wall*; about 7 miles west of *Falkirk*; a tower of 15th century date, which passed from the Baillies to the *Dundases,* is still inhabited.

Castle Douglas (Kirkcudbrightshire). *Burgh of barony* for Douglas of Castle Douglas 1791.

Castle Fraser (Aberdeenshire). Built by Michael Fraser (d. 1588) and his son and completed 1636; retained by Frasers until 1921; made over to *National Trust* 1976.

Casualty. Profits accruing to feudal *superior*: *ward,* the enjoyment of the land during minority of heir; nonentry, enjoyment of land on failure of heir to take possession; marriage, right to dispose of heir in marriage; relief, payment made by heir when he took possession.

Caterans. Highland marauders, especially so called when they descended on Lowlands.

Cathcart Family. Evidently a Breton called Rainald held lands of Cathcart (Renfrewshire) in 12th century and his successors took the name of the place; Alan of C. was a noted supporter of *Robert I*; Robert C. of Killochan, 2nd son of 2nd Lord C., married heiress of Carleton. See also Killochan.

Cathcart, Lordship. Created for Sir Alan C. c. 1452; earldom 1814.

Cathedrals. See Aberdeen, Brechin, Dornoch, Dunblane, Dunkeld, Edinburgh, Elgin, Fortrose, Glasgow, Iona, Kirkwall, Lismore, St Andrews, Whithorn.

Catholic Apostolic Church. Founded by *Edward Irving* and sometimes known as Irvingites, it had a ministry restricted until the expected Second Advent, and has therefore died out.

Catrail. Earthwork, of unknown origin, extending from near *Galashiels* to the western Border.

Caulfield, Major William (d. 1767). Grandson of 1st Viscount Charlemont (Irish); joined *General Wade* in Scotland by 1732 and soon became Inspector of Roads, a post he held until his death; Quartermaster to *Sir John Cope* 1745; advised Perthshire Commissioners of Supply on road-making; Lieutenant-Colonel 1751; built house of Cradlehall outside *Inverness.*

Causeway Mail. Toll or duty levied by magistrates of *Edinburgh* on vehicles entering city and used for upkeep of streets; in force from 17th century until 1878.

Cauvin's Hospital. Founded by Louis Cauvin, French teacher in *Edinburgh* and afterwards farmer at *Duddingston*; on his death (1825) he bequeathed his property for the education primarily of sons of poor teachers or farmers and the hospital was opened in 1833 for 17 boys.

Cavers (Roxburghshire). *Barony* passed from *Balliols* to *Douglases,* who held it until 1878.

Caw, Sir James Lewis (1864-1950). Born *Ayr*; married daughter of *William McTaggart*; Curator of *Scottish National Portrait Gallery* 1895-1907; Director of *National Galleries of Scotland* 1907-30.

Cawdor, Earldom. The ancient family of Cawdor (or Calder), Nairnshire, ended with Muriella, who in 1498 married Sir John Campbell, son of 2nd *Earl of Argyll.* The Campbells were raised to a U.K. baronage 1796 and earldom 1827.

Cellach. Bishops of *St Andrews*: (I) 906; (II) 970-c. 995.

Ceres (Fife). *Burgh of barony* for Hope of Craighall 1620.

Cess (= assessment). Levy on land, especially the land tax of the *Restoration* period, which some *Covenanters* declined to pay.

Cessford (Roxburghshire). Passed from Moubrays to *Douglases* in 14th century and was granted in 1446 to Andrew Ker, ancestor of *Earls of Roxburghe.*

Chalder. See Capacity, Measures of.

Chalmers, Alexander (1759-1834). Son of an *Aberdeen* printer; became journalist in London 1777; edited classics and wrote biographies; published 'History of the Colleges of Oxford' and 'General Biographical Dictionary'.

Chalmers, George (1742-1825). Born *Fochabers*; in Maryland 1763-75; practised as lawyer; settled in London 1775 and published pamphlets on America; edited classics and wrote biographies; compiled 'Caledonia' (1807-24) on Scottish topography and antiquities.

Chalmers Hospital *(Edinburgh).* Founded by bequest of George Chalmers (1773-1836), *Canongate* plumber, and opened 1864.

Chalmers, James (1841-1901). Born *Argyll*; *Congregational minister* 1865; joined London Missionary Society 1861 and served for ten years in Hervey Islands and then in New Guinea, where he was murdered by cannibals.

Chalmers, Patrick (1802-54). Captain of Dragoons; retired to Auldbar; M.P. for *Montrose* burghs 1835-42; wrote 'Ancient Sculptured Monuments . . . of *Angus*' (1848).

Chalmers, Peter MacGregor (1859-1922). Architect noted especially for his churches. See Paisley Abbey.

Chalmers, Thomas (1780-1847). Born *Anstruther; minister* of Kilmany 1803; assisted in mathematics department at *St Andrews*; minister of Tron, *Glasgow,* 1814, and St John's 1819; drew large congregations; with many paupers in his parishes, he was convinced that Christian charity, not poor rates, was the solution; professor of moral philosophy St Andrews 1823 and of divinity *Edinburgh* 1828; published 'Astronomical Discourses' (1817) and 'Political Economy' (1832); took lead in disputes which led to *Disruption;* first principal of *Free Church* College.

Chamberlain. Chief financial officer of the crown from 12th century; supervised *royal burghs,* which he visited on *ayre*; from reign of *James I* his importance diminished, but the office continued until 1705.

Chambers, David (?1530-1592). Studied in *Aberdeen,* France and Italy; *Lord of Session* (Ormond) 1565; implicated in murder of *Darnley*; attainted as supporter of Queen *Mary,* 1568, and went abroad; returned 1582 and restored to bench 1586; wrote 'Abbrégé des Histoires' (1579).

Chambers, Robert (1802-71). Brother of *William Chambers* and associated with him in bookselling and publishing; compiled 'A Biographical Dictionary of Eminent Scotsmen' (1832-4) and 'Domestic Annals of Scotland' (1859-61) and wrote several books, some of them on *Edinburgh.*

Chambers, Robert (1832-88). Son of preceding; took part in publication of the family's 'Encyclopaedia' and became editor of the 'Journal' in 1874.

Chambers, Sir William (1726-96). Studied architecture in Italy and France and practised in London; designed Somerset House.

Chambers, William (1800-83). Moved from *Peebles* to *Edinburgh* 1814 and with his brother Robert set up business as booksellers, then as printers and finally as publishers, responsible for many reference books, including 'Chambers' Encyclopaedia', and for 'Chambers' Journal' (1832). William became Lord *Provost* of Edinburgh 1865 and 1868, initiated many improvement schemes and expended large sums on the restoration of the church of *St. Giles.*

Chancellor. (1) An officer, first heard of under *Alexander I,* who kept the *great seal* and directed the chancery from which various writs were issued. In 16th and 17th centuries usually regarded as being at the head of the administration. (2) Cathedral dignitary who kept *chapter* seal and superintended *grammar school.* (3) Titular head of a university.

Chanter. Part of *bagpipe* on which melody

is played.

Chantor. Scottish equivalent of Latin and English 'precentor'; superintended music of cathedral and its *song school.*

Chapel Royal. The original chapel royal was the *collegiate church* of *St Mary of the Rock, St Andrews.* The chapel at *Stirling* took its place in *James IV's* reign. At *Holyrood,* where there had long been a domestic chapel within the palace, the nave of the abbey church was taken over as a chapel by *James VII.*

Chapman (or **Chepman**), **Walter** (c. 1473-c. 1538). Clerk in office of King's Secretary 1494, but also a merchant who acquired landed property; supplied money for establishment of first Scottish printing press, directed by *Andrew Myllar,* founded a chaplainry in the 'Chapman Aisle' in *St Giles'* Church, *Edinburgh.*

Chapter. Corporate body of dignitaries and canons of cathedral; regulated cathedral services and had to give consent to certain acts of the bishop, including charters.

Charles I (1600-1649). Second son of *James VI,* born at *Dunfermline,* became heir apparent on death of *Prince Henry* 1612; succeeded 27 March 1625 and married Henrietta Maria on 1 May following; visited Scotland for his coronation 1633 and again, in an effort to appease the *Covenanters,* 1641; beheaded at Whitehall 30 January 1649.

Charles II (1630-1685). Eldest son of preceding, proclaimed king at *Edinburgh* on the news of his father's death; the Scots agreed to bring him from his exile in Holland on condition that he would sign the *Covenants;* he was crowned at *Scone* on 1 January 1651, but the Scots, already defeated at *Dunbar,* met with another defeat when they invaded England, at *Worcester.* Charles again fled overseas, to return to England at *Restoration* in 1660, but he did not revisit Scotland; died 6 February 1685.

Charles Edward, 'de jure' **Charles III,** otherwise the Young Pretender (1720-88). Elder son of *'James VIII'*; born Rome 31 December 1720; landed in Scotland 12 July 1745; victorious at *Prestonpans* and *Falkirk*; defeated at *Culloden*; left Scotland 20 September 1746; married Princess Louisa of Stolberg, but had no legitimate children; his illegitimate daughter Charlotte was styled Duchess of *Albany*; died at Rome 31 January 1788.

'Charlotte Dundas'. First steamboat on *Forth and Clyde Canal,* built by *William Symington* in 1802.

Charterhouse. See Perth Priory.

Charteris, Archibald Hamilton (1835-1908). Professor of Biblical Criticism, *Edinburgh,* 1868-98; founded Women's Guild in *Church of Scotland* and established the periodical 'Life and Work'.

Charteris Family. See Kinfauns.

Chaseabout Raid, August-September 1565. Rebellion against Queen *Mary* by *Earl of Moray* after her marriage to *Darnley.*

Châtelard. French poet who was executed in February 1563 for concealing himself in Queen *Mary's* bedroom and forcing his attentions on her.

Châtelherault, Dukedom. Conferred in 1550, with yearly income of 30,000 livres, on *James Hamilton, 2nd Earl of Arran*; restored to Duke of Hamilton in 19th century.

Chepman. See Chapman.

Cherity. Quantity, e.g. of grain, over and above the actual measure stipulated.

Chevalier de St George. See James Francis.

Cheviot Sheep. A Border breed, improved in late 18th century, and subsequently modified to suit Highland conditions.

Chevy Chase, Battle of. See Otterburn.

Cheyne Family. Bernard le Cheyne received lands of *Inverugie* from *William I*; Reginald was *Chamberlain* 1267-9 and his brother Henry was Bishop of *Aberdeen* 1282-1328; Reginald's grand-daughter married a Keith and from his female descendant the lands went by marriage to the Earl *Marischal.*

Chiefs. See Clans.

Chisholm, William (c. 1494-1564). Bishop of *Dunblane* 1527-64 in succession to his brother James, who had been Bishop from 1487; did not accept *Reformation.*

Chisholm, William (d. 1593). Bishop of *Dunblane,* nephew of preceding and his coadjutor from 1561; went to continent and was bishop of Vaison from 1570 until 1585, when he resigned in favour of his nephew, another William.

Choppin. Measure of capacity: = 2 mutchkins = Scots pint = more than an imperial quart.

Christian Knowledge. See Society.

Christianity, Introduction of. See Ninian; Columba.

'Christis Kirk on the Grene'. 15th century poem, of which the scene was probably set in *Leslie,* Fife, describing local festivities; attributed to *James I* and *James V.*

'Christopher North'. See Wilson, John.

Christ's Well *(Doune, Menteith).* This supposed healing well drew such crowds that in 1624 the *Privy Council* threatened with imprisonment those who might attend.

Chrochallan Fencibles. Club formed in *Edinburgh* c. 1778 by *William Smellie,* to meet at Douglas's Tavern in Anchor Close; the landlord entertained his customers by singing a *Gaelic* song, 'Chro Challan'; *Robert Burns* attended 1787; ceased c. 1795.

Chrystal, George (1851-1911). Professor of mathematics at *Edinburgh* 1879; made researches on Ohm's Law.

Church of Scotland. The present *presbyterian* system of government was established by *Parliament* in 1690; it lost many members as a result of *Secessions* and the *Disruption,* but in 1929 the majority of the successors of those who had seceded, now forming the *United Free Church,* united with the Church of Scotland.

Churchill Barriers. Constructed during World War II to seal the eastern approaches to *Scapa Flow*; subsequently formed bases of roads linking Burray and South Ronaldsay to the *Orkney* Mainland.

Ciaran, St. Supposed to have landed from Ireland in Kintyre in 6th century; his church at Dalruadhain, Cill-Chiarain, gave the name *Kilkerran* to the place later called *Campbeltown.*

Cistercian Order. See Balmerino, Coupar, Culross, Deer, Dundrennan, Glenluce, Kinloss, Melrose, Newbattle, Saddell, Sweetheart.

City Guard (*Edinburgh*). Supposed to have been established in the troubled minority of *James V*; reconstructed 1648 with captain, 2 lieutenants and 60 men; another body, numbering 126, was raised in 1689; disbanded early 19th century.

City of Glasgow Bank. Founded 1839; collapsed 1878-82, with debts of over £7,000,000; directors convicted of fraud and imprisoned.

Clach a' Choin. The Dog's Stone, a huge pillar of conglomerate near Dunolly Castle, *Oban*; according to legend the tethering post of *Bran.*

Clachan. Properly speaking a settlement containing a church, like Lowland 'kirktoun', but applied to any hamlet.

Clach-na-Cùdainn. Stone of the Tubs; in front of *Inverness* Town Hall is a fountain on the site of this stone, so named from the fact that women carrying water from the river used to rest their tubs on it.

Clachnaharry, Battle of, 1454. Between Clan Munro and Clan Mackintosh.

Clackmannan. A *royal burgh* mentioned 1165x1171 and the seat of a *sheriff*; *David II* gave the barony to Robert Bruce, a kinsman, and in 1551 the burgh was a *burgh of barony;* an early royal castle was superseded by the existing tower, a *Bruce* possession which dates in part from 14th century.

Claim of Right, 11 April 1689. The *Convention of Estates* declared that *James VII* by his unconstitutional acts had forfeited the crown, and offered the vacant throne to *William of Orange* and his wife Mary, James's elder daughter.

Claimants to the Throne. See Competitors.

Clan. 'Clann' properly means 'children' and thus the descendants of the ancestor to whom a social group attributed its origin; the historic clan took its name from the chief or landlord, but included many clansmen or tenants who shared neither blood relationship nor surname with the chief, who not infrequently was himself descended from an incomer to whom the bulk of the clan could not be related.

Clan Act, 1715. Aimed at breaking down the ties between chief and clansmen; if tenants on the land of a *Jacobite* chief remained loyal they would be excused rents for two years; but if tenants of loyal landlords joined a rebellion their tenancies would be forfeited to the landlord; and settlements in favour of heirs—a device to avoid forfeiture—were forbidden.

Clan Fight at Perth, 28 September 1396. Thirty of the Clan Chattan, with the loss of 19 men, slew 29 out of 30 of the Clan Kay or Quhele, in a battle on the North Inch at *Perth* in presence of *Robert III.*

Clan Line. Shipping Company founded 1845.

Clapperton, Hugh (1788-1827). Born *Annan*; pressed into navy and became Captain and Commander; between 1822 and 1827 led expeditions from Tripoli across the Sahara to the Niger and in various parts of Nigeria.

Clarendon Historical Society. Founded in *Edinburgh* 1882 for publication of historical source material especially from 1440 to 1745; ceased to publish 1889.

Clark's Thread Mills. See Coats.

Clarsach. The ancient Highland harp, of which the Lamont Harp and 'Queen Mary's Harp' survive in the *National Museum of Antiquities.*

Classes, Act of. See Act of Classes.

Clatt (Aberdeenshire). *Burgh of barony* under Bishop of *Aberdeen* 1501.

Claudero. Pen-name of James Wilson, a cripple born in Cumberland, who taught at school in the Cowgate, *Edinburgh,* and commemorated in verse some of the old structures of the town.

Clava, Stones of. Cairns and stone circle in Nairnshire, near *Culloden.*

Clavie. A half-barrel of burning tar, carried on a pole in procession at *Burghead* on 11 January.

Claymore. ('Claidheamh mòr' = 'great sword'.) The two-handed sword of the middle ages.

Cleanse the Causeway, April 1520. Fight in *Edinburgh* between *Douglases* under *6th Earl of Angus* and *Hamiltons* under *1st Earl of Arran,* in association with *James Beaton, Archbishop of Glasgow;* the Hamiltons were defeated.

Clearances. The reorganisation of Highland estates, mainly in the first half of the nineteenth century, involved an expansion of sheep farming at the expense of arable farming, and the consequent removal of tenants from their previous holdings, mostly to other holdings elsewhere on the estate.

Cleaven Dyke (Perthshire). Extends from River Tay to River Isla, in parish of Caputh, abutting on a small Roman fort; one of the supposed sites of *Mons Graupius.*

Cleghorn, Hugh (1757-1834). Professor of civil history at *St Andrews* 1773-93; went to Ceylon 1795 and was instrumental in detaching the mercenaries from the Dutch to whom the island belonged and bringing about its surrender to the British.

Cleish (Kinross-shire). Lands acquired by Colvilles 1530; castle, dating from late 15th century, was ruinous but was restored 1840.

Cleland, James (1770-1840). *Glasgow* cabinet-maker who showed a flair for statistics, first in connection with his own craft and later in connection with the city's vital statistics (in which he had a special interest because, as Superintendent of Public Works from 1814, he was responsible for organisation of burials).

Cleland, William (c. 1661-89). On leaving *St Andrews University* joined militant *Covenanters* and fought at *Drumclog* and *Bothwell Brig,* then fled to Holland and studied at Utrecht; took part in *Argyll's rebellion* 1684 and again fled to Holland; at the *Revolution* was appointed to command the *Cameronian Regiment,* which held *Dunkeld* against the *Jacobite* army which had been victorious at *Killiecrankie* but Cleland was killed in the action.

Clement (d. c. 1257). Bishop of *Dunblane* from 1233; built cathedral.

Clerical Estate. Bishops, abbots, priors and occasionally some lesser clergy formed an estate in *parliament* which was abolished in 1639, restored in 1661 and abolished again in 1689.

Clerk, Sir John, of *Penicuik* (1676-1755). Son of Sir John Clerk, Bart. (d. 1722); *advocate* 1700; member of *parliament* and commissioner for *Union* of 1707, then M.P. at Westminster; wrote on economics and antiquities, which he collected.

Clerk, John (1728-1812). Younger son of preceding; merchant in *Edinburgh;* studied naval tactics although he never went to sea, and wrote an essay on the subject, printed 1782; acquired estate of Eldin, Midlothian.

Clerk, John (1757-1832). Eldest son of preceding; *advocate* 1785; *Lord of Session* (Eldin) 1823.

Clerk Register. From late 13th century there were clerks responsible for keeping the royal or national archives, and the title 'clerk of the rolls, register and council' appears in 14th century; 'clerk register' became usual before 1600; in 16th and 17th centuries usually a trained lawyer, later more often a peer, but retaining responsibility for administration of Scottish archives until 19th century; his last significant function vanished with the abolition of the election of Scottish peers to the House of Lords (1963), but the office still exists.

Clerk-Maxwell, James (1831-79). Born *Edinburgh;* read papers to *Royal Society of Edinburgh* before he was twenty; professor of *natural philosophy* at *Aberdeen* 1856 and at King's College, London, 1860; professor of experimental physics at Cambridge 1871; described as 'the great genius of the 19th century', his researches covered a wide field, but his main discoveries were in electricity and magnetism; wrote 'Theory of Heat' and 'Matter and Motion'.

Clerkington (Midlothian). Otherwise Nicolson, Rosebery or Ancrum; *burgh of barony* for Nicolson of Lasswade 1669.

Clitheroe, Battle of, 9 June 1138. *William FitzDuncan* defeated English.

Clochmaben Stone, Battle of. See Sark, battle of.

Closeburn (Nithsdale). Granted by *Alexander II* to Ivan de Kirkpatrick 1232; Thomas Kirkpatrick became a baronet 1685.

Closeburn, Wallace Hall Academy. Founded 1723 by bequest of John Wallace.

Clova (Aberdeenshire). Only evidence that there had been a monastery there is a reference to a 'monastery of Cloveth' in 1157.

Club. An association formed by the opposition to the ministers of William of Orange (*William II*).
Cluniac Order. See Crossraguel, May, Paisley.
Clunie Castle (Perthshire). On island in loch near *Blairgowrie*; residence of bishops of *Dunkeld* at least from George Brown (1485-1514); acquired by Crichton of Eliok 1562.
Clunies-Ross, George (d. 1854). *Shetland* seaman who acquired the Cocos-Keeling Islands 1825, when they were a kind of no man's land, and developed them; his son became governor when the islands were proclaimed British territory.
Cluny (Aberdeenshire). *Barony* held since 15th century by successive *Gordon* families; the castle is a 19th century castellated mansion on an old site.
Cluny's Cage. A refuge, constructed of trees and brushwood, on the side of Ben Alder, occupied by *Ewen Macpherson of Cluny* after *Culloden* and visited by *Donald Cameron of Lochiel* and Prince *Charles Edward.*
Clyde Company. Formed 1836 by Scottish settlers in Tasmania to develop pastoral farming there and in Victoria.
Clyde, River. Dredged and deepened, to make it navigable, 1770 onwards.
Clyde, Lord. See Campbell, Sir Colin.
Clydebank (Dunbartonshire). *Police 'burgh* 1886.
Clydebank Company. Grew from firm of J. and G. Thomson, founded 1846; merged with John Brown 1899.
Clydesdale Bank. Founded 1838; took over Greenock Union Bank, Edinburgh and Glasgow Bank and Eastern Bank of Scotland; amalgamated with *North of Scotland Bank* 1950.
Clydesdale Horses. Already famous in 18th century and said to derive from six black stallions brought from Flanders by a *Duke of Hamilton.*
Clydesdale, Marquisate. Created 1643 as subsidiary to *dukedom of Hamilton.*
Coal Mining. May have begun in Roman times, but first recorded in monastic charters, e.g. at Carriden (pertaining to *Holyrood*) c. 1200, near *Musselburgh* (*Newbattle*) a little later, and at Pittencrieff (*Dunfermline*) 1291.
Coalstoun. See Colstoun.
Co-Arb. A successor to an abbot in a Celtic monastery, when the office was kept within the members of a family.
Coatbridge (Lanarkshire). *Burgh* created by Parliament 1885.
Coats, Thomas (1809-83). His father founded *Paisley* thread firm 1826; under him and his brother Peter the Ferguslie thread mill prospered and Coats made many gifts to the town—park, playgrounds and an observatory; he was a numismatist of note; firm amalgamated with Clark 1896.
Cochrane, Charles (1749-81). Second son of *Earl of Dundonald*; captain in 4th Regiment, sent to Boston (Massachusetts) 1774; involved in preliminaries to American War of Independence and in various battles; major in British Legion of Loyalists 1778; advocated independence of northern colonies; killed at Yorktown.
Cochrane, Lordship. The lands of C. (Renfrewshire) were held from 14th century by Cochrane family; Sir William C. created Lord C. of Dundonald 1647; lands remained with *Earls of Dundonald* until c. 1760.
Cochrane, Robert (d. 1482). Described as a 'mason' who was a favourite of *James III,* but assumed to have been an architect who designed a great hall at *Stirling Castle*; there is no support for the tale that he was made *Earl of Mar*; hanged at *Lauder Bridge* by indignant nobles.
Cochrane, Thomas, 10th Earl of Dundonald. See Dundonald.
Cockburn, Adam (1656-1735). Inherited estate of Ormiston (East Lothian), on which he carried out improvements; *Justice Clerk* 1692-9, 1705-10 and 1714-35; *Lord of Session* (Ormiston) 1705.
Cockburn, Alison (1710-94). Née Rutherford; married Patrick Cockburn, *advocate*; friend of *Sir Walter Scott*; wrote 'The Flowers of the Forest'.
Cockburn Association (*Edinburgh*). Founded 1875, it claims to be the oldest amenity society in Britain; *H.T. Cockburn* had been much concerned for the preservation of Edinburgh buildings.
Cockburn, Henry Thomas (1779-1854). *Advocate* 1800; supported *Whigs* in campaign for extension of franchise and criticised the wide powers of the *Lord Advocate* in administration; *Solicitor General* 1830; *Lord of Session* 1834; his 'Memorials' and 'Journal' published posthumously.
Cockburn, John (1679-1758). Son of *Adam C*; member of last Scottish *parliament* and a commissioner for *Union* of 1707; sat in British parliament until 1741; continued father's agrarian improvements but they were not a financial success and he had to sell the estate to the

Earl of Hopetoun in 1747.

Cockburnspath (Berwickshire). *Burgh of barony* for Arnot of Cockburnspath 1612; hospital mentioned 1511-81.

Cockenzie and Port Seton (East Lothian). *Burgh of barony* for *Lord Seton* 1591; *burgh of regality* (under name Winton) for *Earl of Winton* 1686. See also Wagonways.

Cocket. See Coquet.

Cock-Fighting. Said to date back to Celtic times; in 17th to 19th centuries a common sport in schools; associated with Shrove Tuesday or Fastern's Eve.

Code of Canons. Introduced by *Charles I* 1635-6; intended to suppress non-liturgical worship and to efface the structure of *presbyteries* which had hitherto co-operated with bishops; reinforced royal supremacy in ecclesiastical matters; ordered registration of baptisms, marriages and burials.

Codex Flotticensis. Term arising from confusion between the Flateyiarbook (= book compiled on flat island) and the Orcadian island of Flotta; a collection of Icelandic literature written c. 1380.

Coel or **Coilus.** A British king in Roman or post-Roman period, associated with *Strathclyde.*

Coilsfield (Ayrshire). A circular mound is pointed out as tomb of *King Coel*; when opened in 1837 it was found to contain cinerary urns.

Coinage. Earliest Scottish coins which are known are silver *pennies* of the reign of *David I.* First gold coin was a *noble* (6s. 8d.) of *David II.* Under *James I* pennies and halfpennies of billon (an alloy of silver with a base metal) came in, and copper farthings appeared under *James III.* See also entries for various coins.

Coinneach Odhar, The Brahan Seer. See Mackenzie, Kenneth.

Coldingham (Berwickshire). In 7th century there was a monastery for monks and nuns, which later became a nunnery and was probably destroyed by Danes; church dependent on Durham was established by *King Edgar,* but it is not clear when a *Benedictine* priory emerged; the priory fell under the domination of the *Home* family in 15th century and was erected into a *temporal lordship* for Alexander Home 1606; the choir, restored, is still in use. Coldingham became a *burgh of barony for* Stewart of Coldingham 1638.

Coldstream Guards. 2nd Foot Guards, raised by *Monck* at Coldstream 1660, out of Fenwick's and Hessellrigg's regiments.

Coldstream Nunnery (*Cistercian*) (Berwickshire). Founded before 1166 by Cospatrick, *Earl of Dunbar*; *temporal lordship* for son of *Earl of Melrose* 1621; nothing remains of buildings.

Colinsburgh (Fife). *Burgh of barony* for Colin, 3rd *Earl of Balcarres.*

Colkitto. See MacDonald, Alastair.

College of Justice. See Justice.

Collegiate Church. So called because it was served by a 'college' or body of clergy, with a head usually called a 'provost'. The objects were to render divine service with ceremonial and music impossible in an average parish church and to provide for the saying of numerous masses.

Collins, Publishers. William Collins, a schoolmaster, started publishing in *Glasgow* 1819; his son, also William, opened London branch 1839.

Colm, St (fl. c. 600). Said to have been associated with *Drostan*; but *Inchcolm* is 'Insula Sancti Columbe', St *Columba's* Isle.

Colman, St (c. 605-76). *Iona* monk who succeeded *Finan* as abbot of Lindisfarne and bishop of the Angles; led Celtic party at *Synod of Whitby* and on his defeat withdrew from England.

Colonel Anne. See Mackintosh, Anne.

Colossus of Roads. See Telford, Thomas.

Colquhoun. Descended from Umfridus (Humphrey) de Kilpatrick who received lands of Colquhoun (Dunbartonshire) from *Earl of Lennox* c. 1241; acquired *Luss* by marriage in mid-14th century.

Colstoun (East Lothian) **Pear.** Magic pear given by the wizard Hugh of *Yester* or Gifford to his daughter on her marriage to a Broun of Colstoun in 13th century; so long as her family held the pear they were to prosper. The pear, shrivelled to the size of a plum, passed by marriage to the 9th *Earl of Dalhousie* and again by marriage to the Bourke family.

Coltness Iron Company. See Houldsworth.

Columba, St (521-97). Born in Donegal of royal race; founded monasteries in Ireland; a quarrel with King Diarmit led to his expulsion from Ireland and settlement at *Iona* (?565); strengthened kingdom of *Dalriada* and visited *Pictish* king at *Inverness*; well known from his 'Life' by his successor, *Adamnan.*

Colville, John (c. 1542-1605). Graduated *St Andrews* 1561; a *minister,* appointed *chantor* of *Glasgow,* but turned to politics; master of requests 1578; had devious career as an English agent, but later renounced protestantism and died in Paris.

'Comes'. Latin term used to translate *mormaer,* but also used to translate the English 'earl', with which mormaer became equated.

'Comet'. Steamboat invented by *Henry Bell;* wrecked at Dorus Mor 1820.

Commendators. Initially a commendator was a cleric appointed to administer and enjoy the revenues of a benefice which he was not qualified to hold; a bishop, for example, could be a commendator of an abbey although he was not a monk. The practice was extended in 16th century to enable laymen to draw revenues without performing religious duties and the office became quasi-hereditary.

Commercial Bank of Scotland. Established in *Edinburgh* 1810, by a deed of partnership on a joint-stock basis; the first bank not established by public authority to assume a national designation; royal charter came 1831; absorbed *Caithness* and *Arbroath* Banking Companies 1825 and 1844; amalgamated with *National Bank* 1958.

Commissary Courts. The jurisdiction of ecclesiastical courts in executry and matrimonial cases was disrupted by the *Reformation,* and in 1564 a new Commissary Court was created for *Edinburgh* with a general jurisdiction over the whole country in matrimonial cases and in testaments above a certain value. Local commissary courts throughout the country had restricted jurisdiction in areas called 'commissariots' based on the old dioceses; most of the business was transferred to *sheriff courts* in 1823.

Commissioners. *Ministers* in the reformed church who combined the tasks of *superintendents* with their parochial duties.

Commissioners for Highland Roads and Bridges. Operated 1803-62; by 1821 had constructed nearly 1000 miles of roads.

Commissioners for Northern Lights. Established 1786.

Commissioners of Supply. Originated with the assessment for land tax in Scottish counties from 1667; through time their functions were widened beyond drawing up valuations and they were the main element in county administration until 1889, when county councils were set up.

Committee of Estates. In 1640-51, 1660-1 and 1688-9 *Parliament* appointed a committee, including lairds and *burgesses* who were not members of Parliament, with wide powers to act on behalf of Parliament but without the need to report to it; from 1640 to 1651 the committee was in effect the government of the country; the committee in office in 1651 was captured by *General Monck* at *Alyth.*

Common Good. The *burgh* fund consisting of profits of burgh lands, fees paid on admission of *burgesses* etc; before the days of rates it was the main revenue of a burgh.

Common Riding. A ceremonial procession maintained or revived in a number of Scottish *burghs*; it was meaningful in earlier times, when, as the Burgh Court Book of *Selkirk,* for example, shows in the 1530s, the boundaries were visited and verified each May or June. Cf. March Ridings.

'Common Sense' Philosophy. In reaction against what some thought to be unrealistic speculations about psychology and perception, some Scots founded a 'common sense' school of thought, expounded by *Dugald Stewart* and *Sir William Hamilton* and influential in France and America.

Commonwealth. Established in England 1649 after execution of *Charles I*; Scotland incorporated in it in October 1651, after Cromwellian conquest. See Cromwellian Administration.

Communion Stones. Near Kirkpatrick-Irongray, *Nithsdale,* marking site where 300 *conventiclers* are said to have held a Communion in 1678.

Communion Tokens. Metal tokens formerly distributed by *elders* and brought to church by communicants to show that they had been found worthy of admission; succeeded by Communion Cards.

Community of the Realm. A phrase used in late 13th and early 14th centuries, apparently meaning the men who counted politically.

Company of Scotland. See Darien Scheme.

Compear. To appear in a court of law, especially when summoned.

Competitors. The thirteen persons who claimed the throne after the death of the *Maid of Norway* in 1290: *Florent V, Count of Holland*; Patrick, *Earl of Dunbar*; William de Vesci; William de Ros; Robert de Pinkeny; Nicolas de *Soules*; Patrick Galithly; Roger de Mandeville; *John Comyn*; John Hastings; *John Balliol*; *Robert Bruce*; Erik, King of Norway.

'Complaynt of Scotland'. Political treatise, favourable to France and hostile to England, printed at *St Andrews* 1548. See Inglis, James.

Comptroller. 'Computorum rotulator' or roller of accounts; shared financial administration with *Treasurer.*

Comyn, Alexander, *Earl of Buchan* (d. 1289). Son of William Comyn and Marjory, Countess of Buchan; married an heiress of *Alan, Lord of Galloway* and *Constable of Scotland,* and became Constable; also a *justiciar* and *sheriff,* and a *Guardian* 1286. His eldest son, John (c. 1260-1308), acted mainly on English side after 1296, but John's wife, Isabella, daughter of Duncan, *Earl of Fife,* is said to have crowned *Robert I.*

Comyn Family. Robert de Comyn (Comines, Flanders), a companion of William the Conqueror, died 1069; his son William was in Scotland but the family remained essentially English until Richard, Robert's great-grandson, married a grand-daughter of *Donald Bane.*

Comyn, John, *Lord of Badenoch* (d. c. 1303). Known as 'the Black Comyn', son of 'the Red Comyn' (I); a *Guardian* 1286; a *Competitor* 1290, on ground of descent from *Donald Bane;* married a sister of *John Balliol.*

Comyn, John (d. 1306). 'The Red Comyn' (II), son of preceding; associated with cause of resistance as long as it was carried on in name of *Balliol,* but could not co-operate with *Robert I,* who murdered him at *Dumfries* 10 February 1306.

Comyn, Walter (c. 1190-1258). Second son of William, *Earl of Buchan*; *Lord of Badenoch*; married Isabella, Countess of *Menteith,* but had no children and his heir was his nephew John, 'the Red Comyn' (I), son of his elder brother, Richard.

Comyn, William, *Earl of Buchan* (d. 1233). Son of Richard Comyn (see Comyn Family) by a grand-daughter of *Donald Bane*; married Countess of Buchan and founded abbey of *Deer* 1219; *justiciar* and *sheriff.*

Conan, St (d. c. 648). Irishman, monk of *Iona,* said to have become a bishop in *Man.*

Conan Doyle, Sir Arthur (1859-1930). Born *Edinburgh*; qualified as physician; creator of 'Sherlock Holmes' and author of many historical novels; knighted 1902.

Concordat of Leith. Agreement between government and a convention of *ministers* in January 1572 approving the appointment to vacant bishoprics of ministers nominated by crown and admitted by church.

Confederate Lords. Party who raised an army against Queen *Mary* after her marriage to *Bothwell* and made her surrender at *Carberry.*

Confession of Faith. Statement of reformed doctrine approved by *Parliament* in 1560 and again in 1567; sometimes known as 'The Scots Confession'; superseded by *Westminster Confession* in 1640s.

Congested Districts Board. Established 1897 to deal with over-population in western isles.

Congregation, Lords of the. Originally the signatories of the *First Bond,* but later the leaders of the rebellion of 1559-60 against the French alliance and the Roman Church.

Congregational Church. There were some 'Old Scotch Independents' in 18th century, but most of the Congregational churches stem from either the missions of *James and Robert Haldane,* which produced the Congregational Union, or the work of *James Morison,* whose followers produced the Evangelical Union; the two merged in 1896.

Connell, John (c. 1765-1831). *Advocate* 1788; legal adviser to *Church of Scotland*; judge of Court of Admiralty 1816; knighted 1822; wrote authoritative 'Treatise on Tithes'.

Conservator. The medieval councils of the Scottish Church, before the appearance of archbishops, selected a bishop as chairman and he was known latterly as 'Conservator of the privileges of the Scottish Church'.

Conservator of the Staple. See Staple.

Constable, Archibald (1774-1827). Born Carnbee, Fife; bookseller's apprentice, Edinburgh; became bookseller and publisher; started '*Edinburgh Review*' 1802; shared in publication of *Walter Scott*'s poems and encouraged him to complete 'Waverley'; entered into London partnership 1808; bankrupt 1826.

Constable of Scotland. The office appears under *Alexander I*; it became hereditary in the *De Morville* family and about 1300 passed to the *Hays,* later *Earls of Errol,* with whom it has remained. The officer's duties were partly in military organisation, partly in securing the peace of the King's court.

Constable, Thomas (1812-81). Son of *Archibald;* entered printing and publishing business; published *Dugald Stewart*'s works, Calvin's 'Commentaries' and an educational series; Queen's printer 1839; joined by his son Archibald 1865; business continued as Thomas and Archibald Constable.

Constance. Abbey, founded 1142, remained in Irish hands until 1518, when a Scottish abbot was appointed from *Ratisbon*; demolished 1533. See Schottenklöster.

Constant Moderators. Permanent chairmen of *presbyteries* and *synods,* introduced 1606-7.

Constant Platt. Scheme prepared by *John Lindsay of Menmuir* to improve stipends of *ministers*; laid aside at the time, but some of its provisions were put into effect later in *James VI*'s reign and in *Charles I*'s.

Constantine (d. 820). King of *Picts* 807; harried by Norse; founded church of *Dunkeld*; possibly ruled *Dalriada* as well.

Constantine I (d. 879). Son of *Kenneth mac Alpin*; King of *Alba* 863; killed in battle against Norse.

Constantine II (d. 952). Son of Aedh; King of *Alba* 900; raided by Scandinavians, but his invasions of Northumbria provoked retaliation from south and he was finally defeated at *Brunanburgh*; abdicated to become monk of *St Andrews* 940.

Constantine III (d. 997). King of *Alba* briefly after killing *Kenneth II* (995); killed by *Kenneth III*.

Conventicles. Unauthorised meetings for worship, especially in *Restoration* period. An act of 1662 declared that none should preach or act as teacher without the licence of a bishop, and an act of 1670 imposed penalties up to death for preaching at conventicles and fines on those attending.

Convention of Estates. Meeting of estates of the realm held with less formality than a *parliament*, without judicial powers but with legislative and tax-imposing powers.

Convention of Royal Burghs. Meetings of the convention, under that name, did not become regular until nearly the middle of the 16th century, but there is ample evidence of concerted action by the *burghs*, or the more important of them, before that date, and the convention is believed to have evolved from the *Court of the Four Burghs* in its non-judicial aspect. The records of the convention begin in 1552 and yearly meetings are recorded from 1578. With the reorganisation of local government in 1975 (see Wheatley Report) a Convention of Local Authorities was set up.

Conveth. Ancient due, rendered to *superior* in lieu of hospitality.

Cope, Sir John (d. 1760). Colonel of foot 1730, of dragoons 1737; Lieutenant-General 1743; commander of the army which *Jacobites* routed at *Prestonpans*.

Coquet or Cocket. Certificate of the payment of customs duty on exports, given under a Coquet Seal.

Corbeil, Treaty of, 1326. Renewal by *Robert I* of the *Franco-Scottish alliance*.

Corbett Tower (Roxburghshire). Burned by English 1522 and 1545; rebuilt 1575; gradually fell into decay, but renovated in early 19th century.

Corbie Steps. Otherwise crow-steps; stepped skew on a gable.

Corgarff Castle (Aberdeenshire). Built before 1550; in 1571 burned down, with Margaret Campbell, wife of the Forbes laird, her family and servants, by *Adam Gordoun of Auchindoun*; burned by *Jacobites* 1689 and 1746.

Coronation Oath. Indications of the content of such an oath emerge in 14th century, when the kings were obliged to undertake to root out heretics and to conserve the patrimony of the crown. These elements survive in the first oath of which we have the full text, that of 1567. This style continued until the *Union*, after which there was an Accession Oath whereby the sovereign undertook to maintain the *presbyterian* settlement of the *Church of Scotland*.

Coroner. Provision was made in 1357 for appointment by crown of coroners, and c. 1600 the coroner or 'crowner' held inquests on murders; until 18th century, when the office became obsolete, coroners arrested persons indicted in the *Justiciary Court*.

Corrichie, Battle of, 28 October 1562. Royal forces led by James *Stewart, Earl of Moray*, defeated *4th Earl of Huntly*.

Corrodie Club (*Perth*). Formed early in 19th century for discussing literature, politics—and whisky; met at Old Ship Inn in High Street.

Corsewall Castle (Wigtownshire). Passed in 1333 from Stewarts of Dreghorn to *Campbells* of Loudoun.

Corstorphine (*Edinburgh*). Lands held from 1376 by *Forrester* family, created Lords Forrester 1633; their castle was occupied until at least 1698, but was destroyed 1790 and no remains are extant.

Corstorphine Collegiate Church. Originated in chapel beside parish church 1426; *collegiate* constitution by 1436; a hospital was attached to it in 16th century.

Cortachy Castle (*Angus*). Home of the *Ogilvies* of *Airlie* since 17th century, but there was a much earlier castle; later accretions have been removed and the oldest portion retained.

Cospatric (fl. 1067). Earl of Northumberland who was forfeited for rebellion against William the Conqueror, and, fleeing to Scotland, received *Dunbar* from *Malcolm III*; his son of the same name (d. 1138) was Earl of Dunbar, followed by a third Cospatric (d. 1166).

Cottar. Tenant holding only a minimum, if any, of arable land and pasture, in addition to a cottage, and presumably earning a wage.

Cotton. The spinning and weaving of cotton developed rapidly from c. 1780 and was the most important single Scottish industry from that period until about the 1860s.

Cotton Mills. First established at *Rothesay, Penicuik* and *Anderston,* 1778-80; see also Dale, David.

Coul (Ross). *Burgh of barony* for Mackenzie of Coul 1681.

Coull (Aberdeenshire). A 13th century castle was seat of Durward family; the property of Corse, within the barony, was granted in 1476 to a *Forbes* family, who built castle dated 1581.

Council. The undifferentiated king's council of the middle ages was the source of *Privy Council, General Council, Parliament* and *Court of Session.*

Council and Session, Lords of. The judges of the *Court of Session.*

Council of Trade. Set up by *Parliament* 1661 to regulate, improve and develop trade and manufactures and to establish companies.

Country Party. See Court Party.

County Councils. Established 1889; abolished 1975. See Commissioners of Supply; Wheatley Report.

County Franchise. In theory, all who held land of the crown could attend *Parliament,* but the smaller men had little desire to exercise their right. An act of 1426 ordered them to come, an act of 1428 authorised each *sheriff*dom to send two representatives, but neither act was observed. In 1587 the act of 1428 was re-enacted and from shortly thereafter shire commissioners appeared regularly in Parliament. In 1681 the franchise was defined in an act which operated until 1832: the right to vote was confined mainly to those holding land or *superior*ity of the crown to the amount of 40s. of *Old Extent* or of £400 of valued rent.

Coupar Angus. (Perthshire). *Cistercian* abbey started by *Malcolm IV* 1159 but not completely organised until 1164; erected into lordship for James Elphinstone, Lord Coupar, 1606; a *burgh of barony* was erected for him in 1607.

Court of Four Burghs. See Burghs.

Court of High Commission. See High Commission.

Court of Justiciary. See Justiciary Court.

Court of Regality. See Regality.

Court of Session. See Lords of Session; Session, Court of.

Court of Teinds. Developed from work of *Charles I* in making arrangements for *ministers'* stipends; its functions transferred to Court of *Session* in 19th century.

Court Party. The party supporting the government, especially 1703-6, while the Country Party was the opposition. Cf. Squadrone Volante.

Coutts, John (1699-1751). Son of an *Edinburgh* merchant and grandson of a *provost* of *Montrose*; founded banking firm in Edinburgh; Lord Provost 1742-4. His fourth son, Thomas (1735-1822) opened branch in London which later became separate bank.

Cove and Kilcreggan (Dunbartonshire). *Police burgh* 1865.

Covenant. See National Covenant, Solemn League and Covenant.

Covenanters. Originally the supporters of the *National Covenant*; split c. 1650 into moderate '*Resolutioners*' and extremist '*Protesters*' or '*Remonstrants*'. After the restoration of episcopal government in 1661, the Protesters formed the core of the opposition, many of them becoming *Conventiclers,* who were prosecuted. At the *Revolution,* although *presbyterian* government was revived, the Covenants were ignored, though adhered to by the *Cameronians.*

Covesea *(Moray). Burgh of barony* for Gordon of Gordonstoun 1698.

Covin Tree. Tree on *Finhaven* estate, *Angus,* believed to have grown from a chestnut dropped by a Roman soldier; on it a 15th century *Earl of Crawford* hanged Jock Barefoot, a gillie who had cut a walking stick from it.

Covington (Lanarkshire). Hospital near parish church endowed 1448x1468.

Cowal. The part of *Argyll* between Loch Fyne and Loch Long, in *Gaelic* 'Còmhall', is supposed to derive its name, like *Lorne,* from an early leader of the Scots of *Dalriada.*

Cowane, John (d. 1633). *Stirling* merchant *(dean of guild* 1624-30), who bequeathed 40,000 merks to found a hospital; the building still exists and the bequest is used to pay pensions.

Cowdenbeath (Fife). *Police burgh* 1890.

Cowie (Kincardineshire). *Burgh of barony* for Earl *Marischal* 1541.

Cowper, William (1568-1619). *Minister* of Bothkennar, then of *Perth* (1595); Bishop of *Galloway* 1612-9; his 'Sermons' are highly rated and he had a part in proposed liturgical revision.

Cowthally Castle (Lanarkshire). Held by *Somerville* family from 12th century; little remains.

Crabstane (or **Craibstane**). Stone built into wall at corner of Bon-Accord Terrace and Hardgate, *Aberdeen,* marking boundary of land which belonged tc John Crab, 14th century *burgess.* In November 1571 *Adam Gordon of Auchindoun* defeated *Forbeses* at 'the Craibstane between the town and the Bridge of Dee'.

Crafts, Craftsmen. Terms applied in middle ages to those now called tradesmen, as distinct from merchants; they had their trade incorporations or guilds. See also Blue Blanket; Merchant Guilds.

Craig (or **St David's**) (Perthshire). *Burgh of barony* for *Lord Madderty* 1626.

Craig, James (?1740-95). Son of William C., an *Edinburgh* merchant; submitted winning plan for *New Town* 1767, but achieved little else of importance; it was on his advice that in 1773 the medieval roof of St Salvator's Chapel, *St Andrews,* was demolished.

Craig, John (1512-1600). *Dominican* friar who fell under suspicion for heresy and went to Italy; narrowly escaped execution in Rome; returned to Scotland 1560 and became *minister* of *Canongate* (1561) and colleague to *John Knox* in *Edinburgh* (1564); compiled a Catechism.

Craig, John (d. 1655). Son of preceding; physician to *James VI* and *Charles I.*

Craig, Sir Thomas (1538-1608). Son of laird of Craigfintray, Aberdeenshire; studied in Paris; *advocate* 1563; author of 'Jus Feudale', a treatise on Scottish land law, and 'De Unione Regnorum Britanniae', written in 1605 to advocate closer union.

Craig, Sir William Gibson (1797-1878). Son of Sir James G.C., *W.S.,* of Riccarton, created baronet; *advocate*; M.P. for Midlothian, then for *Edinburgh*; *Clerk Register* 1862-78.

Craigcrook Castle *(Edinburgh).* 16th century building with later additions; passed through various hands until it became the residence of *Archibald Constable* and then of *Francis Jeffrey* (from 1815); now in use as offices.

Craigie, Sir William (1867-1957). Born *Dundee*; lectured at *St Andrews* and Oxford; editor of 'New English Dictionary' and of an Icelandic-English dictionary; planned '*Dictionary of the Older Scottish Tongue*'.

Craigievar Castle (Aberdeenshire). Built 1626 for a Forbes laird who was also a merchant; remained with *Forbes family* until sold to *National Trust* 1963.

Craigmillar Castle (Edinburgh). An L-plan tower of c. 1374, which is still essentially complete, was much added to; property of *Preston* family, one of whom was Lord *Provost of Edinburgh,* it passed to Gilmours 1661; *John, Earl of Mar,* imprisoned there 1477; the 'Craigmillar Conference', at the end of 1566, was concerned with a discussion of the separation of Queen *Mary* from *Darnley* by one means or another.

Craignethan Castle (Lanarkshire). A 15th-century keep, possibly built by 1st *Lord Hamilton* when he acquired the property on the fall of the *Douglases* in 1455, was much added to until 17th century; sold 1665 by Duchess of Hamilton to Andrew Hay. Cf. Tillietudlem.

Craik, Dr James (1730-1814). Born Kirkbean, *Galloway*; went to America and became friend of George Washington; organised medical service in American army.

Crail (Fife). *Royal burgh* from at latest 1178. Castle, which has completely disappeared, was occasional residence of *David I* and then belonged to *Ada,* mother of *Malcolm IV* and *William I. Collegiate church* founded 1517 by William Myrton, vicar of Lathrisk, and the prioress of *Haddington* (whose house held the *parson*age revenues); property granted to burgh 1587. *Grammar School* evidently developed in association with collegiate church.

Cramond (Midlothian). Site of Roman station, of which remains have been uncovered; Cramond Tower, of 15th-16th centuries, was built by bishops of *Dunkeld* and passed through hands of *Douglases* to the Inglis family, who built a new house 1680.

Cramond, Lordship. Created 1628 for Thomas Richardson; dormant since death of William, 4th Lord, 1735.

Crannogs. Prehistoric dwellings constructed on artificial islands.

Crann-Tàraidh. See Fiery Cross.

Cranston (Midlothian). *Burgh of barony* for Viscount Oxenfoord 1662.

Cranston, Lordship. Created for Cranston family 1609; dormant since death of 11th Lord 1869.

Crathes Castle (Kincardineshire). Built in late 16th century and early 17th by Burnetts, who had received lands of Leys from *Robert I*; retains much of original interior; 19th century addition largely destroyed by fire 1966; presented to *National Trust* 1951.

Craw (or **Crawar** or **Cravar**), **Paul** (d. 1432). Physician who brought Hussite teaching from Bohemia to *St Andrews,* where he was burned. See 'Heretics'.

Crawford (Lanarkshire). *Burgh of barony* for *Earl of Angus* 1511.

Crawford, Alexander Lindsay, 4th Earl of (d. 1454). Called 'The Tiger Earl' or 'Earl Beardie'; entered into bond with *8th Earl of Douglas* against *James II.*

Crawford, Archibald (d. 1480). Abbot of *Holyrood* c. 1450; erected flying buttresses to secure walls against thrust of vaulting.
Crawford, David Lindsay, 5th Earl of (c. 1440-95). High Admiral 1476; supported *James III;* created *Duke of Montrose* 1488.
Crawford, David Lindsay, 28th Earl of (1900-76). Succeeded 1940; Trustee of British Museum, National Gallery, *National Galleries of Scotland, National Library of Scotland,* Pilgrim Trust and Fine Art Commission.
Crawford, Earldom. Created 1398 for Sir David Lindsay of Glenesk (c. 1365-1407). See also Balcarres.
Crawford, James Ludovic, 26th Earl of (1847-1913). Astronomer; erected observatory at Dunecht near *Aberdeen.*
Crawford, Ludovic Lindsay, 16th Earl of (1600-52). In Spanish service; fought for *Charles I*; exiled 1646; resigned earldom in favour of John Lindsay (created Earl of Lindsay 1633).
Crawford Priory (Fife). Mansion built 1813.
Crawford, Thomas, of Jordanhill (?1530-1603). Fought at *Pinkie*; in French service c. 1550-60; after murder of *Darnley* was energetic member of *King's Party*; captured *Dumbarton* Castle 1571.
Crawfordjohn (Lanarkshire). *Burgh of barony* for *Anne, Duchess of Hamilton,* 1668.
Cree (Kirkcudbrightshire). Hospital existed 12th-13th centuries.
Creech, William (1745-1815). Son of William C., *minister* of *Newbattle*; apprentice to Alexander Kincaid, an *Edinburgh* bookseller, and later his partner and (1773) successor; his bookshop a meeting place of the literary men of Edinburgh; published works of *Adam Smith, Burns, Blair* and others; a noted conversationalist; Lord *Provost* of Edinburgh 1811-3.
Creetown (Kirkcudbrightshire). *Burgh of barony* for MacCulloch of Barholm 1791.
Crevant, Battle of, July 1423. French army under *John Stewart, Earl of Buchan* defeated by English under Earl of Salisbury.
Crichton (Midlothian). Castle includes remains of tower of c. 1440, and later additions include a façade inserted by *Francis, Earl of Bothwell,* c. 1590. Crichton became a *burgh of regality* for Viscount *Primrose* 1696. *Collegiate church* founded for William, *Lord Crichton,* 1449.
Crichton Family. Originated with Turstan of C., presumably a Northumbrian, who held lands under *David I.*
Crichton, George (d. 1544). Abbot of *Holyrood;* bishop of *Dunkeld* 1526.
Crichton, James (c. 1560-85). 'The Admirable Crichton'; son of Robert C. of Eliok, *Lord Advocate*; set out on continental travels at age of twenty with, it was said, mastery of a dozen languages as well as skill in swordsmanship, horsemanship and music; issued challenges to competitors in Paris and Padua; tutor to son of Duke of Mantua; possibly killed in duel.
Crichton, Lordship. Created for *Sir William Crichton* 1445.
Crichton, Robert (d. 1585). Nephew of *George Crichton*; contested bishopric of *Dunkeld* with others from 1546 and apparently not in full possession until 1553; took conservative line in 1560 and his later support of Queen *Mary* led to his forfeiture 1571; restored 1584.
Crichton, Sir William (d. 1454). In service of state under *James I*; knighted 1424; governor of *Edinburgh Castle*; *Chancellor* 1439-44 and 1448-53; with *Sir Alexander Livingston* brought about the '*Black Dinner*', but subsequently quarrelled with Livingston.
Crieff (Perthshire). *Burgh of barony* under *Earl of Perth,* then *burgh of regality* for *Lord Drummond* 1687. Crieff Trysts the centre of traffic in Highland cattle from early 18th century to c. 1770. See also Black Cattle; Kind Gallows.
Crinan (d. 1045). Abbot of *Dunkeld*; married Bethoc, daughter of *Malcolm II,* and was father of *Duncan I*; killed in campaign against *Macbeth* on behalf of his grandson, *Malcolm III.*
Crinan Canal. From Ardrishaig on Loch Fyne 9 miles to Crinan, on western seaboard, to avoid voyage round Mull of Kintyre; opened 1801.
Crochallan. See Chrochallan.
Crockett, Samuel Rutherford (1860-1914). Born Balmaghie, Kirkcudbrightshire; educated *Edinburgh,* Heidelberg and Oxford; *Free Church minister* at *Penicuik*; resigned 1895; wrote 'The Stickit Minister', 'The Raiders' and 'The Men of the Moss Hags'; died at Avignon.
Croft. Originally a small piece of arable land; then, especially from later eighteenth century, a holding by an individual tenant, especially in the Highlands and Islands, which superseded the older joint-tenancies and combined a few acres of arable land with rights of pasture on common grazing; since 1886 specifically a holding governed by the Crofters Holdings Act; the use of the term to mean a cottage is

totally wrong.
Crofters Act, 1886. Following on the Crofters Commission, or Napier Commission (appointed 1883), crofters gained security of tenure, the right to inherit, bequeath or assign crofts, fixed rents and the right to compensation for 'improvements' when they removed.
Crofters Commission. Set up by *Crofters Act* to safeguard rights of crofters and deal with disputes, allocation of land, etc. One member had to be a *Gaelic* speaker. Superseded in 1911 by *Land Court,* the Chairman of which has the status of a *Lord of Session.*
Cromartie, Earldom. Created for *Sir George Mackenzie of Tarbat* 1703; *forfeited* by 3rd Earl after '*Forty-Five*; revived 1861 for Anne Hay-Mackenzie, Duchess of *Sutherland,* with limitation to her 2nd son, Viscount Tarbat.
Cromarty. *Royal burgh* by 1264; *burgh of barony* 1672.
Cromdale (Inverness-shire). *Burgh of barony* for Grant of Freuchie 1609.
Cromdale, Battle of, 1 May 1690. *Jacobites* defeated at end of rebellion raised by *Viscount Dundee.*
Cromwellian Administration. The English Parliament appointed 8 commissioners for managing Scottish affairs and they began to act in January 1652; in September 1655 a council of state of 9 members took their place. In 1652 seven commissioners for justice were appointed and later there were up to 11 judges in a 'supreme court of justice'.
Cromwellian Forts. Inverness, Perth, Leith, Inverlochy and Ayr.
Crook of Devon (Kinross-shire). *Burgh of barony* for Halliday of Tullibole 1615.
Crookston (Renfrewshire). Little remains of the castle, which was the property of the *Lennox* Stewarts; there was a hospital in the 12th century.
Cross Keys (or **Cleikum) Inn** (*Peebles*). A 17th century building; a proprietrix, Marion Ritchie, was the original of *Scott's* 'Meg Dods' in 'St Ronan's Well'.
Crossraguel Abbey (*Cluniac*) (Ayrshire). Founded before 1214 by Duncan, 1st *Earl of Carrick*; in 1564 Allan Stewart was *commendator* and in 1570 he was seized by Gilbert, 4th *Earl of Cassillis,* and roasted until he made over abbey property; the revenues were annexed to bishopric of *Dunblane* 1617; remains include part of domestic buildings, church walls and a square *chapter*-house.
Crown. Coin worth 20s; gold from *James IV* to *Mary,* silver under *James VI.*
Crown Jewels. See Regalia.
Crowner. See Coroner.
Cruden, Alexander (1701-70). Son of *Aberdeen* merchant; educated *Marischal College*; amanuensis to Earl of Derby; tutor in Isle of *Man*; bookseller in London 1732; published 'Concordance' 1738; although for a time confined as insane, he won general respect for his erudition.
Cruggleton Castle (Wigtownshire). Massive fortalice of the *Comyns* in 13th century, it passed through various hands and came to Sir Patrick *Agnew* 1642; little remains of it.
Cruisie Lamp. Primitive oil lamp, consisting of two shallow metal basins attached to a suspension hook, with wick hanging from the upper one.
Cruithne. A term for the *Picts*; according to legend the progenitor of the Picts had this name and had seven sons—Fib, Fidach, Flochaid, Fortrend, Got, Ce and Circinn—who gave their names to the provinces of the kingdom.
Crusay. This alleged *Augustinian* foundation arises from a misreading of *Oronsay.*
Crystall, Thomas (d. 1535). As Abbot of *Kinloss* from 1499 he restored the property and buildings, reactivated religious life and patronised learning.
Culbin *(Moray).* The *barony* belonged to Kinnairds; between 1670 and 1695 about 9500 acres were overwhelmed by sand.
Culblain, Battle of. See Kilblain.
Culdees. religious of the Celtic church who seem to have originated as solitaries; the Culdees ('Celi De' = servants of God) known to record were evidently communities, not bound by a monastic rule and serving local churches; their real parallel is in the Old English minster of secular priests; known at *St Andrews, Abernethy, Brechin, Lochleven, Monifieth, Monymusk, Muthil* and elsewhere.
Cullen (Banffshire). *Royal burgh* 1189-1198; *collegiate church* founded by Alexander *Ogilvy* of that *ilk,* the community of Cullen and others, 1543; there was a *grammar school* before foundation of collegiate church; it is not certain that there was a pre-*Reformation* hospital.
Cullen, William (1710-90). Born *Hamilton*; professor of medicine at *Glasgow* 1751 and of chemistry at *Edinburgh* 1756; distinguished exponent of medical science.
Culloden, Battle of, 16 April 1746. *Jacobites* defeated by government army under *Duke of Cumberland.*

Culross (Fife, formerly Perthshire). Formerly *burgh of barony* under abbey of Culross, became *royal burgh* 1592; famed for its old houses, notably the 'Palace' or 'Place', built by *Sir George Bruce* from 1597; now largely in hands of *National Trust.*

Culross Abbey (*Cistercian*). Founded by Malcolm, *Earl of Fife,* 1217; erected into lordship for Sir James Colville 1609; still in use as parish church.

Culross, St Mungo's Chapel. Built 1503 by *Archbishop Blackadder* on traditional site of saint's birthplace; handed over to *National Trust* 1947.

Culzean Castle (Ayrshire). Built by *Robert Adam* for 10th *Earl of Cassillis* on site of ancient castle, 1777-92; handed over to *National Trust* 1945. See also Eisenhower's Flat.

Cumberland, William Augustus, Duke of (1721-65). Third son of George II; commanded government army which defeated *Jacobites* at *Culloden*; called 'the Butcher' from his atrocities after the battle.

Cumbernauld (Dunbartonshire). Lands passed from *Comyns* to Sir Robert *Fleming* under *Robert I*; *burgh of barony* 1649. Cf. New Towns.

Cumbernauld Bond, August 1640. The *Marquis of Montrose* and seventeen others pledged themselves to further the 'public ends' of the *National Covenant* against the 'particular practices' of the *Marquis of Argyll.*

Cumbrae, Little. Light first established 1754.

Cumbria. British kingdom extending from *Dumbarton* to the Derwent and Stanmore; the part south of Solway seems to have been acquired by *Malcolm I* in 945; see also Strathclyde.

Cumbria, Prince of. Title conferred by Shakespeare on *Malcolm,* son of *Duncan I.* His account derives from *Boece,* but there is little evidence to substantiate the idea that the title pertained to the heir apparent to the Scottish throne. Duncan I was 'King of the Cumbrians' in his father's lifetime, and his brother seems to have succeeded to the title when Duncan became king. *David I* was 'Prince of Cumberland' in the reign of *Alexander I.*

Cumine's Camp. Prehistoric fort on *Barra Hill, Buchan,* traditionally associated with *Robert I*'s victory over *Comyns* in 1308.

'Cummy'. See Cunningham, Alison.

Cumnock (Ayrshire). Belonged to Dunbars, *Earls of March,* and passed to a junior branch who held it until 17th century; a *burgh of barony* created for Dunbar of Cumnock 1509; acquired by *Crichton* of *Sanquhar,* created for Dunbar of Cumnock 1509; acquired by *Crichton* of *Sanquhar,* created Viscount Ayr 1622 and *Earl of Dumfries* 1633.

Cunard Shipping Line. Founded 1839 by *George Burns* and *Robert Napier.*

Cunningham(e). Northern division of Ayrshire; held in 12th century by De *Morvilles.*

Cunningham, Alison (1822-1913). Born Torryburn; nurse of *Robert Louis Stevenson.*

Cunningham, William. See Glencairn, Earl of.

Cunninghame-Grahame, Robert Bontine (1852-1936). Born London, son of Dunbartonshire laird and lady of Spanish descent; married in South America, where he spent much time; Liberal M.P. 1886; joined Labour Party but was unsuccessful; president of *National Party of Scotland* 1928; prolific writer; known as 'Don Roberto'.

Cunzie or **Cunzie House.** The *mint.*

Cupar (Fife). *Royal burgh* by 1328; *Grammar School* mentioned 1357; amalgamated with English School to form *Academy* 1822.

Cupar Banking Company. Formed 1802 but gave up business 1811 and was dissolved 1820.

Cupar Friary (*Dominican*). Founded 1348 by Duncan, *Earl of Fife*; decayed by 1517 and friars transferred to *St Andrews.*

Cupbearer. Office of cup-bearer or 'dapifer' to the kings was held by Walter *FitzAlan,* ancestor of the Stewarts, under *David I*; title subsequently changed to more dignified 'senescallus' or steward. See Steward.

Curia Regis. King's Court of 12th and 13th centuries, from which *Parliament, Council* and *Court of Session* ultimately derived; consisted of crown tenants or such of them as the king invited.

Curling. First known club said to have been formed at *Kilsyth* c. 1510; stones survive in *Stirling* from 1511; Royal Caledonian Curling Club formed 1838.

Currie, Sir Donald (1825-1909). Born *Greenock*; founder of Castle Steamship Company; M.P. for *Perth* 1888-1900; benefactor of *Edinburgh University, United Free Church* etc.

Curse of Scotland. No wholly convincing explanation has ever been given of the application of this term to the nine of diamonds playing-card. It has been associated with an order for the massacre of *Glencoe* and with the *Duke of Cumberland*'s 'No Quarter' order at *Culloden,* each alleged to have been written on a card, but neither order was noticeably a 'curse of Scotland'. Attention has also been drawn to the resemblance of the card to the arms of the family of *Stair,* which bear nine lozenges on a *saltire.* It may be that the phrase was originally 'the corse [i.e., cross] of Scotland', in other words St *Andrew's* saltire.

Cursing and Swearing, Acts Against. Act of 1661 imposed penalties on offenders on a scale ranging from £20 for nobleman to 20s for a servant.

Cursiter, Stanley (1887-1976). Born in *Orkney*; Director of *National Gallery of Scotland* and Keeper for five years; H.M. Painter and Limner in Scotland 1948; painted portraits of many notable people and also committed to canvas scenery and historical events of his native islands.

Cushnie (Aberdeenshire). Passed by marriage from Cushnie family to Leslies in 14th century; the Leslies became *Earls of Rothes*; in 1628 it came to the Lumsdens.

Cuthbert, St (?635-687). Supposedly born in Channelkirk and served as shepherd boy at Oxton; monk in Old *Melrose*; prior 661; Bishop of Hexham 684 and of Lindisfarne 685; patron of Durham.

'Cutty Sark'. This famous clipper ship was built in 1870 at *Dumbarton,* to challenge the *Thermopylae.* Her figurehead was witch of same name in *Burns's* 'Tam o' Shanter'.

D

Dairsie (Fife). Of the medieval castle (a seat of bishops of *St Andrews*) little survives; parish church, in an imitation Gothic style, was built by *Archbishop John Spottiswoode* in 1621 as a model rural church.

Dalbeattie (Kirkcudbrightshire). *Police burgh* 1862.

Dale, David (1739-1806). Born *Stewarton*; with a background in *linen* trade, acquired first *cotton* mill in Scotland, at *Rothesay,* in 1778, and in 1785 started the New Lanark Mills, which by 1795 employed 1334 workers; something of a pioneer in employees' welfare; leader of sect known as Old Scotch Independents.

Dalgarnock (Dumfriesshire). *Burgh of regality* for *Earl of Queensberry* 1636.

Dalgattie. See Delgaty.

Dalginross (Perthshire). Site of Roman camp, probably of Agricolan date.

Dalhousie (Midlothian). Belonged to *Ramsays* from 12th century; George Ramsay created Lord R. of Dalhousie 1618 and his son, William, created *Earl of Dalhousie* 1633; hospital of St Leonard (otherwise *Lasswade* or Polton) mentioned 1500-1666.

Dalhousie, Earldom. See preceding entry. The 10th Earl, James Andrew Broun (1812-60), Governor-General of India 1847-56, was created Marquis 1849 but that title died with him. *Fox Maule* (1801-74), 11th Earl, was Secretary for War 1846-52 and 1855-8. John William (1847-87), 13th Earl, was *Secretary for Scotland* 1886.

Dalkeith (Midlothian). *Burgh of barony* for Douglas of D. 1401; *Grammar School* had a national reputation in 18th century; Palace, dating mainly from c. 1700 (see James Smith), incorporated a medieval tower, and was the residence of the *Dukes of Buccleuch,* whose family acquired property from *Douglases* in 1640s.

Dalkeith Collegiate Church. Endowed 1406 by Sir James *Douglas* of Dalkeith; preceded by chapel and hospital 1396; part still stands, roofless.

Dallas, George (1630-?1702). *Writer to the signet*; Deputy Keeper of *Privy Seal*; author of 'A System of Styles' (1697).

Dalmellington (Ayrshire). *Burgh of barony* for *Lord Cathcart* 1607.

Dalmeny (West Lothian). *Burgh of barony* for Thomas, *Lord Binning,* 1616; the fine Norman church, of 12th century, restored between 1926 and 1932, when the tower, which had collapsed centuries before, was rebuilt.

Dalmilling (Ayrshire). Site of the only Scottish house of the Gilbertine order, established 1221 and extinguished 1238.

Dalriada (or **Dal Riata**). An Irish people called 'Scoti' occupied part of north-east Ireland and colonies of them settled in Kintyre and mid-*Argyll,* probably c. 500. Dalriada, the name of their homeland, was transferred to the new settlement and as the kingdom of D. it maintained its existence, sometimes rather tenuously, until *Kenneth mac Alpin* united it to Pictland. See Picts.

Dalry (or **Dalrigh**), **Battle of,** 11 August 1306. *Robert I* defeated by Lord of *Lorne* near Perthshire-Argyll border.

Dalry House *(Edinburgh).* Built by Bailie Walter Chieslie 1661.

Dalrymple (Ayrshire). Originally belonged to family of D., from whom *Earls of Stair* are descended, but passed in late 14th century to Kennedys, ancestors of *Earls of Cassillis.*

Dalrymple, David. See Hailes, Lord.

Dalrymple, James and **John.** See Stair, Viscount and Earls of.

Dalswinton (Dumfriesshire). *Barony* belonged to *Comyns,* then granted by *Robert I* to his son-in-law *Walter Stewart,* and passed to *Maxwells.*

Dalyell (or **Dalziel**), **Sir Thomas,** of the *Binns* (c. 1599-1685). Son of West Lothian laird; taken prisoner when serving with Scottish army at *Worcester,* but escaped and joined royalist rising 1654; in Russian service; commander of forces in Scotland 1666-85; raised *Royal Scots Greys* 1681.

Damian, John (fl. 1504-13). French or Italian alchemist employed by *James IV* and appointed Abbot of *Tongland*; tried to fly from *Stirling Castle.*

Daniel Stewart's College. Daniel Stewart (1741-1814), who held office in the Court of *Exchequer,* left property to found a hospital for poor boys; building erected 1849-53 after design by David Rhind; converted to day school 1870.

Dapifer. See Cupbearer.

Darien Scheme. The Company of Scotland Trading to Africa and the Indies was set up in 1695, with power to establish colonies; one of its projects was a settlement on the isthmus of Darien, and the first expedition went out in 1698, to be followed by a second and third; disaster came because of climate, hostility of Spaniards and refusal of English government to give assistance.

Darnaway (Moray). The castle of 1810, seat of *Earl of Moray,* incorporates a hall said to date from time of *Thomas Randolph*; the place was created a *burgh of barony* for Earl of Moray 1611.

Darnley (Renfrewshire). The *barony* was an early possession of the Stewart family, and in 1460 Sir John S. was created *Lord Darnley*; he became *Earl of Lennox* 1488; in 18th century the property passed to *Duke of Montrose* and then to *Maxwell* of *Pollok.*

Darnley Collegiate Church. Proposed annexation of parish church of *Tarbolton* to a college projected by John Stewart of Darnley in 1421-2 did not take place.

Darnley, Henry Stewart, Lord (1546-67). Son of Matthew, 4th *Earl of Lennox,* by Margaret, daughter of *Margaret Tudor* by 6th *Earl of Angus*; born in England; returned to Scotland 1565; married Queen *Mary* 29 July 1565; participated in murder of *David Riccio*; estranged from Mary; murdered at *Kirk o' Field* 10 February 1567.

Davach. A unit of land-area, used in parts of *Pict*land in place of the *ploughgate*; related to a measure of capacity, it represents either the area sown with a certain quantity of seed or the area yielding a certain quantity of grain; sometimes equated with 4 ploughgates.

David I (c. 1084-1153). Youngest son of *Malcolm III* and *Margaret,* spent youth in England, was brother-in-law of Henry I and married Maud, daughter of Waltheof, Earl of Northumbria, and widow of Earl of Northampton. He ruled southern Scotland as 'Earl' during reign of *Alexander I,* whom he succeeded 1124. Did much to reorganise kingdom on Norman lines, founded many religious houses and established system of diocesan bishops. His intervention in England on behalf of his niece Matilda, against Stephen, led to defeat at the battle of the *Standard*; died at Carlisle 24 May 1153.

David II (1324-71). Son of *Robert I*; married in his fifth year to Joanna, sister of Edward III of England, and succeeded his father 7 June 1329. After Scottish defeats at the hands of *Edward Balliol* and his English supporters, David and his Queen were sent to France for safety 1334. Returning in 1341, he invaded England in 1346 to be defeated at *Neville's Cross,* and remained a prisoner for eleven years. On his release for a ransom of 100,000 merks he seems to have done much to restore the economy after the wars; he pursued plans for peaceful union with England and seems to have governed with vigour. After his Queen died (1362), David married *Margaret Drummond* 1364 and divorced her 1370. He died childless 22 February 1371.

David (1273-81). Younger son of *Alexander III.*

David, Duke of Rothesay. See Rothesay, David, Duke of.

David, Earl of Huntingdon (c. 1144-1219). Younger brother of *Malcolm IV* and *William I,* he married the heiress of the Earl of Chester and his interests were mainly in England. One son, John 'the Scot', survived him, but he died childless in 1237, and Earl David's three daughters—Margaret, Isabella and Ada—were respectively grandmother, mother and grandmother of three of the *Competitors.*

David de Moravia (d. 1326). Bishop of *Moray* 1299; supported *Robert I*; excommunicated 1306 for participation in murder of *Red Comyn* and again 1320 as an abettor of Bruce; his bequest for helping students at Paris is seen as a forerunner of *Scots College* there.

David's Tower (*Edinburgh Castle*). An L-shaped tower, commanding the approach to the castle from the town, begun by *David II* 1366 and completed about ten years later; demolished in siege of 1573 and largely obliterated by *Half-Moon Battery*, but its lower storeys were rediscovered 1912.

Davidson, John (?1549-1603). As a *regent* in *St Leonard's College, St Andrews*, he offended *Regent Morton* by criticising his policy, and fled to England; *minister* of Liberton 1579; exiled in England again for his opposition to episcopacy, 1584-8; mentioned in Marprelate Tracts; minister of Prestonpans 1596; violent opponent of some of *James VI*'s policies; wrote some poetry.

Davidson, John (1857-1909). Born Barrhead; acted as schoolmaster; emigrated to London 1889; wrote plays, including 'The Triumph of Mammon', poems, ballads and songs; committed suicide at Penzance.

Davidson, Randall Thomas (1848-1930). Born near *Edinburgh*; ordained in Church of England 1874; Bishop of Rochester 1891 and Winchester 1895; Archbishop of Canterbury 1903; retired 1928.

Davidson, Robert (1804-94). Born *Aberdeen*; invented printing machine, turning lathe, electro-magnetic locomotive and other devices, but failed to gain recognition.

Davy's Tower. Keep of *Spynie* Palace, *Moray*, built by Bishop David Stewart (1461-76).

Days of Truce. See Truce.

Deacon. (1) One of the seven orders of the medieval church; (2) a lay officer introduced by reformers to control finance, especially alms for the poor, but survived in only certain sections of the *presbyterian* churches; (3) head of a guild of *craftsmen*.

Deacon Brodie. See Brodie, William.

Deaconess Hospital (*Edinburgh*). Opened 11 October 1894 as a memorial to Lady Grizel Baillie, the first deaconess ordained in *Church of Scotland*.

Dean. (1) Of cathedral—president of *chapter* and administrator of diocese during vacancy. (2) Of Christianity—rural dean, parish priest who supervised a group of churches.

Dean (*Edinburgh*). Lands bought 1609 by Sir William Nisbet from John, Lord *Lindsay* of the Byres, and erected into *barony* 1610.

Dean Bridge (*Edinburgh*). Designed by *Telford* to span Water of *Leith* and built 1832.

Dean of Guild. An official, originally the head of the *merchant guild*, known in *Edinburgh* at least from the early 14th century. His court dealt originally with mercantile and maritime causes generally, including weights and measures and disputes over trade, but it was later confined to superintending building operations and anticipated later 'planning authorities'. Abolished 1975.

Dean Orphan Hospital (*Edinburgh*). Charity founded in Bailie Fyffe's Close 1733 and moved to property belonging to Trinity Hospital 1735; new building near *Dean Bridge* designed by *Thomas Hamilton* and erected 1833, accommodating 200 children; building now used to train nurses.

Deans, Jeannie. A fictional character in *Sir Walter Scott's* 'Heart of Midlothian'. Cf. Walker, Helen.

Debateable Land. Territory disputed between England and Scotland, usually said to be between rivers Sark and Esk; for a time it was used only for grazing, and habitation was forbidden; in 1552 the western part (parish of Kirkandrews) went to England and the eastern (parish of *Canonbie*) to Scotland.

Declaration of Arbroath. See Arbroath.

Declaration of Indulgence. See Indulgence.

Decreet. Decree or decision of a court; the Register of Acts and Decreets of Court of *Session* begins 1542.

Dee, Bridge of (*Aberdeen*). Built by *Bishop Gavin Dunbar* 1527, rebuilt 1718-22, widened 1841.

Deed of Demission. See Disruption.

Deer Abbey (*Cistercian*) (Aberdeenshire). No real evidence about Celtic foundation, and the establishment by *William Comyn, Earl of Buchan*, c. 1218, seems to have been made as of new; property erected into lordship of Altrie for Robert Keith, son of Earl *Marischal*, 1587; some ruins remain.

Deer, Book of. MS. discovered in Cambridge University Library 1860, containing St John's Gospel, parts of other gospels and liturgical matter; its importance lies in 'notitiae' in *Gaelic*, dating from 11th and 12th centuries and referring to grants of land to an unnamed religious house, presumably *Deer*.

Deer Raid, 1887. Dispossessed crofters in *Lewis* raided a sheep farm and deer forest but were acquitted after trial.

Degsastan, Battle of, 603. *Aidan*, King of *Dalriada*, defeated by Ethelfrith, King of Angles, perhaps at Dawstane in Liddesdale.

Deil's Dyke. Name given to part of *Catrail*.

Deir Club. Founded in New Maud 1868 for discussion of scientific, literary and other subjects.

Delgaty (or **Delgatie** or **Dalgattie**) (Aberdeenshire). Lands long held by *Hays* as a *barony*; *burgh of regality* created for *Earl of Errol* 1699; 16th century castle, replacing earlier one, has painted ceilings of c. 1592; in 1948 the Countess of Errol made it a 'Clan Hay' centre under Captain John Hay of Hayfield.

Deloraine, Earldom. Named from place in Kirkhope parish, Selkirkshire; created 1706 for Henry Scott, son of Duke of Monmouth; extinct 1807.

Dempster. Court official who repeated sentence after judge and pronounced doom. The office of dempster of *parliament* was held heritably from 1379, if not earlier, until late 15th century by family of Dempster of Caraldstoun, who were also heritable dempsters of abbey of *Arbroath*.

Dempster, George (1732-1818). *Advocate* 1755; M.P. for *Forfar* and for Fife *burghs* 1762-90; Director of East India Company; active in promotion of Scottish fisheries and in agrarian improvement.

Demy. Gold coin introduced under *Robert II*, worth 9s.

Denham, James Steuart, the elder (1712-80). *Advocate* 1735; *Jacobite* in 'Forty-five and, being excepted from Act of Oblivion, was on continent until 1763, when he returned to *Edinburgh*; his 'Inquiry into the Principles of Political Economy' was an exposition of mercantilism and the first systematic study of economics in English.

Denmilne MSS. See Balfour, Sir James.

Dennistoun, James (1803-55). Born Dunbartonshire; *advocate* 1824; collected antiques in Italy and Germany; edited papers on Scottish history and antiquities and wrote 'Memoirs of the Dukes of Urbino'.

Dennys of Dumbarton. Shipbuilding firm established 1817.

Dercongal. See Holywood.

Dere Street. Roman road, originating with *Agricola*, crossing Cheviots and proceeding by Newstead and up *Lauderdale* to *Soutra* Hill, then probably by *Dalkeith* to *Inveresk* and *Cramond*.

Design, Edinburgh School of. Established by *Board of Manufactures* 1760, with support of *Lord Kames*, to assist *linen* production; subsequently other crafts were added—engraving, seal-cutting, coach-painting and wood carving; became a constituent element in *Royal Scottish Academy*; control by Board of Manufactures continued until 1907.

Deskford (Banffshire). *Burgh of regality* for *Ogilvie* of that *ilk* 1698.

Deuchar, David (1743-1808). *Burgess* of *Edinburgh* 1782; seal-engraver and etcher who published two volumes of etchings 1803; encouraged *Raeburn* and was the subject of the earliest extant portrait by that artist.

Devil's Beef Tub. *Reivers* of *Annandale* are said to have concealed their stolen cattle in this hollow in the hills above *Moffat*.

Devil's Dyke. Rampart stretching through part of *Galloway* and *Nithsdale*, of unknown origin and purpose.

Devolution Bill. See Home Rule Bills; Kilbrandon Report.

Devorguilla (c. 1209-1289). Daughter and one of the heirs of Alan, Lord of *Galloway*, by Margaret, eldest daughter of *David, Earl of Huntingdon*; married John *Balliol* and was mother of *King John*. Her husband and she made provision for scholars at Oxford which took shape in *Balliol College*, and she founded New or *Sweetheart Abbey* and a bridge at *Dumfries*.

Dewar (Surname). (1) From 'deoradh', the custodian of a saint's relic, especially the crosier of St *Fillan*. (2) From place in Midlothian.

Dewar, James (1842-1923). Born Kincardine-on-Forth; professor of experimental philosophy at Cambridge and of chemistry at Royal Institute, London; liquefied hydrogen and in his experiments with minimising changes of temperature in liquids discovered the vacuum flask; in association with Sir Frederick Abel he produced cordite.

Dewar Manuscripts. Seven volumes, totalling 750,000 words of *Gaelic* oral tradition, collected 1862-72 by John Dewar, a woodman of Roseneath, on commission from 8th *Duke of Argyll*; in *Inveraray* Castle.

Dick Bequest. See Dick, James.

Dick Institute (*Kilmarnock*). Presented to town by James Dick, who made a fortune out of the commercial use of gutta percha.

Dick, James (1743-1828). Native of *Forres* who in America made a fortune from which he left the 'Dick Bequest' for the benefit of parochial schoolmasters in the counties of *Aberdeen, Banff* and *Moray*.

Dick, Robert (1811-66). *Thurso* baker, self-taught, became a botanist and geologist and furnished information and fossils to *Hugh Miller*.

Dick Veterinary College, Edinburgh. Founded 1823; associated with *University* 1911, affiliated 1934 and incorporated 1951.

Dick, Sir William, of Braid (1580-1655). Lord

Provost of *Edinburgh* 1638-9 and reputed to be its richest merchant; impoverished himself by lending vast sums to the *Covenanters.*
Dick, William (1793-1866). Founder of *Edinburgh (Dick) Veterinary College.*
Dicker. A unit of reckoning: ten of any article.
Dickson, Adam (1721-76). *Minister* of *Whittinghame* 1769; wrote 'The Husbandry of the Ancients' and 'Treatise on Agriculture'.
Dickson, David (1583-1663). Born *Glasgow; minister* at *Irvine* 1618; deposed for opposition to *Five Articles of Perth,* but restored; chaplain to *Covenanting* army 1639; professor of divinity *Edinburgh* 1640 and Glasgow 1650; ejected 1661; wrote 'Treatise on the Promises' (Dublin, 1630) and several works published posthumously or left in MS—'Therapeutica Sacra' (1664), 'Truth's Victory over Error' (1684), 'Commentaries on the Psalms'.
Dickson, Maggie (fl. 1728). Hanged in Grassmarket, *Edinburgh,* 1728; as hearse rattled over cobbles in *Musselburgh* she was jolted back to consciousness and lived to have many children.
Dictionary of National Biography. See Smith, George.
Dictionary of the Older Scottish Tongue. First part published 1931. See Craigie, Sir William.
Diligence. Collective term for processes by which *decreets* of court were made effective. See Arrestment, Caption, Horning, Inhibition, Poinding.
Dingwall (Ross). *Royal burgh* (with a castle) received charter 1227; alienated to *Earls of Ross* in 14th and 15th centuries; recovered status as royal burgh 1498; castle repaired 1507 but ruinous by mid-18th century.
Dingwall, Lordship. Created for Andrew Keith, illegitimate son of *Commendator* of *Deer,* 1584; *forfeited* 1716 in person of 2nd Duke of Ormond.
Dingwall Pursuivant. First mentioned 1460. See Pursuivants.
Dirk. Originally had a blade about the length of a man's fore-arm, with a hilt designed to give firm grip for an upward thrust; could be concealed in folds of plaid.
Dirleton (East Lothian). Castle built by *De Vaux* family in 13th century, and retains work of that period; ranges added by *Haliburtons* in 15th century and *Ruthvens* in 16th. D. was created a *burgh of barony* for *Maxwell* of Innerwick 1631. After the forfeiture of the *Ruthvens* the lands were acquired by Sir Thomas Erskine of Gogar, who was created Lord Dirleton and *Earl of Kellie,* and in 1663 they were bought by *Sir John Nisbet,* who built a new mansion. A *collegiate church,* founded by *Sir Walter Haliburton* c. 1444, was evidently a small foundation, perhaps with only one priest, called 'provost'. A *Trinitarian* friary, founded by Haliburtons in 15th century, had been appropriated to the crown by 1588.
Dirleton, Earldom. Held by Sir James *Maxwell* from 1646 until his death in 1653.
Dirleton Witches, 1649. Some men and women, confined in *Dirleton* Castle, confessed to John McGill, the *minister,* and 'Devil's marks' were found on them by John Kincaid; they were strangled and burned.
Disarming Act (1716). Imposed fines for possessing arms and invited surrender of arms; later act (1725) arranged for search and seizure of weapons.
Discipline, Books of. The First (1560-1) was the reformers' programme for the polity and endowment of their church and for education and poor relief. The Second (1578) proposed the supersession of an episcopal system by a *presbyterian.* Neither Book received the government sanction which would have enabled it to be fully carried out.
Disher and Toyer. The lands on the two sides of Loch Tay.
Disinherited. Lords who lost their Scottish estates because they supported the English against *Robert I.*
Disruption, 1843. After prolonged disputes over the Church's liability to the operation of statute law and judgments of the courts, in May 1843 474 *ministers* (out of about 1200) signed the Deed of Demission and formed the *Free Church.*
Distillers Company Ltd. Formed 1877 by amalgamation of six firms.
'Diurnal of Occurrents'. A collection of jottings covering 1513-75, written (apparently by a minor official in *Edinburgh*) contemporaneously from 1557; published by *Bannatyne* and *Maitland* Clubs 1833.
Dobson, Henry John (1858-1928). Specialist in 'genre' painting, several of whose pictures of Scottish domestic life were reproduced in 'Scottish Life and Character', in which he collaborated with William Sanderson.
Dodds, James (1812-85). Born *Annan; minister* of Humbie; *Free Church* minister of *Dunbar*; friend of *Thomas Carlyle*; wrote 'Famous Men of Dumfriesshire', 'A Century of Scottish Church History' and theology.
Dodds, James (1813-74). Born Softlaw, near *Kelso*; solicitor in London; friend of Leigh

Hunt and *Thomas Carlyle;* wrote 'Lays of the *Covenanters'* and 'The Fifty Years' Struggle of the Covenanters'.

Dods, Marcus (1786-1838). Born *Gifford; minister* of Belford 1818-38; author of 'The Incarnation of the Eternal Word'.

Dods, Marcus (1834-1909). *Minister* of Renfield *Free Church, Glasgow,* 1864-89; professor in *New College,* Edinburgh, 1889, and principal 1907; wrote commentaries on scripture.

Dog Cemetery (*Edinburgh Castle*). Plot below ramparts kept as burial ground for regimental pets.

Dog's Stone. See Clach a 'Choin.

Dollar. Silver coin of *James VI,* worth 53s. 4d.

Dollar (Clackmannanshire). *Burgh of regality* for *Earl of Argyll* 1702.

Dollar Academy. Founded 1818 on bequest by *John McNab,* with building designed by *Playfair.*

Dominican Friaries. See Aberdeen, Ayr, Berwick, Cupar, Dundee, Edinburgh, Elgin, Glasgow, Haddington, Inverness, Montrose, Perth, St Andrews, St Monans, Stirling, Wigtown.

Donald I (d. 863). Succeeded brother, *Kenneth mac Alpin,* as King of *Alba* 859.

Donald II (d. 900). King of *Scots* from 889.

Donald III (or **Donald Bane**) (c. 1031-1100). Younger son of *Duncan I*; spent *Macbeth*'s reign in western isles; on death of *Malcolm III,* his brother, was King 1093-4 and (after defeating *Duncan II)* 1094-7; overthrown and imprisoned by *Edgar* 1097.

Donald Bane. See Donald III.

Donald Breac (d. 642). Son of Eochaid and grandson of *Aidan*; King of *Dalriada* from c. 628; killed fighting against Britons on the Carron.

Donald Dubh (c. 1480-1545). Son of Angus (d. 1490), an illegitimate son of *John, 4th and last Lord of the Isles* (d. 1498), possibly by Angus's wife, a daughter of 1st *Earl of Argyll*; prisoner of the Argyll family for most of his life, but in 1503 and 1545 escaped and endeavoured (on the second occasion with English support) to gain the lordship; died in Ireland.

Donald (Ban) Macwilliam (d. 1187). Son of *William* Fitz Duncan; a pretender against *William I*; defeated and killed at Mam Garbh, an unidentified place near *Inverness.*

Donaldson, James (fl. 1713). Served as soldier until 1690; wrote 'Husbandry Anatomized' (1697) and 'Money increased and credit raised' (1705).

Donaldson, James (fl. 1794). Land surveyor at *Dundee*; prepared county surveys for Board of Agriculture; wrote 'Modern Agriculture' (1795-6).

Donaldson, James (1751-1830). Son of Edinburgh bookseller and publisher; inherited proprietorship and editorship of '*Edinburgh Advertiser*'; left bulk of fortune to found school for 300 poor children, which, as Donaldson's Hospital, was designed by *W.H. Playfair* and erected 1842-51; devoted partly to deaf children from the outset, it amalgamated in 1918 with the Royal Institution for the Education of Deaf and Dumb Children and ultimately became Donaldson's School for the Deaf.

Donaldson Line. Shipping Company founded 1858.

Donan, St (d. 618). Said to have been murdered with 52 followers in island of Eigg.

Donat's Grammar. Latin grammar of Aelius Donatus (4th century), used in Scottish schools until displaced by *Andrew Simson*'s grammar 1587 and *Ruddiman*'s 1714.

Donibristle House (*Aberdour,* Fife). Residence of Earls of Moray, where '*Bonnie Earl*' was killed by *Earl of Huntly* 1592; present house 19th century.

Donn, Rob (1714-78). *Gaelic* poet, commemorated by monument at Durness.

Donnachadh Ban Nan Oran. See Macintyre, Duncan.

Doocot. Dovecot, to house pigeons used for winter feeding.

Doole Weeds (= mourning apparel). Said to have come into general use in Scotland on death of *Queen Madeleine* 1537.

Doomster. See Dempster.

Dornoch *(Sutherland).* Bishopric dates from c. 1146, though there may have been an earlier, Celtic, religious house, and the constitution of the cathedral (dedicated to St Mary and St *Gilbert*) dates from c. 1225, when building started; the building was burned in a local affray 1570 and the nave was then roofless until 19th century restoration. The castle of the bishops, built c. 1250 and rebuilt c. 1550, now restored and modernised as hotel. *Burgh,* originally under Bishop, received royal charter 1628.

Dort, Synod of. Representatives of Calvinist churches, meeting in Holland, upheld the doctrine of the predestined salvation of the Elect against the more liberal views of the Arminians, who believed that Christ died for all men.

Douai (or **Douay**), **Scots College at.** Associated with university of D. in 17th and 18th centuries; relics of St *Margaret* removed there from *Dunfermline*; suppressed at French Revolution. See Scots Colleges.

Douchtie, Thomas (fl. 1533). Hermit who is believed to have founded chapel of Our Lady of Loretto, *Musselburgh*.

Douglas (Lanarkshire). *Burgh of barony* under *Earl of Angus* 1459; *burgh of regality* under *Duke of Douglas* 1707. Petitions for erection of *collegiate church* by Earls of Douglas, 1423, 1448, seem not to have taken effect. A castle which existed in 13th century, and suffered in *War of Independence*, was often repaired, but there are no significant remains.

Douglas, Sir Archibald (d. 1333). Younger brother of '*the Good Sir James*'; *Guardian* in minority of *David II*; defeated *Edward Balliol* at *Annan* 1332, but was killed at *Halidon*.

Douglas, Archibald, Earls of Angus. See Angus.

Douglas, Archibald, 3rd Earl of (c. 1330-1400). Natural son of '*the Good Sir James*'; succeeded 1388, but had already acquired much of *Galloway* by gift and purchase and *Bothwell* by marriage.

Douglas, Archibald, 4th Earl of (c. 1372-1424). Son of 3rd Earl; defeated by English at *Homildon* and taken prisoner fighting with the English rebel Percy at Shrewsbury (1403); returned 1408; took 10,000 men to France to help against English, 1424, was appointed Lieutenant General of the French forces and Duke of Touraine; killed at *Verneuil*; married Margaret, daughter of *Robert III*.

Douglas, Archibald, 5th Earl of (c. 1390-1439). Son of 4th Earl; went to France and was with victorious Scots at *Baugé* but defeated at *Crevant*; associated with government of *James I*, but for a time imprisoned; Lieutenant of kingdom on accession of *James II*; married Euphemia Graham, a descendant of *Robert II*'s second marriage; his sons, William (6th Earl) and David, were the victims of the *Black Dinner* (1440) and were succeeded by their great-uncle, James 'the Gross' (d. 1443).

Douglas, Archibald (fl. 1565-86). *Parson* of *Glasgow*; *Lord of Session* 1565; involved in *Riccio* murder 1566 and *Darnley* murder 1567; supported Queen *Mary* against *James VI*; forfeited 1581, pardoned 1586.

Douglas, Archibald, 3rd Marquis and 1st Duke of Douglas (1694-1761). On his death, childless, the dukedom became extinct. His sister, Lady Jane (1698-1753) had been married secretly in 1746 and in 1748, when she was fifty, twin boys were born. The duke refused to acknowledge them, and on his death ensued the *Douglas Cause*.

Douglas Cause. On death of *1st Duke of Douglas* the claims to his estates of his nephew, Archibald James Edward Douglas (1748-1827) were challenged by the *Duke of Hamilton*, Lord Douglas Hamilton and Sir Hew Dalrymple; the *Court of Session* decided against Douglas by the *Lord President's* casting vote but the House of Lords reversed this verdict (1769); Douglas was created Baron Douglas 1790; the estates he inherited descended through his daughter to Earls of *Home*.

Douglas, David (1798-1834). Native of *Scone*; traveller and botanist; gave his name to 'Douglas Spruce' and introduced to Europe various plants from America and elsewhere; killed by a wild bull in the Sandwich Islands.

Douglas, Earldom, Marquisate and Dukedom. Earldom created 1358 for William (1327-84), nephew of '*the Good Sir James*'; extinct with forfeiture of *9th Earl* 1455; marquisate created for 11th *Earl of Angus* 1633 and now held by *Duke of Hamilton*; dukedom created for 3rd Marquis 1703, extinct with his death 1761.

Douglas Ecossais. Name given to *Royal Scots* when in French service and commanded by Lord George Douglas; he became *Earl of Dumbarton* 1675 and the name was changed to Dumbarton's Regiment.

Douglas Family. William de Douglas, recorded c. 1179, was evidently a Flemish immigrant who took his name from Douglas Water, Lanarkshire.

Douglas, Gavin (1474-1522). Son of *5th Earl of Angus*; *provost* of *St Giles', Edinburgh*, 1503; nominated to archbishopric of *St Andrews* 1514, without success; Bishop of *Dunkeld* 1515; died in London; his poetical works include 'The Palace of Honour' and a translation of Virgil's 'Aeneid'.

Douglas, Sir George, of Pittendreich (1490-1552). Brother of *6th Earl of Angus*; exiled in England with his brother, 1528-43; active in English cause 1544.

Douglas, George (c. 1545-c. 1600). Younger brother of William D. of Lochleven; assisted in Queen *Mary*'s escape from *Lochleven Castle*.

Douglas, George. See Brown, George Douglas.

Douglas, Heron and Co. See Ayr Bank.

Douglas, Sir James (c. 1286-1330), 'the Good Sir James'. Son and heir of William D., 'the hardy', who supported *Wallace*; joined *Robert I* 1306 and was active in all his campaigns; knighted on eve of *Bannockburn*; made several invasions of England; received extensive estates; took Bruce's heart to Spain and was killed there, 25 August 1330.

Douglas, James, 9th Earl of (1426-88). Brother of *William, 8th Earl,* whom he succeeded 1452; withdrew allegiance to *James II*; married brother's widow, descended from second marriage of *Robert II;* when war with the King began in 1455, Douglas fled, leaving his brothers to be defeated at *Arkinholm*; became an English pensioner and joined in *Treaty of Westminster-Ardtornish*; invaded Scotland 1482 and 1484 along with English and *Alexander, Duke of Albany*; captured and confined in abbey of *Lindores.*

Douglas, James, Duke of Hamilton. See Hamilton.

Douglas, James, Duke of Queensberry. See Queensberry.

Douglas, James, Earl of Morton. See Morton.

Douglas, Jane, Lady Glamis. See Glamis.

Douglas, John (1494-1574). Rector of *St Andrews University* 1551; took active part in *Reformation*; first Protestant Archbishop of St Andrews 1572.

Douglas, Katharine. Known only for her alleged action in trying to defend *James I* from his murderers by thrusting her arm through the staples of the door of his room; not mentioned until 100 years later.

Douglas Larder, 7 April 1308. *Sir James Douglas,* capturing his castle of *Douglas* from the English, destroyed it by burning all the food and wine within it, along with the bodies of the slain.

Douglas, Margaret. See Lennox, Matthew Stewart, 4th Earl of.

Douglas, Margaret (c. 1510-72). Margaret Erskine (daughter of 5th *Lord Erskine*) married Robert Douglas of *Lochleven* 1527; mistress of *James V* and mother of *Regent Moray*; gaoler of Queen *Mary* 1567-8.

Douglas, Norman (1868-1952). Born in Germany, with three Scottish grandparents; his novels include 'Unprofessional Tales' (1901), 'South Wind', 'Looking Back' and 'Late Harvest' (1946).

Douglas, Robert (1594-1674). Said to have been grandson of Queen *Mary* through a child borne by her to George Douglas, younger, of *Lochleven*; there is no foundation for the story, but nothing is known of Robert's parentage and early life; chaplain to Scottish regiment in Swedish service; *minister* in *Edinburgh* 1641; preached at coronation of *Charles II* 1651; resigned his charge at *Restoration,* but admitted to *Pencaitland* by *Indulgence* 1669.

Douglas, Thomas, Earl of Selkirk. See Selkirk.

Douglas, Sir William (c. 1300-53). 'The Knight of Liddesdale'; prominent in resistance to *Edward Balliol* in 1330s; received lordship of Liddesdale 1342; captured at *Neville's Cross*; murdered *Alexander Ramsay;* murdered by Lord of Douglas, his kinsman.

Douglas, William, 8th Earl of (c. 1425-52). Son of Earl James 'the Gross'; succeeded 1443; married his cousin, 'The Maid of Galloway', and reunited Douglas inheritance; in 1451 made alliance with *Earl of Crawford* and *Earl of Ross* (Lord of the *Isles*), his refusal to break which caused his murder by *James II* at *Stirling* 22 February 1452.

Douglas, William (d. 1809). Penninghame pedlar who made a fortune in Virginian trade; had Carlingwark erected into *burgh of barony* and re-named it Castle-Douglas; baronet 1801.

Douglas, William, of Fingland. Wrote original version of 'Annie Laurie'.

Douglas, Sir William Fettes (1822-91). Born *Edinburgh*; Curator of *National Gallery of Scotland* 1877; painted 'Hudibras and Ralph visiting the Astrologer' and 'David Laing in his Study'.

Douglas, 'Willie'. Helped Queen *Mary* to escape from *Lochleven* 1568; precise relationship with Douglas family not known.

Doune (Perthshire). Castle built by *Robert, Duke of Albany*; reverted to crown 1425 and was given to successive queens in their marriage-portions; following on a gift by *James V* it passed to Sir James Stewart, created Lord Doune 1570, and, by the marriage of his son to the heiress of the *Regent Moray,* to the Earls of Moray; still retains much of its original character, though with restorations. There was a 'burgh' of D. in 1435, but it is not known to have become a *burgh of barony* (for *Earl of Buchan*) until 1528 and was again created a burgh of barony (for Earl of Moray) 1611.

Dounreay *(Caithness).* Nuclear fast reactor begun 1954.

Dover House. Headquarters of Scottish Office in Whitehall, London.

Dowden, John (1840-1910). Born Ireland; Principal of *Episcopal Church* College, *Edinburgh,* 1880; Bishop of Edinburgh 1886; wrote 'Celtic Church in Scotland', 'Medieval Church in Scotland' and 'Scottish Bishops'.

Doyle. See Conan Doyle.

Drem (East Lothian). Barony belonged to *Knights Templars*; *burgh of barony* for *Lord Binning* 1616.

Drochil Castle (Peeblesshire). Large structure

erected by *Regent Morton* in 1570s; roofless, but walls largely complete.

Drostan, Kings. See Drust.

Drostan, St (fl. 600). Said to have been nephew and disciple of *Columba* and co-founder of abbey of *Deer*.

Drove Roads. Tracks by which cattle were driven largely from West Highlands, to markets at *Crieff* and *Falkirk* and across the Border. See Black Cattle.

Drum, Castle of (Aberdeenshire). Tower which belonged to *Irvines* from 1323 until 1975, when (with addition of 1619) it was bequeathed to *National Trust*.

Drum, House of (Gilmerton, Midlothian). A house built 1584 for *Lord Somerville* was superseded by one built 1724 by *William Adam*.

Drumalban (= the spine of *Alba*). The watershed formed by the hills and mountains extending from south to north, mainly near west coast.

Drumclog, Battle of, 1 June 1679. *Covenanters* defeated *Graham of Claverhouse* in *Avondale* parish, Lanarkshire.

Drumelzier Castle (Peeblesshire). Tweedie stronghold of 16th century, now in ruins.

Drumlanrig Castle (Dumfriesshire). Built by *William Bruce* 1677-89 for 1st *Duke of Queensberry* on site of earlier castle which had belonged to *Douglases* since 14th century.

Drumlanrig, James, Earl of (1697-1715). Heir of 2nd *Duke of Queensberry*; an idiot who murdered and roasted a *Canongate* spit-boy at the fire at *Queensberry House* and was found eating him.

Drumlanrig, Viscountcy and Earldom. The *barony* had belonged to *Douglases* from 14th century; viscountcy created 1628 and earldom 1633; 3rd Earl made *Duke of Queensberry* 1684.

Drumlithie (Kincardineshire). *Burgh of barony* for *Earl of Angus* 1602.

Drummochy (Fife). *Burgh of barony* for Lundy of that *ilk* 1540.

Drummond, Annabella (c. 1350-1401). Daughter of Sir John D. of Stobhall; married *Robert III* 1367.

Drummond Castle (Perthshire). Keep built by 1st *Lord D.* c. 1491; garrisoned by government troops 1715; destroyed by *Jacobite* Duchess of *Perth* to prevent its use by government in 1745; modern house added 1822 and keep restored; passed from Perth family through a daughter to Lord Willoughby de Eresby and then to Earl of Ancaster.

Drummond, George (?1687-1766). Born *Edinburgh*; held various government appointments; Treasurer of city of Edinburgh 1717, *Dean of Guild* 1722 and Lord *Provost* six times between 1725 and 1764; much concerned with improvements and new buildings and proposals which took shape in the *New Town*; laid foundation stone of *North Bridge* 1763.

Drummond, Henry (1851-97). Professor of Natural Science in *Free Church* College in *Glasgow*; his works include 'The Ascent of Man', 'Natural Law in the Spiritual World' and 'In Tropical Africa'.

Drummond, James and John, Earls and Duke of Perth. See Perth.

Drummond, John. See Melfort, Earl of.

Drummond, Lordship. Created 1487 for Sir John Drummond; 4th Lord created *Earl of Perth* 1605.

Drummond, Margaret (d. ? 1375). Daughter of Sir Malcolm D; married Sir John Logie of that *ilk* and after his death became second wife of *David II*, February 1364; divorced March 1370.

Drummond, Margaret (?1472-1501). Daughter of John, 1st *Lord D*; mistress and, according to tradition, privately married, to *James IV*, to whom she bore a daughter, Margaret; poisoned with her sisters, allegedly because she was an obstacle to the King's marriage to *Margaret Tudor*; buried in *Dunblane* Cathedral.

Drummond, William, of Hawthornden (1585-1649). Born *Hawthornden*; educated *Edinburgh,* London, Bourges and Paris, with a view to legal career; on father's death (1610) abandoned professional prospects; his poetry included 'Poems' (1616), 'Forth Feasting' (1617) and 'Flowers of Sion' (1623); his prose 'History of the Five Jameses' published 1655; gave 500 books to Edinburgh University; entertained Ben Jonson at Hawthornden.

Drummond, William Abernethy (1720-1809). His own name was Abernethy but he took his wife's name also; *Episcopalian minister* in *Edinburgh*; Bishop of *Brechin* 1787 and of *Edinburgh* 1788-1805.

Drummondite Schism. David T.K. Drummond, appointed to Trinity Chapel, *Edinburgh,* 1838, was ordered by bishop to discontinue non-liturgical worship; he refused and formed a 'Church of England' congregation; a few others were founded, on a low church and evangelical basis, all quite unconnected with the Scottish *Episcopal Church*.

Drummossie Moor, Battle of. See Culloden.

Drumselch. Royal forest on south side of *Edinburgh*; not to be confused with Drum-

sheugh, which was Meldrumsheugh.
'Drunken Parliament'. The first *Parliament* of the *Restoration.*
Drust (or **Drostan**). Name of several *Pictish* kings from 671 to 835; later associated in romances with Tristan.
Dryburgh. *Burgh of barony* for Abbot of D., 1527.
Dryburgh Abbey (*Premonstratensian*) (Berwickshire). Founded by Hugh de *Morville* 1150; erected, with *Cambuskenneth* and *Inchmahome,* into lordship for John, *Earl of Mar,* 1604; remains of domestic buildings are considerable and the ruins contain the tombs of *Sir Walter Scott* and *Earl Haig.*
Duart Castle (Mull). Possibly dates in part from 13th century; contains substantial tower of 14th; mentioned 1390; after being garrisoned by government troops for a time in 18th century, fell into ruin, to be restored 1912 and become once more a *MacLean* seat.
Dubh. See Duff.
Dubhthach, St. See Duthac.
Ducat. Gold coin valued variously at 40s., 60s. and 80s. from reign of *James V* to that of *James VI.*
Duddingston (Midlothian). Originally called Treverlen, it was renamed after an English proprietor c. 1150; given to abbey of *Kelso*; after *Reformation* passed through *Duke of Argyll* to *Duke of Abercorn,* who built Duddingston House 1768; parish church is partly 12th century.
Dudhope, Viscountcy. Created 1641 for John Scrymgeour (d. 1643); 3rd Viscount was created *Earl of Dundee.*
Duff (or **Dubh**). King of *Alba,* killed 967.
Duff, William, of *Braco* (1693-1763). Son of William D. of Dipple (*Moray*); M.P. for Banffshire 1727-34; Baron Braco 1735; Viscount MacDuff and Earl *Fife* 1759.
Dufftown (Banffshire). *Police burgh* 1863.
Duffus *(Moray).* Lands granted by *David I* to Freskin, a Fleming, who presumably built the 12th century *motte,* which was superseded by a 15th century stone keep of which there are substantial remains although a house was built nearby in 17th century. The line of Freskin ended with heiresses, one of whom married Reginald le Chen c. 1280; the *Cheyne heiress married a son of 4th Earl of Sutherland* c. 1350; property bought by Sir Archibald Dunbar 1705.
Duffus, Lordship. Created for Sutherland of Duffus 1650; *forfeited* by 3rd Lord 1716; restored 1826; extinct or dormant 1875.
Duke of Gordon's Highlanders. See Gordon.
Dull (Perthshire). Site of Celtic monastery; the associated sanctuary survived, marked out by four crosses, one of them still in its original position and two others preserved in old church of Weem.
Dumbarton. Rock of Dumbarton was a capital of kingdom of *Strathclyde*; *royal burgh* 1222; royal castle, mentioned 1238, was held for Queen *Mary* 1568-70 and was specified at time of *Union* as a permanently fortified post, but little remains of dates earlier than 18th century; a medieval *Grammar School* was associated with the parish church.
Dumbarton Collegiate Church. Erected 1454 on petition of Countess of *Lennox*; apparently had an associated hospital.
Dumbarton, Earldom. Created for George Douglas, 2nd son of 1st Marquis of *Douglas,* 1675; extinct on death of 2nd Earl 1748.
Dumbarton's Drums. The 'Scots March' played by drummers of *Hepburn's Regiment* at battle of Leipzig 1631; now a regimental march of *Royal Scots.*
Dumbarton's Regiment. Name for *Royal Scots* when commanded by *Earl of Dumbarton.*
Dumfries. *Royal burgh* by 1178x1188; castle, presumably built then by *William I,* was added to by Edward I and survived in part until 1719. *Grammar School* mentioned 1481.
'Dumfries and Galloway Courier'. Established 1809 by *Henry Duncan, minister* of *Ruthwell.* Amalgamated with 'Herald and Register' 1884.
'Dumfries and Galloway Standard'. Founded 1843.
Dumfries Commercial Bank. Existed 1804-8.
Dumfries, Earldom. Created for William, 9th Lord *Crichton* of *Sanquhar,* 1633; Patrick MacDowall of Freugh succeeded his uncle, 4th Earl, 1768; Earl Patrick's daughter and heiress married John, Lord Mountstuart, and title passed to Marquis of *Bute.*
Dumfries Friary (Conventual *Franciscan*). Founded 1234x1266 by Alan, Lord of *Galloway,* or his daughter *Devorguilla*; revenues granted to *burgh* by 1569.
Dumfriesshire and Galloway Natural History and Antiquarian Society. Founded 1862.
Dun, Finlay (1795-1853). Born *Aberdeen*; edited collections of Scottish songs.
Dunachton (Inverness-shire). *Burgh of barony* for Macintosh of Torcastle 1690; castle burned 1689.
Dunadd (*Argyll*). Rocky outcrop, with traces of artificial fortification, which was a stronghold of the *Scots* after they first arrived from

Ireland, probably in the 6th century, and the place of inauguration of their kings, as certain rock-markings may indicate.

Dunaverty Castle (Southend, *Argyll*). Stronghold of Lords of the *Isles,* captured by *James IV* 1493 and retaken on his departure; garrison slaughtered by *Covenanters* 1647.

Dunbar, Battles of. (1) 27 April 1296. Defeat of Scots by Edward I after *John Balliol* had renounced his allegiance to England. (2) 3 September 1650. Scots under *David Leslie* defeated by Cromwell.

Dunbar, Burgh of (East Lothian). *Burgh of barony* in 13th century and granted by *David II* to *Earl of March* 1370, but received charter as *royal burgh* 1445.

Dunbar Castle. Only fragmentary remains exist of what was a strong fortress commanding an important harbour; figured in *War of Independence* and reign of Queen *Mary,* when it was commanded by *Earl of Bothwell.* See Black Agnes.

Dunbar Collegiate Church. Founded by Patrick, *Earl of Dunbar* and *March,* 1342; hospital or Maison-Dieu associated with it or with friary.

Dunbar, Columba (1370-1435). Son of *George, 10th Earl of March*; *dean* of Dunbar *collegiate church*; Bishop of *Moray* 1422-35; effigy on tomb preserved in *Elgin Cathedral.*

Dunbar, Countess of. See Black Agnes.

Dunbar Drove. See Dunbar, Battle of (3 September 1650).

Dunbar, Earldom. *Cospatrick,* 1st Earl (d. 1138) was descended from Anglian earls of Northumbria and from Scottish royal house. His family held earldom until forfeiture in 1435 of George, 11th Earl of Dunbar and 4th *Earl of March.* Title revived 1605 for George Home of Spott, and in abeyance after his death in 1611.

Dunbar Friary (*Trinitarian*). Founded by Christian Bruce, Countess of Dunbar, 1240-8; revenues transferred to Trinitarians of *Peebles,* 1529.

Dunbar, Gavin (c. 1455-1532). *Dean* of *Moray, archdeacon* of *St Andrews, Clerk Register*; Bishop of *Aberdeen* 1519; built south transept of cathedral, spires on western towers, wooden roof of nave and *Bridge of Dee*; tomb-recess still visible.

Dunbar, Gavin (c. 1495-1547). Nephew of preceding; preceptor to *James V*; Archbishop of *Glasgow* 1524; *Chancellor* 1528-43.

Dunbar, George, 10th Earl of (c. 1370-c. 1455). His daughter was betrothed to *David, Duke of Rothesay,* who married instead the daughter of *3rd Earl of Douglas*; he then deserted to England and fought for Henry IV at Shrewsbury (1403) against 'Hotspur' and the *Earl of Douglas*; restored 1409, forfeited again 1435.

Dunbar, George Home, Earl of (c. 1560-1611). *Treasurer,* 1601; created Earl 1605; acted for *James VI* in his management of the Church.

Dunbar, Naval Battle of. *Sir Andrew Wood* defeated English in Firth of Forth near Dunbar 1489.

Dunbar, Viscountcy. Created 1620 for Sir Henry Constable of Burton Constable; extinct on death of 4th Viscount 1718.

Dunbar, William (c. 1460-1514). A priest, in government service before 1500; celebrated marriage of *James IV* in 'The Thrissill and the Rose'; received pension from crown; author also of 'The Golden Targe', 'The Fenyeit Freir of Tungland', 'The Flyting of Dunbar and Kennedie' and 'Lament for the Makaris'.

Dunblane (Perthshire). First ecclesiastical establishment attributed to St *Blane* c. 590, but no evidence of Celtic monastery or *Culdee* establishment; however, the lower courses of the cathedral tower date from before 1100, long before the first named bishop appeared c. 1150; Bishop Clement (1233-57) started present cathedral (dedicated to St Blane), which was partly ruinous before its restoration in 1889. The bishopric was closely associated with earldom of *Strathearn,* and the earls enjoyed in it the rights normally enjoyed by the king. The place was a *burgh* in 13th or 14th century; later a *burgh of barony* under *Earl of Kinnoull,* and still later a *police burgh.*

Dunblane, Viscountcy. Conferred 1675 on Peregrine Osborne, who in 1712 succeeded his father as Duke of Leeds.

Dunbog (Fife). *Burgh of barony* for George Bannerman 1687.

Duncan I (c. 1010-40). Elder son of *Crinan, Abbot of Dunkeld,* and Bethoc, daughter of *Malcolm II,* whom he succeeded 1034; challenged by *Macbeth* and *Thorfinn*; after incurring heavy losses in a siege of Durham he was twice defeated by Thorfinn and then defeated and killed by Macbeth.

Duncan II (c. 1060-94). Eldest son of *Malcolm III*; hostage to William the Conqueror 1072; assisted to throne of Scotland by William II of England1094, but after six months killed and superseded by his uncle *Donald Bane*; granted first extant Scottish charter.

Duncan, Adam, 1st Viscount Camperdown (1731-1804). Son of Alexander D. of Lundie, Perthshire; entered navy 1745; in action at Cape St Vincent 1780; admiral 1795; patrolled

North Sea until Dutch fleet emerged to be defeated at Camperdown, 11 October 1797; created Baron and Viscount.

Duncan, Earl of Carrick. See Carrick.

Duncan, Earl of Fife. First of name recorded 1139, d. 1154; second, his son and heir, d. 1204; third succeeded c. 1272, d. 1288; fourth, his son and heir, d. c. 1353.

Duncan, Henry (1774-1846). Born Lochrutton; *minister* of *Ruthwell* 1799; energetic in measures to relieve poverty, and started Savings Bank 1810; started '*Dumfries and Galloway Courier*' 1809; reconstructed *Ruthwell Cross*; joined *Free Church* 1843.

Duncan, John (1866-1945). Born *Dundee*; made drawings for illustrations in newspapers and books; studied abroad and took up portrait-painting; professor of art in Chicago 1902-4, but returned and died in *Edinburgh*.

Duncan, Mary Lundie (1814-40). Wife of William Duncan, *minister* of Cleish, son of *Henry D*; wrote ninety-three hymns, including the popular 'Jesus, tender Shepherd, hear me'.

Duncan's Leap. On River Ericht in Rannoch; 'Duncan the Fat', a follower of *Robert I*, is said to have leaped across the river after reconnoitring a camp of the *MacDougals*.

Duncanson, Robert (d. 1705). Major in Argyll's Regiment who gave the immediate order to Captain Robert Campbell of Glenlyon to massacre the MacDonalds of *Glencoe* 1692.

Duncrub, Lordship. Created 1651 for Sir Andrew Rollo, whose ancestors had held *barony* since 1380.

Dundarave Castle (Loch Fyne). Anciently a MacNaughton stronghold; a building mainly of 16th century date, restored by *Sir Robert Lorimer*.

Dundas Family. Remarkable legal dynasty, beginning with Sir James, Lord Arniston (d. 1679); his son Robert was Lord Arniston 1679, d. 1726; his son Robert (d. 1753) was *Solicitor General* 1717, *Lord Advocate* 1721 and *Lord President* 1748; his son Robert (d. 1787) was again a judge as Lord Arniston; his son Robert (d. 1819) was Solicitor General 1784, Lord Advocate 1789 and Chief Baron of Exchequer 1801. See also Melville, Henry and Robert, Viscounts.

Dundee. *Burgh* had charter from *William I* 1178x1182; castle figured in *War of Independence* but hardly thereafter; *Grammar School* dates authentically from 1434 but is supposed to have been much older; the great church of St Mary, enlarged in 15th century, suffered in 16th century wars and from later fires, and only tower survives, with relatively modern churches attached to it. See also Rottenrow.

Dundee and Newtyle Railway. Completed 1832.

Dundee Banking Company. Founded by George Dempster and Co. 1763; united with *Royal Bank* 1864.

Dundee, Caird Hall. Built by bequest of Sir James Caird (d. 1916).

'Dundee Courier and Advertiser'. 'Dundee Weekly Advertiser' established 1801 and 'Dundee Weekly Courier' established 1816; both later became dailies and amalgamated 1926.

Dundee, Earldom. Created for *John Scrymgeour, 3rd Viscount Dudhope,* 1661; on his death (1668) it became dormant, but was successfully claimed by Henry Scrimgeour Wedderburn in 1953.

Dundee Friary (*Dominican*). Founded by Andrew Abercrombie, *burgess,* c. 1521; property bestowed on *burgh* 1567.

Dundee Friary (Conventual *Franciscan*). Said to have been founded by *Devorguilla* before 1289; in existence in 1310, when a declaration of the clergy in favour of *Robert I* was dated here; suffered in English attacks and at hands of reformers; in 1564 Queen *Mary* allowed site to be used as burial ground.

Dundee Friary (*Trinitarian*). Supposed to have been founded by Sir James Scrimgeour c. 1284, but not authenticated before 1390, when Sir James Lindsay granted a tenement in Dundee to Trinitarians for a Maison Dieu which was still in existence in 1548.

Dundee Hospital. There was a medieval leper-house, and possibly a hospital of St John Baptist.

Dundee, Naval Battle off, 1504. *Sir Andrew Wood* defeated English under Stephen Bull and took his three ships into Dundee as prizes.

Dundee New Bank. A reorganisation of Dundee Commercial Bank, which was in disorder in 1802; purchased by *Dundee Banking Company* 1838.

Dundee Nunnery (*Franciscan*). Founded by James Fotheringham 1502; property had gone to *burgh* by 1567.

Dundee Union Bank. Founded 1809; amalgamated with *Bank of Scotland* 1844.

Dundee University. Founded 1883 as University College, Dundee; integrated with University of *St Andrews* in 1890s; styled Queen's College of University of St Andrews 1954; separate university 1 August 1967.

Dundee, Viscountcy. Created 1688 for *John Graham of Claverhouse*; his son James, 2nd Viscount, died at end of 1689; David, 3rd Viscount (brother of 1st) forfeited 1690; right to title passed to Grahams of Duntrune, but it was not restored and that line died out 1759.

Dundonald (Kyle, Ayrshire). Castle of Stewarts from 12th or 13th century; *Robert II* died there; estate bought by Sir William Cochrane 1636 and in 1644 he used the old castle as a quarry from which to build mansion of Auchans. Kirkton of D. was a *burgh of barony* for Cochran of Cowdoun 1638.

Dundonald, Earldom. Created 1669 for William Cochrane.

Dundonald, Thomas Cochrane, 10th Earl of (1775-1860). Served in navy from 1793; M.P. 1806; placed on half-pay for attacking abuses in navy and later expelled from navy and parliament; commander Chilean navy 1817; admiral of Brazilian fleet 1823; admiral of Greek navy 1827; reinstated 1832; British admiral 1851.

Dundrennan Abbey (*Cistercian*) (Kirkcudbrightshire). Founded by *David I* 1142; erected into *temporal lordship* for *John Murray*, later *Earl of Annandale*, 1606; part served as parish church until 1742.

Dunedin. Literary form of Celtic name of *Edinburgh*, which appears as Din Eiddyn as well as Etain and Eden from 7th century.

Dunfermline. *Royal burgh* by c. 1120, but later dependent on abbey until after *Reformation*; *Grammar School*, presumably developed by abbey, authenticated from late 15th century and received further endowments from Queen *Anne* in 1610; there was a pre-Reformation hospital (St Leonard's) which survived into 17th century.

Dunfermline Abbey (*Benedictine*) (Fife). There was a church which Queen *Margaret* enlarged c. 1070 and to which she brought some Benedictine monks from Canterbury; became an abbey under *David I*, c. 1130; some lands granted to Queen *Anne* 1589, others erected into *temporal lordships* for various donatories; nave used as parish church after *Reformation* (as before it), east end ruined by fall of central tower 1753; new church erected on eastern half of site 1822 and nave preserved as ancient monument.

Dunfermline, Alexander Seton, 1st Earl of (1555-1622). Son of George, *Lord Seton*; *advocate* 1577; *Lord of Session* 1586; *Lord President* 1593-1605; *Chancellor* 1605; Lord Urquhart ?1591, Lord Fyvie 1598, Earl of Dunfermline 1605. His son, Charles, 2nd Earl (d. 1673) was a *Covenanter* and supported *Engagement*.

Dunfermline, Earldom. Created 1605 for Alexander *Seton*; 4th Earl forfeited for *Jacobitism* 1690 and died without issue 1694.

Dunfermline Palace. Built partly on site of domestic ranges of abbey, for Queen *Anne*; *Charles I* born there 1600.

Dunfermline Tower. Alleged remains of tower attributed to *Malcolm III*, not far west from entrance to abbey church.

Dunglass (Berwickshire). Charter to *collegiate church* granted by Alexander Home 1423, confirmed by *James II* 1450; building still almost entire; there was an associated hospital, mentioned 1480. D. became *burgh of barony* for *Lord Home* 1489.

Dunkeld. *Burgh of barony* by 1512; *royal burgh* 1704. Royal School, presumably in existence under cathedral auspices in middle ages, had charter from *James VI* 1567. Hospital founded by Bishop George Browne (1484-1515).

Dunkeld, Bishopric and Cathedral. Relics of *Columba* were brought to Dunkeld from *Iona* early in 9th century and it became the seat of an abbot who was also chief bishop of *Pict*land; through *Crinan*, abbot of D., the abbey passed to the royal family and the last abbot was *Ethelred*, son of *Malcolm III*. There is no evidence of *Culdees*. Bishop Cormac, recorded under *Alexander I*, presumably continued an old line and he was followed by Gregory; Richard, consecrated 1170, was the first Norman bishop; diocese included *Argyll* until c. 1190. Most of the cathedral (dedicated to St Columba) is 15th century; choir in use as parish church, nave roofless but almost entire.

Dunkeld, Siege of, 21 August 1689. *Cameronian Regiment* under *Cleland* repulsed attacks of *Jacobite* force.

Dunlop Cheese. Barbara Gilmour, wife of the farmer of Overhill at Dunlop, took refuge in Ireland as a *Covenanter* and brought back a new process of cheese making.

Dunlop, John Boyd (1840-1921). Born Dreghorn, Ayrshire; became veterinary surgeon in Belfast 1867; patented pneumatic tyre 1888; sold patent to William Harvey du Cros 1890 and Dunlop Rubber Company was formed.

Dunlop, William (c. 1649-1700). Son of Alexander D., *minister* of *Paisley*; emigrated to America, but returned 1688; minister of *Ochiltree* and Paisley; principal of *Glasgow University* 1690; a director of *The Company of Scotland*; Historiographer Royal 1693. His son, William (1692-1720), was professor of church history at *Edinburgh*.

Dunmore, Earldom. Created 1686 for Charles Murray, 2nd son of 1st Marquis of *Atholl*; 4th Earl, John (1732-1809), was Governor of New York and Virginia 1770 and of Bahamas 1787; Charles Adolphus, 7th Earl (1841-1907), explored in Tibet and wrote 'The Pamirs'.

Dunmore Pottery. Developed from 1860 by Peter Gardiner, native of *Alloa,* and became noted for teapots, dessert services and ornaments; closed at beginning of 20th century, but ruins of kiln still visible.

Dunnichen. See Nechtansmere.

Dunnideer Castle (*Garioch,* Aberdeenshire). Built in 13th century by John *Balliol,* father of King *John*; little remains.

Dunning (Perthshire). *Burgh of barony* for Rollo of *Duncrub* 1511. Church has tower dating from before 1100.

Dunnottar Castle (Kincardineshire). The promontory was an ancient fortified site, mentioned in 7th century; oldest extant portion built in later 14th century by Sir William Keith, whose family, the *Earls Marischal,* long retained it; Scottish *regalia* brought here 1651 and, when castle was besieged by English, removed to safety in church of *Kinneff*; used as prison for '*Whigs*' rounded up at time of *Argyll's rebellion,* 1685; dismantled from 1720 onwards.

Dunolly Castle *(Argyll).* Ruinous keep, once stronghold of *MacDougals,* Lords of *Lorne,* originating possibly in 12th century; modern house built nearby.

Dunoon *(Argyll).* The castle was *Stewart* property, with *Campbells* as hereditary keepers; *Lamonts* besieged there in 1646 were massacred; only fragmentary remains. D. mentioned as *burgh* 1553; formally *burgh of barony* 1835; later a *police burgh.*

Dunpender. British or Welsh name of *Traprain Law.*

Dunrobin Castle (*Sutherland*). Said to be on very ancient site of habitation, but nearly all present building was erected 1845-51.

Dunrossness Collegiate Church (*Shetland*). Nothing known of it beyond its bare existence.

Duns (Berwickshire). *Burgh of barony* for Home of Ayton 1489 and for Sir James Cockburn 1670; hospital mentioned 1275-1492.

Duns Scotus, John. See John of Duns.

Dunsapie Terraces (*Edinburgh*). *Holyrood* Park contains several series of prehistoric cultivation terraces, of which the range above Dunsapie Loch is only one.

Dunsinane (Perthshire). Hill with remains of ancient fort; traditional association with *Macbeth* not authenticated.

Dunstaffnage Castle (*Argyll*). On site of fortified seat of kings of *Pict*land and *Dalriada,* in which the *Stone of Scone* is said to have been kept for a time; castle dates largely from 13th century, but there were additions until early 18th; passed from *MacDougals* of *Lorne* to *Campbells,* with a branch of whom the captaincy remains; fortified by the government in 1715 and 1745, it was occupied until a fire in 1810, and part was made habitable again in 1902. There are the ruins of a fine 13th century chapel nearby.

Duntreath Castle (Stirlingshire). A tower was built in 15th century by Edmonstone family (who held *barony* from 1452) and other buildings and a curtain wall were added later. Abandoned in 1740, the tower was restored by Sir Archibald Edmonstone in 1863.

Duntrune Castle (*Argyll*). Late 16th century tower-house superimposed on keep of probably 13th century date; sold by *Campbells* in 1792 to Malcolms of Poltalloch, who still live in it.

Dunvegan Castle (Skye). An early fortress was largely effaced by later building, notably sham baronial additions in 19th century, but part of medieval keep and 16th century 'Fairy Tower' survive. Residence of *MacLeod* chiefs. See also Fairy Flag.

Dupplin, Battle of, 12 August 1332. Scots under Donald, *Earl of Mar,* defeated by *Edward Balliol* and his English adherents near *Perth.*

Durham, Treaty of, 1139. King Stephen of England granted to *David I* the whole of Northumberland except Newcastle and Bamborough.

Durie, Andrew (d. 1558). Bishop of *Galloway* 1541; previously Abbot of *Melrose*; said to have died of shock after a protestant riot in *Edinburgh.*

Durie, George (1496-1561). Brother of preceding; Abbot of *Dunfermline, archdeacon* of *St Andrews* and Keeper of *Privy Seal.*

Durie, John (1537-1600). Former monk of *Dunfermline*; became *minister* of *Edinburgh*; opposed crown power over church.

Durie, John (d. 1587). Son of *George Durie*; educated Paris and Louvain; active as Roman Catholic priest in south-western Scotland.

Durie, Robert (1555-1616). Son of *John Durie* (1537-1600); *minister* at Abercrombie and *Anstruther,* then of Scots Kirk in Leyden; banished for attending illegal *General Assembly* at *Aberdeen* 1605.

Durris (Kincardineshire). *Burgh of barony* for Earl *Marischal* 1541.
Durward, Alan (d. 1268). 'Door-ward' ('ostiarius') of Scotland; *Justiciar* before 1246; leader of 'English party' in minority of *Alexander III*; accused of treason and fled to England 1252; *Earl of Atholl* by marriage.
Duthac (or **Dutho**), **St** (?d. 1065). Said to have been native of Scotland educated in Ireland, whence he returned to become chief bishop of Scotland; venerated in *Tain*; his identity with 'Dubthach the Scot, chief confessor of Ireland and Scotland', who died in Armagh in 1065, is not certain.
Dwarfie Stane (Hoy, *Orkney*). Block of sandstone, about 28 feet by 13, ranging in height from 2 to 6½ feet; a chamber with two bunks has been cut into it.
Dyce, William (1806-64). Born *Aberdeen*; painted in *Edinburgh* and London and was in Rome 1827-9; originated 'pre-Raphaelite' school of painting with 'Madonna and Child' (1828); professor at King's College, London, 1844.
Dysart (Fife). Appears as *burgh of barony* under Lord Sinclair 1510; later *royal burgh*; only evidence of *collegiate church* is mention of prebends in 1568.
Dysart, Earldom. Created for William Murray (c. 1600-51), who was educated with *Charles I.*
Dysart, Elizabeth Murray, Countess of (d. 1697). Succeeded her father, the 1st Earl; her second husband was *John Maitland, Duke of Lauderdale.*

E

Eagle's Loup. Chasm in River Mark, Glenesk, where Lindsay of *Edzell,* a fugitive after the murder of Lord *Spynie* in *Edinburgh* in 1607, escaped from a band of men commanded by his uncle, the Earl of *Crawford,* by jumping the river.
Earl of Mar's Greybreeks. *Royal Scots Fusiliers,* raised by *Earl of Mar* and originally wearing grey breeches.
Earls, Earldoms. The Celtic *mormaer* was translated into Latin in the 12th century as 'comes', which was also the equivalent of the English 'earl', and in that century or the next new 'earldoms' also appeared. See also Seven Earls.
Earls Palatine. The *Earls of Strathearn.*
Earlsferry (Fife). The terminus of a ferry from *North Berwick,* distinguished from *Queensferry* and named after *Earls of Fife*; *royal burgh* before 1547, confirmed 1589.
Earlshall Castle (Fife). Built by Sir William Bruce 1546; property passed later to Hendersons of *Fordell;* castle restored by *Sir Robert Lorimer* 1892.
Earlston (Berwickshire). Of old Ercildoun; hospital mentioned c. 1160; *burgh of barony* for Home of Whitrig 1489. See Thomas the Rhymer.
Earlston (Dalry parish, *Galloway*). Tower of 1655 which was stronghold of Gordons of Lochinvar.
East Calder (West Lothian). Conferred by *Malcolm IV* on Randolph de Clere and by *Robert I* on James Douglas, ancestor of *Earls of Morton.*
East Linton (East Lothian). *Burgh of regality* for Stewart of *Traquair* 1631.
East Lothian Bank. Established 1810; wound up 1822.
Easy Club. *Jacobite* association in *Edinburgh* to which *Allan Ramsay* contributed verses.
Ebba, St (d. ?679). Daughter of Ethelfrith, King of Northumbria; Abbess of *Coldingham.* A second abbess of the name held office when the house was destroyed by Scandinavians in 870.
Eccles Nunnery (*Cistercian*) (Berwickshire). Supposedly founded 1156 by Earl *Cospatric* of *Dunbar*, erected into *temporal lordship* for *Sir George Home* 1609; only fragmentary remains.
Ecclesia Scoticana. Term applied in middle ages to the church in Scotland; although it had no archbishop until 1472 it was formally declared to be a separate province, subject directly to the Roman see, 1192.
Ecclesiastical Burghs. *Burghs* established, under licence from the crown, by bishops and abbots on their properties, e.g., *Canongate, St Andrews, Glasgow, Arbroath.*
Ecclesiastical Courts. Before the *Reformation,* had powers in executry and matrimonial causes, as well as in proceedings for fulfilment of contracts; much of their jurisdiction later passed to *Commissary Courts.*
Echt (Aberdeenshire). *Burgh of barony* for *Forbes* of Echt 1698.
Écu (or **Abbey Crown**). Gold coin first issued in reign of Queen *Mary.*
Edderton (Ross). Original site of Abbey of *Fearn.*
Eddleston (Peeblesshire). *Burgh of barony* for Murray of Darnhall 1607.

Edgar (c. 1074-1107). Fourth son of *Malcolm III* and *Margaret*; supported *Duncan II* 1094; supported by William Rufus from 1095 and established on throne by an English army 1097; gave endowments to churches of Durham, *Coldingham, Dunfermline* and *St Andrews.*

Edinample Castle (Loch Earn, Perthshire). Built in early 17th century by *Sir Duncan Campbell of Glenorchy* on site of earlier MacGregor stronghold.

Edinburgh Academy. Erected by private subscription to designs by *W. Burn* 1824, to provide education in the *New Town*; the *High School* had not yet moved to Regent Road.

'Edinburgh Advertiser'. Newspaper first published 1764; owned by Alexander and *James Donaldson* and later by *Robert Chambers*; merged in '*Edinburgh Evening Courant*' 1859.

Edinburgh, Assembly Hall and Rooms. See Assembly.

Edinburgh Bibliographical Society. Founded 1890.

Edinburgh, Bishopric of. Founded by *Charles I* 1633 and, despite the disestablishment of the *Episcopal Church* in 1689, has continued without a significant break except from 1739 to 1776.

Edinburgh, Burgh of. *Royal burgh* by c. 1125.

Edinburgh Castle. Rock mentioned as fortress from 7th century; earliest extant building, 'St *Margaret*'s Chapel', belongs to early 12th century; reconstructed after *War of Independence* and again after siege of 1573. See David's Tower, National War Memorial, Half-Moon Battery, and Scottish United Services Museum.

Edinburgh, Charlotte Square. North side completed by 1808, remainder by 1820. See Adam, Robert.

Edinburgh, City Chambers. See Royal Exchange.

Edinburgh, City Guard. See City Guard.

Edinburgh Club, Old. See Old Edinburgh Club.

Edinburgh, Common Riding at. In 16th century the *bailies* rode the *marches* at All Hallows' Eve.

'Edinburgh Courant'. Folio broadsheet 1705-10. See Watson, James.

Edinburgh, Donaldson's Hospital. See Donaldson, James.

'Edinburgh Evening Courant'. Established 1718.

Edinburgh, Excise Office. Established after *Union,* in building beside Netherbow; later in Cowgate (where southern piers of George IV Bridge stand), in Chessel's Court (see Brodie, William), in what is now head office of *Royal Bank* in St Andrew Square and finally in Bellevue House in Drummond Place, demolished 1846.

Edinburgh Festival. First held 1947.

Edinburgh Fire Brigade. Established 1824, said to be first municipal fire brigade.

Edinburgh, Fires in. A great fire on 3 February 1700 destroyed many of the buildings in Parliament Square; another on 5 November 1824 destroyed the steeple of the *Tron Church,* the east side of Parliament Square and many tenements.

Edinburgh Friary (*Carmelite*). See Greenside.

Edinburgh Friary (*Dominican*). Founded by *Alexander II* 1230; burned 1518 or 1528 but rebuilt; burned by English 1544; property granted to town 1567.

Edinburgh Friary (*Franciscan* Observant). First Scottish Observant house, founded c. 1455 by James Douglas of Cassillis and *burgesses,* but six friars said to have come from Holland 1447; land granted to town as burying-place 1562.

Edinburgh Gates. Six principal gates or ports—West, Bristo, Potterow, Cowgate, New and Netherbow.

Edinburgh, George Square. Dates from 1766.

Edinburgh, Gladstone's Land. See Gladstone's Land.

Edinburgh Golfers, Honourable Society of. Founded at *Leith Links* 1774; moved to *Musselburgh* 1736 and *Muirfield* 1891.

Edinburgh, Greyfriars' Church. Erected 1612-20; New Greyfriars' added (to west) 1721; both burned 1845; reconstructed as single church 1936; the church (*not* churchyard) was the place of signature of *National Covenant* 1638; part of churchyard a prison for *Covenanters* after *Bothwell Brig.*

Edinburgh, High Church. The proper style of the church of *St Giles,* which has not been a cathedral since 1689.

Edinburgh, High School. Usually dated from foundation of abbey of *Holyrood,* with which it certainly had a long association, though managed by town before *Reformation*; first undoubted mention 1503; in Blackfriars' Wynd in 16th century, then in High School Yards, where new school built c. 1780; moved to Regent Road 1829 and to Barnton 1968; lost its identity and became merely a local non-selective school 1973.

Edinburgh, Highland Society. See Highland Society.

Edinburgh, Hospitals. (1) St Andrew and/or St Thomas, mentioned 1561-1666; (2) St Giles mentioned 1541; (3) St John Baptist, mentioned 1392; (4) St Leonard, founded before 1260s, granted to *Holyrood* Abbey and reconstituted 1493-4; (5) Magdalene, see Magdalen Chapel; (6) St Mary the Virgin, founded by community before 1438 and mentioned until 1589; (7) St Paul, an almshouse in *Leith* Wynd, founded by Thomas Spens, Bishop of *Aberdeen,* c. 1459-80, or by *Archibald Crawford,* Abbot of Holyrood, 1469-70, rebuilt 1619 and continued as workhouse until 1750; (8) St Thomas, in the Watergate, founded 1541 by *George Crichton,* Bishop of *Dunkeld,* and buildings survived until 1778.

Edinburgh Institution. Boys' school founded 1832; later renamed Melville College and in 1975 amalgamated with *Daniel Stewart's College.*

Edinburgh, Jenny Ha's Change House. See Jenny Ha's Change House.

Edinburgh, Jewish Cemetery. See Jewish Cemetery.

Edinburgh, John Knox's House. See Knox's House.

Edinburgh, John Watson's Hospital. See John Watson's School.

Edinburgh, Kirk o' Field. *Collegiate church* of St Mary in the Fields, founded 1510; buildings partly destroyed in *Hertford's Invasions* and church ruinous by time of *Darnley* murder 1567; site of *University.*

Edinburgh, Knights Hospitallers. Owned property near top of *Canongate,* where *St John's Cross* stood.

Edinburgh Linen Bank Partnery. Founded c. 1723; formed nucleus of *British Linen Company.*

Edinburgh, Magdalen Chapel. See Magdalen Chapel.

Edinburgh, Merchant Company. Founded by royal charter 1681 and ratified by *parliament* 1693; administers certain schools and charities; see George Watson, James Gillespie, Mary Erskine and Daniel Stewart.

Edinburgh, Mound. Created 1781-1820 by deposit of material excavated during building operations in *New Town.*

Edinburgh, New Town. Originated with the plan prepared by *James Craig* in 1767; see also Drummond, George.

Edinburgh, Nor' Loch. See North Loch.

Edinburgh, North Bridge. Constructed 1763-72; widened 1876. See Mylnes.

Edinburgh Nunnery. See Sciennes.

Edinburgh, Old College. University building on *Kirk o'Field* site; foundation stone laid 1789; *Robert Adam's* design was subsequently modified by *W.H.Playfair.*

Edinburgh Orphan Hospital. See Dean.

Edinburgh, Pleasance. See Pleasance.

Edinburgh, Portsburgh. See Portsburgh.

Edinburgh Regiment. See King's Own Scottish Borderers.

Edinburgh, Reid Concerts and **Reid School of Music.** See Reid, General John.

'Edinburgh Review'. Founded 1802 by *Henry Erskine* and *Francis Jeffrey* in *Whig* interest.

Edinburgh, Royal Burgess Golfing Society. Founded 1735; at first played on Bruntsfield Links; moved to *Musselburgh* 1873 and to Barnton 1891.

Edinburgh, Royal Infirmary. Established 1729; had royal charter 1736; building in Infirmary Street opened 1738; building in Lauriston opened 1880, to design by *David Bryce.*

Edinburgh, St Anthony's Chapel. Remains of chapel, with residence and nearby well, on crag in *Holyrood* Park. See also St Anthony's Chapel.

Edinburgh, St Cecilia's Hall. Erected in Niddry Street 1762 by Musical Society; now owned by *University.*

Edinburgh, St Cuthbert's Church. Church of large parish surrounding the city on west and north; mentioned in *Holyrood* charter c. 1140; present building dates from 1775.

Edinburgh, St Giles, Church of. Existed in 11th century, probably earlier; burned by English 1385; became *collegiate* 1466; a cathedral 1633-8 and 1662-89; divided into three or four churches; underwent two 19th century restorations. See also Thistle Chapel.

Edinburgh, St Mary's Church. Was in the castle, on site of *National War Memorial.*

Edinburgh, St Roque's Chapel. See St Roche.

Edinburgh School of Medicine. The first medical chair was founded in 1685, but the more significant date is the establishment of the faculty in 1726. See Monro, Alexander.

Edinburgh, Sciennes. See Sciennes.

Edinburgh, Trades Maiden Hospital. See Trades Maiden Hospital.

Edinburgh, Treaties of. (1) 17 March 1328. England acknowledged Scottish independence under *Robert I* and provided for marriage of his son to Princess Joanna; see also Northampton. (2) 6 July 1560. Between England and

France: their forces were to withdraw from Scotland; France acknowledged Elizabeth Tudor as Queen of England.

Edinburgh, Trinity College. Founded by *Mary of Gueldres* c. 1460; granted to town 1567; church survived until 1848, when it was demolished to make way for Waverley Station; fragments reassembled in Jeffrey Street 1872; a hospital associated with the *collegiate church* was also demolished, but its endowments continued to provide pensions.

Edinburgh, Tron Church. Begun 1637 but not finished until 1663; styled 'Christ's Kirk at the Tron' (that is, weighing place). A 'Butter Tron' was erected 1660, distinct from 'Salt Tron', and was demolished 1882.

Edinburgh, University. Owes its origin in part to a bequest by *Robert Reid*; after grant from crown in 1582, began to operate in 1583. See Little, Clement; Old College; Robertson, William.

Edinburgh, Weigh House. At head of Lawnmarket and West Bow; demolished by Cromwell 1650.

Edinburgh-Dalkeith Railway. Opened 1831. See also Innocent Railway.

Edinburgh-Glasgow Railway. Opened (Haymarket-Queen Street) 1842.

'Edinburgh's Disgrace'. Term applied to *National Memorial* on Calton Hill, its uncompleted state being held to be a reproach to Edinburgh.

Edinshall (Berwickshire). On Cockburnlaw stands one of the very few *brochs* in southern Scotland.

Edmondston, Arthur (1776-1841). Surgeon in Egypt under *Sir Ralph Abercromby*; settled in his ancestral home in Unst and wrote 'The Zetland Islands' (1809). His brother Laurence (1795-1879), also an M.D., was a noted ornithologist, and a third brother, Thomas, entertained the French savant Biot in Unst in 1817. Thomas, son of Laurence (1825-46), was professor of botany in *Glasgow* at the age of twenty and published a 'Flora' of Shetland. Biot E., another son of Laurence, wrote 'The Home of a Naturalist' with his sister, Jessie M.E. Saxby (1842-1940), who was a voluminous writer of fiction.

Edmund (fl. 1090s). 2nd son of *Malcolm III* and *Margaret*; evidently shared the kingdom with *Donald Bane* 1094-7; became monk in England.

Ednam (Berwickshire). Hospital mentioned from 1178 until after *Reformation.*

Education Acts. (1) Act of *Parliament,* 1496, made it compulsory for men of substance to send their eldest sons to school to learn Latin, arts and law. (2) Act of *Privy Council*, 1616, laid down that there should be a school in every parish. (3) Act of Parliament,1633, reaffirmed the Privy Council act of 1616. (4) Act of Parliament, 1646, transferred responsibility for schools from bishops to *presbyteries*. (5) Act of Parliament, 1696, restored responsibility to presbyteries.

Educational Institute of Scotland. School teachers' organisation, incorporated by royal warrant 1851; became a trade union.

Edward (c. 1070-93). Eldest son of *Malcolm III* and *Margaret*; mortally wounded when his father was killed.

Edzell *(Angus). Burgh of barony* for Lindsay of Edzell 1588.

Egilsay (*Orkney*). Church, probably 11th century, has round tower 48 feet high; scene of murder of St *Magnus.*

Eglinton, Earldom. Created 1507 for Hugh, 3rd Lord *Montgomerie* (d. 1545).

Eglinton Ironworks. Opened 1845.

Eglinton Tournament, August 1839. Romantic revival of medieval practice, organised by 13th *Earl of Eglinton* at Eglinton Castle (built 1798); it was ruined by rain.

Eigg. See Donan, St.

Eileach an Naoimh. Islet in Garvelloch group, *Argyll,* with remains of primitive *bee-hive* cells; said to have been site of monastery founded by St *Brendan* and visited by St *Columba.*

Eilean Donan Castle (Ross). On islet connected to shore by causeway; a vitrified fort preceded a castle built perhaps c. 1230; came into possession of Mackenzies (later *Earls of Seaforth*) but was held by Macraes as constables; badly damaged by fire from warships when held by *Jacobites* in 1719; restored 1932.

Eisenhower's Flat. Flat in *Culzean Castle* placed at disposal of General and President Eisenhower in recognition of his services as allied commander in World War II.

Elcho, Lord. See Wemyss, Earldom.

Elcho Nunnery (*Cistercian*) (Perthshire). Attributed to David Lindsay of Glenesk, before 1241; erected into *temporal lordship* for *Lord Scone* 1606.

Elder. Office introduced by reformers into their congregations before 1560 and included in plans of *First Book of Discipline*; at that stage a lay office, held by annual election; the *Second Book of Discipline* proposed to make it a life-office and quasi-ministerial, and this concept ultimately prevailed.

Elder, John (fl. 1540s). Little is known about this English propagandist except that he was educated at Scottish universities before becoming an agent of Henry VIII.

Eldin, Lord. See Clerk, John.

Elgin (*Moray*). *Royal burgh* by c. 1136; a castle, perhaps previously stronghold of *mormaers* and from 1130s royal, was on Lady Hill and was occupied by Edward I 1296, but only fragments remain; *grammar school*, originally dependent on cathedral, came under town council before *Reformation*, and *song school* mentioned 1594; town council built an '*Academy*' 1791; leperhouse mentioned 1391.

Elgin and Ailesbury, Earldom. Elgin created 1633 for Thomas Bruce, 3rd Lord *Kinloss*; 2nd Earl became Earl of Ailesbury 1664, but that title became extinct on death of 4th Earl without male issue; Elgin passed to his kinsman, 9th Earl of *Kincardine*.

Elgin and Kincardine, Earldom. Kincardine created 1647 for Edward Bruce; 9th Earl succeeded to Elgin title.

Elgin and Kincardine, James Bruce, 8th Earl of (1811-63). Governor General of Canada 1847-54; Viceroy of India 1861.

Elgin and Kincardine, Thomas Bruce, 7th Earl of (1766-1841). Brought 'Elgin Marbles' from Greece 1816.

Elgin Cathedral. The see of the bishops of *Moray* was fixed at Elgin 1224 and cathedral (dedicated to Holy Trinity) founded that year; 289 feet long, it was the third largest in Scotland; burned by *Wolf of Badenoch* 1390; central tower dismantled as unsafe 1506, but rebuilt; lead removed from roof 1568; further damage done by *Covenanters*; central tower collapsed 1711, destroying part of building.

Elgin Friaries. (1) *Dominican.* Founded by *Alexander II* 1233-4. (2) *Franciscan* Conventual. Land granted 1281, but foundation did not endure. (3) Franciscan Observant. Said to have been founded by John Innes of that *ilk* 1479, but possibly by *James IV*; buildings passed to burgh at *Reformation*, lands leased to Robert Innes of Innermarky 1573.

Elgin Literary and Scientific Association. Founded 1836 for study of literature, history, antiquities and science.

Elgin, Maison Dieu. Founded by Andrew, Bishop of *Moray* 1222-42; burned 1390; deserted by 1445; revenues transferred to *Dominicans* 1520; property granted to town for *song school* and poor.

Elibank, Lordship. Created 1643 for Patrick, son of *Sir Gideon Murray*.

Elie (Fife). *Burgh of barony* for Scott of Grangemuir 1599, granted to Sir William Anstruther of that *ilk* 1704.

Elizabeth (d. 1327). Daughter of Aymer de Burgh, Earl of Ulster; second wife of *Robert I* (m. 1302).

Elizabeth, Queen of Robert II. See Mure.

Elizabeth. Daughter of *James VI.* See Winter Queen.

Ell. Unit of linear measurement, usually equal to 37.2 inches.

Elliot, Gilbert (1651-1718). *Lord of Session* (Minto) 1705; his son Gilbert (1693-1766) also a judge with same title; his grandson Gilbert (1722-77) was an M.P., philosopher and poet.

Elliot, Gilbert, Earls of Minto. See Minto.

Elliot, Jane (or **Jean**) (1727-1805). Daughter of *Gilbert Elliot* (1693-1766); wrote 'The Flowers o' the Forest'.

Elliot, Walter (1888-1958). Born *Lanark*; M.P. for Lanark (1918-23), Kelvingrove (1924-45) and Scottish Universities (1946-50); *Secretary of State* for Scotland 1936-8; Minister of Health 1938-40; *Lord High Commissioner* 1956-7.

Ellon (Aberdeenshire). *Burgh of barony* for *Earl of Buchan* 1707.

Elphinstone (East Lothian). Tower, a 15th century three-storeyed structure, rendered unsafe by mineral workings, was demolished in the 1960s; mansion added in 1600 had been demolished in 1865; lands held in 13th century by Elphinstone family, from whom they passed by marriage to Johnstones.

Elphinstone (Stirlingshire). Passed by marriage to Elphinstone family in early 14th century; 15th century tower, sold in 1784 by 11th Lord Elphinstone to *Earl of Dunmore*, still stands; *burgh of barony* for Lord Elphinstone 1673.

Elphinstone, Arthur, James and John. See Balmerino, Lords.

Elphinstone Institute, Bombay. Founded by Mountstuart Elphinstone, Governor of Bombay 1819-27; became part of Bombay University 1857 during governorship of his nephew, Lord E.

Elphinstone, Lordship. Created for Alexander E. 1509.

Elphinstone, William (1431-1514). '*Official*' of *Glasgow* 1471 and of *Lothian* 1478; *Chancellor* of *James III* 1488, but resigned on that king's death; on embassies under *James IV*; Bishop of *Aberdeen* 1483; added to cathedral and founded *King's College*; responsible for *Aberdeen Breviary*; nominated for archbishopric of *St Andrews* 1514.

Emerald Charter, 1324. In token of the extensive jurisdiction which *Sir James Douglas* was to have within his estates, *Robert I* granted him a charter sealed with the king's emerald signet, or, according to another account, placed an emerald ring on his finger.

Emphiteosis (or **Emphyteusis**). Term used as equivalent of *feu-ferm.*

'Encyclopaedia Britannica'. Founded in *Edinburgh* 1768; first published 1781, with Andrew Bell (1726-1809) as half-proprietor and *William Smellie* as editor.

'Encyclopaedia Edinensis'. Edited by *James Millar.*

'Encyclopaedia Perthensis'. Published by Morisons in 18th century.

Engagement, 26-7 December 1647. Representatives of moderate *Covenanters* agreed with *Charles I* at Carisbrooke to invade England on his behalf on condition that he accepted *presbyterianism* in Scotland and gave it a three-year trial in England.

Engagers. See Engagement.

'Englishmen's Syke'. Site near *Galashiels* of a skirmish in 1337 when Englishmen were caught and killed by men of Galashiels as they were gathering plums. Cf. Sour Plums.

Enoch (Dumfriesshire). Castle said to have had date 1281; lands belonged to Menzies family from early 14th century until sold to *Duke of Queensberry* 1703.

Entail. See Tailzie.

Eochaid 'the Venomous' (d. ?733). King of *Dalriada*; an earlier king of the name had died in 697.

Eochaid (d. 889). Grandson of *Kenneth mac Alpin*; apparently king of part of *Alba* from 878.

Eoganan (d. ? 843). The last, or one of the last, kings of the *Picts,* on whose death *Kenneth mac Alpin* united *Dalriada* and Pictland.

Episcopal(ian) Church. As a non-established church originated with those who did not accept the *Presbyterian* system which became statutory in 1690; (see also Rose, Alexander). The *Non-Juring* and *Qualified* congregations united after 1804.

Equivalent. Arrangement made by Treaty of *Union* to compensate Scots for undertaking a share in England's National Debt; consisted of lump sum of nearly £400,000 and funds which were to accrue subsequently from increased customs duties.

Equivalent Company. Formed 1719 in connection with settlement of *Equivalent*; from it grew the *Royal Bank of Scotland.*

Ercildoun(e). Older name of *Earlston,* by which *Thomas the Rhymer* was known.

Erfurt. One of the *Schottenklöster* or monasteries of Irish foundation in Germany; by 1517, when the last Irish abbot died, there was no longer a community and the abbots were appointed by *Ratisbon*; consequently when the Scots obtained the latter they gained control of Erfurt.

Ermengarde (d. 1234). Daughter of Richard de Beaumont; married *William I* 1186; mother of *Alexander II* and three daughters.

Errol (Perthshire). Granted by *William I* to his butler, William de Haya, ancestor of *Earls of E*; *burgh of barony* for Butter of Ardgaith 1648.

Errol, Earldom. Created 1452 for William *Hay* of E. (d. 1462).

Errol, Francis Hay, 9th Earl of (c. 1566-1631). Succeeded his father, 8th Earl, 1585; his participation with *Earl of Huntly* on behalf of the Roman Catholic and Spanish cause led to his being summoned for treason 1594; took up arms against *James VI* and fought at *Glenlivet*; forfeiture reduced 1597, but excommunicated 1608; declared himself a Roman Catholic in his will.

Erskine. For members of the family who held peerages see Buchan, Cardross, Mar, Mar and Kellie, Rosslyn.

Erskine (Renfrewshire). Held from early 13th century by family taking its name from the place; five generations later an Erskine acquired *Alloa*; barony of E. sold to Sir John Hamilton of Orbiston 1638 and in 1703 to Lord *Blantyre.*

Erskine, Charles (1680-1763). Professor of public law, *Edinburgh,* 1707; M.P. for Dumfriesshire, *Dumfries* burghs and *Wick* burghs; *Solicitor General* 1725; *Lord Advocate* 1737; *Lord of Session* (Tinwald) 1744; *Justice Clerk* 1748.

Erskine, Charles (1739-1811). Son of *Earl of Mar* and *Kellie*; held various offices at papal court; Cardinal 1803.

Erskine, David (1772-1837). Natural son of 11th *Earl of Buchan*; professor at Royal Military Academy, Sandhurst; knighted 1830; a founder of Military and Naval Academy, *Edinburgh*; wrote plays on James I and James II and 'Annals and Antiquities of *Dryburgh*'.

Erskine, Ebenezer (1680-1754). Son of *minister* of Chirnside; minister of Portmoak (1703-

11) and then of *Stirling*; took the '*Evangelical*' side in disputes and defended claims of congregations to elect their ministers; after being suspended for a sermon on the latter subject, he, with three other ministers, formed the *Secession Church.*

Erskine, Henry (1746-1817). Son of 10th *Earl of Buchan*; *advocate* 1768; *Lord Advocate* 1783 and 1806; dean of faculty 1785 but lost office 1796 because of his *Whig* principles.

Erskine, James (1679-1754). Brother of *Earl of Mar*; *Justice Clerk* (Lord Grange) 1710; kept his wife (d. 1743) in *St Kilda* for seven years from 1732 to prevent her disclosing his *Jacobite* plotting; resigned office to become M.P. 1734; secretary to Frederick, Prince of Wales.

Erskine, John, 6th Lord. See Mar.

Erskine, John, of Dun (c. 1508-91). An early convert to Protestantism and a signatory of *First Bond* 1557; *superintendent* of *Angus* 1562; supported episcopacy 1571 and 1584.

Erskine, John (1695-1768). *Advocate* 1719; professor of Scots Law, *Edinburgh,* 1737; wrote 'Principles of the Law of Scotland' (1754) and 'Institutes of the Law of Scotland' (1773).

Erskine, Lordship. Created for Robert E., ancestor of *Earls of Mar,* 1438; another lordship created for Thomas Erskine 1806.

Erskine, Margaret (d. 1572). See Douglas, Margaret.

Erskine, Mary (d. 1707). Widow of James Hair, druggist in *Edinburgh*; left 10,000 merks for the education of daughters of *burgesses*; from her foundation developed the *Mary Erskine School* (formerly Edinburgh Ladies' College and Merchant Maiden Hospital), and also the *Trades Maiden Hospital.*

Erskine, Ralph (1685-1752). Brother of *Ebenezer Erskine*; *minister* of *Dunfermline* 1711; joined *Secession* 1737.

Erskine, 'Ruaraidh' (1869-1960). Stewart Erskine, son of 5th Lord E; born Brighton; advocate of 'Gaelic nationalism' or the combination of the revival of the *Gaelic* language with demands for Scottish independence; closely associated with Irish nationalists and later with Marxism. See Maclean, John.

Erskine, Thomas (1750-1823). Brother of 11th *Earl of Buchan* and of *Henry Erskine*; in navy and army before pursuing legal career in England which brought him several offices, including that of Lord Chancellor (1806-7); a Whig-Liberal; Baron Erskine 1806.

Erskine, William (1769-1822). Son of *Episcopalian minister* of Muthill; *advocate* 1790; associated with *Walter Scott* in his early studies in German; *sheriff* depute of *Orkney* 1809; *Lord of Session* (Kinnedder) 1822.

Essie, Battle of, 17 March 1058. *Lulach* killed by *Malcolm III.*

Estates, Committee of. See Committee of Estates.

Estates of the Realm. See Three Estates.

Ethelred (c. 1075- c. 1100). Son of *Malcolm III* and *Margaret*; Abbot of *Dunkeld.*

Ethie *(Angus).* Castle built by *Cardinal David Beaton*; conferred 1596 on Sir John Carnegie, who became Lord Lour 1639, Earl of Ethie 1647 and *Earl of Northesk* 1662.

Ettrick Forest. Hunting reserve (not necessarily to a great extent wooded), including the whole of Selkirkshire and parts of Peeblesshire and Midlothian; often called 'The Forest'; conferred on *Sir James Douglas* by *Robert I* and remained with his family until 1455, when it was resumed by crown.

'Ettrick Shepherd'. See Hogg, James.

Eugenius. Name given to eight 'Kings of Scots', the latest of them dated 761-4; a version of Ewen.

Eugenius (or **Owen**) 'the Bald'. See Owen.

Euphemia Ross. See Ross.

Evangelicals. In early 18th century the theological conservatives, adhering to the strictest Calvinist doctrines; in early 19th century the Evangelical party which caused the *Disruption* did not follow the earlier exclusive line and advocated the expansion of the Church's work by missions at home and abroad.

Eviot Family. Owners of *Balhousie Castle.*

Evoca, St. Name given to house of *Cistercian* nuns in Kirkcudbrightshire, of which little is known except that it was stated in 1423 to be in ruins and deserted by nuns.

Ewart, Charles (1769-1846). Sergeant in *Royal Scots Greys*; captured Imperial standard of 45th Invincibles at Waterloo, for which he was promoted ensign; reinterred on Esplanade of *Edinburgh Castle* 1938.

Ewerislands. See Howieson, John.

Ewing, James Alfred (1855-1935). Born *Dundee*; professor of engineering at Tokyo, *St Andrews* and Cambridge; his discoveries in connection with magnetism were important in development of electrical apparatus; principal of *Edinburgh University* 1916-29.

Exchange and Deposit Bank. Property of John Maberly and Co., an English *linen* manufacturing company with flax spinning mills in Scotland; established 1818; failed 1832.

Exchequer, Court of. Set up after *Union* of

1707 on model of English Court of Exchequer; its jurisdiction merged in *Court of Session* 1856.

Exhorter. According to *First Book of Discipline* an exhorter was authorised to preach, but not to administer the sacraments and was thus intermediate between a *reader* and a *minister*; the office had vanished by 1572, as a result apparently of an enlargement of the function of readers and the promotion of some exhorters to full ministry.

Eyemouth (Berwickshire). *Burgh of barony* for Home of Wedderburn 1598.

Eynhallow. Island in *Orkney* with remains which may be those of a church and associated domestic accommodation; it has been identified, somewhat doubtfully, with a *Benedictine* house supposed to have existed in Orkney, but it is not known to record evidence.

Eythin, Lord. See King, James.

F

Faa, Johnnie. Supposed 'King of the gipsies' whose existence is well authenticated under *James V*; but his supposed exploit in carrying off a Countess of *Cassillis*, for which he was hanged by the Earl, is attached to 17th century and is demonstrably false.

Faed, Thomas (1826-1900). Born *Kirkcudbright*; studied with his brother, John, at Edinburgh *School of Design*; in 1852 went to London and became known for his genre paintings.

Fail (or **Failford**) **Friary** (*Trinitarian*) (Ayrshire). In existence by 1335; maintained some *bedesmen* until 1562.

Fair Isle (*Shetland*). Noted for wreck of Armada ship, 'El Gran Griffon', under Juan Gomez de Medina, 1588; bird observatory started by George Waterston 1948; acquired by *National Trust* 1954.

Fair Maid of Perth. Fictional character in *Walter Scott*'s novel of that name; a house in Perth, known as 'The Fair Maid's House' for no authentic reason, happened to be associated with the incorporation of glovers, the craft which the father of Scott's heroine practised.

Fairfax of Cameron, Lordship. Created 1627 for Thomas Fairfax.

Fairfield Shipbuilding and Engineering Company. Founded 1886, in development of John Elder's business.

Fairlie (Ayrshire). *Burgh of barony* for Fairlie of that *ilk* 1601.

Fairnington (Roxburghshire). Hospital mentioned 1511-94.

Fairy Flag. Preserved at *Dunvegan Castle* and supposed to bring victory to Clan *MacLeod*; said to have been captured from a Saracen on a crusade, and it does appear to have come from the Near East.

Faith, Twopenny. See Twopenny Faith.

Falaise, Treaty of, 8 December 1174. After *William I* had been captured by English he agreed to accept Henry II as his feudal overlord.

Falkirk. *Burgh of barony* for Lord *Livingston* 1600; *burgh of regality* for *Earl of Callendar* 1646. Papal consent for erection of *collegiate church* obtained 1449-50, but subsequently withdrawn and erection not carried out. Falkirk Trysts were main centre for sale of cattle from Highlands, in succession to *Crieff* Trysts about 1770.

Falkirk Banks. Banking Company existed 1787-1825; Union Bank established in opposition 1803 but failed 1816.

Falkirk, Battles of. (1) 22 July 1298. Scots under *William Wallace* defeated by English under Edward I. (2) 17 January 1746. *Jacobites* under Prince *Charles Edward* defeated government troops under General Hawley.

Falkland (Fife). Hunting-seat of kings from perhaps 12th century and the castle was the place of death of *Duke of Rothesay* 1402; palace begun by *James III* or *James IV* and completed by *James V*; south and west ranges still remain; Crichton-Stuart family are hereditary keepers and in 1952 the *National Trust* was appointed as deputy-keeper. A court for 'real *tennis*', established by *James V* and restored in 1890s, is the only one comparable in age and interest to that at Hampton Court (1509). Falkland created *royal burgh* 1458, but did not operate as such.

Falkland Pursuivant. First mentioned 1493-4; revived 1927-39.

Falkland, Viscountcy. Created 1620 for Sir Henry Carey; 2nd Viscount, Lucius, killed in royalist army at Newbury 1643.

Falside. See Fawside.

Falsing of Dooms. Process of appeal.

Farming Banking Company. Proposed for establishment at Kincardine-on-Forth, but although examples of its engraved notes exist it seems never to have engaged in business.

Farnell Castle (*Angus*). Originally residence of Bishops of *Brechin*; passed after *Reformation* to *Earls of Southesk*; enlarged in 19th century as almshouses for estate employees.

Farquharson, Anne. See Colonel Anne.

Farquharson, David (1840-1907). Born *Blairgowrie*; lived in *Edinburgh* 1872-82 and then moved to London; painted landscapes, chiefly of Perthshire and West Highlands.

Farquharson, John, of Inverey. 'The Black Colonel'; his murder of John Gordon of Brackley in 1666 is recounted in a ballad; in *Jacobite* army 1689; defeated troops threatening *Braemar Castle* and burned it to deny its use to them; said to have summoned his servants to table by firing a pistol.

Farquharson, Joseph (1847-1935). Born Finzean; painted landscapes of Scottish and foreign scenes.

Fast Castle (Berwickshire). Previously a *Home* stronghold, it was in 1600 a posession of *Logan* of *Restalrig*, to whom it had passed by marriage 1580; forfeited through Logan's involvement in *Gowrie Conspiracy*; there are persistent legends of a treasure hidden there.

Fastern's Eve. Shrove Tuesday.

Fawside Castle (East Lothian). Lands passed from De *Quincy* family to *Setons*; building dates partly from 15th century but mainly 16th; seized by English before *Pinkie*.

Fearchair Fada (or **Ferchar Fota**) (d. 697). King of *Dalriada*.

Fearn Abbey (*Premonstratensian*) (Ross). Founded by Ferquhard, *Earl of Ross*, at Edderton, in 1220s; moved to Fearn 1238; rebuilt 14th century but described as ruinous 1541; annexed to *Bishopric of Ross* 1609; used as parish church until 1742, when roof fell.

Féileadh-Beag. 'Philabeg' or 'little kilt', formed when *belted plaid* was divided into two portions. See Kilt.

Fencible Men. Men eligible for military service, that is, aged from 16 to 60.

Fencible Regiments. Raised for internal defence 1759-99, twenty-six of them in the Highlands.

Fencing the Court. The Latin 'curia legitime affirmata' was translated 'the court lawfully fencit'. The essence of the proceeding seems to have been to ensure the presence of authorised, and the exclusion of unauthorised, persons and to proclaim that the court must be free from interference.

Fendoch (Perthshire). Roman camp in *Monzie* parish.

Fenella. Said to have been daughter of the *mormaer* of *Angus* and wife of the mormaer of *Mearns* and to have betrayed King *Kenneth II* to his death at *Kincardine* 995.

Fenton, Viscountcy. Created for Sir Thomas Erskine, Lord *Dirleton*, 1606; passed to *Earls of Mar* and *Kellie*.

Fergus. According to legend, 'Fergus I' was the first king of the *Scots* in Scotland in 330 B.C. The first authentic Fergus was a son of Erc, who led a party of Irish to settle in *Argyll* c. 500 A.D. There was a king of *Dalriada* of the name who died c. 780.

Fergus, Lord of Galloway (d. 1161). Married a daughter of Henry I of England; founded religious houses at *Soulseat* and *Whithorn*; rebelled against *Malcolm IV* and retired to abbey of *Holyrood* to die.

Ferguson, David (d. 1598). Said to have been a glover before becoming *minister* of *Dunfermline* 1560; denounced secularisation of church property 1572; compiled collection of 'Scottish Proverbs'.

Ferguson, James (1808-86). Born *Ayr*; after successful career with an indigo factory in India he settled in London and devoted himself to archaeology, especially in relation to Palestine; wrote 'Rude Stone Monuments in all Countries'.

Ferguson, Robert (d. 1714). 'The Plotter'; possibly educated in *Aberdeen*, but his whole career was in England, where he was involved in successive conspiracies on behalf of the Duke of Monmouth, *William of Orange* and the *Jacobites*; arrested for treason 1704 but not tried.

Fergusson, Adam (1723-1816). Born *Logierait*; chaplain in *Black Watch Regiment* 1745-57; Librarian of *Advocates' Library* 1757; tutor in family of *Earl of Bute* 1757-9; professor of *natural philosophy, Edinburgh*, 1759 and of moral philosophy 1764-85; wrote 'Essay on Civil Society' (1766), 'Institutes of Moral Philosophy' (1772) and 'Principles of Political Science' (1792).

Fergusson, Sir James (1688-1759). *Advocate* 1711; *Lord of Session* (Kilkerran).

Fergusson, Sir James (1832-1907). Governor of South Australia 1868-72; of New Zealand 1872-4; and of Bombay 1880-5.

Fergusson, John Duncan (1874-1961). Born *Leith*; studied medicine but turned to art and travelled abroad; in Paris 1905-39, then settled in *Glasgow*; noted for town scenes.

Fergusson, Robert (1750-74) Born *Edinburgh*; educated for ministry; clerk in Commissary Office and Sheriff Clerk's Office in Edinburgh; wrote verses, some of which were published in the 'Weekly Magazine', and a volume of

'Poems' (1773); committed suicide in an asylum; *Burns* acknowledged his debt to F. and erected a monument in *Canongate* Churchyard.

Fer Léginn (or **Ferleyn**). Man of learning, in charge of teaching in Celtic monastery.

Ferm Toun. The group of dwelling houses of the tenants who shared a farm when agricultural operations were collective and holdings intermingled.

Ferms. Roughly equivalent to rents: payments, usually annual or termly, made by tenants (including those in *burghs*) or by proprietors holding lands in *feu.*

Fernaig Manuscript. Compilation by Duncan Macrae of Inverinate, in 1688-93, of *Gaelic* verse reflecting *Jacobite* and *Episcopalian* opinions; in *National Library.*

Fernie Castle (Fife). 16th century tower, with later additions; lands belonged to Fernie family, foresters of *Falkland,* and passed to Arnot of that *ilk* and *Balfour of Burleigh.*

Ferniehirst Castle (Roxburghshire). 15th-16th centuries, possibly replacing an early stronghold of *Kers,* who were in Teviotdale by c. 1350; in 1571, when Ker of F. was a strong supporter of Queen *Mary,* the castle was burned by the Earl of Sussex, but rebuilt 1598; restored by 9th Marquis of *Lothian* and now a Youth Hostel.

Ferrerius, John (fl. 1528-40). Native of Piedmont who spent five years at *Kinloss Abbey* under *Robert Reid*; his continuation of *Boece*'s 'History' published 1574.

Ferrier, Susan Edmonstone (1782-1854). Born *Edinburgh*; contributed to 'Blackwood's Magazine' and wrote novels, including 'Marriage', 'The Inheritance' and 'Destiny'.

Ferry-Port-on-Craig. Old name of *Tayport* (Fife), which came into use when *North British Railway* Company purchased the right to a ferry in 1842.

Fettercairn (Kincardineshire). *Burgh of barony* for Hepburn of Craigs 1504.

Fetterletter (Aberdeenshire). *Burgh of barony* for *Gordon* of Gight 1685.

Fetternear Banner. Pre-*Reformation* banner, belonging to a fraternity of the Holy Blood, perhaps in *St Giles' Church, Edinburgh*; survived in hands of Leslies of Balquhain, to whom the *barony* of Fetternear passed from the bishopric of *Aberdeen.*

Fettes, Sir William (1750-1836). Tea and wine merchant in *Edinburgh*; twice Lord *Provost*; left funds which accumulated until Fettes College was built as boarding school 1865-70 to plans by *David Bryce.*

Feuing. Device whereby property could be conveyed in return for an annual payment (the feu duty) fixed in perpetuity; *superior* retained certain rights, but vassal had complete security in the property; system abolished 1974 and many feu duties now commuted.

Fiars' Prices. Average seasonal prices of grain crops, struck in each *sheriff*dom annually, mainly to determine level of *ministers*' stipends when these were based on value of *teinds* of crops.

Fidra. Supposed *Premonstratensian* foundation not authenticated; the island belonged to *Dryburgh Abbey,* and there was a chapel or chantry on it.

Fiery Cross. Cross charred and dipped in blood, traditionally used to muster a force in the Highlands, but there is little documentary evidence to authenticate it.

'Fiery Face'. Nickname of *James II,* who had a conspicuous birthmark.

Fife Adventurers. Group of Fife merchants and others settled in *Lewis* as part of *James VI*'s policy of infiltrating the Highlands with Lowlanders, 1599; unable to maintain themselves in face of native hostility.

Fife Banking Company. Founded at *Cupar* 1802; stopped payment 1825.

Fife, Earldom and Dukedom. Fife was never a 'Kingdom'; there is not even evidence of *mormaers* of Fife or of '*MacDuff, Thane* (or Earl) of Fife' in mid-11th century. 'Comites' or earls (see 'Comes') appear in 12th century (see Duncan), and a native line continued until 1372, when the Countess resigned. Title went to Robert, later *Duke of Albany,* and on his son's forfeiture (1425) fell to crown. New earldom created 1759 for William Duff of *Braco* and U.K. dukedom conferred 1889.

'Fifteen. See Jacobites.

'Fighting Bishop'. See Sinclair, William.

Fillan, St (d. ? 777). Irish missionary to whom churches were dedicated in *Argyll* and elsewhere; supposed founder of abbey of *Glendochart,* where his crosier, now in *National Museum of Antiquities,* was preserved.

Finan, St (d. 661). *Iona* monk who succeeded *Aidan* at Lindisfarne.

Findhorn (or **Seatoun of Kinloss**). *Burgh of barony* for Abbot of *Kinloss* 1532.

Findlater, Earldom. Created for James, Lord *Ogilvy,* 1638; 4th Earl created *Earl of Seafield.*

Findlay, John Ritchie (1824-98). Born *Arbroath;* proprietor of 'The *Scotsman';* provided money for *National Museum of Antiquities.*

Findon (or **Culbockie**) (Ross). *Burgh of barony* for Mackenzie of Findon 1678.
Fingal (or **Fionn**). Hero of *Gaelic* mythology who is supposed to have ruled a kingdom in Morvern.
Fingask (Perthshire). Estate (with 16th-17th century castle) passed from a *Bruce* family to *Threiplands,* and was *forfeited* after *Jacobite* rebellions of both 1715 and 1745 but restored 1783.
Finhaven Castle *(Angus).* 15th century castle belonged to *Earls of Crawford* and existing remains are mainly of 16th century; sold to *Lord Spynie* 1629, then to Carnegies and in 1773 to *Earl of Aboyne.* See also Covin Tree.
Finlarig Castle (Perthshire). From 16th century a seat of *Campbells* of Glenorchy, later *Earls of Breadalbane*; *Parliament* summoned to meet there 1651, but only three members turned up; near the ruins is the mausoleum of the Breadalbane family.
Finlay, Kirkman (1773-1842). *Cotton* manufacturer; M.P. for *Glasgow burghs*; strong advocate of suppression of radical tendencies c. 1820.
Fintray, Hatton of (Aberdeenshire). *Burgh of barony* for *Forbes* of *Craigievar* 1625.
Fire and Sword, Letters of. When regular criminal justice was weak, the government resorted to commissions of justiciary which gave local officials and landlords powers to proceed with unrestricted force against wrongdoers; such commissions were apt to be abused as instruments of family and clan rivalries and feuds.
Firlot. See Capacity, Measures of.
First Bond, December 1557. A manifesto by certain lords declaring their determination to overthrow the Roman Church; signed by the Earls of *Glencairn, Argyll* and *Morton,* Lord *Lorne* (Argyll's son and later Earl of Argyll) and *John Erskine of Dun.*
Fisher, James (1697-1775). *Minister* of *Kinclaven,* Perthshire; son-in-law of Ebenezer Erskine and with him a founder of *Secession* Church; wrote a Catechism.
Fishery Board. Appointed 1882.
Fishwives' Causeway. Popular name for track from *Musselburgh* to *Edinburgh,* on site of Roman road connecting *Inveresk* and *Cramond.*
Fitzalan, Walter. Son of Alan, *Steward* of Scotland under *David I* and founder of the Stewart family; founded *Paisley Abbey.*
Fitzduncan, William (c. 1090-1151). Son of *Duncan II;* had several children, one of them *Donald MacWilliam.*
Five Articles of Perth. *General Assembly* at *Perth* in 1618 agreed on the observance of the main dates in the Christian Year, private administration of Baptism and Communion, kneeling at Communion and a rite of Confirmation by bishops.
Five Articles of Queen Margaret. Name given to innovations imposed by *Queen Margaret* (d. 1093): abstinence from work on Sunday; commencement of Lent on Ash Wednesday; abolition of a 'barbarous' rite in the Mass; no marriage within the forbidden degrees; and abandonment of reluctance to communicate.
Flanders Moss (Stirlingshire). After the '*Forty-Five,* Highlanders were employed to break up the peat and float it down to the Forth, after which the reclaimed land was cultivated.
Fleming, Sir Alexander (1881-1955). Born Lochfield, Ayrshire; discovered anti-bacterial substance, penicillin, 1928, but it was not exploited until Second World War; shared Nobel Prize 1945.
Fleming Family. Originated with Baldwin, a Fleming who held lands of *Biggar* under *Malcolm IV*; became Lords Fleming c. 1452 and *Earls of Wigtown* 1341 and again 1606; titles dormant on death of 7th Earl 1747.
Fleming, John, 5th Lord (d. 1572). Younger brother of James, 4th Lord, who had been *Chamberlain* and who died 1558 after agreeing in France to marriage contract of Queen *Mary* and the Dauphin; *Chamberlain* 1565; governor of *Dumbarton* Castle; fought in *Queen's Party.*
Fleming, Malcolm (c. 1300-c. 1360). Steward of household to *David II,* whom he accompanied to France 1334; created *Earl of Wigtown* 1341 but his grandsom resigned earldom 1372; captured at *Neville's Cross.*
Fleming, Marjorie (or **Margaret**) (1803-11). 'Pet Marjorie'; daughter of James F., Kirkcaldy.
Fleming, Mary (1542-c. 1600). Daughter of 3rd Lord F. and an illegitimate daughter of *James IV*; one of 'the Queen's *Maries*'; married (1) *William Maitland of Lethington* 1567 and (2) George Meldrum of *Fyvie.*
Fleming, Robert, the elder (1630-94). *Minister* of *Cambuslang,* ejected 1662; went to Rotterdam; wrote 'The Fulfilling of the Scripture'; died in London.
Fleming, Robert, the younger (1660-1716). Son of preceding; born *Cambuslang*; wrote 'Rise and Fall of the Papacy'.

Fletcher, Alexander (1787-1860). Educated for ministry in *Glasgow*; became *minister* of Albion Chapel, London, 1816; involved in breach of promise case; minister of Finsbury Circus Chapel for 35 years.

Fletcher, Andrew (d. 1650). *Lord of Session* (Innerpeffer); member of commission to revise laws 1633; M.P. for *Angus* 1646-8.

Fletcher, Andrew, of *Saltoun* (1653-1716). Member of *Parliament* from 1678 and opposed *Duke of Lauderdale* and Duke of York (later *James VII*); exiled 1681 and associated with more militant English Whigs; involved in Monmouth's rebellion; returned to Scotland at *Revolution* and in last Scottish parliament was leading anti-*Union*ist; interested in commercial and agrarian development.

Fletcher, Andrew (1692-1766). Nephew of preceding; *Lord of Session* (Milton); presided over trial of Captain *Porteous.*

Fletcher, Archibald (1745-1828). Born Glenlyon; *advocate* 1790; acted for political reformers accused of sedition; strong supporter of *burgh reform.*

Flint, Sir William Russell (1880-1970). Born *Edinburgh*; settled in London 1900; famed for water-colours of Scottish and foreign subjects.

Flodden, Battle of, 9 September 1513. Scots under *James IV* defeated by English under Earl of Surrey.

'Flodden Wall'. Probably at least third wall round *Edinburgh*; reputed to have been hastily thrown up after *Flodden* but actually more than a generation in building; parts can still be seen. See also Telford Wall.

Floors Castle (near *Kelso*). Designed by Vanbrugh for *1st Duke of Roxburghe*; started 1718; altered and enlarged by *Playfair* 1838-49.

Florent V, Count of Holland (fl. 1290). Descendant of Ada, daughter of Prince Henry (son of *David I*), who married Florent III of Holland; a *Competitor.*

Flower of Yarrow. Mary Scott, whose beauty caused seven Scott brothers and seven Douglas brothers to fight and perish. See Scott, Mary.

Fochabers (*Moray*). *Burgh of barony* for *Gordon* of Knockespock 1599; for Milne's Free School see Milne, Alexander.

Fogo (Berwickshire). Chapel of St Nicholas given to *Kelso Abbey* 1253x1297; prior mentioned 1465-6, but no other evidence of separate house.

Football. Particularly associated with *Fastern's Eve* in medieval times; forbidden 1424 and 1491, but *James IV* seems to have played in defiance of his own statute.

Forbes, Alexander. See Pitsligo, Lord.

Forbes, Alexander Penrose (1817-75). Son of Lord Medwyn, *Lord of Session*; at Oxford came under influence of Tractarian movement; Bishop of *Brechin* 1848; conspicuous for self-sacrifice and charity to poor and sick, but under displeasure of other bishops for his high-church doctrines; wrote 'Kalendars of Scottish Saints' and edited some 'Saints' Lives'.

Forbes, Duncan (c. 1644-1704). M.P. for Nairnshire, Inverness-shire and again Nairnshire, 1678-1704; supported *Revolution* and his estates of *Culloden* and Ferintosh were ravaged by *Jacobites*; wrote a genealogy of the Innes family and 'A Plan for preserving peace in the Highlands'.

Forbes, Duncan (1685-1747). Son of preceding; *advocate*; *sheriff* of Midlothian 1709; active for government 1715 but opposed trial of Scottish *Jacobites* in England; *Lord Advocate* 1725; *Lord President* 1737 and did much to improve efficiency of *Court of Session*; rendered valuable service to government at times of *Shawfield Riot, Porteous Riot* and *'Forty-Five,* but always tried to maintain Scottish interests; advised *Duke of Argyll* on abolition of *tacksmen* on his estates.

Forbes Family. Named from lands in Aberdeenshire of which they were in possession by late 13th century.

Forbes, John (c. 1568-1634). 3rd son of William F. of Corse; *minister* of *Alford*; banished for denying jurisdiction of *Privy Council* over Church; minister of Middelburg 1611 and of Delft 1621.

Forbes, John (1593-1648). Son of *Patrick F.,* studied on continent; ordained at Middelburg; professor of divinity at *King's College, Aberdeen,* 1620; opposed *National Covenant*; exiled 1644; returned 1646; author of many theological and eirenical works.

Forbes, Lordship. Created by 1445 for Sir Alexander F.

Forbes, Patrick (1564-1635). Son of laird of Corse; lived as a laird after studying for ministry, but became Bishop of *Aberdeen* 1618.

Forbes, Robert (1708-75). *Episcopalian minister* of *Leith* 1735; imprisoned as *Jacobite* 1745; Bishop of *Ross* and *Caithness* 1762; collected Jacobite material in 'The Lyon in Mourning' (1747-75), an important source.

Forbes, William (1585-1634). *Minister* in *Aberdeen* 1618 and *Edinburgh* 1620; first *Bishop of Edinburgh* 1633.

Forbes, Sir William, of *Pitsligo* (1739-1806). Became chief partner in banking firm of *Coutts* and Co. and changed its name to Sir William Forbes, James Hunter and Co; founder member of *Royal Society of Edinburgh* and *Society of Antiquaries of Scotland*; his sons George and William were bankers, John a *Lord of Session* (Medwyn) and Charles a naval officer.

Forbes-Mackenzie Act. See Mackenzie, William Forbes.

Fordell Castle (Fife). 16th century castle, the ancient seat of the Hendersons of Fordell after the lands were acquired by James Henderson in 1511.

Fordell Railway. 18th century wagonway which carried *coal* from the mines at Fordell to the port of St David's.

Fordoun (Kincardineshire). *Burgh of barony* for Bethune of Creich 1554.

Fordoun (or **Fordun**), **John** (c. 1320-c. 1384). Probably a chantry priest at *Aberdeen*; gathered material for the early history of Scotland and his work forms the basis for the '*Scotichronicon*', continued by *Walter Bower.*

Fordyce (Banffshire). *Burgh of barony* for *Bishop of Aberdeen* 1499; school said to have existed before *Reformation,* and recorded from 1574; George Smith, a native of Fordyce and a merchant in Bombay, left £10,000 in 1790 for endowment of an *academy.*

Forest. 'Forests' or hunting reserves are mentioned under *David I,* and special laws, enforced by special courts and officials, operated throughout middle ages. See also Ettrick.

Forfar. *Royal burgh* under *Malcolm IV,* perhaps under *David I.*

Forfar, Earldom. Created for Archibald Douglas, son of *Earl of Angus,* 1661; merged with dukedom of *Douglas* on death of 2nd Earl, 1715, and extinct 1761.

Forfeited Estates. Estates of *Jacobites* forfeited after 1715 and 1745 rebellions; they were mostly sold (cf. York Buildings Company), but some were annexed to crown and administered by commissioners until restored in 1784.

Forgan, Battle of, ?877. *Constantine I* defeated by Scandinavians.

Forgandenny (or **Forgound**) (Perthshire). *Burgh of barony* for Oliphant of Muirhouse 1630.

Forgue (Aberdeenshire). *Burgh of barony* for *Crichton* of Frendraught 1599.

Forman, Andrew (d. 1522). As diplomat negotiated marriage of *James IV* to *Margaret Tudor* but subsequently worked for Scotland's adherence to France against Henry VIII; *Bishop of Moray* 1502; Archbishop of Bourges 1513; Archbishop of *St Andrews* 1514.

Forpit. Quarter of a *peck.*

Forres (*Moray*). *Burgh* and castle probably in existence under *David I* and authenticated under *William I*; leper house mentioned 1564-5.

Forrest, Henry (d. 1533). Born *Linlithgow*; burned as heretic at *St Andrews.* See 'Heretics'.

Forrester of Corstorphine. Sir Adam (d. 1405) acquired *Corstorphine* c. 1374; he was *provost* of *Edinburgh, Chamberlain* and Keeper of the *Great Seal*; built chapel which his son erected into *collegiate church.* Sir John (d. c. 1456) was Chamberlain under *James I.* The 10th of the line was created baronet 1625 and Lord F. of C. 1633. Title passed by marriage to Earls of Verulam.

Forret, Thomas (d. 1540). Canon of *Inchcolm* and *vicar* of *Dollar*; burned for heresy in *Edinburgh.* See 'Heretics'.

Forsyth, Alexander (1768-1843). *Minister* of Belhelvie; invented percussion cap to supersede the flintlock.

Fort Augustus (Inverness-shire). Formerly known as Kilchumin; barracks built 1716, subsequently strengthened and enlarged by *General Wade* and named Fort Augustus; captured by *Jacobites* 1746 but restored and occupied until Crimean War; sold to *Lord Lovat* 1857 and presented by him to *Benedictine* Order 1876; abbey opened 1878.

Fort George. Erected near *Inverness* 1748-69 to designs by William Skinner (b. 1700), extending over 16 acres and accommodating nearly 2000 men; depôt of *Seaforth Highlanders,* later amalgamated with *Cameron Highlanders*; houses regimental museum.

Fort William. A fort built by *General Monck* in 1650s; reconstructed and re-named in reign of *William II;* garrisoned until 1866, after which most of it was demolished.

Forteviot (Perthshire). Residence of Kings of *Pict*land and *Alba,* whose 'palace' is supposed to have been near Halyhill at west end of village.

Forth and Clyde Canal. From *Grangemouth* on the Forth to Bowling on the *Clyde,* a distance of 35 miles; opened 1790; closed to through navigation 1963.

Forth, Earldom. Created 1642 for *Patrick Ruthven*; extinct with his death.

Forth Railway Bridge. Completed 1889, with total length over water of 6,156 feet. See Arrol,

Sir William.
Forth Road Bridge. Completed 1964, with central span of 3,300 feet.
Fortingall (Perthshire). Legend has it that Pontius Pilate was born there when his father was sent on a mission to a local ruler; the Romans were nowhere near F. in those days, but there was a Roman camp later; the yew tree in the churchyard is believed to be 3000 years old.
Fortrenn or **Fortriu.** Province of *Pict*land, lying to west of Fife; sometimes means whole of Pictland.
Fortrose (Ross). *Burgh* under *Bishop of Ross* 1455; *royal burgh* 1590. There was probably a pre-*Reformation* school, and a *Grammar School* is mentioned 1574; *Academy* founded 1791 and united with Grammar School 1810.
Fortrose (or **Rosemarkie) Cathedral.** Bishop Macbeth, mentioned c. 1130, probably continued an old line; cathedral constitution dates from 1255-6 and building (dedicated to St Peter and St Boniface) probably started then; lead removed from roof at *Reformation* and stonework robbed to build Cromwellian fort at *Inverness.*
Fortune (East Lothian). Hospital mentioned 1272; given to *Trinitarian* friars of *Houston.*
'Forty-Five. See Jacobites.
Fothad, Bishop of St Andrews. (1) Early 10th century. (2) 1059-93; married *Malcolm III* and *Margaret.*
Fotheringham Family. Place in *Angus* named from family who came from Fotheringhay in Northamptonshire and were in Angus in 1261. They held Powry by 1476.
Foulis (Ross). Estate held by Monros from 12th century, for the *reddendo* of a snowball in midsummer; original castle burned in mid-18th century and replaced by present one 1754-72; *burgh of barony* for Munro 1699.
Foulis Academy. See Foulis, Robert.
Foulis, Andrew, the elder (1712-75). Brother and partner of *Robert F.*
Foulis, Andrew, the younger (d. 1829). Son of *Robert F.*
Foulis, Sir James, of Colinton (d. 1549). *Lord of Session* 1526 and *Clerk Register* 1532; bought Colinton 1519. Sir James (d. 1688), Lord of Session (Colinton), M.P. for *Edinburgh* and *Justice Clerk.* Sir James (c. 1645-1711), Lord of Session (Reidfurd), eldest son of preceding, opposed *Union.* Sir James (1714-91) wrote treatise on origin of Scots. Sir James (1770-1842), painter and sculptor.
Foulis, Robert (1707-76). With his brother *Andrew* visited Oxford and France collecting rare books, 1738-40; bookseller and printer in *Glasgow*; produced editions of Greek and Latin classics noted for beauty and accuracy; established an 'Academy of Fine Arts' 1759.
Fountainhall, Lord. See Lauder, Sir John.
Four Burghs. See Burghs, Court of Four.
Fowler, William (c. 1560-1610). *Parson* of *Hawick*; secretary to Queen *Anne*; translated 'Triumphs' of Petrarch 1587 and wrote original verse.
Fowlis Easter (*Angus* and Perthshire). Lands, granted by *David I* to William de *Maule,* passed by marriage to Mortimers and then in 1377 to Grays; 9th *Lord Gray* sold them to Murray of Ochtertyre 1699; castle now occupied as farmhouse. The church was made *collegiate* at instance of Lord Gray 1450 and reconstituted 1511.
Fowlis Wester (Perthshire). A cross, originally near mouth of Sma' Glen, with carvings of men and animals, is now in village.
Francis, William. Said to have been a former member of the garrison of *Edinburgh Castle* who led *Randolph, Earl of Moray,* up the rock to capture it, 1314.
Franciscan Friaries. See Aberdeen, Ayr, Berwick, Dumfries, Dundee, Edinburgh, Elgin, Glasgow, Haddington, Inverkeithing, Jedburgh, Kirkcudbright, Lanark, Perth, Roxburgh, St Andrews, Stirling. The older houses of the order, styled 'conventual', were later supplemented by the stricter 'observant' houses.
Franco-Scottish Alliance (the 'Auld Alliance'). Although it appears that in 1168 *William I* offered to help French king against England, first known treaty was made in 1295 and many times renewed; came to an end with *Reformation.* See Corbeil, Rouen.
Franco-Scottish Nationality. In 1558, in preparation for the marriage of Queen *Mary* to the Dauphin, Scottish *Parliament* granted a privilege, reciprocal to one granted by French King to the Scots in 1513, whereby French subjects enjoyed same rights as native Scots.
Fraser, Sir Alexander (d. 1332). Supporter of *Robert I* who married King's sister Mary after death of her first husband, Sir Neil Campbell; killed at *Dupplin.*
Fraser, Alexander (1786-1865). Born *Edinburgh;* studied with *Wilkie* at *Trustees' Academy* and in 1813 joined Wilkie in London.
Fraser, Alexander (1827-99). Born near *Linlithgow*; studied at *Trustees' Academy*; specialised in Scottish landscapes.

Fraser Castle (Aberdeenshire). Lands acquired by Frasers in 13th century; castle built c. 1575-1636 by Michael Fraser (d. 1588) and his son; sold by Frasers 1921; taken over by *National Trust* 1976.

Fraser (or **Frissel**) **Family.** Of French origin; in *Lothian* by c. 1160; held *Oliver* and *Neidpath* castles, which later passed by marriage to *Hays.* See Wardlaw Manuscript.

Fraser, James, of Brea (1639-99). Born *Kirkmichael,* son of 7th *Lord Lovat*; licensed as *Presbyterian* preacher 1670; imprisoned on *Bass* as *Covenanter* 1677-9 and in *Blackness* 1681; member of *General Assembly* 1690 and 1692.

Fraser, Simon. See Lovat, Lord.

Fraser, Simon, Master of Lovat (1726-82). Son of preceding; led clan in support of Prince *Charles Edward* 1745; captured and imprisoned, but pardoned 1750; *advocate* who acted for widow of *Colin Campbell of Glenure* 1752; raised 78th Regiment (Fraser Highlanders) for service in America 1757-61 and 71st Highlanders for service in Canada; M.P. 1761; regained estates 1771.

Fraser, William (d. 1297). *Dean* of *Glasgow*; *Chancellor* 1275; a *Guardian* 1286; Bishop of *St Andrews* 1279; asked Edward I to intervene for sake of peace on reported death of *Maid of Norway* 1290.

Fraser, Sir William (1816-98). Solicitor; Assistant Keeper of *Sasines* 1852; Deputy *Keeper of Records* 1880-92; produced over forty volumes on Scottish noble and landed families; his bequests founded Chair of Scottish History at *Edinburgh* and Fraser Homes at Colinton.

Fraserburgh (Aberdeenshire). *Burgh of barony* for Sir Alexander Fraser of Phillorth 1546; university founded 1592 by Sir Alexander Fraser of Phillorth, received parliamentary ratification 1597, but although a principal was appointed little came of the scheme.

Fraser's Highlanders. (1) 78th Regiment, raised 1757 by *Simon Fraser*; disbanded 1783 but some soldiers elected to settle in America. (2) 71st Regiment, raised 1775 by *Simon Fraser*; disbanded 1783.

Frazer, Sir James George (1854-1941). Born *Glasgow*; Fellow of Trinity College, Cambridge; wrote 'The Golden Bough' (1890) and numerous other works on anthropology.

Frazer, William Miller (1864-1961). Born *Scone*; his paintings, including 'Smack Off Shore' and 'Carradale Shore', were widely exhibited.

Free Church Normal College. Established after *Disruption* by *David Stow* to train teachers for the many Free Church Schools.

Free Church of Scotland. Founded at *Disruption*; majority entered *United Free Church* 1900, minority continued as *'Wee Frees'.*

Free Presbyterian Church. Founded 1893 by those who thought the theology of the *Free Church* too liberal.

Freiceadan Dubh, Am. Gaelic for *The Black Watch.*

Frendraught (Aberdeenshire). Lands acquired in late 15th century by *Crichtons,* who were at feud with the *Gordons* who surrounded them; in 1630 Lord *Aboyne* (son of Marquis of *Huntly*) and other Gordons were burned in the tower, where they had been prevailed on to spend the night by Crichton, whose people escaped.

Frendraught, Viscountcy. Created for James Crichton 1642; extinct on death of 4th Viscount 1698.

Freskin. See Duffus and Sutherland.

Friars of the Sack (or Friars of the Penance of Jesus Christ). Had house in *Berwick* 1267-74.

Friday Club. Met in *Edinburgh* 1803-50, first in Bayle's Tavern, Shakespeare Square, later in Fortune's in Princes Street and Barry's Tavern; included *Dugald Stewart, Sydney Smith, Walter Scott, Henry Brougham* and *Lord Cockburn.*

Friends of the People. Organisation for political reform founded at *Edinburgh* 1772; later associated with French revolutionaries.

Fullarton (Ayrshire). *Burgh of barony* for Fullarton of that *ilk* 1707.

Fullarton, Colonel William (1754-1808). Served as soldier in India; M.P. for *Haddington* 1787-90; immortalised in *Burns*' 'Vision'.

Furnace (Loch Fyne, *Argyll*). *Iron*works operated 1775-1813.

Fyvie (Aberdeenshire). *Royal burgh* under *Alexander III,* but *burgh of barony* for Earl of Dunfermline 1671 or 1673; lands granted by *Robert II* to Sir James Lindsay, from whom they passed to his brother-in-law Sir Henry Preston (who built part of castle c. 1400) and then, through Preston's daughter, to Meldrums, who built a second tower and in 1596 sold property to Alexander Seton, later *Earl of Dunfermline,* who built Seton Tower.

Fyvie, Lordship. See Dunfermline, Earl of.

Fyvie Priory (*Tironensian*). Founded by Reginald le Chen 1285; united to *Arbroath Abbey* 1459; properties went to Alexander Seton, later *Earl of Dunfermline*; no visible remains.

G

Gadderer, James (1655-1733). *Minister* of Kilmacolm 1682; deprived at *Revolution*; spent some years in London; Bishop of *Aberdeen* 1724.

Gadvan Preceptory (*Cistercian*) (Fife). Dependent on *Balmerino*; founded by 1475; granted to James Beaton of Creich 1578.

Gaelic Language. Introduced by Irish emigrants to *Dalriada* c. 500 and perhaps also to *Galloway* about same time (simultaneously with arrival of English in south-east); apparently extended throughout *Pict*land in 9th-10th centuries and made some headway south of *Clyde* and Forth in 11th, but never superseded English in *Lothian* or a Scandinavian tongue in the north; its retreat before English was well under way in 12th century.

Gaelic Society of Glasgow. Founded 1887 for 'the elucidation of Celtic antiquities'.

Gaelic Society of Inverness. Founded 1871 for 'rescuing from oblivion Celtic poetry, traditions, legends, books and manuscripts . . . bearing upon the . . . Highlands and Highland people'.

Gairloch (Ross). *Barony* granted to Eachin Roy, 2nd son of Alexander Mackenzie of Kintail, 1494 and remained with his descendants; *burgh of barony* for Mackenzie of Gairloch 1619.

Gait, Gate. Has same meaning as street or road.

Galashiels (Selkirkshire). *Burgh of barony* for Pringle of Galashiels, 1599.

Galcacus. See Calgacus.

Galloway, Bishopric of. There were bishops at *Whithorn* in 8th century, but thereafter none is known until c. 1125; closely associated with *Lords of Galloway,* who enjoyed in it the rights normally enjoyed by the king.

Galloway Cattle. Developed in early 19th century but did not form a separate class at shows until c. 1860; Galloway Cattle Society formed 1877.

Galloway, Earldom. Created for Alexander Stewart, Lord *Garlies,* 1623.

Galloway, Lordship. Included Kirkcudbrightshire, Wigtownshire, part of Dumfriesshire and in earlier times *Carrick*; first recorded Lord was *Fergus,* succeeded by Gilbert, Roland and *Alan*; fell to heiresses, one of whom was *Devorguilla*; *Robert I* made his brother, *Edward Bruce,* Lord of G. c. 1308; Sir Archibald Douglas bore the title after the lands were conferred on him by *David II* in 1369, and it remained with the *Douglases* until 1455.

Galloway, Maid of. See Douglas, William, 8th Earl of.

Galloway, Patrick (c. 1551-1626). Minister of King's household 1590; *minister* of *St. Giles', Edinburgh,* 1607; while long associated with the opposition to the King's policies, he latterly modified his attitude, but did not become a bishop.

Galston (Ayrshire). *Police burgh* 1862.

Galt, John (1779-1839). Born *Irvine*; customs officer in *Greenock,* then moved to London; wrote novels depicting Scottish life and institutions—'The Ayrshire Legatees', 'The Annals of the Parish', 'The Provost' and the 'The Entail' between 1821 and 1823; his work in London led him to become agent for the organisation of emigration to Upper Canada in connection with the Canada Company, which he founded in 1824; in Canada 1826-9; died Greenock.

Gameline (d. 1271). *Chancellor* 1254; Bishop of *St Andrews* 1255; banished for a time in 1256 because of opposition to predominant faction in country.

Garde Écossaise du Corps du Roi. Scottish bodyguard of French kings, dating from c. 1422 and continuing until Revolution; comprised 100 men-at-arms and 200 archers. See also Gendarmes Écossais; Scottish Archer Guard.

Garden, Francis (1721-93). Born *Edinburgh*; *advocate* 1744; *Lord of Session* (Gardenstone).

Garden, George (1649-1733). *Minister* of Old Machar and then of *St Nicholas, Aberdeen*; professor at *King's College* 1673.

Garden, James (1647-1726). Brother of preceding; professor of divinity at *King's College, Aberdeen* until deprived 1696 for refusal to accept *Westminster Confession.*

Gardiner, James (1688-1745). Native of West Lothian, but lived latterly at Bankton House, Prestonpans; fought at Blenheim; became colonel; killed in government army at *Prestonpans.*

Gargunnock (Stirlingshire). *Burgh of barony* for *Earl of Mar* 1677.

Garioch. District of inland Aberdeenshire; no evidence that it was an administrative division; associated as joint-title with *earldom of Mar* 14th-15th centuries.

Garlies, Lordship. Created for Alexander Stewart 1607.

Garmouth (*Moray*). *Burgh of barony* for Innes

of that *ilk* 1587; later under Duke of Richmond and *Gordon.*

Garnock, Viscountcy. Created 1703 for John Crawford of Kilbirnie; 4th Viscount succeeded to *earldom of Crawford* 1749; dormant 1808.

Gartalunane, Battle of, 11-12 October 1489. *Earl of Lennox* and *Lord Lyle,* in rebellion, were defeated by *James IV* and *Lord Drummond.*

Garth Castle (Perthshire). Ruins of stronghold of *Wolf of Badenoch,* ancestor of Stewarts of Garth; new house built 18th century; birthplace of *David Stewart*: bought by *Sir Donald Currie* 1880.

Garthland Castle (Rhinns of *Galloway*). Said to date from 13th century; owned by MacDowalls until 1803; demolished to erect farm buildings.

Gartly (Aberdeenshire). Ruined castle belonged to Barclays, who held lands from 12th century to 16th.

Gartnait (or **Garnard**). Kings of *Picts,* (1) d. ?597, (2) d. 635, (3) d. 663 or 664.

Gartsherrie Iron Works. Founded by Baird 1826.

Garvelloch Islands (*Argyll*). See Eileach an Naoimh.

Gascon Ha' (or **Hall**). Ruined castle near Aberuthven, on banks of Earn, said to have been a hiding place of *William Wallace.*

Gatehouse of Fleet (Kirkcudbrightshire). *Burgh of barony* for Murray of Broughton 1795.

Gau, John (c. 1495-1553). Graduated at *St Andrews* 1511; possibly chaplain to Scots in Malmö; published 'The Richt Way to the Kingdome of Hevine', translated from Danish work; prebendary of Our Lady Church, Copenhagen.

Gault, David (1867-1936). Born *Glasgow*; worked at newspaper illustration, lithography and stained glass; also a painter.

Ged, William (1690-1749). Born *Edinburgh*; became goldsmith; went to London to develop his invention of stereotyping; returned to Edinburgh 1733.

Geddes, Andrew (1783-1844). Born *Edinburgh*; worked with father in Excise Office but after father's death (1806) went to London to study painting, as a fellow-pupil of *Wilkie*; specialised in portraits, in Edinburgh 1810-14 and then largely in London.

Geddes, Jennie (fl. 1660). There is no contemporary evidence to support her alleged part in the riot in *St Giles', Edinburgh* on 23 July 1637; known to history only as a greengrocer in the High Street who made a bonfire of her stock and equipment to celebrate the *Restoration.*

Geddes, John (1735-99). Educated Scots College, *Rome*; as titular Bishop of Morocco, was coadjutor for Lowland Scotland 1779-97; wrote a 'Life of Queen Margaret'. See also Scots Colleges.

Geikie, Archibald (1835-1924). In Geological Survey of Scotland from 1855 and its Director 1867; professor of geology, *Edinburgh,* 1870; Chief Director of Geological Survey of Great Britain 1881; knighted 1891.

Geikie, James (1839-1915). Brother of preceding, whom he succeeded in *Edinburgh* chair 1882 after serving with the Survey for 21 years.

Geikie, Walter (1795-1837). Born *Edinburgh*; deaf and dumb from second year; noted for sketches and etchings of everyday scenes in and about Edinburgh.

Gemmels, Andrew (1687-1793). The original of *Walter Scott*'s Edie Ochiltree; died in *Roxburgh* at reputed age of 106.

Gendarmes Écossais. Troop of Scottish mercenaries in service of French kings, a forerunner of the *Royal Scots.* See also Garde Écossaise.

General Act Rescissory. See Act Rescissory.

General Assembly. The governing body of the *Church of Scotland;* originated at *Reformation* to represent the *three estates* of the realm and is supposed to have first met in December 1560; through time it came to consist only of *ministers* and *elders* sent up by *presbyteries*; did not meet 1618-38 and 1653-90; now meets annually in May. See also Lord High Commissioner.

General Band (or **Bond**). Device adopted by *James VI* in 1587 to make chiefs and landlords responsible for all dwelling on their estates.

General Council of Estates. A meeting of the *Three Estates* with smaller membership and less formality than a *Parliament* and without judicial powers.

General Council of the Scottish Church. See Provincial Council.

'Gentle Poet'. See Bruce, Michael.

Gentlemen's Cave or Ha'. Cave in *Orkney* island of Westray, where some *Jacobites* sheltered in 1746.

Geographical Society, Royal Scottish. Founded by *J.G. Bartholomew* 1884.

George Heriot's School. See Heriot, George.

George Watson's Colleges. See Watson, George.

Gerard, Alexander (1728-95). Professor of

Philosophy, *Marischal College, Aberdeen,* 1750, and of divinity at *King's College, Aberdeen* 1771; wrote 'Essay on Taste' and 'Essay on Genius'.
Gib, Adam (1713-88). *Secession minister* 1741; served Bristo Street congregation, *Edinburgh*; led *Anti-Burgher* party; called 'Pope Gib'.
Gibb, James. See Gibbs.
Gib(b), 'Muckle John' (fl. 1680). Sailor, called 'King Solomon', who led band of fanatical *Covenanters,* the *'Sweet Singers* of *Borrowstounness'.*
Gibbites. See preceding entry.
Gibbon, Lewis Grassic. See Mitchell, James Leslie.
Gibbs, James (1682-1754). Born *Aberdeen*; completed education in Holland, with exiled *Earl of Mar* as patron; studied in Rome; architect to Queen Anne; designed St Martin's-in-the-Fields, London; Radcliffe Library, Oxford; and part of King's College, Cambridge; rebuilt nave of *St Nicholas', Aberdeen.*
Gibson, Alexander (d. 1644). Bought Durie, Fife, 1614; *Lord of Session* (Durie) 1621; baronet of *Nova Scotia*; published 'Practicks'. His son Alexander (d. 1656) and grandson Alexander (d. 1693) were also noted lawyers, the former a Lord of Session.
Gibson, Walter (fl. 1688). *Glasgow* merchant who pioneered the smoking of red herrings at *Gourock*; Lord *Provost* of Glasgow 1688; his herrings became known as 'Glasgow Magistrates'.
Gibson, William Alfred (1866-1931). Born *Glasgow*; after period as a soldier became self-taught landscape painter.
Gifford. See Yester.
Gight (Aberdeenshire). Ruined castle was seat of a *Gordon* family which ended in an heiress who married John Byron and was mother of Lord *Byron.*
Gilbert, St (d. 1246). Belonged to family of *Duffus* in *Moray* and known as 'de Moravia'; *archdeacon* of Moray; *Bishop of Caithness* 1223; drew up constitution for *chapter* and started cathedral of *Dornoch.*
Gilbertine Order. See Dalmilling.
Gilderoy. Freebooter, apparently named Patrick MacGregor, who in 1636 ravaged lands of Corse, Aberdeenshire, and was taken and hanged.
Giles, St., Feast of. Celebration in *Edinburgh* on 1 September, when there was a procession with statue and relics of saint.
Gill Bells. The signal, from the bells of *St Giles', Edinburgh,* at 11.30 a.m., to the Edinburgh people to have their morning drink.
Gillespie, George (1613-48). Born *Kirkcaldy*; strong opponent of *Charles I*'s innovations in worship and wrote 'English Popish Ceremonies' 1637; *minister* of *Wemyss* 1638, *Greyfriars, Edinburgh,* 1642 and *High Church, Edinburgh,* 1648; at *Westminster Assembly.*
Gillespie Graham. See Graham, James Gillespie.
Gillespie, James (1718 or 1725-1797). Snuff and tobacco merchant in *Edinburgh*; bought estate of Spylaw; left money to found a 'Hospital', which, originally built in 1801-3 to designs by *Burn,* became a day school for boys and girls in 1870; after World War I it was taken over from the *Merchant Company* by the Town Council, who built a new school which became a secondary school for girls, with a junior department for boys and girls; became an ordinary district school 1974.
Gillespie, Patrick (1617-75). Brother of *George G*; *minister* of *Kirkcaldy* and of *High Church, Glasgow*; leader of extreme *Covenanters* 1648-51 and opposed acceptance of *Charles II* as King; nominated by Cromwell's government to principalship of *Glasgow University*; deprived and imprisoned 1660.
Gillespie, Thomas (1708-74). Born *Duddingston; minister* of Carnock 1742; opposed existing church-state relationship and patronage; deposed 1752; with three other ministers formed *Relief Church* 1761.
Gillies, Sir William George (1898-1973). Born *Haddington*; Principal of *Edinburgh* College of Art 1961-6; knighted 1970.
Gillis, James (1802-64). Born Montreal; founded St Margaret's Convent, *Edinburgh,* 1835; vicar apostolic of eastern Scotland 1852.
Gilmorehill. See Glasgow University.
Gilmour, Sir John (d. 1671). Counsel for *Marquis of Montrose* 1641 and for *Argyll* 1663; *Lord President* 1661.
Giric or **Grig** (d. 889). Son of *Donald I*; apparently king concurrently or in rivalry with *Eochaid,* 878-89; known (on grounds unknown) as 'Liberator of the Scottish Church' and inflated in myth as a Scottish 'Gregory the Great'.
Girnigoe Castle (*Caithness*). Place of imprisonment by *George, 4th Earl of Caithness,* of his son John 1576-82; in ruins.
Girth Cross. Stone cross marking boundary of *Holyrood* sanctuary at foot of *Canongate, Edinburgh,* still in existence 1750; boundary still marked on roadway.

Girvan (Ayrshire). *Burgh of barony* for Boyd of Penkill 1668.

Gladsmuir, Battle of. See Prestonpans.

Gladstanes (or **Gledstanes**), **George** (c. 1563-1615). Born *Dundee; minister* of various parishes, finally *St Andrews* 1597; *Bishop of Caithness* 1600; Archbishop of *St Andrews* 1604.

Gladstone, Sir John (1764-1851). Born *Leith*; made fortune in shipping in Liverpool; M.P. for English constituencies; baronet 1846; bought estate of Fasque; his 4th son was William Ewart Gladstone, the Prime Minister.

Gladstone's Land. In Lawnmarket, *Edinburgh*; built by Thomas G. 1620; acquired by *National Trust* 1934; leased to *Saltire Society*.

Glamis (*Angus*). Castle said to date originally from 11th century and to have been scene of murder of *Malcolm II*; present building dates mainly from 18th century, but incorporates 15th century tower. The lands were made into *barony* for John *Lyon* 1372. *Burgh of barony* for *Lord Glamis* 1491.

Glamis, Lady. Jane or Janet *Douglas,* sister of *6th Earl of Angus,* married 6th *Lord Glamis* and then Archibald Campbell of Skipnish; as a result of *James V*'s hostility to the Angus Douglases, she was accused of plotting to kill the King and was burned to death 1537.

Glamis, Lordship. Created for Patrick Lyon 1445; the 8th Lord was *Chancellor* until murdered in 1578 and his brother, *Thomas L., Master of G.,* was a leader of the ultra-protestant party which organised the *Ruthven Raid.* Patrick, 9th Lord, created *Earl of Kinghorne* 1606.

Glas, John (1695-1773). Born *Auchtermuchty*; *minister* of Tealing 1719; critical of principles of established church; deposed 1728 and formed a congregation based on simple apostolic practice; his followers were '*Glassites*'.

Glasgow, Allan Glen's School. See Allan Glen's School.

Glasgow and South-Western Railway. Formed 1851, embracing lines mainly in Ayrshire.

Glasgow and West of Scotland Technical College. See Royal College of Science and Technology.

Glasgow, Anderson's University. See Anderson's University.

Glasgow Archaeological Society. Founded 1856.

Glasgow, Archbishopric. Founded 1492, with *Argyll, Galloway, Dunblane* and *Dunkeld* as suffragans; the last two soon reverted to *St Andrews*.

Glasgow Arms Bank. Founded 1750 as Glasgow agency of *Royal Bank* and became its rival; sequestrated 1793.

Glasgow Art Gallery and Museum. Begun 1893 at Kelvingrove on surplus of income from 1888 Exhibition. See Maclellan, Archibald.

Glasgow Assembly. (1) 1610. Accepted *episcopal* constitution. (2) 1638. Deposed bishops, abolished *High Commission Court* and repudiated *Charles I*'s innovations in worship.

Glasgow Banking Company. Formed 1809; amalgamated with *Ship Bank* 1836 and with *Glasgow Union Banking Company* 1843 to form *Union Bank*.

Glasgow, Bishopric. First authentic information about bishops belongs to second half of 11th century; record evidence continuous from c. 1118.

Glasgow Boys. See Glasgow School of Painters.

Glasgow, Burgh. *William I* authorised bishop to create a *burgh* 1175x1178; received charter as *royal burgh* 1611.

Glasgow Castle. A castle existed in 12th century and a royal castle in 1258, but the castle became the bishop's residence; after it ceased to be so used (late 17th century) it became a prison and then fell into ruin; remains cleared away 1792 for erection of Royal Infirmary.

Glasgow Cathedral. Begun in 12th century (dedicated to St *Mungo*), but choir and crypt 13th century, central tower and *chapter*-house 15th; western towers removed in 19th century, otherwise complete.

Glasgow Chamber of Commerce. Founded 1783.

Glasgow City Bank. Founded 1839; failed 1878 with liabilities of over £6,000,000.

Glasgow, Earldom. Created for David, Lord Boyle, 1703.

Glasgow Ecclesiological Society. Founded 1893; merged in *Scottish Ecclesiological Society*.

Glasgow Educational Society. Founded by *David Stow*; established training college for teachers 1824.

Glasgow, Faculty of Physicians and Surgeons. See Lowe, Peter.

Glasgow Friary (*Dominican*). Probably founded by bishop and *chapter* by 1246; property conferred on *burgh* 1567; church survived until 1670.

Glasgow Friary (Observant *Franciscan*). Founded 1473-9 by bishop and *parson* of

Glasgow; properties granted to *burgh* 1567 and conferred on college by magistrates.

Glasgow Green. Part of it granted to town by *James II* in 1450 and held as common property; enlarged in late 18th century; laid out as park in 1820s and 1870s.

'Glasgow Herald'. 'Glasgow Advertiser' founded 1783; became 'Herald and Advertiser' 1801 and later simply 'Herald'.

Glasgow, High Church. The *Cathedral.*

Glasgow High School. Originated in *grammar school* under auspices of *cathedral* (which also had a *song school*), but administration had passed to *provost* and magistrates before *Reformation*; name changed to High School 1834.

Glasgow, Highland Society School. See Highland Society School.

Glasgow, Hospitals. (1) Blacader's. Roland Blacader, subdean of the *cathedral,* founded hospital by 1525 dedicated to St Nicholas and others; it was still operating 1589. Blacader also made a bequest for a hospital beside the *Collegiate Church (St. Mary and St. Anne's),* but it did not take effect. (2) St Nicholas. Founded by Andrew de Durrisdeer, Bishop of G. c. 1456-71; continued until 18th century. (3) St Ninian. Lepers dwelling there by 1485; continued until later 17th century.

Glasgow, Hutcheson's Schools. See Hutcheson's Hospital.

Glasgow, Merchant Banking Company. Begun 1769; failed after 24 years.

Glasgow Nunnery. Proposed erection, dedicated to St Catharine of Siena, 1510, never carried out.

Glasgow, Paisley and Ardrossan Canal. Planned 1806; reached Johnstone by 1811, but never completed.

Glasgow, Pollok House. See Pollok.

Glasgow Regiment (*Highland Light Infantry*). *MacLeod's Highlanders,* raised by John Mackenzie, Lord MacLeod, 1777, numbered 73rd, later (1796) 71st.

Glasgow Royal Bank. Projected 1793, but never established.

Glasgow, Royal Infirmary. Incorporated 1791; opened 1793.

Glasgow, Royal Philosophical Society of. See Royal Philosophical Society.

Glasgow, St Mary and St Anne's Collegiate Church. Founded by James Houston, subdean of G., by 1549; used as parish church 1592-1793.

Glasgow School of Painters ('The Glasgow Boys'). A group, beginning in 1878, variously trained in London, Paris, Antwerp and Dusseldorf, who were united by two grievances: one with the sentimental and anecdotal paintings of their immediate elders, and the other with the *Royal Scottish Academy* for ignoring artists not living in *Edinburgh.* They wanted 'Art to be Art' and not the 'teacher of religion nor the handmaid of literature'. Included *D. Y. Cameron, James Guthrie, George Henry, E.A. Hornel, William Kennedy,* John Lavery, *Stuart Park, James Paterson* and *E.A. Walton.*

Glasgow, Trinity College. *Free Church* divinity hall, founded after *Disruption*; building completed 1862; passed to *Church of Scotland* through unions of 1900 and 1929.

Glasgow Union Banking Company. Founded 1830; became *Union Bank* 1843.

Glasgow University. Founded 1451 by Bishop *William Turnbull*; old college built in High Street; new buildings by *Sir George Gilbert Scott* at Gilmorehill 1870.

Glasgow-Garnkirk Railway. Opened 1831.

Glassford, John. See Tobacco Lords.

Glassites. Sect founded by John *Glas*; spread to England and America, where it became known as Sandemanians, from *Robert Sandeman.*

Glebe. Piece of land attached to a parochial benefice and forming part of the emoluments of priest or *minister*; at any rate from the *Reformation* the minimum size was understood to be 4 acres.

Glenalmond, Trinity College. Planned 1841 as combined boarding school and theological college for *Episcopal Church*; opened 1847; theological students subsequently moved to *Edinburgh,* but boys' school continues.

Glenbervie Castle (Aberdeenshire). Early 16th century castle, held by Melvilles and by Douglas *Earls of Angus*; altered in 18th and 19th centuries.

Glenbuchat Castle (Aberdeenshire). Built by John Gordon, younger, of Cairnburrow c. 1590; remained with family until sold in 1737 by *John Gordon* of Glenbuchat (d. 1750); ruins preserved.

Glencairn, Alexander Cunningham, 5th Earl of (d. 1574). A signatory of *First Bond*; active in Protestant revolution of 1559-60.

Glencairn, Earldom. Created for Alexander Cunningham, Lord *Kilmaurs,* 1488; extinct with death of 14th Earl 1796.

Glencairn, William Cunningham, 9th Earl of (c. 1610-64). Active as a *Covenanter*; led rebellion against Cromwellian occupation 1653; *Chancellor* 1661-4.

Glencoe, Massacre of, 13 February 1692. The chief of the MacIan MacDonalds of Glencoe was too late in taking an oath to *William of Orange* and the King authorised action against the clan which led to a massacre in which 38 persons were killed by a force led by Campbell of Glenlyon; the *Master of Stair* (*later 1st Earl*) was much blamed. See also Duncanson, Robert.

Glencorse Barracks. Greenlaw House was taken over in 1804 to be used for French prisoners of war and the place continued to be used as a military prison throughout most of the century; it later became the headquarters of the *Royal Scots* and is now the headquarters of the Lowland Brigade.

Glendevon Castle (Perthshire). Said to have belonged to Douglases in 15th century, but much restored by Crawfords in 16th and passed to Rutherfords in 18th; still inhabited.

Glendochart (Perthshire). An 'Abbot of Glendochart' mentioned under *William I* may have been the lay proprietor of the lands of an unrecorded Celtic monastery; the Macnabs are said to be descended from the abbots of G.

Gleneagles (Perthshire). Lands belonged to Haldanes from 12th century; castle built in 14th century was superseded by new house 1624; 12th century chapel was restored by General Sir Aylmer Haldane as a family war memorial in 1925.

Glenfinnan Monument (Inverness-shire). Erected 1815 to commemorate the raising of the *Jacobite* standard there on 19 August 1745; presented to *National Trust* 1938.

Glenfruin, Battle of, 1603. Alastair MacGregor of Glenstrae defeated Alexander *Colquhoun* of *Luss*; added to previous crimes of Clan Gregor, it led to severe measures against them.

Glengarry Fencibles. Formed 1774 from Highlanders who had set out for America and had been shipwrecked and brought to *Greenock*; after disbandment in 1802 most of the men went to Canada and settled with their chief in a new 'Glengarry'; acted as a regiment against United States in 1812.

Glenlivet, Battle of, 3 October 1594. Royal forces under 7th *Earl of Argyll* defeated by *6th Earl of Huntly*.

Glenluce. *Burgh of barony* for *Earl of Stair* by 1705; *burgh of regality* 1707.

Glenluce Abbey (*Cistercian*) (Wigtownshire). Said to have been founded by Roland, *Lord of Galloway*, 1192; dominated by *Earls of Cassillis* before *Reformation* but contested by *Gordons* of Lochinvar; lands erected into *barony* for Laurence Gordon, son of *Bishop Alexander Gordon*, and later acquired by *Earl of Stair*; little remains save chapter-house.

Glenorchy, Willielma Campbell, Lady (1741-86). Daughter of William Maxwell of Preston, *Galloway*; married John Campbell, Viscount Glenorchy, son of 3rd *Earl of Breadalbane*, who died in father's lifetime; founded a church in *Edinburgh* which bore her name and was generous to churches in her husband's country.

Glenshee, Spittal of. Despite name, there is no evidence of a hospital here, but 'Spittale of Glensche' is mentioned in 1542 and there were 'Chapelcrofts'.

Glenshiel, Battle of, 10 June 1719. About 300 Spaniards, who had landed as part of a *Jacobite* scheme, were defeated by government troops.

Glentrool, Battle of, April 1307. Victory of *Robert I* over English force.

Goblin Ha' (or **Hall**). See Yester.

Gododdin. British tribe (otherwise Votadini) who occupied south-eastern Scotland in Roman and post-Roman times, with headquarters on *Traprain Law*.

Godred Crovan (d. 1095). King of *Man* and the *Isles* from c. 1080.

Gogar (Midlothian). Given by *Robert I* to Alexander *Seton*; passed to *Haliburtons* (1409), *Robert Logan of Restalrig* and Adam Couper (1600); house dated 1625.

Gold Coins. First minted in Scotland under *David II*.

Gold Mining. Gold said to have been mined at Crawford Muir (Lanarkshire) under *James IV*, and there was considerable activity under *James V*, who employed Germans as masters of his mines; the King's 'bonnet pieces' were made of Scottish gold and in 1542 35 ounces of it were used to make a crown for the Queen and 46 ounces to re-fashion and embellish the King's crown.

Golden Act, 1592. The act of *Parliament* which first authorised the *presbyterian* system of church government.

Golden Charter. Charter of privileges granted to *Edinburgh* by *James VI* in 1603.

Golden Rose. Ornament of gold and jewels blessed by Pope on 4th Sunday in Lent and presented as mark of papal favour; sent to *William I* by Lucius III 1182, to *James III* by Innocent VIII 1486, to *James IV* by Innocent VIII 1491 and to *Mary* by Pius IV 1560.

Golf. Evidently well established by 1458, when there was a statute against such unprofitable sports, and the prohibition was repeated in

1491, in the reign of *James IV*, who, however, was himself a player; *Mary, James VI, Charles I* and *James VII* also played. See also Royal and Ancient Golf Club.
Good Sir James. See Douglas, Sir James.
Goodall, Walter (c. 1706-1766). Son of Banffshire farmer; assistant librarian in *Advocates' Library* 1730; produced 'An Examination of the Letters said to have been written by Queen *Mary* to the *Earl of Bothwell*' (1754), a two-volume collection of documents; his most important work was an edition of the '*Scotichronicon*' (1769).
Gordon, Adam, of *Auchindoun* (d. 1580). 6th son of *4th Earl of Huntly*; captured at *Corrichie*; in war of *Queen's Men* against *King's Men* he defeated Forbeses at Tullyangus and *Craibstane* (or *Crabstane*) 1571 and burned Towie House with its 27 inmates; pardoned by *Pacification of Perth*.
Gordon, Alexander (c. 1516-75). Brother of *George, 4th Earl of Huntly*; unsuccessful candidate for bishoprics of *Caithness* and the *Isles* and archbishopric of *Glasgow* (for which he was consecrated); titular Archbishop of Athens; joined reformers and reformed his diocese; *Lord of Session* 1566.
Gordon, Alexander, of Auchintoul (1669-1751). General in Russian Army; returned to Scotland 1711 and commanded part of *Jacobite* army in 'Fifteen; wrote biography of Peter the Great.
Gordon Family. First heard of in Berwickshire in 13th century; *Robert I* granted lordship of Strathbogie to Sir Adam de Gordon, from whom sprang the noble house of *Huntly*, and a kinsman of his was progenitor of the Gordons of Haddo, *Earls of Aberdeen*; Sir Adam also acquired the lands of *Kenmure* and Lochinvar, which had belonged to lords of *Galloway*, and a south-western branch of the family, the Gordons of Lochinvar, arose, who became *Viscounts Kenmure*.
Gordon, George, Earls and Marquises of Huntly and **Earl of Aberdeen.** See those titles.
Gordon Highlanders. Duke of Gordon's Highlanders, raised 1759 as 89th Highland Regiment, served in India 1761-5 and were then disbanded. Gordon Highlanders raised 1794 by efforts of Jean, Duchess of Gordon, who offered to kiss recruits; numbered 100th, renumbered 92nd 1798; became 2nd Battalion in 1881, when 75th Stirlingshire Regiment became 1st Battalion.
Gordon, James (1615-86). Son of Robert G. of Straloch; *minister* of Rothiemay; associated with his father in publication of *Timothy Pont*'s maps; prepared detailed surveys of *Edinburgh* and *Aberdeen*.
Gordon, John (1544-1619). Son of *Bishop Alexander G*; briefly *Bishop of Galloway*, perhaps only in name; dean of Salisbury; Lord Glenluce 1611.
Gordon, John, Viscount Kenmure. See Kenmure.
Gordon, Sir John, of Haddo (d. 1644). Active with *Montrose*; imprisoned in 'Haddo's Hole' in *St Giles' Church, Edinburgh*; executed.
Gordon, John (1644-1726). Chaplain in navy; *Bishop of Galloway* 1688; joined *James VII* in France; became Roman Catholic; last survivor of pre-*Revolution* episcopate.
Gordon, John, of *Glenbuchat* (1678-1750). Fought with *Jacobites* in 1715; active in preparation for rising 1737-8; took part in 'Forty-Five at age of 68; died in France.
Gordon, John Watson (1788-1864). Born *Edinburgh*, son of Captain James W. of Royal Artillery; took surname of Gordon 1826; pupil of *Henry Raeburn*, whom he succeeded as leading Scottish portraitist.
Gordon, Lordship and **Dukedom.** Lordship conferred in 1436 on Alexander *Seton*, who married the Gordon heiress and took her name; dukedom conferred on *4th Marquis of Huntly* 1684; on death of 5th Duke the dukedom became extinct. See Huntly. New U.K. dukedom created 1876. See Richmond and Gordon.
Gordon, Sir Patrick, of *Auchindoun* (d. 1594). Participated in murder of *Earl of Moray* 1592; killed at *Glenlivet*.
Gordon, Patrick, of Auchintoul (1635-99). Born *Aberdeen*; one of the foremost commanders of Peter the Great of Russia.
Gordon, Robert, of Straloch (1580-1661). Corrected and completed *Timothy Pont's* maps for the atlas published in Holland by Blaeu.
Gordon, Robert (1665-1732). *Aberdeen* merchant who traded successfully to the Baltic and left a fortune to found a hospital for education of boys in Aberdeen. See Robert Gordon's College.
Gordon, Thomas (d. 1741). Served as commander in Scottish navy from 1705 and then in British navy until 1716; in 1717 took service in Russia, where he became admiral and governor of Kronstadt.
Gordon, William (d. 1577). Son of *3rd Earl of Huntly*; *parson* of *Clatt* and *chancellor* of *Moray*; *Bishop of Aberdeen* 1546; his scandal-

ous life brought him a rebuke from his *chapter* 1559; took a neutral attitude at *Reformation* and retained bishopric until death.

Gordon, William, Viscount Kenmure. See Kenmure.

Gordon-Lennox, Charles, Duke of Richmond. See Richmond.

Gordon's College. See Robert Gordon's College.

Gordonsburgh (*Fort William*). *Burgh of barony* for *Marquis of Huntly* 1618; later Maryburgh.

Gordonstoun (*Moray*). Buildings include tower house of Plewlands of 15th century and later buildings, some of them erected by *1st Marquis of Huntly* 1630; name changed to Gordonstoun when bought by Sir Robert Gordon 1638; school founded 1934 by Kurt Hahn.

Gospatrick. See Cospatric

Gothred (d. 1211.) Son of *Donald MacWilliam,* executed after rebellion.

Gourlay, Norman (d. 1534). Burned for heresy in *Edinburgh.* See 'Heretics'.

Gourock (Renfrewshire). *Burgh of barony* for Stewart of Castlemilk 1694; *police burgh* 1877.

Govan (Lanarkshire). Traditionally there was an early monastery, and certainly there must have been an ecclesiastical establishment about 10th century; *police burgh* 1864.

Governor of the Kingdom. Equivalent to Regent. See Guardian; Regents.

Gow, Nathaniel (1766-1831). Son of *Neil Gow* and like him a fiddler; his son Neil carried on the tradition.

Gow, Neil (1727-1807). Born Inver, near *Dunkeld*; took fiddle lessons from John Cameron of *Perth*; introduced to London society through patronage of ducal family of *Atholl* and became a popular and skilled performer as well as a composer.

Gowk. See Hunt the Gowk.

Gowks' Club. Founded in *Edinburgh* early in 19th century to dine annually on 1 April; seems to have lapsed after 1826.

Gowrie. An ancient district, but no evidence that there was a *mormaer*.

Gowrie Conspiracy, 5 August 1600. *James VI* enticed by Alexander, Master of Ruthven, into *Gowrie House*; the king alleged that he was threatened with death, and when his followers came to his help the Master and his brother the Earl were killed; recent opinion tends on the whole to believe that there was a real plot and that it was not an invention of the King.

Gowrie, Earldom. Created 1581 for William, 4th *Lord Ruthven*; forfeited by 3rd Earl 1600; new U.K. title created 1945.

Gowrie House *(Perth).* Built c. 1520 by Countess of *Huntly* and later bought by *Lord Ruthven*; after *Gowrie Conspiracy* owned by town until presented to *Duke of Cumberland* 1746; town reacquired it and demolished it 1805.

Gowrie, John, 3rd Earl of (c. 1577-1600). Second son of following; succeeded elder brother 1588; studied in Padua; returned 1600 and killed as result of *Gowrie Conspiracy.*

Gowrie, William Ruthven, 1st Earl of (c. 1541-84). Associated with father, *3rd Lord Ruthven,* in *Riccio* murder; *Treasurer* 1571; led *Ruthven Raid*; executed after attempt to regain ascendancy.

Graham, Dougal (1724-79). Bellman of *Glasgow* and writer of chap books; took part in '*Forty-Five* and described it in verse.

Graham Family. William de Graham, mentioned in Scotland 1127, had come from Grantham; his sons founded Dalkeith and Montrose families.

Graham, Henry Gray (1842-1906). Born *North Berwick*; *Church of Scotland minister* in *Glasgow* from 1884; wrote 'Rousseau', 'Social Life in Scotland in the Eighteenth Century' and 'Scottish Men of Letters of the Eighteenth Century'.

Graham, James, Marquis and Dukes of Montrose. See Montrose.

Graham, James Gillespie (1777-1855). Born *Dunblane*; architect who designed Moray Place and adjacent parts of *Edinburgh,* the Tolbooth Church on Castlehill and additions to *Brodick Castle.*

Graham, John, of Claverhouse (1648-89). Served in French and Dutch armies and then in Scotland from 1677; defeated at *Drumclog*; present at *Bothwell Brig*; active against *Covenanters* in south-west 1682-5; called to England by *James VII* after *William of Orange* landed, and created *Viscount Dundee*; withdrew from *Convention* 1689 when it repudiated James and raised army in Highlands; victorious at *Killiecrankie,* but killed there.

Graham, Malise, Earl of Strathearn. See Strathearn.

Graham, Patrick (d. 1478). Nephew of *Bishop James Kennedy*; Bishop of *Brechin* 1463 and *St Andrews* 1465; in trouble with government over papal grant to him of monasteries '*in commendam*', and papal support brought the elevation of his see to an archbishopric 1472; his conduct, which led through megalomania to insanity, led to his deposition 1478; died shortly thereafter.

Graham, Sir Robert (d. 1437). Uncle of *Malise, Earl of Strathearn*; under arrest 1425; continued his opposition to *James I* and led his murderers; executed.

Graham, Thomas, of Balgowan (1748-1843). Raised in 1793 the 90th Regiment of Foot, the *Perthshire Regiment*, and served with it at Quiberon; distinguished himself at Minorca 1798 and Malta 1800; second in command to Wellington in Peninsular War; created Lord Lynedoch of Balgowan 1814.

Grahame, Kenneth (1859-1932). Born *Edinburgh,* but spent whole of working life in London; secretary of Bank of England; wrote 'The Golden Age' (1895), 'Dream Days' (1898) and 'The Wind in the Willows' (1908).

Graham's Act, 1844. Introduced simple procedure for creating '*quoad sacra*' as distinct from 'quoad omnia' parishes.

Graham's Dyke. See Antonine Wall.

Grainger. See Granger.

Grammar Schools. Schools concentrating on teaching Latin. Some existed in 12th century, others developed under auspices of cathedrals or other churches but passed to control of town councils; probably already before *Reformation* (as certainly soon after it) every town of moderate size had a grammar school. See Academies; Donat's Grammar; Song Schools.

Grampian Club. Founded in London 1868 for publication of works illustrative of Scottish literature, history and antiquities; ceased operations 1891. See Rogers, Charles.

Grandtully (Perthshire). Lands held by Stewards from 14th century; first of them was a son of 2nd Lord Innermeath and a descendant of Alexander, 4th High *Steward*; castle dates from 16th century, with additions of 1893.

Grange (or **Grangepans**) (West Lothian). *Burgh of barony* for Hamilton of Grange under *James VI*; burgh of barony for Lord Forrest 1643.

Grange, Lady. See Erskine, James.

Grangemouth (Stirlingshire). Originated with construction of *Forth-Clyde Canal* from 1768 onwards and developed as port at canal's eastern end; within *burgh of barony* of West Kerse, acquired from Hopes by Sir Laurence Dundas 1752; *police burgh* 1872.

Granger, Christian. Wife of James G., *minister* of *Kinneff*; smuggled *Regalia* out of *Dunnottar Castle*.

'Granite City'. Aberdeen.

Grant, Anne (1755-1838). Born MacVicar; married *minister* of Laggan; from 1810 lived in *Edinburgh*; wrote 'Letters from the Mountains' and 'Essays on the Superstitions of the Highlands'.

Grant, Sir Francis (1658-1726). *Advocate* 1691; baronet 1705; *Lord of Session* (Cullen) 1709; supported power of estates to determine succession to throne and wrote on patronage.

Grant, Sir Francis (1803-78). Born *Edinburgh*; painted sporting scenes, but became fashionable portraitist; president of Royal Academy (London) 1866; knighted 1866.

Grant, Sir Francis James (1863-1956). Son of John G., *Marchmont* Herald; *Writer to the Signet* 1887; held various offices in *Lyon* Court from 1886; Lyon 1929-45; wrote on heraldry and genealogy and edited indexes for *Scottish Record Society*.

Grant, James (1822-87). Spent six years of his early life in Newfoundland, with his father, a captain in the *Gordon Highlanders,* and himself served in army for three years; then joined an architect in Edinburgh and became a skilled draughtsman, but turned to literature; his 56 novels included 'The Romance of War' (1845), 'The Yellow Frigate', 'Bothwell' and 'Jane Seton'; other publications were 'Old and New Edinburgh', 'British Battles on Land and Sea' and 'The Tartans and Clans of Scotland'; as a founder of the *National Association for the Vindication of Scottish Rights* he contributed to incipient nationalist movement.

Grant, James (1840-85). *Aberdeen* antiquary; wrote 'History of the Burgh and Parish Schools of Scotland'.

Grant, James Augustus (1827-92). Served in army during Indian Mutiny; explored sources of Nile 1860 and 1869; wrote 'A Walk across Africa' (1864); took part in Abyssinian expedition 1868.

Grant, Patrick (1690-1754). *Lord of Session* (Elchies) 1732; collected 'Decisions of the *Court of Session*', published 1813.

Grant, William (?1701-64). Second son of *Francis Grant*. Lord Cullen: *Lord Advocate* 1746; *Lord of Session* (Prestongrange) 1754.

Granton (Midlothian). 'Grendun' owned by Melvilles in 12th century; divided 1528 into Easter and Wester, held by two branches of family; Easter Granton (re-named *Royston* under Charles II) bought by *Sir George Mackenzie of Tarbat*; in 1739 *Duke of Argyll* bought both Grantons and re-named property Caroline Park; he left it to his eldest daughter, Caroline, who married the Earl of *Dalkeith* and the property thus passed to the *Dukes of Buccleuch.*

Granton-Burntisland Ferry. World's first train ferry 1849.

Grantown-on-Spey (or **Grant,** formerly **Castletoun of Freuchie**) (*Moray*). *Burgh of regality* for Grant of Freuchie 1694; town planned by Sir James Grant of Castle-Grant 1776.

Grassum. Sum paid on entry to or renewal of a lease.

Gray, John (d. 1858). Midlothian farmer who regularly attended Wednesday market in *Edinburgh* with his terrier 'Bobby'; when he died and was buried in *Greyfriars* Churchyard, the dog refused to leave his grave and lived until 1872.

Gray, Lordship. Created c. 1445 for Andrew Gray of Foulis.

Gray, Patrick, 6th Lord (c. 1558-1612). 'The Master of Gray' until 1609; spent many years in France and returned 1584 to win favour of *James VI*; helped to bring about English alliance under *James Stewart, Earl of Arran,* but worked for Arran's overthrow and joined administration which superseded his; on an embassy to England just before the execution of Queen *Mary* he is alleged to have given to Elizabeth the advice 'Mortui non mordent'— 'the dead don't bite'; after the execution, James banished Gray; he was back in 1593 and associated with *Francis, Earl of Bothwell.*

Gray, Robin. Shepherd who lived in cottage in *Balcarres* Park, Fife, immortalised in 'Auld Robin Gray', composed by Lady Ann Barnard 1771.

Great Michael. See Michael.

Great Mother. See Slessor, Mary.

Great North of Scotland Railway. Based on *Aberdeen* and designed to reach *Inverness,* but got no further than *Elgin* and operated mainly in Aberdeenshire, Banffshire and *Moray*; included in London and North Eastern 1923.

Great Seal. The king's principal seal, used to authenticate crown charters and letters patent; earliest example belongs to *Duncan II*; since the *Union* 'a seal appointed by the Treaty of Union to be kept and used in place of the Great Seal of Scotland' has remained in use.

'Greek' Thomson. See Thomson, Alexander.

Green Brigade. Group of Scottish units in service of Gustavus Adolphus, commanded by *Sir John Hepburn.* Cf. Stargate's Corps.

Greenan Castle (Ayrshire). A ruin; once the property of Kennedy of Baltersan.

Greenknowe Tower (Berwickshire). Built 1581 by James Seton of Touch, whose family had acquired estate by marriage with a *Gordon* heiress; bought by Pringle of Stitchel in 17th century.

Greenlaw (Berwickshire). *Burgh of barony* for Home of Spott 1596.

Greenock (Renfrewshire). *Barony* held by *Shaws* from the Prince and *Steward of Scotland*; town a *burgh of barony* for them 1635; Sir John Shaw surrendered his *superiority* of the burgh to the community 1741 and 1751; *parliamentary burgh* 1833.

Greenock Banking Company. Established 1785; absorbed in *Western Bank* 1843.

Greenside Friary (*Carmelite*). Site granted by town council of *Edinburgh* to friars of *Queensferry* 1520; had only brief existence.

Greenwich, Treaties of, 1 July 1543. Provided for Anglo-Scottish peace and for marriage of Queen *Mary* to Edward, heir of Henry VIII; repudiated by Scots before end of year.

Gregory (King). See Girig.

Gregory, David, of Kinnairdie (1627-1720). Practised medicine and had many scientific interests.

Gregory, David (1661-1708). Son of preceding; professor of mathematics at *Edinburgh* 1684; worked in geometry and optics; deprived at *Revolution* and went to Oxford, where be became a professor 1692; did much to popularise work of Isaac Newton.

Gregory, James (1638-75). Brother of *David G. of Kinnairdie*; worked on optics and mathematics; professor of mathematics at *St Andrews* 1668 and *Edinburgh* 1674.

Gregory, James (1753-1821). Son of *John G*; professor of medicine at *Edinburgh.*

Gregory, John (1724-73). Professor of philosophy at *Aberdeen* 1746 and of medicine at *Edinburgh* 1766.

Gregory, William (1803-58). Son of *James G.* (1753-1821); professor of medicine and chemistry at *Aberdeen* 1839 and of chemistry at *Edinburgh* 1844.

Greig, Samuel (1735-88). Born *Inverkeithing*; entered Russian naval service and created a navy manned largely by Scottish officers; took a fleet from the Baltic to the Levant, where he destroyed Turkish fleet at Cheshme in Russo-Turkish War of 1768-84.

Gretna Disaster, May 1915. An express troop train, carrying two companies of *Royal Scots,* collided with a local train standing on the track, and another express crashed into the wreckage, which caught fire; 215 soldiers killed, 191 seriously injured; worst railway disaster in Britain.

Greybreeks. See Earl of Mar's Greybreeks.
Greyfriars Bobby. See Gray, John.
Greys. See Royal Scots Greys.
Grierson, Sir Robert, of Lag (c. 1655-1736). Succeeded to estate of Lag on cousin's death 1667; presided over military courts at *Kirkcudbright* from 1681 and enforced laws against *conventiclers*; three times imprisoned after *Revolution* at instance of victorious *Presbyterians* and heavily fined; baronet 1685.
Grime's Dyke. See Antonine Wall.
Groat. Coin worth 4d., first minted in silver, under *David II.*
Grub, George (1812-92). Librarian to Society of *Advocates, Aberdeen,* 1841; lectured on Scots Law at *Marischal College, Aberdeen,* 1843 and professor 1881; wrote 'Ecclesiastical History of Scotland'.
Gruoch. Grand-daughter of *Kenneth III*; married (1) Gillacomgain, *mormaer* of *Moray,* and had a son *Lulach,* and (2) *Macbeth.*
Guard Bridge (Fife). Bridge built by Bishop *Henry Wardlaw* of *St Andrews* early in 15th century.
Guardian. Term used as equivalent of regent or governor; the best-known Guardians were those appointed in 1286 after death of *Alexander III*—the Bishops of *St Andrews* and *Glasgow,* the *Earls of Fife* and *Buchan,* the *Lord of Badenoch* and the *Steward*—and those appointed after the abdication of *John Balliol,* when, with varying composition, they maintained resistance to England. Cf. Regents.
Gudeman of Ballengeich. See Ballengeich.
Guild, Dean of. See Dean of Guild.
Guild, William (1586-1657). Principal of *King's College, Aberdeen*; accepted *Covenant* with reservations; dedicated his 'Moses Unvailed' to Lancelot Andrewes, 1620.
Gunn, Neil Miller (1891-1973). Born *Caithness;* in civil service until 1937; his novels include 'Grey Coast' (1926), 'Morning Tide', 'The Lost Glen' and 'The Silver Darlings'.
Guthrie (*Angus*). 15th century castle, said to have been built by Sir David Guthrie in 1468, with later additions; still inhabited by Guthrie family; *collegiate church* was founded by Sir David before 1479, when there was a papal bull.
Guthrie, James (c. 1612-1661). *Minister* of *Lauder* 1642 and of *Stirling* 1649; a leader of *Protesters*; in favour with *Cromwellian administration*; executed.
Guthrie, Sir James (1859-1930). Born *Greenock*; first studied law, but abandoned it to study art in Paris and London; joined *Glasgow School*; painted landscapes and figure studies, but later specialised in portraits.
Guthrie, Thomas (1803-73). Born *Brechin*; *minister* of Arbirlot 1830, of Old *Greyfriars, Edinburgh,* 1837, and of St John's, Edinburgh, 1840; joined *Free Church* at *Disruption* and formed Free St John's, Castlehill; took special interest in pauper children and wrote 'Plea for Ragged Schools' 1847; became a recognised authority throughout Britain on the care of criminal and destitute juveniles; also active in cause of temperance; wrote 'The City: its sins and sorrows' (1857).
Gylen Castle (Kerrera). Fortress of *MacDougal* Lords of *Lorne,* possibly going back in part to 13th century, when *Alexander II* died on Kerrera; captured by *General Alexander Leslie's* army 1647; roofless, but walls fairly complete.

H

Habeas Corpus. Cf. Wrangous Imprisonment.
Hackston, David, of Rathillet (d. 1680). Succeeded to estate of Rathillet 1670; one of the murderers of *Archbishop James Sharp*; executed in *Edinburgh.*
Hadden Rig (Roxburghshire), **Battle of,** 24 August 1542. Scots under *Earl of Huntly* defeated English under Sir Robert Bowes and took him and 600 of his men prisoners.
Haddington. *Royal burgh* under *David I.*
Haddington Collegiate Church. Parish church of St Mary (built mainly in 15th century in place of earlier church) mentioned as 'college kirk' 1537; *collegiate* constitution 1540; damaged in English invasions of 1544-5 and siege of 1548; nave used as parish church, crossing and choir roofless until restored 1973.
Haddington, Earldom. Created for *Thomas Hamilton* 1627.
Haddington Friaries. (1) *Augustinian.* On petition of *James IV,* Pope suppressed hospital of St Laurence and erected house of friars or hermits 1511, but the order did not take possession. (2) *Dominican.* Founded sometime between 1297 and 1471, but seems to have had a short life. (3) Conventual *Franciscan.* Founded before 1242; 'the Lamp of Lothian'; burned by English 1355 and again 1544, but church still in existence 1561; property granted to *burgh* 1567 and demolition of church decided 1572.

Haddington Hospitals. (1) Almshouse in Poldrait mentioned 1478. (2) St Mary's, mentioned 1319. (3) St Laurence's, mentioned 1312; refounded as leper house c. 1470; superseded by house of *Augustinian* friars 1511, but friars did not take up residence; annexed to nunnery of *Sciennes* 1532.
Haddington Manuscript. Part of parliamentary register, containing material 1384-1400. Now in *Register House.*
Haddington Nunnery (*Cistercian*). Founded by Ada, mother of *Malcolm IV,* before 1159; burned by English 1336 and 1544-5; fell into hands of *Hepburns*; erected into *temporal lordship* for John Maitland, Master of *Lauderdale,* 1621; no visible remains.
Haddington, School. *Grammar School* existed from at least 14th century, under patronage of abbey of *Holyrood*; an old building in the Nungate was superseded by a new one alongside it in 1578; third building erected in Church Street 1755; absorbed in Knox Institute on its creation in 1879.
Haddington, Treaty of, 7 July 1548. Between Scots and French, engaged in siege of English in Haddington, and concluded at *Nunnery* there; Queen *Mary* was to be sent to France.
Haddington, Viscountcy. Created for *John Ramsay* 1606 and died with him.
Haddo House (Aberdeenshire). Built by *William Adam* for *Earls of Aberdeen*; now used as centre for concerts.
Haddo's Hole. See Gordon, Sir John, of Haddo.
Haggs Castle (near *Govan*). Built by *Maxwells* 1585; a centre of *conventicle* activity in *Charles II*'s reign; now in ruins.
Haig, Douglas, 1st Earl (1861-1928). Born *Edinburgh*; commander on western front 1915-9; Field-Marshal 1917; see Bemersyde.
Haig Family. Appeared with Petrus de Haga in 13th century; one killed at *Halidon,* another at *Otterburn,* another at *Piperden* and another at *Flodden*; others fought at battles from *Stirling Bridge* to *Ancrum.*
Hailes Castle (East Lothian). Dates in part from 13th century; passed from Gourlay family to Hepburns, *Earls of Bothwell,* who added square tower and curtain walls; despite damage by Cromwell, much remains.
Hailes, Sir David Dalrymple, Lord (1726-92). *Lord of Session* 1766; author of important 'Annals'.
Haldane Family. See Gleneagles.
Haldane, James Alexander (1768-1851). Born *Dundee*; served with East India Company but began a career as an evangelical preacher in 1797 and went on many tours in Scotland and England from which *Congregational Churches* developed; with his brother *Robert* opened a Tabernacle in *Edinburgh* 1801.
Haldane, Richard Burdon, 1st Viscount (1856-1928). Son of Robert H. of Cloan; *advocate* 1879; Liberal M.P. 1885; Secretary for War 1905 and formed Territorial Army; Lord Chancellor 1912, resigned 1915; joined Labour Party and again Lord Chancellor 1924.
Haldane, Robert (1764-1842). Brother of James A; born London; served in Royal Navy, then settled on family estate at Airthrey but turned to missionary work.
Half Moon Battery. Constructed in *Edinburgh Castle* by *Regent Morton* on remains of *David Tower* after destruction in siege of 1573.
Haliburton Family. John Haliburton (d. 1355), son of Sir Adam H. of that *ilk,* married heiress of de *Vaux* family and so acquired *Dirleton*; 5th Lord (d. 1505) had three daughters, of whom the eldest married 2nd *Lord Ruthven.*
Haliburton, Lordship. Created for John, son of *Sir Walter H.,* 1450.
Haliburton, Sir Walter (d. 1447). Son of Walter H. and Isobel, daughter of *Duke of Albany*; hostage for ransom of *James I*; *Treasurer* 1438; married Mary, daughter of *Archibald, 3rd Earl of Douglas,* and widow of *David, Duke of Rothesay.*
Halidon, Battle of, 19 July 1333. English under Edward III defeated Scots under *Sir Archibald Douglas.*
Halkerton (Kincardineshire). *Burgh of barony* for Falconer of Halkerton 1611.
Halkhead, Lordship. See Ross.
Halkirk *(Caithness).* Site of an episcopal residence where Bishop Adam was murdered 1222.
Hallforest Castle (Aberdeenshire). *Robert I* granted royal forest of *Kintore* to *Sir Robert Keith* 1309, and he built the castle, which was inhabited until 1639 but is now ruinous.
Halliwell's House (*Selkirk*). Museum of old ironmongery etc., established in early 18th century by George Laurie, an ironmonger.
Halyburton, Andrew (fl. 1500). Conservator of Scottish *Staple*; his 'Ledger', giving a valuable account of Scottish trade, covers years 1492-1503 and has been published.
Hamesucken. Assault on a person in his own house, committed of forethought.
Hamilton (Lanarkshire). Formerly called *Cadzow*; *burgh of barony* 1475; created *royal*

burgh 1549, apparently without effect; *burgh of regality* for *Duchess of Hamilton* 1669. Foundation of *collegiate church* by *Lord Hamilton* ratified by Pope 1451; there was an attached hospital.

Hamilton. For bearers of this surname holding peerages see Abercorn, Arran, Belhaven, Haddington, Hamilton (Marquis and Dukes of), Lanark, Orkney and Selkirk.

Hamilton, Anne, Duchess of (1632-1716). Daughter of *1st Duke* and Duchess in her own right on death of his brother (1651); married William Douglas, *Earl of Selkirk,* son of 1st *Marquis of Douglas,* who was created Duke 1660.

Hamilton, Archibald (d. 1593). Roman Catholic controversialist; had already disputed with *John Knox* 1572, before becoming a Romanist; published work against Scottish Calvinists 1577.

Hamilton, Claud (1543-1622). Fourth son of *James, 2nd Earl of Arran*; *Commendator* of *Paisley*; ancestor of *Dukes of Abercorn.*

Hamilton, David (1768-1843). Born *Glasgow*; architect of *Port Glasgow* Town Hall, Glasgow Nelson monument, Hamilton Palace, *Bothwell* parish church and other churches.

Hamilton Declaration, 13 June 1679. Manifesto issued by less extreme *Covenanters* before battle of *Bothwell Brig,* demanding *presbyterian* government and a free assembly and parliament but expressing loyalty to the King.

Hamilton Family. Possibly originated in place of the name in Northumberland or elsewhere in England; Walter Fitz Gilbert of Hameldone mentioned in Scotland 1295.

Hamilton, Gavin (?1515-71). Son of James Hamilton of Raploch; *Commendator* of *Kilwinning* 1550; *Lord of Session* 1555; coadjutor of archbishopric of *St Andrews* 1551 but died before *Archbishop John Hamilton.*

Hamilton, Gavin (d. 1612). *Minister* of *Hamilton*; *Bishop of Galloway* 1605; consecrated 1610; dean of *chapel royal* 1606.

Hamilton, Gavin (1723-98). Went from *Glasgow* to Rome 1744 and worked as archaeologist and painter, executing large neo-classical pieces; arranged export of several Italian works of art.

Hamilton House (Prestonpans). Built by Sir John Hamilton, brother of 1st *Earl of Haddington,* 1628; acquired by *National Trust* 1937.

Hamilton, Sir Ian (1853-1947). Born Corfu, son of a soldier; spent childhood in *Argyll*; commissioned in *Gordon Highlanders* 1873; served in Afghan and Boer Wars; Commander-in-Chief in Gallipoli 1915; retired 1920.

Hamilton, Sir James, of *Cadzow* (d. 1479). Created *Lord Hamilton* 1445; deserted *Earl of Douglas* 1455 and gained some of his lands; married *Mary Stewart,* sister of *James III* and widow of *Thomas Boyd, Earl of Arran.*

Hamilton, James, 2nd Lord Hamilton and **1st Earl of Arran** (c. 1477-1529). Son of preceding; *Earl of Arran* 1503; played a considerable part in government in minority of *James V,* ultimately aligning himself with pro-English party.

Hamilton, James, 2nd Earl of Arran. See Arran.

Hamilton, Sir James, of Finnart (d. 1540). Natural son of *1st Earl of Arran*; in favour under administration of *Earl of Angus* (1526-8); *master of works* to *James V* and had many gifts bestowed on him; executed 1540 on charge of plotting to kill the King and corresponding with the exiled Angus, but it may be that his real crime was his wealth, which the King appropriated.

Hamilton, James, of Bothwellhaugh (d. 1580). Assassin of Regent *Moray*; escaped to France and worked in cause of Queen *Mary.*

Hamilton, James, 3rd Marquis and **1st Duke of** (1606-49). Son of 2nd Marquis, succeeded 1625; led force to support Protestant cause in Thirty Years' War 1631-3; King's commissioner to *Glasgow Assembly* 1638; opposed Scottish intervention in English civil war 1642-3; created Duke 1643; *Charles I* preferred *Montrose*'s more direct policy and Hamilton was imprisoned 1644; supported *Engagement* and led army into England on behalf of the King, but was defeated at *Preston* and executed.

Hamilton, James Douglas or **Hamilton, 4th Duke of** (1658-1712). Son of *Anne, Duchess of H.,* and her husband the 3rd Duke; spent much of his youth abroad and gained reputation for extravagance and irresponsibility; supported *Jacobite* cause at *Revolution*; defended interests of *Company of Scotland*; an ineffective leader of anti-*Union*ist party 1706; created Duke of Brandon 1711; was planning an arrangement whereby the *Old Pretender* should be recognised as Queen Anne's successor, but killed in a duel.

Hamilton, James Whitelaw (1860-1932). Born *Glasgow*; studied in Glasgow, Paris and Munich; specialised in landscape painting.

Hamilton, John (1512-71). Natural son of *1st Earl of Arran*; *Commendator* of *Paisley* 1525; on continent and believed to incline to Lutheranism; returned 1543 and directed family policy; *Bishop of Dunkeld* 1546; *Archbishop of St Andrews* 1547; conciliatory to reformers and tried measures for reform of discipline; took equivocal attitude 1559-60, but was imprisoned for saying mass 1563; officiated at baptism of *James VI*; suspected of complicity in murders of *Darnley* and Regent *Moray*; active on *Mary*'s side after her deposition; captured in *Dumbarton* Castle and hanged.

Hamilton, John (d. 1609). Roman Catholic controversialist; Rector of Paris University 1584.

Hamilton, John, 1st Marquis of (1532-1604). Son of *2nd Earl of Arran*; *Commendator* of *Arbroath*.

Hamilton, Lordship, Marquisate and Dukedom. Lordship created 1445 for *Sir James Hamilton of Cadzow*; marquisate created 1599 for John Hamilton, son of *2nd Earl of Arran*; dukedom created 1643 for *James, 3rd Marquis*. 4th Duke became Duke of Brandon 1711. 7th Duke inherited Angus titles on death of *1st Duke of Douglas* 1761.

Hamilton, Patrick (1504-28). Son of Sir Patrick H. of Kincavel, natural brother of *1st Lord H.*, and a daughter of *Alexander, Duke of Albany*; *Commendator* of *Fearn*; learned Lutheran doctrines as a student on continent; advocated reformed ideas at *St Andrews*, where he was burned. See 'Heretics'.

Hamilton, Sir Robert, of Preston (1650-1701). In command of *Covenanters* at *Drumclog* and *Bothwell Brig*; escaped to Holland; returned 1688; imprisoned 1692-3.

Hamilton, Robert, of Kilbrachmont (d. 1769). Famous as an eccentric and miser, who tickled the outstretched palms of servants instead of tipping them.

Hamilton, Sir Thomas (1563-1637). 'Tam o' the Cowgate'; *advocate* 1587; *Lord of Session* (Drumcairn) 1592; an *Octavian*; *Lord Advocate* 1596; knighted 1603; *Clerk Register* 1612 and two months later *Secretary of State*; *Lord President* 1616; created *Lord Binning* 1613, *Earl of Melrose* 1619 and *Earl of Haddington* 1627.

Hamilton, Thomas (1784-1858). Born *Edinburgh*; architect of Royal *High School*, Edinburgh, *Burns* monuments at Alloway and Edinburgh, Knox column in *Glasgow*, Orphan Hospital at *Dean*, Edinburgh, and *Royal College of Physicians*, Edinburgh.

Hamilton, William, 2nd Duke of (1616-51). Brother of *1st Duke*; Earl of *Lanark* 1639; mortally wounded at *Worcester*.

Hamilton, William Douglas or **Hamilton, 3rd Duke of** (1635-94). Eldest son of 1st *Marquis of Douglas*; created *Earl of Selkirk* 1646; married *Anne, Duchess of Hamilton*, 1656; created Duke of Hamilton for life 1662; headed opposition to *Duke of Lauderdale* 1673-4 and 1678-9; led support for *William of Orange* 1588-9.

Hamilton, Sir William (1730-1803). British ambassador at Naples 1764-1800; left his collection of geological and archaeological specimens to British Museum.

Hamilton, Sir William (1788-1856). Educated largely in England; studied medicine, then law; *advocate*; professor of civil history at *Edinburgh* 1821; professor of logic and metaphysics at Edinburgh 1836. See 'Common Sense' Philosophy.

Hammer of the Scots. Nickname of Edward I, adopted by himself.

Hand Ba'. Game formerly played annually in several Border towns and villages—Alnwick, *Duns, Jedburgh, Hawick*, Lilliesleaf, *Ancrum, St. Boswell's, Melrose* and Denholm. The teams were east v. west, uppies v. doonies, married men v. bachelors, and so on.

Hand-Fasting. Originally synonymous with betrothal, it became a contract binding a man and woman to live together for a year and a day before they decided on a permanent marriage. If at the end of the year they ceased to live together, no obligation was upon either except that any child was to be the responsibility of the party objecting to further cohabitation. Hand-fasting was often associated with the *Lammas* Fair, and the term 'Handfasting Fair' was used at Eskdalemuir.

Hanna (or **Hannay**), **James** (d. 1661). *Minister* of *Kilmaurs* 1621 and of *Canongate* 1625-35; dean of *Edinburgh* 1633; sent to Durham 1634 to examine the choir there with a view to the reconstruction of *St Giles*' Church, Edinburgh; read the Prayer Book on 23 July 1637, when a riot broke out; deposed by *Glasgow Assembly*.

Hannah Institute. Founded 1931 for dairy research.

Hanoverian Church. Name given to congregations of *Episcopalians* (especially one in the Cowgate, *Edinburgh*) who qualified for toleration under the *Toleration Act* of 1712 and repudiated *Jacobitism*.

Harald the Fairhaired (d.c. 930). King who

united Norway and then led an expedition overseas during which he established the earldom of *Orkney* c. 890.

Harden (Roxburghshire). Acquired by Scotts from *Homes* 1501.

Hardhead. Billon coin worth 2d., introduced under *Mary*.

Hardie, James Keir (1836-1915). Born near Holytown, Lanarkshire; dismissed from *coal*-mining for agitating and took up journalism; organised miners and formed Scottish Labour Party 1888; became first Labour M.P. 1892, but for an English and later a Welsh seat, yet he had *Scottish Home Rule* on his programme; opposed South African War and World War I.

Hare, William (d. c. 1860). Collaborated with *William Burke* in *Edinburgh* in murdering to provide corpses for dissection, but turned King's Evidence against him; believed to have died a pauper in London. See Knox, Robert.

Harlaw. Hospital mentioned 1195-1232.

Harlaw (Aberdeenshire), **Battle of,** 24 July 1411. Highlanders and Islanders under Donald, *Lord of the Isles,* defeated by Lowlanders and *burgesses* of *Aberdeen* under Alexander Stewart, *Earl of Mar.*

Harold's Tower. Erected by *Sir John Sinclair* near *Thurso* to mark supposed grave of Harald Ungi, grandson of *Rognvald, Earl of Orkney,* who was defeated and killed by Harald Maddadson 1196.

Harris. Forms a single island with *Lewis*; belonged to *MacLeods* of *Dunvegan* until 1779; formed part of estate of *Lord Leverhulme.*

'Harry the Minstrel' (or 'Blind Harry') (fl. 1470-92). Author of narrative verses on 'The Acts and Deeds of *Sir William Wallace*', which was a popular work and influential in shaping Scottish hostility to England; it appears that he was not, as formerly believed, blind from birth, that he had a fair education and was of considerable social standing.

'Harry the Ninth'. See Melville, Henry Dundas.

Hart, Andrew (d. 1621). *Edinburgh* printer who published works of *Sir William Alexander, William Drummond of Hawthornden* and *Barbour.*

Hartfell, Earldom. Created 1643 for James Johnstone, Lord J. of Lochwood (1602-53); his son and heir was created *Earl of Annandale.*

Harthill Castle (Aberdeenshire). Built early 17th century on Z-plan by Patrick Leith; abandoned four generations later and now in ruins.

Harvey, Sir George (1806-76). Born *St Ninians*; came to *Edinburgh* 1823 to study at *Trustees' Academy*; painted 'The Covenanters' Communion', 'The Curlers' and 'The Bowlers'.

Hassendean (Roxburghshire). Belonged to branch of the Scotts; the castle is completely ruined.

Hat Piece. Gold coin of *James VI,* worth 80s.

Hatton Castle (*Turriff* parish, Aberdeenshire). Originally 13th century, belonged to Mowats until 1723, when sold to Alexander Duff; present building dates from 1814 but incorporates older work.

Hatton Castle (*Newtyle* parish, *Angus*). Built 1575 by Laurence, 4th *Lord Oliphant*; now in ruins.

Hatton House (Ratho parish, Midlothian). 15th century tower with 17th century additions; estate passed from John de Hatton to Allan de Lauder 1377 and then by marriage to *Lauderdale* family 1653; bought by *Earl of Morton* 1870.

Hawick (Roxburghshire). Lands held by Lovells until forfeited under *Robert I*; granted to *Douglas* of *Drumlanrig* by *James I*; passed to Scotts of *Buccleuch* in 16th century. The town was a *burgh of barony* for Douglas of Drumlanrig 1511 and a *burgh of regality* 1669.

Hawick Archaeological Society. Founded 1856 for dissemination of antiquarian knowledge, preservation of antiquities and formation of museum; published intermittently from 1863.

Hawick Common Riding. Commemorates victory of Scottish youths over party of English from Hexham after *Flodden* and their capture of the banner of the Prior of Durham. See Hexham Pennant.

Hawthornden (Midlothian). The caves below the castle, artificially created, presumably in prehistoric times, were used as retreats by *Sir Alexander Ramsay of Dalhousie* and his men in 1338. The house, built in 17th century on site of earlier castle, was home of *William Drummond,* who entertained Ben Jonson there in 1619.

Hay. For bearers of this surname who held peerages, see Errol, Kinnoull and Tweeddale.

Hay, Alexander (d. 1594). *Lord of Session* (Easter Kennet) 1579; clerk of *Privy Council* 1564; *Clerk Register* 1579. His son Alexander (d. 1616) was also Clerk Register (Lord Newton).

Hay, Edmund (d. 1591). Son of Peter H. of *Megginch*; Jesuit, active as papal agent in

Scotland at various times from 1582; rector of *Scots College* at Port-à-Musson.

Hay Family. Guillaume de la Haye, of Norman origin, was butler to *Malcolm IV* and then or soon after acquired the lands of Errol in Perthshire. Gilbert Hay of Errol became hereditary *Constable* under *Robert I* and the office still remains with the family. See Errol.

Hay, George (d. 1588). *Parson* of Rathven from 1530 and of *Eddleston* from 1552; joined reformers and served as *minister*; disputed with *Quentin Kennedy* 1562; wrote against Jesuit Tyrie 1576; *commissioner* of *Aberdeen* and of *Caithness.*

Hay, George (1729-1811). Vicar apostolic of Lowland Scotland.

Hay, Ian (1876-1952). Pseudonym of John Hay Beith, who wrote many light-hearted novels, beginning with 'Pip' (1907), and successful plays, including 'The Safety Match' (1921), but his best-known work was probably 'The First Hundred Thousand' (1915), arising from his war service.

Hay, John, of *Restalrig* (d. 1784). *Writer to the Signet* and Director of *Bank of Scotland*; became secretary to Prince *Charles Edward*; exiled, he acted for a time as the Prince's major domo, but was dismissed and returned to *Edinburgh* 1771.

Hay, Richard Augustine (1661-1736). Grandson of Sir John Hay, Lord Barra (d. 1654); antiquary; canon of Sainte Genevieve, Paris.

Hay Drummond, Robert (1711-76). Son of George Hay, Viscount Dupplin; assumed name of Drummond as heir of his great-grandfather, William, Viscount of *Strathallan,* 1739; Bishop of St Asaph 1748, of Salisbury 1761, and Archbishop of York 1761.

Heard, William Theodore (1884-1973). Born *Edinburgh,* son of headmaster of *Fettes* College, Edinburgh; became Roman Catholic; held several important appointments in Rome; Cardinal 1959.

Heave Awa' Land (or **House**). Tenement on north side of High Street of *Edinburgh,* above Netherbow, which collapsed in 1863; a boy buried in rubble cried out 'Heave awa', lads, I'm no' deid yet'.

Hebrides. Ceded by Norway to Scotland 1266; properly identical with 'The Isles', as in *Bishopric of the Isles* and *Lordship of the Isles,* though the bishopric included the islands in the Firth of *Clyde,* which were included in the cession of 1266 but are not usually reckoned among the Hebrides.

Helensburgh (Dunbartonshire). *Burgh of barony* 1802.

Helmsdale (*Sutherland*). Castle built 1488 by Countess of Sutherland; scene in 1567 of murder of 11th *Earl of Sutherland* and his Countess by Earl's aunt, Isobel, whose own son also drank the poison and who committed suicide before execution. A hospital bestowed upon *Kinloss Abbey* 1362 has been identified with the hospital of St John at Helmsdale, mentioned 1471.

Hemprigs (*Caithness*). *Burgh of barony* for Dunbar of H. 1705.

Henderson, Alexander (1583-1646). Born Creich (Fife); *minister* of *Leuchars* 1612; one of the authors of the *National Covenant* and *moderator* of the *Glasgow Assembly* 1638; much involved in subsequent negotiations with *Charles I*; a commissioner to the *Westminster Assembly.*

Henderson, Joseph (1832-1908). Born Stanley, Perthshire; settled in *Glasgow* 1852 and painted marine subjects and portraits.

Henderson, Joseph Morris (1864-1936). Son of preceding; born *Glasgow;* painted landscape and seascape.

Henderson, Semple and Company. *Calico printing* firm established at Campsie 1785.

Henry Benedict, Cardinal York (1725-1807). Second son of *James Francis,* titular '*James VIII*'; Bishop of Ostia 1745; Cardinal 1747; styled Duke of York; made no attempt to assert his royal claims after death of *Charles Edward* and by making various bequests to George III implied that he recognised the Hanoverian line.

Henry, Earl (c. 1114-52). Son of *David I*; Earl of Northumberland and *Huntingdon*; married Ada, daughter of Earl of Warenne, and was father of *Malcolm IV* and *William I.*

Henry, George (1858-1943). Born *Irvine*; studied at Glasgow School of Art; designed stained glass, posters etc; travelled in Japan with *Hornel* 1893-4; a member of the *Glasgow School*; later moved to London and specialised in portraits.

Henry, King of Scots. See Darnley.

Henry, Prince of Wales (1594-1612). Eldest son of *James VI*; *Duke of Rothesay* and *Earl of Carrick;* created Prince of Wales 1610; died of typhoid.

Henry the Minstrel. See Harry.

Henryson, Robert (c. 1430-1500). Evidently schoolmaster at *Dunfermline* and possibly teacher of law in *Glasgow University*; his poems include 'The Testament of Cresseid', 'Robene and Makyne' and 'Moral Fabillis'.

Hepburn Family. Named from place in Northumberland; *David II* granted lands of *Hailes* to Adam H., whose descendants became *Earls of Bothwell.*

Hepburn, James, Earl of Bothwell. See Bothwell.

Hepburn, Sir James (d. 1637). Soldier of fortune; succeeded *Sir John Hepburn* as commander of *Scots Brigade.*

Hepburn, John (d. 1522). Brother of *1st Earl of Bothwell*; Prior of *St Andrews*; founder of *St Leonard's College,* St Andrews; built great precinct wall round priory; elected by *chapter* to archbishopric, 1513, but had to give way to *Andrew Forman.*

Hepburn, Sir John, of Athelstaneford (1598-1636). Served under Frederick, Elector Palatine and King of Bohemia, and then under Gustavus Adolphus, commanding *Scots Brigade*; transferred to French service 1632 and formed *Regiment d'Hebron*; became a marshal of France.

Hepburn, Patrick (d. 1573). Son of *1st Earl of Bothwell*; Prior of *St Andrews, Commendator* of *Scone* and (1538) *Bishop of Moray*; notorious for his immorality; took an equivocal attitude at *Reformation* and retained bishopric until his death.

Hepburn's Regiment. See Dumbarton's Drums; Hepburn, Sir John; and Royal Scots.

Heralds. See Albany, Islay, Marchmont, Ross, Rothesay and Snowdon.

Herbertshire (Dunipace). Presumably named after 13th century Herbert de Morham.

Herd, David (1732-1810). Born St Cyrus, Kincardineshire; collector of ancient and modern Scottish songs and ballads and literary adviser to *Archibald Constable.*

'Heretics'. See Buchanan (George), Craw, Forrest, Forret, Gourlay, Hamilton (Patrick), Mylne (Walter), Resby, Straiton and Wishart (George).

Herezeld or **Heriot.** Exacted by *superior* or landlord on death of vassal or tenant; traditionally the best animal among the stock.

Heriot, George (Jinglin' Geordie) (1563-1624). Son of *Edinburgh* goldsmith; followed same craft; goldsmith to Queen *Anne* 1597 and to *James VI* 1601; after 1603 lived mainly in London and built up profitable business, partly in money-lending; bequeathed his fortune for foundation of 'Hospital' in Edinburgh which was built 1628-59 and became George Heriot's School.

Heriot-Watt College, *Edinburgh,* **later University.** Founded 1821 as school of arts, to provide education in mathematics, science and drawing; became 'Watt Institute and School of Arts' 1852 and (with help of funds from *George Heriot*'s Trust) 'Heriot Watt College' 1886; expanded into many branches of engineering and science; constituted a university 1966.

Heritable Jurisdictions. Rights of jurisdictions which were attached to land ownership and transmitted by inheritance, chiefly courts of *regality* and courts of *barony*; many *sheriff*ships were also hereditary. Act of 1747 generally abolished heritable jurisdictions (which had been preserved by the *Union*), but baron courts survived, only to fall into desuetude.

Heritors. Owners of heritable property in a parish, who from 17th century until 1925 were responsible for maintenance of church and *manse* and until 19th century also for school.

Hermitage Castle (Roxburghshire). Originated 13th century with de *Soules family*; acquired by *Douglases* 1338 and exchanged with *Earl of Angus* for *Bothwell Castle* by 1st *Earl of Bothwell*; after forfeiture of *5th Earl of Bothwell,* acquired by Scott of *Buccleuch.*

Herries Family. William de Heriz, who appears in Scotland c. 1152 and is presumed to have been the founder of the family, had probably been a *Bruce* vassal in England. They held *Hoddam* from probably 13th century until 17th.

Herries, Lordship. Held by Maxwells from 1489; attainted 1716 but restored 1848. See Maxwell, John and William.

Herring Industry Board. Established 1935.

Herriot's Dyke. Ancient rampart of unknown origin, running from *Berwick* past *Greenlaw* and Westruther to the valley of the Leader.

Herschip of Buchan. *Robert I,* after defeating *Comyn, Earl of Buchan,* ravaged his lands, 1308.

Hertford's Invasions, 1544 and 1545. Henry VIII's retaliation for the Scots' rejection of the *Treaties of Greenwich.* Edward Seymour, Earl of Hertford, landed at *Leith* on 4 May 1544 and burned and looted from there to the Border; in September 1545 he came by land, to burn the crops ready for harvesting. The Border abbeys and *Holyrood* were devastated in those attacks. Hertford later became Duke of Somerset and defeated Scots at *Pinkie.*

Het Pint. *Earl of Hyndford* provided for a pint of mulled ale yearly to any resident in *Lanark* who applied for it; later the sum of 5s. was offered each New Year's Day instead.

Hexham Pennant. Captured by townsmen of Hawick from English raiders 1514; a replica of the blue and gold flag is borne by the Cornet in the *Hawick Common Riding.*

Hichaten. Supposed *Cistercian* house in *Orkney,* but the only possible site of a medieval monastery there is *Eynhallow.*

High Commission Courts. Established 1610, one for province of *St Andrews* and the other for *Glasgow,* to reinforce the discipline conducted by *Kirk sessions* and to deal with nonconformity. In 1615 a single court was created. It was condemned by the *Glasgow Assembly* 1638 and abolished by *Parliament* 1640.

High Court of Justiciary. See Justice General, Justiciary Court.

Highland and Agricultural Society. Founded at *Edinburgh* 1784; held first show 1822. Ingliston became permanent site of show 1960.

'Highland Host'. Body of troops, including many Lowland Militia as well as Highlanders, who were quartered on the ecclesiastical dissidents of Renfrewshire and Ayrshire in 1678.

Highland Land League. Formed on behalf of crofters 1882. Six candidates stood at the 1885 election and four were elected. After the *Crofters Act* of 1886 agitation died down, but the League continued, to become in 1921 the *Scots National League,* which merged in the *Scottish National Party.*

Highland Light Infantry. Raised 1777 as *Glasgow Regiment*; in 1808 designated Glasgow Highland Regiment, in 1809 Highland Light Infantry; in 1881 it became 1st Battalion of the H.L.I. and the 74th (raised 1787 by Sir Archibald Campbell) the 2nd Battalion; merged with *Royal Scots Fusiliers* to form Royal Highland Fusiliers 1959.

'Highland Mary'. Mary Cameron (d. 1786), *Robert Burns*'s Highland Mary, was born at *Dunoon,* where there is a monument on the Castle Hill; she was buried at *Greenock.*

Highland Railway. From *Perth* to *Wick* and *Thurso*; reached *Inverness* 1863 and Thurso 1874.

Highland Regiment (74th). See Highland Light Infantry.

Highland Regiment (100th). Embodied at *Stirling* 1761 under command of Major Colin Campbell of Kilberry; stationed at Martinique until 1763, when returned to Scotland and disbanded.

Highland Regiment (132nd). Raised by Duncan Cameron of Callart 1794; men soon drafted to other regiments.

Highland Regiment (133rd). Raised by Colonel Simon Fraser 1794; men drafted to other regiments same year.

Highland Regiments. Between 1740 and 1815 there were raised in the Highlands 50 battalions of the line, 3 reserve and 7 militia, besides 23 regiments of '*fencibles*' (embodied for duration of a war) and numerous volunteers.

Highland Roads and Bridges. See Commissioners for.

Highland Society of Edinburgh. Instituted 1784 with objects of improving Highlands and Islands and preserving their language, poetry and music.

Highland Society School, Glasgow. Founded 1727 for children of poor Highlanders in *Glasgow.*

Highland Volunteers, Royal. 113th Regiment, raised 1761 under Major James Hamilton; disbanded 1763.

Highlands and Islands Development Board (*Inverness*). Established by government 1965 to provide financial assistance to a wide range of activities in the area.

Highlands and Islands Emigration Society. Formed 1851 after the distress caused by the potato failures of the late 1840s; enabled several thousands to emigrate, mainly to Australia.

Hill, David Octavius (1802-70). Born *Perth*; landscape and portrait painter who pioneered use of photography in association with portrait-painting.

Hill's Tower. Tower in *Galloway* of unknown antiquity; a later addition has the date 1598.

Hinba. Site of Celtic monastery in 6th-7th centuries, probably identifiable with Jura.

Hind. Farm labourer.

Hislop, James (1798-1827). Born Kirkconnel, *Nithsdale*; shepherd, schoolmaster, tutor and reporter; wrote 'Cameronian's Dream'.

Hoddam (Dumfriesshire). Ecclesiastical centre in 10th century and perhaps later; original castle must have been a *Bruce* stronghold; estate held by *Herries* family from 13th century until 1627, when it was acquired by Murray of Cockfoot; it then passed to 1st *Earl of Southesk* (1653) and to John Sharpe (1690); older buildings were superseded by a 15th century structure enlarged in the 19th.

Hogg, James (c. 1658-1734). Son of *minister* of Larbert; minister of Dalserf 1691 and of Carnock 1699; in 1718 republished 'The *Marrow* of Modern Divinity' and became leader of 'The Marrowmen', the most uncompromising adherents of the doctrine of the predestined salvation of the Elect; denounced by *General Assembly* 1720.

Hogg, James (1770-1835), 'the Ettrick Shepherd'. Born Ettrick; began to publish verses 1800 and his works included 'The Forest Minstrel' (1810), 'The Queen's Wake' and 'Pilgrims of the Sun'. The most important of his many prose works was 'The Private Memoirs and Confessions of a Justified Sinner' (1824). Again and again Hogg made money by a publication and then lost it in a farming venture.

Hogmanay. New Year's Eve.

Holy Island (Arran). Associated with Celtic saint, *Molaise,* and referred to in 1549 as 'ane monastery of friars which is decayit', but there is no evidence of any medieval religious house.

Holyrood Abbey (*Augustinian*). Founded by *David I* c. 1128; sacked by English 1322 and 1385 and again in *Hertford's Invasions*; nave repaired for use of reformed church and served parish of *Canongate* until 1688; roof fell 1758; abbey property erected into *temporal lordship* for John Bothwell 1606; abbey precinct remained sanctuary for debtors until 19th century. See Girth Cross.

Holyrood Font and Lectern. A font of brass, given to the abbey by Abbot *Robert Bellenden,* was carried off by an English commander in 1544 and presented to abbey of St Albans and was apparently removed and melted down in Civil War. A lectern, presented by *George Crichton,* a former Abbot, carried off in similar circumstances, was later discovered in St Stephen's Church at St Albans.

Holyrood, Lordship. Created 1607 for John Bothwell, son of *Adam B*; he died without male heirs.

Holyrood Ordinale. A copy, prepared c. 1450 for abbey of Holyrood, of directions for carrying out certain services as done in some English *Augustinian* houses.

Holyrood, Palace of. *James IV* built a tower adjoining the abbey where his predecessors had resided as guests, but the oldest extant building is a tower of *James V* which, with additions, served until the reign of *Charles II,* when a general reconstruction retained the James V tower but superseded all other buildings by a set of ranges round a courtyard. See Bruce, Sir William.

Holywood Abbey (*Premonstratensian*) (Dumfriesshire). Also known as Dercongal; founded 12th century, but exact date and name of founder unknown; choir used after *Reformation* as parish church, but demolished 1779; property erected as *temporal lordship* for Kirkpatrick of Closeburn 1609, but this did not take effect and it was erected effectively for *John Murray,* later *Earl of Annandale,* 1617-8. A hospital attached to the the abbey was founded by Archibald Douglas, *Lord of Galloway,* before 1362 and was later attached to *collegiate church* of *Lincluden.*

Home Family. Said to be descended from Ada, daughter of Patrick, 5th *Earl of Dunbar,* who was 'Lady of Home' and married William of *Greenlaw,* grandson of 3rd Earl of Dunbar, who took name of Home, in late 13th century.

Home, Sir George, of Spott (d. 1611). See Dunbar, Earl of.

Home, Henry, Lord Kames. See Kames, Lord.

Home, John (1722-1808). Born *Leith*; *minister* of Athelstaneford 1746; after an unsuccessful attempt with a tragedy 'Agis', he wrote 'Douglas', which was produced in *Edinburgh* 1756 and won great praise; suspended by *presbytery*; became secretary to *Earl of Bute,* Prime Minister, and under patronage had some success on London stage; also wrote 'History of the Rebellion of 1745' (1802).

Home, Lordship. Created 1473 for Sir Alexander Home (d. 1491), son of Sir Alexander H. (d. 1456), who had been associated with *8th Earl of Douglas* but did not share in Douglas fall. The 1st Lord was a party to the conspiracy which ended *James III*'s reign. Alexander, 2nd Lord, his grandson (d. 1506), conspired against *James IV* but was *Chancellor* 1488-1506. Alexander, 3rd Lord, his son (d. 1516), *Chamberlain* 1506, commanded a division at *Flodden* but was suspected of playing a dubious part; he rebelled against *John, Duke of Albany,* and was executed. Alexander, 5th Lord (d. 1575), rebelled against *Mary* after *Bothwell* marriage but joined her party after death of *Moray*. Alexander, 6th Lord, his son (?1566-1619), acted with ultra-Protestants in *Ruthven Raid* but was later excommunicated as a papist; he was created Earl of Home 1605.

Home Rule Bills. A series extended from 1908 to 1913, a second from 1926 to 1928; another bill was not presented until 1966; a Devolution Bill came in 1976. See Kilbrandon Report.

Homildon, Battle of, 14 September 1402. Scots heavily defeated by English in Northumberland.

Hommyl, James. A tailor, one of the alleged low-born favourites of *James III*; he did not perish at *Lauder Brig.*

'Honest Toun'. See Musselburgh.

Honeyman, Tom John (1891-1971). Educated *Glasgow*; practised as physician until 1929; Director of Lefevre Gallery, London, 1929-39;

Director of *Glasgow Art Gallery* 1939-54; wrote on art.

Honours of Scotland. The crown, sceptre and sword of state. On view in *Edinburgh Castle.*

Hope, Sir James (1614-61). Sixth son of *Sir Thomas H*; *Lord of Session* 1649; one of Cromwell's judges 1652; ancestor of Earls of *Hopetoun.*

Hope, Sir John (c. 1605-54). Eldest son of *Sir Thomas H*; knighted and raised to bench (Lord Craighall) 1632; president of Cromwell's Committee of Justice 1652. See Cromwellian Administration.

Hope, John. See Hopetoun, Earl of.

Hope, Sir Thomas (c. 1580-1643). *Advocate* 1605; defended *ministers* prosecuted for meeting in *General Assembly* in defiance of King, 1606; acquired many estates, including Craighall in Fife; *Lord Advocate* 1626, baronet 1628, but bent on undermining *Charles I's* policies and acted deviously; declared *National Covenant* not unlawful and refused to defend episcopacy; compiled 'Minor Practicks' (1726) and 'Major Practicks' (1737).

Hopetoun, Earldom. Created 1703 for Charles Hope, grandson of *Sir James Hope*; 7th Earl created *Marquis of Linlithgow* 1902.

Hopetoun House (West Lothian). Built on lands of *Abercorn,* bought by *Hope* family 1678, from designs by *Sir William Bruce* between 1699 and 1703 and later enlarged by *John* and *Robert Adam.*

Hopetoun, John, 4th Earl of (1765-1823). Colonel in *Black Watch*; served in West Indies and Egypt; took command at Corunna on death of *Sir John Moore.*

Hopetoun, John Adrian Louis, 7th Earl of (1860-1908). First Governor General of Australia; *Marquis of Linlithgow* 1902.

Horndean (Berwickshire). Hospital founded c. 1240 by Robert Byseth, lord of Upsetlington; dependent on *Kelso Abbey.*

Hornel, Edward Atkinson (1864-1933). Born Victoria, Australia, of *Galloway* parents, but returned with them in 1866 and settled in *Kirkcudbright*; trained as artist and was a member of the *Glasgow School*; left his 17th-century Broughton House, with its contents, to the inhabitants of the *Stewartry* to be used as public gallery and library.

Horner, Francis (1778-1817). Born *Edinburgh*; *advocate* 1800; English barrister 1807; contributor to '*Edinburgh Review*'; M.P. St Ives and other constituencies and an active politician.

Horning. Process of technical outlawry (by blasts of the horn by a messenger) whereby the goods of a debtor could be escheated to the crown and made available to his creditors; generally a proceeding of *Diligence* for the execution of a court *decreet*; the letters of horning were issued under the *signet.*

Horse Guards. See King's Life Guard of Horse.

Hospitallers. See Knights Hospitallers.

Hot Blast. See Iron Industry.

Houldsworth, Henry (1770-1853). Established *cotton* mills in *Glasgow* and the works to make machinery for them developed into the *Anderston* Foundry (1836). His son John (1807-59) continued machine works and with his uncle Thomas bought Coltness estate and started Coltness Iron Company (1837); later acquired other mines and ironworks.

Houston (East Lothian). *Trinitarian* friary, founded c. 1270 by Christiana, widow of Sir Roger Moubray, granted 1531 to Trinitarian house at *Peebles.* Attached hospital mentioned 1296.

Houston (Renfrewshire). Anciently 'Kilpeter', passed in 12th century from Baldwin of *Biggar* to Hugh of Padvinan (whence 'Houston'), whose descendants retained it until 1740; acquired by *Alexander Speirs* of Elderslie; Houston House demolished 1780. *Burgh of barony* for Houston of that *ilk* 1671. Solitary reference, 1525, points to *collegiate church.*

Houston, George (1869-1947). Born Dalry, Ayrshire; noted mainly for landscapes in water colour, but also etched and painted in oils.

Houston House (West Lothian). 16th-17th century, built by Sir John Shairp, a successful *advocate.*

Howie, John (1735-93). Farmer at Lochgoin, Ayrshire; author of 'Scots Worthies'.

Howie, Robert (1568-c. 1646). Born *Aberdeen*; spent several years at continental universities; *minister* of Aberdeen 1591; principal of *Marischal College, Aberdeen,* 1593-8; minister of *Dundee*; succeeded *Andrew Melville* as principal of *St Mary's College, St Andrews,* 1607.

Howieson, John (or **Jock**). Farmer at Braehead, near *Cramond* Brig, of which his family had been tenants from *James I's* reign, said to have rescued *James V,* when in disguise, from attackers, and the King said to have given him a charter of the land for service by ewer and basin; there were lands called 'Ewerislands', and the service has been rendered from time to time.

Hudson, James, Robert, Thomas and William. English musicians brought to Scotland by the *Lennox* family and appointed to *James VI*'s household 1578.

Humanity. Term used in universities as equivalent of Latin.

Humbie's Wa's. Nickname for *Crichton* Castle after it came into hands of Hepburn of Humbie c. 1649.

Hume. See also Home.

Hume, Alexander (c. 1560-1609). *Minister* of Logie; poet.

Hume, Alexander (1811-59). Cabinet-maker in *Edinburgh* and *Glasgow*; poet and composer who acted as chorus-master in Theatre Royal, Edinburgh.

Hume Castle (Berwickshire). Existed from 13th century; played a part in English invasions 1547 and 1650 and largely demolished; 3rd Earl of *Marchmont* erected walls to mark the site.

Hume, David, of Godscroft (c. 1560-1630). Secretary of *8th Earl of Angus*; wrote a 'History of the House of Douglas and Angus' which drew on the Earl's papers and was later published by his daughter, Anna, and also a 'History of the House of Wedderburn'.

Hume, David, of Crossrig (1643-1707). *Advocate* 1687; *Lord of Session* (Crossrig) 1689; wrote 'Diary of Parliament and Privy Council of Scotland'.

Hume, David (1711-76). Son of laird of Ninewells (Berwickshire); studied at *Edinburgh* and in France and lived at various periods in London and on the continent (as secretary to envoys); Keeper of *Advocates' Library,* Edinburgh, 1752-7; wrote 'Treatise on Human Nature' (1738-40), 'Essays Moral and Political' (1741), other philosophical works and a 'History of England' (1754-61); his religious scepticism and his *Jacobitism* prevented academic appointments, but he was Under-Secretary of State for the Home Department 1767-9.

Hume, David (1757-1838). Nephew of preceding; educated *Edinburgh,* London and *Glasgow*; *advocate* 1779; professor of Scots Law, Edinburgh, 1786; baron of exchequer 1811; his 'Commentaries on the Criminal Law of Scotland' were published from 1797 onwards and his 'Lectures' have been published by the *Stair Society*.

Hume, Grizel. See Baillie.

Hume, Sir Patrick, of Polwarth (1641-1724). Son of Sir Patrick, 1st baronet; as a convinced *Presbyterian* was active in opposition to *Duke of Lauderdale* in *Parliament* 1673-4; twice imprisoned as 'a factious person' and intrigued with English plotters against *Charles II*; on discovery of Rye House Plot he hid for a month in the family vault, attended by his daughter *Grizel Baillie*; fled to Holland, to return and join *Argyll's Rebellion* 1685 and again with *William of Orange*; created *Lord Polwarth* 1690 and Earl of *Marchmont* 1697; *Chancellor* 1696 and King's commissioner to Parliament 1698.

Hunt the Gowk. The observance of 1st April, 'All Fools' Day'; 'gowk' = fool, but also = cuckoo, and there may be a connection with trying to get the first glimpse of the bird.

Hunter, George Leslie (1879-1931). Born *Rothesay*; emigrated to America with family; became illustrator for newspapers and magazines in California; returned to *Glasgow* 1906; best known for still life.

Hunter, John (1728-93). Born Long Calderwood (East Kilbride); brother of *William Hunter,* whom he joined in London 1748; surgeon with army 1761-2 and in London hospitals, where he lectured; surgeon extraordinary to the King 1776; published works on gunshot wounds, venereal diseases and restoration of persons apparently drowned; his collections acquired by London College of Surgeons.

Hunter, William (1718-83). Brother of *John Hunter.* Abandoned divinity studies for medicine and became surgeon at St George's Hospital, London; specialised in midwifery and had lucrative practice; physician extraordinary to the Queen 1764; president of Royal College of Physicians 1781; built up museum and art collection which was acquired by *Glasgow University*; his greatest publication was 'Anatomical Description of the Human Gravid Uterus' (1774).

Hunterian Club. Founded in *Glasgow* 1871 for reproduction of 'works of Scottish writers of Elizabethan times'; final report 1902.

Hunterian Museum (*Glasgow*). See Hunter, William.

Hunters and Co., Ayr. Bank started 1773 by the former cashier of *Douglas, Heron and Co*; acquired *Kilmarnock Banking Co.* 1821; merged with *Union Bank* 1843.

Hunterston Brooch. Discovered 1826 by a shepherd on the hills of the Hunterston estate, West Kilbride; a casting of silver, with amber and gold insets, dating from c. 700 A.D. and believed to reflect Anglian rather than purely Celtic influence; in *National Museum of Antiquities*.

Huntingdon, Earldom of. *David I* enjoyed earldom in right of his wife, whose father had been Earl, and passed it on to his son *Henry*; it was secured to *Malcolm IV* in exchange for his abandonment of claims on the three northern English counties, 1157; *William I* had earldom in 1185 and it passed to his brother *David*.

Huntingtower Castle (Perthshire). See Ruthven Castle.

Huntly (Aberdeenshire). Oldest part of castle dates from 15th century, probably built by 1st *Earl of Huntly*; important Renaissance palace added by *1st Marquis* 1597-1602; family residence until superseded by Gordon Castle, *Fochabers*, 1752. Huntly was a *burgh of barony* for Earl of Huntly 1488 and a *burgh of regality* for 1st *Duke of Gordon* 1684.

Huntly, Alexander Gordon, 3rd Earl of (d. 1524). Shared command of division at *Flodden*; took an active part in minority of *James V* as a member of *council* and lieutenant in the north.

Huntly Castle (near *Longforgan*, Carse of *Gowrie*). Begun by *Lord Gray* of Foulis, master of the household to *James II* in 1452; sold to 1st Earl of *Kinghorne* 1611; the 3rd Earl (also 1st Earl of *Strathmore*) restored it and named it Castle Lyon; but in 1776 the Earl of Strathmore sold it to George Paterson, who married Anne, daughter of 12th Lord Gray, and the old name was restored.

Huntly, Earldom and Marquisate. Earldom created 1455 for Alexander Seton (d. 1470), son of Alexander S. (created *Lord Gordon* 1436) and Elizabeth, sister and heir of Sir John Gordon (d. 1408); 6th Earl created Marquis 1599; 9th Earl created Duke of Gordon 1684, but on 5th Duke's death with no direct male heir (1836) the dukedom became extinct and a distant cousin succeeded as Earl and Marquis.

Huntly Field Club. Founded 1883 to study the geology, botany, natural history and archaeology of the district; ceased to operate 1891.

Huntly, George Gordon, 4th Earl of (c. 1510-62). Grandson of *3rd Earl* by a natural daughter of *James IV*; continued his predecessors' work as lieutenant and, with vast territorial possessions and the office of *sheriff* of *Aberdeen*, was very powerful; on council of regency 1542; *Chancellor* 1546; captured at *Pinkie* but escaped; after long hesitation joined rebellion 1560, but remained essentially conservative; his rebellion against *Mary* in 1562 probably arose mainly from personal reasons; defeated at *Corrichie*, he died suddenly after his capture; Sir John, his third son, was executed and Huntly was posthumously forfeited.

Huntly, George Gordon, 5th Earl of (d. 1576). Son of preceding; *Chancellor* 1566-7; supported *Mary* against *regents* for *James VI*.

Huntly, George Gordon, 6th Earl and 1st Marquis of (1562-1636). Son of preceding; conservative in his political and ecclesiastical outlook, he was favoured by *James VI* even before he married the daughter of *Esmé, Duke of Lennox*; associated with *9th Earl of Errol* in Roman Catholic plots; responsible for murder of *Earl of Moray* 1592; came to terms with King 1596; received into Church of England 1612, but remained under some suspicion for supposed popish sympathies.

Huntly, George Gordon, 2nd Marquis of (c. 1592-1649). Son of preceding; spent most of his early years at the court in England and in France; did not accept *National Covenant* and was prepared to fight for the King in 1639, but was arrested; took up arms 1644 but did not co-operate effectively with *Montrose*; arrested again 1646 and executed 1649.

Huntly, George Gordon, 4th Marquis of (1643-1716). *Duke of Gordon* 1648; Governor of *Edinburgh Castle* and held it for *James VII* 1688-9.

Hurly Haaky. Form of tobogganing said to have been invented by *James V* in his boyhood at *Stirling*; 'haaky' = cow, and a cow's skull may have been used as a toboggan.

Husbandland. One eighth of a *ploughgate*.

Hutcheson, Francis (1694-1746). Received some of his education and did some school teaching in Dublin; professor of moral philosophy at *Glasgow* 1729-46; his 'System of Moral Philosophy' published 1755; influenced '*common sense*' school of philosophy.

Hutcheson's Hospital and Schools (*Glasgow*). George (c. 1580-1639) and Thomas (1589-1641) Hutcheson, lawyers, left money to found a hospital for infirm men and a school for poor boys; in mid-18th century pensions were instituted in place of hospital; in 1872 school was reorganised, to provide secondary school for girls as well as one for boys.

Hutchison, Robert Gemmell (1855-1936). Born *Edinburgh*; seal engraver who studied art and painted both domestic scenes and landscapes in oils, water colours and pastels.

Hutchison, Sir William Oliphant (1889-1970). Trained at *Edinburgh* and Paris; painted portraits and landscapes; Director of Glasgow School of Art 1933-43.

Hutton Hospital (*Berwick*). Mentioned 1296; granted with church of Hutton to *Dunglass collegiate church* 1451; 'Hutton Spital' burned by English 1452.

Hutton, James (1726-97). Born *Edinburgh*; turned from medicine to chemistry and produced sal ammoniac from soot; studying agriculture in England, he realised importance of geology and, after extensive continental travels, settled on a small Berwickshire estate, which he much improved, but occasionally journeyed to Highlands for geological investigations; his 'Theory of the Earth' (1785) was 'the foundation of modern geology'; wrote also 'Physical Dissertations' (1792) and 'Investigations of Principles of Knowledge' (1794).

Hyndford, Earldom. Created 1701 for John, 2nd Lord Carmichael; dormant 1817.

I

Iain Lom. See MacDonald, John.

Icolmkill. See Iona.

Ilk. Means 'same', so that 'Ogilvy of that ilk', for example, would mean 'Ogilvy of Ogilvy'; such a style usually denotes the senior branch of a family and the head of the name.

Improvers. The Honourable Society of Improvers in the Knowledge of Agriculture in Scotland founded 1723.

In Commendam. A benefice (e.g. an abbey) was held 'in commendam' by a person who drew the revenues although he lacked the normal qualifications (e.g. membership of a religious order) for the office. See Commendator.

Inch (Wigtownshire). *Burgh of barony* for *Earl of Stair* 1677.

Inchaffray Abbey (*Augustinian*) (Perthshire). A surviving earlier community is referred to c. 1200, but Gilbert, *Earl of Strathearn,* then provided for the introduction of the Augustinian rule and the house became an abbey in 1220 or 1221; erected into *temporal lordship* for *Lord Madderty,* 1609, and in 1669 for William Drummond, later *Viscount Strathallan*; only fragmentary remains.

Inchbrakie's Ring. A sapphire, set in gold, said to have been spat out by Kate McNiven, a witch of *Monzie,* while being burned at *Crieff,* with a promise that if the laird of Inchbrakie (who had tried to save her) and his descendants kept it they would prosper.

Inchcailloch. Island in Loch Lomond, alleged to be site of nunnery on the strength of the etymology 'island of old women', but no such house is known to record and there seems to have been only a church.

Inchcolm. Island in Firth of Forth. Possibly Celtic foundation before the establishment by *Alexander I,* 1123, of an *Augustinian* priory which became an abbey 1235; with its dedication to St *Columba* and its close association with the ancient see of *Dunkeld* (in which diocese it remained) it was clearly of peculiar significance; erected into *temporal lordship* for Henry Stewart, son of Lord *Doune,* 1609; remains substantial.

Inchgarvie. Island on which middle pier of *Forth Railway Bridge* rests; a fort dates from reign of *James IV* and was used for a time as a prison; re-fortified against *Paul Jones* 1779 and again in 20th century.

Inchinnan (Renfrewshire). Early ecclesiastical centre, as indicated by sculptured stones.

Inchkeith. Island in Firth of Forth. Fortified in 16th and 19th centuries; lighthouse 1804.

Inchkenneth (*Argyll*). Island belonged to nunnery of *Iona,* but no evidence that it contained a religious house.

Inchmahome Priory (*Augustinian*) (Perthshire). Founded soon after 1238 by *Walter Comyn, Earl of Menteith*; *David II* married Margaret Logie there and Queen *Mary* spent a few weeks there after *Pinkie*; erected into *temporal lordship* for *John, Earl of Mar,* 1604 and 1606; remaining buildings in good condition.

Inchmarnock. Island between Bute and Kintyre, reputed to be site of religious foundation, but there is no evidence of anything more than a parish church.

Inchmurrin Castle. Ruins of ancient castle of *Earls of Lennox* on island in Loch Lomond; seized 1424-5 by a son of *Murdoch, Duke of Albany* (whose wife was a daughter of the Earl of Lennox), when in rebellion against *James I*; Sir John Colquhoun and his attendants murdered there 1439.

Inchrye Abbey (near *Newburgh,* Fife). Mansion house built in 19th century; no connection with any abbey.

Inchtavannach. Island in Loch Lomond, reputed to be site of early monastery, but there is no evidence of such.

Inchtuthill (Perthshire). Legionary fortress begun by *Agricola* probably in 83, but used for only a very short period.

'Incident'. During *Charles I*'s visit to Scotland in 1641 there was a rumour of a plot to murder the *Marquises of Argyll* and *Hamilton* and so strengthen the King's position.

Income Tax. Modern Income Tax did not come until 1790s and has been continuous since 1803, but there had been anticipations of it in 17th century Scotland, when taxation was first extended to other property besides land. In 1621 a tax of 5% was imposed on annual rents and interest and in 1625 the rate was raised to 1/16. In 1640 the scope of taxation was defined as 'the yearly worth of every man's rent, in victual, money or other wages' and based on 'everything whereby profit or commodity ariseth'.

Incorporations. See Crafts.

Indemnity, Proclamation of, 1674. As part of a policy of conciliation of ecclesiastical dissidents, an amnesty for those who had broken the laws, except those already condemned or those involved in the *Pentland Rising.*

Independence, Declaration of. See Arbroath, Declaration of.

Independent Companies. See Black Watch.

Independent Labour Party. Formed 1893; remained in being as a minority socialist group outside the Labour Party and held a number of Scottish seats from 1922 to 1945.

Indulf. King of *Alba* 945-62. In his reign *Edinburgh* was added to his kingdom.

Indulgences, Declarations of. Measures designed to conciliate *Presbyterian* dissidents in 1669, 1672, 1679 and 1687: (1) *ministers* deprived in 1662 were allowed to return to their parishes if they were vacant; (2) a number of specified ministers were licensed to preach; (3) laws against those frequenting *conventicles* were suspended, after *Bothwell Brig*; (4) *James VII* conceded a general toleration.

Infeftment. Scottish version of enfeoffment; the investiture of a person who had acquired land, either by inheritance, gift or purchase; almost equivalent to *sasine.*

Infield. The part of a farm nearest to the '*ferm toun*', which was perpetually tilled. See Outfield.

Ingibjorg. Said to have been widow of *Thorfinn, Earl of Orkney,* but that is impossible chronologically and she was presumably his daughter; married *Malcolm III* c. 1060 and had three sons, one of them *Duncan II*; her marriage may have been dissolved on grounds of consanguinity, for Thorfinn was first cousin to Malcolm's father.

Inglis, Elsie Maud (1864-1917). Born India; qualified in medicine and practised in *Edinburgh,* where she was surgeon at Bruntsfield Hospital; founded Scottish Women's Suffrage Federation 1906; active in a Serbian Hospital Unit in World War I.

Inglis, Sir James. Author of the '*Complaynt of Scotland*'; he seems to have been a priest and to have been about the court under *James IV* and *James V.*

Inglis, John (1810-91). Son of John Inglis (1763-1834), *minister* of *Greyfriars*', *Edinburgh*; *advocate* 1835; *Lord Advocate* 1858; *Justice General* (Lord Glencorse) 1867.

Inglismaldie (Kincardineshire). *Burgh of barony* for Falconer of Newton 1682.

Ingliston (*Edinburgh*). See Highland and Agricultural Society.

Inhibition. A proceeding of *Diligence* whereby a debtor was restrained from alienating or burdening his heritable property to the prejudice of his creditors.

Inishail (Loch Awe, *Argyll*). Reputed site of *Cistercian* nunnery, but no evidence of any foundation except a parish church.

Innergelly (Fife). *Burgh of barony* for Barclay of Innergelly 1623.

Innerleithen (Peeblesshire). *Police burgh* 1892.

Innermessan (Wigtownshire). Castle, built by *Agnew* of Lochnaw 1429 and occupied until end of 17th century, was on site of earlier *motte*; two *burgesses* mentioned 1426, but no other evidence of a *burgh* which was said to have been of considerable size and to have been on site of the Rerigonium of the *Novantae* mentioned by Ptolemy in 2nd century.

Innerpeffray (Perthshire). *Collegiate* status of church may go no further back than 1542, though a chapel is mentioned earlier; the library was founded 1691 on bequest by David, 2nd *Lord Madderty.*

Innerwick (East Lothian). *Burgh of barony* for Maxwell of Innerwick 1630.

Innes (*Moray*). Granted by *Malcolm IV* to Berowald, a Fleming, whose descendants took name Innes and held it until 1767, when it was sold to 2nd *Earl of Fife*; Innes House dates from 1640-53; 6th Baronet of Innes succeeded to *dukedom of Roxburghe.*

Innes, Cosmo (1798-1874). Born Durris, Deeside; *advocate* 1832, principal Clerk of Session 1852; professor of constitutional law, *Edinburgh,* 1846; completed 'Acts of the Parliaments of Scotland'; edited many texts for publishing clubs; collected papers published in 'Scotch Legal Antiquities' (1872) and other volumes.

Innes, Lewis (1651-1738). Born Walkerdales, Banffshire; principal of *Scots College* at *Paris* 1682-1713; chief almoner at *Jacobite* court 1714.

'Innes Review'. Published under auspices of Roman Catholic historians since 1950.

Innes, Thomas (1662-1744). Brother of Lewis I; born Drumgask, Aberdeenshire; vice-principal of *Scots College* at *Paris* 1727; priest in Banffshire 1698-1701 and did research in Scotland c. 1722-5; his 'Critical Essay on the Ancient Inhabitants of Scotland' (1729) dismissed the mythology which had been mistaken for early Scottish history; also wrote 'Civil and Ecclesiastical History of Scotland' (1853).

Innes, Sir Thomas, of Learney (1893-1971). *Advocate* 1927; *Carrick Pursuivant* 1926; *Albany Herald* 1935; *Lyon King of Arms* 1945-69; wrote on clans and tartans.

Innis Chonnell Castle. On an islet in Loch Awe, dating partly from 13th century and mentioned 1308; passed from *MacDougals* to *Campbells* and remained their chief seat until superseded by *Inveraray*; existing remains largely 15th century.

Innocent Railway. *Edinburgh* to *Dalkeith*, opened 1831 from St Leonard's; so called from its low speeds and its safety; merged in *North British.*

Insch (Aberdeenshire). *Barony* held by *Balliols* in 13th century; *burgh of barony* under Leith-Hays of Leith Hall.

Interdiction. Bond whereby debtor guaranteed that he would not alienate property to prejudice of creditors; it could be imposed by *Court of Session.*

Inveraray (Argyll). Seat of *Earls and Dukes of Argyll*; old castle of 1520 demolished when present castle built 1773; building remodelled after fire 1877. The town a *burgh of barony* 1474, but *royal burgh* by 1648.

Inverbervie (Kincardineshire). 'Free burgh' 1341, when *David II* landed there on his return from France; *stent*ed as *royal burgh* 1483. *Carmelite* friary said in 1443 to have been recently established; no traces remain.

Invercharron, Battle of. See Carbisdale.

Inveresk (Midlothian). Site of Roman station.

Inverewe. See Mackenzie, Osgood.

Invergarry (Inverness-shire). Castle, stronghold of MacDonnell or MacDonald of Glengarry, destroyed by *Monck* 1654; another castle, burned after *Killiecrankie*, was rebuilt and burned again by *Duke of Cumberland* after *Culloden. Iron* works in operation 1727-36.

Invergordon (Ross). *Police burgh* 1868; naval base until 1956.

Inverkeithing (Fife). *Royal burgh* by 1163. A conventual *Franciscan* friary, founded between 1297 and 1385, conveyed to John Swinton 1559; the hospitium remains. A hospital, mentioned 1196-1453, belonged to *Dryburgh Abbey.*

Inverkeithing, Battle of, 20 July 1651. Cromwellian army defeated Scots supporting *Charles II.*

Inverlochy, Battle of, 2 February 1645. *Montrose* routed *Argyll.*

Inverlochy Castle (Inverness-shire). 13th century castle, built by *Comyn* family, of which substantial remains survive; modern castle nearby.

Inverness. A prominent site may have been a seat of *Pictish* kings; a castle, visited by many sovereigns, of which the keepers were first the chiefs of Mackintosh and then the *Earls of Huntly* (from 1508), was blown up after capture by *Charles Edward* just before *Culloden*; the county buildings occupy the site. *Royal burgh* under *Malcolm IV*. 'Citadel of Inverness' a *burgh of regality* 1666. *Dominican* friary, founded by *Alexander II*, was said to be almost ruined by war (the depredations of the *Lord of the Isles*) 1436. Abertarff House, dating from 1590s and once belonging to Fraser of Lovat, was restored by *National Trust* 1966 and is the northern headquarters of *An Comunn Gaidhealach.*

Inverness Scientific Society and Field Club. Founded 1875 to investigate geology, botany, natural history and archaeology of district.

Inverness, Treaty of, 29 October 1312. *Robert I* gave an undertaking to Haakon V of Norway to observe the terms of the *Treaty of Perth.*

Inverquharity Castle *(Angus).* Belonged from 1420 to an *Ogilvy* family, who received baronetcy 1626; recently restored.

Inverugie Castle (Aberdeenshire). An early castle of *Cheyne* family has disappeared, but a tower of a castle of the Keiths, Earls *Marischal,* dating from 16th century, was known as Cheyne's Tower; after forfeiture in 1716 the lands passed to Ferguson of Pitfour and the castle fell into ruin.

Inverurie (Aberdeenshire). *Burgh* founded by *David, Earl of Huntingdon,* by 1191, but passed to crown; confirmed as *royal burgh* 1558.

Inverurie (or **Barra**), **Battle of,** 22 May 1308. *Robert I* defeated *John Comyn, Earl of Buchan,* and the English.

Inverurie Canal. See Aberdeenshire Canal.

Iona Abbey. The Celtic establishment continued into 12th century, but a house of *Benedictines* was established, probably by *Reginald,* son of *Somerled,* before 1203; existing buildings are mainly 14th century; in 1498 the church was designated the cathedral of the *Isles*; property annexed to bishopric 1615 and subsequently passed to *Dukes of Argyll,* by whom it was in 1900 made over to the *Church of Scotland* and re-roofed.

Iona, Bond and Statutes of, 1609. *Andrew Knox, Bishop of the Isles,* met several West Highland chiefs at Iona and persuaded them to accept certain measures for peace and order in the area, including the advancement of Protestantism, the suppression of bards (who nurtured feuds), the establishment of inns and the reduction of retinues.

Iona Club. Founded in *Edinburgh* 1833 to publish material relating to the Highlands 'as a necessary step towards substituting an authentic history . . . for the fables and errors which have so long prevailed'. It published only one volume and was suspended in 1838 'until a more general desire should be expressed for its continuance'.

Iona Community. Founded 1938 by Rev. George MacLeod, later Lord MacLeod of Fuinary; it has restored some of the residential quarters at the *abbey.*

Iona Nunnery (*Augustinian*). Said to have been founded by *Reginald,* son of *Somerled,* before 1208; lands granted in heritage to Hector MacLean of *Duart* 1574.

Iona, Reilig Odhráin ('The graveyard of [St] Oran'.) Reputed burial place of 48 Scottish, 4 Irish and 8 Norwegian kings.

Ireland, John. A doctor of the Sorbonne who returned to Scotland 1483 to become confessor to *James III*; ambassador to France 1484.

Iron Belt. Worn by *James IV* as a penance for his part in the rebellion which led to his father's death after *Sauchieburn.*

Iron Industry. Little iron smelting in Scotland before 18th century, when several works operated in proximity to the ample timber supplies in the Highlands (see, e.g., Bonawe); *Carron* Works mark beginning of large-scale operations in Lowlands, but it was not until *James Neilson*'s invention of the hot-blast in 1828 facilitated the use of the blackband ironstone of Lanarkshire (the possibilities of which had been discovered by *David Mushet*) that significant expansion began.

Irvine (Ayrshire). *Burgh of barony* under Stewart family, dating from reign of *Alexander II*; *royal burgh* 1372. *Carmelite* friary founded before 1335 by a Fullarton of that *ilk*; property granted in 1572 to Royal School of I., which probably succeeded a pre-*Reformation* school and was in turn succeeded by Irvine *Academy,* erected 1814.

Irvine. Christopher. Surgeon to *Charles II* and to General *Monck*'s army; wrote 'Bellum Grammaticale', 'Medicina · Magnetica' and 'Historiae Scoticae nomenclatura Latina-vernacula'.

Irvine, Earldom. Created 1642 for James Campbell, *Lord Kintyre,* eldest son of 7th *Earl of Argyll* by his second marriage; extinct on his death without issue 1645.

Irvine of Drum, Family of. *Robert I* granted estate of *Drum* to his armour-bearer, Sir William Irvine; Sir Alexander I. was killed at *Harlaw.*

Irvine, Viscountcy. Created 1661 for Henry, son of Sir Arthur Ingram; extinct on death of 9th Viscount 1778.

Irving, David (1778-1860). Born *Langholm*; librarian to Faculty of *Advocates*; wrote 'Lives of the Scottish Poets' and 'Life of *George Buchanan*'.

Irving, Edward (1792-1834). Born *Annan*; after teaching for a time was ordained and in 1821 became *minister* of the Caledonian Church, London, where he built up a large following; his theology—Pentecostalist, sacramentalist and Adventist—led to his deposition 1833; from his London congregation developed the *Catholic Apostolic Church.*

Irvingites. See Catholic Apostolic Church.

Isabella, Countess of Buchan. See Buchan.

Isabella, Queen of Scots. Daughter of Donald, 10th *Earl of Mar*; 1st wife of *Robert I* and mother of *Marjory Bruce,* ancestress of Stewart kings.

Islay Herald. Appears among officers of crown after forfeiture of *Lordship of the Isles* in 1493; perhaps previously a herald of the Lord of the Isles, but an 'Aliszai Herald' had appeared in 1426.

Isle of Man. See Man.

Isles, Bishopric of. In existence from late 9th century and good evidence from c. 1080; had its seat in *Man* and was part of the Norwegian province, even after the Isles became part of Scotland in 1266. In 15th century, partly because Man had now passed to England and partly because England and Scotland differed in their allegiance during the *Papal Schism,* the bishopric fell into two—an English one in Man (still called 'Sodor and Man') and a Scottish bishopric of the Isles for which *Iona* was declared the cathedral in 1498.

Isles, Lordship of. There was a kingdom of the Isles, subject to Norway and with its headquarters in *Man*, from c. 900. In the 12th century magnates of mixed Norse and Celtic blood were dominant, one of them *Somerled*. The territory passed to Scotland in 1266, but the ensuing *Wars of Independence* led to confusion, especially as different branches of the leading family of *MacDonald* took different sides. In 14th century the title 'Lord of the Isles' was assumed by a MacDonald landowner based on Islay, but the title was not officially acknowledged by the crown until 15th century. The turbulence of the lords, and their traitorous dealings with England, caused constant trouble: John, 1st lord (d. 1386), supported *Edward Balliol*; a campaign by Donald, the 2nd (d. 1420), led to battle of *Harlaw*; Alexander, the 3rd (d. 1449), was twice imprisoned by *James I* and in the intervening period burned *Inverness*; for John, the 4th, see John. See also Ross, earldom.

'It Cam' Wi' a Lass'. Remark attributed to the dying *James V*, when he heard of the birth of his daughter *Mary* and supposed to mean that the crown had come to his family through *Marjory Bruce* and would pass from it through Mary; but as she married her cousin, it passed no further than another branch of the house, the *Lennox* Stewarts.

Ius Relictae (or **Relicti**). The right of a surviving spouse to a third ('Terce') of the partner's movables on his or her decease.

Ivory, James (1792-1866). *Advocate* 1816; *Solicitor General* 1839; *Lord of Session* 1840.

J

Jacks, William (1841-1907). Founded *iron* works in Glasgow 1880; M.P. for *Leith* Burghs and for *Stirling*; author of 'Bismarck' and *'James Watt'*; made bequest to *Glasgow University* for chair of modern languages.

Jacobites. Supporters of *James VII* after his deposition in 1689 and subsequently of his son, *James Francis*, and his grandson, *Charles Edward*. In 1708 a French fleet escorted James Francis to the Scottish coast but had to retire before a British fleet. A major rising came in 1715 (see Mar, John, Earl of; Braemar; Sheriffmuir; Preston). In 1719 a small body of Spaniards landed with the Earl *Marischal* and was defeated at *Glenshiel*. For the second major rising, in 1745, see Charles Edward; Culloden; Falkirk; Glenfinnan; and Prestonpans.

James I (1394-1437). Second son of *Robert III*, born *Dunfermline* July 1394; captured on his way to France 1406 and detained in England until 1424 (see London, Treaty of), when he returned with his wife, *Joan*; his enforcement of order, severity against nobles and acquisitiveness made him unpopular, but his murder at *Perth* (21 February 1437) arose at least partly from the claims of the descendants of *Robert II's* second marriage, to *Euphemia Ross*; his heart was taken on a pilgrimage to the east, and, brought back from Rhodes by a Knight of St John, given to the *Charterhouse of Perth*, which he had founded.

James II (1430-60). Son of *James I*, born *Holyrood* 16 October 1430; in 1449 he married *Mary of Gueldres*, dealt ruthlessly with the *Livingston* family who had engrossed the chief offices of state, and assumed personal authority; in his minority the 6th *Earl of Douglas* and his brother had been murdered at the '*Black Dinner*' and the king himself murdered *William, 8th Earl of Douglas* in 1452; in 1455 James finally overthrew the *Black Douglases*; he showed wisdom in raising up families on whom he could rely, but also impetuousness; killed by the bursting of a cannon when he laid siege to *Roxburgh*, 3 August 1460; known as 'James of the Fiery Face' from a birthmark.

James III (1452-88). Son of *James II*, born at *St Andrews* May 1452; in 1469 married *Margaret*, daughter of Christian I of Denmark and Norway, and overthrew the *Boyds*, who had been in control; imprisoned his brothers, the *Duke of Albany* and the *Earl of Mar*; in 1482, when he had set out to meet an English invasion, the nobles turned on his alleged 'low favourites' at *Lauder Bridge* and hanged some of them; trouble revived in 1488 and the King was killed as he fled from the battle field of *Sauchieburn* (11 June). James was a man of culture, and the country was prospering, but there were monetary problems with which the administration could not cope and he was personally acquisitive.

James IV (1473-1513). Born 17 March 1473, probably at *Stirling*; figurehead of the rebellion which overthrew his father, *James III*; as he was fifteen, no regency was necessary, and he soon assumed power in person and on the whole exercised it wisely, with the extension of civil and criminal justice, expeditions to the Highlands and a treaty of 'perpetual peace' with England to accompany his marriage to *Margaret Tudor*; patronised men of science and literature and encouraged education and printing; when France and England went to war, the moral obligation of the traditional French alliance proved stronger than the legal obligation of the new English treaty, and James was killed at *Flodden* (9 September 1513).

James V (1512-42). Son of *James IV*, born at *Linlithgow* 10 April 1512; the capriciousness of his mother, *Margaret Tudor*, and her tempestuous relations with her second husband, the *6th Earl of Angus*, were the background to his early years, and when Angus finally gained control and kept the king a prisoner (1526-8) he was imbued with hatred of the Angus Douglases, who had represented the English interest. His own preference was probably for a French marriage and his negotiations with England and the Emperor Charles V designed to stimulate Francis I of France into conceding his daughter *Madeleine*, which he did in 1537; on her death James married *Mary of Guise*. Meantime, by playing on the fears of the Pope at a time when Henry VIII had rejected the papacy, he gained financial concessions from the Scottish church which enabled him to finance the *College of Justice* (1532). James's vindictiveness towards troublesome subjects, and the suspicion that he attacked the wealthy with trumped-up charges, as well as distrust of the French and papal alliance, divided the nation and led to the rout of *Solway Moss*, three weeks after which the King died, at *Falkland* (14 December 1542).

James VI (1566-1625). Son of *Mary*, Queen of Scots, and *Darnley*, born in *Edinburgh Castle* 19 June 1566. Four regencies (of *Moray*, *Lennox*, *Mar* and *Morton*) were followed by the ascendancies of various factions, but in 1585 the King began to direct policy. His aim was to bring about the conciliation of the various factions by pursuing a middle course in religion and a judicious mixture of suppression and leniency towards nobles and *ministers*. By 1597 he was substantially in control and ruled the country perhaps more effectively than it had ever been ruled before; royal authority was extended in Borders, West Highlands and northern isles; James grafted on to a *presbyterian* system an episcopate which was a useful instrument in secular as well as ecclesiastical affairs. James's literary attainments were not negligible, and his patronage of poets did much to encourage literature. Acceded to English throne 1603. Cf. Union with England.

James VII (1633-1701). Second son of *Charles I*, born 14 October 1633; was in Scotland 1679 and 1680-2, when he acted as his brother's commissioner to the Scottish *Parliament*; on his accession in 1685 the country was effusively loyal, but James almost at once showed a determination to gain toleration for his Roman Catholic co-religionists, which was fatal to his position; when *William of Orange* landed in England, there was a general revulsion against James's government and a *Convention* declared that he had forfeited the throne (4 April 1689).

James, Duke of Berwick (1670-1734). Illegitimate son of *James VII* by Arabella Churchill; proved a very able general and was ultimately ennobled in Spain.

James Francis ('James VIII'), **The Old Pretender** (1688-1766). Only son of *James VII* by his second wife, Mary of Modena; born at Whitehall, London, 10 June 1688; sent off to France after *William of Orange* landed in England in November; in 1708 aboard a French fleet which approached the Scottish coast, but not put ashore; landed at *Peterhead* December 1715 to join *Earl of Mar*, but left from *Montrose* 4 February; spent most of his remaining life in Rome, where he died 1 January 1766.

James of the Glens. See Stewart, James.

Jameson, Andrew (1845-1911). *Advocate* 1870; *Lord of Session* (Ardwall) 1905.

Jameson, Robert (1774-1854). Born *Leith*; professor of natural history, *Edinburgh*, 1808; founded Wernerian Society 1808 and began 'Philosophical Magazine' 1819.

Jamesone, George (1589/90-1644). Born *Aberdeen;* apprenticed to decorative painter in *Edinburgh;* was painting portraits in Aberdeen from 1620; Aberdeen remained the centre of his life, but he painted a good deal in the south of Scotland, especially in the 1630s; the first of a continuous succession of Scottish portraitists.

Jamieson, John (1759-1838). Born *Glasgow*; *Anti-Burgher minister* there and in *Edinburgh*; published sermons and theology, produced outstanding 'Etymological Dictionary of the Scottish Language' (1808-9) and edited *Barbour* and *Blind Harry*; followed *Pinkerton* in believing that the *Picts* were Teutonic.

Jardine, Matheson and Company. Founded by Dr William Jardine (1784-1843), surgeon on an East Indiaman, who began trade in Canton c. 1829 and entered into partnership with *James Matheson* (1796-1878) c. 1827; trading in tea, the company was the first to establish a warehouse in Hong Kong.

Jarl. Scandinavian equivalent of Earl, in use particularly for rulers of *Orkney*.

Jarlshof (*Shetland*). The name, invented by

Walter Scott for a house at Sumburgh built by Earl *Robert Stewart*, is applied to a site which contains a remarkable series of layers of civilisations from the Stone Age, including round-houses and wheel-houses as well as a *broch* and houses of Scandinavian settlers.

Jedburgh. *Royal burgh* under *David I*; *mediatised* to Douglases in 14th century and resumed by crown 1455.

Jedburgh Abbey (*Augustinian*) (Roxburghshire). Founded by *David I* c. 1138 as a priory (following an earlier foundation at Old Jedburgh); an abbey c. 1154; suffered in English invasions, but most of the walls of the church remain; erected into *temporal lordship* for Alexander, *Lord Home*, 1606; *Blantyre*, *Canonbie* and *Restennet* were dependencies.

Jedburgh Castle. Existed in 12th century and was one of the fortresses handed over to England by *Treaty of Falaise*; place of death of *Malcolm IV* and of second marriage of *Alexander III*; demolished 1409 to deny its use to the English; jail erected on site 1823.

Jedburgh Friary (Observant *Franciscan*). Founded before 1505 by local nobles or *burgesses*; burned by English 1544, 1545.

Jedburgh Grammar School. Possibly originated in abbey, but supported by town council by 1557 and in 1638 the council ordained that boys should attend no other school.

Jedburgh Hand Ba'. Said to date from a Scottish victory over English when the victors used the heads of their enemies as footballs; between 'Uppies' and 'Doonies', according to residence above or below site of *mercat cross*; play extends from Castlehill to Townfoot.

Jedburgh Hospitals. The master of a Maison Dieu is mentioned 1296 and the institution mentioned as late as 17th century. There was another hospital or almshouse dependent on abbey, mentioned 1296-1575.

Jedburgh, Queen Mary's House. Associated with a visit in 1566 when *Mary* fell dangerously ill; a museum.

Jeddart Axe or Staff. Stout pole, 7 or 8 feet long, with an iron head formed into a hook and a hatchet.

Jeddart Justice. Hanging first and trying afterwards; said to date from 1608, when freebooters were executed at *Jedburgh* without trial.

Jeffrey, Francis (1773-1850). Born *Edinburgh*; *advocate* 1794; turned to literature and was one of the founders of the '*Edinburgh Review*', for which he wrote over 200 articles; as *Lord Advocate* (1830) had some responsibility for the *Reform Act* of 1832 and *Burgh Reform Act* of 1833; *Lord of Session* 1834.

Jenny Geddes. See Geddes, Jenny.

Jenny Ha's Change House. Tavern in *Edinburgh* in 18th century kept by Jenny Hall and frequented by John Gay, the English poet, when he was in Edinburgh under patronage of Duchess of *Queensberry*.

Jervise, Andrew (1820-78). Born *Brechin*; Examiner of Registers 1856; wrote 'Memorials of *Angus* and *Mearns*' (1861), 'The Land of the Lindsays' (1863) and other works on local history.

Jewish Cemetery, Old. In Braid Place, off Causewayside, *Edinburgh*, opened 1816.

Jinglin' Geordie. See Heriot, George.

Joan, Queen (1210-38). Daughter of King John of England and first wife of *Alexander II* (1221); had no children.

Joan, Queen (1321-62). Daughter of Edward II of England and first wife of *David II* (1328); in France with her husband 1334-41; had no children.

Joan, Queen (c. 1400-45). Daughter of John Beaufort, Earl of Somerset; married *James I* 1424; after his death married *James Stewart*, '*the Black Knight of Lorne*'.

Jocelin (d. 1199). Abbot of *Melrose*; *Bishop of Glasgow* 1175; obtained Glasgow's charter as a *burgh* and started new cathedral after one had been destroyed by fire.

'The Jocks'. See Scots Guards.

Jocteleg. Folding clasp-knife, introduced in Queen *Mary's* time by a Belgian, Jacques de Liège, of whose name 'jocteleg' is a corruption.

John (d. 1147). Possibly native of France; tutor to *David I* before his accession; *Bishop of Glasgow* probably 1118.

John de Sacro Bosco (fl. 1230), otherwise John of Holywood or Halifax; his identification as a monk of *Holywood* is doubtful; a distinguished mathematician at Paris University.

John, King of Scots (c. 1250-1313). Of Picard descent (see Balliol); son of *Devorguilla*; selected by Edward I from among the *Competitors* for the throne 1292; rebelled against Edward's overlordship 1296 and after battle of *Dunbar* resigned the kingdom; known then as 'Toom Tabard' or empty coat; captive in England for three years, then allowed to retire to his French estates.

John, 4th (and last) Lord of the Isles (d. 1498). The first of the line to hold title by direct royal grant (1476); son of Alexander, 3rd Lord (d. 1449); joined *Earls* of *Douglas* and *Crawford* against *James II* 1452 and in 1462 made *Treaty of Westminster-Ardtornish* with Edward IV;

forfeited 1475; restored to lordship but not to *earldom of Ross* 1476; gave trouble again in early years of *James IV*, but surrendered 1494 and ended his days in *Paisley Abbey*; had no lawful issue, but an illegitimate son, Angus Og, was killed about 1490, and Angus's posthumous son, *Donald Dubh*, survived until 1545 to become a 'Lord of the Isles' under Henry VIII's patronage.

John of Duns or **Duns Scotus** (c. 1265-c. 1308). Supposed to have been born at *Duns* and to have entered *Franciscan* order at *Dumfries*; captured by English and on his release went to Oxford, then to Paris and finally Cologne; won great renown as 'the subtle doctor', but philosophers of other schools held him in contempt and the word 'dunce' derives from his name.

John o' Groat. A Dutchman (Groot) who is said to have settled at the extremity of *Caithness* in the reign of *James IV*.

John Scotus or **Erigena** (fl. 850). Presumably an Irish 'Scot' and not a Scotsman; distinguished as a philosopher mainly at court of Emperor Charles the Bald.

John 'The Scot' (d. 1237). Son of *David, Earl of Huntingdon*; succeeded mother's brother as Earl of Chester; had no issue.

John Watson's School. Founded under bequest of John Watson, *Writer to the Signet*, 1759; was a foundling hospital but became a school housed in a building erected near *Dean Bridge* by *William Burn* 1825-8; later a co-educational school with both boarders and day pupils; closed 1975 as a result of government action.

'Johnnie Walker'. Named from a grocer who founded a whisky bottling firm in Kilmarnock in 1820.

Johnston, Alexander Keith (1804-71). Born Kirkhill, *Penicuik*; with his brother William (1802-88) founded map-producing firm of W. and A.K. Johnston 1826.

Johnston, Alexander Keith (1844-79). Son of preceding; continued geographical and cartographic work; explored in S. America and Africa.

Johnston, Archibald, of Wariston (1611-63). Born *Edinburgh*; *advocate* 1633; religious to verge of mania, but accepted existing church establishment until appearance of *Scottish Prayer Book* of 1637; a principal framer of the *National Covenant*; *Lord of Session* (Wariston) 1641; at *Westminster Assembly; Lord Advocate* 1646; *Clerk Register* 1649; opposed *Engagement* and acceptance of *Charles II* as King 1650; took part in *Cromwellian administration* and sat in last two *Protectorate* parliaments; condemned to death 1661, but had fled abroad; arrested in Rouen 1663 and executed at Edinburgh.

Johnston, Arthur (1587-1641). Son of laird of Caskieben, Aberdeenshire; graduated M.D. at Padua 1610; after twenty-four years' absence returned to Scotland and became rector of *King's College, Aberdeen*, 1637; Latin poet and scholar.

Johnston, James (1655-1737). Son of *Archibald J*; *Secretary of State* 1692-6.

Johnston, John (1570-1611). Educated *Aberdeen* and Rostock; professor of divinity at *St Andrews* 1593-1611; poet.

Johnston, Thomas (1882-1965). Born *Kirkintilloch*; Labour M.P. 1922-45; editor for 27 years of periodical 'Forward'; founder of *Scottish Home Rule Association* 1917; Regional Commissioner for Scotland 1939; *Secretary of State* for Scotland 1941-5; Chairman of Scottish Forestry Commission 1945-8; a founder of *Scots Ancestry Research Society*; wrote 'A History of the Working Classes in Scotland'.

Johnstone (Renfrewshire). *Police burgh* 1892.

Johnstone, James (1719-1800). 'The Chevalier de Johnstone'; born *Edinburgh*; aide-de-camp to *Charles Edward* 1745-6; wrote 'Memoirs' of the rising; escaped to continent after *Culloden* and joined French army, in which he served at Louisbourg and Quebec.

Johnstone's Highlanders. Five companies embodied at *Perth* as the 101st Regiment 1760; while under orders for Portugal in 1763 peace was made and the regiment disbanded.

Jolly, Alexander (1756-1838). Born *Stonehaven*; *Episcopalian minister* at *Turriff* and *Fraserburgh*; *Bishop of Moray* 1798.

Jones, John Paul. See Paul Jones, John.

Jougs. Iron collar, hung by chain in public place, often a church wall, to be fastened round the neck of a culprit; use abolished 1837.

Judicial Factor. An administrator appointed by *Court of Session* when, for example, a father has died without a settlement leaving his children in *pupil*larity ('factor loco tutoris'), when a party is resident abroad ('factor loco absentis'), or when a person is incapacitated from managing his affairs ('curator bonis').

Jura. See Hinba.

'Juridical Review'. Established *Edinburgh* 1889.

Juridical Society. Founded in *Edinburgh* 1773 for study of law and literature.

Jury. The sworn inquest was in use from *David*

I's reign and the jury for criminal cases is found under *Alexander II.*

Jury Court. Court for civil cases, on English model, established 1815, to act on remit from *Court of Session* or *Admiralty Court*; abolished 1830 and its functions transferred to Court of Session.

Justice Clerk. By the late 15th century the criminal courts, presided over usually by peers, had professional lawyers as clerks; when the High Court of Justiciary (see Justiciary Court) was organised in something like its present form in 1672, the Justice Clerk was second-in-command to the *Justice General*, and he has so continued; with the re-organisation of the *Court of Session* in the early nineteenth century he became also president of the Second Division of that court.

Justice, College of. *Court of Session* endowed as College of Justice 1532, on application by *James V* to the pope; from 1535 judges of the court have been *Senators* of the College, and the College nominally includes counsel practising in the court and others.

Justice General. The chief judge in criminal cases; the office, usually held by peers, was hereditary in the *Argyll* family 1514-1628; with the re-organisation of the court in 1672 the Justice General became usually a professional, and the office has been held in combination with that of *Lord President* from 1837.

Justices of the Peace. Foreshadowed 1587 and set up generally throughout the country 1609, but they were comparatively ineffective—except during the *Cromwellian administration*—until after the *Union.*

Justiciar. The officer to whom the King chiefly delegated jurisdiction in 12th century; there were sometimes two or three, for different areas (e.g., *Lothian, Scotia, Galloway*); justiciars went on *ayre* to supervise work of *sheriffs* and hear suits both in the first instance (if *Pleas of the Crown*) and on appeal; in the later middle ages the office passed into that of *Justice General.*

Justiciary Court. As organised in 1672, the court, supreme in criminal justice, consisted of the *Justice General, Justice Clerk* and five Commissioners of Justiciary (who were also *Lords of Session*); later all Lords of Session became Commissioners of Justiciary; the court still goes on circuit to hear cases elsewhere than in *Edinburgh.*

Jute. After some experiments from 1824, pure jute fabrics began to be woven in 1835, and the industry developed rapidly in *Dundee.*

K

Kames Castle (Bute). 14th century tower, belonging to Bannatyne family; later passed to Marquis of *Bute*; modern house added 1799.

Kames, Henry Home, Lord (1696-1782). Son of Berwickshire laird; *Lord of Session* (Kames) 1752; produced many books on legal and antiquarian subjects, but entered on philosophy with 'Essays on the Principles of Morality and Natural Religion' (1751); took practical interest in agrarian improvements, especially after succeeding to estate of Blair Drummond through his wife, and wrote 'The Gentleman Farmer' (1776).

Kay, Archibald (1860-1935). Born *Glasgow*; studied in Glasgow and Paris; painted chiefly Scottish scenes.

Kay, James (1858-1942). Born Arran; studied in *Glasgow*; exhibited in Paris and painted scenes in France and Scotland.

Kay, John (1742-1826). *Edinburgh* barber who turned his acquaintance with Edinburgh society to account through his talent for drawing, and etched in all some 900 caricatures from 1784; many of them published in 'Kay's Edinburgh Portraits'.

Keelie. A word for a kestrel or hawk, but some derive it from 'ghillie' (= outdoor servant); applied to rough townsmen.

Keeper of the Records. Nearly all the functions previously vested in the Lord *Clerk Register* were transferred in 1879 to the Deputy Clerk Register, an office which had existed since 1806; subsequently effective headship passed to the Deputy Keeper, who in 1928 became Keeper of the Registers and Records; last holder of office of Deputy Clerk Register died 1919; offices of Keeper of Records and Keeper of Registers created 1948, on division of functions of Keeper of Registers and Records. See also Register House.

Keil School. Independent boarding and day school for boys, originally situated in Kintyre and removed, after fire, to *Dumbarton* 1924.

Keir (Stirlingshire). Passed in 1488 from Leslies to a Stirling family, now *Stirling-Maxwell.*

Keiss Castle (Caithness). Remains survive of small 16th century tower, home of a *Sinclair* family which in 1681 succeeded to *earldom of Caithness*; later acquired by Sinclair of Dunbeath and new house built nearby.

Keith (Banffshire). *Burgh of regality* under *abbey of Kinloss*; new town laid out by *Earl of Findlater* c. 1750.

Keith Family. See Marischal.

Keith, George (c. 1639-1716). Born *Aberdeen*; became Quaker and missionary, associated with *Robert Barclay*; accompanied George Fox and William Penn to Holland and Germany.

Keith, George, 10th Earl Marischal. See Marischal.

Keith, George Skene (1752-1823). Born Aquhorsk, near *Aberdeen*; *minister* of Keith-Hall and Kinkell 1778-1822; wrote 'Weights, measures and coins' and 'General View of the Agriculture of Aberdeen'.

Keith House (East Lothian). Once a seat of Earls *Marischal*; passed to *Earls of Hopetoun*; timber used in its construction said to have been a gift from King of Denmark in late 16th century.

Keith, Field-Marshal James (1696-1758). Younger brother of 10th Earl *Marischal*; in *Jacobite* expeditions of 1715 and 1719; served in armies of Spain, Russia, and Prussia, where Frederick the Great made him a Marshal; killed at Hochkirch.

Keith, Sir John (d. 1714). 4th son of William, 6th Earl *Marischal*; held *Dunnottar Castle* against Cromwellian army; created Knight Marischal at *Restoration* and *Earl of Kintore* 1677.

Keith, Sir Robert (d. 1346). Received lands of *Keith* from King *John* 1294; joined *Robert Bruce* 1308 and became *Justiciar* and *Marischal*; latter office remained in his family; commanded cavalry at *Bannockburn*; killed at *Neville's Cross.*

Keith, Robert (1681-1756). Born near *Dunnottar*; tutor to 10th Earl *Marischal* and his brother *James* (*Field-Marshal*); ordained in *Episcopal Church* 1713; pastor to congregation in Edinburgh; consecrated 1727 to assist *Bishop of Edinburgh*; *Bishop of Caithness* and then of Fife (1733); *Primus* 1743; produced 'History of the Affairs of Church and State in Scotland' (1734) and 'Catalogue of Scottish Bishops' (1755).

Keith, Sir Robert (d. 1774). Son of laird of Craig, Kincardineshire; ambassador at Vienna 1748-58 and later at St Petersburg.

Keith's Highlanders. 87th Regiment, raised 1759, disbanded 1763; commanded by Robert Murray Keith and fought in Germany.

Keithhall Castle (Aberdeenshire). Earlier called Caskieben; purchased from Johnstone family by John Keith, later *Earl of Kintore*; a 16th century house later enlarged.

Keithick (Perthshire). *Burgh of barony* under *Coupar Angus Abbey* 1492.

Kelburne Castle (Ayrshire). Belonged to *Earls of Glasgow*, whose ancestors had held lands since reign of *Alexander III*; 17th century tower was enlarged by 1st Earl.

Kelheim. 'Scottish' abbey in Germany; in Irish hands until 1515; a Scottish monk there in early 17th century; in hands of *Ratisbon* until 1862. See Schottenklöster.

Kellach. See Cellach.

Kellie Castle (Fife). Mainly 16th and 17th centuries, but some earlier traces; belonged to *Oliphant* family for 250 years until acquired by *Erskines* 1613; restored by Professor James Lorimer and his son *Sir Robert*; Robert's son, Hew, turned it over to *National Trust.*

Kellie, Earldom. Created 1619 for Thomas Erskine of Gogar (1566-1639), grandson of John, 4th *Lord Erskine*; he had killed the Master of Gowrie at the time of the *Gowrie Conspiracy* and acquired lands of *Dirleton*; he became *Viscount Fenton* and Baron Dirleton 1604-6; on death of 10th Earl title passed to *Earl of Mar.*

Kello, John (d. 1570). *Minister* of Spott; strangled his wife one Sunday morning and hanged her on a hook in the *manse,* then preached his sermon as usual in church; he was not suspected, but a few weeks later he confessed and was hanged.

Kelly Castle (*Angus*). Belonged to Auchterlonies 1444-1630; aquired by *Earl of Panmure* 1679; 19th century mansion nearby.

Kelly House (Renfrewshire). Held by Bannatynes from 15th century until 1792, when it was purchased by John Wallace.

Kelso. Mentioned as *burgh* under abbey of K. 1237, but in 14th century as only a 'villa' or township; *burgh of barony* for Lord *Roxburghe* 1614.

Kelso Abbey (*Tironensian*) (Roxburghshire). Founded at *Selkirk* by Earl David (later *David I*) c. 1113 and moved to Kelso 1128; frequently damaged in war; erected into *temporal lordship* for Robert, *Earl of Roxburghe*, 1607.

Keltie Castle (Perthshire). Built in 16th century by Bonar family, who had held lands since 1454; purchased by John Drummond 1692; passed by marriage to *Earl of Airlie* 1812; still occupied.

Kelton (Dumfriesshire). *Burgh of barony* for Robert Johnstone 1705.

Kelvin, Lord. See Thomson, William.

Kemp, George Meikle (1790-1844). Son of shepherd at Ninemileburn, Midlothian; architect of *Scott* monument in *Edinburgh.*

Kenmore (Perthshire). There is no evidence to support the idea that there was a nunnery on an island at the east end of Loch Tay. Kenmore became a *burgh of barony* for *Earl of Breadalbane* 1694.

Kenmure Castle (New Galloway). A mainly 16th century structure on site of earlier stronghold of *Lords of Galloway*; held by *Gordons* of Lochinvar; a ruin since World War II.

Kenmure, Viscountcy. Created 1633 for Sir John Gordon (c. 1559-1634); 6th Viscount executed after the '*Fifteen*; his descendants bought the estates back and title was restored 1824, to become dormant 1847.

Kennedy Castle (Wigtownshire). Built by Kennedy family, *Earls of Cassillis*, 1607; passed to *Earls of Stair*; destroyed by fire 1716 and replaced by modern castle completed 1867.

Kennedy, Gilbert and John, Earls of Cassillis. See Cassillis.

Kennedy, James (c. 1408-65). Son of James Kennedy of Dunure and a daughter of *Robert III*; studied at *St Andrews* and Louvain; *Bishop of Dunkeld* 1437 and of St Andrews 1440; engaged on various diplomatic missions and as an adviser of *James II*; influential in *James III's* minority; founded College of St Salvator, *St Andrews*.

Kennedy, Kate. Reputed niece of preceding, she figures in students' festivity at *St Andrews*; behind the figure may really lie a bell called 'Katharine' which the bishop presented to his college.

Kennedy, Quentin (1520-64). Son of 2nd *Earl of Cassillis*; *Commendator* of *Crossraguel* 1548; condemned abuses in church in 'Ane Compendious Tractive' (1558), but disputed with Protestant reformers, including *John Knox*, whom he encountered at *Maybole* in 1562.

Kennedy, Thomas. *Kilmarnock* gunsmith who invented a meter for accurate measurement of water, 1852, and with John Cameron, clockmaker, founded firm of Glenfield and Kennedy, specialists in that field.

Kennedy, Walter (c. 1460-1508). Nephew of *James Kennedy*; poet who inspired *William Dunbar's* 'Flyting of Dunbar and Kennedy'.

Kennedy, William (1859-1918). Born *Paisley*; studied art in Paris; worked in *Stirling* and in *Glasgow*; painted many military subjects; a member of the *Glasgow School*.

Kennedy-Fraser, Marjorie (1869-1932). Daughter of David Kennedy; married A.Y. Fraser, headmaster of *Allan Glen's School, Glasgow*; spent much of her life collecting and editing songs from the Western Isles (published from 1909 onwards) and in giving recitals.

Kenneth mac Alpin (d. 858). Succeeded father as King of *Scots* 841 and later became King of *Picts* in circumstances which remain obscure; seems to have gained acceptance in Pictland from 843 onwards; invaded *Lothian* six times; moved headquarters of church from *Iona* to *Dunkeld*.

Kenneth II (d. 995). Brother of *Dubh*, a previous king; succeeded 971; acknowledged Edgar of England as his lord and received *Lothian*; killed near *Fettercairn*. See Fenella.

Kenneth III (d. 1005). A king, or at least a claimant, from 997, when he killed *Constantine III*; overthrown by *Malcolm II*, it is said at Monzievaird.

Kennoway (Fife). *Burgh of barony* for Preston of *Airdrie* 1663.

Kentigern (c. 520-?612). Legend relates that his mother was *Theneu* ('St Enoch'), daughter of a king of *Lothian*, and that he was brought up at *Culross* by St *Serf*. His missionary work seems to have been chiefly among the *Britons* of Wales and *Cumbria* (which included south-western Scotland), and he is the alleged founder of the church of *Glasgow*. His alternative name, 'Mungo', means 'dear friend'.

Keppoch (Inverness-shire). *Burgh of barony* for Mackintosh of Torcastle 1690.

Ker(r) Family. Name first appears c. 1190. The *Cessford* branch began with Andrew (d. c. 1482), previously known as 'of Altonburn'; Sir Andrew (d. 1526) fought at *Flodden* and became a *Warden of the Marches*; Sir Walter (d. c. 1582), also a Warden, was banished to France for his part in the murder of Walter Scott of *Buccleuch* (1552) and was active against *Mary*, Queen of Scots 1568-72. The *Ferniehirst* branch is authenticated from Thomas (d. 1484); the best known of this line was Sir Thomas (d. 1586), who supported Queen Mary's party, was *provost* of *Edinburgh* 1570 when that party was in the ascendant there, and, after a period of banishment, returned to join in the administration of *James Stewart, Earl of Arran*. The Cessford branch ultimately attained the *Earldom and Dukedom of Roxburghe* and the Ferniehirst branch the lordship of *Jedburgh* and the *Earldom and Marquisate of Lothian*.

Kerr, Henry Wright (1857-1936). Born *Edinburgh*; painted mainly in water colours, but also in oils, producing portraits and character studies.

Ker(r), John, of Kersland (1673-1726). Spy who acted for both the government and the *Jacobites*; died in prison.
Ker(r), John, Duke of Roxburghe. See Roxburghe.
Ker(r), Mark (d. 1584). Son of Sir Andrew K. of *Cessford* (d. 1526); *Commendator* of *Newbattle Abbey* 1557. His son, also Mark (d. 1609), was created Lord Newbattle 1591 and *Earl of Lothian* 1606.
Kerr, Philip Henry, 11th Marquis of Lothian. See Lothian.
Ker(r), Robert. See Ancram, Earl of, Lothian, Marquis of, and Roxburghe, Earl of.
Ker, Schomberg Henry. See Lothian, Marquis of.
Kerelaw Castle (Ayrshire). Belonged to *Earls of Glencairn*; sacked by *Montgomeries* of Eglinton in 15th century, and Eglinton Castle burned in retaliation; now a ruin.
Kessog, St (fl. c. 600). Traditionally an Irish follower of St *Columba* who was martyred near *Luss*.
Kettins (*Angus*). Parish church appropriated to *Trinitarian* friars, but not in itself a friary.
Kidd, Captain William (1650-1701). Born *Greenock*, son of a *minister*; skippered merchant vessels and settled in New York, where he married; commissioned as a privateer, he turned to piracy; captured and hanged at Wapping.
Kilbarchan (Ayrshire). *Burgh of barony* for Cunningham of Craigends 1704; a weaver's cottage of 1723 was acquired by *National Trust* 1957.
Kilberry Castle (*Argyll*). Built 1497; rebuilt and enlarged in 19th century.
Kilbirnie (Ayrshire). Passed by marriage from Barclays to Crawfords 1470, Lindsays 1661 and 4th *Earl of Glasgow* 1833; a *burgh of barony* for Crawford of K. 1642; a 14th century tower, with addition of 1627, accidentally burned 1757.
Kilblain, Battle of, 30 November 1335. Scots under *Sir Andrew Moray* defeated *Earl of Atholl* and other supporters of *Edward Balliol*.
Kilbrandon Report, 1973. Royal commission under Lord Kilbrandon recommended establishment of separate Scottish legislature.
Kilbride (Arran). *Burgh of barony* for *Duchess of Hamilton* 1668.
Kilbryde Castle (Perthshire). Seat of *Earls of Menteith* from c. 1460; bought by Campbell of Aberuchill 1669.
Kilbucho (Peeblesshire). *Burgh of regality* for Dickson of Hartree c. 1650.
Kilchurn Castle (Loch Awe, *Argyll*). Consists of tower erected by Sir Colin Campbell of Glenorchy (d. 1475), hall built by Sir Duncan Campbell of Glenorchy (d. 1513) and a number of later buildings, which received a certain unity at the hands of the *1st Earl of Breadalbane* in the 1690s; garrisoned by government 1745-6; abandoned as residence about that time.
Kilconquhar House (Fife). Originally L-shaped 16th century tower, added to later; probably built by *Sir John Bellenden, Justice Clerk*; later acquired by *Earls of Lindsay*.
Kildrummy (Aberdeenshire). A great 13th century castle of *Earls of Mar* came into hands of *Robert I* as guardian of the young Earl, his nephew; Robert's Queen sent there 1306 in care of King's brother Nigel, but the castle was taken, the queen imprisoned and Nigel executed. Suffered damage in 1640s, and largely dismantled after 1715. Kildrummy was a *burgh of barony* for Alexander Elphinstone 1509 and received another charter 1594.
Kilkerran (*Argyll*). Old name of *Campbeltown* (Cill Chiarain, church of Chiaran); Kintyre acquired early 17th century by *Campbells*, who changed name.
Killearnan, Hospital (Ross). Said to have been foundation of *Knights of St John*, but of this there is no evidence.
Killeith. Old name of Currie, Midlothian.
Killiecrankie, Battle of, 27 July 1689. *John Graham* of Claverhouse, Viscount Dundee, on behalf of *James VII*, defeated *General Mackay*, on behalf of *William of Orange*, but was mortally wounded.
Killin (Perthshire). *Burgh of barony* for *Earl of Breadalbane* 1694.
Killing Time. The years 1681-5, when the prosecution of the *Covenanters* reached its height.
Killochan Castle (Ayrshire). An earlier castle, built by *Cathcarts* of Carleton, to whom the lands were granted by *Robert I*, was replaced by another 1586; still occupied.
Kilmarnock (Ayrshire). *Burgh of barony* for *Lord Boyd* 1592; see also Dick Institute.
Kilmarnock Bank. Founded 1802, absorbed 1821 by *Hunters and Co.*, bankers of *Ayr*, and that firm amalgamated with *Union Bank* 1843.
Kilmarnock Bonnets. In 17th and 18th centuries *Kilmarnock* was famous for the weaving of bonnets, referred to by Richard Frank, an English visitor, in 1658.
Kilmarnock, Earldom. Created for William, 10th *Lord Boyd*, 1661; 4th Earl was *Privy*

Councillor to Prince *Charles Edward* in the '*Forty-Five*, Colonel of the Prince's Guard and later General; captured at *Culloden*, he was executed and his estates *forfeited*. The 5th Earl recovered the estates 1751 and in 1758 succeeded his great-aunt as 15th *Earl of Errol*, when he took the name *Hay*. Title remains dormant.

Kilmaurs (Ayrshire). *Burgh of barony* for *Earl of Glencairn* 1527. *Collegiate church* probably originated with endowment of three chaplainries in the parish church by William, Lord of Kilmaurs, 1413.

Kilmun (*Argyll*). *Collegiate church* founded by Sir Duncan Campbell of Lochawe 1441; *burgh of barony* for *Earl of Argyll* 1490.

Kilpatrick (Dunbartonshire). *Burgh of barony* for Hamilton of Orbiston 1672.

Kilpeter. See Houston, Renfrewshire.

Kilravock Castle (Nairnshire). Built c. 1460 by Hugh Rose of K; lands of K. made into *barony* 1474; additional house erected in 17th century.

Kilrenny (Fife). *Burgh of regality* 1578, but *royal burgh* by 1592.

Kilrimont. Old name for *St Andrews*.

Kilspindie (Perthshire). A reference to an 'abbot' in early 13th century points to earlier existence of a Celtic monastery.

Kilsyth (Stirlingshire). Belonged to cadet branch of *Livingstons* of Callendar from early 15th century; their castle now a ruin; *burgh of barony* for Livingston of K. 1620.

Kilsyth, Battle of, 15 August 1645. *Montrose* routed *Covenanters* under *William Baillie*.

Kilsyth, Viscountcy. Conferred on Sir James *Livingston* 1661; his second son, 3rd Viscount, *forfeited* after the '*Fifteen*.

Kilt. Now used to mean the '*feileadh-beag*' or 'little kilt', the lower portion of the older *belted plaid*. A garment of that general nature may have been used in the western isles from very early times, and its adoption by the Norwegian King *Magnus* in the 1090s would explain his name of 'Barelegs'. But the 'little kilt', consisting of 7 or 8 yards of cloth, pleated to fit round the waist, does not seem to be older than the late 17th century. There is no evidence to support the story that it was invented by an English employer of labour in the Highlands who saw the inconvenience of the voluminous belted plaid.

Kilwinning (Ayrshire). Formerly *burgh of barony*; *police burgh* 1889.

Kilwinning Abbey (*Tironensian*) (Ayrshire). Founded by Hugh de *Morville*, lord of *Cunningham*, 1140×1191; property erected into *temporal lordship* for *Earl of Eglinton* 1603; church used for parish purposes until 1775.

Kincardine (Kincardineshire). In parish of *Fordoun*; a castle, of which slight traces remain, was said to have been scene of murder of *Kenneth II* in 995; it was used as a residence by kings from 12th century to 14th, and in it *John Balliol* abdicated; it was demolished 1646. The town, still called 'the chief *burgh* of the county' when made a *burgh of barony* for Earl *Marischal* 1532, dwindled out of existence; the *mercat cross* was removed to *Fettercairn* c. 1730, and *Stonehaven* became the county town.

Kincardine [on Forth]. *Burgh of barony* for *Earl of Kincardine* 1663.

Kincardine [on Forth] **Bridge.** Built 1936 as part of a compromise scheme (in association with improved ferry at *Queensferry*) in place of a *Forth Road Bridge* at Queensferry.

Kincardine Castle (Perthshire). Near *Auchterarder*, originated with *Earls of Strathearn*, who were *Grahams*, and passed to another Graham family, *Earls of Montrose*; dismantled by *Earl of Argyll* 1645; new mansion built nearby in 19th century.

Kincardine, Earldom. (1) Conferred on *Earl of Montrose* 1644. (2) See Elgin.

Kincardine O' Neil (Aberdeenshire). Hospital founded c. 1231 and conferred on *Aberdeen Cathedral* as prebend 1330; *burgh of barony* 1511.

Kinclaven Castle (Perthshire). 13th century castle, held by English under Edward I and again under Edward III; captured by *Wallace* 1297; seems to have been neglected from 14th century and became a ruin.

Kind Gallows of Crieff. *Crieff* was the chief town of *Strathearn* and therefore the seat of justice of the Earls, and later Stewards, of Strathearn; the gallows still stood in 1796.

Kindly Tenants. Tenants, both numerous and widespread, who, without a formal long lease, in practice held their land for life and by hereditary succession, as a matter of well recognised custom. The term 'kindly' is associated with 'kin' and means hereditary. 'The King's kindly tenants' were a relatively insignificant group of such tenants in villages round *Lochmaben*.

Kindrochit Brooch. Dating from c. 1500, found in 1925 in the 'pit' of Sir Malcolm Drummond's tower at Kindrochit Castle, Aberdeenshire; about 3 inches across, it has an inscription in French translated 'Here am I in place of a friend'. Now in *National Museum of Antiquities.*

Kinfauns (Perthshire). Lands given by *Robert I* to Thomas de Longueville, '*The Red Rover*', who founded the family of Charteris, many of whom became *provosts* of *Perth*; passed to Carnegies, then Blairs, whose heiress married 12th *Lord Gray* 1741. Present castle, on site of earlier one, dates from 1822.

King, General James (1589-1652). Returned from service in Swedish army to join King's forces 1639; created Lord Eythin (or Ythan) 1642; returned to Sweden, where he died.

King's Advocate. See Lord Advocate.

King's Bedesmen. Privileged beggars, called 'Blue Gowns' from the colour of their garb; received cloaks, badges and alms from the king; entitled to beg throughout Scotland and not only in their own parishes like ordinary beggars.

King's Bishop. See Sinclair, William.

King's Cadger. Allegedly an officer who carried fish from *Earlsferry* to royal residence at *Falkland*, with a house in Newburn and rights of grazing for cow, pig, goose and gander. The 'King's Cadgergait' is well attested, but it was a king's highway like any other, used by cadgers or fish-carriers, and does not prove the existence of the office.

King's Cave, Larder and Stables. Caves in Arran, associated with *Robert I.*

King's College. See Aberdeen.

King's Confession. The 'Negative Confession' of 1581, drawn up during a 'Popish Scare' and vigorously denouncing all kinds of papistry; formed first part of *National Covenant.*

King's Covenant. Royal riposte to *National Covenant*, reciting *King's Confession* but omitting the new bond incorporated in the National Covenant.

King's Guard. A Guard, at least partly of archers, raised for *Mary* in 1561 and revived under *James VI*. See Archers.

King's House. Places in *Glencoe*, Balquhidder and Letterfinlay, said to be named from their use as bases by *Marshal Wade* when he was making his roads.

King's Kindly Tenants. See Kindly Tenants.

King's Life Guard of Horse. 'The private gentlemen of the King's Life Guard', raised on *Leith Links* 1661 under *Earl of Newburgh*; after 1707 became 4th Troop of Life Guards, but disbanded 1746.

King's Limner. Official painter to the King in Scotland.

King's Own Scottish Borderers. Raised 1689 by *Earl of Leven* to secure *Edinburgh* for *William of Orange*, and known as 'Leven's' or 'The Edinburgh' Regiment; after being the Sussex Regiment and the King's Own Borderers, received present title 1887.

King's Party. Supporters of *James VI* against those of Queen *Mary* 1568-73.

King's Quair (Book). Poem attributed to *James I* and written during his captivity in England, telling of his love for *Joan Beaufort*.

Kingcase Hospital (Ayrshire). May be of 14th century origin (see Bruce's Well), though not recorded until 1452; dedicated to St *Ninian* and originally a leper-house; later hospital for poor and infirm and was in existence until 18th century.

Kinghorn (Fife). *Royal burgh* 1165x1172; royal castle from same period, granted by *Robert II* to his son-in-law Sir John *Lyon*, whose descendant was in 1606 created Earl of Kinghorn and later of *Strathmore*; the castle has disappeared. A hospital, founded before 1478 and dedicated to St James, was further endowed by Robert Peirson, *burgess*, 1478.

Kinghorn, Battle of, c. 1040. Alleged defeat of Scandinavians by *Macbeth.*

Kingston, Viscountcy. Created for Alexander Seton, 4th son of 3rd *Earl of Winton*, 1651; extinct on death of 3rd Viscount 1726.

Kingussie (Inverness-shire). 13th century castle of the Comyn Lords of *Badenoch* passed to *Wolf of Badenoch* and then to *Earls of Huntly*, who built new castle in later 16th century. The place became a *burgh of barony* for Earl of Huntly 1464. *Ruthven* Barracks on site of castle.

Kingussie Friary (*Carmelite*) Founded by *Earl of Huntly* before 1501, but not recorded after 1531.

Kinkell Castle (Ross). 16th century tower of Mackenzies of *Gairloch*; became farmhouse and was later abandoned; restored as a home 1968.

Kinloss (*Moray*). *Burgh of barony* for Abbot of K., 1497.

Kinloss Abbey (*Cistercian*) (*Moray*). Founded by *David I* c. 1150; erected into *temporal lordship* 1601 for *Edward Bruce*, who became Lord Kinloss 1604; in 1650 the then owner, Alexander Brodie, sold the stones for erection of Cromwellian fort at *Inverness*.

Kinmont Willie. See Armstrongs.

Kinnaird (*Gowrie*, Perthshire). Granted in 1170s to Radulfus Rufus, whose descendants presumably took their name from the place and received title of Lord Kinnaird 1682; castle dates from 14th or 15th century, was renovated externally 1855 and, after being long roofless, has recently been restored; it was bought from Kinnairds by Threipland of Fingask 1674.

Kinnaird Castle (*Angus*). Built by Carnegie family, who acquired lands at beginning of 15th century; Sir Robert Carnegie created Lord C. of Kinnaird 1616 and *Earl of Southesk* 1633; estates and title *forfeited* after *'Fifteen*, but estates subsequently bought back and title restored 1855; castle mostly rebuilt at beginning of 19th century and enlarged 1854-60 by *David Bryce*.

Kinnaird (or **Kinnaird's**) **Head** (Aberdeenshire). A castle built by Sir Alexander Fraser of *Philorth* c. 1570 was made the base of a lighthouse 1787.

Kinnaird, Lordship. Created 1682 for George Patrick Kinnaird (d. 1689), a member of *Parliament* and *Privy Councillor*; 10th Lord (1814-87) was M.P. for *Perth* and a philanthropist.

Kinnear, Thomas, and Sons, Bankers. Began business 1748; joined in 1831 by Douglas Smith and Co. to become Kinnears, Smith and Co., but closed 1834.

Kinneff (Kincardineshire). The castle, of some importance in minority of *David II*, is represented only by some fragments. In the church the *Regalia*, smuggled out of *Dunnottar Castle* by Christian *Granger*, were buried for nine years.

Kinneil (West Lothian). The lands belonged to the Hamiltons from *Robert I's* reign; the house enlarged by *2nd Earl of Arran* and has mural paintings from his period; later *Anne, Duchess of Hamilton*, enlarged it again; part now roofless. *Dugald Stewart* lived there 1809-28 and *James Watt* made some of his experiments with the steam engine nearby.

Kinnoull (or Bridgend of Tay) (Perthshire). *Burgh of regality* for Viscount Dupplin 1706.

Kinnoull, Earldom. Created 1633 for George *Hay*.

Kinnoull, George Hay, 1st Earl of (1572-1634). Second son of Peter H. of *Megginch*, a descendant of the *Errol* family; gentleman of the bedchamber to *James VI*; knighted 1609; had patent for glass manufacture; *Chancellor* 1622; Viscount Dupplin and Lord Hay of *Kinfauns* 1627; Earl of Kinnoull 1633; buried in old church of Kinnoull, where there is a remarkable monument to him.

Kinross. Lands long belonged to *Douglases* (*Earls of Morton*), but acquired by *Sir William Bruce*, who built Kinross House 1685-92. The town was a *burgh of barony* for Douglas of *Lochleven* 1541 and a *burgh of regality* for Bruce of Kinross 1685. A hospital of either St Thomas or St Mary mentioned before 1184.

Kintore (Aberdeenshire). Castle used as royal hunting centre in 12th and 13th centuries; forest granted by *Robert I* to *Robert Keith*, his *Marischal*, 1309; a *royal burgh* under *William I* (1187x1200) received new charter 1506.

Kintore, Earldom. Created 1677 for Sir John Keith, 3rd son of 6th Earl *Marischal*; on death of 4th Earl, unmarried, title passed to distant kinsman, Anthony Adrian, 8th Lord Falconer of *Halkerton*.

Kintyre, Lordship. Created for James, son of 7th *Earl of Argyll*, 1626; he became *Earl of Irvine* 1642 and died without issue 1645.

Kintyre, Mull of. Lighthouse established 1787.

Kintyre Pursuivant. Possibly title had belonged to an officer of the *Lord of the Isles*, for a royal officer of the name is first mentioned 1494, after forfeiture of lordship in 1493. See Pursuivants.

Kirk o'Field. See Edinburgh, Kirk o'Field.

Kirk, Robert (c. 1641-1692). Succeeded father as *minister* of Aberfoyle; wrote 'The Secret Commonwealth of Elves, Faunes and Fairies' and was said to have been transported to Fairyland; made first complete translation of metrical psalms into *Gaelic* 1684.

Kirk Session. Composed of *elders* of congregation, with *minister* as *moderator*; responsible for exercise of discipline over members and in many instances for the general organisation of the congregation's affairs.

Kirkcaldy (Fife). *Burgh* under *Dunfermline Abbey* by 1304, but made its way into tax-roll of burghs and into *Parliament* by 1450 and received charter as *royal burgh* 1644; *Grammar School* under town council by 1569, possibly of pre-*Reformation* origin.

Kirkcaldy, Sir William, of Grange (c. 1520-73). Eldest son of Sir James K., who was *Treasurer* 1537-42 and an opponent of *Cardinal Beaton*; himself involved in Beaton's murder; captured and sent to France, where he distinguished himself as a soldier; returned to help reformers in their campaign 1559-60; joined rebellion against *Mary* and *Bothwell* 1567 and pursued Bothwell to *Shetland*, but did not approve of Mary's deposition and held *Edinburgh Castle* for her 1571-3; hanged after its fall.

Kirkcudbright. Apparently a *royal burgh* in 13th century and paid its *ferms* to exchequer 1330, but evidently *mediatised* to the *Douglases* until their fall in 1455, when it became a royal burgh again. A *Grammar School* is claimed to date from 1455, when it was started by the *Friary*, and its first record, 1576, shows that it was not new then; a new building of 1815 was called an *academy*. The *tolbooth*, of 16th-17th century date, is now used as a memorial to *Paul Jones*.

Kirkcudbright Castle. There are remains near the *burgh* (Castledykes or Castlemains) of what was probably a castle of the *Lords of Galloway* which passed to the *Balliol* family and then to the *Douglases* until their forfeiture in 1455; a castle was given by *James IV* to the burgh in 1508. But within the burgh a castle, still a massive ruin, was built in 1582 by Sir *Thomas Maclellan* of Bombie, whose ancestors had long held the *barony*.

Kirkcudbright Friary (Conventual *Franciscan*). Founded probably 1449x1458; property granted 1569 to *Thomas Maclellan* of Bombie, who turned it over to town council, and the church became the parish church.

Kirkcudbright, Lordship. Created 1633 for Sir William Maclellan of Bombie; dormant on death of 9th Lord 1832.

Kirkcudbright, Stewartry of. See Stewartry.

Kirkintilloch (Dunbartonshire). *Burgh* granted by *William I* to *William Comyn* 1211x1214; granted (with the lands) by *Robert I* to *Malcolm Fleming*, from whom it passed to Sir Gilbert *Kennedy* under *Robert II*, but it seems to have lost burghal status; re-erected a *burgh of barony* 1526.

Kirkintilloch Railway. From *Forth and Clyde Canal* to *Monkland*, 10 miles, opened 1826.

Kirkliston (West Lothian). *Burgh of regality* for *Earl of Winton* 1621. See also Liston.

Kirkmichael (otherwise Kirkhill, Kirkton or Tomlachan) (Perthshire). *Burgh of barony* for Wemyss of that *ilk* 1511.

Kirkton (or **Kirktoun**). The '*toun*' in the vicinity of the parish church. Cf. Clachan.

Kirkton, James (c. 1620-99). *Minister* at *Lanark* 1655, then at Mertoun; deprived 1662 and later had to flee to Holland; minister of Tolbooth, *Edinburgh* 1691; wrote 'Secret and True History of the Church of Scotland'.

Kirkwall (Orkney). Received charter as city and *royal burgh* 1486. The castle was built by Henry St Clair, *Earl of Orkney* from 1379, and demolished after failure of rebellion on behalf of *Earl Patrick Stewart* 1615 (see under Orkney); remains used to build town hall in 1745. Schools existed by 1486 and provision for both a *grammar school* and a *song school* was made when Bishop *Robert Reid* reorganised the cathedral constitution 1544.

Kirkwall Cathedral. Dedicated to St *Magnus* by its founder, his nephew Earl *Rognvald*; started 1137 and largely romanesque of 12th century; later additions, especially at west end, made until 16th century; skulls and some bones of both Magnus and Rognvald entombed in pillars.

Kirkwall Palaces. Bishop's Palace existed in 13th century and King Haakon the Old died there 1263; its ruins contain work so late as the period of Bishop *Robert Reid*. Earl's Palace was built by *Earl Patrick Stewart* (see under Orkney) and, though roofless, is a structure of outstanding quality.

Kirkwood, James (fl. 1700). Master of schools of *Linlithgow* (1675-90) and *Kelso*, from both of which he was dismissed in circumstances of which he published accounts; his edition of Despauter's Latin Grammar went through several editions.

Kirkwood, James (?1650-1708). Born *Dunbar*; *minister* of *Minto*, deprived for refusing *Test Oath* 1685; rector of Astwick, Bedfordshire, deprived as *non-juror* 1702; advocated parish libraries in 'An Overture for founding and maintaining Bibliothecks in every Paroch throughout the Kingdom' (1699).

Kirn. The usual Scots term for a churn, but the name was used also for the festival associated with the completion of the harvest, when at a kirn-feast the decorated last sheaf occupied a place of honour and dancing and singing followed.

Kirriemuir (Angus). *Burgh of barony* for *Earl of Angus* 1459 and *burgh of regality* for *Marquis of Douglas* 1670. The birthplace of *Sir James Barrie* was presented to *National Trust* 1937.

Kisimul Castle (Barra). Origin of this MacNeil stronghold now assigned to 13th century, but most of existing building is probably 15th century and later; abandoned as residence in mid-18th century, but in 1937 the ruins were acquired by a successful claimant to the MacNeil chiefship, and restoration carried out.

Kitchen of Angus. Nickname for *Edzell* Castle, owing to hospitality of Lindsay family.

Knight Marischal. See Keith, Sir John.

Knights Hospitallers. Had their headquarters in Scotland at *Torphichen.* See also Liston, Maryculter.

Knights of St John. See Knights Hospitallers.

Knights Templars. First established in Scotland at *Temple* by *David I*; on suppression by Pope in 1312 the property of the order passed to the *Knights Hospitallers.* See also Maryculter.

Knock Castle (Aberdeenshire). Simple tower in Glenmuick, probably late 15th century with some later modifications; belonged to a *Gordon* family and figured in their feuds with the *Forbeses*; roofless, but fairly complete.

Knock Castle (Ayrshire). Z-shaped structure of late 16th or early 17th century, owned by *Frasers* who had married the Knock heiress and then by *Montgomeries* (from 1640s) and others; partly restored.

Knockhall Castle (Aberdeenshire). Built 1565 by Henry, Lord Sinclair of *Newburgh;* sold 1633 to *Udny* family; captured by *Covenanters* 1639; accidentally burned 1734; roofless, but walls fairly complete.

Knox, Andrew (1559-1633). *Minister* of *Paisley*; *Bishop of the Isles* 1605-18; played part in government action for pacification of the Isles and in Bond and Statutes of Icolmkill (see under Iona, Bond etc.); Bishop of Raphoe 1611-33.

Knox Institute. See Haddington, School.

Knox, John (?1512-72). Priest who attached himself to *George Wishart* and then joined murderers of *Cardinal Beaton* in *St Andrews Castle*; on fall of castle sent to French galleys; on his release (1549) became a preacher of note in the Protestant England of Edward VI, and escaped when Mary Tudor succeeded, to settle in Geneva; returned to Scotland 1559 to take part in the anti-French and anti-papal revolution and became *minister* of *Edinburgh*; his 'History of the *Reformation*' constitutes his Memoirs, and contains many documents.

Knox, John (1720-90). Became a bookseller in London, published works on Scottish fisheries and was active in fostering fisheries and manufactures in Scotland.

Knox, John (1778-1845). Painted many scenes in *Glasgow* and the *Clyde* estuary, including 'At Glasgow Cross' (1826), 'Old Glasgow Bridge' (1816-7) and 'The First Steamboat on the Clyde'.

Knox, Robert (1791-1862). Born *Edinburgh*; after medical service with the army, became keeper of the Anatomy Museum in Edinburgh 1825; his responsibility for the purchase of corpses for dissection led him into dealings with *Burke* and *Hare*, who committed murders to sell corpses, and he incurred much odium, but was exonerated by Burke in his confession and by a committee of enquiry; failed to gain a chair in Scotland and was latterly pathologist at Cancer Hospital, Brompton, London.

'Knox's House'. A house near the Netherbow, *Edinburgh*, dating from late 16th century; it seems at some date to have belonged to one Knox, and became popularly known as 'Knox's House' and so associated with the reformer; but the reformer's *manse* was near his church of *St Giles* and there is no evidence that he ever lived in this building at the Netherbow. See Mossman, John.

Krames. Wooden booths erected between the buttresses of *St Giles' Church, Edinburgh*, for the sale of wares of all kinds.

Kyle. The middle district of Ayrshire, between *Cunningham* and *Carrick*; the River *Ayr* divided it into Kyle Stewart on the north and King's Kyle on the south; a bailiary in the middle ages.

Kyle, James Francis (1788-1869). Born *Edinburgh*; professor at college at *Aquhorthies* 1808; vicar apostolic in the Highlands 1827; made a collection of documents relating to Roman Catholicism in Scotland.

L

Labour Party. The Scottish Labour Party founded 1906 from Scottish Workers' Parliamentary Election Committee (1900); merged with British Labour Representation Committee 1909; obtained two Scottish seats 1906. Cf. Independent Labour Party.

Ladle Duty. Ladleful of meal or grain taken from each load brought to market for sale; lasted until c. 1846.

Lady Mary Fair (*Dundee*). Held on week beginning 15 August, the feast of the Assumption of the B.V.M.

Lady's Rock. Between *Oban* and Mull. Lachlan *MacLean* of *Duart* attempted to drown his wife, a daughter of the 2nd *Earl of Argyll*, by marooning her on this tidal rock, but she was rescued.

Ladykirk (Ayrshire). The so-called 'preceptory' was only a chapel (founded 1446), not connected with *Knights Templars*.

Ladykirk (Berwickshire). Said to have been founded c. 1500 by *James IV* to commemorate his escape from drowning in the Tweed and to have been built wholly of stone to make it immune from fire; tower by *William Adam* 1743.

Laigh. Low. The Laigh of *Moray* is the fertile coastal plain.

Laigh Parliament Hall (*Edinburgh*). Undercroft of *Parliament Hall*; used to house prisoners after *Dunbar* (1650), as place of torture by *Privy Council* after 1660 and to house some of the records from 1661 until they found a home in the *Register House*; became part of *Advocates' Library* 1870.

Laing, Alexander (1787-1857). The 'Bard of Brechin'; son of agricultural labourer in *Brechin*; a flax dresser until disabled by an accident; edited *Burns* and *Tannahill* and published his own songs and verses in 'Wayside Flowers' 1846.

Laing, David (1793-1878). Son of *Edinburgh* bookseller and joined his father's business; Librarian of *Signet Library* 1837; secretary of *Bannatyne Club*; edited many volumes for that club and others; his MSS. now in Edinburgh University Library.

Laing, Eppie (fl. 1630). Native of *Anstruther*; burned as witch for raising storm which drowned the architect of the first lighthouse on the *May* Island.

Laing, Malcolm (1762-1818). Son of *Orkney* laird; *advocate* 1785; wrote 'History of Scotland' 1800, with appendix attacking authenticity of *Macpherson's 'Ossian'*; in 'The participation of *Mary*, Queen of Scots, in the Murder of *Darnley*' (1804) he adjudged Mary guilty; M.P. for Orkney.

Laing, Samuel (1780-1868). Brother of preceding; served in army and travelled in Scandinavia; translated 'Heimskringla', the sagas of the Norse kings (1844).

Laird's Loft. Part of a church, either specially constructed or set apart to accommodate the principal *heritor* and family, often with an ornate pew and sometimes with a retiring room.

Laird's Stable. Cave on coast of *Moray*, once the home of a hermit; used as stable by Sir Robert Gordon of *Gordonstoun* in the *'Forty-five*.

Lamb, Andrew (fl. 1560). *Leith* merchant, to whose house *Mary*, Queen of Scots, was taken when she landed at Leith in 1561; the building now known as 'Andrew Lamb's House' is, however, of later date, though a splendid example of burghal architecture. See Leith, Lamb's House.

Lamberton, William (d. 1328). *Chancellor* of *Glasgow* 1292; *Bishop of St Andrews* 1297; assisted at coronation of *Robert I*.

Lamington (Lanarkshire). Named from Lambin, a Fleming who held it under *Malcolm IV*; granted 1368 to William Baillie, whose descendant became Lord L. 1880. Lamington Tower, traditionally associated with *William Wallace*, occupied until c. 1750.

Lammas. Celtic autumn festival, on 1 August; identified with feast of St Peter ad Vincula; associated with *hand-fasting*. See Term Days.

Lamond, William (1857-1924). Born *Newtyle;* worked in *Dundee* painting portraits, marine subjects and landscapes.

Lamont Family. Name derived from Norse word for a 'lawman'; occurs as Christian name in 13th century and as surname in 15th; powerful in *Cowal* until massacred by *Campbells* 1646. See also Dunoon.

Lamont Harp. A *clarsach* dating from 15th century, now in *National Museum of Antiquities.*

Lamont, John. Author of Diary for 1649-71, sometimes called 'The Chronicle of Fife'.

Lamont, John (1805-79). Native of *Braemar*; educated at Scots monastery at *Ratisbon*; member of Munich Academy of Sciences 1827; astronomer to King of Bavaria and ennobled as Von Lamont; commemorated by monument at Inverey, between Braemar and Linn o' Dee.

Lamp of Lothian. Apparently originally the *Franciscan Friary* at *Haddington*, though this has been disputed; name apt to be used of parish church of Haddington (*St Mary's*).

Lanark. Possibly *royal burgh* under *David I* and certainly under *William I*; castle, presumably dating from same period and visited by 12th century kings, was occupied by English in *War of Independence* until recovered by *Robert I* 1310, but has long disappeared. Lanark became a member of *Court of Four Burghs* after loss of *Berwick* and *Roxburgh*. The *Grammar School* was apparently in existence in 12th century.

Lanark Common Riding. On 'Lanimer Day', early in June, men and boys marched to one of the *burgh* boundaries, where novices were ducked in a river and boughs of birch cut to carry in procession which returned to cross; later town council and others rode the marches (see March Ridings). A 'Lanimer Queen' was elected to take part.

Lanark Friary (*Franciscan* Conventual). Founded by *Robert I* 1325-9; lands leased to James Lockhart of *Lee*.

Lanark Hospital. Dedicated to St Leonard, mentioned under *Alexander II*; property granted by *Robert III* to Sir John Dalziel 1392, but preceptorship continued and in 1636 some of the lands were acquired by town.

Lanark Silver Bell. Said to have been presented to *burgh* by *William I*, but hallmarks on it do not go back beyond 16th century and the oldest shield attached to it, with the name of the owner of the winning horse, is dated 1628.

Lanark Spurs. On Lanimer Day (see Lanark Common Riding) a race is run for this trophy by horses belonging to *burgesses.*

Land. Tenement or house in *burgh*, usually of several storeys.

Land Court. See Scottish Land Court.

Land League. See Highland Land League.

Lang, Andrew (1844-1912). Native of *Selkirk* who after a long university education and the offer of a Fellowship at Merton turned to journalism and lived mainly in London, where he poured out books on an astonishing variety of subjects, from folklore and classical scholarship to biographies and other historical works, including a four-volume 'History of Scotland' (1900-7) and 'The Mystery of *Mary* Stuart' (1901).

Lang, Cosmo Gordon (1864-1945). Son of John Marshall Lang (1834-1909), Principal of *Aberdeen University*; born Tyrie *Manse*, Aberdeenshire; Bishop of Stepney 1901, Archbishop of York 1908, Archbishop of Canterbury 1928; Lord Lang of Lambeth 1942. His brother, Marshall Lang (1868-1964), *minister* of *Whittinghame*, was *Moderator* of the *General Assembly* of the *Church of Scotland* 1935.

Lang Dykes or **Lang Gaitt.** Road running along north side of *Nor' Loch*, *Edinburgh*, on site of modern Princes Street.

Lang Herdmanston (East Lothian). Fight in which Sir David *Fleming* of *Cumbernauld* was killed by Sir James *Douglas*, 14 February 1406.

Langholm (Dumfriesshire). *Burgh of barony* for *Earl of Nithsdale* 1621; *burgh of regality* for Duchess of *Buccleuch* 1687.

Langside, Battle of, 13 May 1568. *Regent Moray* defeated supporters of *Mary*, Queen of Scots.

Langton (Berwickshire). *Barony* granted to Sir Alexander Cockburn 1394, with erection of *burgh* which does not seem to have operated; *burgh of barony* again created for Cockburn of L. 1510 and 1542.

Lanimer Day. See Lanark Common Riding.

Lantern of the North. *Elgin Cathedral*.

Larg (Kirkcudbrightshire). Granted 1619 to Sir Patrick McKie, with burgh of *Minnigaff.*

Largo (Fife). *Barony* conferred by *James III* on *Sir Andrew Wood* 1482; *burgh of barony* for Wood of L. 1513; passed in 1663 to Sir Alexander Durham, with whose family it remained until 1868.

Largs (Ayrshire). *Burgh of barony* for *Alexander* of *Menstrie* 1629. See also Skelmorlie.

Largs, Battle of, 2 October 1263. A detachment from the Norwegian fleet was defeated by Scots when some of their ships were driven ashore; King Haakon, the Norwegian leader, returned to *Kirkwall*, where he died.

Lasswade (Midlothian) **Hospitals.** (1) St Mary's, founded by *Robert Blackadder*, *parson* of L., 1478; (2) St Leonard's, see Dalhousie.

Lauder (Berwickshire). *Royal burgh* under *William I.* Hospital, founded by Richard de *Morville* 1175x1189, absorbed in *Dryburgh Abbey* in early 15th century.

Lauder Bridge. Scene of murder of some of *James III*'s favourites in 1482, by nobles led by *Archibald, 5th Earl of Angus*; the victims included *Robert Cochrane* and William Roger, a musician, but *Sir John Ramsay* and *James Hommyl* were not killed.

Lauder Family. Named from place, where they were established in 13th century; one of them held the *Bass* by 1297.

Lauder, Sir Harry Maclennan (1870-1950). Born *Portobello*; worked as flax-spinning hand in *Arbroath* (where he first appeared on the stage in 1882) and as miner in *Hamilton*; gained great popularity first as an amateur in *Glasgow* and its vicinity and became an international figure who typified the stage Scotsman; did much to entertain troops in World War I; knighted 1919.

Lauder, Sir John, of Fountainhall (1646-1722). *Advocate* 1668; counsel of *9th Earl of Argyll* 1681; *Lord of Session* (Fountainhall) 1689; M.P. for East Lothian 1685-1707; opposed *Union*; wrote 'Diary', printed 1840; compiled 'Decisions of Court of Session'.

Lauder, Robert Scott (1803-69). Born Silvermills, *Edinburgh*; married daughter of *John Thomson* of *Duddingston*; studied art in Edinburgh and abroad; in London 1838-52, then settled in Edinburgh; chiefly noted for historical paintings.

Lauder, Thomas (1395-1481). *Bishop of Dunkeld* 1452; finished nave of cathedral, built *chapter* house and part of tower; built bridge at Dunkeld 1461; wrote biography of Bishop John the Scot and a volume of sermons; was preceptor to *James II*; at one stage Highland *caterans* made him retire to *Perth* and administer his diocese from there.

Lauder, Sir Thomas Dick (1784-1848). Son of Sir Andrew L. of Fountainhall; served in *Cameron Highlanders*; lived in the Grange,

Edinburgh; secretary of *Board of Trustees for Manufactures* 1839 and encouraged foundation of technical and art schools; wrote 'The Wolfe of *Badenoch*' (1827), 'Morayshire Floods' (1830) and other works.

Lauder, William (1520-73). Priest who joined reformers and became *minister* at *Forgandenny*; wrote several volumes of poetry.

Lauderdale. Granted by *David I* to de *Morville* family, by *Robert I* to *Sir James Douglas* and returned to crown on fall of Douglases 1455.

Lauderdale, Earldom and Dukedom. Earldom created 1624 for John Maitland, 2nd Lord *Thirlestane*; dukedom conferred on *2nd Earl* 1672 and extinct on his death, but earldom passed to his brother, Charles Maitland of Haltoun (d. 1691), who held many offices in the Duke's administration and was denounced for corruption.

Lauderdale, John Maitland, 2nd Earl and 1st Duke of (1616-82). Son of 1st Earl, succeeded 1645; joined *Covenanters* against *Charles I*; a framer of *Solemn League and Covenant* 1643 and a Scottish commissioner to *Westminster Assembly*; a party to *Engagement* and after death of Charles I persuaded *Charles II* to come to terms with Scots; captured at *Worcester* and a prisoner until 1660; *Secretary of State* for Scotland 1661-80 and King's commissioner to *parliaments* from 1669; personally inclined to *presbyterianism*, but attempted to destroy opposition to episcopal settlement by alternate measures of conciliation and repression; the corruption of his regime, and the venality of his second wife, the *Countess of Dysart*, strengthened the political opposition to him and when the ecclesiastical opposition erupted in the *Bothwell Brig* rising he was superseded (1680).

'Laud's Liturgy'. Term erroneously applied to the *Scottish Prayer Book* of 1637, which owed most of its characteristics to *Charles I* personally and two Scottish bishops—*John Maxwell* of *Ross* and *James Wedderburn* of *Dunblane*; Laud had pressed for the adoption in Scotland of the English Prayer Book.

Laurence of Lindores (c. 1372-1437). Presumably born at *Lindores*; distinguished graduate of Paris; lectured at *St Andrews* from the opening of the university there; dean and rector; his lectures famous on continent; Inquisitor of Heretical Pravity, under whom *Paul Craw(ar)* was burned. See 'Heretics'.

Laurencekirk (Kincardineshire). *Burgh of barony* for Lord Gardenstone 1779.

Lauriston Castle (*Edinburgh*). Incorporates 16th century tower (built by *Sir Archibald Napier of Merchiston*) in a modern mansion which was presented to the city in 1926. The lands had belonged to a family which took its name from them, before passing to *Forresters of Corstorphine* (1456) and Napiers; in late 17th century acquired by *John Law*.

Lauriston Castle (Kincardineshire). An early castle, captured by the English 1336, belonged to Straton family until 1695; almost entirely superseded by 19th century house.

Law, Andrew Bonar (1858-1923). Born in New Brunswick, of Ulster father and Scots mother; educated *Glasgow*; became *iron* merchant; M.P. from 1900; Unionist leader 1911; Chancellor of the Exchequer 1916; Prime Minister 1922-3.

Law, James (c. 1560-1632). *Minister* of *Kirkliston* 1585; *Bishop of Orkney* 1605 and played an important part in integrating the islands into the Scottish administration; *Archbishop of Glasgow* 1615.

Law, John, of *Lauriston* (1671-1729). Descendant of preceding and son of an *Edinburgh* goldsmith; after a turbulent youth emerged as writer on economic subjects 1700, advocating reliance on paper currency; his schemes were not accepted in Scotland, but he was influential on the continent and, besides making a fortune by gambling, he induced the Regent Orleans to establish the Bank of France 1716 and a West India Company, to exploit the Mississippi area, 1717; Comptroller General of France 1720, but his schemes led to confusion and bankruptcy.

Law Society of Scotland. Founded 1815.

Lawson, James (1538-84). A *regent* in *St Andrews University*; succeeded *John Knox* as *minister* of *Edinburgh*; supported *presbyterian* programme and in 1584, at the time of the '*Black Acts*', fled to England, where he died.

Lead Mining. Possibly started by Romans and certainly carried on in 13th century; systematic work went on from 16th century and mining was carried on at Wanlockhead (Dumfriesshire) 1680-1959; in 1810, 1400 tons of lead were produced.

Leadhills (or Hopetoun) (Lanarkshire). *Burgh of barony* for *Duke of Hamilton* 1661.

Leckie House (Stirlingshire). Land belonged to Leckies from 14th century until 1659, when it was bought by David Moir, with whose family it remained until early 20th century; the house, built in 16th century, was visited by Prince *Charles Edward* when his army encamped nearby in 1745.

Lee (Lanarkshire). Lands acquired by Flemish family of Loccard (Lockhart) in 12th century; the old castle rebuilt 19th century.

Lee, John (1779-1859). Born Stow; professor of church history at *St Andrews* 1812-21; *minister* of *Canongate*, Edinburgh, 1821; professor of divinity 1843-59 and principal of *Edinburgh University* 1840-59.

Lee Penny. A red heart-shaped jewel, set in a shilling of Edward I, said to have been brought back by *Simon Lockhart of Lee* after his expedition with *Sir James Douglas* to carry *Robert I*'s heart to Spain, or perhaps in an earlier crusade when it had been given by a Saracen woman as her son's ransom; it was supposed to have curative powers.

Lee, Robert (1804-68). Born Tweedmouth, educated *Berwick* and *St Andrews*; *minister* of Inverbrothock 1833, Campsie 1836 and *Old Greyfriars, Edinburgh*, 1843; his attempts to enrich public worship and his preparation of a service-book (1857) led to proceedings against him; he was professor of biblical criticism in Edinburgh from 1847 and was one of the founders of the Church Service Society in 1864.

Leechman, William (1706-85). Born Dolphinton; *minister* of Beith 1736; professor of divinity at *Glasgow* 1743, principal 1761; followed the trend towards a more liberal theology.

Legerwood Hospital (Berwickshire). Apparently founded by 1177, and mentioned 1296 but not otherwise known.

Leighton, Alexander (1568-1649). After education at *St Andrews* and Leyden, practised as physician in England and wrote ultra-puritan works, including 'Zion's Plea against Prelacy' (1630), for which he had an ear cut off by order of the Star Chamber.

Leighton, Alexander (1800-74). Born *Dundee*; editor of 'Tales of the Borders' and author of 'Romance of the Old Town of *Edinburgh*'.

Leighton, Henry (d. 1440). *Bishop of Moray* 1415 and of *Aberdeen* 1422; built nave, western towers and north transept of *Aberdeen Cathedral*.

Leighton Library (*Dunblane*). Some 1400 volumes bequeathed by *Robert Leighton* for use of the clergy of diocese and added to since.

Leighton, Robert (1611-84). Son of *Alexander Leighton*; *minister* of *Newbattle* 1641; antipathetic to *Covenanting* extremes; principal of *Edinburgh University* 1653; *Bishop of Dunblane* 1661; his attempts at 'accommodation' with the *Presbyterians* had little result, and his translation to *Glasgow* (1669) did nothing to conciliate the extremists of south-west; resigned 1674 and retired to England.

L'eine-Chròich. The saffron-coloured shirt which was formerly part of the Highlander's dress.

Leishman, Thomas (1852-1904). Born *Govan*; *minister* of Linton, Teviotdale, 1855-95; active in movement to enrich public worship and with *G. W. Sprott* published edition of '*The Book of Common Order*'.

Leith. Land and harbour granted to *Holyrood Abbey* by *David I*; rights in harbour granted to *burgh* of *Edinburgh* by *Robert I* 1329; South Leith held by *Logans* of *Restalrig* under Holyrood, North Leith directly under abbey; *burgh of barony* with Edinburgh as *superior* 1636; independent *parliamentary burgh* 1833; amalgamated with Edinburgh 1920.

Leith Academy. *Grammar School* mentioned 1521 and presumably associated with St Mary's Church (founded c. 1486); governed by *kirk session* from 1560; new buildings 1806; name changed to Leith *Academy* 1888; present building 1931; became a non-selective district school 1973.

Leith Bank. Established 1792; had many branches, but failed 1842.

Leith, Citadel of. Cromwellian fort in North Leith was known as the Citadel; area erected into *burgh of regality* for *Earl of Lauderdale* 1662.

Leith Docks. East and West Old Docks created just before and after 1800; Victoria, Albert and Edinburgh followed, and the Imperial 1910.

Leith Family. Established in Aberdeenshire from 13th century; in 1650 James Leith built Leith Hall, which remained with the family (latterly Leith-Hay) until 1945, when it was presented to *National Trust*.

Leith Fort. Built 1779 for defence against descent of *Paul Jones*; used as barracks until mid-twentieth century.

Leith, House of St Anthony. Hospital erected 1418 for *Augustinian* friars, probably by Sir Robert *Logan* of *Restalrig*; designed for treatment of sufferers from 'St Anthony's disease' (erysipelas); some of the property went to John Hay 1591, but charity continued.

Leith, Lamb's House. See Lamb, Andrew. Bought by 4th *Marquis of Bute* 1938, presented to *National Trust* 1958.

Leith Links. Originally the grass-covered sand behind the shore to the east of the town, they were the nearest natural golf course to the capital and were used by kings down to *James VII*; the Company of *Edinburgh Golfers*, founded 1744, played there, and golf continued until late 19th century. In 1560, when the Scots and English were besieging the French in Leith, they raised artificial artillery mounds on the Links, remains of which can still be seen.

Leith Races. Held on Leith Sands, east of the town, from reign of *James VI* and annually from 1665, until 1856 (except between 1816 and 1836), when they were transferred to *Musselburgh*; patronised and presumably organised by *Edinburgh* town council.

Leith, St Nicholas Chapel and Hospital. The chapel of St Nicholas mentioned 1488, but there is no evidence of supposed associated hospital.

Leith, Siege of. See Leith Links.

Leith, Treaty of. See Edinburgh, Treaty of (2).

Leith, Trinity House. In existence from 14th century as charitable foundation, receiving dues from vessels known as '*prime gilt*' and disbursing charity to mariners; sculptured stones of 1555 still to be seen; present building dates from 1816. For a time it had extensive powers in licensing pilots, but latterly has been again reduced to the administration of charitable funds, now (since abolition of prime gilt in 1862) derived from property and investments.

Lekprevik, Robert (d. 1588). Printer in *Edinburgh* in 1560s and King's Printer 1568.

Lennox Castle (Midlothian). A castle, now in ruins, in the parish of Currie, which at one time belonged to *Earls of Lennox* and later to *George Heriot*.

Lennox, Earldom and Dukedom. The district, of old Levenax, consisted mainly of the later Dunbartonshire; there was a Celtic earldom or *mormaer*dom; Earl Malcolm supported *Robert I* and was killed at *Halidon*; a later Earl Malcolm was executed with his son-in-law *Murdoch, Duke of Albany*; Sir John Stewart of Darnley, grandson of a sister of Duke Murdoch's wife, was created Earl 1473 and died 1495; Matthew, 2nd Stewart Earl, killed at *Flodden* in command of right wing; John, 3rd Earl, killed in attempt to free *James V* from *Earl of Angus*, 1526. Dukedom created 1581 for *Esmé Stewart* and on death of 6th Duke without surviving heirs (1672) reverted to *Charles II*, who bestowed it in 1675 on one of his natural sons, who was already (1672) Duke of Richmond. The 6th Duke of Richmond and Lennox was created Duke of Gordon 1876.

Lennox, Esmé Stewart, 1st Duke of (c. 1542-83). Son of John, 3rd son of *3rd Earl of Lennox,* and so a first cousin of *Lord Darnley*; his father had succeeded to the lordship of Aubigny in France, where he spent most of his life c. 1544-67; Darnley's younger brother, Charles, died 1576, leaving only a daughter, Arabella, and King *James VI's* nearest kinsman on the male side, after an aged great-uncle, *Robert Stewart, Bishop of Caithness*, was Esmé; when the latter arrived in Scotland in 1579 he was welcomed by the King, Bishop Robert resigned the *earldom of Lennox* to him and in 1581 he was created Duke; suspected of being a Roman Catholic agent, his influence raised a kind of Popish Scare which produced the *Negative Confession*; overthrown by *Ruthven Raid* and died in France. His son Louis, or Ludovick (1574-1624), came to Scotland, and Esmé's daughter married *1st Marquis of Huntly*.

Lennox, Matthew Stewart, 4th Earl of (1516-71). Succeeded his father, 3rd Earl, 1526; spent some years in France, but returned 1543 as rival to *2nd Earl of Arran*, who was governor, and when the latter abandoned the English alliance Lennox became an English agent; his activities led to his forfeiture (1545) and exile in England for nearly twenty years; married 1544 Margaret Douglas (1515-78), daughter of *Margaret Tudor* by *6th Earl of Angus*, and their son, *Lord Darnley*, thus stood next to *Mary*, Queen of Scots, in the English succession; Lennox was allowed to return to Scotland 1564; after Darnley's murder he went back to England, but became Regent with English backing 1571; shot in an affray at *Stirling* 4 September 1571.

Lennoxlove (East Lothian). Formerly Lethington, a home of the Maitland family from 14th century and incorporating a medieval tower; bought in 18th century by Lord Blantyre, who changed the name; acquired by *Duke of Hamilton* 1947.

Lerwick (*Shetland*). *Burgh of barony* for inhabitants 1818.

Leslie (Aberdeenshire). Granted in 12th century to a Flemish family who took name Leslie; from them it passed by marriage to Forbes of *Monymusk*, who built a castle 1661, and then to the *Leiths* of Leith Hall; *burgh of barony* for Forbes of Leslie 1649.

Leslie (Fife). Of old called Fettykil; held by Leslie family (later *Earls of Rothes*) from *Alexander III's* reign; Leslie or Leslie Green became *burgh of barony* 1457 and was confirmed as such to Earl of Rothes 1539; house built by *Duke of Rothes* was largely burned down 1763, but remainder of it preserved as dwelling house.

Leslie, Alexander, Earl of Leven. See Leven.

Leslie, Andrew, George and John, Earls of Rothes. See Rothes.

Leslie, David, Lord Newark. See Newark.

Leslie, George (d. 1637). Capuchin friar, called Father Archangel; sent from Scots College, *Rome*, on mission to Scotland c. 1624 and, after a period when he had to flee to France, returned to Scotland 1631.

Leslie (or Lesley), John (?1527-96). Son of priest who was an ecclesiastical judge, and followed in his footsteps, with training at Toulouse, Poitiers and Paris; *Lord of Session* 1564; *Bishop of Ross* 1566; supported Queen *Mary* and acted for her at York and Westminster 1568-9, but was equivocal in religion; involved in plot against Elizabeth and imprisoned for a time; went to France; Bishop of Coutances 1592; wrote 'A Defence of the Honour of.... Mary' (1569) and 'History of Scotland' (1578).

Leslie, John (1766-1832). Born *Largo*; his researches into heat and other topics ultimately brought him the chair of mathematics and *natural philosophy* at *Edinburgh*, after a prolonged dispute about his orthodoxy which was famous as 'The Leslie Case'.

Leslie, Norman (d. 1554). Master of *Rothes*; a leader of the murderers of *Cardinal Beaton*; sent as prisoner to France, but escaped to England; killed at Cambrai.

Leslie, Walter, Count Leslie (1606-67). Soldier of fortune and diplomat.

Lesmahagow (Lanarkshire). *Burgh of barony* for *Anne, Duchess of Hamilton*, 1668.

Lesmahagow Priory (*Tironensian*). Founded by *David I* 1144 as dependency of *Kelso Abbey*; included in erection of Kelso for *Earl of Roxburghe* 1607 but transferred to *Marquis of Hamilton* 1623; church served as parish church until 1803.

Lethington. See Lennoxlove.

Letters of Fire and Sword. See Fire and Sword.

Letters of Horning. See Horning.

Leuchars (Fife). No vestiges remain of castle on site known as Castle Knowe, where the de *Quincy* family had their seat in 12th century after marrying local heiress. The church has some of the finest Norman work in Scotland.

Levellers. In 1724, after landlords in Dumfriesshire and *Galloway* had evicted tenants and enclosed their holdings as grazing for cattle, bands of men pulled down the dykes; the episode seems to have retarded agrarian 'improvement' in the area.

Leven (Fife). *Burgh of barony* for *Lauder* of the *Bass* 1609; *police burgh* 1867.

Leven, Alexander Leslie, 1st Earl of (c. 1580-1661). Illegitimate son of George L., captain of *Blair Atholl* Castle; became Field-Marshal in Swedish army; joined *Covenanters* 1638 and commanded their armies against *Charles I*; on a pacification created Earl of Leven 1641, but led Covenanting army into England 1644; opposed *Engagement* but supported agreement with *Charles II* 1650; captured by English 1651 but liberated on parole 1654; succeeded by grandson, Alexander (c. 1637-64) and then by two great-granddaughters.

Leven, David Melville, 3rd Earl of. See Melville, Earl of.

Leven, Earldom. Created 1641 for *Alexander Leslie*; on death of his great-granddaughter title passed to David, son of *George, 1st Earl of Melville*, by sister of Alexander, 2nd Earl of Leven.

Leverhulme, William Hesketh Lever, 1st Lord (1851-1925). Born Lancashire; entered father's grocery business; took up soap manufacture 1884 and developed it and many other projects on an enormous scale; bought *Lewis* from Duncan Matheson 1917 and *Harris* in 1919; his many schemes for improvement of agriculture and fishing were nearly all thwarted by local opposition and when he withdrew in 1923 he had lost £1,500,000.

Lewis. Belonged to branch of *MacLeods* until 1599, when *James VI* annexed it and attempted its 'plantation' by Lowlanders, but this was not a success and in 1610 the '*Fife Adventurers*' sold out to the Mackenzies of Kintail, from whom it was bought in 1844 by *Sir James Matheson*. See also Leverhulme.

Lewis Grassic Gibbon. See Mitchell, James Leslie.

Leyden, John (1775-1811). Born Denholm, Roxburghshire; contributed to 'Edinburgh Literary Magazine' and assisted *Walter Scott* with 'Border Minstrelsy'; assistant surgeon at Madras 1803-5; died in Java.

Liddell, Duncan (1561-1613). Born *Aberdeen*; had distinguished career at Danzig, Frankfurt-on-Oder, Breslau, Rostock and Helmstadt, in logic, mathematics and astronomy, but his chief reputation was in medicine; his 'Ars Medica' (Hamburg 1607) reissued 1624 and 1628; returned to Scotland c. 1607; bequeathed to *Marischal College, Aberdeen* property to found bursaries and chair of mathematics and also his books and instruments.

Liddesdale, Knight of. See Douglas, Sir William.

Lifters. *Ministers* in the late 18th century who caused controversy by elevating the elements in the Communion.

Lifting. Return of cattle to outdoor grazing in the spring, when, it was said, some were so weak after their winter starvation diet that they had to be lifted to their feet.

Limner. See King's Limner.

Lincluden (Kirkcudbrightshire). *Benedictine* nunnery founded by Uchtred, *Lord of Galloway*, before 1174; suppressed 1389 in favour of *collegiate church* at instance of *Archibald Douglas, Lord of Galloway and Earl of Douglas*; annexed to *chapel royal* 1508-29; property passed to William *Douglas* of *Drumlanrig* and Robert *Gordon* of *Lochinvar*; for attached hospital, see Holywood.

Lindores Abbey (*Tironensian*) (Fife). Founded c. 1191 by *David, Earl of Huntingdon*; *9th Earl of Douglas* was confined there for his last years; erected into *temporal lordship* for Patrick Leslie, who had become *commendator* on death of *John Leslie, Bishop of Ross*.

Lindores. Lordship. Created 1600 for Patrick Leslie (see preceding); 2nd Lord died unmarried and was succeeded by his brother; dormant on death of 8th Lord 1813.

Lindsay, Alexander, 1st and 2nd Lord Spynie. See Spynie.

Lindsay, Alexander, 4th Earl of Crawford. See Crawford.

Lindsay, Lady Anne (1750-1825). Eldest daughter of 5th *Earl of Balcarres*; wrote ballad of 'Auld Robin Gray' 1771.

Lindsay, Colin, 3rd Earl of Balcarres. See Balcarres.

Lindsay, David, 5th Earl of Crawford and Duke of Montrose. See Crawford.

Lindsay, Sir David (?1486-1555). Son of David Lindsay of the Mount, near *Cupar*; a 'familiar' of the court under *James IV* and in childhood of *James V*; herald from 1530, *Lyon* and a knight by 1542; employed in various embassies; his works mostly satirical, with a moral purpose, and combine castigation of abuses in church and state with an appeal to the King and others to use their offices worthily: '*The Satire of the Three Estates*', 'The Dreme', 'The Complaynt', 'The Tragedy of the Cardinal', 'The Testament of the Papyngo', 'Kitteis Confessioun' and 'Squire Meldrum'.

Lindsay, David (c. 1531-1613). Related to *Earls of Crawford*; member of English congregation at Geneva in 1550s; *minister* of *Leith* 1560; superintended various districts and was six times *moderator* of the *General Assembly*; a mediator, he approved of episcopal government in 1572 and 1584; officiated at marriage of *James VI*; received revenues of *bishopric of Ross* 1600 and consecrated 1611.

Lindsay, Earldom. Created 1633 for *John, 10th Lord Lindsay* of the Byres; combined with *Earldom of Crawford* 1644-1808.

Lindsay, James Bowman (1799-1862). Lecturer on mathematics and physics at Watt Institute, *Dundee*; patented wireless telegraphy system.

Lindsay, James Ludovic, Earl of Crawford. See Crawford.

Lindsay, John (1552-1598). 2nd son of 9th *Earl of Crawford*; held revenues of *parson*age of Menmuir, but was not in orders; *Lord of Session* (Menmuir) 1581; *Secretary of State* 1596; an '*Octavian*'; prepared '*Constant Platt*'.

Lindsay, John, 1st Earl of Lindsay (1596-1678). 10th Lord L. of the Byres; created Earl 1633; joined *Covenanters* and fought at Marston Moor 1644; succeeded to *Earldom of Crawford* 1644.

Lindsay, Ludovic, 16th Earl of Crawford. See Crawford.

Lindsay, Patrick, 6th Lord Lindsay of the Byres (d. 1589). Supported *Reformation*; in plot to murder *Riccio*; took active part in compelling Queen *Mary* to abdicate; a party to *Ruthven Raid*.

Lindsay, Robert, of Pitscottie (c. 1532-80). Laird of estate near *Ceres*, Fife, but a very obscure figure; his 'Historie and Cronicles of Scotland', extending from 1436 to 1575, begins with a translation of *Boece's* 'History' for 1436-60, continues as a compilation from other writings and narratives the author had heard from his seniors and finally, from 1542, is a valuable contemporary account, reflecting his Protestant standpoint.

Linen. Industry already important before 1707, but much fostered in 18th century by *Board of Trustees for Manufactures*; though largely driven from the west by *cotton*, it remained important in Fife and *Angus* until after the First World War. See also Design.

Linklater, Eric (1899-1975). Son of Robert L. of Dounby, *Orkney*; studied medicine at *Aberdeen*; wounded in World War I; his many works included novels like 'Poet's Pub' and

'Juan in America', a biography of '*Mary*, Queen of Scots', accounts of his experiences in both World Wars and 'The Survival of Scotland'.

Links. Grass-covered sand, especially on east coast, the natural home of golf.

Linktown (Fife). *Burgh of barony* for Ramsay of Abbotshall 1663.

Linlithgow. *Royal burgh* c. 1138; became member of *Court of Four Burghs* 1369. Burgh school existed 1187 and in 16th century had as its master *Ninian Winzet* (or Winyet).

Linlithgow Almshouses. (1) In existence before 1448, identifiable with one in the Kirkgate in 1578 which was destroyed in Cromwellian period: (2) Founded by Henry Livingston 1496 outside the east port; nothing known of its operation. See also Hospital.

Linlithgow (or Linlithgow Bridge), Battle of, 4 September 1526. 3rd *Earl of Lennox*, trying to rescue *James V* from 6th *Earl of Angus*, was defeated and killed.

Linlithgow Common Riding. In early June; formerly associated with appointment by magistrates of a *baron bailie* of *Blackness*; now mainly a ride to the Bridge and to Blackness, where a 'head court' is held on the Castlehill.

Linlithgow Convention. Meeting of clergy 1606 which approved *James VI's* plans for *Constant Moderators*.

Linlithgow, Earldom. Created 1599 for Alexander, 7th Lord *Livingston*; 4th Earl succeeded by his nephew, 4th Earl of *Callendar*, who was *forfeited* after the '*Fifteen*.

Linlithgow Friaries. (1) *Augustinian*: donations recorded to Augustinian friars 1503, but no evidence of settlement. (2) *Carmelite*: founded c. 1401 by Sir James Douglas of *Dalkeith*. (3) *Dominican*: possibly, but not certainly, in existence for brief period c. 1500.

Linlithgow, George Livingston, 3rd Earl of (1616-90). Sat in Cromwellian parliament 1654; major-general of Scottish forces; *Justice General* 1684-9. See Cromwellian Administration.

Linlithgow, George Livingston, 4th Earl of (c. 1652-95). Supported *James VII* at *Revolution*.

Linlithgow Hospital. First mentioned 1335; dedicated to St Mary Magdalene, for the poor; master mentioned 1563-4 but lands alienated before 1591. See also Linlithgow Almshouses.

Linlithgow, Marquisate. Created 1902 for 7th *Earl of Hopetoun*, Governor General of Australia 1900; 2nd Marquis was Viceroy of India 1936-43.

Linlithgow Palace. Castle and royal residence in 12th century; occupied by English but retaken 1313 by stratagem of William Binnock; building operations by most kings from *James I* to *James VI*, especially *James V* (who erected great hall) and James VI (who erected north range); James V and Queen *Mary* born there; burned by government forces after Battle of *Falkirk* 1746.

Linlithgow, St Michael's Church. *Collegiate* constitution proposed by *James I* 1430, but not carried out.

Linlithgow, Wheat Firlot. Measure of capacity, made of wood and hooped with brass, containing (in 1754) 21 pints and 1 mutchkin of the *Stirling* jug, or 73 lbs. ¾ oz. French Troyes weight of *Edinburgh* fountain water.

Linoleum Manufacture. Started at *Kirkcaldy* by Michael Nairn 1847.

Linton (Roxburghshire). *Barony* belonged to *Somervilles* from reign of *Malcolm IV* if not *David I*; Tower, which stood near parish church, destroyed in *Hertford's Invasions*.

Lion. There is no evidence that the Lion was adopted as a heraldic device by *William I*, but it appears on the seal of the *Guardians* in 1286 and shortly thereafter it was explicitly used to symbolise the Scottish monarchy.

Lion. Gold coin from *James II's* reign, increasing in value from 5s. to 44s; Lion Noble = 75s; also equivalent to '*hardhead*' under *Mary* and *James VI*.

Lion of Glamis. Loving cup in shape of rampant lion, at *Glamis* Castle.

'Lion of the Covenant'. See Cameron, Richard.

Lippy. Measure of capacity varying from 1 to 2 pints.

Lipton, Sir Thomas (1850-1931). Born *Glasgow*; founded grocery business with small shop at Finniston 1870; it grew into Liptons Ltd. (1885); acquired tea and rubber estates; owned racing yachts; knighted 1898; baronet 1902.

Lismore. Island in Firth of *Lorne* associated with *Moluag*; cathedral (dedicated to Moluag) erected for bishopric of *Argyll* in 13th century; choir, much altered, survives as parish church.

Lismore, Dean of. See MacGregor, James.

Lispund. Weight in *Orkney and Shetland*, varying between 12 and 32 lbs.

Liston (Mid and West Lothian). *Barony* held by *Knights Hospitallers*; see also Kirkliston.

Liston, Sir Robert (1742-1836). Born *Kirkliston*; tutor to sons of *Gilbert Elliot*; had notable career in diplomatic service, at Madrid (1785-88), Stockholm (1788-93), Constantinople (1793-6) and Washington (1796-1802).

Liston, Robert (1794-1847). Son of Henry L. (1771-1836), *minister* of Ecclesmachan and inventor of a type of organ; surgeon at *Royal Infirmary, Edinburgh*; professor of clinical surgery, London, 1834.

Lithgow, Sir James (1883-1952). Son of William L., shipbuilder at *Port Glasgow*, and with his brother Henry took charge of firm 1908; Director of Merchant Shipping 1917; reorganised firm after 1919, took control of *Beardmores* (steelworks) and *Fairfields* (shipbuilding) 1936-7; baronet 1925; member of Scottish Development Council (see Scottish Council); Controller of Merchant Shipbuilding and Repair in World War II.

Lithgow, William (c. 1582-1650). Born, educated and buried at *Lanark*; known as 'lugless Will' because his ears had been cut off as a punishment; travelled widely in Europe and Near East and wrote account of his travels, published 1614.

Little, Clement (d. 1580). *Advocate* 1560; one of the original *commissaries* of *Edinburgh* 1564; left his library to *ministers* of Edinburgh and it formed the nucleus of the library of *Edinburgh University*.

Livingston (West Lothian). Named from an Englishman who settled there in early 12th century; its proprietors, the Livingston family, became *Earls of Callendar* and *Linlithgow*; *burgh of barony* for *Earl of Linlithgow* 1604.

Livingston, Sir Alexander (d. 1450). Rose to sudden eminence in minority of *James II*, at first in association with *Sir William Crichton*, whom he subsequently displaced from the leadership of affairs; he and his family gained many offices in the later years of the minority and were suddenly overthrown 1450.

Livingston, George, 3rd Earl of Linlithgow. See Linlithgow.

Livingston, James, 1st Earl of Callendar. See Callendar.

Livingston, Mary (c. 1535-c.1585). Daughter of Alexander, 5th Lord L; one of 'the Queen's *Maries*'; married John Sempill, a son of *Robert, 3rd Lord Sempill*, 1565.

Livingstone Family. A totally different name from the Lowland Livingston: anglicised version of name of people in *Appin* and *Lismore*.

Livingstone, Charles (1821-73). Brother of *David L*; emigrated to America; joined his brother on African expedition 1857-63.

Livingstone, David (1813-73). Born *Blantyre*; worked in *cotton* mill; educated *Anderson's College* and *Glasgow University*; joined London Missionary Society; carried out exploration from Cape of Good Hope 1840-3, as far as Zambesi, and from 1852 to 1856 worked northwards into west-central Africa; consul at Quilimane 1858; further expedition to Lakes Shirwa and Nyasa; published 'Zambesi and its Tributaries' 1864; from 1865 preoccupied with search for sources of Nile, and, after being once brought back by Stanley (1871), returned and died in Africa.

Lix (Perthshire). Name does *not* derive from the 59th milestone on General *Wade*'s or any other road, but means 'the hard slope'. Lands belonged to *Charterhouse*, passed to a *Campbell* family 1573, were sold to *Earl of Perth* 1684, *forfeited* 1746 and acquired by *Earl of Breadalbane* 1766.

Lizars, John (c. 1787-1860). Professor of surgery, Royal College of *Surgeons*, Edinburgh, 1831; wrote 'A system of anatomical plates of the human body'. His brother, William Home (1788-1859), was a painter and engraver.

Loanhead (Midlothian). *Burgh of barony* for Sir John Nicolson of Lasswade 1669; *police burgh* 1884.

Loch an Eilean Castle (Inverness-shire). Once a stronghold of the *Wolf of Badenoch*.

Loch Arkaig Treasure. A store of 40,000 louis d'ors which arrived on 3 May 1746, too late to help the '*Forty-Five*; buried at Loch Arkaig, its ultimate disposal remains mysterious.

Loch, David (d. 1780). Inspector General of Woollen Manufactures in Scotland, and later of Fisheries; wrote pamphlets and essays on trade, commerce etc. of Scotland.

Loch Doon (Ayrshire-Kirkcudbrightshire). On an island was a castle which was a *Balliol* stronghold in 13th century and passed to *Bruces*; when the water-level was raised for hydro-electric purposes it was taken down and re-erected on the shore.

Loch, James (1780-1855). *Advocate* 1801; M.P. for *Wick* 1830-52; as an estate manager, engaged on reorganisation of *Sutherland* estates, in which he devolved a good deal on *Patrick Sellar* and others.

Loch Ness Monster. First mentioned by *Adamnan* in 7th century; recent series of reported sightings date from 1932.

Loch Tay. Island granted to priory of *Scone* by *Alexander I* 1122-4, but no evidence of religious house on island.

Lochaber. Ancient district in south Inverness-shire, bounded by Perthshire, *Argyll*, the Great Glen and *Badenoch;* never an administrative district.

Lochaber Axe. Weapon like a halberd, with a

long cutting edge on one side and a hook on the other, which could be used to pull horsemen from their mounts.

Lochgilphead (*Argyll*). *Police burgh* 1892.

Lochindorb Castle (*Moray*). A castle of round towers and linking curtain walls, held by *Comyns* in 13th century; occupied by English 1303 and again 1335, when *Andrew Moray* besieged it unsuccessfully; stronghold of *Wolf of Badenoch*; later held by *Douglases* and destroyed on their fall 1455.

Lochkindeloch. Parish in which *Sweetheart Abbey* is situated.

Lochleven Castle (Kinross-shire). Tower dates from 14th century, with 16th century additions; held by Scots against English troops 1335; Queen *Mary* imprisoned there June 1567-May 1568, when it was the property of Sir William Douglas of Lochleven. See Douglas, George and 'Willie'.

Lochleven Priory (*Augustinian*). A Celtic foundation, to which gifts were made in 11th century, was transferred to Augustinian canons by *David I* c. 1150; dependent on *St Andrews Priory*; property conferred on *St Leonard's College, St Andrews*, 1580; also known as Portmoak; a hospital nearby which existed in 13th century became known as *Scotlandwell*.

Lochmaben. Took place of *Annan* as chief *burgh* of *Bruces'* lordship of *Annandale* and had a castle (presumably *motte-and-bailey*) in 12th century; passed to *Randolph,* Earl of Moray, as Lord of Annandale, then to *Douglases*; returned to crown by 1447; some ruins of castle remain; *barony* and keepership of castle conferred on *John Murray,* afterwards *Earl of Annandale*, 1612.

Lochmaben (Dumfriesshire), Battle of, 22 July 1484. Alexander, Duke of *Albany*, and *James, 9th Earl of Douglas*, invaded Scotland but were defeated.

Lochnaw Castle (Wigtownshire). Original castle on island in loch, later one on the shore; Patrick *Agnew* appointed constable of King's castle of Lochnaw 1330, and the family were hereditary *sheriffs* of *Wigtown* 1451 to 1747.

Lochore Castle (Fife). On an island in a loch, which has been drained; said to date from Duncan of Lochore c. 1160, and later held by Wardlaws. The place has been claimed as the site of a battle between Romans and Caledonians in 79 A.D.

Lochryan (Wigtownshire). *Burgh of barony* for *Agnew* of Lochnaw 1701.

Lochwarret, Locherworth, Lochorwart. Old name of *Borthwick*.

Lochwinnoch (or Semple). *Collegiate church* founded 1504.

Lockhart Family. See Lee.

Lockhart, Sir George, of *Carnwath* (c. 1630-89). Son of Sir James L. (d. 1674), *Justice Clerk*; *advocate* 1656; 'sole attorney' (equivalent of *Lord Advocate*) under *Cromwellian administration* 1658; knighted 1663; associated with opposition to *Lauderdale* 1674, 1679; defended *James Mitchell* and Archibald Campbell, *9th Earl of Argyll*; *Lord President* 1685; murdered by John Chiesley of Dalry.

Lockhart, George, of *Carnwath* (1673-1731). Son of preceding; opposed *Union* and supported *Jacobite* and *Episcopalian* causes; a commissioner for Union, but did not sign the Articles; M.P. for *Edinburgh* 1708-15; arrested as Jacobite 1715; later fled to Holland; killed in duel; wrote 'Memoirs concerning the Affairs of Scotland', which give Jacobite point of view on Union.

Lockhart, John Gibson (1794-1854). Born Cambusnethan; *advocate*, but his uselessness as a speaker made him turn to literature; married *Sir Walter Scott's* daughter, Sophia; contributed to '*Blackwood's Magazine*' and edited 'Quarterly Review'; wrote 'Life of *Burns*', 'Life of Scott' and a novel, 'Adam Blair'.

Lockhart, Sir Simon, of Lee (fl. 1330). Accompanied *Sir James Douglas* on his mission with *Robert I's* heart.

Lockhart, Sir William, of Lee (1621-75). Brother of *Sir George L.* (d. 1689); fought against *Charles I*, but was knighted by him 1646 and joined the *Engagement*; fought at *Preston* and *Worcester* but submitted to *Commonwealth* 1652 and appointed a commissioner for justice in Scotland; married Cromwell's niece and sat in *Protectorate* parliaments; ambassador to France, commander of English troops at siege of Dunkirk and governor of Dunkirk; played little part after *Restoration*, but was ambassador to France again 1674.

Logan Family. First appear c. 1200, mainly in south-west; a Logan acquired barony of *Restalrig* by marriage in early 14th century.

Logan, John (1748-88). Ordained 1773 to parish of South *Leith*; composed some paraphrases, edited *Michael Bruce's* poems and wrote 'Ode to the Cuckoo'.

Logan, Sir Robert and Sir Walter (fl. 1330). Companions of *Sir James Douglas* on his mission with *Robert I's* heart.

Logan, Sir Robert, of *Restalrig* (d. 1606). Forfeited after his death for his part in the *Gowrie Conspiracy*; owned *Fast Castle* and was reputed to have buried a treasure there.
Logie, Margaret. See Drummond.
Logierait (Perthshire). *Burgh of regality* for *Earl of Atholl* 1671.
Lollius Urbicus. Roman commander who built *Antonine Wall*.
London and Edinburgh Shipping Company. Founded 1809; operated ships until 1959.
London, Treaty of, 4 December 1423. Provided for release of *James I* from his English captivity, for a ransom of £40,000 payable in six annual instalments, and for the cessation of reinforcements to Scottish troops in France.
Longforgan (Perthshire). *Burgh of barony* for Earl of *Kinghorn(e)* 1672.
Longmuir, John (1803-83). Born *Stonehaven*; schoolmaster; ordained in *Aberdeen* 1840; compiler of revised edition of Scottish Dictionary of *Jamieson*.
Longnewton (Roxburghshire). *Burgh of barony* for *Earl of Lothian* 1634.
Lord Advocate. Chief law-officer of crown, with complete discretion over prosecution for crimes; also advises government on Scottish legal matters and for a considerable period in 18th and 19th centuries was in effect the head of the Scottish administration. The office dates from 1478 and the officer was long known as 'King's Advocate'. See Solicitor General.
Lord Angus Regiment. See Scottish Rifles.
Lord Chancellor. See Chancellor.
Lord High Commissioner. The representative of the sovereign, formerly at both *Parliament* and *General Assembly*, and still appointed each year to the latter.
Lord Justice Clerk. See Justice Clerk.
Lord Justice General. See Justice General.
Lord Lyon King of Arms. See Lyon King of Arms.
Lord of the Isles. See Isles, Lordship of.
Lord President. The presiding judge of the *Court of Session* since its endowment as the College of *Justice* in 1532; initially he had to be a cleric, but this restriction was abolished by *Parliament* 1579; office combined with that of *Justice General* since 1837.
Lords of Parliament. From the reign of *James I*, when it proved impracticable for all the King's tenants to attend *Parliament* and it was proposed that lesser tenants should be represented, it became the practice to summon individually certain greater tenants, so constituting in effect a new grade of peers, below the rank of earls.
Lords of Session. The judges of the *Court of Session*. Originally there were fifteen ordinary lords, but extraordinary lords were appointed until 1723. Seven of the original fifteen, as well as the *Lord President*, were to be 'spiritual men', but this distinction did not long survive the *Reformation*, and a statute of 1640 (rescinded in 1661) ordained that all ordinary lords were to be laymen. The last clerical lord was Archbishop *Alexander Burnet*, an extraordinary lord, 1664-8. By reforms of the early 19th century the number of judges was reduced to thirteen, composing an Outer House of five (each hearing cases individually) and an Inner House of Two Divisions (to hear appeals). The number was increased again to fifteen in 1948, and other increases have been made since, to bring the total to 21.
Lords of the Articles. See Articles.
Lords of the Congregation. Dated from the *First Bond* of December 1557; term generally applied to the leaders of the revolution of 1559-60.
Loretto. See Musselburgh.
Lorimer, James (1818-90). *Advocate*; professor at *Edinburgh*; wrote 'The Institutes of Law' and 'The Institutes of the Law of Nations'.
Lorimer, Peter (1812-79). Professor of theology in English Presbyterian College, London; wrote '*John Knox* and the Church of England'.
Lorimer, Sir Robert Stoddart (1864-1929). Son of *James L*; apprenticed to Sir Robert Rowand *Anderson*; his architectural work lay largely in restoration, especially of castles, but also of churches (see Paisley Abbey and Perth, St. John's); his most notable original works were the *Thistle Chapel*, *Edinburgh* (1911), and the Scottish National War Memorial, *Edinburgh Castle* (1928); knighted 1911.
Lorne. Ancient district of North *Argyll*, said to have been named from Loarn, one of the sons of *Fergus, son of Erc*. Gives titles of Baron and Marquis to *Dukes of Argyll*.
Lorne, Brooch of. See Brooch of Lorne.
Lost Clan. After defeat of Francis I of France at Pavia (1525), the remnants of his Scots Guard, in retreat, are said to have been snowed up in the Simplon Pass and settled down in the area, where their descendants still live. See Garde Écossaise.
Lothian. Originally the whole territory between Firth of Forth and River Tweed, but later the land north of the Lammermoors.
Lothian, Earldom and Marquisate. Earldom created 1606 for *Mark Ker*, Lord *Newbattle*;

3rd Earl (who married daughter of 2nd) was son and heir of 1st *Earl of Ancram*, and the *4th Earl of Lothian* was also Earl of Ancram; marquisate created 1701.

Lothian, Philip Henry Kerr, 11th Marquis of (1882-1940). Adviser of Lloyd George's government 1916-21, but criticised Versailles settlement; worked for good relations with U.S. and Commonwealth in 1920s and 1930s and sought appeasement with Germany; ambassador to U.S. 1939-40.

Lothian Regiment. See Royal Scots.

Lothian, Robert Kerr, 4th Earl and 1st Marquis of (1636-1703). Supported *Revolution*; succeeded to *Earldom of Ancram*; Commissioner to *General Assembly* 1692; created Marquis 1701.

Lothian, Schomberg Henry Kerr, 9th Marquis of (1833-1900). *Secretary for Scotland* 1886-92, after career as diplomat.

Loudoun, Earldom. Created 1641 for John Campbell, Lord L.

Loudoun Hall (Ayr). Built c. 1513; acquired by Campbells of Loudoun, *sheriffs* of *Ayr*, then (1632) by James Chalmers of Gadgirth; restored by *Marquis of Bute* from 1938 and presented to *Saltire Society*.

Loudoun Hill, Battle of, 10 May 1307. *Robert I* defeated English under Earl of Pembroke.

Loudoun, John Campbell, 1st Earl of (1598-1663). A leading *Covenanter*; created Earl 1641; *Chancellor* 1641-60.

Loudoun, John Claudius (1783-1843). Born *Cambuslang*; studied botany and landscape gardening; went to London 1803; farmed in Oxfordshire and after touring continent published periodicals on gardening and architecture.

Loudoun's Highlanders. Regiment, raised mainly in the Highlands from clans loyal to the government, by *Earl of Loudoun* at *Inverness* 1745; held Inverness until defeated by *Jacobites* at Rout of *Moy*; in Flanders 1747; disbanded 1748.

'The Lounger'. News-sheet published weekly by former staff of '*The Mirror*' from 1785 to 1787; contained one of the earliest notices of the poems of *Burns*.

Lovat, Lordship. Created for Hugh Fraser 1456 × 1464; *forfeited* 1747; estates restored 1774; U.K. peerage conferred 1837; Scottish peerage restored 1857.

Lovat Scouts. Raised 1900 by 14th Lord Lovat, from among stalkers and gamekeepers, for service in South Africa; also served in both World Wars. Cf. Yeomanry Regiments.

Lovat, Simon Fraser, 11th Lord (c. 1667-1747). Cousin of 9th Lord and son of 10th; pursued devious and violent action to acquire title and estates; active *Jacobite* 1702, but played the French King false and was imprisoned in France; supported government in 'Fifteen; under suspicion again 1737; played dubious part in 'Forty-Five; tried in London, he conducted an able defence, but was condemned and beheaded.

Love, John (1695-1750). Master of *Dumbarton* Grammar School 1721 and Rector of *Dalkeith* Grammar School 1739. Cf. Grammar Schools.

Love, John (1757-1825). Born *Paisley*; *Presbyterian minister*; went to London 1788; helped to found London Missionary Society 1795; returned to *Glasgow* 1800.

Low, David (1768-1855). *Minister* of *Episcopalian* congregation at *Pittenweem* 1789; *Bishop of Ross*, *Argyll* and the *Isles* 1819.

Low, George (1747-95). Wrote 'Tour through the Islands of *Orkney and Shetland* in 1774' and 'Fauna Orcadensis' (published 1813).

Lowe, Peter (c. 1550-1612). Founder of Faculty of Physicians and Surgeons of *Glasgow* 1599; had studied in Paris.

Luce, Abbey of. See Glenluce.

Luckenbooth Brooches. The Luckenbooths were the premises between the church of *St Giles* and the north side of the High Street of *Edinburgh*; silversmiths there made silver love-tokens or betrothal brooches, sometimes decorated with small crystals or amethysts and engraved with messages of endearment.

Luffness Friary (*Carmelite*) (East Lothian). Founded before 1293; referred to until 1560.

Lulach (d. 1058). Son of *Gruoch*, wife of *Macbeth*, by her first husband; known as 'The Simple', he was raised to the throne on Macbeth's death in 1057 but was defeated and killed by *Malcolm III* at Essie in Strathbogie 17 March 1058.

Lumphanan (Aberdeenshire). Scene of battle in which *Malcolm III* defeated and killed *Macbeth*, 15 August 1057; large *motte* nearby represents site of 12th-13th century castle, associated with Durward family.

Lumsden, Andrew (1720-1801). In service at *Jacobite* court; secretary to *Charles Edward* in 1745 and subsequently to his father; returned to Scotland 1768 and wrote 'Antiquities of Rome and its environs'.

Lumsden, James, of *Innergellie* (c. 1598-c. 1660). Served under Gustavus Adolphus; returned to support *Covenanters*; fought at

Marston Moor; captured at *Dunbar*, but later released. His brother Robert, of *Mountquhanie*, who had likewise served under Gustavus, defended *Dundee* against *Monck* and was killed on its surrender (1651). A third brother, William, also fought for Gustavus and the Covenanters.

Lumsden's Musketeers. Unit in service of Gustavus Adolphus, no doubt named from one of the brothers named above.

Lunardi, Vicenzo (1759-1806). Balloonist who came to *Edinburgh* 1787 and crossed Firth of Forth in his balloon.

Luncarty, Battle of, ? c. 973. Alleged defeat of Scandinavian invaders by *Kenneth III*.

Lundin Tower (Fife). Erected in reign of *David II*; belonged to family of Lundie, supposed to be descended from a *Chamberlain* of *William I*; passed to Drummonds by marriage and remained with them until forfeiture after 1745. Cf. Forfeited Estates.

Luss (Dunbartonshire). In hands of *Colquhoun* family from at least 14th century; *burgh of barony* for Colquhoun of L. 1642.

Lyell, Charles (1767-1849). Born Kinnordy, *Angus*; lived for many years in England; returned 1826; botanist who studied mosses and also published translation of Dante; his son, Sir Charles (1797-1875), was a geologist.

Lyle, Lordship. Estate in Kilmacolm parish, Renfrewshire, belonged to Lyles from 13th century; the seventh of the line created Lord Lyle 1446; 4th Lord sold estate to Porterfields in 16th century.

Lyle, Robert, 2nd Lord (d. c. 1497). *Justice General* 1488; ambassador to England on several occasions and to Spain 1491; supported *James IV* 1488 but rebelled against him 1489.

Lynedoch, Lord. See Graham, Thomas.

Lyon (or Lion) Chamber. In *Linlithgow Palace*, of reign of *James V*.

Lyon Family. First mentioned in Scotland c. 1320; John L., clerk and secretary of *David II*, married a daughter of *Robert II* and received *barony* of *Glamis*; he was *Chamberlain* 1377 and died 1382. Sir Patrick was created *Lord Glamis* 1445, and descendants became Earls of *Strathmore and Kinghorne*. The 9th Earl married the heiress of George Bowes of Streatlam and assumed additional surname of Bowes. The 14th Earl was the father of Queen Elizabeth, consort of George VI.

Lyon, John, Lord Glamis. See Glamis.

Lyon King of Arms. Title first found 1318 and a Lyon first named 1399; has for centuries had supreme jurisdiction in Scotland in matters armorial; his court contains *heralds* and *pursuivants* and Lyon Clerk. The Lyon Office has Registers, including the Public Register of all arms and bearings from 1672.

Lyon, Thomas (c. 1546-1608). Son of 7th Lord Glamis (d. 1559) and known as Master of Glamis; acquired Baldukie 1576; a leader of the *Ruthven Raid*; exiled in England 1584-5; *Treasurer* 1585; *Lord of Session* 1586; knighted 1590.

M

MacAdam, John Loudon (1756-1836). Born *Ayr*; after emigrating to America 1770, returned as a loyalist 1783; took part in various enterprises, including tar and coke and the victualling of the navy, but his interest turned increasingly to roads, partly as a result of his experience with the Volunteers during the French wars; it was only in 1816, when he was sixty, that he became Surveyor General of the Bristol Turnpike Trust and a professional road-engineer; his method of road-construction, based on a layer of small stones, laid on a drained surface, which pressure would bond together, was widely adopted.

MacAlpine (or Machabeus), John (d. 1557). Prior of *Dominicans* at *Perth*; adopted reforming views and had to flee from Scotland; became professor in Copenhagen and assisted in translating Bible into Danish.

Macaulay Institute (*Aberdeen*). Founded 1930 for soil research.

Macaulay, James (1817-1902). Qualified in medicine; strenuously opposed vivisection; travelled abroad as a tutor; edited 'Leisure Hours' and 'Sunday at Home'; founded 'Boys' Own Paper' and 'Girls' Own Paper'.

Macaulay, John (d. 1789). *Minister* of South Uist, *Lismore, Inveraray* and *Cardross*.

Macaulay, Robertson M. (1833-1915). Born *Fraserburgh*; went to Canada 1854; as General Manager of Sun Life Assurance Company of Montreal built up a business in which he was succeeded by his son, Thomas Bassett M. (1860-1942).

Macaulay, Thomas Babington (1800-59). Son of *Zachary M*; born Leicestershire; M.P. for *Edinburgh* 1839-47 and 1852-6; Secretary for War 1839-41; contributed to '*Edinburgh Review*'; best known for his 'History of England'; created baron 1857.

Macaulay, Zachary (1768-1838). Son of *John Macaulay*; managed estate in Jamaica and became prominent in anti-slavery movement.

MacBain, Alexander (1855-1907). Rector of Raining's School, *Inverness,* 1881; wrote 'Celtic Mythology and Religion' and compiled *Gaelic* Dictionary.

Macbeth (c. 1005-57). Son of Finlay, *mormaer* of *Moray*, possibly by a daughter of *Malcolm II*; married *Gruoch*; asserted his claims to throne by killing *Duncan I* in battle, 1040; maintained his position against *Crinan*, father of Duncan I, and *Malcolm III*, son of Duncan I, until 1057, and went on pilgrimage to Rome; defeated and killed by Malcolm at *Lumphanan* in *Mar* 15 August 1057; left no issue.

McBey, James (1883-1959). Born *Newburgh*, Aberdeenshire; as an etcher was employed by *North of Scotland Bank* until 1910, when he took up art professionally; travelled much abroad and became U.S. citizen 1942.

MacBrayne, David. Nephew of shipowners G. and J. *Burns* and a partner with David and Alexander Hutcheson in the firm David Hutcheson & Co., formed 1851; after the retirement of the Hutchesons, MacBrayne carried on the business in his own name from 1879.

McCallum, Orme and Co. Formed 1929 by amalgamation of John McCallum & Co. and Martin Orme & Co., which had operated from about the 1870s; incorporated in David *MacBrayne* 1947.

MacCalzean, Euphame (d. 1591). Daughter of Thomas M., *Lord of Session* and *provost* of *Edinburgh*; burned for conspiring to destroy *James VI* by witchcraft.

MacCombie, William (1805-80). Made study of cattle-breeding and wrote 'Cattle and Cattle-Breeders'; M.P. for West *Aberdeen* 1868-76.

MacCombie, William (1809-70). Farm labourer who took up journalism; on staff of 'North of Scotland Gazette' 1849; editor of 'Aberdeen Daily Free Press' 1853.

MacCormick, John (1904-61). *Glasgow* lawyer; leader in *National Party of Scotland* and *Scottish National Party*; parliamentary candidate 1929; devised *Covenant* 1930; founded *Scottish Convention* 1942; wrote 'The Flag in the Wind' (1955).

MacCormick, Joseph (1733-99). *Minister* 1758; principal of *United College, St Andrews*, 1783; dean of *chapel royal* 1788; edited 'State Papers and Letters of William Carstares'.

MacCosh, James (1811-94). *Minister* of *Arbroath* and *Brechin*; joined *Free Church*; professor of logic at Queen's College, Belfast 1851-68; president of Princeton College, New Jersey, 1868; wrote 'Scottish Philosophy', 'Psychology' and 'Laws of Discursive Thought'.

McCrie, Thomas (1772-1835). *Anti-Burgher minister* 1796; joined '*Auld Lichts*' 1806; edited 'Christian Magazine'; wrote lives of *John Knox* (1811) and *Andrew Melville* (1819).

McCrie, Thomas (1797-1875). Son of preceding; professor of church history and systematic theology in English Presbyterian College, London.

MacCrimmon Family. Hereditary pipers to *MacLeods* of *Dunvegan*; supposed to have had a 'school' or 'college' of piping at Boreraig, Skye; Donald Ban MacCrimmon, who composed 'Cumha Mhic Cruimein' ('MacCrimmon's Lament') was killed at Rout of *Moy*; John Dubh MacCrimmon (1731-1822) was the last of the line.

MacCulloch, Horatio (1805-67). Born *Glasgow*; pupil of W.H. *Lizars*; landscape painter distinguished for Highland scenes.

MacCulloch, John (1773-1835). Geologist of Trigonometrical Survey 1814; commissioned to prepare geological map of Scotland 1826; wrote 'Description of Western Isles' and 'Geological Classification of Rocks'.

MacCunn, Hamish (1869-1916). Born *Greenock*; composed 'Land of the Mountain and the Flood' at age of 18; other works include 'Lord Ullin's Daughter', 'Lay of the Last Minstrel' and an opera 'Jeannie Deans'.

MacDonald, Alexander (or **Alastair**) (d. 1647). Son of M. of Colonsay (who bore name Coll 'ciotach' or 'left-handed'—a name sometimes given to the son); brought force from Ireland and joined with *Montrose* in his campaigns 1644-5; killed in Ireland.

MacDonald, Alexander (or **Alasdair Mac Mhaighstir Alasdair**) (c. 1700-70). Son of *Episcopalian minister;* teacher with *Society in Scotland for Propagating Christian Knowledge*; compiled *Gaelic* vocabulary; joined *Jacobites* 1745; published first book of Scottish Gaelic secular poetry 1751.

MacDonald, Alexander (1736-91). Sent from *Scots College* in *Rome* to be priest in Barra 1765; vicar apostolic of Highlands 1780.

MacDonald, Alexander (1755-1837). Roman Catholic priest who collaborated in production of *Gaelic* dictionary in 1828.

MacDonald Family. Several Highland chiefs claimed descent from Donald, eldest son of

Reginald, but of course the surname, like other patronymics, could arise anywhere at any time down to the 17th century and ideas of kinship among those who bear it are fanciful.

MacDonald, Flora (1722-90). Daughter of Ranald M. of Milton in South Uist; assisted *Charles Edward* to avoid capture after *Culloden*; imprisoned in *Dunstaffnage*, then on board ship off *Leith* and finally in London, but released; married Allan MacDonald of Kingsburgh 1750; emigrated to America 1774 but returned 1779.

MacDonald, George (1824-1905). *Minister* at Arundel and Manchester after education at *Aberdeen*; his novels, mostly dealing with Scottish life, include 'Robert Falconer' and 'The Marquess of Lossie'; also wrote children's books, and poems.

MacDonald, Sir George (1862-1940). Born *Elgin*; taught in Kelvinside *Academy, Glasgow*; lectured in Greek at *Glasgow University*; Assistant Secretary to Scottish Education Department 1904, later Secretary; authority on Romano-British history and on numismatics; wrote 'The Roman Wall in Scotland' (1911); K.C.B. 1927.

MacDonald, Sir Hector Archibald (1853-1903). Born near *Dingwall*; joined *Gordon Highlanders* as private and, with service in Afghanistan, Egypt and South Africa, rose to be Major General 1900; committed suicide on his way home to face court martial over private scandal.

MacDonald, James Ramsay (1866-1937). Born Lossiemouth; Labour politician from 1900 and M.P. from 1906; Prime Minister 1924 and 1929-35; formed National Government in crisis of 1931.

MacDonald, John (or Iain Lom) (c. 1624-1710). A kinsman of the chief of MacDonalds of Keppoch, but little is known of his life, though he was in close touch with political events, to which much of his poetry relates; almost 3000 lines are extant, dealing with *Montrose*'s Wars, the *Restoration*, the *Revolution* and the *Union* and coloured by his hatred of Clan *Campbell* and the Lowland nobility.

MacDonald, John (1779-1849). Ordained 1806; joined *Free Church* 1843; 'The Apostle of the North'; wrote *Gaelic* poems and published sermons.

MacDonald, Sir John Hay Athole (1836-1919). *Solicitor General* 1876-80; *Lord Advocate* 1885-6; *Justice Clerk* (Lord Kingsburgh) 1888.

MacDonald's Highlanders. 76th Highland Regiment, raised 1777 by MacDonald of Sleat and commanded by MacDonald of Lochgarry; served in America 1779; disbanded at *Stirling* 1781.

MacDonell, Alastair Dubh, of Glengarry (d. 1724). Joined Viscount Dundee 1689 (see Graham, John, of Claverhouse) and *Earl of Mar* 1715.

MacDonell, Alastair Ruadh, of Glengarry (c. 1725-61). Joined a Scottish regiment in France 1743; sent to Highlands during the *'Forty-Five*, he was captured and imprisoned in London; became a spy for the government ('Pickle the Spy'); chief of clan 1754.

MacDonell, Alexander (1762-1840). Ordained Roman Catholic priest 1787; helped to raise regiment of Glengarry *Fencibles* and after its disbandment in 1801 obtained land in Canada for the men; appointed vicar apostolic of Upper Canada 1819 and Bishop of Kingston (Canada) 1826.

MacDougal Family. Claims descent from eldest son of *Somerled*; Lords of *Lorne* from 13th century, but lost ground to *Campbells* of Lochawe in reign of *Robert I* and later; *Dunolly Castle* remains with the family.

MacDowal, Andrew, of Logan (1685-1760). *Lord of Session* (Bankton) 1755; wrote 'Institutional Laws of Scotland'.

MacDowal(l) Family. The name is clearly the same in origin as MacDougal, but there is no evidence either that the MacDowalls in *Galloway* had a connection with *Lorne* or that they are descended from the Lords of Galloway; they held estates of *Garthland*, Freugh, Logan and others.

MacDowall, William (1815-88). Edited '*Dumfries* and *Galloway* Standard'; wrote 'History of Dumfries', 'The Man of the Woods' and 'Mind in the Face'.

Macduff (Banffshire). *Burgh of barony* 1783 for *Earl of Fife*, whose family developed the harbour.

'Macduff, Thane of Fife'. There is no historical support for this character in Shakespeare's 'Macbeth', or indeed for any '*Thane* of Fife', but a family name 'Macduff' was associated with the rulers of Fife, who appear as earls in 12th century.

Macduff's Law. According to tradition, a kinsman of Macduff to the ninth degree could obtain pardon for premeditated murder by taking sanctuary at Macduff's Cross at *Newburgh* in Fife and compensating the kinsmen of his victim.

MacEwan, Elspeth (d. 1698). Last witch to be put to death in *Kirkcudbright*.
MacEwen, Sir John Blackwood (1868-1948). Became principal of the Royal Academy of Music in London 1924; wrote a violin concerto and chamber music.
Macfarlan, James (1832-62). Pedlar who walked from *Glasgow* to London to have a volume of his lyrics published, 1853; other volumes followed.
Macfarlane, Walter (d. 1767). Industrious antiquary, whose genealogical and topographical collections have been of great value.
MacGibbon, David, and **Ross, Thomas.** Authors of the magisterial 'Castellated and Domestic Architecture of Scotland' (1887-92) and 'Ecclesiastical Architecture of Scotland' (1896-7). See also Ross, Thomas.
MacGill, James, of Nether Rankeillor (d. 1579). *Advocate* 1550; *Clerk Register* 1554.
MacGill, James (d. 1663). *Lord of Session*; Viscount Oxfuird 1651.
McGill, James (1744-1813). Born *Glasgow*; attended *Glasgow University* and then emigrated to Canada, where be became a fur trader; left fortune to found McGill University, Montreal.
MacGillivray, Charles (c. 1804-67). Lecturer in *Gaelic* at Glasgow Institution 1859; translated 'Pilgrim's Progress' into Gaelic.
MacGillivray, James Pittendreigh (1856-1938). Born *Inverurie*; King's sculptor in Scotland 1921; works include *Gladstone* Memorial, *Edinburgh* and *Byron* Statue, *Aberdeen*; wrote 'Bog Myrtle and Peat Reek' (1922).
MacGillivray, John (1822-67). Son of *William M*; employed as naturalist on government expeditions.
MacGillivray, William (1796-1852). Assistant to professor of natural history, *Edinburgh,* 1823; conservator of Royal College of *Surgeons*' Museum, Edinburgh, 1831; professor of natural history, *Aberdeen*, 1841; wrote 'A History of British Birds'; called 'father of British Ornithology'.
McGonagall, William (1825-1902). Born *Edinburgh*, son of hand-loom weaver; family moved to *Dundee*; took to stage and in 1877 started writing verse; 'Poetic Gems' published 1890.
MacGregor, Gregor, of Glenstrae (d. 1570). After taking vengeance on two *Campbell* agents who had killed two of his kinsmen, he was pursued by Campbells and eluded them by a famous leap across River Lyon; captured 1569, he was beheaded at Balloch (later *Taymouth*).
MacGregor, James (d. 1551). *Vicar* of *Fortingall*; dean of *Lismore* (or *Argyll*) 1514; buried in *Kenmore*; made collection of *Gaelic* verse known as '*The Book of the Dean of Lismore*', including items of various dates from early 14th century.
MacGregor, James Mhor (d. 1789). Son of *Rob Roy M*; *Jacobite* in 1745 but managed to make his peace; sentenced to death for his part with his brother, *Robin Oig*, in the abduction of Jean Kay, a wealthy widow, from her home at Edinbellie, Stirlingshire; escaped from *Edinburgh Castle* with the help of his daughter, who disguised herself as a cobbler and changed clothes with him; died in France.
MacGregor, Rob Roy (1671-1734). Took his mother's name of *Campbell*; had farm in Balquhidder, and operated as a cattle-dealer, but indulged in illicit pursuits and levied blackmail; with *Jacobite* army at *Sheriffmuir* but did not fight; more than once arrested, but his escapes are legendary; when in Newgate in 1726 he was saved from transportation by a pardon.
MacGregor, Robin Oig (d. 1754). Son of preceding; condemned and executed for abduction of Jean Kay (see MacGregor, James Mhor).
MacGregor's Leap. See MacGregor, Gregor.
MacGrigor, Sir James (1771-1858). Qualified in medicine at *Aberdeen* and *Edinburgh*; as surgeon of Connaught Rangers saw service in Flanders, West Indies and India; Inspector General of Hospitals 1809; chief of medical staff of Duke of Wellington in Peninsular War.
MacIan, Robert Ronald (1807-56). Produced a series of paintings illustrating Highland costume and weapons which were reproduced as the 'MacIan prints'.
Macintosh. See Mackintosh.
Macintyre, Duncan (or Donnachadh Ban Nan Oran) (1724-1812). Born Glenorchy; gamekeeper; fought in Campbell Regiment 1746; married Mary Macintyre (Mairi Bhan Og); became member of Edinburgh *City Guard*; although not literate, he composed thousands of lines of poetry, which he dictated and which were published, first in 1768; the most widely acclaimed of *Gaelic* poets.
Macintyre, Robert Douglas (1913-). Physician; first Scottish Nationalist M.P., elected at a by-election 1945 and almost immediately unseated at general election; *provost* of *Stirling* 1967.

Mackail, Hugh (c. 1640-66). Ordained 1661; arrested as a *Covenanter* 1662, but escaped to Holland; returned 1666 and joined *Pentland Rising*; captured, tortured and executed.

Mackail, Matthew (d. 1734). Son of Matthew M. (fl. 1657-96), a medical writer; professor of medicine at *Aberdeen* 1717.

MacKay, Aeneas James George (1839-1911). *Advocate* 1864; professor of constitutional law, *Edinburgh*, 1874; *sheriff* of Fife; wrote 'History of Fife and Kinross', 'The Practice of the *Court of Session*', '*William Dunbar*' and other historical works.

MacKay, Alexander (1815-95). *Free Church minister* of *Rhynie* 1844; wrote 'A Manual of Modern Geography'.

MacKay, Alexander (1833-1902). Editor of 'Educational News' 1878; president of *Educational Institute of Scotland* 1881.

MacKay, Andrew (1760-1809). Keeper of *Aberdeen University* Observatory 1781; examiner in mathematics to Trinity House and to East India Company; wrote on navigation.

MacKay, Archibald (1801-83). Wrote 'My first Bawbee', 'My ain couthie wife', 'Drouthy Tam' and a 'History of *Kilmarnock*'.

MacKay, Donald, 1st Lord Reay. See Reay.

MacKay, General Hugh, of Scourie (c. 1640-92). Served on continent from 1660 and entered service of States General 1673; commanded government forces at *Killiecrankie*; returned to Holland to fight in King William's wars and was killed at Steinkirk.

MacKay, John (d. 1896). Son of John MacKay, *Leith* (d. 1865); as 'Ben Reay' wrote 'An Old *Scots Brigade*', 'The Royal Burgh of *Canongate*' and 'The Barony of *Broughton*'.

MacKay, Mackintosh (1800-73). Superintended production of *Gaelic* Dictionary for *Highland and Agricultural Society* 1828; joined *Free Church*, went to Australia and became *minister* of Gaelic Church at Melbourne 1854 and Sydney 1856; returned home.

MacKay's Highlanders. Served in *Scots Brigade* in army of Gustavus Adolphus.

MacKellar, Mary (1834-90). Née Cameron; married John MacKellar, a sea captain; wrote poems and songs in *Gaelic* and English.

MacKelvie, William (1800-63). Ordained 1829; wrote 'Annals and Statistics of the *United Presbyterian Church*'.

Mackenzie, Sir Alexander (?1763-1820). Born *Stornoway*; emigrated to Canada when he was sixteen and entered service of North-West Company, whose work led him into exploration; in 1789 went on a canoe voyage by the Slave Lake and down the River Mackenzie to the northern ocean; in 1792-3 made his way across the Rockies to the Pacific; wrote an account of his 'Voyages' (1801); knighted 1802; returned to Scotland.

Mackenzie, Sir Alexander Campbell (1847-1935). Born *Edinburgh*; principal of Royal Academy of Music in London; wrote operas, oratorios, violin and piano concertos.

Mackenzie, Colin (?1753-1821). Born *Stornoway*; joined East India Company 1783; as a cartographer and collector of antiquities, as well as a surveyor and engineer, he earned a knighthood.

Mackenzie, Sir Compton (1883-1973). Born and educated in England; served in South African and First World Wars; director of intelligence in Aegean 1917; his wide range of novels includes several with Scottish settings, notably 'Whisky Galore'.

Mackenzie, George, 2nd Earl of Seaforth. See Seaforth.

Mackenzie, Sir George, of Rosehaugh (1636-91). Nephew of *Earl of Seaforth*; *advocate* 1659; justice for criminal cases, 1661; *Lord Advocate* 1677; as a prosecutor of *Covenanters*, earned name 'Bluidy Mackenzie'; out of sympathy with *James VII*'s policy of toleration, he was dismissed 1686 but restored 1688; opposed deposition of James and withdrew to England; wrote on many topics, including 'Institution of the Law of Scotland' (1684), 'Vindication of the government of Scotland during the reign of *Charles II*' (1691) and 'Jus Regium' (1684); remembered as the founder of the *Advocates' Library*, established by the Faculty in 1682, when he was dean.

Mackenzie, Sir George, of Tarbat (1630-1714). Son of laird of *Tarbat;* active royalist against Cromwellian occupation; *Lord of Session* 1661-3, but out of office, owing to his opposition to *Lauderdale*, until 1678, when he became *Justice General*; *Clerk Register* 1681; at *Revolution* made peace with King William, became *Secretary of State* 1702 and Justice General 1705; supported *Union*; created Viscount Tarbat 1685 and *Earl of Cromartie* 1703; versatile in his writings, which include 'A Vindication of *Robert III* from the imputation of bastardy' (1695), 'The Mistaken Advantage of Raising of Money' (1695) and 'Daniel's Prophecy and St John's Revelation' (1707).

Mackenzie, George (1777-1856). From 1802 made systematic study of the weather and in 1819 wrote 'Primary Cycle of the Winds'; also compiled various reports on meteorology.

Mackenzie, Sir George Stewart, of Coul (1780-1848). Discovered composition of diamond and its identity with carbon; studied mineralogy and geology in Iceland and the Faroes.

Mackenzie, Henry (1745-1831). Born *Edinburgh*; wrote 'The Man of Feeling', 'The Man of the World' and 'Julia de Roubigné'.

Mackenzie, John (1727-89). Captured as *Jacobite* 1746; pardoned but deprived of estates 1748; went to Sweden 1750; aide de camp to Marshal *Keith*; returned to Scotland 1777; raised regiment of Highlanders; served in India; estates restored 1784; Count of *Cromarty* in Swedish peerage.

Mackenzie, John (1806-48). Book-keeper in *Glasgow University* printing office; collected popular songs and published 'Beauties of *Gaelic* Poetry'; translated theological works into Gaelic.

Mackenzie, Kenneth (Coinneach Odhar) (c. 1610-c. 1670). 'The Brahan Seer'; born Uig, *Lewis*, but named from Brahan Castle near *Dingwall*, seat of his patron, the Mackenzie *Earl of Seaforth*; credited with many prophecies relating to a wide area, especially Ross and Skye.

Mackenzie, Kenneth, 4th Earl of Seaforth. See Seaforth.

Mackenzie, Murdoch (d. 1797). Admiralty Surveyor; surveyed *Orkney and Shetland*; wrote treatise on 'Marine Surveying'. His nephew Murdoch (1743-1829) followed him as Admiralty Surveyor.

Mackenzie, Osgood (d. 1922). 3rd son of laird of *Gairloch*; on the estate of Inverewe, bought for him in 1862, he started planting in 1865 and created a remarkable garden about which he wrote in 'A Hundred Years in the Highlands'; his daughter, Mrs Sawyer, presented it to the *National Trust*.

Mackenzie, Roderick (d. 1746). Officer in *Lord Elcho*'s troop of Prince *Charles Edward*'s Life Guards who closely resembled the prince; said to have died to save him from pursuit by government forces; commemorated by monument in Glenmoriston.

Mackenzie, Thomas (1807-69). *Lord of Session*; *Solicitor General* 1851; wrote 'Studies in Roman Law', comparing Scots law with other systems.

Mackenzie, William, 5th Earl of Seaforth. See Seaforth.

Mackenzie, William (1791-1868). Ophthalmic surgeon who lectured in *Glasgow University*; surgeon-oculist to Queen Victoria 1838; wrote 'Practical Treatise on the Diseases of the Eye'.

Mackenzie, William Forbes (1807-62). *Advocate* 1827; M.P. for Peeblesshire 1837-52; Lord of the Treasury 1845-6; responsible for 'Forbes-Mackenzie Act', 1852, regulating public houses in Scotland.

Mackenzie, William Lyon (1795-1861). Born *Dundee*; emigrated to Canada 1820; ran 'The Colonial Advocate' at Toronto 1824-34; mayor of Toronto 1834; advocated radical political reform and had a turbulent career as a member of the legislative assembly of Upper Canada, culminating in a rebellion in 1837; fled to United States.

Mackerstoun. See Makerstoun.

Mackie, James (1816-91). Bookseller at *Kilmarnock*; founded 'Kilmarnock Journal' and 'Kilmarnock Weekly Post'; collected editions of *Burns.*

Mackinnon, Daniel (1791-1836). Joined *Coldstream Guards* 1804 and became colonel; wounded at Waterloo; wrote 'Origin and History of the Coldstream Guards'.

Mackinnon, John (d. 1500). Abbot of *Iona* whose tomb is still to be seen.

Mackinnon, Sir William (1823-93). Founded firm for coasting trade in India and British India Steam Navigation Company 1856; in 1878 leased part of East Africa from Sultan of Zanzibar and founded British East Africa Company; founded East African Scottish Mission 1891.

Mackintosh, Anne (1723-87). Daughter of James Farquharson of Invercauld; married Aeneas Mackintosh of Mackintosh, who in 1745 raised a company for King George while his wife, 'Colonel Anne', raised one for Prince *Charles*; helped to secure *Jacobite* success in Rout of *Moy*; briefly imprisoned after *Culloden.*

Mackintosh, Charles (1766-1843). Born *Glasgow*; son of *George M*; investigated by-products of tar, chiefly naphtha, and by combining naphtha with rubber produced the water-proofing process which bears his name; started alum works 1797; connected with *St Rollox* chemical works until 1814; patented water-proofing process 1823 and started works in Manchester; firm taken over by North British Rubber Company 1895.

Mackintosh, Charles Rennie (1868-1928). Born *Glasgow*; studied at Glasgow School of Art; travelled in France and Italy; won competition for new Glasgow School of Art 1894; designed Cranston's Tea Rooms; exhibited widely on continent; moved to London 1913; turned to painting.

Mackintosh, Donald (1743-1808). *Gaelic* language expert for Society of *Antiquaries* 1785; ordained in *Episcopal Church* 1789 and, refusing to abandon traditional allegiance to Stewarts, was consecrated as the last *non-juring* bishop; keeper of Gaelic records for *Highland Society* 1801.

Mackintosh, George (1739-1809). In business in *Glasgow* in shoe-making and dyeing and was partner of *David Dale* in *cotton* mill in *Sutherland.*

Mackintosh, Sir James (1765-1832). Educated *Aberdeen* and *Edinburgh*, where he qualified in medicine, but turned to law and political philosophy; barrister in England and judge in India; M.P. for *Nairn* 1813; wrote defence of French Revolution in 'Vindiciae Gallicae' (1791), but later adopted Burke's views; author of several historical works.

Mackintosh, John (1833-1907). Wrote 'History of Civilisation in Scotland'.

Mackintosh, William, of Borlum (1662-1743). Commanded part of *Jacobite* army in 1715 and led it south to join English rebels; captured and imprisoned but escaped 1716; returned to Scotland 1719 and again arrested.

MacLaren, Charles (1782-1866). First editor of '*Scotsman*' 1817; edited 6th edition of '*Encyclopaedia Britannica*'.

MacLaren, Duncan (1800-86). *Edinburgh* draper from 1824; Lord *Provost* 1851-4; member of *National Association for Vindication of Scottish Rights* 1853; Liberal M.P. for Edinburgh 1865-81; referred to as 'the member for Scotland'.

MacLaren, Ian (1850-1907). Real name John MacLaren Watson; educated *Stirling* and *Edinburgh*; *Free Church minister* in Edinburgh, *Glasgow* and Liverpool; wrote 'The Stickit Minister', 'Kate Carnegie', 'The Days of Auld Lang Syne' and other books.

MacLaren's Loup. Another name for the *Devil's Beef Tub*, from the escape of an arrested *Jacobite* in 1746 by wrapping his body in his plaid and rolling down the steep hillside in the mist.

MacLauchlan, Thomas (1816-86). Ordained 1837; joined *Free Church*; edited '*Book of the Dean of Lismore*' and supported authenticity of James *Macpherson's* '*Ossian*'.

MacLaurin, Colin (1698-1746). Born *Argyll*, son of a *minister*; professor of mathematics at *Marischal College, Aberdeen* at age of 19; assistant professor of mathematics at *Edinburgh* 1725, professor 1726; prepared to defend Edinburgh against *Jacobites* 1745, and when city surrendered took refuge in York.

MacLean Family. The name is a patronymic from Gillean, 'servant of [St] John'; recorded in Perthshire 1296; in *Duart* and Lochbuie in 15th century.

MacLean, John. Native of Port Logan, Wigtownshire, who, as a skipper of clipper ships who beat the '*Cutty Sark*', was known as 'Hellfire Jack'.

MacLean, John (1828-86). Born *Portsoy*; clerk in London; ordained in Church of England 1858; became first Bishop of Saskatchewan (1874) and founded Alberta University.

MacLean, John (d. 1923). *Glasgow* teacher; Marxist revolutionary influenced by Irish nationalism and associated with *Gaelic* political movement led by *Ruaraidh Erskine*; after the Bolsheviks appointed him their 'consul' in Britain he was imprisoned (1918).

MacLean's Highlanders. Raised by Allan MacLean of Torloisk 1761; saw no active service, but provided replacements; disbanded 1763.

Macleay, Kenneth (fl. 1819). *Glasgow* physician who wrote 'Historical Memoirs of *Rob Roy* and the Clan MacGregor' (1818); his son, also Kenneth (1802-78), was a miniature painter and one of the original members of the *Royal Scottish Academy.*

Maclehose, Agnes (1759-1841). Married to James Maclehose, a Glasgow lawyer, 1776, but separated from him and moved to *Edinburgh* 1782; the 'Clarinda' of the letters of *Burns*.

Maclellan, Archibald (1797-1854). Coachbuilder in *Glasgow* who collected works of art which formed nucleus of *Glasgow Art Gallery*.

Maclellan, Sir Thomas, of Bombie (c. 1540-97). *Provost* of *Kirkcudbright*; built Kirkcudbright Castle with stones from friary and older castle.

Maclellan, Sir William, of Bombie. See Kirkcudbright, Lordship.

MacLeod, Donald. Stonemason, born in Strathnaver, who was evicted with his family 1831; wrote letters to press denouncing the Sutherland *Clearances* and a 'History of the Destitution in *Sutherland*'.

MacLeod Family. Two families, owners of *Dunvegan* (with *Harris*) and of *Lewis*, claimed common origin in Scandinavian Liot; more than one bearer of that Christian name does in fact occur in 12th century Scotland; the Lewis branch was dispossessed in 16th century, the other continues.

MacLeod, John (1757-1841). Ordained 1779; helped in publication of *Gaelic* Bible and Dictionary.

MacLeod, Mary (or Mairi Nighean Alasdair Ruaidh) (c. 1615-1705). Born *Rodel, Harris*; associated with *MacLeod* lairds, to whom she was a servant; the best-known *Gaelic* poetess; her work includes twelve eulogies or laments, mainly for MacLeod chiefs and members of the family.

MacLeod, Norman (1780-1866). Born Assynt; his inability to conform prevented his acceptance as either *minister* or schoolmaster; emigrated to Pictou; Nova Scotia, and formed a community under his domination, which in 1820 moved to St Ann's, Cape Breton, and in 1851 to Australia and New Zealand.

MacLeod, Norman (1783-1862). Son of *minister* of Morvern; minister of *Church of Scotland* 1806; wrote religious books in *Gaelic* and English. His son, also Norman (1812-72), edited the 'Christian Instructor' and wrote 'Reminiscences of a Highland Parish'.

MacLeod, Sir Roderick, of *Dunvegan* (d. 1626). Known as 'Rory Mor'; in 1595 led 500 men to Ulster to help Hugh O'Donnell against the English; knighted by *James VI*.

MacLeod's Highlanders. Raised by Lord MacLeod as 73rd Regiment, later 71st, in 1777; served in India and at Gibraltar; 2nd Battalion disbanded 1783; another 2nd Battalion, formed 1804 and recruited mainly in *Glasgow*, was known as 'The Glasgow *Highland Light Infantry*'.

MacMillan, Alexander (1818-96). Grandson of Malcolm MacMillan, who farmed in Arran; with his brother Daniel (1813-57) founded publishing firm of MacMillan & Co., London.

MacMillan, Hugh, Lord (1873-1952). Son of Hugh M. (1833-1903), *Free Church minister* at *Glasgow* and *Greenock*; *Lord Advocate* 1924; Lord of Appeal (Lord M. of Aberfeldy) 1930; Minister of Information 1939-40.

MacMillan, John (1670-1753). Ordained 1701 and joined the *Cameronians*, who were sometimes known as MacMillanites.

MacMillan, Kirkpatrick. Blacksmith at Keir, Dumfriesshire; applied pedals to tricycle 1834 and to two-wheeled velocipede 1840.

MacMorran, John (d. 1595). Wealthy *Edinburgh* merchant, whose house still exists in Riddell's Court in the Lawnmarket; shot by *William Sinclair* in an affray at the *Edinburgh High School*.

Macnab, Archibald (?1781-1860). Nephew of *Francis* M., whom he succeeded as chief; fled from his creditors to Upper Canada, where he settled some of his former tenants in a quasi-feudal establishment.

Macnab Family. See Glendochart.

Macnab, Francis, of Macnab (1734-1816). Best known for his striking portrait in Highland dress by *Raeburn*; despite poverty and pressing debts, he lived in a pretentious manner in the family home at Kinnell and was regarded as an eccentric.

Macnab, John (1732-1802). Dollar herd-boy who became a sea-captain and shipowner and amassed a fortune, half of which he left to found *Dollar Academy*.

McNaught, John. In business as engineer in *Glasgow* by 1833; between 1825 and 1830 he had improved the engine indicator; moved to Bury, Lancashire; in 1845 devised method of 'compounding' existing engines.

MacNeill, Duncan (1794-1874). Son of Sir John M. (1795-1883), who studied medicine and became a diplomat; *Solicitor General* 1834-5 and 1841-2; *Lord Advocate* 1842-6; *Lord of Session* (Oronsay) and *Justice General* 1852-67; created Baron Colonsay and *Oronsay*.

MacNeill, Sir John Benjamin (c. 1793-1880). Assistant to *Telford*; professor of civil engineering at Trinity College, Dublin, 1842-52; engaged in railway construction in Scotland and Ireland.

MacNicol, Donald (1735-1802). *Minister* who wrote 'Defence of the Highlands against Dr Johnson'.

Maconochie, Alexander (1777-1861). Son of *Allan M*; *Lord Advocate* 1816; M.P. 1817-9; *Lord of Session* (Meadowbank) 1819; assumed additional surname of Welwood 1854.

Maconochie, Allan (1748-1816). Professor of public law, *Edinburgh*, 1779; *Lord of Session* (Meadowbank) 1796; wrote on law and on agriculture.

Macpherson, Ewen, of Cluny (d. 1756). Joined *Jacobites* 1745; helped Prince *Charles Edward* to escape and himself escaped to France, where he died. See Cluny's Cage.

Macpherson, James (d. c. 1701). Son of a chief and a gipsy woman; freebooter in Banffshire; his targe and two-handed sword are preserved in Duff House; an expert fiddler, he played, on his way to execution, a tune known by his name ever since.

Macpherson, James (1738-96). Born *Kingussie*; schoolmaster at *Ruthven*, Inverness-shire; published 'The Highlander' in 6 cantos when he was twenty, and began travelling through Highlands to collect ancient verses; in 1760 issued 'Fragments of Ancient Poetry . . . translated from the *Gaelic* or Erse language' and followed that by 'Fingal' (1762) and 'Temora' (1763); the works were at first enthusiastically acclaimed, but scepticism arose and there was prolonged controversy; the 'originals' which Macpherson produced turned out to be translations from English, but he had used certain old material as a basis; later he wrote historical and political works and was employed in colonial and Indian affairs.

Macpherson, Sir John, Bart. (1745-1821). Went from *Edinburgh University* to join East India Company as clerk; M.P. 1779-82, 1796-1802; Governor General of India 1785-6; Baronet 1786.

Macpherson, Paul (1756-1846). Educated at *Scots Colleges* at *Rome* and *Valladolid*; first Scottish Rector of Scots College at Rome, previously ruled by Italians.

Macpherson's 'Ossian'. See Macpherson, James.

MacQuarrie, Lachlan (1761-1824). Entered army 1777; became major-general; Governor of New South Wales 1809-21.

MacQueen, Robert. See Braxfield, Lord.

MacRae, Duncan (d. 1967). Actor who was notably successful in Scots pieces like 'Jamie the Saxt' and 'The Three Estates'.

MacRae, James (1677-1748). Born *Ochiltree*; emigrated to India; Governor of Madras 1725; returned 1731 and used fortune to buy several estates, including *Houston*, Ochiltree and Orangefield; adopted family of MacGuires, to whom he left the estates.

MacRaes, Affair of the Wild. In August 1778 the *Seaforth Highlanders*, newly raised, received orders to embark for India, but mutinied and entrenched themselves on Arthur's Seat, *Edinburgh* until a settlement was reached.

MacRobert Trust. Sir Alexander MacRobert, Bart., went from *Aberdeen* to India, where he made a fortune; he bought estate of Cromar in 1918 and died in 1922. His eldest son and heir, Sir Alasdair, was killed in a flying accident in 1933, and two younger brothers, Sir Roderick and Sir Ian, were killed in action in the R.A.F. in 1940. Lady MacRobert made over her house of Cromar as a guest-house for R.A.F. officers and later presented the MacRobert Centre to *Stirling University*.

Mactaggart, Ferchar. Created *Earl of Ross* 1215 after helping *Alexander II* to put down an insurrection in *Moray*.

Mactaggart, James (1791-1830). Born Borgue, Kirkcudbrightshire; emigrated to Canada for three years; wrote 'Three Years in Canada' and 'Scottish Gallovidian Encyclopaedia'.

Mactaggart, William (1835-1910). Born Kintyre; studied in *Glasgow* and *Edinburgh*; went home to *Campbeltown* and painted genre pictures, landscapes and seascapes as well as scenes from Scottish song and poetry; after 1870 turned more to the open sea, and figures disappear from his later pictures; though his base was Edinburgh, and later Broomieknowe, 6 miles away, he occasionally visited Kintyre.

Macer. Officer of court, responsible for maintaining order.

Machar, St (fl. c. 600 ?). Said to have been one of twelve monks who came with *Columba* to *Iona* and to have built a church in *Aberdeen*, where the later *Cathedral* was dedicated to him; supposed to have died as Bishop of Tours in France.

Machute, St (6th century ?). Gave his name to *Lesmahagow*—'the church of Machute'.

Madderty, Lordship. Created 1609 for James Drummond (c. 1540-1623).

Madeleine (1521-37). Daughter of Francis I of France; married *James V* in Paris 1 January 1537; died 7 July following.

Madras College, St Andrews. Founded 1833 by *Dr Andrew Bell* and using his system of education.

Madrid, Scots College at. Founded 1613 by *William Sempill* (1546-1633), who bought a mansion to be used for students drawn from Scottish gentry; transferred to *Valladolid* 1772 when Bishop *John Geddes* arrived with a dozen Scottish students.

Maeatae. Tribe which in Roman times inhabited Strathmore and central Scotland down to near *Stirling*.

Maelrubha, St (7th century). Said to have founded monastery at Applecross 673 and to have been buried there.

Maeshowe. The most splendid chambered tomb in Scotland, in Stennes parish, *Orkney*; it was raided in 12th century by Scandinavians who left runic inscriptions on the walls; opened up 1861.

Magdalen Chapel, in Cowgate, *Edinburgh*. Endowed 1547 by Michael MacQuhen, an Edinburgh *burgess*, and Janet Rynd, his wife; long the hall of the *Incorporation* of Hammermen; contains some pre-*Reformation* stained glass.

Magnus Barelegs. King of Norway, who according to his saga led an expedition down the west coast and made a treaty with King

Edgar ('Malcolm' in the saga) whereby he was to have all the islands off the west coast; he took his ship across the isthmus at *Tarbert*, Loch Fyne, and claimed Kintyre as an island; his nickname is said to derive from his adoption of the earlier equivalent of the *kilt* as a dress.

Magnus, St (d. ? 1117). Son of Erlend, joint *Earl of Orkney*, and himself joint Earl with his cousin Haakon, who murdered him on *Egilsay*; buried in *Birsay* and subsequently *Kirkwall Cathedral*.

Magus Muir. Between *Ceres* and *St Andrews*; scene of murder of Archbishop *James Sharp*.

Maid of Norway. See Margaret.

Maiden. Instrument of execution, a form of guillotine, used in *Edinburgh* (from late 16th century) and *Aberdeen*; the Edinburgh one is in the *National Museum of Antiquities*.

Maiden Castle (or Castle of the Maidens). See Castellum Puellarum.

Maiden's Leap. A daughter of *1st Earl of Gowrie* is said to have jumped the 9 feet between two buildings of the castle of *Huntingtower*, 60 feet above the ground, to avoid discovery when being courted by a suitor of whom her parents disapproved.

Maidment, James (c. 1795-1879). *Advocate* who specialised in peerage cases and turned to antiquarian studies; edited a number of historical texts.

Mails (or Maills). Rents.

Maitland, Charles and John, Earls and Duke of Lauderdale. See Lauderdale.

Maitland Club. Founded in *Glasgow* 1828 'to print works illustrative of the antiquities, history and literature of Scotland'; operated until 1859.

Maitland, Edward Francis (1803-70). Brother of *Thomas Maitland*, Lord Dundrennan; *Solicitor General* 1855-8 and 1859-62; *Lord of Session* (Barcaple) 1862.

Maitland, Sir Frederick Lewis (1777-1839). Son of Frederick Lewis M. (d. 1786), a rear-admiral; commanded the 'Bellerophon' when Napoleon surrendered after Waterloo; commanded in East Indies and China; built Lindores House, Fife.

Maitland, Sir John, of *Thirlestane* (1543-95). Son of *Sir Richard M*. and brother of *William*; *Commendator* of *Coldingham* and Keeper of *Privy Seal* 1567; in Queen *Mary*'s party in civil war, and out of favour during regency of *Morton*; *Lord of Session* 1581; *Secretary* 1584; *Chancellor* 1587 and head of the administration; created Lord Thirlestane 1590.

Maitland, Sir Richard, of *Lethington* (1496-1586). *Lord of Session* and Keeper of the *Privy Seal*; compiled Dictionary of Decisions of *Court of Session* and 'History of the House of *Seton*'; formed collection of Scottish verse and wrote some poetry.

Maitland, Sir Thomas (c. 1759-1824). Lieutenant-general; served in India; Commander-in-Chief Ceylon 1806-11; Governor of Malta 1813; M.P. for East Lothian 1794-6 and 1800-6.

Maitland, Thomas (1792-1851). *Solicitor General* 1840; M.P. for Kirkcudbrightshire 1845-50; *Lord of Session* (Dundrennan) 1850.

Maitland, William, of *Lethington* (c. 1525-73). Son of *Sir Richard M*; *Secretary of State* 1558; joined reformers because of his devotion to Anglo-Scottish amity; married *Mary Fleming*; implicated in murder of *Darnley*; sided with *Regent Moray* after *Mary*'s abdication, but later joined *Queen's Party*; captured when *Edinburgh Castle* fell and possibly hastened his death by poison.

Major (or Mair), John (1467-1550). Born Gleghornie, East Lothian; studied at Cambridge and Paris; professor of theology at *Glasgow* 1518 and *St Andrews* 1522; again in Paris 1525-33, then settled at St Andrews; his 'History of Greater Britain' (Paris, 1521), written to support the cause of Anglo-Scottish amity, was much more critical than earlier histories; some of his other writings, on philosophy, were old-fashioned, but he was critical of abuses in the church.

Makerstoun (Roxburghshire). A farm named Charterhouse had no connection with the *Carthusian* order.

Malcolm I (d. 954). Son of *Donald II*; King from 943; killed by men of *Moray* in battle, perhaps at Fetteresso.

Malcolm II (c. 954-1034). Son of *Kenneth II*; for ten years after father's death he had to contend with rivals, but established himself by 1005; possibly besieged Durham 1006; his victory at *Carham* (1018) is held to have finally secured *Lothian* to Scotland; the succession of his grandson, *Duncan I*, to a king of *Strathclyde* who died in 1018 in effect incorporated the south-west also in the kingdom; one of his daughters married Earl *Sigurd* of *Orkney*; his eldest daughter, Bethoc, married *Crinan* and was mother of *Duncan I*; died 25 November 1034.

Malcolm III (c. 1031-93). Called 'Canmore' (that is, great head or chief); son of *Duncan I*; in England during reign of *Macbeth*; possibly acquired southern Scotland 1054, then overthrew Macbeth 1057 and *Lulach* 1058; married *Ingibjorg*, daughter of Earl *Thorfinn* of *Orkney*, and then (c. 1069) *Margaret* of England; invaded England five times (1061-93), sometimes in association with English rebels against William the Conqueror (who made Malcolm submit to him in 1072); killed at Alnwick 13 November 1093; had three sons by Ingibjorg, including *Duncan II*, and six by Margaret—*Edward, Ethelred, Edmund, Edgar, Alexander I* and *David I*—as well as two daughters, one of whom married Henry I of England.

Malcolm IV (1141-65). Son of Earl *Henry*, son of *David I*; succeeded grandfather 1153; internal troubles arose with native earls who possibly resented the Normanising policy of the ruling house and Malcolm's obvious subordination to England, as well as with chiefs in *Moray* and the *Hebrides* who may have represented separatism; surrendered northern English counties to Henry II 1157; founded *Coupar Angus* Abbey 1162; died unmarried 9 December 1165; the idea that he had a son seems to derive from a scribal error.

Malcolm Macheth. Possibly illegitimate son of *Alexander I*; led rebellion in *Moray* with *Angus*, the *mormaer*; captured 1134; *Earl of Ross* 1157; died 1168.

Malcolm's Tower. See Dunfermline.

Malignants. Term applied by *Covenanters* to their Royalist opponents.

Mallet, David (c. 1705-65). Born *Crieff*; tutor to Earl of *Home*'s family; friend of *James Thomson*; wrote ballad, 'William and Margaret'.

Malsnectai (d. 1085). Son of *Lulach*; *mormaer* of *Moray* until ousted by *Malcolm III* 1078; ended his days as a monk.

Malt Tax. Tax of 3d. per bushel on malt led to rioting in 1725, especially in *Glasgow*, where the house of Campbell of Shawfield, the local M.P., was wrecked; the captain whose troop fired on the mob was condemned to death but received a royal pardon.

Malvoisine (d. 1238). *Bishop of Glasgow* 1200; translated to *St Andrews* 1202; *Chancellor* 1199-1211.

Mam Garvia (or Garvyach), Battle of, 1187. Forces of *William I* defeated *Donald* MacWilliam.

Man, Isle of. Ceded by Norway to Scotland by *Treaty of Perth*; inhabitants defeated by Scots 8 October 1275; seized by England 1290, restored 1293, fell to England again about 1296 and was the scene of operations 1310-5 which resulted in its acquisition by the Scots, who lost it again 1333; inherited by *Duke of Atholl* 1735; his rights purchased by British government 1765 and 1829.

'Manager for Scotland'. The individual who, by his use of patronage and other means, controlled Scottish parliamentary elections and the votes of Scottish M.P.s. See Melville, Henry Dundas, 1st Viscount, and Melville, Robert Saunders, 2nd Viscount.

Manderston House (Berwickshire). Built c. 1770, probably to design by *Sir William Chambers*: reconstructed by John Kinross for Sir James Miller, whose father bought estate in 1855.

Manrent, Bond of. See Bonds.

Manse. The residence for the parish priest in medieval times and for the *minister* later; traditionally it was, with the *glebe*, inalienable church property.

Mansfield, Earldom. Created 1776 for William Murray (1705-93), of the *Scone* family, who was educated mainly in England, where he became Lord Chief Justice 1756; he was succeeded by his nephew, David (1727-96), noted as a diplomat.

Manson, Sir Patrick (1844-1922). Son of John M. of Fingask, *Aberdeen*; founded London School of Tropical Medicine; medical adviser to Colonial Office; discovered association of malaria with mosquito.

Manuel Nunnery (*Cistercian*) (West Lothian). Founded by *Malcolm IV* before 1164; *James IV* proposed substitution of *Augustinian* friars 1506, but nunnery continued; property fell mainly to Lord *Livingston*; only a fragment remains.

Manufactories Act, 1661. Granted privileges to persons erecting manufactories; forbade export of raw materials fit for manufacture and encouraged import of raw materials by granting them freedom from dues; goods of foreign manufacture were restricted as imports. A similar act was passed in 1681.

Manufactures, Board of. See Board of Trustees.

Maol (or **Moil**) **Castle** (near Kyleakin, Skye). Ruins of what is said to have been a fortress where a Scandinavian princess levied tolls on ships passing through the Sound of Sleat.

Mar, Donald, Earl of (d. 1332). Nephew of *Robert I;* captured and taken to England 1306; exchanged after *Bannockburn* but chose to live in England until 1327; appointed *Guardian* 1332; defeated and killed at *Dupplin*.

Mar, Earldom. Mar was a province of the *Pictish* kingdom, and a *mormaer* fought at the battle of Clontarf in Ireland 1014; Ruadri, mormaer of M., was a witness 1131-2. The Celtic line of earls ended with Thomas, died 1374; his niece married Alexander, natural son of the '*Wolf of Badenoch*', who was styled Earl of Mar and died 1435. *James I* then annexed it and it was bestowed on John, son of *James II*, c. 1459; on his death it fell to the crown once more and was granted to *James III's* brother, Alexander, Duke of *Albany*, in 1482; John, 3rd son of James III, next held it, c. 1486-1503. *James Stewart*, son of *James V*, was created Earl of M. 1562 but resigned the title next year and became *Earl of Moray*. In 1565 Queen *Mary* granted earldom to 6th Lord *Erskine*, a descendant of the earlier line, and it remained with his descendants, though under forfeiture 1716-1824. In 1835 the then Earl succeeded to the earldom of *Kellie*, but on his death Kellie passed to the next male heir, his cousin, Walter Coningsby; as a result of a celebrated case, it was established that there were two earldoms, one created 1404 and the other 1565, the second now held with the earldom of Kellie.

Mar, John Stewart, Earl of (c. 1456-79). Younger son of *James II*; imprisoned in *Craigmillar Castle* and died mysteriously either there or in *Edinburgh*.

Mar, John Erskine, Earl of (c. 1510-72). Succeeded father as 6th Lord *Erskine* 1555; *Commendator* of *Dryburgh*, *Inchmahome* and *Cambuskenneth*; keeper of *Edinburgh Castle*, which he held in a kind of neutrality in the revolution of 1559-60; created Earl of Mar 1565; relieved of Edinburgh Castle 1567, but as governor of *Stirling Castle* he had the custody of the young *James VI*; appointed Regent 5 September 1571; died 28 October 1572.

Mar, John Erskine, Earl of (1562-1634). Son of preceding; educated with *James VI*, who called him 'Jockie o' the sclates'; joined party of *Ruthven Raiders* and in exile 1583-5; *Treasurer* 1616; built *Braemar Castle* to dominate his vassals the Farquharsons 1628.

Mar, John Erskine, 11th Earl of (1675-1732). Called 'Bobbing John' from his facility in changing sides; *Secretary of State* 1705 and commissioner for *Union* 1706; prepared to welcome George I 1714, but when he was repulsed he planned a rebellion; raised standard for '*James VIII*' on the Braes of Mar 1715; raised to a *Jacobite* dukedom; singularly inept as a leader; after the tactically drawn battle of *Sheriffmuir* he retreated and slipped off to France; later abandoned Jacobitism.

Mar's, Earl of, Greybreeks. *Royal Scots Fusiliers*, originally raised by Earl of Mar and uniformed in grey breeches.

Mar's Work. Remains of a town house in *Stirling* built by *Regent Mar* in 1570; most of the building stones are said to have come from *Cambuskenneth Abbey*, which Mar owned; occupied until time of 11th Earl.

March, Earldom. Alternative style of *Earls of Dunbar*, 1290-1455; held by Alexander, 2nd son of *James II*, 1455 until his death and by *Robert Stewart*, Bishop of Caithness, 1580-86; new creation for William Douglas, 2nd son of 3rd *Earl of Queensberry*, 1697; on death of 2nd Earl 1731 passed to *Earl of Wemyss*.

March Pursuivant. First mentioned 1515.

March Ridings. Before there were maps, plans and expert surveys, boundaries were defined by physical features and stones or other artificial marks. It was therefore important that individuals and communities should know their 'marches' or boundaries, and the custom developed of solemnly riding round the marches of a *burgh* annually, halting at various significant points and carrying out certain ceremonies to impress their importance on those present. Some pageantry carried out in certain towns derives from those ancient operations. Cf. Common Riding.

Marches. The areas of Scotland adjoining England were divided into the East, Middle and West Marches, each governed by a warden appointed by the crown (though two or even three wardenries were sometimes held by one man). The Marches had their own laws and customs, and during the 15th century the custom grew of holding Days of *Truce* when wardens from both sides of the frontier collaborated.

Marchmont. A name associated with *Roxburgh*, and later with *Kelso*; it appears on the royal signet from *James I* to *James V* and it gave a style to a herald from 1438.

Marchmont, Earldom. Created 1697 for *Sir Patrick Hume* of Polwarth; dormant on death of Hugh, 3rd Earl, 1794.

Margaret, St (c. 1046-93). Daughter of Edward 'the Exile', son of King Edmund Ironside and grandson of Ethelred II; Edward was an exile while the Danish Kings held the English throne and Margaret may have been born in Hungary; she was in England under Edward the Confessor, her great-uncle, but exiled again after William the Conqueror excluded her brother, Edgar the Atheling, from the throne; she came to Scotland and married *Malcolm III*. c. 1069; according to her biographer, *Turgot*, Prior of Durham, she eliminated out-dated usages in the Scottish church, and, after correspondence with Lanfranc, Archbishop of Canterbury, brought *Benedictine* monks to *Dunfermline*, but she patronised existing *Culdee* communities and made no changes in church organisation; it is assumed that she was in general an important agent of southern influence; buried at east end of Dunfermline Abbey, on site outside present church; her Gospel Book is in the Bodleian Library, Oxford. See Five Articles of Queen Margaret.

Margaret (1240-75). Daughter of Henry III; married *Alexander III* 1251; mother of *Alexander, David* and *Margaret,* all of whom predeceased their father.

Margaret (1261-83). Daughter of *Alexander III*; married Erik, King of Norway, 1281; mother of '*Maid of Norway*'.

Margaret, 'The Maid of Norway' (?1283-1290). Daughter of *Margaret*, daughter of *Alexander III*, by King Erik of Norway; acknowledged heir 5 February 1284; succeeded her grandfather 19 March 1286; her marriage to Prince Edward of England was arranged, but she died in or near *Orkney*, on her way to Scotland, on or about 26 September 1290; buried in Bergen.

Margaret (d. c. 1375). Wife of *David II*; see Drummond.

Margaret (1425-45). Daughter of *James I*; married Dauphin, later Louis XI.

Margaret (c. 1457-86). Daughter of Christian I of Denmark and Norway; married *James III* 1469.

Margaret Tudor (1489-1541). Daughter of Henry VII; married *James IV* 1503; married Archibald Douglas, *6th Earl of Angus*, 1514, and divorced him 1526; married Henry Stewart, later *Lord Methven*, 1526; played a significant, but capricious, part in affairs in the minority of *James V*—driven out of Scotland with Angus 1515, soon allowed to return, allied with John, Duke of *Albany*, 1521, and with *Earl of Arran* 1524, helped James to escape from Angus 1528.

Marianus Scotus (or Moelbrigte) (1028-c. 1082). Irish pupil of Tigernach who entered Cologne abbey 1056; wrote a universal history.

Marianus Scotus (or Muiredach) (d. 1088). First (Irish) abbot of St Peter's, *Ratisbon*.

Maries, The Queen's. The four companions chosen for *Mary, Queen of Scots*, not later than 1548, when she was sent to France. See Beaton, Fleming, Livingston and Seton.

Marischal. This office existed from 12th century; under *Robert I* it became hereditary in the Keith family, who became Earls Marischal in 1458 and continued until their extinction in 18th century.

Marischal College. See Aberdeen, Universities. Original buildings were those of *Franciscan* Friary; replaced after fire in 17th century; present building, designed by Archibald Simpson, dates from 1836-41.

Marischal, George Keith, 5th Earl (1553-1623). Grandson of 4th Earl, whom he succeeded 1581; spent several years on continent and became aligned with ultra-Protestants, partly under influence of Theodore Beza at Geneva; founded *Marischal College* in *Aberdeen* 1593.

Mark. Weight in *Orkney and Shetland*, 1/24 of a *lispund*, approximating to 1½ lbs. See also Merk.

Markinch (Fife). Church mentioned 11th century and existing tower perhaps late 11th century; *burgh of barony* for Law of Brunton 1673.

Markle (East Lothian). Some evidence that there existed a provost and prebendaries, but no proof of *collegiate* constitution.

Marr, Charles Kerr (1855-1919). Born *Troon*; in 1895 went to London and left £330,000 for education in Troon; Marr College opened 1935.

Marriage of the Thistle and the Rose. Marriage of *James IV* to *Margaret Tudor*, at *Holyrood*, 8 August 1503.

Marrow Bone Club. Whig club which met at Cameron's Tavern in Fleshmarket Close, *Edinburgh*, from 18th century until 1877.

Marrow Controversy. 'The Marrow of Modern Divinity', published 1646, was a puritan work emphasising the place of Grace as opposed to Works; in 1718 *James Hogg* of Carnock republished it and it encouraged the *Evangelical* wing in the *Church of Scotland*, who were censured by the *General Assembly* because their teaching could lead to moral laxity.

Marshall, William (1807-80). Born in Perthshire; secession *minister* at *Coupar Angus* 1830; advocated Free Trade; took leading place in union of *Relief* and *Secession* Churches 1847; also wrote historical works.

Marsiliers, Pierre de. Frenchman who taught Greek in *Montrose* in late 16th century.

Marston Moor, Battle of, 2 July 1644. *Charles I* defeated by parliamentarians and

Covenanters.

Martin, David (1737-98). Pupil and assistant of *Allan Ramsay*; engraved in mezzotint and painted portraits in Ramsay's style.

Martin, Martin (d. 1719). Factor of laird of *MacLeod*; wrote 'Voyage to St Kilda' (1698) and 'Description of Western Isles' (1703).

Martin, Sir Theodore (1816-1909). Practised as solicitor in *Edinburgh*; moved to London 1846 and became parliamentary agent; contributed to magazines under name of 'Bon Gautier' and collaborated with *William Edmonstone Aytoun*.

Martine, George (1635-1712). Secretary of Archbishop *James Sharp*; commissary clerk of *St Andrews*, deprived as *Episcopalian* 1690; wrote 'Reliquiae Divi Andreae'.

Martinmas. 11 November, called 'St Martin in Winter' to distinguish it from the feast of another Martin on 4 July (15 July by modern reckoning). See Term Days.

Marts. Carcasses of cattle slaughtered and salted at *Martinmas*.

Martyrs. See 'Heretics'.

Marwick, Sir James David (1816-1908). Born *Leith*, son of *Orkney* merchant; town clerk of *Edinburgh* 1860-73 and then of *Glasgow*; responsible for publication of many volumes of municipal records and a founder of the *Scottish Burgh Records Society*.

Mary de Coucy. Daughter of Enguerand III, Baron of Coucy in Picardy; married *Alexander II* 1239 and was mother of *Alexander III;* returned to France 1251 and later married Jean de Brienne, son of a king of Jerusalem.

Mary Erskine School (*Edinburgh*). More recent name of *Merchant Maiden Hospital*; see Erskine, Mary.

Mary of Gueldres (d. 1463). Daughter of Arnold, Duke of Gueldres; married *James II* 1449; founded *Trinity College, Edinburgh*, 1462.

Mary of Gueldres Hospital (*Stirling*). Founded by Mary of Gueldres before 1462, but apparently lapsed on her death.

Mary of Guise (1515-60). Daughter of Claude, Duke of Guise; married Duke of Longueville, who died 1537, and then *James V* (1538); took active part in the struggle for power in minority of her daughter, *Mary*, supporting the French cause against the English party; became *Governor* 1554 and pursued a policy of French domination which became unpopular; lenient to reformers until 1559, when her action against them provoked the rebellion which ultimately, with English help, brought the French regime in Scotland to an end; Mary died 11 June 1560.

Mary, Queen of Scots (1542-87). Daughter of *James V* and *Mary of Guise*; born *Linlithgow* 8 December 1542 and succeeded her father six days later; proposed as bride of Prince Edward of England 1543, but in 1548 sent to France as prospective bride of the Dauphin Francis, whom she married 1558 and who became King 1559; he died in December 1560 and Mary returned to Scotland in August 1561; she pursued a statesmanlike policy until her marriage to Henry, Lord *Darnley*, 1565; her son was born 19 June 1566, but she was soon estranged from her husband, who was murdered in February 1567; she married James, Earl of *Bothwell*, on 15 May, surrendered to rebels 15 June and abdicated 24 July; imprisoned in *Lochleven Castle*, but escaped 2 May 1568 and was defeated at *Langside*; fled to England, where she was imprisoned until her execution, 8 February 1587.

Maryculter (Kincardineshire). House of *Knights Templars* founded by Walter Bisset, 1221×1236; passed to *Knights Hospitallers* and became one of the *baronies* of the order.

Marymass Fair. Held yearly at *Irvine* in August; said to date from visit of Queen *Mary* in 1563, but it would seem to have pagan origins, with a bonfire around which the people made merry, and to have been associated in middle ages with Feast of the Assumption of the B.V.M. (15 August).

Marywell *(Angus). Burgh of barony* for Mill of Kincardine 1740.

Masons' Walk. In *Melrose* a procession takes place by torchlight from the Cross to the Abbey and back on St John's Day, 27 December.

Massacre of Glencoe. See Glencoe, Massacre of.

Masson, David (1822-1907). Born *Aberdeen*; professor of English literature, University College, London, 1853, and of Rhetoric and English Literature, *Edinburgh*, 1865-95; wrote 'Life of Milton' and *'Drummond of Hawthornden'* and edited many volumes of the Register of the *Privy Council* of Scotland; Historiographer Royal 1893.

Master Mason. Office first recorded 1532.

Master of Works. Office first mentioned 1507; but masters of works for individual buildings appear in 14th century.

Matheson, Sir James (1796-1878). Son of Donald M. of Shiness; became head of trading firm at Canton; purchased island of *Lewis* 1844. See Jardine, Matheson and Co.

Matilda (d. 1130). Grand-niece of William the Conqueror; daughter of Waltheof, Earl of Northumbria; married Simon de St Liz, Earl of Northampton; inherited *Earldom of Huntingdon*; married *David I* 1113-4.

Mauchline (Ayrshire). Lands belonged to *Melrose Abbey*, but there was no monastic establishment other than a grange; property erected into lordship of Kylesmuir 1606. References to a 'hospice' do not signify a hospital, but only a residence for the supervisor of the Melrose property and for visitors from Melrose. *Burgh of barony* under abbey 1510 and *burgh of regality* for *Earl of Loudoun* 1707.

Maule Family. Of Norman origin, first mentioned in Scotland c. 1141.

Maule, Fox (1801-74). Son of William, Baron *Panmure*, younger brother of George, 9th *Earl of Dalhousie*; served in army 1820-32; M.P. for various Scottish constituencies 1835-52; Secretary at War 1846-52 and 1855-8; 2nd Baron Panmure 1852; 11th Earl of Dalhousie 1860.

Maule, Harry and Patrick, Earls of Panmure. See Panmure.

Maurice (d. 1347). Abbot of *Inchaffray* who blessed Scottish army before *Bannockburn*; Bishop of *Dunblane* 1322.

Mavor, Osborne Henry. See Bridie, James.

Maxton (Roxburghshire). *Burgh of barony* for Ker of Littledean 1588.

Maxton, James (1885-1946). Born *Pollokshaws*; school teacher; joined *Independent Labour Party* 1904; imprisoned 1916 for calling general strike on *Clyde*; M.P. for Bridgeton 1922-46 and chairman of the I.L.P. 1926-31 and 1934-9; wrote 'Lenin' and 'If I were Dictator'.

Maxwell Family. Name derives from 'Maccusweel' ('pool of Maccus' in Anglo-Saxon) in Tweed; individuals named 'de Maccuswell' appear soon after 1200, and before 1300 held office as *sheriff* of *Peebles* and as *Chamberlain.*

Maxwell, James Clerk. See Clerk-Maxwell.

Maxwell, Sir John, of *Terregles* (c. 1512-83). 2nd son of *5th Lord Maxwell,* and in right of wife 4th Baron *Herries*; warden of west *marches* 1552; rallied to Queen *Mary* after murder of *Riccio* and commanded her cavalry at *Langside*.

Maxwell, John, 8th Lord Maxwell (1553-93). Created *Earl of Morton* on death of *Regent Morton*; denounced rebel 1582 and 1585 but after he helped to capture *Stirling Castle* in 1585 with the lords of the ultra-Protestant faction he received an indemnity; warden of west *marches* 1592; killed in fight with Johnstones.

Maxwell, John, 9th Lord Maxwell (c. 1586-1612). Son of preceding; at feud with Johnstones, and also with *Douglases* over *Earldom of Morton*; after once escaping from *Edinburgh Castle* (1607) he was captured and executed for killing the laird of *Johnstone*.

Maxwell, John (c. 1590-1647). *Bishop of Ross*, *Privy Councillor* and Extraordinary *Lord of Session* 1633; one of the compilers of the 1637 *Prayer Book*, which he used in his cathedral for some months; deposed by *Glasgow Assembly* 1638; Bishop of Killala and Achonry in Ireland and Archbishop of Tuam 1643.

Maxwell, Lordship. Created by 1445 for Herbert M. of *Caerlaverock*.

Maxwell, Robert, 5th Lord Maxwell (d. 1546). Warden of west *marches* 1517; *provost* of *Edinburgh* 1524; surrendered to English at *Solway Moss* and agreed to assist them in Scotland; again warden of west marches 1547.

Maxwell, William, 5th Lord Herries (d. 1603). Warden of west *marches*; at feud with Johnstones; submitted feud to arbitration 1597.

Maxwell, William, 5th Earl of Nithsdale. See Nithsdale.

Maxwell, Winifred, Countess of Nithsdale. See Nithsdale.

Maxwelltown (Kirkcudbrightshire). *Burgh of barony* for *Maxwell* of Terregles 1810.

May. Island reputed to have been abode of St *Adrian*; *Benedictine* or *Cluniac* priory founded by *David I*; dependent on Reading until 1318; then associated with *Pittenweem* and probably removed to mainland. A *coal* beacon was established 1635 and a lighthouse 1816.

Maybole (Ayrshire). Chief town of *Carrick* and its castle the headquarters of the Kennedy family, later *Earls of Cassillis*; a chapel beside the parish church, founded by John Kennedy of Dunure 1371, developed into *collegiate church* which had a constitution by 1382; town became *burgh of barony* for Earl of Cassillis 1516; scene of a debate in 1561 between *John Knox* and *Quentin Kennedy*.

Meal Monday. Holiday given to Scottish students half-way through the long term, to enable the poorer of them to return home and acquire a new supply of meal.

Mearns. Province of *Pict*ish kingdom, corresponding to modern Kincardineshire; there was a *mormaer*, but the area did not become an earldom.

Mearns (Renfrewshire). Lands and *barony* passed by marriage from family styled 'of Mearns' to *Maxwells* of *Caerlaverock*, later *Earls of Nithsdale*; sold c. 1648 to Sir George Maxwell of Nether Pollock and later acquired by Sir Archibald Stewart of Blackhall.

Mears, Sir Frank Charles (1880-1953). Designed *David Livingstone* Memorial, *Blantyre*, and carried out restorations in old town of *Edinburgh*; served widely as consultant for local authorities and other bodies.

Mediatise. To insert an intermediate *superior* over a *vassal*, e.g. by granting a *burgh*, hitherto royal, to a baron.

Medina, Sir John Baptist de (1659-1710). Of Spanish parentage, and Flemish by birth; came to Scotland 1688 under patronage of *Earl of Leven* and became fashionable portrait painter.

Medina, John (1721-96). Grandson of preceding; employed to restore pictures at *Holyrood;* made copies of the 'Ailsa' portrait of *Mary,* Queen of Scots.

Medraut. Traditionally a king of the *Picts* who defeated and slew King Arthur at Camelon, near *Falkirk*; not known to history.

Meggernie Castle (Glen Lyon, Perthshire). Built by Colin Campbell of Glenlyon c. 1585; later held by Menzies of Culdares, who was active in the '*Fifteen*; descended to Stewarts of Cardeny, who adopted name Stewart-Menzies and sold estate 1885.

Megginch Castle (Carse of *Gowrie*, Perthshire). Probably built by Peter *Hay* (d. before 1496) and altered by another Peter 1575; sold by Sir George Hay, last of the family, to the Drummonds, who still have it.

Meigle (Perthshire). *Burgh of barony* for Fullarton of *Ardoch* 1608. The Museum of Sculptured Stones, of Celtic Christian period, one of most notable assemblages of Dark Age sculpture in Western Europe.

Meikle, Andrew (1719-1811). Son of James M., who invented 'fanners' for winnowing grain 1710 and a barley-mill; mill-wright at Houston, near *Dunbar*; patented machine for dressing grain 1768; experimented with threshing machinery from 1768 and started producing it 1789; *Sir John Sinclair* raised £1500 for his relief in his old age.

Meikle Dalton (Dumfriesshire). *Burgh of barony* for Carruthers of Holmains 1755.

Meikle, George (d. 1811). Son of *Andrew M*; invented water-raising wheel which was used in draining Kincardine Moss 1787.

Meikleour (Perthshire). *Burgh of barony* for *Mercer* of Meikleour 1665.

Melba, Dame Nellie (c. 1860-1931). Helen Porter Mitchell; born Melbourne; daughter of an *Angus* farmer who emigrated to Australia; first trained in Australia but after a visit to London in 1886 went on to further study in Paris; became a world-famous opera singer.

Meldrum, William, of *Cleish* and *Binns* (c. 1485-1550). 'Squire Meldrum' of verses by *Sir David Lindsay*, son of Archibald M; took part in naval expedition to France 1513; wooed Marjory Lawson, widow of Sir John Haldane of *Gleneagles* (d. 1513); was attacked on road to *Leith*, probably by her brothers, 1517, and left for dead; *sheriff* depute of Fife 1522.

Melfort (Argyll). *Burgh of regality* for Countess of Melfort 1688.

Melfort, Earldom. Created 1686 for John Drummond, 2nd son of James, 3rd *Earl of Perth*; he accompanied *James VII* to France and was *forfeited*; title restored 1853 to George, titular 6th Earl, who was also Earl of Perth, but dormant on his death.

Mellerstain House (Berwickshire). Designed by William and Robert *Adam*; originally built by George Baillie (husband of *Grizzell Baillie*) 1725; now property of *Earl of Haddington*.

Melrose. *Burgh of barony* 1605; created afresh for *Viscount Haddington* 1609; *burgh of regality* for *Earl of Melrose* 1621.

Melrose Abbey (*Cistercian*) (Roxburghshire). Founded by *David I* c. 1136; suffered in English attacks, especially 1385 and 1544-5; much of the extant building is late 15th century; erected as *temporal lordship* for *John Ramsay,* Viscount Haddington, 1609.

Melrose and Company. *Edinburgh* firm which started importing tea from Canton to *Leith* in 1833.

Melrose, Battle of, 24 July 1526. Unsuccessful attempt by *Walter Scott* of *Branxholm* to rescue *James V* from *Earl of Angus*.

Melrose, Earldom. Created 1619 for *Sir Thomas Hamilton*, who changed the title to *Earl of Haddington*.

Melrose,. Old. Site of early monastery, associated with *Aidan,* c. 635; first three priors were Eata, *Boisil* and *Cuthbert.*

Melville, Andrew (1545-1622). Born Baldovie, *Angus*; after ten years on the continent, largely at Geneva, Melville came to Scotland 1574 to be principal first of *Glasgow* and then (1580) of *St Andrews*; a scholar, especially in languages, he did much to reorganise university education and was a powerful influence on his students, but his main importance was his advocacy of a *presbyterian* system of church government, with *ministers* of equal rank and administration in the hands of courts, and he also argued for the exclusion of lay authority in the Church; in conflict with the state, he was exiled 1584-5 and, summoned to London in 1606, was not allowed to return to Scotland and ended his career as a professor at Sedan.

Melville, Andrew (1624-1706). After some time on the continent, he joined the *Covenanters* 1647 and fought at *Worcester*; escaped to Holland and served in France, Sweden and Brandenburg; wrote an autobiography.

Melville, Arthur (1855-1904). Born *Guthrie, Angus;* studied in Scotland and then travelled in Near East, painting in oils and water colours.

Melville Castle (Midlothian). *Barony* took its name from a Norman de Malavilla in 12th century; it passed to Sir John Ross of Halkheid in late 14th century; purchased 1705 by David Rennie, through whose daughter it passed to Henry Dundas, 1st. *Viscount Melville*; present castle built on site of earlier one 1786, to designs by James Playfair, father of *W.H. Playfair.*

Melville College. See Edinburgh Institution.

Melville, David, 3rd Earl of Leven and 2nd Earl of Melville (1660-1728). Son of *George, 1st Earl of Melville*; succeeded to *Earldom of Leven* 1681; raised regiment of Scottish refugees 1688 and fought at *Killiecrankie* and in Ireland; served in Flanders 1692; commander-in-chief in Scotland 1706; dismissed 1712.

Melville, Earldom. Created 1690 for *George, 4th Lord M.*

Melville, George, 4th Lord and 1st Earl of Melville (1636-1707). Succeeded father 1643; acted against *Covenanters* 1679 but associated with Rye House plot 1683 and fled to Holland; assisted Monmouth's Rebellion (1685) financially, and was forfeited; returned 1689; *Secretary of State* 1689, Commissioner to *General Assembly* 1690, President of Council 1696; deprived of office 1702.

Melville, Henry Dundas, 1st Viscount (1742-1811). Son of Robert *Dundas*, Lord Arniston, *Lord President*; *Solicitor General* 1766; M.P. for Midlothian 1774 and later for *Edinburgh*; *Lord Advocate* 1775-83; member of administration of William Pitt the younger as Treasurer of the Navy, Home Secretary, President of the Board of Control for India, Secretary for War and First Lord of the Admiralty; extended his influence over the Scottish electoral system until he controlled the elections in 36 constituencies and was referred to as 'Harry the Ninth, uncrowned King of Scotland'; he became unpopular when radical tendencies arose in the 1790s and resigned in 1805 after accusations of malversation.

Melville House (Fife). Built 1692 by *Earl of Melville*.

Melville, Sir James, of Halhill (1535-1617). Son of Sir John M. of Raith, who joined the reforming and pro-English party and was executed for treason in 1548; went to France 1550 and remained mostly on the continent until 1564, as courtier and soldier; employed on diplomatic missions to England 1564 and later; wrote 'Memoirs of his Own Time', with vivid but sometimes misleading narrative.

Melville, James (1556-1614). Nephew of *Andrew Melville*, of whom he was a colleague at *Glasgow* and *St Andrews*; exiled in England 1584-5 and again from 1606; *minister* of *Anstruther* 1586; wrote 'Autobiography and Diary'.

Melville, Robert (1527-1621). Son of Sir John M. of Raith; served in France, returned 1559; in Queen *Mary's* army at *Langside*; *Treasurer-*Depute 1581; *Lord of Session* (Murdocairny) 1594; created Baron M. of Monimail 1616.

Melville, Robert Saunders, 2nd Viscount (1771-1851). Son of *Henry, 1st Viscount*; M.P. for English constituencies and then for Midlothian (from 1800); President of Board of Trade, Secretary for Ireland and First Lord of the Admiralty; became 'manager for Scotland' as the controlling influence in Scottish elections.

Melville, Thomas (1726-53). Studied divinity at *Glasgow*; wrote 'Observations of Light and Colours', with notes on experiments in spectrum analysis, and 'Refrangibility of the Rays of Light'.

Melville, Viscountcy. Created 1802 for Henry Dundas. See Melville, Henry Dundas.

Menstrie Castle (Clackmannanshire). 16th century building, recently restored as housing accommodation; birthplace of *Sir William Alexander* and *Sir Ralph Abercromby*; two rooms commemorate the connection of Alexander with *Nova Scotia*.

Menteith. Evidently an early province, but there is no evidence of its organisation before an *Earldom* is mentioned in 1164. When the earldom fell to the crown Menteith was a *stewartry*.

Menteith, Earldom. First recorded 1164, it descended deviously until it came, in right of his wife, to Robert, Duke of *Albany*; after the execution of his son, *Murdoch*, it was conferred on Malise Graham, formerly Earl of *Strathearn*, and remained with his descendants until the death without issue of Earl William in 1694.

Menteith, Sir John (d. c. 1329). Captured by English 1296 but released 1297 and made governor of castle and *sheriffdom* of *Dumbarton*; captured *William Wallace* and handed him over to English; created *Earl of Lennox*; joined *Robert I* 1307 and was one of the barons whose names were attached to the Declaration of *Arbroath*.

Menteith, Robert (fl. 1621-60). Educated at *Edinburgh*; professor of philosophy at Saumur; *minister* of *Duddingston* 1630; exiled 1633; became Roman Catholic; secretary to Cardinal de Retz and canon of Notre Dame, Paris; wrote 'Histoire des Troubles de la Grande Bretagne'.

Menteith, William Graham, 7th Earl of (1591-1661). His claim to the *Earldom of Strathearn*, with its implied right to seniority in the royal line, led to his demotion to the *Earldom of Airth*.

Menzies Castle (Perthshire). Built c. 1570 and later enlarged, as seat of Menzies family, who originated in Normandy and came from Durisdeer in Dumfriesshire to settle at Comrie Castle in 13th century.

Menzies, John (1756-1834). Gave his estate of *Blairs*, Aberdeenshire, to Roman Catholic Church for education of priests, 1827; also helped to found St Margaret's Convent, *Edinburgh*.

Menzies, Michael (d. 1766). *Advocate* who invented a threshing machine and machinery for *coal* mines.

Mercat (or **Market**) **Cross.** A law attributed to *William I* commanded all goods for sale in burghs to be presented at the 'mercat and mercat cross'; as the focal point of the *burgh* it became the place where proclamations were made and punishments inflicted; in form it varied from a simple cross or pillar to an elaborate platform type.

Mercer, Andrew (1775-1842). Born *Selkirk*; studied for church and turned to miniature painting; wrote articles, poems and a 'History of *Dunfermline*'.

Mercer Family. In 1478 Robert Mercer was a *burgess* of *Perth* and he acquired *Balhousie Castle*; the family provided several *provosts* of Perth and are said to have given the *North and South Inches* to the town; also acquired estates of *Aldie* and *Meikleour*.

Mercer, Hugh (c. 1726-77). Born *Aberdeen*; as medical student joined *Jacobite* army 1745; took up soldiering in America; in command at Fort du Quesne; drilled Virginia militia; fatally wounded at Princetown; county and town in Pennsylvania named after him.

Merchant Banking Company of Glasgow. See Glasgow.

Merchant Banking Company of Stirling. See Stirling.

Merchant Company of Edinburgh. See Edinburgh.

Merchant Guilds. The merchants in a *burgh*, who were the wealthiest and most influential element in a community whose primary purpose was trade, formed themselves into a guild which very often controlled the burgh administration, to the exclusion of the *craftsmen*. Cf. Dean of Guild.

Merchant Maiden Hospital. Founded 1695 by contributions from the *Merchant Company of Edinburgh* and a donation from *Mary Erskine*; originally at corner of Bristo Place and Lothian Street, it acquired a building in Lauriston 1816; converted from boarding establishment to day school and moved to Queen Street 1871; moved to Ravelston House 1966.

Merchiston Castle (Edinburgh). 15th century tower, home of Napier family, who provided *provosts* of *Edinburgh* in 15th century; birthplace of *John Napier*; restored as nucleus of Napier College 1962.

Merchiston Castle School. Founded 1833 by Charles Chalmers (brother of *Thomas C.*) at Merchiston Castle; moved to Colinton 1924.

'Mercurius Caledonius'. News-sheet published by *Thomas Sydserf*, with comments on Scottish affairs, 1661.

'Mercurius Politicus'. Started in London 1650; reprint produced in *Leith* 1653 for Cromwellian troops; ceased publication at *Restoration*, but reappeared as 'Mercurius Publicus' with new management and policy.

Merk. Rarely a coin, but much used in reckoning; = 13s.4d.

Merkland Cross (*Dumfries*). Said to mark spot where Master of Maxwell was murdered 1484.

Merlin. The magician of Arthurian legend is reputed to have been buried at Drummelzier.

Merse. The eastern part of the Scottish Border or *March*, comprehending roughly the country between the Lammermoors and the Tweed, but later identified with Berwickshire.

Merton (Wigtownshire). *Burgh of barony* for MacCulloch of Merton 1504.

Messuage. House or mansion; the chief messuage of an extensive property was usually designated as the place where *sasine* was to be given.

Methil (Fife). *Burgh of barony* for archbishop of *St Andrews* 1662.

Methven (Perthshire), **Battle of,** 19 June 1306. *Robert I* defeated by English under Earl of Pembroke.

Methven Collegiate Church. Founded in parish church by *Walter Stewart, Earl of Atholl,* 1433; new erection 1516.

Methven, Lands and Castle of. Belonged in 13th century to Moubray family, who were forfeited by *Robert I* and the lands conferred on Walter, the High *Steward,* whose son succeeded as *Robert II*; that King granted Methven to his son, *Walter Stewart, Earl of Atholl,* forfeited 1437, and the lands were then used as dower for successive queens. An earlier castle (used as a residence by royal dowagers including *Margaret Tudor,* who died there) was superseded by present building 1680.

Methven, Lordship. *Margaret Tudor* married as her 3rd husband Henry Stewart, a descendant of *Robert II,* and he was created Lord Methven 1528; 3rd Lord died without issue c. 1580 and the property was then granted to Ludovick, *Duke of Lennox.* It was bought in 1664 by Patrick Smythe of *Braco.*

Methven, Paul (d. 1606). Said to have been a *Dundee* baker; *minister* of *Jedburgh* 1560; deposed for adultery 1562; took refuge in England, where he became a prebendary of Wells and ancestor of the noble family of Methuen.

'Michael, The Great'. Ship built for *James IV* in 1511, said to have been 240 feet long, with 300 sailors, 120 gunners and 1000 soldiers; lent to France 1513 and later sold, she rotted away at Brest. See Wood, Sir Andrew.

Michaelmas. Feast of St Michael the Archangel, 29 September; various celebrations associated with it, especially horse-racing; date of elections in *sheriff*doms and *burghs.* See St Michael's Struan.

Mickle, William Julius (1735-88). Born *Langholm*; owned brewery in *Edinburgh*; wrote 'There's nae luck aboot the hoose', a ballad 'Cumnor Hall', which suggested to *Scott* the plot of 'Kenilworth', and 'The Concubine'.

Middleton, Earldom. Created 1660 for *John Middleton*; *forfeited* when his son, Charles (d. 1719) followed *James VII* into exile; titular 3rd Earl, John, his son, died unmarried 1746 and no claim has since been made.

Middleton, John, 1st Earl of (c. 1608-74). Returned from French service to join *Covenanters* 1639; for a time in English parliamentary army, but rejoined Covenanters and was second in command at *Philiphaugh*; Lieutenant-General of cavalry at *Preston,* where he was taken prisoner, but escaped, and after being captured at *Worcester* escaped again, to join the King in France and lead a royalist rising in Scotland 1653; created Earl by exiled King 1656, ratified 1660, when he was made Commander-in-Chief in Scotland and Commissioner to the Scottish *Parliament*; deprived of office 1663, he was made governor of Tangier, where he died.

Midmar Castle (Aberdeenshire). Built on Z-plan in 16th century, with later additions; not at present occupied; passed through various families, including *Gordons* for a period after 1422, and was sold to Gordon of *Cluny* 1842.

Mile. Scots mile was 1,984 yards.

Militia. Act for raising militia passed 1797 in expectation of French invasion; partly because of fear that enlistment would lead to overseas service, there were riots which led to 11 deaths in an encounter with soldiers at *Tranent.*

Mill, James (1773-1836). Son of shoemaker at Logiepert, *Angus*; ordained 1798; went to London 1802; contributor to various journals and to '*Encyclopaedia Britannica*'; assisted in foundation of London University 1825. His son was John Stuart Mill (1806-73).

Mill, Walter. See Mylne.

Millar, James (1762-1827). Edited 'Encyclopaedia Edinensis'.

Millar, John (1735-1801). Born Shotts; professor of law at *Glasgow* 1761; opposed slave trade; wrote 'The Origin of the Distinction of Ranks' and 'Historical View of the English Government'.

Miller, Andrew. See Myllar.

Miller, Betsy (d. 1864). For 24 years master of the brig 'Clitus'.

Miller, George (1771-1838). Erected first East Lothian printing press in *Dunbar* 1795; removed to *Haddington* 1804 and published 'Cheap Magazine'.

Miller, Hugh (1802-56). Born *Cromarty*; began life as stone-mason, but educated himself, became a banker and in 1835 wrote 'Scenes and Legends of the North of Scotland'; he then embarked on geology—'Old Red Sandstone' (1841), 'Footprints of the Creator' (1847) and 'Testimony of the Rocks' (1857); supported *Free Church* and edited its periodical 'Witness'; probably tension between orthodoxy and science caused him to take his life; wrote an autobiography, 'My Schools and Schoolmasters'. His wife, Lydia Falconer Fraser (c. 1811-76), edited his works and wrote stories for the young under name 'Harriet Myrtle'.

Miller, Patrick, of *Dalswinton* (1731-1815). Brother of *Sir Thomas M*; *Edinburgh* merchant, a director and later deputy governor of *Bank of Scotland*; shareholder in *Carron Company*; experimented with methods of propelling ships by paddle-wheels, with *James Taylor* and *William Symington*.

Miller, Sir Thomas (1717-89). *Solicitor General* 1759; *Lord Advocate* 1760; Lord *Justice Clerk* (Glenlee) 1766; *Lord President* 1788.

Miller, Sir William (1755-1846). Son of preceding; *Lord of Session* (Glenlee) 1795-1840.

Miller, William (1796-1882). Born *Edinburgh*; engraver of Turner's paintings and others; of a Quaker family, descended from a master gardener at *Holyrood*; lived at Millerfield House, south of the Meadows in Edinburgh.

Miller, William (1810-72). Wrote 'Wee Willie Winkie' and other nursery rhymes.

Millers Acre. Site of *Edward Balliol's* encampment before the battle of *Dupplin*; legend had it that it took its name from a miller whose daughter was the mother of *Malcolm III*.

Milligan, William (1821-93). *Minister* of Cameron and Kilconquhar; professor of biblical criticism at *Aberdeen* 1860; assisted in revision of New Testament Translation 1870; first president of Scottish Church Society.

Millport (Bute). *Police Burgh* 1864. *Collegiate Church* of Holy Spirit founded 1849-53 by G.F. Boyle, later *Earl of Glasgow*.

Mills, George (1808-81). Born *Glasgow*; shipbuilder and stockbroker; founded 'Glasgow Advertiser and Shipbuilding Gazette' 1857; established Milton Chemical Works 1866; founded 'Northern Star' in *Aberdeen* 1869; was literary critic of 'Glasgow Mail' and wrote several novels.

Milne. See Mylne.

Milne, Alexander (1742-1838). Born *Fochabers*; emigrated and settled in 1776 in New Orleans, where he died; left 100,000 dollars to Fochabers for erection of a 'Free School', opened 1846.

Milne-Home, David (1805-90). Son of Admiral Sir David Milne (1763-1845); founded Scottish Meteorological Society and proposed an observatory on *Ben Nevis*.

Milngavie (Stirlingshire). *Police burgh* after 1862.

Mingary Castle (Ardnamurchan). Possibly as early as 13th century, but with later insertions in courtyard; may have been seat of MacIans of Ardnamurchan; occupied by *James IV* 1493 and 1495; captured by *Montrose's* ally, *Alexander MacDonald*, 1644; garrisoned 1745.

Minister. In reformed church, cleric authorised to preach and to administer the sacraments.

Minnigaff (Kirkcudbrightshire). *Burgh of barony* for McKie of *Larg* 1619.

Mint. In early times coins were minted at various places, but by 15th or 16th century coining was concentrated in *Edinburgh*; in 1547 the mint was in South Gray's Close, adjoining the Cowgate. By the Treaty of *Union* a Scottish mint was to continue, but it ceased to exist in the later 18th century.

Minto (Roxburghshire). *Burgh of barony* for Scott of Haychester 1695.

Minto, Earldom. The lands passed from Turnbulls (14th century) to Stewarts and were sold to Sir Gilbert *Elliot* (1722-77), whose son, Sir Gilbert (1751-1814) was created Baron Minto 1797 and Earl of Minto and Viscount Melgund 1813. Gilbert John Murray Kynynmond, 4th Earl (1845-1914), who succeeded 1891, was Governor General of Canada 1898-1904 and Viceroy of India 1905-10.

Minto, William (1845-93). Went from *Aberdeen University* to London, where he edited the 'Examiner' and was leader writer to 'Daily News' and 'Pall Mall Gazette'; professor of logic and literature, Aberdeen, 1880-93.

Mirin, St. Celtic monk who settled at *Paisley* in 6th century.

'The Mirror'. Periodical produced in *Edinburgh* by social club for legal and literary men, 1779-80; succeeded by '*The Lounger*' 1785-7.

Mitchell, Alexander Ferrier (1822-99). *Minister* of *Dunnichen* 1847; professor of Hebrew at *St Andrews* and later of divinity and ecclesiastical history.

Mitchell, Sir Andrew (1708-71). Born *Edinburgh*, son of *minister* of *St Giles*; left Scotland c. 1730; Under-*Secretary for Scotland* 1741-7; M.P. for Aberdeenshire 1747 and for *Elgin burghs* 1755 and 1761; ambassador to Prussia 1756.

Mitchell, Sir Arthur (1826-1909). Born *Elgin*; Commissioner in Lunacy 1870-95; wrote 'The Past in the Present', edited *Macfarlane*'s 'Geographical Collections' and made important contributions to the bibliography of Scottish history.

Mitchell, James (d. 1678). Joined *Pentland Rising*; escaped to Holland; returned 1668 and attempted to murder *Archbishop James Sharp*; again escaped; arrested 1673 and confessed but retracted the confession; executed.

Mitchell, James Leslie (1901-35). 'Lewis Grassic Gibbon'; journalist, soldier, airman and archaeologist; his varied writings include 'Hanno, or the Future of Exploration', 'The Thirteenth Disciple', 'The Calendar of Cairo', 'Egyptian Nights' and 'The Conquest of the Maya', but he is best known for his trilogy which formed 'A Scots Quair' (Book).

Mitchell, John Murray (1815-1904). Born *Aberdeen*; went to Bombay as *Presbyterian* missionary and founded *Free Church* mission at Poona 1843; in Bengal 1867-73; *minister* of Scots church at Nice 1888-98; wrote 'Hindustan Past and Present' and 'The Great Religions of India'.

Mitchell Library, Glasgow. Founded on bequest by Stephen Mitchell (d. 1874); opened 1877 and moved to present building 1891.

Mitton (or Myton), Battle of, 20 September 1319. Scots under *Thomas Randolph, Earl of Moray*, defeated English in Yorkshire; so many clergy were killed that the encounter was known as 'The Chapter'.

Mochrum (Wigtownshire). Lands belonged to Dunbars, then *MacDowalls*, and passed by marriage to the *Bute* family, who restored the Castle or 'Old Place', which had long been ruinous, to its medieval character.

Mod. An annual festival of *Gaelic* song and poetry, organised by *An Comunn Gaidhealach.*

Moderates. Party in *Church of Scotland* in 18th century who favoured a more liberal theology and distrusted 'enthusiasm'; they later came to support *patronage*. See also Evangelicals.

Moderator. The chairman of each court of the reformed church, from the *kirk session* to the *General Assembly*.

Modwenna, St (d. 518). Irish princess baptized by St Patrick; travelled with some companions to Scotland, where she founded churches; died at *Dundee*.

Moffat (Dumfriesshire). *Burgh of regality* for Johnstone of Corhead 1648; *Grammar School* founded by Robert Johnstone (1557-1659), brother-in-law of *George Heriot*, and in 1834 united with the old parish school to form Moffat *Academy*.

Moffat, Graham (1866-1951). Son of a *Glasgow* teacher of elocution; became famous for his portrayal of Scottish life and character in a series of plays—'Bunty pulls the strings', which lasted for 16 months at the Haymarket in London (then a record), 'Susie tangles the strings', 'A scrape o' the pen' and 'Granny'.

Moffat, Dr Robert (1795-1883). Born Ormiston; went to southern Africa under London Missionary Society and penetrated what is now Rhodesia; followed by *David Livingstone*, his son-in-law.

Moidart. One of the old districts of the West Highlands, bounded north and north-east by Arisaig, south-east and south by Loch Shiel and Loch Moidart. It was in Moidart that Prince *Charles Edward* landed in 1745, with companions known as 'The Seven Men of Moidart'—the *Marquis of Tullibardine*, Aeneas MacDonald, a banker, Francis Strickland, of a Westmorland family, Sir Thomas Sheridan, who had been the prince's tutor, George Kelly, a *non-juring* clergyman, Sir John MacDonnell, a soldier who had been in the Spanish service, and *John William O'Sullivan*, who had been a professional soldier in France.

Moir, David Macbeth (1798-1851). 'Delta' of *Blackwood's Magazine*; a *Musselburgh* physician who wrote on medical subjects, including cholera; first essays published in 'Cheap Magazine' at *Haddington* 1812; wrote 'The Bombardment of Algiers, and other Poems' (1816), 'The Legend of Genevieve' (1824) and 'The Autobiography of Mansie Wauch' (1828).

Molaise, St (d. c. 639). Said to have been born in Scottish *Dalriada* and educated in Ireland; set up cell or community on *Holy Island*, Arran; returned to Ireland and was abbot of a monastery there.

Moluag, St (d. 592). Came from Ireland and established himself on *Lismore*, to the chagrin of his rival *Columba*; associated also with *Rosemarkie* and *Mortlach*; his pastoral staff preserved in Lismore.

Monan, St (d. c. 875). Traditionally a companion of *Adrian*, whose martyrdom he shared.

Monboddo, James Burnett, Lord (1714-99). Born Monboddo; as *advocate*, prominent in *Douglas Cause*; *Lord of Session* (Monboddo) 1767; learned and eloquent, he was prominent among *Edinburgh* literati, and was noted for eccentricities; wrote 'Ancient Metaphysics' (1779-99) and 'The Origin and Progress of Language' (1773-92), in which he emphasised the possible relationship between men and monkeys and was therefore credited with the belief that humans were born with tails.

Monck, General George (1608-70). In Dutch

service 1629; returned to join royal army against *Covenanters* 1639; fought against Irish rebels 1642-3 and then on King's side in England until he joined Parliament 1646; in Ireland again 1648; with Cromwell in Scotland 1650; Commander-in-Chief in Scotland 1651 and 1654-60; in naval actions 1652-3 during Dutch War; took forces from Scotland to bring about *Restoration*.

Moncreiff(e) (Perthshire). On summit of hill was a fort which may have been an important *Pict*ish centre; the lands have been held since early 13th century by a family taking its name from them; Moncreiffe House built 1679 by *Sir William Bruce*.

Moncreiff, Sir Henry (1750-1827). 8th Baronet; *minister* of *Blackford* 1771 and of *St Cuthbert's, Edinburgh*, 1775.

Moncreiff, Henry James, Lord (1840-1909). 2nd Lord M. of *Tulliebole*; *Lord of Session* 1888.

Moncreiff, Sir Henry Wellwood (1809-83). 10th Baronet; son of *Sir James Wellwood M*; *minister* of Free St Cuthbert's, *Edinburgh*, 1852.

Moncreiff, James, 1st Lord M. of *Tulliebole* (1811-95). Son of *Sir James Wellwood M*; *advocate* 1833; M.P. for various constituencies 1851-68; *Lord Advocate* 1851; *Justice Clerk* 1869.

Moncreiff, Sir James Wellwood (1776-1851). Son of *Sir Henry M*; *advocate* 1799; *Lord of Session* (Moncreiff) 1829.

Moniaive (Dumfriesshire). *Burgh of barony* for *Earl of Dumfries* 1636.

Monifieth *(Angus). Culdee* settlement referred to as extinct 1243; *police burgh*.

Monimail (Fife). Lands belonged to bishops of *St Andrews*, and the castle (with a 'Beaton's Tower') was occupied by *David Beaton* and *John Hamilton*; property acquired by Balfours and later passed to Melvilles.

Monivaird. See Monzievaird.

Monkland Canal. Constructed 1761-90 to link *Glasgow* with the *iron* and *coal* fields of the *Airdrie-Coatbridge* district.

Monks of St Giles. Social club in *Edinburgh*, founded 1852; the office-bearers have monastic titles and the members use monkish names.

Monmouth, Anne Scott, Duchess of (1651-1732). Younger daughter of Francis, 2nd Earl of *Buccleuch*, and Countess of Buccleuch 1693; married James, Duke of Monmouth, illegitimate son of *Charles II*, 1663; Duchess in her own right after his execution 1685.

Monreith Tower (Wigtownshire). Belonged to *Maxwells*, who acquired *barony* 1481; ruinous and superseded by modern mansion.

Monro, Alexander (d. c. 1715). Professor of divinity at *St Andrews* 1682; principal of *Edinburgh* 1683; deprived at *Revolution*.

Monro, Alexander (1697-1767). Son of naval surgeon who later practised in *Edinburgh*; professor of anatomy at Edinburgh 1719-69; real founder of *Edinburgh School of Medicine*; wrote 'Anatomy of Human Bones and Nerves' (1726).

Monro, Alexander (1733-1817). Youngest son of preceding; joint professor with father 1754; succeeded father and held chair until 1808; wrote 'Treatise on the Lymphatics' (1770), 'The Structure and Functions of the Nervous System' (1783), 'The Bursae Mucosae of the Human Body' (1788) and 'The Brain, the Eye and the Ear' (1797).

Monro, Alexander (1773-1859). Son of preceding; joint professor with father 1798 and held chair 1808-46; was criticised for merely reading his grandfather's lectures, and the anatomy class shrank to a third of what it had been under his father; wrote several volumes on anatomy and in particular 'The Anatomy of the Brain' (1831).

Monro, Donald (c. 1500-c. 1575). *Archdeacon* of the *Isles* c. 1548; wrote 'Description of the Western Isles'; *commissioner* of Ross and *minister* of Kiltearn and Lymlair after *Reformation*.

Monro, Robert (d. 1633). 'The Black Baron'; chief of Clan Munro; joined Scottish Corps in German wars 1626 and was colonel with Gustavus Adolphus; fatally wounded at Ulm.

Monro, Robert, of Opisdale (d. 1680). Served in continental armies as general, and later in Ireland.

Mons Graupius, Battle of, A.D. 84 or 85. *Agricola* defeated *Caledonians* at unknown site, between Strathmore and *Moray* coast; possibly at Bennachie or near *Huntly*.

Mons Meg. Believed to have been forged locally for siege of *Threave* in 1455, but now considered to have been imported from Flanders, where a similar gun exists at Ghent; 13′ 4″ long with bore of 1′ 8″; burst when firing salute for *James VII*; taken to London 1754 but returned 1829.

Montgomery, Alexander (c. 1550-c. 1602). One of the poets of the court of *James VI*, best known for 'The Cherry and the Slae' (1597).

Montgomery, Alexander, Archibald and Hugh, Earls of Eglinton. See Eglinton.

Montgomery (or **Montgomerie) Family.**

Robert de Montgomerie (1103-78) married a daughter of Walter the *Steward* and obtained from him a grant of the lands of Eaglesham in Renfrewshire. Sir John, 9th of Eaglesham, married heiress of Sir Hugh de Eglinton and acquired *Eglinton* and *Ardrossan*; at *Otterburn* he captured Percy 'Hotspur'. His grandson, Sir Alexander (d. c. 1470), was made Lord Montgomery 1444, and the 1st Lord's grandson became Earl of Eglinton 1508.

Montgomery, Sir James (d. 1694). 10th baronet of *Skelmorlie*; imprisoned for harbouring *Covenanters* 1684; M.P. for Ayrshire 1689; organised a political body called 'The *Club*'; became a *Jacobite* and died in Paris.

Montgomery, Sir James William (1721-1803). *Lord Advocate* 1766; Chief Baron of *Exchequer* 1775.

Montgomery, Robert (d. 1609). *Minister* of *Cupar* 1562, *Dunblane* 1567 and *Stirling* 1572; Archbishop of *Glasgow* 1581, but appointment strenuously opposed by *General Assembly*; deprived 1585; minister of *Symington* 1588 and of *Ayr* 1589.

Montgomery, Sir Robert (1680-1731). 11th Baronet of *Skelmorlie*; served in War of Spanish Succession; received grant of land in South Carolina.

Montgomery's Highlanders. Raised 1757 as 77th Regiment by Archibald Montgomery; embarked for Halifax to fight against French in America, later served in West Indies; at end of war some chose to remain in America; many rejoined the colours as Loyalists and as members of 84th or Royal Regiment of Highland Emigrants.

Montrose. *Royal burgh* under *David I*; castle occupied by *William I* and captured by Edward I 1296; according to some accounts it was in the castle that *John Balliol* abdicated. *Dominican* friary, said to have been founded by Sir Alan Durward c. 1275, was refounded 1516 and the properties were granted to burgh 1571. A hospital, dedicated to B.V.M., mentioned c. 1245, was recovered from lay hands 1512 and handed over to friary 1517. The *Academy* or *Grammar School* existed by 1549; Greek was taught there by Pierre de *Marsiliers* and *Andrew Melville* was a pupil.

Montrose, Dukedom, Earldom and Marquisate. Dukedom created for *David Lindsay, 5th Earl of Crawford*, 1488, but died with him 1495. Earldom created 1503 for William, 3rd Lord Graham; 5th Earl created Marquis 1644; 4th Marquis created Duke 1707.

Montrose, James Graham, 5th Earl and 1st Marquis of (1612-50). Succeeded father 1626; joined *Covenanters* 1638, but alienated by extremists and self-seekers; opposed Scottish intervention in English civil war; conducted brilliant campaign against Covenanters 1644-5; defeated at *Philiphaugh*; went to continent and returned 1650 to land in *Orkney* and march south, but was defeated at *Carbisdale* and hanged in *Edinburgh* on 21 May.

Monymusk (Aberdeenshire). *Culdee* establishment mentioned 1170; an *Augustinian* priory, mentioned 1245, fell into hands of *Forbes* family, to whom property passed after *Reformation*. The place became a *burgh of barony* for Forbes of Monymusk 1589 and a *burgh of regality* 1612. A 16th century tower house, altered and enlarged, on the former priory property, was sold to *Sir Francis Grant* 1713.

Monymusk Reliquary. Casket containing relics of St *Columba*, carried before Scottish army at *Bannockburn*; now in *National Museum of Antiquities*.

Monzie (Perthshire). Lands held by Campbells and remained with descendants of Archibald, 5th son of *Sir Duncan C. of Glenorchy*, until 1869; an early 17th century castle was restored by *Sir Robert Lorimer*.

Monzievaird (Perthshire), **Burning of.** In 1511 120 members and followers of the Murray family were burned in the church by Drummonds and *Campbells*.

Moore, James (1763-1834). Son of John M. (1729-1802), a physician who wrote novels and an account of the French Revolution; wrote accounts of his brother, *Sir John*.

Moore, Sir John (1761-1809). Born *Glasgow*; eldest son of John Moore (see preceding); served in American War; M.P. 1784-90; served in Corsica, West Indies and Egypt 1794-1801; lieutenant-general 1805; commanded in Portugal 1806; advanced to aid Madrid, and then made winter retreat to Corunna, where he was mortally wounded.

Moravia, de. See Gilbert, St.

Moray. Anciently a vast area extending far on all sides of *Inverness* and evidently a *Pict*ish province, with *mormaers*, one of whom was father of *Macbeth*. There were strong separatist tendencies and although the mormaerdom was suppressed after *David I* defeated *Angus* in 1130, and the property annexed to the crown, rebellions continued until reign of *William I*.

Moray, Alexander Stewart, 5th Earl of (1634-1701). *Justice General* 1674; *Secretary of State*

1680-8; active against *Covenanters* and supporter of *James VII*; King's Commissioner to *Parliament* 1686.

Moray, Sir Andrew. See Murray.

Moray, Bishopric. 'Bishop Gregory', later styled 'of Moray', appears c. 1114, but the see may well have been older. See also Elgin.

Moray, Earldom. Conferred by *Robert I* on *Thomas Randolph*; on death of 3rd Earl (1346) the title went to Patrick Dunbar, husband of one of his daughters, and then to John Dunbar, of the same family; this line died out in the male succession c. 1430 and the earldom then passed through an heiress to Archibald, 3rd son of 7th *Earl of Douglas*; after forfeiture of Douglases in 1455 it was conferred on 3rd son of *James II*, who died in infancy, and then on illegitimate sons of *James IV* and *James V* (see below).

Moray House, Edinburgh. Built by widow of 1st Earl of *Home*; passed by marriage to Lord *Doune*, later *Earl of Moray*; occupied by the *Marquis of Argyll*, Cromwell and Cromwell's general, Lambert; taken over 1752 by *British Linen* Company; in 1848 became premises of *Free Church* Training College for Teachers and in 1907 a general Training College; now Moray House College of Education.

Moray, James Stewart, Earl of (1500-1544). Son of *James IV* by Janet Kennedy; Earl of Moray 1501; warden of east and middle *marches* 1532-6; lieutenant general 1535; member of council of regency 1543; had no male issue and his daughter married John Stewart, Master of *Buchan*.

Moray, James Stewart, Earl of (1531-70). Son of *James V* by *Margaret Erskine*; *Commendator* of *St Andrews Priory* 1538; in France 1548 and 1550; joined insurgents 1559; prominent in government of Queen *Mary* until her marriage to *Darnley*, and created *Earl of Mar* 1562 and Earl of Moray 1563; raised rebellion against Darnley marriage and fled to England but returned to join Darnley against *Riccio*; almost certainly had foreknowledge of the Darnley murder, but kept out of the way and went abroad; returned to assume regency for *James VI* 1567; murdered by *James Hamilton of Bothwellhaugh* 23 January 1570.

Moray, James Stewart, Earl of (c. 1560-92). Eldest son of Sir James Stewart of *Doune*; married elder daughter of preceding by Agnes Keith, daughter of Earl *Marischal*, 1580, and styled Earl of Moray; this 'Bonny Earl' became a favourite with the ultra-protestant faction and his religious leanings exacerbated his family's feud with the *Earl of Huntly*, who murdered him at Donibristle, 7 February 1592.

Moray, Sir Robert (c. 1600-73). Son of Sir Mungo Moray of Craigie; served in Royalist forces in 1640s; *Justice Clerk* 1650; resisted Cromwellian occupation and joined *Charles II* in Paris, but spent part of his exile in Holland, studying chemistry; Justice Clerk again 1662, and Deputy *Secretary* 1663, but withdrew from public employment to devote himself to his scientific interests; one of the founders of the Royal Society and highly esteemed in London.

Mordington, Lordship. Created for 2nd son of 10th *Earl of Angus* 1641; 4th and last Lord died 1741.

More, Jacob (1740-93). Born *Edinburgh*; studied art and specialised in landscape; spent twenty years in Rome, assisting in decoration of Villa Borghese; died in Rome.

Morison, James (1762-1809). *Perth* bookseller who seceded from the *Glassites* and founded new sect.

Morison, James (1770-1840). Born Bognie, Aberdeenshire; merchant who called himself 'The Hygeist'; cured himself and sold his 'Morison's Pills'; died in Paris. His son, James A.C. Morison (1832-88), wrote lives of St Bernard, Gibbon and Macaulay.

Morison, James (1816-93). Born *Bathgate*; *minister* of *Kilmarnock* 1840; suspended 1841 and with three other ministers founded 'The Evangelical Union' of *Congregational* churches.

Morison, Robert (1620-83). Born *Aberdeen*; studied science at Paris and medicine at Angers; physician to Gaston, Duke of Orleans; physician and botanist to *Charles II*; professor of botany at Oxford 1669; wrote 'Praeludia Botanica' and 'Historia Plantarum Oxoniensis'.

Mormaer. Head of a province; the office is now thought to be of *Pict*ish origin and to have meant 'great steward'; survived into 12th century and, with the title translated into Latin as 'comes', became 'earl' in English.

Morocco Land (*Edinburgh*). Tenement on north side of Canongate, now rebuilt, with a half-figure of a turbaned moor, supposed to represent the story of one Andrew Gray, who fled from justice in Scotland and returned with wealth gained from service with the Sultan of Morocco.

Morris, Tom (1821-1908). Winner of Open Golf Championships 1861, 1862, 1864, 1866; green-keeper at *St Andrews* 1863-1908.

Morrison's Academy (*Crieff*). Founded by bequest from Thomas Morrison (d. 1820), a native of *Muthill* who made a fortune as a master builder in *Edinburgh*; school opened 1860; received further endowment 1937 from John Smith of Giffnock.

Mortimer's Deep. The sound between *Inchcolm* and Fife, said to derive its name from Alan de Mortimer, who gave lands to the abbey of Inchcolm and was to be buried in it but whose body, in its leaden shroud, fell or was thrown overboard on its way to the island.

Mortlach (Banffshire). There is no reason to accept that either *Malcolm II* in 1011 or *Malcolm III* in 1063 established a monastery, but there is no need to doubt that there was an ecclesiastical establishment before 1100 and that bishops for the area had their seat there before moving to *Aberdeen* after 1100.

Morton Castle (Dumfriesshire). Possibly built c. 1250 and an important stronghold in 14th; still an impressive ruin, with remains of hall and gatehouse; occupied until 1715.

Morton, Earldom. Created 1456 for James Douglas, Lord of *Dalkeith*, a descendant of Archibald of Douglas (fl. 1198-1239), ancestor of *Earls of Douglas*; the 3rd Earl (d. 1548) had three daughters, one of whom married *James Douglas*, who became 4th Earl. On his execution *John, 8th Lord Maxwell*, was Earl 1581-6, but Earl James's heir was his nephew, the *Earl of Angus*, on whose death in 1588 the earldom passed to the Douglases of *Lochleven*.

Morton, James Douglas, 4th Earl of (c. 1516-81). Second son of Sir *George D. of Pittendreich*, brother of *6th Earl of Angus*; Earl of Morton in right of his wife, 1550; controlled Angus estates during minority of his nephew, 1557-75; committed himself to the *Reformation* in the '*First Bond*' and was a lifelong supporter of the English alliance; *Chancellor* 1563; dismissed for his part in *Riccio* murder; had foreknowledge of the *Darnley* murder; leading man in *King's Party* after death of Regent *Moray*; Regent 1572-8 and still in control of administration until 1580; executed as an accessory to Darnley murder.

Morton, Thomas (1783-1862). Born *Kilmarnock*; invented machinery for carpet making.

Morville, de, Family. Received lands from *David I* in *Lauderdale*, *Cunningham* and elsewhere; held office of *Constable* in 12th and 13th centuries; Sir Hugh (d. 1162) endowed *Dryburgh* and *Kilwinning* Abbeys and Sir Richard (d. 1189) was a benefactor of *Melrose*.

Mossman, John (d. 1573). Goldsmith who made crowns for *James V* and his Queen; captured on surrender of *Edinburgh Castle* and hanged; supporter of Queen *Mary*; apparently the true owner of the alleged 'John *Knox's House*' in *Edinburgh*.

Mote. See Motte.

Motherwell and Wishaw (Lanarkshire). *Police burgh* 1893.

Motherwell, William (1797-1835). Born *Glasgow*; *sheriff*-clerk of Renfrewshire 1819; edited 'Paisley Advertiser' 1828 and 'Glasgow Courier' 1830; wrote 'Poems, Narrative and Lyrical' and collaborated in edition of *Burns*.

Motte-and-Bailey Castles. Wooden structures consisting of tower on lofty mound surrounded by palisaded enclosure at lower level; over 200 sites of such erections, dating from 12th century, have been identified in Scotland.

Motte Hill of Scone. See Scone.

Motte of Mark (near *Dalbeattie*). Site of ancient hill fort.

Motte of Urr (Kirkcudbrightshire). Perhaps the finest example of a *motte-and-bailey* structure, covering nearly 5 acres.

Mounth. The mountain barrier running east and west from south of *Aberdeen* to Ben Nevis; significant in arrangements made for administration of Scotland.

Mountquhanie Castle (Fife). A Balfour castle in 15th and 16th centuries; bought by Major-General Robert *Lumsden*, who had served with Gustavus Adolphus, fought at *Dunbar* 1650 and was killed when *Dundee*, of which he was governor, fell to *General Monck*; ruins now belong to Wedderburns.

Mount-Stuart House (Bute). A house built 1712-18 by 2nd *Earl of Bute* was superseded, after destruction by fire, by a Gothic pile designed by Rowand *Anderson* in 1879. The name had been given to a *burgh of regality* for the Earl of Bute 1703.

Mousa, Broch of (*Shetland*). The finest example of those towers, built with circular cavity walls, which are so numerous in the north and west; it stands some 45 feet high. See also Brochs.

Moy, Rout of, 16 February 1746. Government forces under Lord *Loudoun* came out from *Inverness* and attempted to capture Prince *Charles Edward* at Moy Hall, but were surprised and routed.

Moysie, David (fl. 1582-1603). *Edinburgh burgess* who wrote 'Memoirs of the Affairs of Scotland 1577-1603'.

Muckle Mou'ed Meg. Agnes, daughter of *Sir Gideon Murray*, whom *William Scott of*

Harden agreed to marry as an alternative to being hanged.

Mugdock (Stirlingshire). Lands acquired by David de Graham, ancestor of *Earls of Montrose*, from Malduin, *Earl of Lennox*, in 13th century; the castle, possibly of 13th century origin, became residence of Earls of Montrose but is now ruinous; *burgh of regality* for Marquis of Montrose 1680.

Muir, Alexander (1830-1906). Native of *Lesmahagow*; emigrated to Canada as a child; graduated at University of Toronto; composed 'The Maple Leaf Forever'.

Muir, Edwin (1887-1959). Orcadian who was a clerk and took up journalism and literature; Director of British Institute at Rome 1949; Warden of *Newbattle Abbey* College 1950-5; Professor of Poetry at Harvard 1955; best known for his poems, but also wrote a biography of *John Knox* and an autobiography.

Muir, John (1810-82). Born *Glasgow*; in service of East India Company 1829; principal of Queen's College, Benares, 1844; judge at Fatehpur 1845-53; Sanskrit scholar; founded chair of Sanskrit at *Edinburgh* 1862.

Muir, John (1838-1914). Born *Dunbar*; emigrated to America with parents; fought for preservation of forests and was instrumental in creating National Parks, the first of them at Yosemite 1864; founded Sierra Club 1892.

Muir, Thomas (1765-98). Born *Glasgow*; *advocate* 1787; associated with radicals and corresponded with French revolutionaries; after war started with France 1793 he went there and was outlawed; on his return tried for exciting disloyalty and recommending seditious writings; sentenced to 14 years' transportation to Australia; rescued by U.S. ship 1796 and after many adventures reached France, where he was welcomed, but died at Chantilly.

Muir, Sir William (1819-1905). Born *Glasgow*; brother of *John M*; joined East India Company 1837; Lieutenant Governor of North-West Provinces 1868; founded Muir College and University at Allahabad; principal of *Edinburgh University* 1885.

Muirfield (East Lothian). Since 1891 the home of the Company of *Edinburgh Golfers*.

Muirhead, James (1742-1808). Born *Buittle*; *minister* of *Urr* 1770; naturalist and mathematician; wrote 'Bess the Gawkie' and other songs.

Muirhead, James (1831-89). *Advocate* 1857; professor of civil law, *Edinburgh*, 1862; *sheriff* in chancery 1885; wrote on Roman Law.

Muirhead, Roland Eugene (1868-1964). A tanner who founded 'Scottish Secretariat' in *Home Rule* cause.

Mulroy, Battle of. *MacDonalds* of *Keppoch* defeated Mackintoshes in *Charles II*'s reign, in what has been called the last clan battle.

Multure. Proportion of corn brought for grinding in a mill which was retained by miller or proprietor of mill as his due. See Thirlage.

Muness Castle (*Shetland*). Built by Laurence Bruce of Cultmalindie and bearing date 1598: roofless, but walls almost complete.

Mungo. See Kentigern.

Munro, Sir Hector (1725-1805). General, served mainly in India; suppressed mutiny at Patna; captured Pondicherry 1778.

Munro, Hector Hugh (1870-1916). Under name of 'Saki' wrote fiction, especially short stories, e.g. 'Reginald' and 'The Chronicles of Clovis'; killed in First World War.

Munro, Neil (1864-1930). Native of *Inveraray*; wrote 'John Splendid', 'The New Road', 'The Daft Days', 'Para Handy' and other works.

Munro, Sir Thomas (1761-1827). Major-general; fought against Hyder Ali 1780-4; Governor of Madras.

Murchison, Charles (1830-79). Physician; migrated to India 1853; professor of chemistry at Calcutta; wrote on 'Continued Fevers' and 'Diseases of the Liver'.

Murchison, Sir Roderick Impey (1792-1871). Born Tarradale; entered army 1807 and served until 1814; took up geology; wrote 'The Silurian System' (1838); Director General of Geological Survey 1855.

Murdock, William (1754-1839). Born *Auchinleck*; went to London and Cornwall; returned to Ayrshire 1784 to build a locomotive and perfect his invention of coal-gas lighting; managed Soho works of Boulton and *Watt*, where he first experimented with coal-gas.

Mure, Elizabeth (d. c. 1353). Daughter of Sir Adam M. of Rowallan; married *Robert II* after issue of papal dispensation 22 November 1347, when she already had had several children by him, including the future *Robert III*, Robert, Duke of *Albany*, and '*The Wolf of Badenoch*'.

Mure Family. Held estate of Rowallan in *Cunningham* from 13th century to 18th; estate passed by marriage to Earl of *Loudoun*.

Mure, Sir William, of Rowallan (1594-1657). Wrote a 'Historie' of the family and some verse and translated psalms; he and his son and grandson were *Covenanters*.

Murray, Agnes. See Muckle Mou'ed Meg.

Murray, Alexander (1775-1813). Born *Minni-*

gaff; self-taught in many languages and became professor of oriental languages 1812; wrote account of *James Bruce*'s travels in Abyssinia and a 'History of European Languages'.

Murray, Sir Andrew (d. 1297). Son and heir of Sir Andrew M., Lord of *Petty* in Inverness-shire, *Avoch* in the Black Isle and *Boharm* in Banffshire, *justiciar* of Scotland 1289; captured on John *Balliol*'s fall, he escaped to start a rising in *Moray* and joined with *Wallace* to defeat English at *Stirling Bridge*, where he probably received wounds which proved fatal.

Murray, Sir Andrew (d. 1338). Posthumous son of preceding; *Guardian* of Scotland 1332; captured *Kildrummy Castle* 1335 and *Bothwell Castle* 1336.

Murray, Charles, Earl of Dunmore. See Dunmore.

Murray, Sir David, of Gorthy (1567-1629). Held various appointments, but best known as poet who wrote 'The Tragical Death of Sophonisba' and 'Coelia'.

Murray, Sir David, of Gospertie. See Scone, Lord.

Murray, David, Earl of Mansfield. See Mansfield.

Murray, Elizabeth, Countess of Dysart. See Dysart.

Murray, Lord George (c. 1700-60). Son of *1st Duke of Atholl*; took part in 'Fifteen and in *Jacobite* effort in 1719; fled to France but pardoned 1726; joined Prince *Charles Edward* 1745 and became Lieutenant-General, but was regarded with some suspicion and was opposed to Prince's Irish followers; he had some marked successes, not least on the retreat from Derby; opposed decision to fight at *Culloden* and resigned next day; died in Holland.

Murray, Sir George (1772-1846). Entered army 1789; served in Flanders, Egypt and West Indies and was Quartermaster-General in Peninsular War; Governor of Canada 1814; M.P. for Perth 1823.

Murray, Sir Gideon (d. 1621). *Minister* of Auchterless 1585; chamberlain to Walter Scott of Buccleuch; received lands of Elibank 1594; knighted 1605; *Lord of Session* 1613; *Treasurer* Depute 1612 and managed revenues well; his son Patrick created Lord Elibank 1643.

Murray, James (c. 1690-1770). 2nd son of 5th Viscount *Stormont*; served with *Jacobites* 1715; escaped to France; negotiated marriage of *Old Pretender* and was created 'Earl of Dunbar' in Jacobite peerage.

Murray, James (c. 1719-94). Served in army in West Indies, Flanders and Brittany; Governor of Quebec and Minorca.

Murray, Sir James Augustus Henry (1837-1915). Born Denholm; head-master of *Hawick* Subscription *Academy* 1857; settled in Oxford and initiated New English Dictionary; edited *Sir David Lindsay*'s Works, 'The Complaynt of Scotland' and other Scottish literature.

Murray, John (d. 1640). Groom of *James VI*'s bedchamber; appointed governor of *Lochmaben* Castle and received *barony* of Lochmaben; created Earl of *Annandale* 1625; served on Border commissions.

Murray, John, of Broughton (1715-77). Son of Peeblesshire laird; educated *Edinburgh* and Leyden; visited Rome and made contacts with *Jacobite* court; became agent for Scottish Jacobites; secretary to Prince *Charles Edward* 1745-6; remained in Scotland to look after *Loch Arkaig Treasure*; captured and gained liberty by giving evidence against *Lord Lovat*.

Murray, John (1778-1843). Went to London as agent for *Constable*, the *Edinburgh* publishers, 1803; founded publishing house; his son John (1808-92) wrote many guide books.

Murray, Sir John Archibald (1779-1859). *Lord of Session* 1839; M.P. for *Leith* 1832; *Lord Advocate* 1835; instrumental in promoting *Reform Act* 1832; wrote for '*Edinburgh Review*'.

Murray, John, Earls, Marquises and Duke of Atholl. See Atholl.

Murray, John, Earl of Dunmore. See Dunmore.

Murray, Sir Patrick. Made a great collection of plants in his garden at *Livingston*, West Lothian; after his death Sir Andrew Balfour took the specimens to *Edinburgh*, where they formed the Old *Physic Gardens* near the *Nor' Loch*.

Murray, Sir Thomas (c. 1630-84). *Lord of Session* (Glendoick) 1674; *Clerk Register* 1662-81; licensed to print the Statutes 1679.

Murray, Thomas (1792-1872). Printer in *Edinburgh* 1841; wrote 'Literary History of *Galloway*'.

Murray, Sir William, of *Tullibardine* (d. 1583). *Comptroller* 1565-82; supported Queen *Mary*'s marriage to *Darnley*, but joined opposition after her marriage to *Bothwell*.

Murray, William, Earl of Dysart. See Dysart.

Murray, William, 1st Earl of Mansfield. See Mansfield.

Murray, William, Marquis of Tullibardine. See Tullibardine.

Murthly Castle (Perthshire). Contains tower of late 16th century date, seat of Stewarts of Murthly, descended from Alexander, 4th High *Steward*.

Museum of Science and Art. Earlier name of *Royal Scottish Museum*.

Mushet, David (1772-1847). Born *Dalkeith*; at Calder Ironworks discovered value of black-band iron-stone 1801; went to England 1805; wrote on iron and steel. See Iron Industry, and Neilson, James.

Musselburgh (Midlothian). The bridge, reputedly Roman, is in fact a typical medieval bridge, though there is a Roman camp nearby at Inveresk; it remained the main route until 1806, when *Rennie*'s bridge was built, and as such was used by many armies. The place was apparently a *burgh* in 12th century, but its status was indeterminate until *Robert I* made it a burgh under *Dunfermline Abbey*; it was a *burgh of regality* under Dunfermline in 1562. A hospital is mentioned 1386, when it was ruinous because of war, and was still in existence in 1561; it was dedicated to Mary Magdalene, and was for poor and lepers.

Musselburgh Festival. The riding of the *marches* took place on 15 August, the Feast of the Assumption, obviously associated with Our Lady of Loretto; an 'Honest Lad' and 'Honest Lass' were the chief characters, the town deriving its reputation as 'The Honest Toun' from a remark attributed to *Thomas Randolph*, Earl of Moray, who died there 1332.

Musselburgh Links. Home of Company of *Edinburgh Golfers* 1836-91.

Musselburgh, Loretto Chapel. Dedicated to Our Lady of Loretto, it was in existence by 1536; suffered in English attacks and razed after *Reformation*, when stones from it are said to have been used to build Town Hall. See Douchtie, Thomas.

Musselburgh, Loretto School. Boarding school for boys, founded 1778.

Musselburgh Races. Racing held from 1817; *Leith* races transferred to M., 1856.

Musselburgh Silver Arrow. Originally presented by *burgh*; medals bearing the names of winners begin 1603; now shot for by Royal Company of *Archers*.

Mutchkin. Measure of capacity equalling a pint.

Muthill (Perthshire). There was a *Culdee* foundation, mentioned c. 1180; the tower is presumably 11th century.

Myllar, Andrew (fl. 1503-5). *Edinburgh* bookseller who brought in books printed abroad and then associated with *Walter Chepman* to set up the first Scottish printing press 1507

Mylne, Alexander (1474-1548). Canon of *Dunkeld*; Abbot of *Cambuskenneth*; first *Lord President* of College of *Justice* 1532; wrote 'Lives of the Bishops of Dunkeld'.

Mylne, Alexander. See Mylnes, master masons.

Mylne, Andrew (1776-1856). Teacher and *minister* who became cashier of Trust set up by *John Macnab* and first rector of *Dollar Academy*.

Mylne, John. See Mylnes, master masons.

Mylne, Robert. See Mylnes, master masons.

Mylne, Thomas. See Mylnes, master masons.

Mylne (or Mill), Walter (c. 1478-1558). Parish priest of Lunan who, when over eighty, was put to death for heresy, the last of the protestant martyrs. See 'Heretics'.

Mylne, Walter. See Mylnes, master masons.

Mylnes, Master Masons. This remarkable dynasty of masons, architects and engineers began with John (d. 1621), great-nephew of *Alexander M., Lord President*; he repaired *Dundee* harbour works and built a bridge at *Perth*. John (d. 1657), his son, built the tolbooth steeple in *Aberdeen* and fortifications at Dundee. He had two sons: John (1611-67) designed *Tron Church, Edinburgh*, and built part of *Heriot's Hospital*; and Alexander (1613-43) specialised in sculpture and assisted his brother. Alexander's son, Robert (1633-1710) reconstructed *Leith* pier, superintended the rebuilding of *Holyrood Palace* (1670-9) and built a number of houses in Edinburgh, as well as *Mylne's Mount*; he was associated with *Sir William Bruce*. Robert's son, William (1662-1728), carried on the craft, and in the next generation Thomas (d. 1763) was city surveyor in Edinburgh. Thomas had two sons: William (d. 1790), as architect to the city of Edinburgh, designed the *North Bridge*, 1765-72; Robert (1734-1811), after studying on the continent, built Blackfriars Bridge in London, designed the Gloucester and Berkeley Canal, was engineer to the New River Company and surveyed St Paul's Cathedral. Robert's son, William Chadwell (1781-1863), succeeded his father as engineer to the New River Company and undertook other projects in connection with water and drainage, and his son, Robert William (1817-1890), besides being engineer to the Limerick Water Works, turned to geology

and wrote on artesian wells and the geology of London.
Mylne's Mount. Bastion on north side of *Edinburgh Castle*, named after *Robert Mylne*, who was associated with John Drury in repairing Edinburgh Castle after the *Revolution*.
Myres Castle (Fife). Built about 1530 by a branch of the *Scrymgeour* family who had acquired the lands by marriage in 1453 from Sir Robert Coxwell; passed to Pattersons in 17th century, and acquired by Fairlies 1887.
Myrtoun Castle (*Galloway*). Built on an older *motte*; once the home of the MacCullochs, from whom the lands were acquired by the Maxwells of *Monreith* in 1685; a modern house was built but much of the castle survives.

N

Nairn. There was a *sheriff* of Invernairn by 1204 and a *royal burgh* was mentioned before 1214; granted by *Robert I* to *Randolph*, Earl of Moray, 1312 and passed to *Earls of Ross*; reverted to crown 1475; castle, mentioned 13th century, said to have been 'cast doun' 1581.
Nairn(e), Lordship. Created 1681 for Sir Robert Nairn of Strathurd (c. 1620-83), *Lord of Session*, descended from Nairns of Mukkersy; his daughter married William Murray (d. 1726), son of John, 1st Marquis of *Atholl*, who was captured at *Preston* 1715 and sentenced to death but reprieved; John, 3rd Lord, was with *Jacobites* in 1715 and 1745 and died in France (1770); peerage *forfeited* 1716, restored 1824.
Nairn, Michael. See Linoleum.
Nairne, Caroline, Lady (1766-1845). Caroline *Oliphant* of Gask, married 1806 William Murray Nairne (1757-1830), who became Lord N. 1824; from 1821 to 1824, as 'Mrs Bogan of Bogan', she contributed lyrics to 'The Scottish Minstrel'; few of her songs were printed in her lifetime, but in 1846 'Lays from Strathearn' included popular items like 'Wi' a hundred pipers' 'The Laird o' Cockpen' and 'Caller Herrin".
Napier, Sir Alexander, of *Merchiston* (d. 1473). *Burgess* of *Edinburgh*; *provost* 1457; *Comptroller* 1449-61, with intermissions; ambassador to England and continent.
Napier, Sir Archibald, of *Merchiston* (1534-1608). Son of Alexander N. (died at *Pinkie*); Master of the *Mint* 1576; built *Lauriston Castle*.
Napier, Admiral Sir Charles (1786-1860). Grandson of 5th Lord N; born near *Falkirk*; took part in West Indian campaign 1806-8; commanded Portuguese fleet and created Count St Vincent; captured Sidon in Syrian war of 1840; in command against Russia in Baltic 1854.
Napier, General Sir Charles James (1782-1853). Grandson of 5th Lord N; conquered Sind. His despatch read 'Peccavi'.
Napier Commission. See Crofters Commission.
Napier, David (1790-1869). Cousin of *Robert N*; invented steeple engine; established steam communication between *Greenock* and Belfast 1820.
Napier, John, of *Merchiston* (1550-1617). Born Merchiston; son of *Sir Archibald N*; moved from an interest in the scriptures and the production of 'A Plaine Discovery of the Whole Revelation of St John' (1593) to a series of technical inventions and then to mathematics; his discovery of logarithms incorporated in 'Mirifici Logarithmorum Canonis Constructio' (written 1614, printed 1619) and 'Rabdologiae seu Numerationes per Virgulas Duo' (1617), which explained his calculating device, 'Napier's Bones'; acquired reputation for necromancy, as a result of his retired, studious life.
Napier, Mark (1798-1879). Son of *Edinburgh W.S*; *advocate* 1820; wrote 'The Law of Prescription' and works on the *Napiers*, *Montrose* and *Graham* of Claverhouse.
Napier of Merchiston, Lordship. Created 1627 for Sir Archibald Napier (1576-1645), son of *John N. of Merchiston, Treasurer* Depute 1622 and *Justice Clerk* 1624; Archibald, 2nd Lord (d. 1658), fought with *Montrose* and died in Holland.
Napier, Robert (1791-1876). Born *Dumbarton*; cousin of *David N.*, constructed his first marine engine 1823; began shipbuilding 1841; built for *P. & O.* Company and for various foreign governments; patented numerous improvements in ships and engines.
Napier, Sir William Francis Patrick (1785-1860). Brother of *Sir Charles James N*; served in Napoleonic Wars; wrote 'History of the War in the Pyrenees' and 'History of the Conquest of Scinde'.
'Napier's Bones'. See Napier, John.
Nasmyth, Alexander (1758-1840). Born *Edinburgh*; pupil of *Allan Ramsay*; worked in Italy on landscapes and architectural subjects; on his return set up as a portrait-painter and executed a famous painting of *Burns*, but

turned again to landscapes; also did some architectural work and associated with *Patrick Miller* in his steamboat experiments.

Nasmyth, David (1799-1839). Founded *Glasgow* City Mission 1826 and similar missions elsewhere.

Nasmyth, James (1808-90). Born *Edinburgh*; son of *Alexander N*; constructed steam carriage 1828; started making machine-tools in Manchester 1834; invented steam hammer 1839 and other devices.

Nasmyth of Dawyck, Family. John N., a lawyer (d. 1706), known as 'Deil o' Dawyck', bought estate from the Veitches; his son, created Baronet 1706 and died 1779, was a botanist and arboriculturalist.

Nasmyth, Patrick (1787-1831). Born *Edinburgh*; son of *Alexander N*; landscape painter, mainly in England.

National Association for the Vindication of Scottish Rights. Founded 1853 to demand financial and terminological justice for Scotland.

National Bank of Scotland. Established 1825; absorbed Commercial Banking Company of Aberdeen 1833 and *Perth Union Bank* 1836.

National Commercial Bank. Formed 1958 by amalgamation of *National* and *Commercial* Banks.

National Covenant. Manifesto drawn up by *Alexander Henderson* and *Archibald Johnston* and first signed in *Greyfriars' Church, Edinburgh*, at end of February 1638, to consolidate opposition to *Charles I*'s innovations in worship, the 'corruptions of the public government of the Kirk' and the 'civil places and power of kirkmen'. The concept of a 'Covenant' was revived by a Nationalist movement in the 20th century: one in 1930 was a pledge to restore 'the independent national status of Scotland' and 'an independent parliament'; a second, in 1949, pledged the signatories to support a Scottish parliament 'within the framework of the United Kingdom'. See also Solemn League and Covenant.

National Galleries of Scotland (*Edinburgh*). National Gallery begun 1850 to designs by *W.H. Playfair*; National Portrait Gallery founded 1882 with endowment from *John Ritchie Findlay* and opened 1889. Board of Trustees for National Galleries formed 1907 from old *Board of Trustees for Manufactures.* National Gallery of Modern Art opened 1960.

National Library of Scotland (*Edinburgh*). *Advocates' Library* made over to nation 1925; new building opened 1956. Now has about 3,000,000 volumes.

National Memorials. (1) For Napoleonic Wars, on Calton Hill, *Edinburgh*, begun to design of *W.H. Playfair* 1824 and never completed ('Edinburgh's Disgrace'). (2) For First World War, in *Edinburgh Castle*, designed by *Sir Robert Lorimer* and completed 1928.

National Museum of Antiquities of Scotland *(Edinburgh).* Collection made over to nation by Society of *Antiquaries* 1851; Queen Street building erected 1885-90, to design by Sir Robert Rowand *Anderson*.

National Party of Scotland. Founded 1927. Superseded by *Scottish National Party* 1930.

National Trust for Scotland. Founded 1931.

National War Memorial. See National Memorials.

Nationality, Franco-Scottish. See Franco-Scottish.

Natural Philosophy. Term used in universities as equivalent to physics.

Nau, Claude, de la Boisselière. Secretary to Cardinal of Lorraine and then to his niece, *Mary*, Queen of Scots, from 1575 until her death; wrote a biography of Mary.

Navigation Acts. English Act of 1660 generally forbade the import of goods to England except in English ships or ships of the country of origin, prohibited 'aliens' from trading with the colonies and laid down that certain exports from the colonies were to be carried only to English ports. Scottish Act of 1661 replied with similar terms in favour of Scotland's own nationals.

Neaves, Charles (1800-76). Born *Edinburgh*; *Solicitor General* 1852; *Lord of Session* 1853; published 'The Greek Anthology' 1870.

Nechtan (d. 732). Son of Derelei or Dergard, King of *Picts*; accepted Roman usages and invited Anglian architects to build a church in his kingdom.

Nechtansmere, Battle of, 20 May 685. At Dunnichen, near *Forfar, Brude*, King of *Picts*, defeated Angles under Egfrith.

Negative Confession. See King's Confession.

Neidpath Castle (Peeblesshire). Mainly 15th century, built by Sir William *Hay*, descendant of Sir Gilbert H., who acquired the property by marriage with heiress of the Frasers who owned it under *Robert I*; Hay's descendant became *Earl of Tweeddale*; sold 1686 to 1st *Duke of Queensberry*; now belongs to *Earl of Wemyss*.

Neilson, James Beaumont (1792-1865). Born Shettleston; engine-wright at *Irvine*; foreman of *Glasgow* Gas Works 1817; introduced use of hot blast for smelting iron 1828. See Iron Industry, and Mushet, David.

Nelson, Sir Hugh Muir (1835-1906). Born *Kilmarnock*; emigrated with his father to Queensland 1853; minister of railways 1888; President of Legislative Council 1898.

Nelson, Thomas (1822-92). Son of Thomas N. (1780-1861), an *Edinburgh* publisher; entered father's business; invented rotary press 1850; in partnership with his brother William (1816-87).

Nesbit, Battles of (1) August 1355. Scots defeated English and took Sir Thomas Gray prisoner; (2) 22 June 1402. English defeated Scots.

Ness. Landowner at *Leuchars* in 12th century.

Neville's Cross, Battle of, 17 October 1346. *David II* defeated and captured by English.

New Abbey. See Sweetheart Abbey.

New Club (*Edinburgh*). Founded 1787 as dining club; bought premises at No. 4 Princes Street 1803; moved to present site 1837.

New Club (*Paisley*). Founded 1877 to print works illustrative of Scottish history and literature.

New College (*Edinburgh*). The theological college of *Free Church*, established 1843; present building on *Mound* opened 1850; since union of *Church of Scotland* and Free Church in 1929 the building has housed the Faculty of Divinity of *Edinburgh University*.

New Galloway (Kirkcudbrightshire). *Royal burgh* 1630.

New Lanark. See Dale, David.

New Lights. The *Burgher* and Anti-Burgher sections of the *Secession* each split about 1800 into 'Old Light' and 'New Light' sections, the latter being less insistent on the duty of the state to maintain the church.

New Towns. Designated as follows: East Kilbride 1947, Glenrothes 1948, Cumbernauld 1955, Livingston 1962, Irvine 1966.

New Year's Day. The official beginning of the year was 25 March until 1600, when *James VI* substituted 1 January; in England it was 25 March until 1753, after the Gregorian Calendar had been adopted for Britain as a whole in 1752.

Newark Castle (Fife). Ruins near *St Monans*; belonged to Sandilands family, created Lords *Abercrombie*; sold by 2nd Lord 1649 to *David Leslie*, created Lord Newark; passed to Anstruthers and to Bairds of *Elie*.

Newark Castle (Renfrewshire). Lands passed from family of Danyelstoun by marriage to *Maxwells* 1402; 15th century tower was added to and bears date 1597; handed over to nation by Sir Hugh Shaw Stewart 1909.

Newark Castle (Selkirkshire). Built early 15th century, when a charter to *Earl of Douglas* mentioned the 'new werk'; passed with other Douglas properties to crown 1455; granted to Queens of *James III* and *James IV*; later passed to Scotts of *Buccleuch*, and still belongs to Duke of Buccleuch; burned by English 1548; after battle of *Philiphaugh*, nearby, a hundred of *Montrose*'s men were butchered by *Covenanters*.

Newark, David Leslie, Lord (d. 1682). Grandson of *5th Earl of Rothes*; served under Gustavus Adolphus; joined army of *Covenanters* 1643; fought at *Marston Moor* and defeated *Montrose* at *Philiphaugh*; defeated by Cromwell at *Dunbar*; taken prisoner at *Worcester* and spent nine years in Tower of London.

Newark, Lordship. Created 1661 for *David Leslie*; dormant on death of 4th Lord 1791.

Newbattle Abbey (*Cistercian*) (Midlothian). Founded by *David I* and possibly his son Earl *Henry* 1140; burned by English 1385, 1544, 1548; erected into *temporal lordship* for *Mark Ker* 1587. Mansion, of various dates from 17th century and incorporating crypt of church, was given to nation by 11th *Marquis of Lothian* and is now a residential college. Newbattle became *burgh of barony* for Earl of Lothian 1634.

Newbigging (Fife). *Burgh of barony* for Kirkcaldy of Grange 1541.

Newburgh (Aberdeenshire). Existed in 1261; received charter as *burgh of barony* for Lord Sinclair 1509. A hospital was founded by *Alexander Comyn*, Earl of Buchan, c. 1261.

Newburgh (Fife). *Burgh* dependent on *Lindores Abbey* by 1266; *royal burgh* 1631.

Newburgh (Wigtownshire). *Burgh of barony* for *Earl of Galloway* 1638.

Newburgh, Earldom. Created 1660 for Sir James Livingston of Kinnaird, who was granted a viscountcy 1647; the title went by marriage to an Italian family.

Newmill of Strathisla (Banffshire). *Burgh of barony* for *Gordon* of Glengarrock 1673.

Newmilns (Ayrshire). *Burgh of barony* for *Campbell* of Loudoun 1491; *burgh of regality* for *Earl of Loudoun* 1707. In the castle some *Covenanters* were imprisoned and the townsmen, led by John Law, rescued them, but Law was killed in the action.

Newport-on-Tay (Fife). Created *burgh* by act of Parliament 1822 as southern terminus of Tay ferry.

Newton Castle (*Ayr*). In existence c. 1200; captured by Norwegians 1263; passed from Wallace family to Hamiltons in reign of *James V*, later to Craigie family; demolished 1701.
Newton Castle (Perthshire, near *Blairgowrie*). Belonged to Drummond family; still occupied.
Newton Castle (Perthshire, *Doune*). Dates from 16th century; belonged to Edmonstones, who received lands from *James V*; sold 1858 to John Campbell, a *Glasgow* merchant; still occupied.
Newton Mearns (Renfrewshire). *Burgh of barony* for *Earl of Nithsdale* 1621.
Newton of Gogo (Ayrshire). *Burgh of barony* for Brisbane of Bishopton 1595.
Newton-Stewart (Wigtownshire). *Burgh of barony* for Stewart of Castle Stewart 1677.
Newton upon Ayr. *Burgh of barony* c. 1314x1371, under Stewarts; re-erected 1600 as burgh of barony for community.
Newtyle (*Angus*). *Burgh of barony* for Sir George *Mackenzie of Rosehaugh* 1682.
Nichol, John Pringle (1804-59). Born *Brechin*; rector of *Montrose Academy* 1827; professor of astronomy at *Glasgow* 1836.
Nichol, John (1833-94). Son of preceding; professor of English Language and Literature at *Glasgow* 1862.
Nicholson, Brinsley (1824-92). Born *Fort George*; as army surgeon served in Africa, China and New Zealand; edited 'The best plays of Ben Jonson', 'Donne's Poems' and 'Henry the Fifth'.
Nicholson, John (1777-1866). Brother of *William N*; publisher in *Kirkcudbright*.
Nicholson, William (1783-1849). Born Borgue; 'the pedlar-poet of *Galloway*'; encouraged by *James Hogg* and Dr *Alexander Murray*.
Nicol, Erskine (1825-1904). Born *Leith*; studied art in *Edinburgh*; taught in Dublin 1846-50; returned to Edinburgh; moved to England 1862; painted 'Irish merry-making', 'Donnybrook Fair' and 'Unwilling to School'.
Nicol, James (1810-79). Son of James N., *minister* of Traquair (1769-1819); professor of geology at Cork 1849 and at *Aberdeen* 1853-78; wrote on mineralogy.
Nicol, John (d. 1667). A *Writer to the Signet* whose 'Diary' extends from 1637 to 1657.
Nicol, William (c. 1744-97). Master at *High School, Edinburgh*; friend of *Robert Burns*, whom he accompanied to the Highlands and who commemorated him in 'Willie brewed a peck o' maut'.
Nicoll, Sir William Robertson (1851-1923). Born Lumsden, Aberdeenshire; *Free Church minister* at *Dufftown* 1874, *Kelso* 1877; moved to London for health 1885; edited 'British Weekly' from 1886; knighted 1909.
Nicolson, Alexander (1827-93). Born Skye; *advocate* and journalist; *sheriff* substitute of *Kirkcudbright* and *Greenock*; collected *Gaelic* proverbs and revised Gaelic Bible.
Nicolson Family. The name, like other patronymics, arose in many parts of the Lowlands, and there were also Highlanders, especially in Skye and *Lewis*, who adopted it as an English form of MacNicol. John N. of that *ilk* and Lasswade was created Baronet 1629, and the title continued, in a family based mainly on Fetlar in *Shetland*, until 1961.
Nicolson Institute (*Stornoway*). Founded 1873 in terms of will of Alexander Morison Nicolson (d. 1865), native of Stornoway and marine engineer; further endowed by *Sir James Matheson*.
Niddry Castle (West Lothian). 15th century L-shaped tower, with later additions on top, now roofless; was property of *Lord Seton*, who received Queen *Mary* there on her escape from *Lochleven*; now property of *Marquis of Linlithgow*.
Nimmo, James (1654-1709). *Covenanter* who escaped to Holland after *Bothwell Brig*; returned later and after *Revolution* served in Customs; his 'Narrative' has been published.
Ninian, St (fl. c. 400). First missionary to Scotland whose name is known; a Briton by birth and instructed at Rome; said to have converted 'southern *Picts*' and to have built church at *Whithorn*, where he was bishop.
Nisbet, Alexander (1657-1725). Son of N. of that *ilk*; practised as solicitor; author of 'System of Heraldry' (1722).
Nisbet, Charles (1736-1804). Son of schoolmaster of Long Yester; *minister* of *Montrose* 1764; supported cause of American Colonies; principal of Dickinson College, Pennsylvania, 1785.
Nisbet, Sir John (c. 1609-87). *Lord Advocate* 1664-77; *Lord of Session* (Dirleton) 1664; bought *Dirleton* 1663 and built Archerfield to replace castle.
Nisbet, Pollok Sinclair (1848-1922). Born *Edinburgh*; as a landscape painter travelled widely in Italy, Spain and Morocco, but he left many Scottish scenes.
Nisbet, William (d. c. 1808). Practised as physician in *Edinburgh* before settling in London 1801; wrote on scrofula, cancer and venereal diseases; published 'The Clinical Guide' (1793) and 'General Dictionary of Chemistry'.

Nithsdale. Called Strathnith or Stranit in 12th century, when it was held by a native called Dunegal, said to have had four sons; he certainly had two, Donald and Ralph or Randolph, the latter claimed as the ancestor of *Thomas Randolph*.

Nithsdale, Earldom. Created 1620 for Robert, 10th *Lord Maxwell*; 5th Earl *forfeited* 1716 and title in abeyance.

Nithsdale, William Maxwell, 5th Earl of (1676-1746). Taken prisoner at *Preston* 1715; escaped from Tower of London with help of his wife; died at Rome.

Nithsdale, Winifred, Countess of (d. 1749). Wife of 5th Earl; allowed to visit her husband in the Tower of London, she changed clothes with him and he escaped; she later joined him in Rome.

Noble. Gold coin originally worth 6s.8d. under *David II;* worth £3 or £4 under *James VI*. See also Rose noble.

Noltland Castle (Westray, *Orkney*). Probably built by Gilbert Balfour, who acquired lands from Bishop *Adam Bothwell* 1560; some of *Montrose*'s followers took refuge there and the castle was taken by Cromwellian forces.

Non-Jurors. *Episcopalians* who refused to take oaths to post-*Revolution* sovereigns until after 1788 and therefore did not qualify for toleration under *Toleration Act* of 1712.

Nordreys. As the *Sudreys* were the Western Isles, Nordreys can be applied to *Orkney and Shetland*, the Northern Isles.

Norman's Law. Hill in Ochil range, above Firth of Tay, crowned by remains of hill fort, Dunmore; said to derive name from burials by Scandinavian invaders.

Norries Law. Tumulus on *Largo-Ceres* road. In 1817 a tinker who had heard that it was the burial place of a chief began to dig and found a hoard of Celtic silver ornaments, most of which were sold and melted down. Later General Durham of Largo excavated and found further ornaments, now in *National Museum of Antiquities*.

Norse Law. Preserved in *Orkney and Shetland* by *Parliament* 1504 and 1567, but abolished by *Privy Council* 1611. See Udal Law.

North Berwick (East Lothian). *Barony* held by *Earls of Fife*, then by *Black Douglases* 1371-1455; granted 1479 to *Earl of Angus*, whose family retained it (including *Tantallon*) until bought by Sir Hew *Dalrymple* in early 18th century. *Burgh* was baronial under Douglases in 14th century, but is said to have been made *royal burgh* by *Robert III* and was certainly one by 1426. *Cistercian nunnery* founded by Duncan, Earl of Fife, c. 1150; its property granted to Alexander *Home* 1587; little remains of buildings. Hospital, founded before 1154 by Duncan, Earl of Fife, was granted by his successor to the nunnery and is not heard of after 1214. Almshouse, distinct from that hospital and in patronage of *Lauder* of the *Bass*, mentioned 1542-73.

North Berwick Witches. In 1591, according to witch trials, the devil appeared in the pulpit of the church (that is, the old church beside the harbour) to 100 witches.

North British Locomotive Company. Formed by amalgamation of 13 companies 1903.

North British Railway. Began as *Edinburgh-Berwick* line 1846, but gradually took over lines to *Glasgow*, *Dundee*, Carlisle etc. and expanded to *Fort William* and Mallaig as well as *Aberdeen*.

North, Christopher. See Wilson, John.

North Inch. See Perth.

North (or Nor') Loch (*Edinburgh*). North of *Castle*; drained in part at various dates and completely 1763; site occupied by Princes Street Gardens.

North of Scotland Bank. Established at *Aberdeen* 1836; amalgamated with *Clydesdale Bank* 1950.

North of Scotland Hydro-Electric Board. Established 1943.

North of Scotland Shipping Company. As *Aberdeen, Leith* and *Clyde* originated 1790; North of Scotland and *Orkney and Shetland* Steam Navigation Company 1875; North of Scotland, Orkney and Shetland Shipping Company 1953; absorbed by Coast Lines 1961 and by *P. & O.* 1971.

North Queensferry. See Queensferry, North.

Northampton, Treaty of, 1328. The treaty by which England acknowledged the independence of Scotland was concluded at *Edinburgh* on 17 March and ratified at Northampton on 4 May. See also Edinburgh, Treaties of.

Northern Association for the Promotion of Science and Literature. Founded in *Inverness* 1825 to investigate the antiquities and natural history of Highlands and Islands; published one volume.

Northern Association of Literary and Scientific Societies. Founded at *Elgin* 1887 for joint action in the counties from *Aberdeen* to *Shetland*; issued some transactions to 1899 and continued to meet thereafter.

Northesk, Earldom. Title assumed 1666 by John Carnegie (1579-1667), previously Earl of

Ethie, younger brother of 1st *Earl of Southesk*.

Northfield House (East Lothian). Built by Joseph Marjoribanks, an *Edinburgh* merchant, 1611, on ground acquired from George Hamilton, *portioner* of Saltpreston; still occupied.

Nórway, Annual of. See Perth, Treaty of.

'Not Proven' Verdict. Apparently the practice of permitting juries to return this verdict in criminal cases originated in *Charles II*'s reign.

Notary Public. Authorised by Pope, Emperor or King; authenticated and recorded legal transactions of all kinds, issuing instruments and noting their substance in protocol books; since *Reformation* admitted by *Court of Session*.

Nova Scotia. In 1629 *Sir William Alexander* organised a small colony, but the territory was ceded to France 1632; restored to Britain 1713.

Nova Scotia Baronets. Projected by *James VI* and instituted by *Charles I* 1625, these baronetcies were conferred on persons contributing to the settlement in Nova Scotia; in all about 280 were created, down to reign of Anne.

Novantae. Tribe who in Roman times occupied modern *Galloway*.

Nunraw Abbey. *Cistercian* house, founded 1946; no medieval religious house on site. See next entry.

Nunraw Castle. Nunnery of *Haddington* had a 'place and fortalice' at Nunraw in 1548; it was added to and modernised as a house, but retained some 15th century features; property passed to *Hepburns*, then to *Dalrymples* and in 1880 to Walter Wingate Hay; bought 1946 by *Cistercian* order.

O

Oban (Argyll). *Burgh of barony* for *Duke of Argyll* 1811 and for Duke and Campbell of Combie 1820; *police burgh* 1862.

Ochiltree, Barony of (Ayrshire). Belonged to Colvilles from 14th century to 16th; exchanged for East Wemyss with Sir James *Hamilton of Finnart* 1530 and exchanged again with Andrew, 3rd Lord *Avondale*, who in 1543 was created Lord Stewart of Ochiltree, a title which became dormant 1675.

Octavians. Eight administrators employed by *James VI* to reorganise royal finances in 1596: *John Lindsay*, *Alexander Seton* (see Dunfermline), *Thomas Hamilton*, *David Carnegie*, *James Elphinstone* (see Balmerino), *Sir John Skene*, *Walter Stewart* and *Peter Young*.

Oengus. See Angus.

Officers of State. Officials to the number of about eight were entitled to sit in *Parliament* ex officio, and they also formed one element in the Committee of *Articles*.

Official. Judge in ecclesiastical courts before *Reformation*; usually one for each diocese, but two in *St Andrews* (St Andrews and *Lothian*) and *Glasgow* (Glasgow and Teviotdale).

Og(h)am Inscriptions. Formed by combinations of short lines connected at varying angles with a long base line; in use in many parts of Scotland c. 500-800 and, when they can be read intelligibly, containing elements of *Pict*ish as well as *Gaelic*.

Ogilvie, David and James. See Airlie, Earldom, and Findlater, Earldom.

Ogilvie (or Ogilvy) Family. Named from place in parish of *Glamis*, Angus; first occurs in 12th century.

Ogilvie, John (1579-1615). Born Banffshire; as Jesuit worked in *Edinburgh*, *Renfrew* and *Glasgow*; hanged for denying royal supremacy; beatified 1929; canonised 1976.

Ogilvie, John (1733-1813). Born *Aberdeen*; *minister* of Midmar 1759; served on commission for revising translations and paraphrases of scriptures.

Ogilvie, John (1797-1867). Born Marnock, Banffshire; after working as ploughman graduated M.A. at *Aberdeen* 1828; mathematics teacher at Gordon's Hospital, Aberdeen, 1831-59; compiled several English dictionaries.

Ogilvie, William (1736-1819). Son of laird of Pittensear, near *Elgin*; professor of philosophy at *King's College, Aberdeen*, 1762, and of *humanity* 1765; wrote 'The Right of Property in Land', which advocated common ownership.

Ogilvy. See Ogilvie.

Ogilvy, Sir George, of Barras (d. after 1679). Defended *Dunnottar Castle* against Cromwellian troops and helped to save *regalia*; baronet of *Nova Scotia* 1660.

Ogilvy, Marion (d. 1575). Daughter of James, 1st Lord O., mistress of *Cardinal Beaton* and mother of several of his children.

Olaf the Black (d. ? 1238). King of the *Isles*; imprisoned by *William I* c. 1208-14; contested Isles with his brother, Reginald, whom he finally defeated at *Dingwall* 1230.

Old Aberdeen. *Burgh of barony* for *Bishop of Aberdeen* 1489.

Old Edinburgh Club. Founded 1908 for publication of material on history of *Edinburgh*.

Old Extent. A valuation of lands, supposedly based on figures for 13th century, used in the qualification for electing members of parliament until 1832.
Old Lights. See New Lights.
Old Meldrum (Aberdeenshire). *Burgh of barony* for Urquhart of Meldrum 1671.
Old Melrose. See Melrose.
'Old Mortality'. See Paterson, Robert.
Old Pretender. See James Francis.
'Old Q.'. The *4th Duke of Queensberry*.
Old Roxburgh. See Roxburgh.
Oldcambus (Berwickshire). Leper hospital existed 12th-13th centuries.
Oliphant Family. Otherwise Olifard; appeared in Scotland with a Northamptonshire vassal of *David I*, c. 1140; obtained lands of Gask and Aberdalgie from *Robert I*.
Oliphant, Lordship. Created c. 1458 for Laurence Oliphant; dormant on death of 11th Lord 1751.
Oliphant, Margaret (1828-97). Née Wilson; married Francis Wilson Oliphant; novelist and historical writer.
Oliphant, Sir William (d. 1329). Defended *Stirling Castle* against English 1304; on its fall sent to London; released by Edward II and received land from *Robert I*.
Oliver Castle (Peeblesshire). Original seat of *Frasers*, from whom it passed to Tweedies; razed to the ground.
Orchardson, Sir William Quiller (1832-1910). Born *Edinburgh*; fellow student of *John Pettie* and Tom Graham at *Trustees' Academy*; went to London 1862; visited Venice 1870; painted portraits and many historical and Shakespearian subjects, including 'Napoleon on board the Bellerophon'; knighted 1907.
Orchardton Tower (Kirkcudbrightshire). 15th or 16th century tower-house which is possibly unique in being entirely circular; built by Cairns family.
Order of St John. See St John of Jerusalem.
Ordiquhill, Kirkton of (Banffshire). *Burgh of barony* for Gordon of Inverbucket 1617.
Ordnance Survey. Begun by Major-General *William Roy* 1784; primary triangulation completed 1858; one-inch map of Scotland completed 1887.
Original Secession. The first *Secession*, originating in 1733. See Erskine, Ebenezer and Ralph.
Orkney and Shetland. The Norwegian crown's lands and rights were pledged by Christian I on 8 September 1468 and 20 May 1469 for 58,000 florins of the Rhine remaining unpaid of the dowry of Princess *Margaret* on her marriage to *James III*; in 1470 the Earl made over his rights to the Scottish crown, and the *earldom* and lordship were annexed to the Scottish crown in 1472; efforts to redeem the islands were made on several occasions, down to 1749. See Norse Law, Udal Law.
Orkney and Zetland Antiquarian and Statistical Society. Founded in *Edinburgh* 1831 to investigate the antiquities and the capabilities of improvement of the islands.
Orkney, Antiquarian and Natural History Society of. Founded in *Kirkwall* 1844 for studies implied in its title and for the formation of a museum; published only a Report. The later Orkney Antiquarian Society issued several volumes, and the Orkney Record and Antiquarian Society issued a few publications after the Second World War.
Orkney, Bishopric of. Presumably founded by Earl *Thorfinn*, with its seat at *Birsay*, c. 1060.
Orkney, Dukedom. Created for *James, 4th Earl of Bothwell*, in May 1567 and forfeited December following.
Orkney, Earldom. The Norse earldom, dating from late 9th century, passed in 13th to a succession of Scottish earls, finally (1379) the St Clairs or Sinclairs—(1) Henry (d. c. 1400), son of William Sinclair (d. c. 1358), who is said to have seized both Shetland and Faroe and to have voyaged to Greenland; (2) Henry (d. 1418), son of (1), who was captured by English at *Homildon* and who, as *Admiral of Scotland*, accompanied *James I* on voyage which led to his capture; (3) William (c. 1404-80), who as Admiral conveyed *Princess Margaret* to France 1436, founded *collegiate church* of *Roslin* and was created Lord Sinclair 1449 and *Earl of Caithness* 1455. The earldom was resigned to the crown 1470, revived for *Robert Stewart*, lapsed on the execution of his son, *Patrick*, and revived again in 1696 for George Hamilton (1666-1737), a son of the 3rd *Duke of Hamilton*, whose wife was a mistress of *William of Orange*.
Orkney, Patrick Stewart, Earl of (d. 1615). Second son of Earl Robert (see Stewart, Robert), *Commendator* of *Whithorn* 1581; received charters of *Earldom* and *Bishopric* 1600; remembered as an oppressor of the natives of the islands, but he has had his defenders; his palace at *Kirkwall* is an outstanding building and his castle at *Scalloway* is an exceptionally fine tower-house; after *James Law* was appointed to the bishopric, Patrick made an agreement with him (1607), but the

bishop continued to complain, and Patrick was imprisoned 1609; after his son had raised a rebellion in the islands, he was executed.

Orkney, Robert Stewart, Earl of. See Stewart, Robert.

Ormond(e), Earldom. Named from castle, now in ruins, near *Avoch* in Black Isle; created c. 1445 for Hugh Douglas, 4th son of James, 7th *Earl of Douglas*; he was executed and forfeited 1455.

Ormonde, Marquisate. Created for James, 2nd son of *James III*, 1476; he died 1504 without heirs and the title lapsed. See Stewart, James.

Ormonde Pursuivant. First mentioned 1501. See Pursuivants.

Oronsay Priory (*Augustinian*). On tidal island off Colonsay; said to have been founded by Lords of the *Isles* in 14th century and first recorded 1353; property assigned to Bishopric of Isles 1616; the remains are considerable.

Orphan Institution (*Edinburgh*). See Dean Orphan Hospital.

Orpheus Choir. Established *Glasgow* by *Sir Hugh Roberton* and dissolved on his death.

Orr, John Boyd, Lord (1880-1971). Born *Kilmaurs*; graduated at *Glasgow* in medicine and science; specialised in human and animal nutrition; wrote 'History of the Scots Church Crisis of 1904', 'Food, Health and Income', 'Food and the People' and 'Minerals in Pastures and their Relation to Animal Nutrition'; created baron 1949.

'Ossian'. See Macpherson, James.

O'Sullivan, John William (1700-?). Served in French army in War of Austrian Succession; adjutant to Prince *Charles Edward* 1745-6; escaped to France. *Jacobite* knight and baronet.

Otterburn, Sir Adam (d. 1548). *Provost* of *Edinburgh* 1529; *King's Advocate* 1524; served as ambassador.

Otterburn, Battle of, 5 August 1388. Scots under James, 2nd *Earl of Douglas*, and George Dunbar, *Earl of March*, defeated English under Henry Percy ('Hotspur'), son of Earl of Northumberland; Douglas was killed and Hotspur captured.

Outfield. Until 18th century, the arable land further away from the *'ferm toun'* was cropped in portions, each for a series of years, with periods of fallow intervening. Cf. Infield.

Outlawry, or **Fugitation.** A person failing to appear in High Court of *Justiciary* was disqualified from bearing testimony or holding a place of trust or taking part in any legal process, and his moveables were escheated; if he remained rebel for a year his heritage also was forfeited.

Owen, Robert (1771-1858). Born Montgomeryshire; owned *cotton*-mill in Manchester; son-in-law of *David Dale*; manager of New Lanark factory 1800; his social experiments in the mill and village attracted much attention; went to U.S.A. 1828 and established a colony in New Harmony.

Owen the Bald (d. 1018). King of *Strathclyde*; succeeded by *Duncan*, grandson of *Malcolm II*.

Oxenfoord Castle (Midlothian). Older castle remodelled by *Robert Adam* 1780-5 and enlarged by *William Burn*.

Oxfuird, Viscountcy. Name identical with Oxenfoord; created 1661 for James MacGill (d. 1663); dormant with death of 2nd Viscount 1705; a descendant married Sir John *Dalrymple* and their son succeeded to *Earldom of Stair* 1853. Sir Donald Makgill successfully claimed the Viscountcy in 1977.

Oxgang. One eighth of a *ploughgate*.

Oysel, Henri Cleutin, Sieur d' (d. 1566). French ambassador or resident in Scotland 1546-60 and chief adviser of *Mary of Guise*.

P

P. & O. See Peninsular and Oriental.

Paisley. *Burgh of barony* for Abbot 1488; *burgh of regality* for Lord *Claud Hamilton* 1587.

Paisley Abbey (*Cluniac*) (Renfrewshire). Founded by Walter, *Steward of Scotland*, c. 1163, at *Renfrew*, transferred to Paisley by 1169; erected into *temporal lordship* for Lord *Claud Hamilton* 1587; church still in use, and restored 1897-1928, by MacGregor *Chalmers* and *Sir Robert Lorimer*.

Paisley Banking Company. Established 1783; amalgamated with *British Linen* Company 1836.

Paisley, Black Book of. Ms. volume in British Library, containing a copy of the *Scotichronicon* and some other material, written at *Paisley Abbey* c. 1542.

Paisley Grammar School. Had charter 1576, but probably existed before *Reformation*.

Paisley Union Bank. Founded 1788; merged with *Glasgow Union Bank* 1838.

Palladius, St (fl. 432). Sent by Pope Celestine I to the '*Scots*' as their first bishop; the 'Scots' were then in Ireland, but the church of *Fordoun* in Kincardineshire was dedicated to 'St Paldy'.

Palmer, Thomas Fyshe (1747-1802). Born Bedfordshire; Unitarian minister at *Montrose* 1783 and *Dundee* 1785; associated with radical or revolutionary societies and was sentenced to twelve years' transportation to Botany Bay.

Panmure *(Angus).* Lands acquired by marriage by Peter de *Maule* in early 13th century; *burgh of barony* for Maule of Panmure 1541.

Panmure, Earldom and Lordship. Earldom created 1633 for Patrick *Maule* (d. 1661); *forfeited* 1716. U.K. Lordship created for 2nd son of *Earl of Dalhousie* 1831.

Panmure, Fox Maule, 2nd Lord. See Maule.

Panmure, Harry Maule, Earl of (d. 1734). Took part in '*Fifteen* and escaped to Holland; on his return collected chronicles, cartularies and documents.

Pannanish Wells (Aberdeenshire). Their medicinal properties discovered 1760 and led to development of *Ballater* as a spa.

Panter, David (d. 1558). Nephew of *Patrick P*; secretary to *James V*; *Bishop of Ross* 1545.

Panter, Patrick (c. 1470-1519). Secretary to *James V*; active at French court; Abbot of *Cambuskenneth*.

Papa Stour (*Shetland*). The name means 'great island of the priests'; but no traces have yet been discovered of an early ecclesiastical settlement; there was an eighteenth-century 'leper house' for sufferers from elephantiasis, but no reference to a medieval hospital.

Papal Schism. From 1378 Scotland, with France and other countries, acknowledged the Pope at Avignon, while England and other countries acknowledged his rival at Rome; later France abandoned the cause of Benedict XIII, who took refuge in Spain, but Scotland adhered to him until 1418, when Martin V, appointed by the Council of Constance, was acknowledged.

Papingo, Festival of. See Popinjay.

Papingo Medal. Competed for by Royal Company of *Archers*.

'Paraffin Young'. See Young, James.

Paris, Scots College at. In 1325 David, *Bishop of Moray*, bought a farm for the support of poor Scottish scholars in Paris; the college was established by Archbishop *James Beaton* (II) after 1569 and a house bought in the Rue des Amandiers; new college built 1662; buildings sold and turned into private school 1846.

Park Castle (Wigtownshire). Built 1590 by Thomas Hay of Park, son of last abbot of *Glenluce*, partly, it is said, from the stones of the abbey.

Park, Mungo (1771-1806). Born Foulshiels near *Selkirk*; qualified as physician; went to Africa 1795 and journeyed from Senegal to the Niger; practised in *Peebles* 1801-3; returned to Africa 1805 and travelled from Gambia to the Niger, where he was drowned in an attack by natives.

Park, Patrick (1811-55). Stone-cutter who was sent by *Duke of Hamilton* to study under Thorvaldsen, the Danish sculptor; well known for his portrait busts.

Park, Stuart (1862-1933). Born Kidderminster, of Scottish parents, who returned to *Glasgow* in his childhood; studied in Glasgow and Paris; painted portraits and figure subjects, but became noted for flower painting; a member of the *Glasgow School*; lived in *Kilmarnock* from 1896.

Parliament. Term first recorded 1293, but neither the word nor the institution was then a novelty; although its membership expanded from the original barons and prelates, it remained unicameral. See Articles, Lords of the; Clerical Estate; Convention of Estates; Council; County Franchise; Lords of Parliament; Three Estates.

Parliament House (or **Hall**), *Edinburgh.* Begun 1632, finished 1639; since *Union* of 1707 used by *Court of Session*.

Parliamentary Burghs. Centres of population which had not previously been *burghs* but which became entitled to elect M.P.s under the *Reform Act* of 1832 and were now equipped with town councils.

Parson. Scottish equivalent of Latin and English 'rector': the incumbent of a parish retaining its entire revenues. Cf. Vicar.

Paterson, James (1854-1932). Born *Glasgow*; studied art in Glasgow and Paris; worked in several continental countries, then settled in *Moniaive* and later *Edinburgh*; joined the *Glasgow School*; painted landscapes, portraits and flowers.

Paterson, John (1632-1708). Son of John P. (c. 1604-79), *Bishop of Ross*; *minister* of *Ellon* 1660, *Tron* (*Edinburgh*) 1663; *Bishop of Galloway* 1674 and *Bishop of Edinburgh* 1679; *Archbishop of Glasgow* 1687.

Paterson(e), John (fl. 1681). Partnered *James VII* (when Duke of York) at golf.

Paterson, John (1776-1855). Born Duntocher; influenced by *Haldanes*; missionary in Denmark, Sweden and Russia (1812); received pension from Czar; secretary of London

Missionary Society.

Paterson, Robert (1715-1801). Born Haggisha, near *Hawick*; *Walter Scott*'s 'Old Mortality'; stone-cutter who spent forty years renovating monuments of *Covenanters*; himself a *Cameronian.*

Paterson, William (1658-1719). Born Tynwald, but spent most of early life in England; traded with West Indies; a projector of Bank of England and one of its directors 1694; involved himself in Company of Scotland and advocated establishment of emporium at *Darien*; accompanied first expedition to Scottish colony there, returned 1699; prepared scheme for Sinking Fund and Consolidation of National Debt.

Paton, John Gibson (1824-1907). Born Kirkmahoe, of *Cameronian* stock; missionary with City of *Glasgow*; went with wife as missionary to New Hebrides.

Paton, Sir Joseph Noel (1821-1901). Born *Dunfermline*; brother of *Walter Hugh P*; had little formal training in art except for a short time at the Royal Academy Schools in London, where he became a friend of Millais; Queen's *Limner* 1865; knighted 1867; noted for historical and mythological painting, e.g. 'Luther at Erfurt', 'The Quarrel of Oberon and Titania'.

Paton, Walter Hugh (1825-95). Brother of preceding; landscape painter.

'Patrick's Places'. Theses circulated by *Patrick Hamilton*.

'Patrimony of the Kirk'. Term used in late 16th century, by reformers and *Presbyterians*, to denote in particular the *teinds*, but sometimes other ecclesiastical property, to which the reformed church was held to have the right to succeed.

Patronage. Abolished 1649, restored 1661; in 1690 the right was transferred to *heritors* and *elders*, but individual rights were restored in 1712 and abolished 1874; contributed to *Secessions* and *Disruption*.

Paul, Sir James Balfour (1846-1931). *Lyon* King of Arms 1890-1927; K.C.V.O. 1926; editor of 'The Scots Peerage' and of record publications; wrote 'History of the Royal Company of *Archers*'.

Paul Jones or **John Paul Jones** (1747-92). Born Kirkbean, Kirkcudbrightshire, son of gardener called Paul; became a sailor engaged in slave trade and smuggling and trading with West Indies; settled in Virginia; entered American navy 1775 as Jones and carried out various exploits in British waters during American War of Independence; served also in French and Russian navies and died in Paris.

Paul's Work. See Edinburgh, Hospitals (7).

Peace and War, Act Anent, 1703. Provided for independent Scottish foreign policy after the death of Anne without heirs of her body.

Pearson, Charles John (1843-1910). *Lord Advocate* 1891; *Lord of Session* 1896.

Peck. A quarter of a *firlot*; usually = about 5.8 pints.

Pedagogy (St Andrews). Original building of *St Andrews University*.

Peden, Alexander (1626-86). Born Ayrshire; after being schoolmaster at *Tarbolton*, became *minister* at New Luce 1660; deprived 1662 and preached at *conventicles*; declared a rebel 1665 and went to Ireland; returned 1673 and was sentenced to imprisonment on *Bass Rock*; liberated 1678; preached in Ayrshire and Ireland; took refuge in cave at *Sorn*.

Peden's Stone (near Shotts, Lanarkshire). By tradition a preaching place of the *Covenanters.*

Peebles. Apparently *royal burgh* in reign of *David I*; castle existed from about that time until 1685, after which it was used as a quarry and a parish church built on its site.

Peebles, Collegiate Church. College founded in parish church by John Hay of *Yester* and the community 1541; said in 1560 to have been destroyed by English about 12 years before.

Peebles, David (d. 1579). Canon of *St Andrews*; composed Latin motets; after 1560 commissioned by Lord James Stewart (see under Moray) to set the psalms of reformed church to music. See St Andrews Psalter.

Peebles Friary (*Trinitarian*). Allegedly founded by *Alexander III* in 1261 on the finding of a cross and the relics of 'St Nicholas the Bishop', but not mentioned until 1296; dedicated to Holy Cross; used as parish church 1561-1784; lands belonging to house erected into *barony* for Lord Hay of *Yester* 1624.

Peebles, Hospitals. (1) and (2): Grants of lands for almshouses, one in connection with the chapel of Our Lady and the other in connection with the *Trinitarian* friary, referred to 1462 and 1464; they seem still to have existed in 1540s. (3): St Leonard's, founded before 1305 at Chapel Yards near Horsburgh about 2 miles east of *burgh*, for the poor; appointment of *preceptor* recorded 1558.

Peebles, Parish Church of St Andrew. Founded 1195 by Bishop *Jocelin* of *Glasgow*; destroyed by English in 1540s.

Peebles, School. Existed 1464, when *bailies*

appointed schoolmaster, and management by town council was continuous.

Peel (or **Pele**). Usual term for a tower, especially in the Borders, but it is sometimes applied to larger structures, e.g. *Linlithgow Palace*.

Peel Castle (Renfrewshire). Belonged to Lord Sempill.

Peers' Elections. Held, in terms of Treaty of *Union*, until 1963.

Peffermill House (*Edinburgh*). Built 1636 by Edgar family, from whom it passed to Osborns, Alexanders, Nelsons and Gilmours; still occupied.

Penal Laws. Laws against *Non-jurors* in 1718, 1746 and 1748.

Pencaitland (East Lothian). *Burgh of barony* for Sinclair of Herdmanston 1505.

Pend. Generally speaking an access through the ground floor of a tenement; but particularly the elaborate vaulted structure which formed approach to a religious house, still to be seen at *Dunfermline* and *St Andrews* and formerly at *Holyrood*.

Penicillin. See Fleming, Sir Alexander.

Penicuik (Midlothian). Lands bought 1646 from Dr Alexander Penicuik by John Clerk (1611-74), son of a *Montrose* merchant who had made a fortune in Paris; his son John was created a baronet 1679; Penicuik House built 1761 by Sir James Clerk. Town was formerly a *burgh of barony* and became a *police burgh* 1892.

Peninsular and Oriental Steam Navigation Company. Founded largely by Arthur Anderson (1792-1868), a Shetlander, who acquired mail contracts in 1837.

Penny. Appears as silver coin under *David I*; nominally 1/240 of a pound of silver, but actually 252 were coined from a pound and the number increased to 1680 in 1482, and as its value dwindled the penny was made of billon and then copper.

Penny Post. Started in Edinburgh 1777 by *Peter Williamson*, who undertook to deliver letters and parcels anywhere within a mile of the *mercat cross* for 1d. The government later took over the business and paid Williamson £25 a year.

Penny Weddings. Originally each neighbour contributed 1d. towards festivities; later they brought gifts in kind.

Pentland Rising, 1666. *Covenanters* in south-west captured government commander, *Sir James Turner*, and marched towards *Edinburgh* in the vain hope of getting support; falling back, they were routed at *Rullion Green*.

Peploe, Samuel John (1871-1935). Born and died in *Edinburgh*; studied in Paris; associated with *Cadell, Hunter* (George Leslie) and *Fergusson* (J.D.) as 'The Scottish Colourists'.

Percussion Cap. Invented by *Alexander Forsyth*.

Perth. *Royal burgh* existed in 1120s, but the earliest extant charter is of 1210; a castle stood at end of Skinnergate; it was captured by Edward I 1298, recovered by *Robert I* 1311, changed hands again in 1330s but after that disappears from history. Perth was something of a chief town in Scotland in the middle ages, especially under *James I*, who held many *parliaments* and *general councils* there.

Perth Academy. Founded by town council 1760; combined 1807 in one building with older *Grammar School* (descendant of school mentioned c. 1150).

Perth Banking Company. Established 1787 as an amalgamation of several small companies; amalgamated with *Union Bank* 1857.

Perth Charterhouse. See Perth Priory.

Perth, Collegiate Church. Referred to 1548, but no evidence that the *burgh* church ever became *collegiate*.

Perth, Earldom and Dukedom. Earldom created for James, *Lord Drummond*, 1605; 4th Earl (James, 1648-1716) became 1st Duke in *Jacobite* peerage; 2nd Duke (James, 1675-1720), commanded Jacobite cavalry at *Sheriffmuir*; 3rd Duke (James, 1713-47), commanded left wing of Jacobite army at *Culloden*, and his brother John (d. 1747), who succeeded him, was also in that army. Earldom restored 1853 for George (1807-1902), 14th titular Earl.

Perth, Fair Maid of. See Fair Maid.

Perth, Five Articles of. See Five Articles.

Perth Friaries. (1) *Carmelite*, established at *Tullilum* by Richard, *Bishop of Dunkeld*, 1262. (2) *Dominican*, said to have been founded by *Alexander II* 1231 and in existence 1240; scene of murder of *James I*; attacked by mob 1543 and 1559; lands granted to *burgh* 1569. (3) Observant *Franciscan*, said to have been founded 1460 by Laurence, 1st *Lord Oliphant*, but it probably did not exist until 1480×1492; looted 1559; buildings demolished 1580 to make way for cemetery.

Perth, Hospitals. (1) St Anne's, founded before 1488, apparently by Rollo of *Duncrub*; inmates removed to new hospital 1586. (2) St Katharine's, founded 1523 by John Tyrie, provost of *collegiate church* of *Methven*, for poor travellers; associated with St Katharine's chapel and probably included with property disposed to Patrick Murray of Tibbermuir 1567. (3) St Leonard's, mentioned 1184; later attached to St Leonard's nunnery and transferred with it to Charterhouse; in being as late as 1543. (4) St Mary Magdalen's, founded before 1327; associated with *Dunfermline Abbey* until 1466, when transferred to Charterhouse; still in being 1543. (5) St Paul's, founded 1434 by John Spens of Glendouglas, *burgess* of Perth, for strangers, poor and infirm; possibly destroyed 1559 and an attempt to re-establish it in 1583 did not succeed. (6) King *James VI*, founded by Regent *Moray* 1569; endowed with revenues of friaries; original buildings destroyed to build Cromwellian fort 1652; new building begun 1749 on site of *Charterhouse*.

Perth, Literary and Antiquarian Society. Founded 1784 for study of antiquities and records, particularly of area round Perth.

Perth, North and South Inches. The North Inch was the scene in 1396 of a *Clan Fight*. The South Inch was the site of a Cromwellian citadel, soon demolished. Both Inches said to have been given to the town by the *Mercer* family.

Perth Nunnery (*Cistercian*). Dedicated to St Leonard; suppressed in favour of *Carthusian* priory 1438.

Perth, Pacification of, 23 February 1573. Most of the *Queen's Party* agreed to acknowledge *James VI*.

Perth Priory (Carthusian). Founded by *James I* 1429; Scotland's only Carthusian house; known as house of 'The Vale of Virtue'; James I, his Queen and *Margaret*, widow of *James IV*, buried there; sacked by mob 1559; last prior was Adam Forman and much of the property went to town.

Perth, St John's Church. Mainly 15th century; restored 1923-6 by *Sir Robert Lorimer*.

Perth, St Ninian's Cathedral. Built 1850, first post-*Reformation* cathedral built in Scotland. Architect William Butterfield.

Perth, Salutation Hotel. Dates from 1699; a room is shown in which Prince *Charles Edward* spent the night in 1745.

Perth, Sandeman Library. Founded 1896 by Archibald Sandeman of Tulloch, professor of mathematics and natural science, Owen's College, Manchester; opened 1898.

Perth, Treaty of, 2 July 1266. Magnus IV, King of Norway, ceded the *Hebrides* and *Man* in return for a payment of 4000 merks in four annual instalments and 100 merks in perpetuity—'the annual of Norway'.

Perth Union Banking Company. Established 1810; amalgamated with *National Bank* 1836.

Perthshire Regiment. (1) Raised at *Perth* 1780 by Norman MacLeod, Chief of *MacLeod*, as the 73rd, a second battalion for the *Black Watch*; in 1881 became territorial regiment; now called 'The Royal Regiment, the Black Watch'. (2) Raised 1794 by Major Alexander Campbell as the 116th; men soon drafted to other units; disbanded 1794.

Perthshire Society of Natural Science. Published Proceedings and Transactions and a magazine called 'The Scottish Naturalist'.

Peterhead (or **Keithinch**) (Aberdeenshire). *Burgh of barony* for *Commendator* of *Deer* and Earl *Marischal* 1587.

Petilius Cerialis. Roman commander in Britain (71-74) who appears to have crossed present Border into Annandale.

Petrie, Alexander (c. 1594-1662). Son of *Montrose* merchant; *minister* of Rhind 1632; minister of Scottish Church at Rotterdam 1643; wrote 'History of the Catholick Church in Scotland 600-1600'.

Pettie, John (1839-93). Born *Edinburgh*; trained at *Trustees' Academy* under *Robert Scott Lauder*; painted mostly historical scenes, a few of them Scottish, and aimed at colour as well as subject; settled in London 1862.

Petty (Inverness-shire). *Barony* passed from Moray family to *Douglases* until 1455, when it was resumed by crown; later granted to Ogilvie of *Findlater*, who sold it to *Earls of Moray*. The *burgh* (otherwise Fishertoun of Petty) became *burgh of barony* for Earl of Moray 1611.

Phantassie Doocot (Dovecot) (East Lothian). Presented to *National Trust* 1961.

Philabeg. See Féileadh-beag.

Philiphaugh, Battle of, 13 September 1645. *Marquis of Montrose* defeated by *David Leslie*.

Phillip, John (1817-67). Born *Aberdeen*; studied art in England from 1837; travelled much in Spain and became known as 'Phillip of Spain' or 'Spanish Phillip' for his studies of Spanish life; died in London.

Philorth (Aberdeenshire). *Barony* belonged to *Frasers*; 7th laird, Alexander, built a harbour 1546 and had town of Faithlie erected into *burgh of barony* as *Fraserburgh*.

'Philosophical Magazine'. Begun by Professor *Robert Jameson* 1819.

Philosophical Society of Edinburgh. Founded

by *Thomas Ruddiman* 1739; originally for advancement of medical knowledge; became *Royal Society* after 43 years.

Physic Gardens. Forerunners of *Botanic Gardens* in *Edinburgh*: first of them in 1656 at Surgeons' House, another at *Heriot's* Hospital 1661 and a third at *Holyrood* 1670.

Physicians, Royal College of, Edinburgh. Founded by *Sir Robert Sibbald* 1681; its hall was formerly in George Street but since 1845 has been in a building in Queen Street designed by *Thomas Hamilton*.

Piccolomini. See Aeneas Sylvius.

'Pictish Chronicle'. Probably originally written at *Abernethy* or *Brechin* in late 10th century; in present form may date from reign of *William I*.

Picts. Their origin uncertain; identifiable with the *Caledonians* whom the Romans encountered in 1st century A.D; had their own mysterious language but some of them adopted a form of British akin to Welsh; joined with *Scots* in kingdom of *Alba*. See also Cruithne, Dalriada.

'Picts' Dyke'. Part is traceable near Buckney Burn in Clunie parish, Perthshire.

Piershill Barracks, Edinburgh. Built 1793 as cavalry barracks; demolished in 1930s.

Pilrig House (*Edinburgh*). Built 1638 by Gilbert Kirkwood, goldsmith; acquired 1718 by James Balfour, a director of the *Company of Scotland* and an ancestor of *R.L. Stevenson's* grandfather, the *minister* of Colinton; bequeathed 1941 by Miss Balfour-Melville to Edinburgh Corporation, who neglected it and allowed it to be much damaged.

Pinkerton, Alan (1819-84). Son of *Glasgow* policeman; emigrated to U.S.A. and in Chicago in 1850 founded detective agency which was carried on by his sons.

Pinkerton, John (1758-1826). Born *Edinburgh*; law apprentice; moved to London 1781; his early publications were of verse, but he turned to numismatics and anthologies and then to history; his 'Dissertation on the Scythians or Goths' (1787) and 'History of Scotland preceding the reign of *Malcolm III*' (1790) were coloured by admiration for the Teutonic peoples (who, he believed, included the *Picts*) and contempt for the Celtic; his most important historical work was a 'History of Scotland from the accession of the House of Stewart to that of *Mary*' (1792).

Pinkie, Battle of, 10 September 1547. Duke of Somerset (formerly Earl of Hertford) defeated Scots under *Earl of Arran*.

Pinkie House (*Musselburgh*). Erected round 16th century tower by *1st Earl of Dunfermline*; has very fine painted gallery; now part of *Loretto School*.

Pinkie Pin. Prize for archery, to be competed for in grounds of Pinkie House, instituted 1965 by Trustees of *Loretto School*, *Musselburgh*.

Pint. Equalled 2 choppins or 4 mutchkins.

Piperden, Battle of, 15 September 1436. Scots under William, 2nd *Earl of Angus*, defeated English under Percy and Sir Robert Ogle, near *Berwick*.

Pirrie, William (1807-82). Born *Huntly*; professor of surgery at *Marischal College, Aberdeen* 1839.

Pistole. Gold coin minted 1701, worth £12.

Pitcairlie House (Fife). Home of Patrick Leslie, 1st *Lord Lindores* (1600); bought by Cathcart of Carbiston in mid-18th century; originally a 16th century tower on Z-plan, it was added to and modernised.

Pitcairn(e), Archibald (1652-1713). Born *Edinburgh*; qualified in medicine; professor at Leyden 1692-3; returned to Edinburgh; wrote 'The Assembly', a play satirising the *Church of Scotland,* and some verse.

Pitcairn, David (1749-1809). Born in Fife; brother of *Robert P*; became physician at St Bartholomew's Hospital, London, 1780.

Pitcairn, Robert (c. 1747-c. 1770). Brother of preceding; midshipman; first to sight Pitcairn Island 1767.

Pitcairn, Robert (1793-1855). Born *Edinburgh*; *writer to signet* 1815; assistant to *Thomas Thomson* in *Register House*; edited 'Criminal Trials' for *Bannatyne* and *Maitland* Clubs.

Pitcaple Castle (Aberdeenshire). 15th century tower-house on Z-plan, built by *Leslie* family who held lands from 1457; *Mary*, Queen of Scots, and *Charles II* visited it and *Montrose* was imprisoned there in 1650; passed by marriage to Professor John Lumsden of *King's College, Aberdeen*; a wing was added in 19th century.

Pitcullo Castle (Fife). 16th century L-plan castle, built by Sibbalds and passed to Balfours; roofless, but recently restored.

Pitcur Castle *(Angus).* Remains of ancient seat of *Haliburtons*.

Pitfichie Castle (Aberdeenshire). Early 16th century, on Z-plan; passed from family of Hurry or *Urry* to Forbes of *Monymusk* c. 1657.

Pitfirrane Castle (Fife). Tower house built by Halkett family, who had held lands since at least 1437 and were often *provosts* of *Dunfermline*; passed by marriage to Wedderburns of Gosford, who took name of Halkett; enlarged 1573 and again in 18th century; now club-house of a golf course.

Pitkeathly, Sir James Scott (1882-1948). Born *Dunkeld*; went to India in service of electrical firm 1903; Electrical Inspector in United Provinces 1909; Director of Electrical and Engineering Works in Mesopotamia campaign in First World War.

Pitlessie. *Burgh of barony* for Lord *Lindsay* of the Byres 1541.

Pitlochry (Perthshire). Developed from mid-19th century; hydropathic built 1875.

Pitlochry Festival Theatre. Established 1951.

Pitmedden Gardens (Aberdeenshire). 17th century garden re-created by *National Trust*.

Pitreavie Castle (Fife). Built by Henry Wardlaw, son of Sir Cuthbert W. of Balmule, *chamberlain* to *Anne*, Queen of *James VI*, who acquired lands 1608; much altered and enlarged, it is now naval headquarters.

Pitsligo Castle (Aberdeenshire). Ruins go back to keep built 1424 by Sir William Forbes.

Pitsligo, Lordship. Created for Forbes of Pitsligo 1633; 4th Lord, Alexander (1678-1762), joined *Jacobites* in 'Fifteen and, at age of 67, in the 'Forty-Five; after *Culloden* lived on estate in disguise and in hiding; title *forfeited*.

Pittenweem (Fife). *Burgh of barony* 1526; *royal burgh* 1541.

Pittenweem Priory (*Augustinian*). Lands of Pittenweem granted to priory of *May* by *David I* c. 1143; it appears that, probably in 14th century, priory was transferred from May to Pittenweem; property granted to *burgh* and confirmed 1593; *temporal lordship* for Frederick Stewart 1606.

Pittheavlis Castle (*Perth*). L-shaped tower of 16th century, still occupied; probably built by Robert Stewart, who acquired property from John Ross of Craigie before 1586; belonged to Patrick Oliphant of Bachilton 1636.

Pittodrie House (Aberdeenshire). Built by Erskine family early 17th century.

Plack. Billon coin in reign of *James III*, later made of copper; worth 4d. or 8d.

Plantation of Ulster. See Ulster.

Play-Days. Festivals in medieval *burghs* when the principal feature was a procession or pageant called a 'play'.

Playfair, Sir Hugh Lyon (1786-1861). Son of James Playfair (1738-1819), principal of *St Andrews University*; served in Indian army; returned 1834; *provost* of St Andrews 1842-6; did much to restore town and university buildings and revived the *Royal and Ancient Golf Club*; knighted 1856.

Playfair, John (1748-1819). Son of *minister* of Benvie; lectured while still a student at *St Andrews* and at age of 18 applied unsuccessfully for chair of mathematics at *Marischal College, Aberdeen*; minister of Benvie 1773; assistant to professor of mathematics at *Edinburgh* 1785; professor of natural philosophy at Edinburgh 1805; published edition of Euclid's 'Elements', 'Analysis of the Volcanic Theory of the Earth' (1802) and 'Outlines of Natural Philosophy' (1814).

Playfair, Sir Lyon (1818-98). Born Bengal; grandson of James P., principal of *St Andrews*; professor of chemistry, *Edinburgh*, 1858-69; Liberal M.P. for Universities; Postmaster-General 1873; Baron Playfair of St Andrews.

Playfair, William Henry (1789-1857). Born London, son of James P., architect, and nephew of *Professor John P*; went to *Edinburgh* 1794; architect of *National Gallery of Scotland*, *Royal Scottish Academy*, National Monument on Calton Hill, *Donaldson's Hospital, Surgeons' Hall* (all in Edinburgh), and part of *New Town* of Edinburgh.

Pleas of the Crown. Already by late 12th century restricted to murder, rape, robbery and fire-raising, along with treason.

Pleasance (*Edinburgh*). In an absurd attempt to explain the name, a nunnery of 'St Mary of Placentia' was invented on the analogy of *Sciennes*.

Plockton (Ross). *Burgh of barony* 1808.

Ploughgate. A denomination of land area, related to the amount of land which a plough-team could cultivate over a period; clearly variable, but has been equated with 104 acres.

Pluscarden, Book of. A history based on the work of *Bower*, probably written in *Pluscarden Priory* by Maurice Buchanan.

Pluscarden Priory (*Valliscaulian*, later *Benedictine*) (*Moray*). Founded by *Alexander II* 1230; in 1454 joined with *Urquhart* to become dependency of *Dunfermline*; erected into lordship for *Alexander Seton* (see Dunfermline) 1587. In 1943 the buildings were presented to the Benedictine Order, who have occupied them and done some restoration.

Poinding. Process of *diligence* whereby movables of a debtor were appropriated in favour of a creditor.

Poker Club. Founded in *Edinburgh* 1762, to

stir up agitation in Scotland for the raising of a *militia*; lasted until 1784.
Police Burghs. Burghs set up under 'Police Acts', especially those of 1850 and 1862; by 1892 there were over 100 such burghs.
Polish School of Medicine (Edinburgh). The Polish Army, which was reorganised in Scotland after the fall of France in 1940, included medical teachers and students and in February 1941 they were formed into a School of Medicine in *Edinburgh University* which existed until March 1949.
Pollok (Renfrewshire). Hospital of St Mary Magdalene mentioned 1417; castle, built round an early tower of the Pollok family, burned down 1882; Pollok House built by Maxwells 1747-52. Part designed by *William Adam*. Given to City of *Glasgow* 1967. Fine collection of paintings, esp. Spanish, acquired by Sir William *Stirling-Maxwell*.
Pollokshaws (Renfrewshire). *Burgh of barony* for Maxwell of *Pollok* 1813.
Polmadie Hospital (Lanarkshire). St John's; existed under *Alexander III*; revenues diverted to a prebend of *Glasgow* and *collegiate church* of *Dumbarton*.
Polmont (Stirlingshire). *Burgh of regality* for *Marquis of Hamilton* 1611.
Polton Hospital. See Dalhousie.
Polwarth, Lordship. Created 1690 for *Sir Patrick Hume*, who became *Earl of Marchmont* 1697. Earldom extinct 1794, lordship claimed successfully by Hugh Scott of Harden 1835.
Pont (or **Kylpont, Kynpont**), **Robert** (1524-1606). *Minister* of *Dunblane* 1562 and *Dunkeld* 1563; *commissioner* of *Moray, Inverness* and *Banff*; *provost* of *Trinity College, Edinburgh*; minister of *St Cuthbert's, Edinburgh*, 1573; *Lord of Session 1573*.
Pont, Timothy (c. 1565-1614). Son of preceding; *minister* of Dunnet, *Caithness*, 1601; evidently spent most of the period 1583-1601 in travelling over Scotland and making the first survey of the country; compiled maps which were used in the atlas of Blaeu of Amsterdam. See Gordon, Robert.
Pontius Pilate. See Fortingall.
'Pontius Pilate's Bodyguard'. The *Royal Scots* Regiment, so called because of its antiquity; reputed oldest British regiment.
Poor Law. 16th century legislation incorporated three principles which long guided Scottish poor relief: the responsibility for a pauper lay with his parish of origin; there was to be no assistance for the able-bodied; and parishes could impose an assessment. An act of 1672 proceeded on those principles and remained the law until 1845, though even by that date few parishes had assessments and the main source of the poor fund came from church collections and charitable endowments. See also Board of Supervision.
Poors Roll. The *Faculty of Advocates* appointed six of their number to be available as counsel for the poor, and *Writers to the Signet* and *Solicitors to the Supreme Court* likewise provided four of their members to act for the poor. See also Advocate for the Poor.
Pope Gib. See Gib, Adam.
Popinjay, Festival of. This shooting match, which provided the opening for *Scott's* 'Old Mortality', was still observed at *Maybole* in 1870 and at *Kilwinning* even later.
Port. Meant gate in town wall.
Port Glasgow. (Renfrewshire). Became a port for *Glasgow*, with harbour and *tolbooth*, 1668.
Port of Menteith (Perthshire). *Burgh of barony* for *Earl of Menteith* 1467; *burgh of regality* for *Marquis of Montrose* 1680.
Porteous, John (d. 1736). Born *Canongate*; professional soldier, who had served in Holland, employed 1715 to train *City Guard* in *Edinburgh*; as Captain of the guard at execution of Andrew Wilson, a smuggler, ordered his men to fire on a crowd who made a tumult, and killed or wounded some thirty people; tried and sentenced to death, but reprieved; the mob then broke into the *tolbooth*, seized him and hanged him.
Porteous Riot. See Porteous, John.
Porteous (or **Portuous**) **Roll**. Roll of cases to be heard in High Court of *Justiciary*.
Portincraig Hospital (Angus). Founded by Gillebride, *Earl of Angus* (d. 1187-9), and not mentioned after early 13th century.
Portioner. Normally an estate gave its name to a sole proprietor, but when it was divided (e.g. among co-heiresses) the proprietor of each part was styled a portioner.
Portmahomack (or **Castlehaven**) (Ross). *Burgh of barony* for Mackenzie of *Tarbat* 1678.
Portmoak Priory. See Lochleven Priory. There was also a hospital in 12th century.
Portobello (Midlothian). Named from a cottage built 1742 by sailor who had served at capture of Portobello near Panama in 1739; brick works started 1765; seaside resort in 19th century; pier built 1871; amalgamated with *Edinburgh* 1896 after being *police burgh* under act of 1862.

Portobello Pottery. Founded 1770 and expanded 1786, to manufacture china and other ware, stone jugs and jars; bought in 1867 by Buchan family, who owned it until after 1945.
Portpatrick (Wigtownshire). *Burgh of barony* for Montgomerie of Newton 1620.
Portpatrick Railway. 'British and Irish Grand Junction Railway' was intended to join *Glasgow* and South-Western line to the packets from Portpatrick and to extend from *Castle Douglas*; there was a branch from *Newton Stewart* to *Whithorn*; taken over 1885 by a joint committee of larger companies.
Portsburgh (*Edinburgh*). An area immediately outside the West *Port*, south of present West End; *superiority* purchased from Sir Adam Hepburn by City of Edinburgh 1647 and *burgh of barony* erected under city.
Portsoy (Banffshire). *Burgh of barony* for Ogilvy of Boyne 1550.
Pound Scots. Starting as of the same value as £ sterling, had fallen to 1/5 of that by 1560 and 1/12 by 1600, at which value it remained.
Prayer Book of 1637. See Scottish Prayer Book.
Precept. Writ commanding an officer or deputy to take legal action, e.g. a precept of *sasine* instructed a *bailie* to give actual possession of heritable property.
Precept of Clare Constat. Issued by *superior* for *infeftment* of a vassal who was 'clearly understood' to be the heir of his predecessor.
Preceptor. Term used of heads of certain religious houses, especially the *Knights Hospitallers*.
Prelacy. Pejorative term for *episcopal* government, much used by *Covenanters* in reigns of *Charles II* and *James VII*; Act abolishing Prelacy passed 1689.
Premier Peerages. Duke—*Hamilton*; Marquis—*Huntly*; Earl—*Crawford*; Viscount—*Earl of Mar and Kellie* as *Viscount Fento(u)n*; Baron—*Forbes*.
Premonstratensian Order. See Dryburgh, Fearn, Holywood, Soulseat, Tongland, Whithorn.
Presbyterian Government. Implied, if not fully defined, in Second Book of *Discipline* and advocated by *Andrew Melville*; authorised by *Parliament* 1592, 1639 and 1690. Oversight is vested not in individual bishops or *superintendents* but in courts or councils, of which there is a hierarchy—*kirk session, presbytery, synod*, and *General Assembly*.
Presbytery. An organ of church government, representing a kind of corporate episcopacy, introduced c. 1580 and now consisting of *ministers* and *elders*.
Preston (Berwickshire). *Burgh of barony* for *Earl of Angus* 1602.
Preston (*East Linton*). Mill, probably the oldest working mill in Scotland, was presented to *National Trust* 1950.
Preston (East Lothian). *Burgh of barony* for *Commendator* of *Holyrood* 1552. L-shaped tower, built before 1491 for Hamilton family, had two storeys added 1628, was burned by English 1650 and again accidentally 1663. *Mercat cross* dates from 1617. Preston House, which succeeded the tower, was residence of Lord Grange (see Erskine, James); it passed to a Dr Schaw, who used it as a charity school for boys c. 1780-1832; yet another house was then built, which became the Mary Murray institution for the training of girls. *Barony, burgh* and harbour confirmed to Sir Thomas Hamilton 1663. See also Hamilton House, Northfield House.
Preston (Kirkcudbrightshire). *Burgh of regality* for *Earl of Nithsdale* 1663.
Preston (Midlothian). *Burgh of barony* for Preston of that *ilk* 1663.
Preston, Battle of, 17-19 August 1648. Scots under *Duke of Hamilton* defeated by Cromwell, on invading England in support of *Engagement*.
Preston, Sir Simon, of *Craigmillar* (d. 1570). *Provost* of *Edinburgh* 1538-43, 1544-5 and 1560; Queen *Mary* was lodged in his house in Edinburgh, opposite the *Tron*, after her surrender at *Carberry*.
Prestonfield House (*Edinburgh*). Built 1687 by *Sir William Bruce* for Sir James Dick of Braid; now an hotel.
Prestongrange (East Lothian). House dates in part from 16th century, but most of it is 19th century; estate passed from *Newbattle Abbey* to *Earl of Lothian*, to John Morrison, father of Alexander M., who was a *Lord of Session* (Prestongrange), 1626, and to *William Grant, Lord Advocate*.
Prestonpans, Battle of, 21 September 1745. *Jacobites* under Prince *Charles* routed government forces under *Sir John Cope*.
Prestwick (Ayrshire). *Burgh* under Stewart family, but in 1600 became *burgh of barony* for inhabitants.
Pretenders. See Charles Edward; James Francis.
Prime Gilt. Levy of 12d. on every ton of goods loaded or unloaded by Scottish ships at *Leith*,

for maintenance of the charities of *Trinity House*; in force from at latest mid-fifteenth century until 1862.

Primrose, Sir Archibald (1616-79). Son of *James Primrose*; *Clerk Register* 1661; *Lord of Session* (Carrington) 1661.

Primrose, Archibald, Earl of Rosebery. See Rosebery.

Primrose, James (d. 1641). Son of David P. in *Culross*; Clerk of *Privy Council* 1599.

Primus. Presiding bishop of Scottish *Episcopal Church* since 1720.

Princess Stone (near Dulsie Bridge, *Nairn*). Stone with runic inscriptions, supposed to commemorate a Celtic princess who was drowned with her Scandinavian lover.

Printing. *Walter Chepman* and *Andrew Myllar* set up a printing press in *Edinburgh* 1507.

Prison Commissioners. Appointed 1877.

Privy Council. Developed from undifferentiated *council* in early 16th century; its separate Register begins 1545; abolished 1708.

Privy Kirks. Protestant congregations which met, without official recognition and in semi-secrecy, in a number of Scottish *burghs* in late 1550s, before there was 'the face of a public kirk' in the realm.

Privy Seal. First known under *Alexander III*; used for *precepts* commanding the keeper of the *great seal* to prepare and authenticate charters and for various gifts of pensions, appointments to offices, presentations to benefices and so forth. Discontinued 1898.

Procurator Fiscal. Nowadays the official prosecutor in *sheriff courts*; he also investigates sudden and suspicious deaths (like English coroner). In earlier times several courts and institutions had their procurators fiscal.

Prophet's Grave. Grave of *William Smith* (d. 1644), *minister* at *Largs*.

Prosecutions. Conducted by *Lord Advocate* and *procurators fiscal* or their deputies, on behalf of the crown; private prosecutions, except for poaching, are now almost unknown.

Protectorate. The government of Oliver Cromwell and his son Richard, in terms of the Instrument of Government of December 1653; usually included in *Commonwealth*.

Protesters. Extreme *Covenanters*, who protested against *General Assemblies* of 1650 and 1651 in which they were in a minority.

Provand's Lordship (*Glasgow*). House dating from 1471, town residence of prebendaries of Barlanark in the cathedral.

Provincial Council. Legislative body of medieval church, convened in terms of papal bull of 1225; previous councils had been held from time to time by papal legates. Some 20 councils are known to have been held between 1225 and 1560, but the records are very imperfect and there may well have been many more.

Provost. (1) Originally the officer appointed to have charge of any royal estate, but came to be applied especially to officer in charge of a *burgh*, who in time was elected by the community. (2) Head of *collegiate church*.

Pupils. Pupillarity is the period before the age of 12 in females and 14 in males; it is followed by the state or period of minority.

Purdie, Tom. First employed by *Sir Walter Scott* when he acquired *Ashestiel* in 1804; there is no support for the tale that he made Scott's acquaintance when he appeared as a poacher before the *sheriff*; buried in *Melrose Abbey*.

Pursuivants. Officers of Lyon Court (see *Lyon* King of Arms), inferior to *heralds*. See Bute, Carrick, Dingwall, Kintyre, March, Ormonde and Unicorn.

Q

Quair (Book), **The King's.** See King's Quair.

Quakers. First heard of in Scotland in 1653, at East Kilbride, Glassford in Lanarkshire and *Kirkintilloch*.

Qualified Chapels or Congregations. Organised by *Episcopalians* qualified for toleration under *Toleration Act* of 1712.

Quarrier, William (1829-1903). Began work at age of seven in pin factory; started his own business when he was twenty, and devoted his attention to orphans; the homes he founded were established at Bridge of Weir 1876.

Quarter Days. Candlemas (2 February); Whitsunday (formerly moveable, now 15 May); Lammas (1 August); Martinmas (11 November).

Queen Mary's House (Jedburgh). See Jedburgh.

Queen Mary's House (*St Andrews*). House of Hugh Scrymgeour, a merchant, used by Queen *Mary* 1564; now owned by *St Leonard's School*.

Queen Mary's Mount. Site of Queen *Mary's* surrender at *Carberry*.

'Queen of Hearts'. See Winter Queen.

Queen Victoria School (*Dunblane*). Founded (as memorial to dead of South African War) for sons of Scottish servicemen, 1908; the architect was John A. Campbell.

Queen's Cairn. Hillock near Stichell (or Stitchell) House (Roxburghshire), where *Mary of Gueldres* is said to have received news of death of *James II*.

Queen's Highlanders. Raised by Colonel David Graeme of Gorthie as 105th Regiment 1762; disbanded after service in Ireland 1763.

Queen's Maries. See Maries.

Queen's Own Cameron Highlanders. Raised by *Alan Cameron of Erracht* 1793 as 79th Regiment (Cameron Volunteers); amalgamated with *Seaforth Highlanders* as Queen's Own Highlanders 1961.

Queen's Own Highlanders. See preceding entry.

Queen's Party. Supporters of Queen *Mary* against those of her son, *James VI*, 1567-73.

Queensberry, Earldom, Marquisate and Dukedom. Earldom created 1633 for William Douglas, *Viscount Drumlanrig*; marquisate created 1682 for 3rd Earl and dukedom created for him two years later. On death of 4th Duke in 1810 dukedom passed to *Duke of Buccleuch*; marquisate passed under separate destination, to Charles Douglas of Kelhead, descended from 1st Earl.

Queensberry House (*Canongate*, *Edinburgh*). Built 1681 for Charles Maitland, later *Earl of Lauderdale*; bought by *Duke of Queensberry* and later sold to government for use as barracks; later a hospital.

Queensberry, James Douglas, 2nd Duke of (1662-1711). Son of 1st Duke, whom he succeeded 1695; King's commissioner to *Parliament* 1700, 1702 and 1705; 'The *Union* Duke'.

Queensberry, William Douglas, 4th Duke of (1724-1810). Succeeded cousin, Charles, 1778; famed for his interest in horse-racing and notorious for his dissolute life and association with the Prince of Wales (later George IV); known as 'Old Q'.

Queensferry (West Lothian). *Burgh* under *Dunfermline Abbey* from early 14th century; *royal burgh* 1636. *Carmelite* friary founded by James Dundas of Dundas c. 1441; after 1583 it was leased by Sir Walter Dundas to town for use as church and school; since 1889 used by *Episcopal Church*.

Queensferry, North (Fife). Hospital in existence by 1153×1165; not mentioned after 1233.

Queensferry Paper. A manifesto of extreme *Covenanters*, found on *Cargill* when he was arrested at *Queensferry*; repudiated any responsibility of the church to the state or to the majority of the community.

Quincy, de, Family. Robert de Q. married heiress of *Ness*, son of William, an important landowner in Scotland, and acquired lands of *Leuchars*; their son, Saher de Q. (c. 1153-1219), completed church of Leuchars and became Earl of Winchester 1207; Saher's son, Roger (c. 1195-1273), married Helen, daughter of *Alan*, *Lord of Galloway*, and was *Constable of Scotland* in right of his wife; on his death the earldom of Winchester lapsed. The family was forfeited under *Robert I* and its East Lothian lands given to Alexander *Seton*.

Quitclaim of Canterbury. See Canterbury.

Quoad Sacra Parishes. Parishes established in 19th century to provide additional church accommodation; their functions were purely ecclesiastical and they did not have the civil functions, e.g. in education and poor relief, of the 'quoad omnia' or 'quoad civilia' parishes.

R

Raban, Edward (d. 1658). Started printing in *Edinburgh* 1620 but later settled in *Aberdeen*.

Radar. See Watson-Watt.

Radical Road. Footpath round Salisbury Crags, *Edinburgh*, made in 1820 to give work to unemployed at time of radical agitation.

'Radical War', April 1820. Strikes and riots arising from economic distress led to a skirmish with troops at *Bonnymuir*.

Rae, Sir David (1724-1804). *Lord of Session* (Eskgrove) 1782; *Justice-Clerk* 1799.

Rae, John (1813-93). Born *Stromness*; surgeon with Hudson's Bay Company; member of first expedition to search for Sir John Franklin 1847 and in command of second expedition 1851.

Rae, Sir William (1769-1842). Born *Edinburgh*; son of *Sir David R*; *Lord Advocate* 1819.

Raeburn, Sir Henry (1756-1823). Born Stockbridge, *Edinburgh*; apprenticed to a goldsmith, then to an engraver and etcher; pupil of *David Martin*; became a leading portrait painter in Edinburgh; went to London and to Rome for further training; practised in Edinburgh from 1787; knighted 1822; produced about 600 portraits, including all the notables of the day.

Ragged Schools. The first of these, founded by Dr *Thomas Guthrie*, was in Ramsay Lane, *Edinburgh*.

Ragman Rolls. Rolls of names of the many

Scots who did homage or gave allegiance to Edward I 1296.

Raid of Ruthven. See Ruthven Raid.

Railways. See Wagonways, and the names of individual companies. In 1923 the Scottish lines were absorbed by the London and North Eastern and the London Midland and Scottish. Nationalised 1947.

Rainy, Robert (1826-1906). Born *Glasgow*; *Free Church minister* at *Huntly* 1851 and at Free High Church, *Edinburgh*, 1854; professor of church history at *New College*, Edinburgh 1862 and principal 1874; did much to preserve unity of Free Church in a time of new theological thought and debate about the authority of the Bible; an architect of the union of the Free and *United Presbyterian* Churches 1900.

Ralph the Rover. Reputed to have been a pirate who cut away the warning bell placed on the *Bell Rock* by the Abbot of *Arbroath* and was himself afterwards wrecked on the rock.

Ramsay, Sir Alexander, of *Dalhousie* (d. 1342). Relieved *Dunbar Castle* 1338 and captured *Roxburgh Castle* from English 1342; taken prisoner by *Sir William Douglas of Liddesdale* and starved to death in *Hermitage Castle*.

Ramsay, Alexander (1822-1909). Editor of 'Banffshire Journal' from 1847; edited '*Aberdeen-Angus* Herd Book' and wrote 'History of the Agricultural Society of Scotland'.

Ramsay, Allan (1686-1758). Wig-maker in *Edinburgh*; contributed verses to meetings of the *Easy Club* from 1712; studied work of earlier Scottish poets and decided to revive vernacular; became bookseller and publisher; best known for 'The Gentle Shepherd' (1st part 1720) and 'The Tea Table Miscellany'; built a playhouse but it probably never operated; the site of his house commemorated in Ramsay Garden, Edinburgh.

Ramsay, Allan (1713-84). Son of preceding; studied painting in *Edinburgh*, London and Italy; worked from 1738 in Edinburgh and from 1756 in London, where he became portrait painter to King and Queen; he was so much in demand that he had to delegate a good deal of work to other hands; active in literary life in London and published essays and pamphlets.

Ramsay, Andrew (1574-1659). Professor at Saumur; *minister* at *Arbuthnot* 1606 and *Edinburgh* 1614; professor of divinity at Edinburgh 1614; became prominent, but moderate, *Covenanter*.

Ramsay, Sir Andrew (c. 1620-88). Son of preceding; *Lord of Session* (Abbotshall) 1671; Lord *Provost* of *Edinburgh* 1654-7 and 1662-3.

Ramsay, Edward Bannerman (1793-1872). Born *Aberdeen*; after serving in *Edinburgh* at St Paul's, York Place, and Old St Paul's, became incumbent of St John's 1830; Dean of Edinburgh 1841; wrote 'Reminiscences of Scottish Life and Character'.

Ramsay Family. Presumed to have come from Huntingdonshire under *David I* and mentioned in *Lothian* under *Malcolm IV*. In 1618 George Ramsay was created Lord R. of Dalhousie and in 1633 his son was created *Earl of Dalhousie*.

Ramsay, James Andrew Broun, Earl of Dalhousie. See Dalhousie.

Ramsay, Sir John (d. 1513). One of *James III*'s favourites; created *Lord Bothwell*; forfeited by *James IV* and went to England.

Ramsay, Sir John (c. 1580-1626). Favourite of *James VI*, whom he helped at the time of the *Gowrie Conspiracy* by killing Earl of *Gowrie*; accompanied James to England; created *Viscount of Haddington* and Earl of Holderness.

Ramsay, John William, Earl of Dalhousie. See Dalhousie.

Ramsay, Sir William (1852-1916). Born *Glasgow*; professor of chemistry at University College, Bristol, 1880-7, and at London 1887-1912; associated with discovery of argon and helium; Nobel Prize-winner.

Ramsay, Sir William Mitchell (1851-1916). Born *Glasgow*; professor of *humanity* at *Aberdeen* 1886-1911; from his archaeological work, especially in Asia Minor, he wrote 'The Church in the Roman Empire' and 'St Paul, the Traveller and the Roman Citizen'.

Ramsays, Bonars and Company, Bankers. Founded 1738 by James Mansfield, a draper; became Mansfield, Hunter and Co. 1760 and Ramsays, Bonars and Co. 1807; taken over by *Bank of Scotland* 1837.

Ramsay's Library. Circulating library founded by *Allan Ramsay* in Lawnmarket, *Edinburgh*.

Randolph, Charles (1809-78). Born *Stirling*; apprenticed to *Robert Napier*; joined by John Elder, 1852, in a business which developed into Fairfield Shipbuilding Company.

Randolph, John, 3rd Earl of Moray (d. 1346). Younger son of *Thomas R*; succeeded elder brother 1332; defeated *Edward Balliol* at *Annan* 1332; joint-*Guardian* of the realm 1334; captured by English 1335 and imprisoned until 1341; killed at *Neville's Cross*.

Randolph, Thomas (d. 1332). Nephew of *Robert I* (probably grandson of Robert I's mother by her first husband); captured at *Methven* and co-operated with English; captured by *Sir James Douglas* and returned to Scottish allegiance; *Earl of Moray* 1312, Lord of *Man* 1315; captured *Edinburgh Castle* 1314 and commanded left wing at *Bannockburn*; invaded England; *Guardian* 1329; died at *Musselburgh* when leading army against *Edward Balliol*; his son and heir died three weeks later.

Rathven Hospital (*Banff*). Founded for lepers 1224-6; became prebend of *Aberdeen Cathedral* 1445, but still with provision for *bedesmen*, and the hospital continued.

Ratisbon, Scots Abbey at. Abbey of St James founded by Irish '*Scots*' c. 1110 and had an Irish community until 1515, when a Scot became abbot; reconstituted after *Reformation* as monastery and college for Scottish exiles; dissolved 1862. Priory of St Peter given to *Marianus Scotus* 1075-6; Scottish priors from 1515; demolished 1552. See Schottenklöster.

Rattray (Aberdeenshire). *Burgh of barony* in 14th century; had charter as *royal burgh* 1564; O.S. Map shows 'site of burgh of Rattray' about a mile west of Rattray Head, and the site of a castle of 'Old Rattray'.

Rattray, Thomas (1684-1743). Laird of Craighall, Perthshire; *Bishop of Dunkeld* 1727; *Primus* 1739; his liturgical studies had much to do with the re-shaping of the *Scottish Liturgy*.

Ravelston House (*Edinburgh*). 17th century house, built by George Foulis, largely destroyed by fire; now the core of modern buildings of *Mary Erskine School.*

Ravenscraig Castle (Fife). Built by *James II* as a strong fortification against cannon; granted to William Sinclair, 1470, on his resignation of *Earldom of Orkney*.

Rayne (Aberdeenshire). *Burgh of barony* for *Bishop of Aberdeen* 1493.

Reader. In reformed church, authorised to read prayers and homilies. Cf. Exhorter.

Reay (*Caithness*). *Burgh of barony* for *Lord Reay* 1628.

Reay, Donald MacKay, 1st Lord (1591-1649). Son of MacKay of Farr; recruited many bodies of Scotsmen to serve under Christian IV of Denmark and Gustavus Adolphus of Sweden from 1626 onwards; knighted 1616, created Lord Reay 1628; joined *Charles I* 1639; brought troops and money for the King from Denmark 1643; defended Newcastle and was captured when it fell; released 1645; returned to Denmark 1649 and died in Bergen.

Reay, Donald James MacKay, 11th Lord (1839-1921). Born at the Hague, where his family had settled; Governor of Bombay 1885-90.

Reay, John MacKay, 2nd Lord (d. c. 1680). Son of *1st Lord;* active in royalist cause 1639-54.

Reay, Lordship. Created for Donald MacKay 1628.

Rector (of parish). Correctly rendered *parson* in Scotland.

Rector (of University). At one time the active head; since 1858 the students' representative and often (though not always) merely titular.

Red Castle (Lunan Bay, *Angus*). Castle on site under *William I*; 15th or 16th century castle held by Lords Innermeath and in 1544 burned by Grays of Dunninald; occupied by an *Episcopalian minister* after 1688.

Red Comyn. See Comyn, John.

Red Douglas. The junior branch of the Douglas family, who became *Earls of Angus.*

Red Fox. See Appin Murder.

Red Friars. See Trinitarians.

Red Hackle. Worn on left of the bonnet; granted to *Black Watch* 1795.

Red Hall. Building in *Berwick* occupied by Flemish merchants, who defended it to the last man against Edward I in 1296.

Red Parliament. *Parliament* at *Perth* in July 1606, when the nobles wore the red robes recently prescribed by the King for them.

Red Rover. Thomas de Longueville, after killing a nobleman in the presence of Philip IV of France, was exiled and took to piracy, being known as the Red Rover from the colour of his sails. *William Wallace*, on his way to France in 1301 or 1302, captured him and interceded for him with Philip, who pardoned and knighted him. De Longueville then attached himself to Wallace and subsequently joined *Robert I.* In reward for his services at the capture of *Perth* in 1313 he received a grant of lands and married the heiress of Charteris of *Kinfauns*, whose name he assumed. His two-handed sword was preserved at Kinfauns Castle.

Red Sox Race. Instituted at *Carnwath* by 3rd Lord Carnwath about the end of the 15th century; a pair of hose containing half an ell of English cloth was the prize for a race from the east end of the town to the cross.

Redcastle (Ross). Ancient but modernised house, one of many claimants to be the oldest inhabited house in Scotland and to have been built by *David, Earl of Huntingdon*, in 1179.

The place became a *burgh of barony* for Mackenzie of Redcastle 1680.
Reddendo. The opening word of the clause in a charter which specified the consideration (e.g. service, articles, money) for which the lands granted were held; hence the consideration itself.
Redford Barracks (*Edinburgh*). Cavalry and infantry barracks constructed 1907-12.
Redhouse (East Lothian). 16th century tower with slightly later additions, roofless but almost complete; passed from John Laing (whose initials appear on it) to his son-in-law Sir Andrew Hamilton, with whose family it remained until the '*Forty-Five*.
Redpath, Anne (1895-1965). Born *Galashiels*; studied at *Edinburgh* Art College; lived in France for 15 years; returned 1934.
Redswire (or **Redeswire, Reidswire), Raid of,** 7 July 1575. A dispute arose between English and Scottish *Wardens* of the Middle *Marches* over one Harry Robson, a noted freebooter; Scots under laird of Carmichael defeated English under Sir John Foster.
Reform Act, 1832. Franchise extended to £10 householders in towns, £10 owners and £50 leaseholders in shires; Scottish M.P.s increased from 45 to 53.
Reform Act, 1868. Franchise extended to all rate-paying householders and lodgers paying £10 rent for unfurnished rooms in towns and to £5 owners and £14 occupiers in shires; Scottish M.P.s increased to 60.
Reform Act, 1885. Household and lodger franchise extended to shires; Scottish M.P.s increased to 72.
Reform Act, 1918. See Representation of the People Act.
Reformation. Lutheran thought had reached Scotland by 1525, when there was a statute against it; Tyndale's English translation of New Testament found its way to Scotland by 1530; Henry VIII's proceedings, from 1532, stimulated a desire for similar moves in Scotland; reading of Bible in vernacular authorised 1543; 'conservative reform' embodied in statutes of *Provincial Councils* 1549, 1552 and 1559; '*First Bond*' of Protestant lords 1557; armed revolt against French and papal domination began May 1559; Latin mass and papal supremacy abolished and reformed *Confession of Faith* authorised by a *parliament* (of somewhat doubtful legality) August 1560.
Reformed Presbyterian Church. See Cameronians.
Regalia. See Honours.
Regality. Lands and accompanying rights of jurisdiction constituted a 'little kingdom' in which the landlord's courts tried all cases except treason and royal *justiciars* and *sheriffs* did not operate; abolished 1747.
Regality, Burgh of. Not a distinct type of *burgh*, but simply a non-royal burgh which happened to be within a *regality*.
Regality Club. Founded in *Glasgow* 1885 'to preserve a record of old Glasgow buildings and relics'.
Regent. University teacher.
Regents. See Moray, James Stewart, Earl of; Lennox, Matthew Stewart, Earl of; Mar, John Erskine, Earl of; and Morton, James Douglas, Earl of. See also Guardian.
Regiam Majestatem. Compilation of law, dating from c. 1200 and owing much to English jurist Glanvil; recognised as authoritative for Scottish practice from 1425 or earlier.
Regiment de Douglas. See Royal Scots.
Regiment d'Hebron. The remainder of the *Green Brigade* was amalgamated in 1632 with a number of other Scottish units in the French service to form a regiment under *Sir John Hepburn*. See also Royal Scots.
Reginald. Son of *Somerled*, *Lord of the Isles*; founded *Saddell Abbey* c. 1207.
Register House (*Edinburgh*). Traditional name for the repository where the national archives were kept; applied to premises in *Edinburgh Castle* c. 1540; after *Restoration* records were mainly in *Laigh Parliament Hall* until the present (Old) Register House (architect *Robert Adam*) was built at the east end of Princes Street (foundation stone 1774); New Register House built alongside, 1859-63, to house *Registrar General*'s Department; and the former St George's Church in *Charlotte Square* became the West Register House in 1971.
Register of Sasines. See Sasines.
Registrar General. Official in charge of Birth, Marriage and Death Registers.
Regulus (or **Rule), St.** According to legend, brought relics of St *Andrew* from Mediterranean and founded *St Andrews*; his name is attached to 11th century tower which formed part of the predecessor of the later cathedral.
Reid Concerts, Reid School of Music. See Reid, General John.
Reid, Sir George Houston (1845-1918). Born *Johnstone*; went to Australia at age of seven; barrister; premier of Australian Commonwealth 1904-5.
Reid, Hugo (1809-72). Born *Edinburgh*; son of

Peter Reid (1777-1838), an educational reformer; migrated to U.S.A. 1858; principal of Dalhousie College, Halifax, *Nova Scotia*; wrote textbooks on scientific subjects.

Reid, General John (1721-1807). Changed name from Robertson to Reid on inheriting estate of Straloch, Perthshire; student at *Edinburgh* 1743-4; in Loudoun's Regiment 1745; served in America; flute player; composed 'The Garb of Old Gaul' and other pieces; left his fortune to *Edinburgh University* to endow a chair of music, with a concert on his birthday (13 February) at which one of his own compositions was to be performed; the chair was founded 1839 and the first concert given 1841.

Reid, Sir John Watt (1823-1909). Born *Edinburgh*, son of naval surgeon; himself a naval surgeon; medical director-general of the navy.

Reid, Robert (d. 1558). *Vicar* of *Kirkcaldy*; ecclesiastical lawyer; *Commendator* of *Kinloss* 1526 and of *Beauly* 1530; *Bishop of Orkney* 1541; *Lord President* of *Court of Session* 1549; died at Dieppe when on mission connected with marriage of Queen *Mary* to the Dauphin; left legacy for a college in *Edinburgh* which was later applied to the university.

Reid, Robert (1776-1856). Architect who continued work of *Robert Adam*, with St George's Church, Edinburgh, and completion of *Register House*. Also designed *Signet Library*.

Reid, Thomas (1710-96). Born Strachan, Kincardineshire; Librarian of *Marischal College, Aberdeen* 1733; *minister* of New Machar 1737; professor of philosophy at Marischal College 1751; wrote 'Inquiry into Human Mind'; professor of moral philosophy at *Glasgow* 1764.

Reith, John Charles Walsham, Lord (1889-1971). Qualified as civil engineer; Director General of B.B.C. 1927-38; Minister of Information and of Transport 1940 and of Works and Planning 1940-2.

Reiver. Marauding Borderer.

Relief. Feudal *casualty* paid by vassal to *superior* on taking up his inheritance.

Relief Church. The 'Second Secession'; in 1761 *Thomas Gillespie*, *minister* of Carnock, and two others, established a *presbytery* 'for the relief of Christians oppressed in their Christian privileges' as a result of disputes over *patronage*.

Remonstrance, Remonstrants. In 1650 the extreme *Covenanters* denounced the *Resolutions* which undermined the policy of the *Act of Classes*, which they thought had not been severely enough applied; the 'Remonstrants' were virtually identical with *Protesters*.

Renfrew. *Royal burgh* under *David I*; *barony* and *burgh* granted by him to Walter, the High *Steward*; property remained with his descendants, who became the Stewart kings, and the title Baron Renfrew is still borne by Prince of Wales. A *motte-and-bailey* castle was built by *David I* or Walter the Steward, and it was the object of attack by *Somerled* when he met his death in 1164; a stone castle took its place, and is mentioned so late as the reign of *James IV*, but no traces remain. A *Cluniac* priory established here was soon moved to *Paisley*. The *Grammar School* is mentioned in 1396.

Renfrewshire Bank. Otherwise New *Greenock* Bank, founded 1785; failed 1842.

Rennie, George (1749-1828). Elder brother of *John Rennie*; as owner of estate of *Phantassie*, East Lothian, was a notable agriculturist.

Rennie, George (1791-1866). Eldest son of *John R*; partner with his brother, Sir John (1794-1874) as a civil engineer; with him completed London Bridge and Plymouth Breakwater.

Rennie, John (1761-1821). Born *Phantassie*, East Lothian; employed by *James Watt* 1784; began business as civil engineer 1791; designed Waterloo, London and Southwark Bridges and Plymouth Breakwater.

Renwick, James (1662-88). Born *Moniaive*; ordained in Holland 1683 and returned to minister to *Cameronians* as a field preacher; captured and executed.

Representation of the People Act, 1918. Increased Scottish M.P.s to 74; gave vote to men over 21 and women over 30; in 1928 the age for women was reduced to 21.

Resby, John (d. 1407). Follower of English preacher John Wyclif; burned at *Perth*; reckoned the first of the Protestant martyrs. See 'Heretics'.

Rescissory Act, 1661. Annulled all acts of *Parliament* since 1633.

Resolutioners. Moderate *Covenanters* who supported the Resolutions which rescinded the exclusive policy of the *Act of Classes*.

Resolutions. See Resolutioners.

Restalrig (*Edinburgh*). Belonged until 13th century to Lestalric family; passed by marriage to *Logans* early 14th century and remained with them until their forfeiture after the *Gowrie Conspiracy*; acquired by *Lord Balmerino* 1604 and held by his family until their forfeiture 1746, after which it passed to the *Earl of Moray* by purchase. *Burgh of barony* (Restalrig and Calton, or Easter and Wester Restalrig) created for Master of Balmerino 1673;

Calton or Wester Restalrig sold by Lord Balmerino to Edinburgh 1725. Part of 16th century Restalrig House survives in 'Lochend House' above the loch; a new Restalrig House, built 1815-7, was demolished c. 1960.

Restalrig Collegiate Church. Founded by *James III* 1487 and in 1497 styled a 'chapel royal'; partly demolished 1560, restored as parish church 1836; the hexagonal aisle of St *Triduana*, wrongly called a 'well', survives. The churchyard was used as burial place by *non-juring* Episcopalians in 18th century.

Restennet Priory (*Augustinian*) (*Angus*). Tower may include work of early 8th century done by an Anglian architect sent from Jarrow at request of *Nechtan*, King of the *Picts*; the church, dedicated to St Peter, was granted by *Malcolm IV* to *Jedburgh Abbey* 1153-60 and became a dependent priory of that house; used as parish church until 1591; erected into lordship for *Viscount Fenton*, later *Earl of Kellie*, 1606.

Restitution, Act of, 1606. Restored to bishops the *temporalities* of which they had been deprived by Act of *Annexation* of 1587.

Restoration. *Charles II* returned to England in May 1660 and the institutions of monarchical government were restored in both England and Scotland.

Retour. The findings of an inquest, made in obedience to a *brieve* from chancery, and most commonly relating to inheritance, were returned or 'retoured' to chancery and engrossed in a record volume from which an official extract was issued; the official extract is usually called a retour.

Revocation, Act of. By recognised law and custom, a king could, before reaching his 25th birthday, revoke all grants made during his minority, and such revocations were made by *James V* and *James VI*; *Mary* was compelled to abdicate before she reached the critical age; *Charles I* revoked all grants made since 1540, including the erection of church properties as *temporal lordships;* his main object was to recover the *teinds* for the use of the reformed church, but the sweeping scope of the measure occasioned such alarm that it had much to do with his downfall.

Revolution. In 1689 (not 1688 as in England) the Scottish *Convention* declared that *James VII* had forfeited the crown and offered it to William and Mary.

Rhind, Alexander Henry (1833-63). Born Lybster, *Caithness*; devoted antiquary who, owing to ill-health, had to spend much time abroad, and wrote 'Thebes, its Tombs and their Tenants'; bequeathed funds to Society of *Antiquaries* of Scotland for the institution of Rhind Lectures, the first series of which was delivered in 1876.

Rhind Lectures. See Rhind, Alexander Henry.

Rhydderich Hael. King of *Strathclyde*, with his seat at *Alclut* or *Dumbarton*; won battle of *Arderydd* 573.

Rhymer, Thomas. See Thomas.

Rhynd. See Rindalgros.

Rhynie (Aberdeenshire). *Burgh of barony* for *Duke of Gordon* 1684.

Riccio (or Rizzio), David (c. 1533-66). Born Turin; came to Scotland with Savoy ambassador and was employed by Queen *Mary* as a singer, then as her French secretary; his advancement roused jealousy and it was alleged that he had an improper relationship with the Queen; her husband, *Darnley*, leagued with other nobles to murder him at *Holyrood* 9 March 1566.

Richmond, Alexander Bailey (d. c. 1834). Weaver who was reputed to be a government spy and 'agent provocateur' in the unrest from 1812 onwards.

Richmond and Gordon, Charles Henry, 6th Duke of R. and 1st Duke of G. (1818-1903). A.D.C. to Duke of Wellington 1842; created Duke of Gordon 1876; *Secretary for Scotland* 1885.

Riddell Family. Associated with district round Lilliesleaf (Roxburghshire), beginning with Gervase c. 1120, who may have come from Gascony.

Riddell, Henry Scott (1798-1870). Born *Langholm*; *minister* of Teviothead; wrote 'Scotland Yet' and 'Oor ain folk'.

Riddell, John (1785-1862). Son of *Glasgow* merchant; *advocate*; outstanding expert on peerage law, on which he wrote several books.

Rider. Gold coin from *James II* to *James VI* varying in value from 23s. to £6. 13s. 4d.

Riding of Parliament. The members rode in state from *Holyrood* to the *Tolbooth* of *Edinburgh* or later the *Parliament House*, clad in dress appropriate to their estate, as defined in 1606; the '*Honours*' or *Regalia* were borne in the procession, and the King or his Commissioner was attended by the *Chancellor*, bearing the *great seal,* and the *Marischal* and *Constable*.

Riding School (*Edinburgh*). 'Royal Academy for Teaching Exercises' founded 1763 by a number of peers and others; had royal charter 1766; premises in Nicolson Street, on site of later *Surgeons' Hall* (see Surgeons, Royal College of); lasted until 1828.

Riding the Stang. A husband who beat his wife was set by the women of the community on a wooden beam, with his legs tied underneath it, carried round and then ducked in a pond.

Ridpath, George (d. 1726). *Whig* journalist; imprisoned 1681 for burning an effigy of the Pope in *Edinburgh*; went to London and wrote *Presbyterian* propaganda as 'Will Laick'.

Ridpath, George (c. 1717-72). Son of *minister* of *Ladykirk*; minister of Stitchell 1742; wrote 'History of the Borders', edited by his brother Philip (1721-88).

Rig. A strip of cultivated land. See also Runrig.

Right and Wrong Club. Founded in *Edinburgh* at a jovial dinner in 1814, according to *James Hogg*; the club was pledged to support any suggestion made by a member, however wrong or ridiculous; it was short-lived.

Rindalgros (or **Rhynd**) (Perthshire). Lands granted by *David I* to Reading Abbey with a view to establishment of a *Benedictine* house there; there was subsequently a cell dependent on the priory of *May*.

Rintoul, Robert Stephen (1787-1858). Born Tibbermuir; apprenticed to printer in *Edinburgh*; moved to *Dundee* 1809; edited 'Dundee Advertiser' 1811-25; moved to London and founded 'Spectator'.

Ripon, Treaty of. See Bishops' Wars.

Ritchie, David. See Black Dwarf.

Ritchie, John (1778-1870). Founder of '*Scotsman*' newspaper and eventually sole proprietor.

Ritchie, William (1781-1831). Younger brother of preceding; joined *Charles MacLaren* and his brother in founding '*Scotsman*'.

Rizzio. See Riccio.

Rob Roy. See MacGregor.

Robert (d. 1159). Prior of *Scone* under *Alexander II*; nominated to *Bishopric of St Andrews* 1124; consecrated 1127; began the building of the *Cathedral*.

Robert I (1274-1329). Grandson of *Robert Bruce* the *Competitor* and son of Robert, *Earl of Carrick* in right of his wife, Marjory; probably born at *Turnberry*; was on English side against *Balliol*, but joined *Wallace*'s rising and thereafter maintained resistance for a time; submitted to Edward 1302; renewed resistance 1306 after murdering *John Comyn*; inaugurated as King at *Scone* 25 March; defeated at *Methven* and *Dalry*; out of the country for a time; returned 1307; victorious at *Loudoun Hill* and in *Pass of Brander*; recovered various castles; defeated Edward II at *Bannockburn*; supported his brother *Edward* in Ireland, and invaded England; overcame papal opposition by 1323; made Treaty of *Corbeil* with France; gained English recognition of independence by Treaty of *Edinburgh-Northampton*; died at *Cardross* 7 June 1329; married (1) *Isabella*, daughter of *Earl of Mar*, by whom he had a daughter, Marjory, and (2) *Elizabeth*, daughter of the Earl of Ulster, who bore *David II*. See also Bruce's Heart.

Robert II (1316-90). Son of Walter, 6th High *Steward of Scotland*, and *Marjory*, daughter of *Robert I*; shared in military commands and in regency during *David II*'s absence in France and later captivity; aged 55 when he succeeded David 1371, his reign brought increasing infirmity and incapacity, with power passing to his eldest son, John, *Earl of Carrick*, and then his next son, *Robert*, afterwards *Duke of Albany*; married (1) *Elizabeth Mure*, whose family some thought of doubtful legitimacy, and (2) *Euphemia Ross*.

Robert III (c. 1337-1406). Eldest son of *Robert II*; baptized John; *Earl of Carrick* 1368; a kick from a horse left him permanently lame; assumed name of Robert on accession; lacked energy to rule effectively, and power lay with his younger brother, *Robert, Duke of Albany*, though *David, Duke of Rothesay*, the King's elder son, was appointed Lieutenant 1399; Rothesay's death in 1402 was attributed to Albany; the King arranged for his younger son, James (see James I), to be sent to France, but he was captured by the English and the King died in Rothesay (where he may have gone for security); married *Annabella Drummond*.

Robert Gordon's College, Aberdeen. Charitable foundation for education of boys; founded on bequest of 1729 by *Robert Gordon*; opened 1750; further endowed by Alexander Simpson of Collyhill 1816; became fee-paying school for day boys, with foundationers, 1881.

Roberton (Roxburgh-Selkirk shires). *Burgh of regality* for *Earl of Angus* 1631.

Roberton, Sir Hugh (1874-1952). Born *Glasgow*; founded Glasgow *Orpheus Choir* 1906; composed and arranged many songs and wrote 'Choir Training'; knighted 1931.

Roberton, James (c. 1590-1664). Professor of *humanity* at *Glasgow* 1618; Judge of *Admiralty Court* 1626; *Lord of Session* (Bedlay) 1661.

Robertson, Alexander, of Struan (c. 1670-1749). Active on *Jacobite* side at *Killiecrankie* and in the 'Fifteen; captured at *Sheriffmuir* but escaped to France and was pardoned 1731; 'out' again in 1745, at age of 75; wrote some verse.

Robertson, Andrew (1777-1845). Born *Aberdeen*; brother of *Archibald R*; miniature painter in Aberdeen and from 1801 in London.

Robertson, Archibald (1765-1835). Born *Monymusk*; brother of preceding and like him a miniaturist; went to London 1786 and then to America, where he painted Washington and other leading Americans.

Robertson, James Patrick Bannerman (1845-1909). *Solicitor General* 1885; *Lord Advocate* 1889; *Lord President* 1891; Lord of Appeal 1899; created Baron Robertson of *Forteviot*.

Robertson, Joseph (1810-66). Born *Aberdeen*; Curator of Historical Records, *Register House*, 1853; a founder of *Spalding Club*; edited 'Concilia Ecclesiae Scoticanae'.

Robertson, William (1721-93). Son of *minister* of *Borthwick*, who moved to Old *Greyfriars'*, *Edinburgh*, 1733; spent several years in study; minister of Gladsmuir 1743 and of Lady Yester's, Edinburgh, 1756; a leading '*Moderate*' in the *General Assembly*; principal of *Edinburgh University* 1762; wrote 'History of Scotland during the reigns of *Mary* and *James VI*' (1759), 'History of Charles V' (1769) and 'History of America' (1791); as principal he furthered the plans for a new building, now the Old College, of which the foundation stone was laid in 1789.

Robertson, William (1740-1803). Born *Fordyce*; secretary of *Earl of Findlater* and *Seafield* 1766; deputy *Keeper of the Records* 1773; published a volume of 'Parliamentary Records' which, however, was suppressed as inadequate.

Robinson Crusoe. See Selkirk, Alexander.

Rochead, John Thomas (1814-78). Born *Edinburgh*; apprenticed to *David Bryce*; architect in *Glasgow* 1841-70; designed many *Free Churches* and *Wallace Monument* at *Stirling*.

Rodel (or **Rowadill**) (*Harris*). Supposed *Augustinian* monastery, but in truth no more than an elaborate parish church.

Roebuck, John (1718-94). Born Sheffield; studied medicine at *Edinburgh* and Leyden; established sulphuric acid plant at Prestonpans 1749; partner in *Carron Company*.

Rogers, Charles (1825-90). Born Denino, Fife; clergyman who was chaplain to garrison at *Stirling* 1855-63; founded *Grampian Club* and edited many of its publications; secretary to Royal Historical Society.

Rognvald, Earl of Orkney (d. 1158). Nephew of St *Magnus*; baptised Kali, but took name Rognvald; founded *Kirkwall Cathedral* 1137; went on pilgrimage to Mediterranean; canonised 1192 (?).

Rollock, Hercules (d. c. 1619). Brother of *Robert R*; rector of *Edinburgh High School* 1584; wrote some verse.

Rollock, Peter (d. c. 1626). *Advocate*; *Bishop of Dunkeld* 1585; Ordinary *Lord of Session* 1598.

Rollock, Robert (c. 1555-99). Brother of *Hercules R*; first principal of *Edinburgh University*; wrote Sermons and Commentaries.

Rome, Scots College at. Founded 1600 by Pope Clement VIII, and endowed partly from revenues of a medieval Scottish Hospice in Rome. New buildings were opened in Via Cassia 1964.

Ronnel Bell. Celtic bell preserved in church of *Birnie*, *Moray*.

Rood. (1) = cross. (2) = area of 1440 square ells, about one third of an acre.

Rory More's Horn. Drinking horn preserved at *Dunvegan Castle*, holding 2 quarts; the heir of the *MacLeods* was expected to drain it at one draught.

Rose (or Ross), Alexander (?1647-1720). Born Kinnairnie, Aberdeenshire; *minister* of *Perth* 1672; professor of divinity at *Glasgow* 1683; principal of *St Mary's College*, *St Andrews*, 1686; *Bishop of Moray* 1687 and of *Edinburgh* 1688; represented Scottish bishops in London on arrival of *William of Orange*, and refused to give up allegiance to *James VII*; his action went a long way to bring about the disestablishment of *episcopal* government; said to have founded congregation in Carrubber's Close, Edinburgh.

Rose Noble. Coin worth 46s. 8d.

Rosebery, Archibald Primrose, 1st Earl of (1661-1723). Son of *Sir Archibald Primrose*; opposed *James VII*'s policy; a commissioner for the *Union*.

Rosebery, Archibald Philip Primrose, 5th Earl of (1847-1929). Succeeded grandfather 1868; married daughter of Baron Meyer de Rothschild; Foreign Secretary 1886, 1892-4; Prime Minister 1894-5; supported Scottish *Home Rule*; wrote many historical works.

Rosebery, Earldom. *Barony*, in *Temple* parish, Midlothian, formerly known as Nicolson, bought by Archibald Primrose of *Dalmeny* 1695; he became Viscount Rosebery 1700 and

Earl 1703.

Rosehearty (Aberdeenshire). *Burgh of barony* for Lord Forbes of *Pitsligo* 1681.

Rosemarkie and Fortrose. Rosemarkie had a charter as *royal burgh* from *Alexander II* or *Alexander III*; charter of *James II*, 1455, made *Fortrose* a royal burgh and united it with Rosemarkie.

Roslin (or **Rosslyn**) (Midlothian). *Barony* belonged to *St Clair* family from late 13th century if not earlier; earliest part of castle assigned to William St Clair (d. 1330); Henry St Clair or Sinclair, who became *Earl of Orkney* 1379, built the great keep c. 1390; there were 15th century additions and a residence was added in 1622, but much destruction was done by English in 1544 and 1650. Near the site the English under Sir John Segrave were defeated on 24 February 1303 by *John Comyn* and Simon *Fraser*. See also Rosslyn.

Roslin Collegiate Church (Rosslyn Chapel). Founded by William, *Earl of Caithness* and *Orkney*, 1446, and described as *collegiate* 1456, but no *provost* is mentioned until 1523-4, when it formally received collegiate status; dedicated to St Matthew; damaged by mob 1688, but preserved and now used by Scottish *Episcopal Church*.

Ross, Arthur (d. 1704). *Minister* at Kinernie; Bishop of *Argyll* 1675, of *Galloway* 1679; *Archbishop of Glasgow* 1679, of *St Andrews* 1684.

Ross, Bishopric of. There is some evidence of bishops at *Rosemarkie* in *Pict*ish times, and the first bishop to appear on record, c. 1130, bore the unmistakeably native name of Macbeth.

Ross, Earldom and Dukedom. There were *mormaers* of Ross, who were styled 'comites' or earls in 12th century; the earldom was for a time in the hands of the crown, but was bestowed c. 1226 on Ferquhard; it passed by marriage to Leslies 1372 and then to the *Lords of the Isles*; reverting to crown 1476, the title of Duke was granted to *James Stewart*, 2nd son of *James III*, Alexander, posthumous son of *James IV* (d. 1515) and Henry, Lord *Darnley*; held with dukedom of *Albany* by Prince James 1566-7 and by Prince Charles 1600-25.

Ross, Euphemia (d. c. 1387). Widow of *John Randolph,* 3rd *Earl of Moray*; married *Robert II* 1372; her sons—David, *Earl of Strathearn*, and *Walter, Earl of Atholl*—were thought by some to have a stronger claim to the succession than their half-brothers by Robert II's first marriage to *Elizabeth Mure*.

Ross, Euphemia, Countess of (c. 1343-95). Succeeded her father, Earl William, 1372; married Walter Leslie 1366 and after his death in 1382 married *Alexander Stewart*, 'Wolf of Badenoch'.

Ross, Family of. (1) A Norman family who arrived in Scotland by way of Yorkshire in 12th century and acquired lands in Ayrshire and Renfrewshire; Hawkhead, near *Paisley*, gave its name to their *barony*; (2) individuals named from the district of Ross in the north.

Ross Herald. Title first appeared 1476, after forfeiture of *Earldom of Ross* by *Lord of the Isles*.

Ross, Sir John (1777-1856). Born near *Stranraer*; served in navy in French wars; began exploring for North-West passage 1818 and traversed Baffin Bay; led expedition in search of Sir John Franklin 1850; published accounts of his voyages; K.C.B. 1834.

Ross, Lordship. Created 1490 for Sir John Ross of Halkhead; extinct with death of 14th Lord 1754; lands passed to his daughter's son, the 4th *Earl of Glasgow*, and in 1815 a new U.K. barony of Ross of Hawkhead was created for him.

Ross Priory (on east side of Loch Lomond). A modern name, invented in 19th century.

Ross, Thomas (d. 1930). Architect responsible for reconstruction of *Church of Holy Rude, Stirling*; see also MacGibbon.

Ross, William, 12th Lord Ross of Halkhead (c. 1656-1738). Fought against *Covenanters* in *Charles II*'s reign; supported *Revolution*; Commissioner to *General Assembly* 1704; Commissioner for *Union*.

Ross, William Stewart (1844-1906). Born Kirkbean; began journalism as student at *Glasgow*; wrote as 'Saladin'; went to London and in 1872 began publishing educational works; prominent in 'free thought' movement.

Rossend Castle (Fife). Contains remains of structure of 13th or 14th century, but most of it of 16th century date or later; it was there that *Châtelard* made one of his attempts on Queen *Mary*; acquired by Melvilles of Murdocairny from Durie family, later passed to Wemyss of Caskieberry; named Rossend when purchased by Murdoch Campbell from Skye; much neglected and damaged, but painted ceilings were preserved and despite attempts by the town council to have it demolished it has survived.

Rossie (Perthshire). Acquired by *Kinnaird* family through marriage to an heiress in late 14th century; in grounds of Rossie Priory is the *mercat cross* of the village of Rossie, destroyed when mansion was built 1807-17; name 'Priory' is fanciful, but it is possible that there had been an early establishment, for an 'abbacia de Rossin' is mentioned c. 1150-53.

Rosslyn, Earldom. Created 1801 for *Alexander Wedderburn*, who was succeeded by his nephew, Sir James St Clair Erskine. See also Roslin.

Ross-shire Buffs, Duke of Albany's. Sub-title of *Seaforth Highlanders* (78th), from the yellow or buff facings to their uniforms.

Rosyth Castle (Fife). Bears date 1561; on rock formerly connected to shore by causeway, but the whole area was reclaimed when the naval base was constructed in the early 20th century; belonged to Stewarts from 1435 until 18th century, when it passed to *Earl of Rosebery*, then to *Earl of Hopetoun*; damaged by Cromwellian troops 1650, but repaired and remains fairly complete.

Rothes (*Moray*). Belonged in 14th century to Polloks, from whom it passed by marriage to Leslies, who sold it c. 1700 to Grant of Elchies; thereafter it passed through several hands until it came to *Earls of Seafield*; castle completely ruined; *police burgh* 1884.

Rothes, Andrew Leslie, 5th Earl of (d. 1611). Son of *4th Earl*; joined insurgents 1559; supported *Mary*, Queen of Scots, after 1568.

Rothes, Earldom. Created 1457 for George, Lord Leslie.

Rothes, George Leslie, 4th Earl of (d. 1558). *Lord of Session* 1541; acquitted of participation in murder of *Cardinal Beaton* (in which his eldest son, *Norman Leslie*, took part); ambassador to Denmark 1550 and France 1558; died at Dieppe.

Rothes, John Leslie, 6th Earl of (c. 1600-41). Grandson of *5th Earl*; voted against *Five Articles of Perth* 1621; complained of *Charles I*'s manipulation of *Parliament* 1633; a leader of *Covenanters* 1638.

Rothes, John Leslie, 7th Earl and 1st Duke of (1630-81). Supported royalist wing of *Covenanters* 1650-1; captured at *Worcester* and remained in prison until 1658; President of *Privy Council* 1660; *Treasurer* and Commissioner to *Parliament* 1663; repressed Covenanters; *Chancellor* 1667; associated with opposition to *Lauderdale* 1673-4; created Duke 1680, but as he had no son the dukedom died with him, while the earldom continued through his daughter.

Rothesay (Bute). Origin of castle assigned to so early as 1098; certainly existed c. 1240; round towers may have been added to original oval curtain wall in later 13th century; possessed by Stewart family; *Robert III* died there; burned in *Argyll's Rebellion* 1685; renovated 1871-7. The town was termed '*royal burgh*' 1401. The church of St Mary was only a parish church except when it served as a cathedral for the *Isles* in 17th century.

Rothesay, David, Duke of (1378-1402). Son of *Robert III*, created Duke 28 April 1398; appointed Lieutenant 1399 because of father's incapacity, but evidently unfitted to exercise authority; betrothed first to sister of *Earl of Crawford*, then to daughter of *Earl of March*, but married daughter of *Archibald, 3rd Earl of Douglas*, which led March to transfer his allegiance to England; his irresponsibility was presumably the reason for his confinement in *Falkland* Castle on the advice of his uncle the *Duke of Albany* and of Douglas; his death there (26 March 1402) was attributed to Albany.

Rothesay, Dukedom. Created 1398 for *David*, elder son of *Robert III*; from 1469 it has been held by the eldest son of the sovereign from birth.

Rothesay Herald. First mentioned 1479; perhaps originally a *herald* of the Stewart family, before accession of *Robert II*.

Rothiemay, Kirkton of (Banffshire). *Burgh of barony* for Gordon of Rothiemay 1617.

Rottenrow (or Hilltown of Dundee). *Burgh of barony* for Maitland of Halton 1672.

Rouen, Treaty of, 26 August 1517. Concluded by *Duke of Albany, Governor* of Scotland, with France: Scotland and France were to give each other mutual support against England, and prospects were held out that *James V* might marry a daughter of Francis I; ratified by France 13 June 1522.

Rough Castle (Stirlingshire). One of the forts on the *Antonine Wall*, near Bonnybridge, covering about an acre.

Rough, John (d. 1557). *Dominican* friar at *Stirling*; chaplain to *Earl of Arran* 1543; preacher to garrison holding *St Andrews Castle* after murder of *Cardinal Beaton* 1546; entered service of Duke of Somerset 1547; burned as heretic in London.

'Rough Wooing'. Otherwise *Hertford's Invasions*; so called because the Scots had broken off the betrothal of Queen *Mary* to Prince Edward, afterwards Edward VI, and the English tried to bring about the marriage by force.

Round Table Club. Founded in *Edinburgh* 1868 by Dr Robert James Blair Cunynghame for encouraging discussion and good fellowship; died out 1895.

Rout of Moy. See Moy.

Row, John (c. 1526-80). Born near *Stirling*; ecclesiastical lawyer; Scottish agent at Rome in 1550s; returned to be a leading *minister* 1560; appointed to *Perth*.

Row, John (1568-1646). Son of preceding; *minister* of Carnock 1592; wrote 'Historie of the Kirk of Scotland'.

Row, John (c. 1598-1672). Son of preceding; master of *grammar school* of *Kirkcaldy* 1619; rector of grammar school, *Perth*, 1632; *minister* of *St Nicholas', Aberdeen*, 1641; compiled Hebrew grammar and dictionary.

Row, William (1563-1634). Son of *John R.* (c. 1526-80) and brother of *John R.* (1568-1646); *minister* of *Forgandenny*.

Rowadill. See Rodel.

Rowallan Castle (Ayrshire). Built c. 1562 by Mure family, to which *Elizabeth Mure* belonged.

Rowett Institute (*Aberdeen*). Founded 1920 for animal research.

Roxburgh. *Royal burgh* in existence c. 1120 and castle a favourite royal residence in 12th and 13th centuries; castle changed hands many times, including its capture by *Sir James Douglas* 1313, and remained with English from 1330s until 1460, when it was taken after *James II* had been killed while besieging it; *burgh* one of the '*Four Burghs*', but town and castle alike decayed and were abandoned, though the place later became a *burgh of barony*.

Roxburgh(e), Earldom and Dukedom. Earldom created 1616 for Robert *Ker* (c. 1570-1650), who had become Lord R. in 1600; dukedom created 1707 for 5th Earl.

Roxburgh Friary (*Franciscan* Conventual). Said to have been founded by *Alexander II* 1232-4; burned by English 1545 and partly restored for military purposes 1547.

Roxburgh, Hospitals. (1) Hospital endowed by *David I* may be identical with Maison Dieu mentioned 1545 and 1696. (2) St John's, possibly founded under *Alexander III*, referred to 1330. (3) St Mary Magdalene's, mentioned 1319. (4) St Peter's, appears to have been founded in reign of Alexander III and mentioned 1426.

Roxburgh, Old. Church, mentioned under *Malcolm IV*, had possibly been a minster of some importance. *Barony* granted to Robert *Ker*, later Lord R., 1574.

Roxburgh, Schools. Mentioned in foundation charter of Abbey of *Kelso*; rector mentioned 1241.

Roxburghe Club. See Roxburghe, John Ker, 3rd Duke of.

Roxburghe, John Ker, 5th Earl and 1st Duke of (c. 1680-1741). *Secretary of State* 1704; created Duke 1707.

Roxburghe, John Ker, 3rd Duke of (1740-1804). Noted book collector, after whom the Roxburghe Club, for the printing of rare books, was named.

Roy, John. See Stewart, John.

Roy, Major-General William (1726-90). Born near *Carluke*; possibly acquired knowledge of surveying from father, who was a factor; employed in *Ordnance* Office; Assistant Quartermaster to David Watson, engaged from 1747 in surveys for making military roads from base at *Fort Augustus*; survey extended to whole north of Scotland 1749 and to south 1752; Lieutenant Colonel 1763; Inspector General to Board of Ordnance 1765; besides his maps, produced 'Military Antiquities of the Romans in North Britain' (1793).

Royal and Ancient Golf Club (*St Andrews*). St Andrews had been called 'the metropolis of golfing' as early as 1691; Society of St Andrews Golfers was founded 1754 and became the Royal and Ancient 1834, under the patronage of the Duke of St Andrews (one of the titles of the later William IV). See Playfair, Sir Hugh Lyon.

Royal Bank of Scotland. Founded 1727, as offshoot of Company set up to manage the *Equivalent*.

Royal Blind Asylum (*Edinburgh*). Founded 1793, first in Shakespeare Square, whence it moved to Nicolson Street.

Royal Botanic Garden (*Edinburgh*). See Botanic Gardens, Physic Gardens.

Royal Burgess Golfing Society. Began on Bruntsfield Links, *Edinburgh* 1735.

Royal Burghs. See Burghs, Royal, and Convention.

Royal Caledonian Ball. Held annually in London in aid of Royal Caledonian Schools and Scottish Corporation of London.

Royal Caledonian Hunt. Established 1777.

Royal College of Physicians (*Edinburgh*). Established 1681. Its hall was in George Street 1775-1845 and then moved to building in Queen Street designed by *Thomas Hamilton*.

Royal College of Science and Technology. Glasgow and West of Scotland Technical College founded 1886, partly from *Anderson's University* and other institutions; became

Royal Technical College 1912 and R.C.S.T. 1956. See Strathclyde, University of.

Royal College of Surgeons (*Edinburgh*). See Surgeons.

Royal Company of Archers. See Archers.

Royal Exchange. Built in High Street, *Edinburgh*, 1753-61, for the accommodation of merchants, but soon taken over by the corporation as the City Chambers.

Royal Highland Emigrant Regiment (84th). Raised 1775 by Lt.-Col. Allan MacLean, late of 104th Regiment, among emigrants in Canada and men disbanded in Canada after peace had been made in 1783.

Royal Highland Fusiliers. Formed 1959 by merging of *Highland Light Infantry* and *Royal Scots Fusiliers.*

Royal Institution (*Edinburgh*). Built between 1823 and 1836 to designs by *W.H. Playfair*, to accommodate Royal Institution for the Encouragement of the Fine Arts, the *Board of Trustees,* the *Royal Society of Edinburgh,* the *School of Design,* and galleries; now the *Royal Scottish Academy*.

Royal Medical Society of Edinburgh. Student society founded 1737; obtained royal charter 1778.

Royal Observatory (*Edinburgh*). Established on Calton Hill 1776; new building 1818 to designs by *W.H. Playfair*; moved to Blackford Hill 1893.

Royal Philosophical Society of Glasgow. Founded 1802 for 'discussion of subjects bearing upon the trade and manufactures of the country and the improvement of the arts and sciences'; historical and philosophical section added 1902.

Royal Scots (or **Royal Regiment**). The 1st Regiment of Foot; descended from regiments in French service, known variously as *Regiment d'Hebron*, Regiment de *Douglas*, *Douglas Écossais*, the *Earl of Dumbarton*'s Regiment of Foot, the Royal Regiment of Foot, the Lothian Regiment, or '*Pontius Pilate's Bodyguard*'.

Royal Scots Fusiliers. Raised by *Earl of Mar* 1678 for service against *Covenanters*; known variously as the 'Earl of Mar's Greybreeks', Royal North British Fusiliers Regiment of Foot, 21st Regiment of Foot; amalgamated with *Highland Light Infantry* 1959.

Royal Scots Greys. Raised 1681; known variously as Royal Regiment of Scots Dragoons, Royal Regiment of North British Dragoons, The Greys, 'The Bubbly Jocks', 'The Bird Catchers'; their motto is 'Second to None' and they wear the grenadier bearskin headdress as a reward for capturing the standard of the Regiment du Roi at Ramillies (1706); mechanised 1941. Cf. Dalyell, Sir Thomas.

Royal Scottish Academy (*Edinburgh*). Founded 1826; held first exhibition 1827; amalgamated with artists of *Royal Institution* and received charter 1838 as the Royal Scottish Academy of Painting, Sculpture and Architecture. Housed in former Royal Institution. Cf. Glasgow School.

Royal Scottish Corporation. Founded 1611 by Scots in London for charitable purposes; received royal charter 1665.

Royal Scottish Museum (*Edinburgh*). Opened 1866; took over natural history collections formed by university. Departments: Art and Archaeology; Geology; Natural History; Technology. Also administers *Scottish United Services Museum*.

Royal Society of Edinburgh. Founded 1783; the 'literary class' disappeared after a time and the society became purely scientific, but literary side revived 1977.

Royston (Midlothian). In 1661 Patrick Nicoll, merchant, bought lands of Easter Granton, which in 1661 were erected into a *barony* called Royston. See Granton.

Ruddiman, Thomas (1674-1757). Born Boyndie, Banffshire; after graduating at *King's College, Aberdeen*, was schoolmaster at *Laurencekirk*; found employment in *Advocates' Library* and then, in 1706, with the printer and bookseller Robert Freebairn; associated with editions of *Gavin Douglas* and *William Drummond*; set up own printing and publishing business, which produced *Allan Ramsay's* works, 'Rudiments of the Latin Tongue', the works of *George Buchanan* and 'Epistolae Regum Scotorum'; Keeper of Advocates' Library 1730; published *James Anderson's* 'Diplomata'.

Ruglen, Earldom. Created 1697 for John, 4th son of 3rd *Duke of Hamilton*; 2nd Earl became 4th *Duke of Roxburghe*, but on his death in 1810 the earldom became extinct.

Rule, Gilbert (c. 1629-1701). Sub-principal of *King's College, Aberdeen*, 1651; studied and practised medicine; imprisoned on *Bass Rock* as a *Covenanter*; *minister* of *Greyfriars', Edinburgh*, 1688; principal of *Edinburgh University* 1690.

Rulemouth (or **Spittal-on-Rule**) (Roxburghshire) **Hospital.** Founded by 1426; burned 1545.

Rullion Green, Battle of, 28 November 1666. *Covenanters* defeated by *Sir Thomas Dalyell.*

Run (fl. c. 850). King of *Strathclyde*, married daughter of *Kenneth mac Alpin*.
Runciman, Alexander (1736-85). Son of *Edinburgh* builder; apprenticed to a firm which painted panels above fireplaces, in current fashion; studied in Italy with his brother *John*; appointed master in *Trustees' Academy*; executed paintings in St Patrick's Church, Cowgate, Edinburgh, and 'Ossian's Hall' at *Penicuik* House.
Runciman, John (1744-68). Brother of preceding; painted mainly scriptural scenes, like 'Road to Emmaus' and 'Belshazzar's Feast'.
Runrig. Down to 18th century it was a common practice for the *rigs* of individual tenants to be intermingled with each other, and even to be reallocated from time to time; the practice survived until very recently, on a miniature scale, in some *croft*ing townships.
Rutherford (Roxburghshire). Hospital mentioned 1276, dedicated to B.V.M. or St Mary Magdalene; given to *Jedburgh Abbey* 1395; mentioned 1444. As 'Rutherford' or 'Capehope' or 'Hunthill' a *burgh of barony* for Lord Rutherford 1666.
Rutherford, Samuel (c. 1600-61). Born Crailing, Roxburghshire; *regent* in *Edinburgh University* 1623-5; *minister* of *Anwoth* 1627; suspended 1636; returned to Anwoth 1638 as *Covenanter*; professor of divinity at *St Andrews* 1639; *commissioner* to *Westminster Assembly*; principal of *St Mary's College, St Andrews*, 1648; deprived at *Restoration*; his 'Letters', though not in accordance with modern taste, provided spiritual excitement at the time and later; his other works included defences of the *presbyterian system* and 'Lex Rex', which advocated the right to depose kings.
Rutherglen (Lanarkshire). *Royal burgh* from 1120s, but first extant charter dated 1324; castle (commemorated in 'Castle Wynd') was used by 12th and 13th century kings and in time was alienated to Hamiltons of Ellistoun, whose support of Queen *Mary* caused it to be burned by *Regent Moray*; *Covenanters* affixed a copy of a Declaration or manifesto to the cross in 1679; castle abandoned 18th century and no traces remain. A supposed 'hospital' derives from the name of land called 'Spittall' and 'Spittalquarter', which probably belonged to hospital of *Polmadie*.
Ruthven (Inverness-shire, near *Kingussie*). On site of castle which belonged to Comyn Lords of *Badenoch* and a later castle built by *6th Earl of Huntly*, the government built barracks 1718; they were blown up by *Jacobites* after *Culloden*. The place was a *burgh of barony* for *Marquis of Huntly* 1684.
Ruthven Castle (Perthshire). Otherwise Hunting tower; built by *Lord Ruthven* in 15th century; on forfeiture of *Gowrie* family it was bestowed on Murrays of *Tullibardine*, ancestors of *Dukes of Atholl*.
Ruthven, Family and Lordship. Family descended from Swan, who held lands of Ruthven in 12th century; lordship created 1488 for William Ruthven of that *ilk*.
Ruthven, Patrick, 3rd Lord (c. 1520-66). Eldest son and heir of 2nd Lord, by Jonet, an heiress of *Haliburton* of *Dirleton*; succeeded 1552; took part in *Riccio* murder and died in England.
Ruthven, Sir Patrick (c. 1573-1651). In Swedish army from 1612; knighted by Gustavus Adolphus; returned to Scotland 1638 to join *Charles I*; created Lord Ruthven of Ettrick 1639; held *Edinburgh Castle* for King February-July 1640; fought at Edgehill; created Earl of Forth 1642 and Earl of Brentford 1644; accompanied Prince Charles to France 1646 and returned with him to Scotland 1650.
Ruthven Raid. The ascendancy of *Esmé, Duke of Lennox* was ended when a group of ultra-Protestants, led by *1st Earl of Gowrie*, invited *James VI* to *Ruthven Castle*, where he was detained and remained in the hands of the 'Raiders' for ten months.
Ruthven, William, 4th Lord. See Gowrie, Earl of.
Ruthwell (Dumfriesshire). *Burgh of barony* for Murray of Cockpool 1508. Ruthwell Cross is thought to date from c. 680 and to reflect Anglian occupation of area; stood outside parish church until, after *Reformation*, it was broken to pieces; reassembled by Rev. *Henry Duncan* in *manse* garden; now housed inside church. The Parish Bank Friendly Society of Ruthwell, the first regularly organised savings bank in Scotland, was established by Duncan 1810.
Ryal (or **Rial**). French coin worth 60s; also Scottish silver penny under *Mary* and *James VI*.
Rymour Club. Founded in *Edinburgh* 1793 for collection of verse and music illustrating Scottish dialect, character and manners of earlier days.

S

Saddell Abbey (*Cistercian*) (Kintyre). Founded before 1207 by *Reginald*, Lord of the *Isles*; said in 1507 to be decayed, and was united to bishopric of *Argyll*.

Saddell Castle. About 1000 yards from the *Abbey*; incorporates tower of early 16th century and some later buildings; tower restored in late 19th century; evidently built by a *Bishop of Argyll*, but later held of him by MacDonalds, from whom it passed to *Earl of Argyll* in early 17th century.

Sage, John (1652-1711). Born Creich; *minister* in *Glasgow*; deprived as *Episcopalian* at *Revolution*; while acting as private chaplain and suffering much hardship, Sage wrote 'The Fundamental Charter of Presbytery' (1695) and 'The Reasonableness of Toleration to those of the Episcopal Persuasion' (1703); consecrated Bishop 1705; collaborated with *Thomas Ruddiman* in editions of works of earlier Scottish writers.

Saighdearan Dearga. 'Red soldiers' or government troops, with red tunics.

Sailors' Walk (*Kirkcaldy*). Group of 17th century merchants' houses at harbour, restored by *National Trust*.

St Andrew Society. Founded in *Edinburgh* 1906 to foster study of Scottish history, literature and the arts.

St Andrews, Archbishopric. Created 1472.

St Andrews, Bishopric. Names of bishops presumed to have had their seat at St Andrews are known from 906; the last of the native line died in 1093, and after a period of confusion a regular succession began with the election of *Robert* 1124.

St Andrews, Burgh. *David I* licensed bishop to create *burgh* 1144; represented in *General Council of Estates* 1357 and *Parliament* 1456 and taxed from 1483; *burgh of regality* for Archbishop 1614; *royal burgh* 1620.

St Andrews Castle. Built c. 1200 by Bishop Roger; held by English under Edward I and Edward III; largely rebuilt in 14th century and altered in late 16th; occasional royal residence; in 'Bottle Dungeon' Protestants including *George Wishart* were imprisoned; *Cardinal Beaton* murdered in castle 1546 and murderers were then besieged until captured by French fleet; largely ruinous since 17th century.

St Andrews Cathedral. There was a church at St Andrews from 8th century; early cathedral, of which part still stands, including tower of St *Regulus* (St. Rule's Tower), of Anglian type, built in 11th century; medieval cathedral founded c. 1160 and consecrated 1318; suffered from accidental fire c. 1378 and from insecure foundations; fell into decay after *Reformation*, until little remains.

St Andrews, Church of St Mary of the Rock (or **Kirkheuch**). The *Culdee* community of St Andrews was intended to be superseded by *Augustinian* canons in 12th century, but their properties retained their identity and were used as the endowment of a *collegiate church* and *chapel royal* which for a time kept the Culdee name; only foundations remain.

St Andrews, Culdees. See preceding entry and also St Andrews Priory.

St Andrews, Friaries. (1) *Dominican*. Said to have been founded by Bishop Wishart, but not mentioned until 1464 and seems thereafter to have developed in association with *University*; buildings damaged 1559 and largely cleared away later, leaving fragment in grounds of *Madras College*; property granted to *burgh* 1567. (2) Observant *Franciscan.* Founded 1463×1465 by Bishop *James Kennedy*; property granted to burgh 1567.

St Andrews, Hospitals. Hospital of *Culdees* mentioned 1144, hospital of St Andrew 1183 and 'new hospital' 1158-62. St Leonard's Hospital, first so named 1248, was attached to *St Leonard's College* 1512. Hospital of St Nicholas, mentioned before 1127, appears as lepers' hospital and poor's hospital; attached to *Dominican Friary* 1529; still in use 1583.

St Andrews, Links. See Royal and Ancient Golf Club of St Andrews.

St Andrews, Madras College. See Madras College.

St Andrews, Pedagogy. Established 1430 on site adjoining *St John's College.*

St Andrews Priory (*Augustinian*). Founded 1144 by Bishop *Robert* and acquired right of electing Bishop 1147—a right long contested by canons of the *collegiate church* of *St Mary of the Rock* as successors of *Culdees*; erected into *temporal lordship* for *Duke of Lennox* 1592.

St Andrews Psalter. Composed by *David Peebles*. Metrical psalms set to music.

St Andrews, Queen Mary's House. See Queen Mary's House.

St Andrews, Queen's College. See Dundee University.

St Andrews, St John's College. Existed in 1416 and endowed in 1419 by Robert of *Montrose,* *parson* of Cults; later identified with *Pedagogy*.

St Andrews, St Leonard's College. Founded 1512 by Archbishop *Alexander Stewart* and Prior *John Hepburn*.

St Andrews, St Leonard's School. Private school for girls, founded 1877. In grounds formerly occupied by *St Leonard's College*. See United College.

St Andrews, St Mary's College. Founded 1538 by Archbishop *James Beaton*, especially for teaching theology; foundation amplified by Archbishops *David Beaton* and *John Hamilton*; continued to be associated with divinity faculty.

St Andrews, St Salvator's College. Founded 1450 by *Bishop James Kennedy*; the church is almost intact. See Craig, James; United College.

St Andrews, Schools of. Mentioned in early 13th century, probably then a titular survival from Celtic times.

St Andrews, Tower of St Regulus (or **St Rule**). See St Andrews Cathedral.

St Andrews, United College. In 1747 the colleges of *St Salvator* and *St Leonard* were united and the buildings on the St Leonard's site abandoned.

St Andrews University. Teaching began 1410, formal establishment was granted by Bishop *Henry Wardlaw* 1412 and confirmation came in a papal bull 1413.

St Andrews, University College. See Dundee University.

St Andrew's House. Built in Regent Road, *Edinburgh*, on site of Calton Jail, in 1938, to house headquarters of Scottish government departments. New St Andrew's House on St James Square site 1974.

St Anthony, Baron Bailie of. Official appointed by South *Leith kirk session* to administer property of *St Anthony's monastery* and hospital; abolished 1833.

St Anthony's Chapel (*Holyrood* Park, *Edinburgh*). Supposed to have been founded c. 1435 by *Logan* of *Restalrig* in association with *St Anthony's monastery in Leith*, but nothing is certain about its history except that chaplains are mentioned in 16th century.

St Boswell's (Roxburghshire). Named after *Boisil*.

St Bothans. See Abbey St Bathans.

St Clair. See Sinclair.

St Evoca (Kirkcudbrightshire). *Cistercian* nunnery mentioned as decayed 1423.

St Germain's Hospital (East Lothian). Only Scottish house of the order of the Star of Bethlehem; founded c. 1170; described as ruinous 1496 and its property transferred to *King's College, Aberdeen*.

St John of Jerusalem, or Hospitallers, Order of. House at *Torphichen* founded in reign of *David I*; on suppression of order of *Knights Templars*, their properties were transferred to *Knights Hospitallers*, 1312. A Scottish branch of the order was revived in 1947.

St John's Cross (*Canongate*, *Edinburgh*). Cross which stood outside the house of the Order of St John; probably identical with 'loplestane' [i.e., hospital stone]; not identical with Canongate *Mercat Cross*.

St Johnstoun. *Perth*, of which the patron saint was St John Baptist.

St Johnstoun's Tippet. Rope used in gallows at *Perth*.

St Kessog's Bell. Until early 19th century rested on hill-top on island of *Inchtavannoch* in Loch Lomond.

St Kilda. There was no such saint, and the name of the island-group is a misunderstanding of 'Skildar', which appears on an early map; Hirta is the name of the principal island; the population was evacuated 1930 and the islands acquired by *Bute* family and bequeathed to *National Trust* by 5th Marquis 1957.

St Luke's School or Academy. See School of St Luke.

St Magnus Hospital (*Caithness*). Possibly existed 1290, and certainly identified 1440; mentioned as late as 1644.

St Margaret's Chapel (*Edinburgh Castle*). Possibly built by *Edgar*, son of *Margaret*, c. 1100, perhaps as part of a square stone keep.

St Martin, Alexander de. *Sheriff* of Haddington c. 1150; gave property to *Haddington Nunnery*.

St Mary's College. See St Andrews.

St Mary's Isle (or **Traill**) (Kirkcudbrightshire). Founded before c. 1190, possibly by *Fergus, Lord of Galloway*; described 1512 as cell of *Holyrood* though virtually independent, but threatened with ruin.

St Michael's Struan. Cake prepared at *Michaelmas* from all the cereals grown on a farm, carried to church to be blessed and then eaten in a feast.

St Monans (Fife). Church founded by *David II* and transferred to *Dominicans* by *James III* 1471; attached to *St Andrews Friary* 1519. *Burgh of barony* for Sandilands of St Monans 1596.

St Ninians (Stirlingshire). Proposal to make church *collegiate* 1528 did not take effect; tower survives of church blown up in 1746.

St Ninian's Cave (Glasserton, near *Whithorn*). Crosses incised on walls and on loose stones suggest early Christian occupation.

St Ninian's Chapel (near *Whithorn*). 13th century structure on site of earlier chapel.

St Ninian's Isle (*Shetland*). A small church, dating from perhaps 11th century, has been excavated, but there was an earlier building below it; a 'treasure' of silver objects was found 1958 and, despite much opposition and even litigation, was appropriated by *National Museum of Antiquities*.

St Obert's Play. Festival in *Perth* in honour of the patron saint of the bakers.

St Orland's Stone (*Glamis*). Stone with cross on one side and four horsemen on the other, said to commemorate alleged murder of *Malcolm II*.

St Roche. St Roch or Rocco (c. 1295-1327) was a native of Montpellier who cured many people in Italy of the plague. Chapels dedicated to him existed at *Edinburgh, Stirling, Dundee* and *Paisley* and it is assumed that *St Rollox* in *Glasgow* represents the same dedication. A bone of the saint was brought by a French friar to *James IV*.1502. The Edinburgh chapel (sometimes called St Roque's) was on the *Burghmuir*.

St Rollox (*Glasgow*). See preceding entry. A chapel dated from 1506, but disappeared at *Reformation*. Chemical works founded by *Charles Tennant* 1800; absorbed by United Alkali Company 1890.

St Serf's Priory. See Lochleven.

Sair Sanct for the Croun. Name given to David I by *James I* as a reproach for his excessive generosity to the church.

Saki. See Munro, Hector Hugh.

Salisbury, Treaty of, 6 November 1289. Erik, King of Norway, agreed with Edward I of England that the *Maid of Norway* should be brought to Scotland 'free of all contract of marriage'; but Edward had already asked for a dispensation with a view to her marriage to his son Edward.

Salt Manufacture. Making of salt by evaporation of sea-water was established in Firth of Forth area by 12th century if not before, and reached its peak in the 17th.

Salt Tax. Imposed 1712 in violation of Treaty of *Union*; detrimental to fish-curing.

Saltcoats (Ayrshire). *Burgh of barony* for *Earl of Eglinton* 1529.

Saltire. Diagonal cross of St *Andrew*, the Scottish national flag.

Saltire Society. Founded 1936 to encourage preservation of Scottish culture; has headquarters in *Gladstone's Land*.

Saltoun or **Salton** (East Lothian). Passed from de *Morvilles*, who held it in 12th century, to Abernethy family before 1300; the Abernethy proprietor was created Lord Saltoun 1445, a title which subsequently passed to *Frasers* (1670); 9th Lord Saltoun sold property in 1643 to Sir Andrew *Fletcher*, *Lord of Session*, with whose descendants it remained.

Salvesens. Firm founded by John Theodore S., a Norwegian who entered a *Glasgow* merchant's office in 1842; engaged in great variety of enterprises, notably whaling in Antarctic, where *Leith* Harbour, S. Georgia, was established 1909.

Sandeman, Archibald. See Perth, Sandeman Library.

Sandeman, Robert (1718-71). Son of *Perth* merchant; married daughter of *John Glas*; went to America and died in Connecticut.

Sandemanians. Another name for *Glassites*, from *Robert Sandeman*.

Sandford, Daniel (1766-1830). Born near Dublin; Oxford graduate 1791; *minister* of St John's Episcopal Chapel, *Edinburgh* (then in West Register Street), 1792; *Bishop of Edinburgh* 1806—the first Englishman to be appointed to a Scottish bishopric since early times; did much to facilitate the acceptance by *Qualified Chapels* of the jurisdiction of bishops.

Sandilands, James (d. 1579). *Preceptor* of *Torphichen*; property of Order of *St John* erected as *temporal lordship* for him 1564.

Sandy, George (d. 1853). As an apprentice *W.S.* he kept a meticulous diary about his visits to places of interest; became secretary of *Bank of Scotland*.

Sang Schules. See Song Schools.

Sanquhar (Dumfriesshire). *Burgh* mentioned 1325; created *burgh of barony* for Crichton of Sanquhar 1484; created *royal burgh* 1598. Castle was seat of *Crichtons* from 15th century until 1639, when it was acquired by *1st Duke of Queensberry*; original building enlarged in 16th and 17th centuries.

Sanquhar, Common Riding. At different dates in August; the cornet or standard-bearer led a procession round the *marches* and the *burgh* piper paraded from the Thorn Tree to the Gallows Knowe. Cf. Common Riding.

Sanquhar Declaration, 1680. *Richard Cam-*

eron and his associates renounced allegiance to the King and declared war on him and his agents.

Sanquhar Protestation, 1685. Protest by *Cameronians* against proclamation of *James VII* as King.

Sark, Battle of, 23 October 1448. Scots under Hugh Douglas, *Earl of Ormond*, defeated English under Percy at Clochmaben Stone.

Sasine (of old **Seisin**). Transaction whereby property was transferred by handing over of symbols—earth and stone, hasp and staple and so forth. A *notary* recorded the action in an Instrument of Sasine, which constituted the title to the property.

Sasines, Register of. A Register under the direction of the *Secretary* was instituted 1599 and discontinued 1609; the existing Register, under the *Clerk Register*, began in 1617. The *burghs*, however, had their own registers from various dates until the 20th century. All sasines must be recorded and the registers constitute an unparalleled record of the transmission of heritable property.

'Satire of the Three Estates'. By *Sir David Lindsay*; first produced 1535; fuller version 1540. See Three Estates.

Sauchie Tower (Clackmannanshire). Built in late 15th century by Schaws of Sauchie, who had acquired the property by marriage from the Annands; now a ruin.

Sauchieburn, Battle of, 11 June 1488. *James III* was defeated by nobles with his heir at their head, and murdered after battle.

Savings Banks. See Ruthwell.

'Scalachronicon'. Written by Sir Thomas Gray, who was taken prisoner at battle of *Nesbit* 1355 and imprisoned in *Edinburgh Castle*; covers period 1274-1364.

Scalloway Castle (*Shetland*). Fine tower-house erected by Patrick Stewart, *Earl of Orkney*, c. 1600; still almost complete, though roofless.

Scapa Flow. Anchorage used by Grand Fleet in World War I and World War II; German fleet scuttled after surrender, 1919; after 'Royal Oak' was torpedoed by German submarine in 1939 the eastern approaches to the Flow, hitherto obstructed by blockships, were sealed by '*Churchill Barriers*'.

Sceptre. Part of *Regalia*, presented to *James IV* by Pope Alexander VI 1494.

Schaw, William (1550-1602). *Master of works* to *James VI*, whom he accompanied to Denmark 1589-90; executed work at *Dunfermline*, where he is commemorated in the abbey.

Schevez, William (d. 1496). Physician to *James III* and noted as astronomer and book-collector; *Archbishop of St Andrews* 1476.

Schism, Papal. See Papal Schism.

School of Design. Founded in *Edinburgh* 1760 and much used in 19th century by pupils in art; its gallery contained many casts of sculptures.

School of St Luke. Formed in *Edinburgh* 1729 for encouragement of the arts, but lasted for only two years. Cf. Winter's Academy.

Schottenklöster. Monasteries of Irish foundation in Germany. See Constance, Erfurt, Kelheim, Ratisbon, Wurzburg.

Sciennes (*Edinburgh*). *Dominican* nunnery, dedicated to St Catharine of Siena, founded 1517 by Sir John Crawford and others; largely destroyed at *Reformation* and property passed to town.

Sciennes Hill House. In Braid Place, off Causewayside, *Edinburgh*, entered through passage at No. 7; built c. 1740; place of meeting of *Robert Burns* and *Walter Scott*.

Scone Abbey (*Augustinian*) (Perthshire). Founded as priory by *Alexander I* c. 1120; abbey 1164; pillaged by English 1298 and by reformers 1559; erected into *temporal lordship* for *Earl of Gowrie* 1581 and after his family's forfeiture for David Murray, *Lord Scone*, 1606; no visible remains of abbey buildings. The *Stone of Scone* was kept in the abbey until Edward I carried it off in 1296, but the inauguration ceremony took place on the *Moot Hill* (see Scone, Moot Hill of). Some later kings were crowned in the abbey, and *Charles II* was crowned in the new parish church nearby on 1 January 1651.

Scone Ball Game. Football game played on Shrove Tuesday, said to have originated when an Italian challenged the parishes around *Perth* to the game and Scone won the ensuing match; the opposing sides were bachelors and married men; fell out of use in 19th century.

Scone Hospital. Mentioned 1206×1227.

Scone, Lordship. Created 1606 for David Murray of Gospertie, *Comptroller* 1599-1608, later *Viscount Stormont*.

Scone, Moot Hill of. Low mound in grounds of present *Scone Palace*, near site of *Abbey*; created as the scene of royal inaugurations, it was said to consist of soil brought from various parts of the realm and it has been suggested that it was a substitute for a natural rock fortress like *Dunadd* where earlier inaugurations had been conducted. A parish church was built on it c. 1620 and on its site is now the mausoleum of the *Earls of Mansfield*.

Scone Palace. Sometimes mistakenly believed to be a former royal residence, it is nothing more than a residence of the *Earls of Mansfield*, built 1803-8 to supersede an earlier home of the family.
Scotch Education Department. So styled 1872-1918.
Scotia. Name applied to Ireland until about the end of the 10th century, but 'Scoti' (or *Scots*) who colonised *Argyll* from Antrim had brought the name to Scotland, to which it was applied from 11th century and for some time meant specifically Scotland north of the Forth.
'Scotichronicon'. See Bower, Walter, and Goodall, Walter.
Scotlandwell Friary (*Trinitarian*) (Kinross-shire). Founded as hospital of St Mary before 1251, when it was granted by Bishop de *Bernham* to Trinitarians; secularised for son of last '*minister*' or head, 1592.
Scots. Irish immigrants who settled in *Dalriada*, the modern *Argyll*, under *Fergus*, son of Erc, c. 500; united with *Picts* in kingdom of *Alba*.
Scots Ancestry Research Society. Founded 1945, largely by *Thomas Johnston* and the *Earl of Rosebery*, as a non-profit-making company to continue the work of pedigree-hunting which had long been carried on by private searchers.
Scots Brigade. Scottish mercenaries in the employment of the United Provinces of the Netherlands; originated in 1570s; ultimately comprised up to 6 regiments; ended 1784, when Dutch government required soldiers in its pay to renounce foreign allegiance; name given to 94th British Regiment 1793.
Scots Colleges. Seminaries for Roman Catholic ordinands on the continent. See Douai, Madrid, Paris, Rome and Valladolid.
Scots Confession. See Confession of Faith.
Scots Greys. See Royal Scots Greys.
Scots Guards. Wrongly believed to have originated in 1642 when *Charles I* commissioned *1st Marquis of Argyll* to raise a royal regiment; actually formed 1662; known successively as 'Scots Regiment of Guards', '3rd Foot Guards' and 'Scots Fusilier Guards' and nicknamed 'The Jocks'.
'Scots Intelligencer'. Newspaper published in *Edinburgh* 1643.
Scots Language. A branch of English, introduced to the south-east by Anglian settlers in the 6th century and spreading rapidly through most of Scotland from the 12th century.
'Scots Magazine'. First published 1739; ceased 1826; resumed 1888-93 and 1927-76.
Scots National League. Founded 1921; absorbed *Highland Land League*; later merged in *Scottish National Party*.
'Scots Spy' (or **'Critical Observer'**). First published March 1776 by *Peter Williamson* as weekly paper.
'Scotsman'. Newspaper founded 1817. See Findlay, John Ritchie; MacLaren, Charles; and Thomson, Roy.
Scotstarvet Tower (Fife). Dated 1627 but had existed 1579; home of *Sir John Scott*; still complete.
Scott, Alexander (?1530-84). Author of 'Ane New Yeir Gift to the Quene Mary quhen scho come first hame' and other poems.
Scott, Archibald (1837-1909). Born Cadder; *minister* in *Glasgow*, *Linlithgow* and *Edinburgh* (St George's, from 1890); author of 'Endowed Territorial Work' and 'Buddhism and Christianity'.
Scott, Lord Charles Thomas Montagu-Douglas- (1839-1911). Son of *5th Duke of Buccleuch*; served in navy; Commander-in-Chief Australian Station 1889-92 and Plymouth 1900-3.
Scott, David (1806-49). Born *Edinburgh*; studied at *Trustees' Academy;* painted imaginative scenes from history and literature, e.g. 'The Traitors' Gate', 'Puck fleeing before the Dawn' and 'Ariel and Caliban'.
Scott, Sir George Gilbert (1811-78). Worked mainly in England, but designed St Mary's *Episcopal* Cathedral, *Edinburgh* and *Glasgow University* buildings, Gilmorehill.
Scott, Henry (1676-1703), **Earl of Deloraine.** See Deloraine.
Scott, James, Duke of Monmouth and Buccleuch. See Monmouth, Anne Scott, Duchess of.
Scott, Sir John, of Scotstarvet (1585-1670). Director of chancery 1611 in succession to father and grandfather; knighted 1617; *Lord of Session* (Scotstarvet) 1632; involved in *Charles I's* negotiations with nobles over church property; became *Covenanter*; edited 'Delitiae Poetarum Scotorum', an anthology of Latin verse by Scots (1637); assisted with *Blaeu's* Atlas; wrote, among other works, 'The Staggering State of Scots Statesmen' (published 1754), with illuminating comments on contemporary politicians and administrators.
Scott, John (1830-1903). Born *Greenock*; son of Charles S., head of family firm of *Clyde* shipbuilders; succeeded as head of firm and developed many improvements in marine

engines.

Scott, Mary or **Marion** (c. 1550-c. 1587). The 'Flower of Yarrow'; daughter of John S. of Dryhope; married *Walter Scott of Harden*.

Scott, Michael (c. 1160-c. 1235). Very little is known of his life, and he may not even have been born in Scotland; said to have studied at Oxford, Paris and Padua; in Toledo 1217; translated works of Aristotle; in Bologna and Rome and reputedly associated with Emperor Frederick II; lives in legend as a wizard.

Scott, Michael (1789-1835). Born *Glasgow*; in business in Jamaica; contributed to '*Blackwood's Magazine*' and wrote 'Tom Cringle's Log' and 'The Cruise of the Midge'.

Scott, Thomas (c. 1480-1539). Son of *William S., Lord Balwearie*; *Lord of Session* (Petgormo); *Justice Clerk* 1535.

Scott, Sir Walter (c. 1490-1552). Fought at *Flodden, Ancrum* and *Pinkie*; supported Governor Albany (see Albany, John Stewart) 1515 and in 1526 tried to rescue *James V* from *Angus*; killed in feud with *Kers* of *Cessford*.

Scott, Walter (1565-1611). Rescued *Kinmont Willie* from Carlisle 1596; served under Prince of Orange against Spaniards in Netherlands; created 1st Lord S. of *Buccleuch* 1606.

Scott, Walter, of *Harden* (d. 1629). 'Auld Wat'; associated with *Francis, Earl of Bothwell*, in some of his escapades and with *Walter Scott of Buccleuch* in rescue of *Kinmont Willie*.

Scott, Walter, of Satchells (c. 1614-c. 1694). Served in Holland with 1st Earl of *Buccleuch* 1629; wrote metrical history of Scott family.

Scott, Walter (1644-93). Grandson of Sir *William S. of Harden* (d. 1655); married Mary, Countess of *Buccleuch*, 1659; created Earl of Tarras for life 1660.

Scott, Sir Walter (1771-1832). Born *Edinburgh*, son of *W.S*; spent boyhood in Borders and at Royal *High School*, Edinburgh; *advocate* 1792; *sheriff* of *Selkirk* 1799; married Charlotte Charpentier 1797; after some translations from German, published 'Minstrelsy of the Scottish Border' (1802) and then his own narrative poems, beginning with 'The Lay of the Last Minstrel' (1805); the novels began with 'Waverley' (1814); other prose works included 'Life of Napoleon'; created baronet 1820; faced financial disaster 1826, but undertook to pay off a debt of nearly £100,000, in doing which he ruined his health.

Scott, Walter Francis, Duke of Buccleuch. See Buccleuch.

Scott, William (d. 1532). Fought at *Flodden*; named *Lord of Session* (Balwearie) 1532, but had long been active as judge.

Scott, William, of *Harden* (d. 1655). Son of *Walter S. of Harden*; captured on a raid by *Sir Gideon Murray* of Elibank, he was offered his life if he would marry Murray's daughter, '*Muckle Mou'd Meg*', which he did (1611).

Scottish Archer Guard. Force in service of kings of France, said to date back to time of Crusades; did exist in 15th century. See also Garde Écossaise.

Scottish Burgh Records Society. Founded 1868 and published records until its dissolution in 1908.

Scottish Clergy Society. Founded in *Dundee* 1888 to promote 'the national element in the life of the Scottish Church' and to print material relating especially to the *Episcopal Church* at and after the *Revolution*.

Scottish College of Textiles. Established *Galashiels* 1909.

Scottish Convention. Established by one section of Nationalists 1942.

Scottish Council (Development and Industry). Formed 1946 by merging Scottish Development Council and Scottish Council on Industry; financed by voluntary contributions to promote industrial development.

Scottish Ecclesiological Society. Founded 1903 by union of *Aberdeen* and *Glasgow Societies*, for study of Christian worship and allied arts; published Transactions until its dissolution 1971.

Scottish Education Department. See Scotch Education Department.

Scottish Fisheries Museum. Opened at *Anstruther* 1969.

Scottish Football Association. Founded 1873. Scotland play at Hampden Park, *Glasgow*.

'Scottish Historical Review'. Published 1904-28 and from 1947.

Scottish History Society. Founded 1886.

Scottish Home Rule Association. Existed 1886-1914 and 1917-29. See Home Rule Bills; Johnston, Thomas.

Scottish Horse. Founded on suggestion of Caledonian Society in South Africa, under *Marquis of Tullibardine* (later 8th *Duke of Atholl*), in 1899; recruited in Natal, Britain and Australia; disbanded 1902 but re-formed in Britain 1903; served in World Wars and finally became unit of Transport Corps. Cf. Yeomanry Regiments.

Scottish Land Court. Established 1911 in succession to *Crofters Commission*; chairman has status of *Lord of Session*.

Scottish Literary Club. Name adopted by

Thomas G. Stevenson, an antiquarian bookseller and publisher in *Edinburgh*, with a view to publication of rare books.

Scottish Liturgy. See Scottish Prayer Book.

Scottish National Convention. Summoned by Home Rulers to City Hall, *Glasgow*, 1924.

Scottish National Dictionary. Completed 1976 in 10 volumes.

Scottish National Gallery of Modern Art. See National Galleries.

Scottish National Party. A National Party of Scotland existed 1928-34; S.N.P. founded 1934.

Scottish National Portrait Gallery. See National Galleries.

Scottish Patriotic Society. Founded 1846 to assist crofters and fishermen and subsidise emigration.

Scottish Prayer Book. Published 1637, reprinted 1712. The Communion Office or Liturgy was frequently reprinted in 18th century as 'Wee Bookies' and revised until it attained a stable form in 1764. A 'Book of Common Prayer (Scotland)' was issued 1912 and a new Scottish Prayer Book in 1929.

Scottish Record Society. Founded 1898 for printing indexes and abstracts of Scottish records.

Scottish Regiments in British Army. Highland—*Black Watch, Gordon Highlanders, Argyll and Sutherland Highlanders, Queen's Own Cameron Highlanders, Highland Light Infantry*; Lowland—*Royal Scots, King's Own Scottish Borderers, Cameronians, Royal Scots Fusiliers*; Cavalry—*Royal Scots Greys;* Guards—*Scots Guards, Coldstream Guards*.

'Scottish Review'. Vehicle of Nationalist opinion 1914-20.

Scottish Rifles. See Cameronian Regiment.

Scottish Rugby Union. Founded 1873. Scotland play at Murrayfield, *Edinburgh*.

Scottish Text Society. Founded in *Edinburgh* 1882 for printing and editing texts in early and middle *Scots*.

Scottish Tourist Board. Established by *Thomas Johnston*.

Scottish Trades Union Congress. Constituted 1897.

Scottish United Services Museum. Established 1930 in *Edinburgh Castle* as Scottish Naval and Military Museum. Administered by *Royal Scottish Museum*.

Scougal, Henry (1650-78). Son of *Patrick S*; professor of divinity in *King's College, Aberdeen*, 1673-8; wrote 'The Life of God in the Soul of Man'.

Scougal, John (c. 1645-1730). Had studio in Advocates' Close, *Edinburgh*; died at Prestonpans; his self-portrait is in *National Gallery*; painted among others *Sir Archibald Primrose* and *Sir John Clerk* and his wife.

Scougal, Patrick (c. 1605-85). *Minister* of Dairsie 1636, *Leuchars* 1644 and *Saltoun* 1658; *Bishop of Aberdeen* 1664-82.

Scouler, John (1804-71). Born *Glasgow*; surgeon and naturalist with Hudson's Bay Company 1824-5; professor of geology at *Anderson's Institute* 1829.

Scrabster (*Caithness*). Castle built by *Bishop of Caithness* in 12th century; only vestiges survive. *Burgh of barony* for Bishop, 1527.

Scrymgeour Family. Alexander Skyrmeschur, mentioned 1293, was grandson of Carun and had charter from *William Wallace* conferring offices of Constable of *Dundee* and *Standard Bearer*, 1298.

Scrymgeour, Henry (1505-72). Son of *Provost* of *Dundee*; studied at *St Andrews* and in France; secretary to Bishop of Bourges; became Protestant and was appointed professor of philosophy and civil law at Geneva.

Scrymgeour, Sir James, of *Dudhope* (c. 1550-1612). Constable of *Dundee* and hereditary *Standard-Bearer*; banished for complicity in *Ruthven Raid*; *Provost* of Dundee 1588.

Scrymgeour, James and John, Viscounts of Dudhope and Earl of Dundee. See Dudhope, Dundee.

Sea (or **Maritime**) **Laws**. *Sir James Balfour* of Pittendreich compiled 'Sea Laws' 1580; Alexander King wrote 'Tractatus Legum et Consuetudinem Navalium' about same time; *William Welwood* published 'The Sea Laws of Scotland' 1590.

Seabury, Samuel (1729-96). As medical student in *Edinburgh* became acquainted with Scottish *Episcopal Church*; in 1784, on refusal of English bishops to consecrate an American bishop, Seabury was consecrated by Scottish bishops in *Aberdeen*.

Seafield, Earldom. Created 1701 for James Ogilvy, 4th *Earl of Findlater* (1664-1730), *Chancellor* 1702-4, 1705-8 and a Commissioner for *Union*. On death of 4th Earl in 1811 he was succeeded by his cousin, Sir Lewis Alexander Grant (1767-1840), who assumed additional surname of Ogilvy.

Seaforth, Earldom. Created 1623 for Colin Mackenzie, 2nd Lord Mackenzie of Kintail; 5th Earl, William (d. 1740), was a *Jacobite* 1715 and 1719 and the estates *forfeited* 1716; he was pardoned 1726 but although the estates were later restored the earldom was not.

Seaforth, George Mackenzie, 2nd Earl of (d. 1651). Played a vacillating part in events of 1640s, but finally joined *Charles II* in Holland and died at Schiedam.

Seaforth Highlanders. In 1881 the 72nd (Duke of Albany's Own Highlanders) amalgamated with 78th (Seaforth Highlanders) which had been raised by de jure 7th Earl of Seaforth (1744-81).

Seaforth, Kenneth Mackenzie, 4th Earl of (d. 1701). Followed *James VII* to France and was created by him Marquis of Seaforth.

Secessions. The first or *Original Secession* dates from 1733; for Second, see Relief Church.

Secretary of State. The office of Secretary existed in the Scottish kingdom from at latest the reign of *David II;* after the *Union* a Secretary continued intermittently until 1747; in 1885 a Secretary for Scotland was again appointed and the office became that of Secretary of State in 1926.

Security, Act of, 1704. This act, passed by the estates in 1703 but not approved by Queen Anne until 1704, provided that in certain circumstances Scotland would on Anne's death choose a different successor from that of England. See Alien Act.

Security, Act of, 1707. Provided for continuance of *Church of Scotland* under its *presbyterian* government after the *Union.*

Sederunt, Acts of. Ordinances made by the *Court of Session*, originally as empowered by a statute of 1540, for the ordering of the business of the Court; later statutes have given express power to pass such acts.

Segden Hospital (Berwickshire). Founded 13th century, dedicated to St Mary, at Follydean, 2 miles north of *Berwick*; seems to have been moved to Berwick by 1367 and annexed to chapel of St Mary Magdalene there in 1437.

Seingie Fair. Held at *St Andrews* in the fortnight beginning a week after Easter; originally associated with meetings of the synod or 'seinyie'.

Select Society of Edinburgh. Founded by *Allan Ramsay*, younger, 1754, with a view to raising standard of design by offering prizes.

Selkirk. *Royal burgh* from end of 13th century, but said to have been erected as *burgh of barony* for *Earl of Angus* 1602. There was a royal castle in 12th and 13th centuries, probably on Peel Hill; in decay by 1300, it was repaired by English 1302, but retaken by Scots, who demolished it. There is very slight evidence of the existence of a *Dominican* friary.

Selkirk Abbey (*Tironensian*). Founded by Earl David (later *David I*) 1113; moved to *Kelso* 1128.

Selkirk, Alexander (1676-1721). Born *Largo*; when sailing master of the 'Cinque Ports', quarrelled with officers and was marooned on island of Juan Fernandez for four years; accounts of his adventures were printed and inspired Daniel Defoe to write 'Robinson Crusoe'; later a lieutenant in Royal Navy.

Selkirk Arrow. Silver trophy now shot for by Royal Company of *Archers*; has existed since early 17th century.

Selkirk Common Riding. On Thursday evening the ceremony of 'bussing' the colours takes place; on Friday the standard-bearer leads a procession, part of which rides the *marches* and part takes up a position to view the other's return; then in the Market Square takes place the 'casting of the colours' to the tune of 'Up wi' the Soutars o' Selkirk'. The tradition is said to date from the fate of the Selkirk detachment at *Flodden*, when only one man out of eighty returned, with a captured banner.

Selkirk, Earldom. Created 1646 for William, 3rd son of 1st *Marquis of Douglas*; he became *Duke of Hamilton* by marriage and in 1688 resigned the earldom in favour of his 3rd son; in 1885 the title fell to the Duke of Hamilton, and in 1940 it devolved under special destination to the 2nd son of the 13th Duke, who became 10th Earl.

Selkirk, Thomas Douglas, 5th Earl of (1771-1820). From 1803 onwards organised several migrations of Highlanders to various parts of Canada, most ambitiously (and least successfully) in the Red River area between 1812 and 1815.

Sellar, Patrick (1780-1881). Son of Thomas S. of Westfield (*Moray*); had legal education in *Edinburgh*; factor on *Sutherland* estates who arranged reorganisation which involved substitution of large sheep-farms for small *crofts*; accused of brutality in the consequent *Clearances*, he was tried and unanimously acquitted.

Sellar, William Young (1825-90). Son of preceding; taught at *Glasgow* and *St Andrews* universities and became professor of *humanity* at *Edinburgh*.

Selvach (or **Selbach**) (d. 729). Son of Ferchair Fota or Fada (d. 697); killed his brother 719 and became king of *Dalriada*; defeated in sea battle and became monk 723.

Sempill, Sir James, of Beltrees (1566-1625).

Educated with *James VI*; ambassador to France 1601; collaborated with King in preparing *'Basilikon Doron'*.

Sempill, Robert, 3rd Lord (d. 1572). Supported *Mary of Guise* against *Lords of the Congregation*, and later supported Queen *Mary* after her marriage to *Darnley*, but joined *Confederate Lords* 1567.

Sempill, Robert (c. 1530-95). Spent some years in Paris, but escaped back to Scotland at massacre of St Bartholomew's Eve 1572; supported reformers and wrote ballads.

Sempill, Robert (c. 1595-1665). Son of *Sir James S*; wrote 'Life and Death of *Habbie Simpson*'.

Sempill, William (1546-1633). Soldier of fortune; emissary of Spain to Scottish Roman Catholics 1588; arrested but escaped; in 1613 endowed college in *Madrid* to train Scots as missionaries. See Scots Colleges.

Semple (or **Lochwinnoch) Collegiate Church** (Renfrewshire). Founded by John, Lord Sempill, 1504.

Senators of the College of Justice. Title given to judges of *Court of Session* in terms of papal bull of 1535.

Septimius Severus (d. 211). Roman Emperor 193; came to Britain to press campaigns against *Caledonians* 208-211; evidently penetrated far up east coast, but did not attempt to add to the empire territory north of Hadrian's Wall.

Serf, St. According to tradition educated *Kentigern* at *Culross*; associated with island in *Loch Leven*.

Serfdom. Last reference to serfs in Scotland was in 1364. The servile status of colliers and salters, which went on until late 18th century, seems to have originated in 17th and was not connected with medieval serfdom.

Service, James (1823-99). Born Ayrshire; emigrated to Melbourne and founded commercial firm of John Service and Co. 1883; premier of Victoria 1883-5.

Service, John (1833-84). Born Campsie; *minister*; edited *'Dumbarton* Herald'; minister in Hobart, Tasmania, 1866-70; returned to charges in Scotland.

Service, Robert William (1874-1958). Born Lancashire, of Scottish father; emigrated to Canada 1894 to serve in bank in Victoria, British Columbia; published 'Songs of a Sourdough' 1907 and other ballads, verses and novels; in Canadian Army Medical Corps in World War I.

Session, Court of. Sessions' of parliamentary committees for civil justice were held under *James I* and *James II*, but conciliar sessions took their place and by *James IV's* reign something like a permanent judicature had taken shape. It received endowment as the College of *Justice* in 1532, when fifteen judges were nominated. See Lords of Session.

Seton (East Lothian). The 'villa' of Seton was granted to Sir Alexander Seton as a 'free *burgh*' in 1321, but it does not seem to have operated as such. A residence was erected by George, 4th *Lord Seton*, on site of castle destroyed by English in 1544; it was much enlarged and adorned by the early 17th century and was frequently visited by royalty; damaged during the '*Fifteen* (after which Lord Seton was *forfeited*), it was replaced by mansion built by *Robert Adam* 1790. The *collegiate church*, founded 1492 on earlier petition by George, Lord Seton, was looted and burned by English 1544; restored, it was defaced by government forces 1715.

Seton, Alexander (c. 1621-91). Son of 3rd *Earl of Winton*; excommunicated for refusing to take *Covenant* 1644; attended Prince Charles (later *Charles II*) in France; created *Viscount Kingston* at king's coronation at *Scone* 1651.

Seton, Sir Alexander (c. 1639-1719). *Advocate* 1661; baronet 1684; *Lord of Session* (Pitmedden) 1677; removed from office by *James VII*.

Seton, Alexander, Earl of Dunfermline. See Dunfermline.

Seton, Charles, Earl of Dunfermline. See Dunfermline.

Seton, Sir Christopher (c. 1278-1306). Married Christina, sister of *Robert I*; captured and executed by English.

Seton Family. Appear c. 1150; assumed to have been of Norman origin, but whether they took their name from or gave their name to Seton in East Lothian seems uncertain. Sir Alexander S., by deserting the English for *Robert I* on the eve of *Bannockburn*, earned lands in and around *Tranent*. Cf. Quincy, de.

Seton, George, 5th Lord (c. 1530-85). *Provost* of *Edinburgh* 1557 and 1559; strongly supported Queen *Mary*; captured at *Langside*.

Seton, George, 5th Earl of Winton. See Winton.

Seton, Lordship. Created for George Seton 1448.

Seton, Mary. Daughter of *George, 5th Lord S*; one of *Queen's Maries*; never married, but remained with *Mary* until her execution and then retired to French nunnery.

Sett. (1) The constitution of a *burgh* under the

unreformed system before 1833. (2) The pattern of a tartan.

Seven Earls. According to legend, the kingdom of *Alba* was divided into seven provinces—*Angus, Atholl, Strathearn, Fife, Mar, Moray* and *Caithness* (or *Argyll*)—each with a sub-king, who was thought to have been the forerunner of the *mormaer*. But there is no foundation for the real existence of such a sevenfold structure. Nor is it evident whether there was any foundation for the 'Protest of the Seven Earls' who in 1290 claimed to have a voice in the selection of a king.

Seven Men of Moidart. See Moidart.

Seven Sisters of Borthwick. Guns cast for *James IV* by the master gunner, James Borthwick, and lost at *Flodden*.

Sgian Dubh. Small dagger carried by Highlanders, formerly concealed about the person, now displayed in the stocking.

Shairp, John Campbell (1819-85). Born Houston, West Lothian; taught at Rugby, *Glasgow* and *St Andrews*; professor of Latin at St Andrews 1861-72; principal of *United College*, St Andrews 1868; wrote 'Kilmahoe and Other Poems' and 'Studies in Poetry and Philosophy'.

Shale Mining. Started 1860. See Young, James.

Sharp, James (1618-79). Born *Banff*; went to England on *Covenanters*' triumph in 1638; *minister* of *Crail* 1649; joined moderate *Resolutioners* and represented them in discussions with Cromwell; *Archbishop of St Andrews* 1661; his murder attempted 1668; murdered at Magus Muir 3 May 1679.

Sharp, John (c. 1572-c. 1648). *Minister* of Kilmany, Fife, 1601; clerk of illegal *General Assembly* at *Aberdeen* 1605; banished; professor at Dauphiné, France, 1608-30; professor of divinity, *Edinburgh*, 1630.

Sharp, William (1855-1905). Born *Paisley*; law apprentice in *Glasgow*; in Australia 1876-8; clerk in London, but never settled down; as 'Fiona MacLeod' wrote poems, biographies and novels.

Shaw, Christian. Of the Bargarran family; started *Paisley* thread industry c. 1720.

Shaw Family. There are two distinct surnames, a Lowland one of territorial origin (John de Schau appears 1284) and a Highland one derived from Sythach and other spellings. Shaws claimed to be hereditary *cupbearers* to the King.

Shaw, Farquhar (d. 1405). Led one of the forces at the *Clan fight at Perth* 1396.

Shaw, Lachlan (1692-1777). *Minister* of *Elgin* 1734-74; wrote 'History of the Province of *Moray*'.

Shaw, William (1749-1831). Born Arran; *minister* of Ardclach 1779; travelled in Scotland and Ireland; compiled *Gaelic*-English Dictionary 1780; criticised *James Macpherson's* 'Ossian'; rector of Chelvey 1795.

Shawfield Riots, 1725. See Malt Tax.

Sheriff. Office first recorded in 1120s; originally the sheriff was the general executive officer of the crown in the localities, with administrative and financial duties, but his judicial functions included the hearing of appeals from courts of *barony*. In later middle ages the office was generally hereditary, and the duties were often carried out by deputies. The heritable sheriffships were abolished 1747 (see Heritable Jurisdictions) and the country subsequently organised into principal sheriffships, with sheriffs substitute in every county town and several other places.

Sheriff Courts. Have jurisdiction in almost all civil actions except those affecting status (e.g., divorce) and in criminal cases except treason, murder and rape.

Sheriffmuir, Battle of, 13 November 1715. *Jacobites* under *Earl of Mar* encountered government forces under *Duke of Argyll*; tactically indecisive, the battle was a strategic defeat for the Jacobites, who retreated.

Shetland. See Orkney and Shetland.

Shetland Bank. Founded by Hay and Ogilvie 1821; failed 1842.

Shiel, Tibbie. Eponymous hostess of 'Tibbieshiels Inn', by St Mary's Loch; said to have married Westmorland mole-catcher named Richardson. The hostess when the inn was a haunt of literary figures was indeed a Mrs Richardson (1781-1878).

Shields, Alexander (c. 1660-1700). Born *Earlston*; *Covenanter* arrested in London 1685 and imprisoned on *Bass Rock*; appointed chaplain to *Cameronians* 1691; went to *Darien* settlement 1699; died of fever in Jamaica; wrote 'Hind let Loose' and 'Life and Death of *James Renwick*'.

Shieling. Hill pasture to which cattle were taken in summer months to give them fresh fodder and remove them from proximity to crops on cultivated ground.

Shinty. Formerly played, from at latest 17th century, throughout most of Scotland, but now almost confined to Highlands; organised by Camanachd Association.

Ship Bank, Glasgow. Founded 1749; merged

1837 with *Glasgow Banking Co.* to form Glasgow and Ship Bank, and with Glasgow *Union Bank* 1838.

Shirts, Battle of, 3 July 1544. *Frasers* defeated by Clanranald in parish of Kilmonivaig; *Lord Lovat* and 300 *Frasers* killed.

Shorter Catechism. Drawn up by *Westminster Assembly* and adopted by *Church of Scotland*; used as vehicle of instruction in schools until 20th century.

Shorthorn Cattle. Originated in County Durham in late 18th century; Shorthorn Society founded 1822.

Shotts (Bertramshotts) **Hospital** (Lanarkshire). Dedicated to St Catharine and founded before 1476 by James Hamilton.

Sibbald, Sir Robert (1641-1722). Born *Edinburgh*; graduated M.D. at Leyden; settled in Scotland and studied botany, founding a *Physic Garden* 1667; founder member of *Royal College of Physicians* of Edinburgh 1681; first professor of medicine in Edinburgh 1685; King's physician and geographer in Scotland 1682; produced 'Scotia Illustrata' (1684) and planned a series of county surveys or histories, only a few of which appeared; also wrote 'The Liberty and Independency of the Kingdom and Church of Scotland' (1703) and other papers; became a Roman Catholic under *James VII* and reverted to Protestantism later.

Signet. Earliest example of this royal seal dates from 1359; it became the seal associated with the 'executorials' or '*Diligence*' by which the *decreets* of the *Court of Session* were put into effect.

Signet Library. Founded 1722 by *Writers to the Signet*, all of whom contributed to funds on entry; became a more general library, as opposed to a narrowly professional one, 1778; housed in building (designed by *Robert Reid*) adjacent to *Parliament House* from 1815.

Signet, Writers to. See Writers.

Sigurd, Earl of Orkney (d. 1014). Supposed to be converted to Christianity by King Olaf Trygvasson c. 995; married a daughter of *Malcolm II* and was father of *Thorfinn*; killed at battle of Clontarf in Ireland.

Silver. Has been mined in the *Leadhills* since the 12th century if not earlier.

Silver Arrow. See Selkirk.

Silver Gun of the Seven Trades. Presented by *James VI* to *craftsmen* of *Dumfries* 1617, to be shot for on Kingholm Merse; in the form of a cannon 10 inches long.

Simpson, Habbie. 16th century piper, commemorated in a poem by *Robert Sempill*; in 1822 a wooden statue was erected to his memory at *Kilbarchan*, where he was buried; it has since been replaced by a bronze replica.

Simpson, Sir James Young (1811-70). Born *Bathgate*; professor of midwifery at *Edinburgh* 1839; introduced use of chloroform 1847; baronet 1866; wrote several works on obstetrics and anaesthesia.

Simpson Memorial Hospital, Edinburgh. Erected in memory of *Sir James Young Simpson*; planned 1870 and amalgamated with Maternity Hospital dating from 1843.

Simson, Andrew (d. 1590). Master of *Perth Grammar School* 1550 and of *Dunbar* Grammar School 1564; *minister* of *Dalkeith* 1582; wrote Latin grammar, 'Rudimenta Grammatica'. Cf. Donat's Grammar.

Simson, Andrew (1638-1712). *Minister* of Kirkinner, then of *Douglas*; wrote 'A Large Description of *Galloway*'.

Simson (or **Simpson**), **Sir George** (1792-1860). Native of Lochbroom; entered Hudson's Bay Company service 1826; Governor of Company.

Simson, John (c. 1668-1740). Son of minister of *Renfrew*; *minister* of Troqueer 1705; professor of divinity at *Glasgow* 1708; suspended 1729 because of his unorthodox opinions.

Sinclair, Catharine (1800-64). Daughter of *Sir John S*; wrote 'Holiday House', 'Scotland and the Scots' etc.

Sinclair (or **St Clair**) **Family.** From St Clair in Normandy; in south-east Scotland under *David I*; acquired *Roslin*, *Orkney* and *Caithness*, and *Ravenscraig*.

Sinclair, George (d. 1696). Professor of philosophy at *Glasgow* 1654-66, professor of mathematics 1691-6; associated with invention of diving-bell and laying of water-pipes in *Edinburgh*; wrote on hydrostatics, mathematics, natural philosophy and astronomy; author of 'Satan's Invisible World Discovered'.

Sinclair, George, 4th and 5th Earls of Caithness. See Caithness.

Sinclair, Henry (1508-65). Brother of *Oliver S*; *Lord of Session* 1537; *Lord President* 1558; *Commendator* of *Kilwinning* 1541; dean of *Glasgow* 1550; *Bishop of Ross* 1561; died in Paris.

Sinclair, Henry, Earls of Orkney. See Orkney.

Sinclair, James, Earl of Caithness. See Caithness.

Sinclair, John (d. 1566). Brother of *Henry S*; *Bishop of Ross* 1540; officiated at marriage of Queen *Mary* to *Darnley*.

Sinclair, John, 7th Lord Sinclair (1610-76).

Covenanter; joined *Charles II* 1650; captured at *Worcester* and imprisoned until 1660.

Sinclair, Sir John, of Ulbster (1754-1835). Succeeded to extensive estates 1770; M.P. 1780-1811; toured northern Europe; president of Board of Agriculture 1798, 1806-13; baronet 1786; did much to improve agriculture and published 'Code of Agriculture' (1819); instrumental in preparation of first 'Statistical Account of Scotland' (1791-8). Cf. Statistical Accounts.

Sinclair, Oliver, of Pitcairns (d. 1560). Favourite of *James V*; in command at *Solway Moss*.

Sinclair, Sir William, of *Roslin* (d. 1330). Son of Sir Henry S; accompanied *Sir James Douglas* on his expedition with *Robert I's* heart; killed in Spain.

Sinclair, William (d. 1337). Elected *Bishop of Dunkeld* 1309, consecrated 1312; active on behalf of *Robert I*, who is said to have called him 'my Bishop'; also known as 'the fighting Bishop'; in 1317 rallied Scots against English attack on *Dunfermline*; crowned *Edward Balliol*.

Sinclair, William (c. 1584-c. 1647). Eldest son of George Sinclair of Mey, chancellor of *Caithness*; as *Edinburgh High School* boy shot Bailie *MacMorran* 1595; later Sir William S. of Cadboll.

Sinclair, William, Earl of Orkney. See Orkney.

Singer Works. Opened at *Clydebank* 1884.

Skara Brae (*Orkney*). Stone Age village on Bay of Skaill, buried by sand and rediscovered in recent times.

Skelbo (Sutherland). *Barony* held by *Lords of Duffus* and *forfeited* when last Lord Duffus took part in '*Fifteen*; acquired by *Sutherland* family and in 1835 incorporated into earldom.

Skelmorlie Castle (near *Largs*, Ayrshire). A *Montgomery* castle, of which the oldest part dates from 1502; restored 1852. The 'Skelmorlie Aisle', in a churchyard in *Largs*, contains a very decorative monument to Sir Robert Montgomery (d. 1651).

Skelton, John (1831-97). *Advocate* 1854; Secretary of *Board of Supervision* and Vice-President of Local Government Board; wrote for periodicals and was author of a book, '*Maitland of Lethington*'.

Skene Castle (Aberdeenshire). North wing has been assigned to 13th century. The *barony* was created 1317 for the Skene family who had a legendary origin in the time of *Malcolm Canmore* and who held the property until 1827.

Skene, Gilbert (c. 1522-99). Physician to *James VI*; wrote 'Breve Description of the Pest' (1568).

Skene, Sir James (d. 1633). Son of *Sir John S*; *Lord President* 1636; baronet 1630.

Skene, James, of Rubislaw (1775-1864). *Advocate*; friend of *Sir Walter Scott* and made sketches to illustrate Waverley Novels; Secretary to *Board of Trustees for Manufactures*; edited *Spalding*'s 'History of the Troubles'.

Skene, Sir John (c. 1543-1617). *Advocate* 1575; *Clerk Register* 1594; *Lord of Session* (Curriehill) 1594; accompanied *James VI* to Denmark; an *Octavian*; prepared revision of laws and compiled legal dictionary, 'De Verborum Significatione', besides editing '*Regiam Majestatem*'.

Skene, William Forbes (1809-92). Son of *James S*; clerk of bills in *Court of Session*; wrote 'The Highlanders of Scotland' (1837) and 'Celtic Scotland' (1876-80); Historiographer Royal 1881.

Skene's House (Aberdeen). See Aberdeen, Provost Skene's House.

Skerryvore Lighthouse. Constructed 1838-44. See Stevenson, Alan.

Skinner, John (1721-1807). After acting as schoolmaster and tutor, became *Episcopal minister* of Longside 1742 and remained there for 65 years; wrote 'A Preservative against Presbytery' and 'Dissertation on John's Prophecy'; composed 'Tullochgorum' and 'The Ewie wi' the Crookit Horn'.

Skinner, John (1744-1816). Son of preceding; *Bishop of Aberdeen* 1786.

Skinner, John (1778-1857). Son of preceding; *Bishop of Aberdeen* 1816; *Primus* 1841.

Skipness Castle (Kintyre). Oldest part assigned to early 13th century, but with many later accretions; abandoned in 17th century; apparently mainly in hands of *Lords of the Isles* or their cadets until 1493, when granted to Sir Walter Forrester and then to *Campbells*.

Skire Siller. Equivalent of Maundy Money, distributed by the sovereign to paupers on the Thursday of Holy Week.

Skirling (Peeblesshire). Belonged to Cockburn family, whose castle was demolished in 1568 because they supported Queen *Mary*; *burgh of barony* created for the family 1592.

Skirving, Archibald (1749-1819). Son of Adam S. (1719-1803), a *Jacobite* song-writer; portraitist, best known for sketch of *Burns*.

Slains (Aberdeenshire). Property of *Hays* from reign of *Robert I*; 9th Hay of Slains became *Earl of Errol* 1452; the old castle was destroyed by *James VI* in 1594 because the Errol of the time plotted with Spain; a new one built 1664 and rebuilt with extensions 1836 but now ruinous.

Slessor, Mary (1848-1915). *Dundee* mill-girl who trained as missionary and went to Calabar, West Africa, 1876; known among natives as 'Great Mother'.

Slezer, Captain John (d. 1714). Dutchman who served as royal engineer in Scotland under *Charles II* from 1669; compiled 'Theatrum Scotiae', published 1693, containing views of castles and towns.

Slioch (Aberdeenshire), **Battle of,** 25 December 1307. *Robert I* defeated John Comyn, *Earl of Buchan*.

Smailholm (Roxburghshire). Tower dates from 14th or 15th century and was originally owned by Pringles, from whom it passed by marriage to a Scott family and then by purchase to *Sir Walter Scott of Harden*; tower now ruinous. *Burgh of barony* for Don of Smailholm 1687. Hospital founded before 1429 and granted to *Dryburgh Abbey*; burned by English 1544.

Small, James. *Dalkeith* man who in 1763 patented swing plough, which required only one man and one pair of horses, in place of several men and team of eight or more oxen.

Smellie, William (1697-1763). Born *Lanark*; went to London 1739 and made a great reputation by his practice in midwifery.

Smellie, William (1740-95). Born *Edinburgh*; printer and publisher; first editor of '*Encyclopaedia Britannica*'; wrote on natural history and edited *Burns'* poems.

Smeton, Thomas (1536-83). After a period in Paris and Geneva became schoolmaster at Colchester; *minister* of *Paisley* 1577; principal of *Glasgow University* 1580.

Smibert, Thomas (1810-54). Edited '*Chambers's Journal*' 1837-42; wrote a play, 'Condé's Wife', and 'Clans of the Highlands'.

Smiles, Samuel (1812-1904). Born *Haddington*; in medical practice; wrote 'Self-Help' and 'Physical Education'.

Smith, Adam (1723-90). Born *Kirkcaldy*; educated *Glasgow* and Oxford; lectured in *Edinburgh* on rhetoric and belles lettres 1748-51; professor of logic at Glasgow 1751 and of moral philosophy 1755-64; wrote 'Theory of Moral Sentiments' (1759); frequently visited Edinburgh and toured continent 1764-6; settled at Kirkcaldy 1766; produced 'An Inquiry into the Nature and Causes of the Wealth of Nations' (1776), which was at once influential.

Smith, Alexander (1830-1867). Lace-pattern designer in *Glasgow*; secretary to *Edinburgh University* 1854; wrote 'A Life Drama', 'A Summer in Skye', 'City Poems' and 'Edwin of Deira'.

Smith, Colvin (1795-1875). Born *Brechin*; studied at Rome and London; settled in *Edinburgh* as portraitist.

Smith, Donald Alexander, Lord Strathcona. See Strathcona.

Smith, Donald, and Company. Banking firm in *Edinburgh* 1773.

Smith, George (1824-1901). Born *Elgin*; joined firm of Smith and Elder, publishers, founded by his father; founder and proprietor of 'Dictionary of National Biography'.

Smith, George (1870-1934). Born Midcalder; studied at *Edinburgh* and Antwerp; painted mostly landscapes, frequently with domestic animals; died in Edinburgh.

Smith, James (d. 1731). Son-in-law of *Robert Mylne* (d. 1710); Overseer of King's Works under *James VII*; architect of *Dalkeith* Palace, *Melville* and *Yester* Houses and *Canongate* parish church.

Smith, James (1789-1850). Invented reaping-machine; practised thorough draining and deep ploughing on his farm at Deanston.

Smith, John (1747-1807). Born Glenorchy; wrote '*Gaelic Antiquities*' and 'Life of St *Columba*'.

Smith, Sir Robert Murdoch (1835-1900). Commissioned in Royal Engineers 1855; accompanied an archaeological expedition in Asia Minor, where he discovered site of Mausoleum of Halicarnassus, 1856-9; Director of *Museum of Science and Art, Edinburgh*, 1885.

Smith, Sir Sydney Alfred (d. 1969). Educated New Zealand and *Edinburgh*; Medical Officer of Health to New Zealand Government; medico-legal expert of Egyptian government; professor of forensic medicine in Edinburgh 1928-53.

Smith, William (d. 1644). *Minister* of *Largs* who faithfully attended his parishioners during an outbreak of plague and died of it; his grave is known as '*The Prophet's Grave*'.

Smith, Sir William Alexander (1854-1914). Born *Thurso*; founder of *Boys' Brigade* 1883.

Smith, William Robertson (1846-1894). Born Keig, Aberdeenshire; studied in Germany; professor at *Free Church* College, *Aberdeen*, 1870; edited 9th edition of '*Encyclopaedia Britannica*'; censured for some of his views; professor of Arabic at Cambridge 1883.

Smollett, Tobias George (1721-71). Born Dunbartonshire; studied medicine at *Glasgow*; left for London when he was eighteen; surgeon's mate on warship 1741; first success was 'Roderick Random' (1748), and others were 'Peregrine Pickle' (1751) and 'Humphrey Clinker' (1771); also wrote 'History of England' (1748); did much periodical writing, especially satire on political issues.

Snell, John (1629-79). Educated at *Glasgow University*; fought on Royalist side at *Worcester*; left his estate for foundation of Exhibitions at *Balliol College*, Oxford.

Snowdon Herald. First found 1448, but if the name derives from an ancient term for *Stirling* it may be older.

Sobieski Stuarts. Two brothers, John (c. 1795-1872) and Charles (c. 1799-1880), who claimed to be legitimate grandsons of Prince *Charles Edward*; received in Scotland by *Earl of Moray* and *Lord Lovat* and settled on island in River *Beauly*; turned their attention to many dubious pseudo-scholarly activities and published 'Vestiarium Scoticum', a work on 'clan tartans' professing to be based on an ancient manuscript which was never produced.

Society in Scotland for Propagating Christian Knowledge. Founded 1709 for advancement of education in Highlands and Islands; its second charter, 1738, widened scope of its schools to include instruction in practical subjects; in 1826 it had 134 schools; after 1872 its funds were used to provide bursaries.

Society of Antiquaries of Scotland. See Antiquaries.

Society of Eight. See Cadell.

Sodor. See Sudreys.

Solemn League and Covenant. Scottish *Covenanters* agreed to assist English Parliament against *Charles I* on condition that England would, in effect, adopt a *Presbyterian* church system; drawn up by Scots in August 1643 and accepted, with some modification, by English in September.

Solicitor General. First appointed 1587 as the King's agent in actions before the civil courts; the appointment came to be made on party-political grounds and the Solicitor became the second law officer of the government of the day, after the *Lord Advocate*.

Solicitors to the Supreme Court. Formed into a society 1784 and incorporated by charter 1797.

Solway Moss, Battle of, 24 November 1542. Scottish force commanded by *Oliver Sinclair* routed and many Scottish notables surrendered.

Somerled (d. 1164). Obviously of mixed ancestry, but emerged as leader of native people of western isles against Norse supremacy; conquered isles 1156-8 and recognised by Norway as 'King of the Isles'; defeated and killed at *Renfrew*; succeeded by his sons, *Reginald* in Kintyre and Islay, Dugald in *Lorne,* Mull and Jura and Angus in Bute, Arran and North Argyll (Ardnamurchan to Glenelg).

Somerville, Alexander (1811-85). Son of *Lothian* carpenter; served in army, then took up study of economics; wrote 'The Autobiography of a Working Man'.

Somerville College, Oxford. See Somerville, Mary.

Somerville, James, 10th Lord Somerville (1632-1693). Fought in *Covenanting* army at *Dunbar*; wrote 'Memorie of the Somervilles', published 1815.

Somerville, Lordship. The family, originating in a place near Caen in Normandy, received land in Lanarkshire from *David I* and made their headquarters at *Cowthally Castle,* near *Carnwath*; a member received *Linton* (Roxburghshire) from *Malcolm IV.* Lordship created 1445 for William S., Lord of Carnwath and Linton. John, 2nd Lord, fought at battle of *Sark;* Hugh, 6th Lord, built house of *Drum* (1584) and repaired Cowthally; James, 13th Lord, was aide-de-camp to *Cope* at *Prestonpans* and Hawley at *Falkirk*; on death of 18th Lord, unmarried, in 1870, title became dormant.

Somerville, Mary (1780-1872). Born *Jedburgh,* daughter of Admiral Sir William Fairfax; educated in various schools, finally an academy for young ladies opened in *Edinburgh* by *Nasmyth,* the artist, and developed interest in mathematics and science; married (1) Captain Samuel Greig and (2) her cousin, Dr William Somerville, with whom she moved from Edinburgh to London; died at Sorrento; gave her name to Somerville College, Oxford.

Song Schools. Some cathedrals and other large churches in the middle ages had schools where choristers were trained, and in 1474 town councils were ordered by *Parliament* to set up schools for instruction in music. After *Reformation,* if not before it, song schools widened their scope and provided a more general education than the *grammar schools.* Cf. Academies.

Sorn Castle (Ayrshire). Before 1406 it came into the hands of Andrew Hamilton, 3rd son of Sir David H. of *Cadzow*; later passed by marriage to *Earls of Winton* and then purchased by *Earls of Loudoun* and by *Somervilles* at end of 18th century.

Souden. See Southdean.

Soules, de, Family. Normans who first appeared in Scotland in the company of *David I* before his accession; acquired hereditary office of butler; Nicholas de S. was a *Competitor* as descendant of an illegitimate daughter of *Alexander II*; Sir John was a *Guardian*; his great-nephew, William, plotted against *Robert I* in 1320 and was condemned to perpetual imprisonment.

Soulseat (*Premonstratensian*) (Wigtownshire). Possibly a *Cistercian* house preceded it before its foundation in late 12th century, perhaps by *Fergus, Lord of Galloway*; said to be ruinous 1386; annexed to *parson*age of *Portpatrick* 1630.

Souming. The number or proportion of cattle which each tenant was entitled to keep on the common grazing.

Sour Plums. Motto of *Galashiels,* commemorating a Border raid in 1337, when a band of Englishmen were surprised while gathering wild plums.

Souter Johnnie's House (Kirkoswald). Home of John Davidson, a village cobbler from 1786 to 1806, the original of 'Souter Johnnie' in *Burns*' 'Tam o' Shanter'; contains Burns relics.

Souters. People of *Selkirk,* once famous as shoemakers.

Southdean Church. In this church, now ruined, James, 2nd *Earl of Douglas*, and other Scots made their plans for the campaign which led to battle of *Otterburn.*

Southesk, Earldom. Created 1633 for Sir David Carnegie of Culluthie and *Kinnaird* (*Angus*); 5th Earl, James, *forfeited* after '*Fifteen*; James, de jure 9th Earl, recovered title 1855.

Soutra, Hospital (Midlothian). Founded on top of Soutra Hill by *Malcolm IV* c. 1164; *Mary of Gueldres* had its properties annexed to *Trinity College, Edinburgh*; a fragment of the church remains; it had become the burial vault of the Pringles of Beatman's Acre.

Spalding Club. Named after following; founded in *Aberdeen* 1839 to print material relating to north-east; dissolved 1870 but a New Spalding Club was founded in 1886 and a Third Spalding Club, founded 1929, continued to publish until 1960. See Robertson, Joseph; Stuart, John.

Spalding, John (d. c. 1650). *Aberdeen* man who wrote a 'History of the Troubles and Memorable Transactions in Scotland', covering 1624-45.

Spanish Blanks. Papers signed 1592 by *Earls of Huntly, Errol* and *Angus,* found in possession of George Ker, a Roman Catholic about to sail for Spain; it was assumed that they represented offers by the signatories to support a Spanish invasion.

Speirs, Alexander, of Elderslie (1714-82), the 'mercantile god of *Glasgow*'. A prominent *tobacco lord,* son of a *burgess* of *Edinburgh.* Bought a series of estates in Renfrewshire, Stirlingshire and Lanarkshire. Cf. Houston (Renfrewshire).

Spence, Sir Basil (1907-1976). Born India, educated *Edinburgh*; studied in London; associated with Sir Edwin Lutyens; set up practice in Edinburgh; best known for reconstruction of Coventry Cathedral but designed many other buildings in Scotland as well as in England.

Spens, Sir John, of Condie (c. 1520-73). *Advocate*; *Lord of Session* 1560; Queen's Advocate 1555. See Lord Advocate.

Spens, Thomas (c. 1415-80). Sub*chantor* of *Moray*; *Bishop of Galloway* 1448; acted on various embassies; Keeper of *Privy Seal*; *Bishop of Aberdeen* 1459.

Spirituality. Consisted mainly of *teinds*; the spirituality of a bishopric or an abbey consisted of the teinds of parish churches appropriated to it.

Spittal. The term means 'hospital', but some of the occurrences of the name must signify no more than some kind of shelter, and the name is not evidence of the existence of an institution.

Spottiswood(e) Family. Named from lands in Berwickshire; first mentioned 1296; lands remained with them, except 1620-1700, until in 1836 the heiress married Lord John Douglas-Montagu-Scott.

Spottiswoode, John (1510-85). Went to England to escape prosecution as a heretic and was ordained there; *parson* of *Calder* 1548; *superintendent* of *Lothian* 1561.

Spottiswoode, John (1565-1639). Son of preceding; assistant at *Calder* 1583; accompanied *James VI* to London 1603; *Archbishop of Glasgow* 1603 and of *St Andrews* 1615; consecrated 1610; energetic in defence of episcopacy, but cautious in enforcing *Five Articles of Perth*; *Chancellor* 1635; critical of *Charles I's Code of Canons* and *Prayer Book*; fled to England 1638; wrote 'History of the Church of Scotland' (published 1655).

Spottiswoode, John (1660-1728). *Advocate*; professor of law in *Edinburgh* 1703; edited 'Practicks of the Law of Scotland' compiled by

his grandfather, *Sir Robert*.
Spottiswoode, Sir Robert (1596-1646). Son of *Archbishop S*; *Lord of Session* 1622; *Lord President* 1633; supported *Montrose*; captured at *Philiphaugh* and executed.
Spottiswoode Society. Founded in *Edinburgh* 1843 for publication of works by members of the *Episcopal Church* and other material relating to Scottish history.
Sprott, George (d. 1608). Notary in *Eyemouth*; convicted of having forged letters purporting to be by *Robert Logan of Restalrig* to *3rd Earl of Gowrie* and executed for being privy to *Gowrie Conspiracy*.
Sprott, George Washington (1829-1909). Born Nova Scotia; educated in *Glasgow* for ministry of *Church of Scotland*; chaplain to Scottish troops in Ceylon 1857-65; *minister* of *North Berwick* 1873; edited '*Book of Common Order*'.
Spynie (Moray). The church served as cathedral of *Moray* before the see was settled at *Elgin* in 1224. A bishop's castle existed by 1224, and a palace built largely in 15th century, by Bishops George Innes (1406-14) and David Stewart (1461-76). The *4th Earl of Bothwell* spent part of his youth here with his uncle, the Bishop, and Queen *Mary* visited it in 1562. Bishop Guthrie (1623-38) garrisoned it against the *Covenanters* 1638, but it changed hands in 1644 and again in 1645. In 1690 it was taken possession of by the crown (with other episcopal *temporalities*) and then dismantled. Spynie was made a *burgh of barony* for *Bishop of Moray* 1451.
Spynie, Alexander Lindsay, 2nd Lord (d. c. 1646). Served under Gustavus Adolphus 1628-33; commanded forces in Scotland on behalf of *Charles I*.
Spynie, Lordship. Created 1590 for Alexander Lindsay (d. 1607), 4th son of 10th *Earl of Crawford* and vice-*chamberlain* to *James VI*.
Squadrone Volante. A 'third party' at the time of the making of the *Union*, in addition to the *Court* and *Country* parties; for a time uncommited, as its name suggests, its ultimate decision to support Union ensured its passing.
Stair, Earldom. Created 1703 for *John Dalrymple, 2nd Viscount*. See below.
Stair, James Dalrymple, 1st Viscount (1619-95). Son of laird of Drummurchie; served in army of *Covenanters* 1639-41; *regent* in *Glasgow University* 1641; *advocate* 1648; a Cromwellian commissioner for administration of justice in Scotland (see Cromwellian Administration); *Lord of Session* 1661; baronet 1664; *Lord President* 1671; resigned 1681 rather than take the *Test Oath*, and fled to Holland; returned with *William of Orange*; reappointed Lord President and made Viscount 1690; his 'Institutions of the Law of Scotland' (1681) was an important contribution to making of Scots law into a system.
Stair, John Dalrymple, 1st Earl of (1648-1707). Son of preceding; knighted 1667; *advocate* 1672; despite father's attitude, he came to terms with *James VII*, who made him *Lord Advocate* 1687, *Justice Clerk* 1688; Lord Advocate again 1689; joint *Secretary of State* 1691; had heavy responsibility for Massacre of *Glencoe*, but King defended him and he was Secretary until 1695; created Earl 1703.
Stair, John Dalrymple, 2nd Earl of (1673-1747). Son of preceding; ambassador to several continental countries; fought in war against France 1702-13 and again 1742; Field-Marshal.
Stair Society. Founded 1934 to publish material related to history of Scots law.
Standard, Battle of, 22 August 1138. *David I* heavily defeated near Northallerton.
Standard Bearer. Office held heritably by family of *Scrymgeour of Dudhope* from time of *William Wallace*, though contested by *Earl of Lauderdale* in Standard Bearer Case of 1902-8.
Staple. From 1347, if not earlier, the Scots had a port on the continent through which their staple goods, especially the exports of *linen* and woollen cloth and *salt*, passed and where a Conservator, rather like a consul, looked after the interests of Scottish merchants. The staple was first at Middelburg, but in 1359 it was at Bruges, and, after much negotiation in early 16th century, finally at Veere or Campvere on island of Walcheren.
Stargate's Corps. One of the regiments in the service of Gustavus Adolphus which formed the *Green Brigade*.
Start. In 1650, when *Charles II* was in the hands of the *Covenanters*, he left them for *Cortachy Castle* and went up Glen Clova, where he was overtaken and compelled to return.
Statistical Accounts of Scotland. The first was the work of *Sir John Sinclair*, compiled 1791-8. A second was produced in the 1840s. A third, started after the Second World War, proceeded so far but was abandoned. Each account gives a description of the country parish by parish.
Steeds Stalls. On slope of Gourdie Hill, Clunie

parish, Perthshire, a standing stone is associated with eight parallel mounds and trenches, said to have been formed by *Caledonians* as defence against Romans.
Steelbow. Form of tenure in which landlord equipped tenant with implements and seed.
Steell, Gourlay (1819-94). Born *Edinburgh*; artist who specialised in animal painting; curator of *National Gallery* in *Edinburgh.*
Steell, Sir John (1804-91). Born *Aberdeen*; brother of preceding; among his sculptures are the statue of the Duke of Wellington in *Edinburgh* ('the Iron Duke, in bronze, by Steell'), 'Alexander taming Bucephalus' at the City Chambers, Queen Victoria, *Sir Walter Scott* and Prince Albert.
Stent. Derived from 'extent'; an assessment or taxation. either national or local.
Stephen, George (1829-1921). Born *Dufftown*; pioneer of Canadian Pacific Railway; created Lord Mountstephen.
Stevenson, Alan (1807-1865). Son of *Robert S*; as engineer to Lighthouse Commission designed *Skerryvore* and other lighthouses.
Stevenson, David (1815-86). Son of *Robert S*; lighthouse engineer; his reports led to improvements in rivers of Scotland and northern England.
Stevenson, Robert (1772-1850). Son of a *Glasgow* merchant; his widowed mother married Thomas Smith, engineer to the Commissioners for Northern Lights, whom Robert assisted and ultimately succeeded (1807); responsible for *Bell Rock* (1807-11) and other major lights.
Stevenson, Robert Louis (1850-94). Son of *Thomas S*; *advocate* 1875 but did not practise; ill-health drove him to various parts of the world and he settled in 1890 in Samoa, where he died; his principal works were 'Treasure Island' (1882), 'Jekyll and Hyde' and 'Kidnapped' (1886), 'The Master of Ballantrae' (1889) and 'Catriona' (1893).
Stevenson, Thomas (1818-87). Son of *Robert S*; lighthouse engineer.
Stevenston (Ayrshire). Town mentioned in charter of 1240.
Steward. See Stewartry.
Steward of Scotland. Office held by family of Breton origin from mid-12th century: Walter *FitzAlan* 1147-77; Alan 1177-1204; Walter, 1204-46; Alexander 1246-83; James 1283-1309; Walter 1309-28; Robert 1328-90. The last-named became King as *Robert II* and from that time the office has been vested in the crown and it still pertains to the heir apparent, who is 'Prince and High Steward of Scotland'. Prince Charles is reckoned the 29th High Steward. See Cupbearer.
Stewart. See the following titles: Albany, Arran, Atholl, Bothwell, Buchan, Galloway, Lennox, Moray, Orkney, Strathearn and Traquair.
Stewart, Adam (c. 1535-75). Illegitimate son of *James V* by Elizabeth, daughter of John, *3rd Earl of Lennox*; supposed to have become *Commendator* of the *Charterhouse*, but this is not certain; buried in *Kirkwall Cathedral*.
Stewart, Alan (d. c. 1587). *Commendator* of *Crossraguel* 1565; in 1570 he was roasted before the fire in Dunure Castle by the *Earl of Cassillis* to make him sign a charter in the Earl's favour.
Stewart, Alan Breck (d. c. 1789). Foster brother of *James Stewart* of the Glens; *Jacobite* agent; accused of *Appin Murder* but escaped.
Stewart, Alexander, 'The Wolf of Badenoch' (c. 1342-1406). 4th son of *Robert II*; *Lord of Badenoch* and *Earl of Buchan* 1382; King's Lieutenant in the north 1372, but his record as a ringleader of disorder caused his removal from office; in 1389, after deserting his wife, he was excommunicated by the *Bishops of Moray* and *Ross* and in revenge burned the town of *Forres* and the town and cathedral of *Elgin*; subsequently did penance, but his illegitimate sons were rebellious; his tomb. with an effigy, is in *Dunkeld Cathedral.*
Stewart, Alexander (c. 1375-1435). Son of preceding; forcibly married widowed Countess of *Mar* and thus obtained that earldom; led 'Lowland' army at *Harlaw*; acted as ambassador to England and warden of the *marches* and led a force to France.
Stewart, Alexander (1493-1513). Son of *James IV* by Margaret Boyd; *Archbishop of St Andrews* 1505; studied at Padua under Erasmus; *Chancellor* 1510; founded *St Leonard's College, St Andrews*; killed at *Flodden*.
Stewart, Alexander, of Invernahyle (d. 1795). Served with Stewarts of *Appin* in 1715 and 1745; wounded at *Culloden*; later pardoned; introduced *Sir Walter Scott* to the Highlands 1787.
Stewart, Andrew, Lord Avondale (d. 1488). Illegitimate son of Murdoch, Duke of *Albany*; created Lord *Avondale* 1456; *Chancellor* 1460-82; ambassador to Denmark 1468 and to France 1484.
Stewart, Archibald (1697-1780). Lord *Provost* of *Edinburgh* 1744-6; for his weakness in not resisting the *Jacobite* occupation in 1745 he

was tried for treason; though found not guilty, he moved to London, where he prospered.

Stewart, Bernard, of Aubigny (c. 1447-1508). Grandson of *Sir John S.* of Darnley; Lieutenant General of French army; sent on mission to Scotland and died there.

Stewart, Bernard (c. 1623-45). Youngest son of Esmé, 3rd *Duke of Lennox* (d. 1624); fought for *Charles I* at Edgehill and Naseby; killed at Chester.

Stewart, David, of *Garth* (1772-1829). Succeeded father and elder brother in Perthshire estate; served in *Black Watch* in Flanders, West Indies, Gibraltar, Minorca, the Peninsula and Italy; retired owing to wounds; Governor of St Lucia 1825; made study of psychology and outlook of Highlanders and wrote 'Sketches of the Character, Manners and Present State of the Highlanders of Scotland'. (1822), which was designed as propaganda against emigration and was the foundation of other books on 'The Clans'.

Stewart, Sir Donald Martin (1824-1900). Born near *Forres*; served with East India Company in 9th Bengal Infantry from 1840; took part in Mutiny campaign, the Abyssinian expedition and the Afghan War; Commander-in-chief in India 1880; Field Marshal 1894.

Stewart, Dugald (1753-1828). Son of Matthew S., professor of mathematics at *Edinburgh*; was his father's assistant and successor (1785) but succeeded *Adam Fergusson* as professor of moral philosophy in same year; also taught economics, natural philosophy, Greek and logic; wrote 'Philosophy of the Human Mind' (1792-1827), 'Outlines of Moral Philosophy' (1793) and 'Philosophical Essays' (1810); retired 1810. See 'Common Sense' Philosophy.

Stewart, Henry, Lord Methven. See Methven, Lordship.

Stewart, James (d. 1309). *Steward* of Scotland from 1283; a *Guardian* 1286; supported *Wallace* and *Bruce*; envoy to France 1295 and 1302.

Stewart, Sir James, 'The Black Knight of *Lorne*'. Married *Joan,* widow of *James I*, 1439; their sons were Sir John, of Balveny, *Earl of Atholl*, James, *Earl of Buchan*, and Andrew, *Bishop of Moray*.

Stewart, James (c. 1475-1504). 2nd son of *James III*; created *Marquis of Ormond* 1476 and *Duke of Ross* 1488; *Archbishop of St Andrews* 1497 and *Chancellor* 1501.

Stewart, James (1500-1544). Son of *James IV*. See Moray, Earl of.

Stewart, James (d. 1558). Son of *James V* by Elizabeth Shaw of *Sauchie*; *Commendator* of *Kelso* and *Melrose*.

Stewart, James (c. 1531-70). Son of *James V* by *Margaret Erskine*. See Moray, Earl of.

Stewart, Sir James, of Goodtrees (1635-1713). Son of Sir James S., Lord *Provost* of *Edinburgh* (d. 1681); associated with *Presbyterian* dissidents and political opposition to *Lauderdale*; outlawed for part in *Argyll's Rebellion*; pardoned by *William of Orange*; *Lord Advocate* 1692-1709 and 1711-13.

Stewart, James, 'of the Glens' (d. 1752). Illegitimate son of laird of Ardshiel and half-brother to the Ardshiel whose activities in the '*Forty-Five* led to forfeiture of the estate (See Forfeited Estates); Colin Campbell of Glenure was appointed factor, with power to evict tenants, including James, and was murdered (the *Appin Murder*); James was hanged, protesting his innocence.

Stewart, James (1701-96). Born Glenfinlas; *minister* of *Killin* 1737-96; translated Bible into *Gaelic* (1767).

Stewart, Sir John, of Bonkill (d. 1298). Son of Alexander, High *Steward*; killed at battle of *Falkirk*; among his seven sons, Alexander was *Earl of Angus,* Alan *Earl of Lennox*, Walter the progenitor of the *Earls of Galloway* and James the progenitor of the *Earls of Atholl, Buchan* and *Traquair* as well as the Lords of *Lorne* and Innermeath.

Stewart, John. Illegitimate son of *Robert II*; created heritable *sheriff* of Bute; ancestor of noble family of *Bute*.

Stewart, Sir John, of *Darnley* (c. 1365-1429). Son of Sir Alexander S. of Darnley; commanded force in French service which defeated English at *Baugé* 1421; created Comte d'Evreux and Seigneur d'Aubigny.

Stewart, John (1459-79). 4th son of *James II*; created *Earl of Mar* 1459; died in mysterious circumstances, at *Craigmillar Castle* or in *Edinburgh*.

Stewart, John (1479-1503). 3rd son of *James III*; created *Earl of Mar* 1486.

Stewart, John (d. 1563). Son of *James V* by Elizabeth, daughter of Sir John Carmichael; *Commendator* of *Coldingham*; married Jean, daughter of Patrick, 3rd *Earl of Bothwell.*

Stewart, John (1700-52). *Gaelic* poet, known as John Roy; officer in *Scots Greys* but resigned; fought with French at Fontenoy; commanded 'The Edinburgh Regiment' in '*Forty-Five*; escaped after *Culloden* to France.

Stewart, Mary (c. 1450-c. 1490). Elder daughter of *James II*; married (1) Thomas, Lord

Boyd, *Earl of Arran*, 1467 and (2) James, Lord *Hamilton*, 1474; her son by Lord Hamilton was created Earl of Arran and her daughter by him married Matthew, 2nd *Earl of Lennox*.

Stewart, Sir Robert (d. 1437). Grandson of *Walter, Earl of Atholl*; an assassin of *James I*; executed.

Stewart, Robert, of Aubigny (c. 1470-1543). Brother of Matthew, 2nd *Earl of Lennox*; served with Scots in France and as a marshal of France fought at Marignano and Pavia.

Stewart, Robert (c. 1520-86). Son of 3rd *Earl of Lennox*; administrator of *Bishopric of Caithness* 1542; joined reformers; *Commendator* of *St Andrews Priory* 1570; Earl of Lennox 1578; *Earl of March* 1580.

Stewart, Robert (1533-93). Son of *James V* by Euphemia Elphinstone, daughter of 1st *Lord E.* (who later married John Bruce of Cultmalindie); *Commendator* of *Holyrood* 1539; received from Queen *Mary* a *tack* of *Orkney and Shetland* 1564 and a feu charter 1565; compelled *Adam Bothwell* to exchange the *Bishopric of Orkney* for the abbey of Holyrood 1568; created *Earl of Orkney* 1581; from time to time accused of treasonable dealings with Denmark and of tyrannical proceedings against the islanders.

Stewart, Walter (1293-1326). Son of *James, High Steward*; fought at *Bannockburn*; married *Marjory*, daughter of *Robert I*, 1315; took part in continuation of English wars.

Stewart, Walter (d. 1617). Son of Sir John S. of Minto; educated with *James VI*; *Commendator* of *Blantyre* 1566; Keeper of *Privy Seal* 1582; *Lord of Session* 1593; an *Octávian*; created Lord Blantyre 1606.

Stewart, William (1479-1545). Son of Sir Thomas Stewart of Minto; *dean* of *Glasgow* 1527; *Treasurer* 1530-7; *Bishop of Aberdeen* 1532; built library of *King's College, Aberdeen*; also *provost* of *Lincluden*.

Stewart, William (c. 1481-c. 1550). Wrote a metrical version of *Boece* and other verses; pensioned by *James V*.

Stewart, Sir William, of Houston (c. 1555-c. 1604). Son of Thomas S. of *Galston*; in Dutch service 1575; Captain of *King's Guard* 1582; ambassador to England 1583; *Commendator* of *Pittenweem* 1583; engaged in other missions abroad; his son Frederick created Lord Pittenweem 1609.

Stewarton (Ayrshire). *Burgh of barony* for *Lord Garlies* 1623; *police burgh* under act of 1862. A 'Hospital' has been inferred from references to lands called 'Spetale', but there is no supporting evidence.

Stewartry. Term formerly applied to any area which was crown property and therefore administered by a steward rather than a *sheriff*, e.g. *Strathearn* and *Menteith* after the annexation of those earldoms to the crown by *James I*, and *Orkney and Shetland* later; but the term continued to be applied to Kirkcudbright, which became 'The Stewartry' par excellence.

Stirling, Allan's Hospital. See Allan's Hospital.

Stirling Archaeological Society. Founded 1878 as 'Stirling Field Club' to study geology, natural history and archaeology of district.

Stirling, Argyll's Lodging. See Argyll's Lodging.

Stirling Bridge, Battle of, 11 September 1297. *William Wallace* and *Andrew Moray* defeated English under John de Warenne.

Stirling, Burgh. *Royal burgh* in 1120s; one of four burghs which had their Court. See Burghs, Court of Four.

Stirling Castle. Already a major fortress in 12th century, if not earlier; changed hands several times in *War of Independence*; held by *Sir William Oliphant* for three months 1304; surrendered to Scots after *Bannockburn* (when English had hoped to relieve it); important royal residence from *James II* to *James VI*, and residential buildings erected especially by *James III* and *James V* (see *Stirling Heads*); captured by General *Monck* 1651.

Stirling, Chapel Royal. Founded 1501; deanery attached to *Bishopric of Galloway* 1504 and to *Bishopric of Dunblane* after *Reformation*; new building 1594. Cf. Chapel Royal.

Stirling, Collegiate Church of Holy Rude. Parish church erected as *collegiate church* by magistrates and community before 1546; Queen *Mary* and *James VI* crowned there.

Stirling, Cowane's Hospital. See Cowane, John.

Stirling, Earldom. Created for *Sir William Alexander* 1633; dormant on death of 5th Earl 1739 and subsequent claims disallowed.

Stirling Engine. See Stirling, Robert.

Stirling, 'Field' or **Battle of.** See Sauchieburn.

Stirling Friaries. (1) *Dominican*. Founded by *Alexander II* 1233; prior and convent granted their property to Alexander Erskine of Cangnoir 1560 and his family retained it until 1652, when it went to town in terms of grant by Queen *Mary* in 1567. (2) *Franciscan* Observant. Founded by *James IV* c. 1494; property granted to town 1567.

Stirling Grammar School. 'Schools of Stirling' mentioned in 1150s; *Grammar School* came to be administered by town council, who paid the master in 1641.
Stirling Heads. Series of effigies, carved in oak, formerly in Palace in *Stirling Castle*; dispersed 1777 and some destroyed, but many have been reassembled in Stirling Castle. Three in *National Museum of Antiquities.*
Stirling Hospitals. (1) Almshouse or Over Hospital (St Peter's) existed before 1482 and was described as ruinous 1610. (2) Leperhouse mentioned 1464-1513. (3) St James's, at Causewayhead, mentioned 1221x1225, granted to *Cambuskenneth Abbey* 1403 and said to have been destroyed at *Reformation.* (4) Nether Hospital founded by Robert Spittal, tailor to *James IV*, 1530, fell into ruin by 1738. (5) Hospital founded by *Mary of Gueldres* 1462 was short-lived.
Stirling Jug. Standard measure of pint, in keeping of town 1457; now in *Smith Institute, Stirling*.
Stirling Merchant Banking Company. Established 1784; failed 1813.
Stirling Natural History and Archaeological Society. See Stirling Archaeological Society.
Stirling, Raid of, April 1584. An unsuccessful attempt by *Ruthven Raiders* to regain power.
Stirling, Smith Institute. Founded on bequest by T.S. Smith of Glassingall (1817-69) to house his collection of paintings; other pictures and objects have been added; erected 1873-4.
Stirling University. Founded 1967; buildings erected on Airthrey estate.
Stirling, James (1692-1770). Born Garden, Stirlingshire; expelled from Oxford for *Jacobitism*; in Venice discovered secret of Venetian glass-making; returned to London 1725; manager of mining company in *Leadhills* 1735.
Stirling, Sir James (1791-1865). Son of Andrew S. of Drumpellier, Lanarkshire; admiral; commander in China and East Indies 1854-6; first Governor of Western Australia.
Stirling, James Hutchison (1820-1909). Born *Glasgow*; practised medicine but turned to philosophy; wrote 'The Secret of Hegel', 'Text Book to Kant' and a critique of *Sir William Hamilton*'s theory of perception.
Stirling, Robert (1790-1878). Born in Perthshire; *minister* of *Galston* 1834-78; invented a heated-air engine and constructed scientific instruments.
Stirling, Sir Thomas (1733-1808). Son of Sir Henry S. of Ardoch; served in *Scots Brigade* in Holland 1747-57; captain in *Black Watch* 1757; served in conquest of Canada and commanded Black Watch in American War; succeeded to baronetcy of Ardoch.
Stirling, Sir William Alexander, Earl of. See Alexander, Sir William.
Stirling-Maxwell, Sir William, of *Pollok* (1818-78). Born Kenmure, son of Archibald S. of *Keir*; married daughter of Sir John Maxwell of *Pollok*; interested in art and archaeological work; M.P. for Perthshire; wrote many historical works, incl 'Annals of the Artists of Spain'.
Stirling's Library (*Glasgow*). Founded by Walter Stirling, a merchant, 1791; amalgamated with Public Library 1871.
Stob Cross (Fife). Rough-hewn stone marked with cross; thought to have been a '*girth*' or sanctuary cross associated with church of *Markinch*.
Stobhall (Perthshire). Said to have been granted by *Robert I* to Sir Malcolm Drummond after *Bannockburn*, but more likely acquired by Drummonds through marriage with a Montifex heiress c. 1360; castle said to date originally from 13th century, but oldest part of present building belongs to 1578. Sir John Drummond, created *Lord D.* 1487, began *Drummond Castle*, but building went on at Stobhall by David, Lord D., in 16th century and John, 2nd *Earl of Perth*, in 17th. Castle still belongs to Earl of Perth and has a chapel with a 17th century painted ceiling.
Stobo (Peeblesshire). Probably site of an early minster or even diocesan centre.
Stoddart, Thomas Tod (1810-80). Lived in *Kelso* from 1836; wrote 'The Death-Wake', 'Angler's Companion to the Rivers and Lakes of Scotland' and 'Songs of the Seasons'.
Stone of Destiny. See Stone of Scone.
Stone of Scone. The stone used for inaugurating Scottish kings (see Scone) was said to have been brought from Ireland to *Argyll* (possibly *Dunadd* and then *Dunstaffnage*) and later to Scone, whence it was removed by Edward I to Westminster Abbey 1296. In 1950 a group of young Scots recovered it and deposited it at *Arbroath Abbey*, but it was taken back to London. It seems that the stone now at Westminster is probably of Perthshire sandstone, but it has often been asked whether that stone is the stone which was at Scone before 1296.
Stonehaven (Kincardineshire). *Burgh of barony* for Earl *Marischal* 1587.
Stonehouse (Lanarkshire). *Burgh of barony* for Lockhart of *Lee* 1667.

Stormont, Viscountcy. Created for Sir David Murray of Gospertie, *Lord Scone*, 1621.
Stornoway (*Lewis*). *Burgh of barony* for Lord *Balmerino* and others 1607.
Stornoway, Nicolson Institute. See Nicolson Institute.
Story, Robert Herbert (1835-1907). Son of Robert S. (1790-1859); succeeded father as *minister* of Roseneath, 1860-86; professor of church history at *Glasgow* 1886-98; principal 1898; wrote '*Robert Lee*' and '*William Carstares*'.
Stoup. Measure of capacity varying from 1 pint to 1 or more gallons.
Stow, David (1793-1864). Born *Paisley*; established Sunday evening school for general instruction; associated with *Thomas Chalmers* in his parochial work; founded *Glasgow Educational Society*; joined *Free Church* and founded its college for training teachers; wrote 'Physical and Moral Training' (1836).
Stracathro *(Angus).* In 1130 Angus, *mormaer* of *Moray*, was defeated by royal army under Edward, the *Constable*, in absence of *David I*. In 1296 John *Balliol* surrendered his kingship to Edward I in the churchyard. In 1452 the *Earl of Crawford* was defeated by *Earl of Huntly*.
Strachan, Alexander (d. 1652). Served under Cromwell at *Preston* 1648; joined Scottish *Covenanters* 1649; defeated *Montrose* at *Carbisdale* and fought at *Dunbar*.
Strachan, John (1778-1867). Born *Aberdeen*; teacher; went to Kingston, Ontario, 1799; ordained as Episcopalian *minister* 1806; Bishop of Toronto 1839; first president of Canadian Board of Education 1823.
Straiton, David, of Lauriston (d. 1534). Burned as *heretic* at *Edinburgh*.
Strange, Sir Robert (1721-92). Born *Kirkwall*; joined *Jacobites* in 'Forty-Five; studied engraving in Paris; settled as engraver in London 1759.
Stranraer (Wigtownshire). *Burgh of barony* 1595; *royal burgh* 1617.
Strathallan School. Founded 1912 by Harry Riley (d. 1942) at *Bridge of Allan*, but removed to *Forgandenny* 1920; boarding school on English 'public school' model.
Strathallan, Viscountcy. Created 1686 for William Drummond, 4th *Lord Madderty*; *forfeited* 1746 but restored 1824.
Strathaven (Lanarkshire). *Burgh of barony* for *Earl of Douglas* 1450.
Strathclyde. Kingdom of *Britons* in south-west Scotland, often joined with north-west England in a kingdom more appropriately known as *Cumbria*; on death of last king in 1018 he was succeeded by Duncan, son of *Malcolm II*, who became king of *Alba* 1034.
Strathclyde University (*Glasgow*). Formerly *Royal College of Science and Technology*; became university 1964.
Strathcona, Donald Alexander Smith, 1st Lord (1820-1914). Born *Forres*; joined uncle in service of Hudson's Bay Company and became Governor of Company; M.P. in Canadian parliament after confederation 1867; prime mover in construction of Canadian Pacific Railway; knighted 1886; High Commissioner for Canada in London 1896; Lord Strathcona (= Glencoe) and Mount Royal 1897.
Strathdon (Aberdeenshire). *Burgh of regality* for *Earl of Mar* 1677.
Strathearn, Earldom. Malise, Earl of S., named c. 1130; descended in male line until 1333, when *Edward Balliol* granted it to John de Warenne, Earl of Surrey (d. 1347); a Scottish creation for Maurice Moray, 1344, expired with his death 1346; Robert Stewart, afterwards *Robert II*, was Earl 1357 and on his accession he transferred it to his 5th son, David; from David's daughter, Euphemia, it passed to Malise Graham, her son; Malise was deprived 1427 in favour of *Walter*, *Earl of Atholl*; on his death in 1437 the title remained in abeyance until it was claimed in 1631 by William, *Earl of Menteith*, but he was compelled to relinquish it in 1633 and accept *Earldom of Airth*.
Strathendry Castle (Fife). 16th century tower, built by Forresters who had acquired lands from Strathendry family by marriage in 1496; subsequently passed to *Douglases* and Clephanes.
Strathfillan Priory (*Augustinian*) (Perthshire). Founded by *Robert I* 1318; revenues conferred on Campbell of Glencarradale 1607.
Strathgryfe. Ancient name for Renfrewshire.
Strathmiglo (Fife). *Burgh of barony* for Scott of *Balwearie* 1510. The proposed erection of a *collegiate church* by Sir *William Scott* in 1527 did not materialise.
Strathmore and Kinghorne, Earldom. Created 1677 for Patrick *Lyon*, 3rd Earl of Kinghorne and 11th *Lord Glamis*.
Strathspey Regiment (97th). Raised 1794 by Sir James Grant and embodied at *Elgin*; men drafted to other regiments 1795.
Streeking of the Plough. At first ploughing each year, special foods were eaten with blessings on the fields.
Stromness (*Orkney*). *Burgh of barony* for

freeholders 1617.

Struthers Castle (Fife). At one time a large fortress, home of the Lords *Lindsay* of the Byres, and in 18th century still a large house, but little remains.

Struthers, John (1776-1853). Born Long Calderwood; cowherd and shoemaker, but took up literary work; librarian of *Stirling*'s *Library* in *Glasgow* 1833; wrote 'The Poor Man's Sabbath', 'Anticipation' and 'Dychmont'.

Struthers, Sir John (1823-99). Born Brucefield, *Dunfermline*; professor of anatomy at *Aberdeen* 1863; president of *Royal College of Surgeons* 1895-97.

Stuart or **Crichton Stuart, Earls and Marquesses of Bute.** See Bute.

Stuart, Sir Alexander (1825-86). Emigrated from *Edinburgh* to New South Wales 1851 and became premier there 1883.

Stuart, Sir Charles (1753-1801). 4th son of 3rd Earl of *Bute*; captured Minorca from Spaniards.

Stuart, Sir Charles (1779-1845). Son of preceding; ambassador to Paris 1815-30, to St Petersburg 1841-5; Baron Stuart de *Rothesay* 1828.

Stuart, Frances Theresa, 'La Belle Stuart' (1647-1702). Granddaughter of Walter, 1st *Lord Blantyre*; maid of honour to Catharine of Braganza, wife of *Charles II*; married 3rd Duke of Richmond; bought Lethington 1682 and re-named it *Lennoxlove*.

Stuart, Gilbert (1742-86). Born *Musselburgh*; wrote 'History of Scotland', 'Dissertation on the English Constitution' and 'A View of Society in Europe'.

Stuart, James (1775-1849). *Writer to the signet*; killed *Sir Alexander Boswell* in duel 1822.

Stuart, John (1743-1821). Born *Luss*; completed translation of Old Testament into *Gaelic*.

Stuart, John (1813-77). *Advocate* in *Aberdeen*; secretary of *Spalding Club* 1839-70; produced 'The Sculptured Stones of Scotland', 'The Book of *Deer*' and 'A Lost Chapter in the History of *Mary*, Queen of Scots'.

Stuart, John McDowall (1815-1866). Born *Dysart*; emigrated to Australia 1838; explored interior of continent 1858-62.

Subchantor. Deputy of *chantor* in some cathedrals; Scottish equivalent of English and Latin 'succentor'.

Succession Acts. (1) 1315. Designated *Edward Bruce*, *Robert I*'s brother, as heir in preference to his daughter *Marjory*. (2) 1318. After death of Edward and Marjory, Marjory's son, Robert Stewart, was designated, failing issue of the King. (3) 1373. The succession to *Robert II* was entailed on his sons and the heirs male of each of them, to the exclusion of females, but when all the male lines were extinguished *Mary* succeeded without challenge in 1542.

Sudreys. The Hebrides, designated 'sudreyar' or southern isles from the point of view of *Orkney*; the name is perpetuated in the English diocese of Sodor and *Man*.

Sugar Manufacture. Started in Scotland in early 17th century and developed greatly in *Glasgow* and *Greenock* after 1783.

Sumburgh Head (*Shetland*). Lighthouse erected 1821.

Superintendents. Officers of the reformed church, instituted 1561, with administrative but not sacramental powers of bishops, each with oversight of a diocese; ten were proposed, but only five were appointed, the functions being performed elsewhere by bishops who joined the reformed church or by *ministers* acting as '*commissioners*'. They were superseded from 1572 by Protestant bishops as they took over various dioceses, and then by *presbyteries*.

Superior. In feudal law, the vassal held the lands, the superior retained the right to *casualties* and received the *reddendo*.

Supplication. Document in which leading noblemen proposed to approach *Charles I* complaining of his manipulation of *parliament* in 1633 and his heavy taxation; one of the supplicants, *Lord Balmerino*, was tried for treason; the document anticipated the *National Covenant*.

'Surfaceman'. See Anderson, Alexander.

Surgeons' Hall. See Surgeons, Royal College of.

Surgeons, Royal College of. Founded 1505 and received charter from *James IV* 1506; now housed in Surgeons' Hall in Nicolson Street, *Edinburgh*, built 1833 after design by *W.H. Playfair*.

Sutherland. 'The southern land', so named from the point of view of *Orkney*, of which earldom it formed a part until the late 12th century.

Sutherland, Earldom and Dukedom. Earldom existed c. 1230, in hands of William of *Duffus*, grandson of Freskin, a Fleming, who was granted lands in *Moray* by *David I*; continued in that family until 1514, when it passed through marriage to a son of the *Earl of Huntly*; in 1766 this line also ended in an heiress who married the Marquis of Stafford, who was created Duke of S. 1833; in 1963 the line again ended in an heiress, who became Countess, while the U.K. dukedom fell to a kinsman.

Sutherland Highlanders. Raised 1799 as 93rd regiment by Major-General Wemyss of Wemyss, nephew of late *Earl of Sutherland*, and sometimes known by his name. Formed '*Thin Red Line*'. Amalgamated 1881 with 91st Argyllshire Highlanders to form *Argyll and Sutherland Highlanders*.

Swan, Annie S. (d. 1943). Born Gorebridge; married Dr Burnett Smith; successful author of romantic novels.

Sweet Singers of Bo'ness. Followers of Muckle John *Gibb*, otherwise 'King Solomon', who in 1681 marched to the Pentland Hills, singing, in expectation of seeing 'the smoke and utter ruin of the sinful, bloody city of *Edinburgh*'.

Sweetheart Abbey (*Cistercian*) (Kirkcudbrightshire), otherwise New Abbey. Founded 1273 by *Devorguilla*; erected into *temporal lordship* for *Sir Robert Spottiswoode* 1624.

Sweno's Stone (*Forres*). Sandstone slab, 23 feet high, with carvings depicting warriors on horse and foot, all arrayed in order; derives name from supposed victory of Sweno, son of King Harald of Denmark, over *Malcolm II* in 1006, but it may be associated with a victory c. 900 by Sigurd, *Earl of Orkney*, over Maelbrigde, a Scottish 'earl'.

Swinton (Berwickshire). Edulf de Swinton held lands before 1100 and founded a family which continued for centuries, including *Alexander Swinton* and John S. (d. 1799), a *Lord of Session* (Swinton).

Swinton, Alexander (c. 1625-1700). Taken prisoner at *Worcester*; *advocate* 1671 and *Lord of Session* (Mersington) 1688.

Swinton, John (1621-79). Brother of preceding; joined *Cromwellian administration* after *Dunbar*.

Sword of State. One sent to *William I* by Innocent III 1202, another to *James IV* by Julius II 1506 and a third to *James V* by Paul III 1537. See Honours of Scotland.

Sybilla (d. 1122). Illegitimate daughter of Henry I; married *Alexander I*.

Sydserf, Thomas (1587-1663). *Bishop of Brechin* 1634 and of *Galloway* 1635; deposed 1638; *Bishop of Orkney* 1661.

Sydserf, Thomas (b. 1624). Son of preceding; published news-sheets 'Mercurius Criticus' in 1651 and '*Mercurius Caledonius*' in 1660; also a dramatist.

Syme, David (1827-1908). Born *North Berwick*; became proprietor of newspaper 'The Age' in Melbourne.

Symington (Lanarkshire). Named from Simon Loccard, progenitor of the Lockharts of *Lee*, a Fleming; from 14th century the proprietors were known as Symington of that *ilk*.

Symington, William (1763-1831). Born *Leadhills*; educated for church but became civil engineer; invented method of applying steam power to a road carriage by chains and ratchets and then a rotary engine; patronised by Duke of Bridgewater; devised first practical steamboat, the '*Charlotte Dundas*', which was put on *Forth and Clyde Canal* 1802. See also Miller, Patrick and Taylor, James.

Synod. Court of reformed church, first mentioned 1562; originally the court of bishop or *superintendent*; when the *presbyterian* system took shape it took intermediate place between *General Assembly* and *presbytery*.

T

Tables. Committee, consisting of four members from each estate (see Three Estates), set up by organised opposition to *Charles I* after introduction of 1673 *Prayer Book*; its work led to *National Covenant*.

Tack, Tacksman. A tack was a lease, and a tacksman a leaseholder; the term tacksman was applied particularly to a Highland tenant who leased a large area of the chief's lands and sublet to a number of subtenants.

Tailzie. Entail whereby the succession to heritable property was determined beyond, or despite, the normal rules of heritage.

Tain (Ross). *Royal burgh* from 1457, probably earlier, but not, as supposed, under *Malcolm III*. 'The *collegiate church* of St *Duthac*' mentioned 1457, when *James II* endowed a chaplainry in it; there was a fuller erection of a collegiate church by *James III* in 1487; the building was used as a parish church until 1815, and restored in 1849 and 1882 for monumental and memorial purposes.

Tait, Archibald Campbell (1811-82). Born *Edinburgh*; succeeded Dr Arnold as headmaster of Rugby; dean of Carlisle 1849; Bishop of London 1856; Archbishop of Canterbury 1868.

Tam o' the Cowgate. See *Thomas Hamilton*, 1st Earl of Haddington.

Tanistry. By Celtic practice a 'tanaist' or successor to a king or chief could be designated from among the kindred group.

Tannach Moor, Battle of, 1464. Family of Gunn fought against Keiths and Mackays.
Tannahill, Robert (1774-1810). Born *Paisley*; *cotton*-weaver; published 'Poems and Songs' 1807, including 'Gloomy winter's noo awa" and 'Jessie the Flower o' Dunblane'; embarrassed by popularity; finally burned his MSS and committed suicide.
Tantallon Castle (East Lothian). Of 14th century date, with alterations and additions in late 15th and early 16th; probably originated with 1st *Earl of Douglas*, and fell to *Earl of Angus*; besieged by *James IV* 1491 (when property of '*Bell the Cat*') and by *James V* 1528 (when property of his stepfather, *6th Earl of Angus*); occupied by *Covenanters* 1639 and taken by *Monck* 1651; fell into decay after 1699.
Tarbat (Ross). *Burgh of barony* for Mackenzie of Tarbat 1678; *burgh of regality* for Viscount Tarbat 1686.
Tarbat, Viscountcy. See Mackenzie, Sir George, of Tarbat.
Tarbert (Knapdale, *Argyll*). *Magnus Barelegs*, King of Norway, took a vessel across the isthmus c. 1098, and *Robert I* performed the same feat to symbolise his possession of the *Isles*. Royal castle existed from late 13th century and was repaired by Robert I and strengthened by *James IV*. The place was a *royal burgh* from c. 1329.
Tarbolton (Ayrshire). *Burgh of barony* for Cunningham of Enterkin 1671. Lordship of T. was included in creations of dukedom of *Lennox*, 1581 and 1675.
Tarland (Aberdeenshire). *Burgh of barony* for *Irvine of Drum* 1683.
Tarras, Earldom. Title bestowed for his lifetime on *Walter Scott* (1644-93) on his marriage to Countess of *Buccleuch*.
Tarves (Aberdeenshire). *Burgh of barony* for *Gordon* of Haddo 1673. A hospital, probably of post-*Reformation* origin, was said to have been founded by Forbes of *Tolquhon*.
Tarvet, Tarvit (Fife). See Scotstarvet.
Tassie, James (1735-99). Born *Pollokshaws*; apprenticed as stonemason but studied art in *Foulis Academy*; in 1763 went to Dublin, where with Dr Henry Quin he produced a special vitreous paste for making portrait-medallions; later moved to London and produced many such medallions.
Tassie, William (1750-1860). Joined his uncle *James T.* in his business; left his stock to *National Galleries of Scotland*.
Tay Bridges. First railway bridge, designed by Sir Thomas Bough, was opened 31 May 1878 and blown down 28 December 1879, with a loss of about 90 passengers in a train; new bridge, with double line of rails, begun 1883, completed 1888. Road bridge opened 1966.
Taylor, James (1753-1825). Born *Leadhills*; as tutor to sons of *Patrick Miller* he collaborated with him in fitting paddle-wheels to a vessel, and then collaborated with *William Symington* in applying steam power to a vessel.
Taylor, John (?1637-1770). Buried in churchyard of *Leadhills* after, so it was said, working as a miner for about a hundred years and enjoying a long retirement.
Taylor's Institution (*Crieff*). Founded by William Taylor of Cornton, tallow chandler in Crieff, for children of poor.
Taymouth Castle (Perthshire). Original castle of 'Balloch' built by Colin *Campbell* of Glenorchy c. 1580; present castle built by *Breadalbane* family 1801-42; became hotel 1920 and later used for other purposes.
Tayport (Fife), otherwise *Ferryport-on-Craig* or South Ferry. *Burgh of barony* for Robert Durie 1599; *burgh of regality* for *Douglas* of *Glenbervie* 1725.
Teinds. Tithes, the tenths of produce rendered by parishioners for the upkeep of the local priest and church. In later medieval times the bulk of teinds were appropriated to larger institutions, leaving little for the parishes, and attempts after the *Reformation* to recover them bore some fruit in the work of *Charles I*, who provided machinery for the payment of *ministers*' stipends which lasted with little change until 1925.
Telephone. See Bell, Alexander Graham.
Television. See Baird, John Logie.
Telford, Thomas (1757-1834). Born Westerkirk, Dumfriesshire; trained as stone-mason; went to *Edinburgh* 1779 and London 1782 and was employed on building Somerset House; studied civil engineering and started a professional career which included bridges of stone and iron, canals, roads and docks; leading engineer in *Caledonian Canal*; built *Dean Bridge*, Edinburgh; designed harbours at *Aberdeen*, *Wick* and elsewhere; engineer to *Commissioners for Highland Roads and Bridges* from 1803; called 'The Colossus of Roads'.
Telford Wall (*Edinburgh*). An extension to the *Flodden Wall* constructed in early 17th century, taking in the area round *Heriot*'s Hospital.
Templars. See Knights Templars.
Temple (Midlothian). Formerly *Balantro-*

doch, it became the principal Scottish seat of the *Knights Templars*, probably in reign of *David I*; on suppression of that order the property passed to *Knights Hospitallers*; the 13th century church remained in use until early 19th, and the walls are still complete.

Temporal Lordship. From 1564 onwards the properties of various religious houses were converted into hereditary lordships, often for those who had previously held them as *Commendators*.

Temporality. The portion of ecclesiastical revenues consisting of lands and their rents, as opposed to *Spirituality*.

Ten Years' Conflict. The struggle within the *Church of Scotland* which preceded the *Disruption*, beginning with the *Veto Act*.

Tennant, Charles (1768-1838). Born Ochiltree; as a silk manufacturer, studied bleaching; patented use of chloride of lime 1798; established chemical works at *St Rollox*, *Glasgow*, 1800.

Tennant, Sir Charles (1823-1906). Grandson of preceding; partner in *St Rollox* works and other industrial undertakings; Liberal M.P; art patron.

Tennant, William (1784-1848). Born *Anstruther*; professor of Hebrew and Oriental languages at *St Andrews*; wrote 'Syriac and Chaldee Grammar' and also 'Anster Fair' (1812).

Tennis Courts. Kings evidently played tennis from at least the reign of *James I*, and there were tennis courts at various royal residences. The one at *Holyrood* is shown on *James Gordon* of Rothiemay's map of 1647 and mentioned as the scene of plays in 1705 and 1714 but has now disappeared. The one at *Falkland*, restored by the *National Trust*, alone survived, but one was constructed at *Troon* in the old style in 1909.

Terce. Right of a widow to a third of her husband's heritage.

Term Days. See Candlemas, Lammas, Martinmas, Whitsunday.

Ternan (d. c. 431). Said to have been a disciple of *Palladius* and to have died at Banchory on Deeside.

Terpersie Castle (Aberdeenshire). Built on Z-plan by William *Gordon* 1561; the 5th and last Gordon laird was executed after the *'Forty-Five*; the castle is now roofless.

Terregles (or **Herries**) (Kirkcudbrightshire). *Burgh of barony* for *Lord Herries* 1510.

Test Act and **Oath,** 1681. The act imposed on all office-holders an oath adhering to the Protestant religion as defined in the *Confession of Faith* of 1560 and accepting royal supremacy.

Testoon. Silver coin of *Mary*'s reign, worth 4s.

Teviot, Viscountcy. Created 1685 for Robert Spencer, brother of 1st Earl of Sunderland; extinct on his death 1694.

Thane (or **Thegn**). Anglo-Saxon term denoting either status or office; introduced into Scotland, in early 12th century if not earlier, and equated with *Toisech.*

'Theatrum Scotiae'. See Slezer.

Theneu. Daughter of Loth, King of Southern *Picts,* and mother of *Kentigern.*

'Thermopylae'. This famous clipper ship was built at *Aberdeen* in 1868; her run from Gravesend to Melbourne in 62 days constituted a record which still stands for sailing vessels. Cf. Cutty Sark.

'Thin Red Line'. 93rd *Sutherland Highlanders,* part of the Highland Brigade in the Crimea in 1854 under *Sir Colin Campbell,* formed a line two-deep to repulse a charge of Russian cavalry.

Thirds of Benefices. By arrangements made in January 1562 all holders of benefices were to continue to draw their revenues, less one third, which was to be uplifted by the crown, partly for its own needs and partly to pay stipends to reformed clergy. The system operated until early 17th century.

Thirlage. Obligation on a holding or its occupier to have grain ground in a particular mill, to which *multure* was paid.

Thirlestane (Berwickshire). There was probably a fortress of the de *Morville* family, to whom *David I* granted *Lauderdale,* and Edward I built a fort there; residence built by *John Maitland of Thirlestane* c. 1590 and enlarged by 1st Duke of Lauderdale, with *Sir William Bruce* as architect; widow of 15th Earl of L. (d. 1953) left it to her grandson, who took name of Maitland-Carew. Lands of Spittale mentioned 1541 may point to medieval hospital under abbey of *Dryburgh,* and there was a hospital on Lauderdale estate in late 17th century. A *burgh of regality* for Lady Mary Maitland 1661.

Thistle Bank. Founded 1761 by Sir Walter Maxwell of *Pollok* and other Glasgow merchants; absorbed in *Glasgow Union Bank* 1836.

Thistle Chapel. See Thistle, Order of the.

Thistle, Order of the. Origin assigned in mythology to *Achaius*; seems to have existed under *James V,* but would disappear at *Refor-*

mation; revived by *James VII* 1687 and re-established by Queen Anne 1703; consists of sovereign and 16 knights. Thistle Chapel added to *St Giles' Cathedral, Edinburgh* by *Sir Robert Lorimer* 1911.

Thom, James (1802-50). Born *Tarbolton*; builder's apprentice who turned to sculpture; made figures of 'Tam o' Shanter' and 'Souter Johnnie'; moved to Australia and then New York.

Thom, William (c. 1798-1848). Weaver; contributed 'The Blind Boy's Pranks' to the 'Aberdeen Herald' 1841; published 'Rhymes and Recollections'.

Thomas the Rhymer (Thomas of Ercildoun) (c. 1210- c. 1294). Mentioned in charter of 1260x1270; no authority for supposed surname of Learmonth; evidently wrote 'Romance of Sir Tristram'; his reputation as a prophet was referred to from 14th century onwards; alleged to have spent seven years in Elfland.

Thomson, Alexander (1817-75). Born Balfron; entered architect's office in *Glasgow* 1834; acquired distaste for Gothic style and his enthusiasm for Grecian models earned him the nickname 'Greek Thomson'; his work included a number of *United Presbyterian* churches, such as those in St Vincent Street and Caledonia Road, the Egyptian Hall in Union Street, most of Gordon Street, and Great Western Terrace—all in Glasgow.

Thomson, Sir Charles Wyville (1830-82). Born Bonnyside; professor of natural history at *Edinburgh* 1870; scientific director of the expedition of H.M.S. 'Challenger' 1872-6; wrote 'The Depths of the Sea'.

Thomson, George (1757-1851). Born Limekilns; clerk to *Board of Trustees for Manufactures*; collected Scottish music and published collections.

Thomson, James, of Ferniehill (1700-48). Born *Ednam*, son of parish *minister;* intended for church, but associated with others who shared his interest in literature and in 1725 went to London, with a poem 'Winter' which was published in 1726; other 'Seasons' followed; also wrote tragedies and 'The Masque of Alfred', which included 'Rule Britannia'.

Thomson, James (1768-1855). Born *Crieff*; co-editor of 3rd edition of '*Encyclopaedia Britannica*'; wrote articles on 'Scripture', 'Septuagint' etc.

Thomson, James (1822-92). Son of James T. (1786-1849), a mathematician; professor of civil engineering at Belfast 1857-73 and at *Glasgow* 1873-89; invented Vortex water-wheel.

Thomson, James (1834-82). Born *Port Glasgow*; became an army schoolmaster; wrote 'The City of Dreadful Night' and other verses.

Thomson, James Bruce (1810-73). Surgeon to *Perth* Prison 1858; expert on criminology and wrote papers in 'Journal of Mental Science'.

Thomson, James Charles (1887-1960). Born Eastertown of Gagie, *Angus*; son of a builder and nephew of inventor of pneumatic tyre; joined navy and was discharged on health grounds; studied nature cure in Chicago, then returned to Scotland 1912 and started practice; founded Kingston Clinic, *Edinburgh*, 1939.

Thomson, John (1778-1840). Brother of *Thomas Thomson; minister* of Dailly in succession to father 1800, and of *Duddingston* 1805; studied under *Alexander Nasmyth* and became successful landscape painter.

Thomson, Sir John Arthur (1861-1933). Born in East Lothian; studied at *Edinburgh*, Jena and Berlin; lecturer in biology at Edinburgh; professor of natural history, *Aberdeen*, 1899; wrote 'Secrets of Animal Life', 'Outline of Biology' and 'Science and Religion'.

Thomson, Joseph (1858-95). Born Penpont; explorer in central and east Africa, succeeding *A.K. Johnston* 1880.

Thomson, Robert William (1822-73). Born *Stonehaven*; merchant in Charleston, U.S.A., but returned home to become an engineer; took out patents for rubber tyres 1845 and fountain-pen 1849; devised machinery for sugar-manufacture, a steam-crane, hydraulic dock gates and a traction engine; while engaged on demolition work at *Dunbar Castle*, hit on idea of firing mines by electricity and undertook blasting operations on Cliffs of Dover.

Thomson, Roy Herbert, Lord Thomson of Fleet (1894-1976). Born Canada; British citizen 1963; acquired chain of newspapers, including 'Times' and '*Scotsman*'.

Thomson, Thomas (1768-1852). Son of *minister* of Dailly and brother of *John T*; *advocate* 1793; Deputy *Clerk Register* 1806; entered on ambitious plans for arranging, repairing, binding and indexing the Scottish archives, and pursued policy of publication, including 'Acts of the Parliaments of Scotland'; edited volumes for *Bannatyne Club*, of which he was President 1832; Principal Clerk of Session 1828; his casualness in finance led to his dismissal from his record appointment 1839.

Thomson, Thomas Napier (1798-1869). *Minis-*

ter at Maitland, New South Wales, 1831; returned home to edit *Robert Chambers*'s 'Biographical Dictionary of Eminent Scotsmen'.

Thomson, William (1824-1907). Brother of *James T*; born Belfast, where his father was professor of mathematics; moved to *Glasgow* when his father became professor there 1832; professor of *natural philosophy*, Glasgow, 1846-99; made outstanding discoveries in thermodynamics, electricity and navigation; created Lord Kelvin 1892.

Thomson, William, and Co. See Ben Line.

Thorburn, Grant (1773-1863). Nail-maker in *Dalkeith*; said to be original of *John Galt*'s 'Lawrie Todd'; emigrated to New York 1794 and became seed merchant; wrote 'Forty Years' Residence in America'.

Thorfinn (c. 1009-1065). Eldest son of *Sigurd, Earl of Orkney*, by daughter of *Malcolm II*; fought against his cousin, *Duncan I*, and perhaps partitioned Scottish kingdom with *Macbeth*; went to Rome c. 1050 and built cathedral at *Birsay* for bishop of his earldom of Orkney; his two sons fought with Harald Hardrada, King of Norway, at Stamford Bridge in 1066; his daughter *Ingibjorg* married *Malcolm III*.

Thornhill (or New Dalgarno) (Dumfriesshire). *Burgh of regality* for William, Lord *Drumlanrig*, 1664.

Thornton (Kincardineshire). Lands passed in early 14th century, by marriage, from a family of Thornton to Strachans, who held them for thirteen generations, until 1683; then passed through various hands until re-acquired by a Thornton 1893. Tower bears date 1531, but probably incorporates older work, and the building has been well preserved.

Threave Castle (Kirkcudbrightshire). Built on island in River Dee by *Archibald, 3rd Earl of Douglas*; captured by royal forces from *James, 9th Earl,* 1455; keepership vested in *Maxwells*, who became *Earls of Nithsdale*.

Three Estates. Took shape in 14th century as clergy, nobility and *burgesses*, the constituents of Scottish *Parliament* and *General Council* or later *Convention*; representatives of lesser crown tenants, below the rank of peers, came in after 1587 to form in effect a fourth estate; see *Clerical Estate*.

Threipland Family. Originated in *Kilbucho*, Peeblesshire, but in 1672 bought estate and castle of *Fingask*, Perthshire; Patrick was *provost* of *Perth* 1665 and was made a baronet 1687; his son Sir David (1666-1746) was active as a *Jacobite* in the 'Fifteen and the estates were *forfeited*, but his wife bought them back; Sir Stuart T. (1716-85) lost them again after the 'Forty-Five but was able to buy them back in 1783; baronetcy restored to his son Patrick (1762-1837) in 1826.

Thumbikins or **Thumbscrews.** Instrument of torture in use at least as early as 1491.

Thurso (*Caithness*). A castle of Norse *jarls* was destroyed in late 12th century, but a castle on the site (now in grounds of *manse* of St Andrew's Church) was occupied in 1612 by Sir John Sinclair of Greenland and Rattar and a later castle, built in 1640 and now roofless, was the home of *Sir John Sinclair* of Ulbster. Thurso became a *burgh of barony* for *Earl of Caithness* 1633.

Tibbermore. See Tippermuir.

Tibbers Castle (Dumfriesshire). Only vestiges remain of a castle which was allegedly built by the Romans and named after the Emperor Tiberius (who was dead long before the Romans reached Scotland); garrisoned by English in *War of Independence* and captured by *William Wallace* and later by *Robert I*, who destroyed it.

Tibbie Shiel. See Shiel, Tibbie.

Tillicoultry (Clackmannanshire). *Burgh of barony* for *Earl of Stirling* 1634.

Tillietudlem Castle. Scene of much incident in *Scott*'s *'Old Mortality'*; fictitious, but clearly based on *Craignethan*.

Tillyangus (*Clatt*, Aberdeenshire), **Battle of,** 1571. *Gordons* defeated Forbeses.

Tippermuir, Battle of, 1 September 1644. Victory of *Montrose* over *Covenanters*.

Tiree, Riot in, 1886. Crofters, resentful of rack-renting and insecurity, formed a Land League and seized a farm; the proprietor, the *Duke of Argyll*, obtained assistance of marines and police, in large numbers, and the offenders were jailed.

Tironensian Order. Monks of the order of Tiron, founded c. 1105 as a reform of the *Benedictine* order. See Arbroath, Fogo, Fyvie, Kelso, Kilwinning, Lesmahagow, Lindores and Selkirk.

Tobacco Lords. After the *Union* the tobacco trade with America developed rapidly in the *Clyde* area and it flourished until the American War of Independence. The 'Tobacco Lords' were the merchants who prospered accordingly. John Glassford, one of them, owned 25 ships and traded to the extent of £500,000 yearly.

Tobar Nan Ceann. See Well of Seven Heads.

Tobermory (Mull). Founded by *British Fisheries Society* 1788; *police burgh* under Act of 1862.

Tobermory Treasure. The 'Florida', ship of Spanish Armada, sank in Tobermory Bay 1588; rights of salvage granted by *Charles I* to *Earl of Argyll*; many attempts at salvage have recovered a number of articles, but not the expected treasure.

Toft. Plot of land, usually one of a series of such plots laid out in a *burgh* on a uniform plan.

Toisech. Dignitary referred to occasionally in early days; possibly either the head of a family group or an official at a lower level than the *mormaer*; the English term '*thane*' was introduced as its equivalent.

Tolbooth. Originally the booth where tolls or customs were collected; later the town house of a Scottish *burgh*, meeting place of town council and burgh court and often incorporating a prison.

Toleration Act, 1712. Toleration conceded to *Episcopalian* clergy who used 'the liturgy of the Church of England', provided that they prayed for the sovereign and royal family by name and fulfilled certain other conditions; the act led to the appearance of a number of '*Qualified*' congregations, sometimes called 'English' because they had to draw their clergy from England (or Ireland) and completely separate from the *non-juring* or *Jacobite* congregations under the Scottish bishops.

Tolquhon Castle (Aberdeenshire). Incorporates a tower built by Preston family who held lands until c. 1420, but mainly of late 16th century date, built by William, 7th *Forbes* laird; ruins in charge of Department of the Environment.

Tongland Abbey (Kirkcudbrightshire) *(Premonstratensian).* Founded by *Alan, Lord of Galloway*, c. 1218; held *in commendam* by *Bishop of Galloway* 1510-25 and annexed to bishopric from 1529 (when it was said to be ruinous), except when held by William Melville as *Commendator* 1588-1606.

Toom Tabard (= Empty Cloak). *John Balliol*, who was stripped of his royal insignia by Edward I in 1296.

Tore, Adam (fl. c. 1350). *Edinburgh burgess*; moneylender and master of the *mint*; engaged in negotiations in Low Countries 1348 and in England for release of *David II*.

Torfness, Battle of, 14 August 1040. *Thorfinn, Earl of Orkney*, defeated *Duncan II*, probably not far from *Burghead*.

Torhouse Standing Stones (Wigtownshire). Group of about 19 on circumference of circle and 3 in centre; alleged memorial to a king Galdus who conquered *Galloway* from Romans.

Torphichen, Preceptory. Headquarters of Knights of *St John of Jerusalem* in Scotland, established probably by *David I*; transepts, crossing and fragment of nave of church survive; property erected into *temporal lordship* for last *preceptor*, *Sir James Sandilands*, 1564.

Torrance Hospital (Stirlingshire). Dedicated to St Leonard; existed 1296; annexed to *collegiate church* of *Restalrig* by 1532.

Torry (Kincardineshire). *Burgh of barony* for abbey of *Arbroath* 1495.

Torry, Patrick (1763-1852). *Episcopalian minister* at *Peterhead*; Bishop of *St Andrews, Dunkeld* and *Dunblane* 1808.

Torthorwald (Dumfriesshire). Belonged to Kirkpatricks from 13th century, passed by marriage in 1418 to William Carlyle, who built a tower, surrounded by earthworks and now in ruins. Village made a *burgh of barony* for Lord Carlyle of Torthorwald 1473.

Torthorwald, Lordship. Sir John Carlyle created Lord C. of T. 1473-4. See Carlyle.

Tory. First applied to upholders of the traditional monarchy in *Charles II*'s reign; applied to conservative (sometimes *Jacobite*) faction in the 18th century and then to the generally conservative party which opposed reform in the early 19th; superseded by 'Conservative' in later 19th.

Touch (Stirlingshire). Belonged to Bernard *Fraser*, *sheriff* of Stirlingshire in 1234, and known as Touch Fraser; in hands of *Seton* family from 1510; 15th century tower had mansion added in late 16th.

Touraine, Duke of. Title conferred on *4th Earl of Douglas* and held by 5th and 6th Earls.

Towie Barclay Castle (Aberdeenshire). Built c. 1570, probably on site of 12th century fortress, by family of Barclay of Towie, on L-plan; restored as a residence 1970.

Town and County Bank. See Aberdeen.

Trades Maiden Hospital. Founded by *craftsmen* of *Edinburgh* in conjunction with *Mary Erskine*, originally in Horse Wynd, 1704; moved later to Argyle Square, then in 1855 to Rillbank House and in 1892 to Ashfield, Grange Loan; unlike other similar foundations it did not run its own school.

Trail. See St Mary's Isle.

Trail, Robert (1642-1716). Son of *minister* of *Elie*; associated with extreme *Covenanters*;

fled to Holland after *Pentland Rising*; wrote 'A Vindication of the Protestant Doctrine'.

Trail, Walter (d. 1401). Doctor of civil and canon law; *Bishop of St Andrews* 1385; ambassador to France 1391.

Trailtrow Hospital (Dumfriesshire). Dedicated to St James; first mentioned, as hospital for poor, 1455; extinct before 1609.

Train, Joseph (1779-1852). Born *Sorn*, Ayrshire; excise officer; wrote 'Poetical Reveries', 'Strains of the Mountain Muse' and 'Account of the Isle of *Man'*; supplied information to *Sir Walter Scott*, to *Lockhart* for his 'Life of *Burns*' and to *George Chalmers* for his 'Caledonia'.

Tranent (East Lothian). *Burgh of barony* for *Lord Seton* 1542; burgh of barony for *Earl of Winton* 1619. Cf. Militia.

Traprain (East Lothian). 'Dunpender' in early times. Surmounted by extensive hill-fort, a stronghold of the *Votadini*; the treasure of Traprain, found 1919, consisted of 160 articles of silver, much of it Roman work, probably looted from the continent in 4th century, and is now in *National Museum of Antiquities*.

Traquair, Earldom. Created 1633 for John Stewart of Traquair (d. 1659), who had been created Lord Stewart of T. 1628 and became *Treasurer* 1636; extinct on death of Charles, 8th Earl, 1861.

Traquair House (Peeblesshire). A residence in Traquair was used by 12th century kings; lands granted by *Robert I* to *Sir James Douglas* and subsequently passed through various hands, finally to Stewart *Earls of Buchan* in 1478, with a cadet of which family they long remained; present building claims exceptional antiquity but is mainly of 16th-17th century date. The Bear Gates have been closed for over two hundred years: one story is that they were closed after *Charles Edward* passed through them, not to be opened again except to a Stewart king; another that the 7th Earl closed them on the death of his wife, until another countess should pass through.

Treasurer. (1) Of kingdom: shared financial responsibility with *Comptroller*. (2) Of cathedral: had care of vestments, sacred vessels etc.

Treaty of Union. See Union with England.

Trefontains (Berwickshire). Supposed house of *Cistercian* nuns, but all that seems to have existed was a 'church or hospital' which in 1437 belonged to *Dryburgh Abbey*; in 1452 the lands were bestowed on *Dunglass collegiate church*.

Triduana, St. Supposed to have lived part of her life at Rescobie, *Angus*; the legend is that she was a Christian who, to escape the importunity of a pagan prince who admired her eyes, plucked them out and sent them to him on a skewer; devotion to her was believed to be efficacious against blindness; there were dedications to her at *Restalrig* and elsewhere, the name appearing as Trodwin and Tredwell.

Triennial Act, 1640. *Charles I* had to agree that *Parliament* should meet at least every three years even if the King did not summon it; annulled by *Act Rescissory* 1661.

Trimontium. Roman camp at Newstead, near *Melrose*, taking its name from the three peaks of the Eildon Hills.

Trinitarian Order, or **Red Friars.** Founded 1198 to redeem slaves and ransom captives. See Aberdeen, Berwick, Dirleton, Dunbar, Fail, Houston, Peebles, Scotlandwell. See also Kettins.

Trinity College. See Edinburgh and Glenalmond.

Trinity House. See Leith.

Tron. A weighing-beam in a market. For Tron Church, see Edinburgh.

Troon (Ayrshire). Developed as port by Duke of Portland from 1808; *police burgh*.

Troquhen (or Troquhain) (Kirkcudbrightshire). *Burgh of barony* for *Gordon* of Troquhen 1688.

Trot of Turriff, 14 May 1639. Opening engagement in the Covenanting Wars: Aberdeenshire royalists drove out small force of *Covenanters*.

Truce, Days of. On the Borders, the English and Scottish *wardens* held periodical meetings at which grievances by the subjects of one kingdom against those in the other could be redressed and prisoners found guilty on previous days of truce but who had escaped punishment were handed over. See Marches.

Trumwin. Bishop established by Angles at *Abercorn* in 681 for the part of *Pict*land subject to them; he had to retire after *Nechtansmere*.

Trustees' Academy. School of art founded in *Edinburgh* 1760.

Trysts. See Crieff, Falkirk.

Tudor, Margaret. See Margaret.

Tuitean Tarbhach, Battle of, 1397. Between *MacLeods* and MacKays near Kincardine, Ross.

Tulchan Bishops. Bishops appointed at instance of crown, from about 1540 onwards, under an arrangement whereby a large part of the revenues was diverted to lay hands in the shape of 'pensions'. A 'tulchan' was a kind of dummy calf placed beside a cow to persuade her to give milk.

Tullibardine Collegiate Church (Perthshire). Said to have been founded by Sir David Murray of Tullibardine 1446, but it may be doubted if this became effective and if the building (still well preserved) was ever more than a private chapel.

Tullibardine, Earldom and Marquisate. Earldom created 1606 for Sir John Murray of Tullibardine; his eldest son became *Earl of Atholl* and resigned earldom of Tullibardine to his brother Patrick 1628, but the title later reverted to Earl of Atholl. When the 2nd Marquis of Atholl became a Duke, in 1703, he was created also Marquis of Tullibardine.

Tullibardine, William Murray, Marquis of (1689-1746). 2nd son of John Murray, 1st *Duke of Atholl*; his eldest brother was killed at Malplaquet; took active part in *Jacobite* activities in 1715, 1719 and 1745; on his father's death the ducal title passed, through his forfeiture, to a younger brother, but in Jacobite eyes he was Duke of Atholl, and 'King James' (see James Francis) made him Duke of Rannoch 1717; after *Culloden* he surrendered and was sent to the Tower of London, where he died.

Tullibardine's Regiment. Raised 1694 as 'John, Lord Murray's, Regiment of Foot'; Murray became *Earl of Tullibardine* 1696 and his name passed to the regiment; disbanded 1697.

Tulliebole Castle (Fife). Built c. 1608 by John Halliday, son of an *advocate* who bought the estate 1598; property passed by marriage to Moncreiffs 1705.

Tullilum Priory (*Carmelite*) (*Perth*). Founded by Richard, *Bishop of Dunkeld*, 1262; first Carmelite house in Scotland.

Tulloch, John (1823-86). Born Dron; *minister* at *Dundee* 1844 and *Kettins* 1849; professor of theology at *St Mary's College*, *St Andrews*; principal 1854.

Tun. Measure of capacity for wine, standardised at 60 gallons.

Turgot (d. 1115). Prior of Durham 1087; confessor to *Queen Margaret*, a biography of whom is attributed to him; appointed *Bishop of St Andrews* by *Alexander I* 1109, but could not agree to repudiate obedience to York and was in effect displaced.

Turnberry Bond, September 1286. Bond by supporters of claim of *Robert Bruce* to Scottish throne after death of *Alexander III*.

Turnberry Castle (Ayrshire). Ruins remain of a castle which belonged to the *Earls of Carrick* and may have been birthplace of *Robert I*; King Robert started from there in 1307 on his ultimately successful campaign.

Turnbull, William (c. 1410-54). *Parson* of *Hawick*, *archdeacon* of *Lothian*, *Secretary* (1441-2) and Keeper of *Privy Seal*; *Bishop of Glasgow* 1447; obtained bull for foundation of *Glasgow University* 1451; doctor of canon law, probably of Pavia.

Turner. Copper coin worth 2d.

Turner, Sir James (1615-?1686). Son of *minister* of *Borthwick* and *Dalkeith*; entered Swedish army 1632; returned to join army of the *Covenant*; sided with *Engagers* 1648; captured at *Preston* and again at *Worcester*; joined *Charles II* in Paris; in charge of operations against *Covenanters* 1666; captured by them at *Dumfries*, escaped after *Rullion Green*; spent later life in retirement; wrote 'Pallas Armata' (essays on the art of war) and also 'Memoirs'; thought to be the original of Dugald Dalgetty in *Scott*'s 'Legend of Montrose'.

Turnpike Acts. The first was for Midlothian 1714, and there were 350 between 1750 and 1844; tolls were levied on the roads and administered by Turnpike Trusts for road maintenance.

Turriff (Aberdeenshire). Abbot of 'Turbruaid' mentioned c. 1150, but no other evidence of Celtic abbey. Hospital founded by *Alexander Comyn, Earl of Buchan*, 1273; revenues annexed to prebend of *Aberdeen Cathedral* 1412. *Burgh of barony* for *Earl of Errol* 1512.

Turriff, Trot of. See Trot.

Tusculan Society. Founded in *Edinburgh* 1822 for discussion of legal and speculative questions.

Tushielaw Tower (Selkirkshire). Ruin which was the stronghold of Adam Scott, 'The King of Thieves' or 'King of the Border', who was executed 1529.

Tweeddale, Earldom and Marquisate. Earldom created 1646 for John, 8th Lord Hay of *Yester* (c. 1593-1654); marquisate created for 2nd Earl 1694.

Tweeddale, John Hay, 2nd Earl and 1st Marquis of (1625-97). Son of 1st Earl, whom he succeeded 1654; fought against *Charles I* at *Marston Moor* and with *Engagers* at *Preston*; sat in *Commonwealth parliaments*; President of *Council* 1663 and joined moderate party against *Lauderdale*; dismissed 1674, readmitted 1680; *Chancellor* 1692-6.

Tweeddale, John Hay, 2nd Marquis of (1645-1713). Son of preceding; *Treasurer* 1695; associated with *Jacobites* 1703, but Commissioner for the Queen to the *Parliament* of 1704 and *Chancellor* 1704-5; headed *Squadrone Volante* and led it to support *Union*.

Tweedsmuir, Lord. See Buchan, John.

Twopenny Faith. Brief exhortation on the Eucharist issued by the *Provincial Council* of 1559 for instruction of the people.

Tyepers Well, Foray at, c. 1544. Party of Stewarts of *Appin*, marauding through Menteith, seized the provisions ready for a wedding feast; the *Earl of Menteith*, one of the guests, pursued them and engaged them at Tyepers Well, in the Trossachs, and the Earl was killed.

Tyninghame (East Lothian). A monastery supposed to have been founded by St *Baldred* was sacked by Scandinavians 941; a very fine parish church was built in 12th century and parts of it survive, though it was superseded by another building. Lands and barony granted to George *Lauder* of the *Bass* 1591, but in 1628 granted to 1st *Earl of Haddington*; his successors built Tyninghame House, which was much enlarged 1829 by *Burn*.

Tyrie, James (1543-97). Joined Jesuits in Rome 1563; wrote a 'Refutation' against *John Knox* and publicly disputed with *Andrew Melville* in Paris in 1574.

Tytler, Alexander Fraser (1747-1813). Elder son of *William T;* professor of universal history in *Edinburgh* 1780-1802; *Lord of Session* (Woodhouselea) 1802; compiled 'Decisions of Court of *Session*' and wrote 'Life of Lord *Kames*'.

Tytler, James (c. 1747-1805). Son of *minister* in *Brechin*; studied medicine in *Edinburgh*; tried to set up laboratory in Newcastle; returned to Edinburgh and was in debtors' sanctuary at *Holyrood*; made successful balloon flight 1784; wrote for 2nd and 3rd editions of '*Encyclopaedia Britannica*', 'Pamphlet on the Excise' and 'Historical Register'; emigrated to America and died there.

Tytler, Patrick Fraser (1791-1849). Son of *Alexander T*; associated with *Thomas Thomson* and *Sir Walter Scott* in historical work and wrote 'History of Scotland' in 9 volumes (1828-43).

Tytler, William (1711-92). Wrote 'An Inquiry into the Evidence against *Mary*, Queen of Scots' (1759).

U

Udal Law. In *Orkney and Shetland* udal tenure persisted at least until the 17th century: land was held in absolute property, not of a *superior*, and was divisible among heirs instead of passing by primogeniture; property also extended below high-water mark, down to the lowest stone in the ebb, and this rule has continued to affect fishing and other rights down to the present.

Udny (Aberdeenshire). Property belonged to family of Udny from 1426 if not earlier until the 20th century when the line died out and it passed to Lord *Belhaven* and Stenton. The castle consisted of a massive three-storeyed tower, probably of 14th century date, with 19th century additions.

Ugadale Brooch. Said to have been given by *Robert I* to Gilchrist MacKay and preserved by MacNeals of Ugadale at Lossit Park.

Ulster, Plantation of. Hugh *Montgomerie* and James Hamilton were pioneers in the settlement of County Down in 1605. In 1610 the six counties came into the hands of the crown by the forfeiture of native landlords, and the settlement of English and Lowland Scots (mainly from the south-west) went on on a considerable scale.

Umfraville, Family of. A Norman of this name, settled in England, was associated with *David I*, from whom he received lands probably in Stirlingshire. Gilbert married Matilda, Countess of Angus, c. 1240 and that earldom was held by their son, Gilbert (c. 1244-1307) and their grandson (1277-1325), who fought against *Robert I*, was taken prisoner at *Bannockburn*, and lost his Scottish lands; in the next generation another Gilbert supported *Edward Balliol* and was recognised in England as *Earl of Angus*.

Unicorn. Gold coin from reign of *James III*, worth 18s. or 23s.

Unicorn, Order of the. The unicorn was the supporter of the Scottish royal arms from the reign of *James II*, if not earlier. There is some reason to believe that the Order of the *Thistle* was foreshadowed by an Order of the Unicorn, conferred by *James III* on Anselmo Adorno, his agent in Bruges, whose arms, on his tomb in Bruges, are surrounded with the collar of such an order.

Unicorn Pursuivant. First mentioned 1426. See Pursuivants.

Union Bank of Scotland. Name adopted in 1843 by *Glasgow Union Banking Company*; amalgamated with *Bank of Scotland* 1955.

Union Canal. Completed 1822, linking a basin at Lothian Road, *Edinburgh* (Port Hopetoun and Port Hamilton), with the *Forth and Clyde Canal* at *Falkirk*, to which it descended by a series of locks; otherwise its whole course was level.

Union Duke. See Queensberry, 2nd Duke of.

Union with England. *James VI*'s accession to the English throne in 1603 produced only a personal link, for there were still two kingdoms, each with its own institutions of government. There was a legislative and incorporating union (by compulsion) under the *Commonwealth* and *Protectorate* in the 1650s. The Union of 1707, drawn up by commissioners and subsequently approved after debate in the two parliaments, was legislative and to a large extent administrative, and came into effect on 1 May 1707, when the kingdoms of England and Scotland alike ceased to exist and were incorporated in a United Kingdom of Great Britain. In the 19th century separate Scottish boards began to be set up for various functions, and in the 20th separate Scottish departments took over most Scottish administration, in a process of administrative devolution. See Dover House; St Andrew's House; Home Rule Bills; Kilbrandon Report.

United Alkali Company. Formed 1890 by the chemical companies founded by *Charles Tennant* in 1800, with other companies.

United Free Church. Formed 1900 by union of *Free Church* (with a dissenting minority) and *United Presbyterian Church*. In 1929 it joined the *Church of Scotland*, though a minority continued the U.F. Church.

United Industrial School (or Dr Guthrie's School). Instituted in *Edinburgh* in 1847 by *Thomas Guthrie* and some wealthy supporters to educate destitute juveniles; first situated in Blackfriars Street, it later moved to Liberton.

United Original Secession. Formed 1842 from two groups of *Old Light* Seceders; joined *Free Church* 1852 but minority continued to 1956.

United Presbyterian Church. Formed 1847 by union of most of the *New Light* Seceders and the *Relief Church*. See United Free Church.

United Scotsmen. Revolutionary society, in imitation of United Irishmen, founded 1796 and suppressed 1799.

United Secession. Union of most of the *New Light* Seceders, formed 1820; joined *Relief Church* 1847, to form *United Presbyterian Church*.

United Thread Manufacturing Company. Was formed 1896 by amalgamation of firms of *Coats* and Clark.

United Turkey Red Company. Formed 1898 by chief dyeing companies of Vale of Leven.

Universities. See Aberdeen, Dundee, Edinburgh, Fraserburgh, Glasgow, Heriot-Watt, St Andrews, Stirling, Strathclyde.

Up Helly Aa. Festival held annually in *Lerwick* on last Tuesday in January. At one time no more than the burning of a tar-barrel, a rite known elsewhere, it has since the beginning of this century become invested with a lot of 'Viking' ceremonial: replica of a longship, manned by a Guiser *Jarl* and his crew, in appropriate costume, is drawn through the streets accompanied by a procession of hundreds of torch-bearers, then burned. The festival is held to mark the end of the Christmas festivities and the point at which men looked forward to resuming seafaring in the longer days of spring.

Upsetlington Hospital. See Horndean.

Ure, Andrew (1778-1857). Professor of chemistry at *Anderson's College*, *Glasgow*, 1804; director of Glasgow Observatory 1809 and inaugurated popular lectures; wrote 'Dictionary of Chemistry' and 'Dictionary of Arts, Manufactures and Mines'.

Urie (Kincardineshire). Land passed from *Frasers* to Keiths, by whom it was sold in early 15th century to Hays, Lords of *Errol*; returned to Keith, Earl *Marischal*, 1640 and sold 1647 to *David Barclay*.

Urquhart Castle (Loch Ness, Inverness-shire). Began as royal fortress c. 1200; captured by Edward I 1297 and 1303; *James IV* conferred lordship and castle on John Grant of Freuchie; part blown up by powder 1691 and since then a ruin.

Urquhart Priory (*Benedictine*) (*Moray*). Founded by *David I* c. 1136; dependency of *Dunfermline* by c. 1153; united to *Pluscarden* 1454; erected into *temporal lordship* for Alexander Seton, *Earl of Dunfermline*; very few remains.

Urquhart, Sir Thomas, of *Cromarty* (1611-60). Fought for *Charles I* against *Covenanters*; knighted 1641; taken prisoner at *Worcester*, released on parole and went to continent, where he died; wrote 'Epigrams, Divine and Moral' (1641), 'Treatise on Trigonometry' (1645) and 'An Introduction to the Universal Language' (1653), besides more quaint and eccentric works, and he translated Rabelais.

Urr (Kirkcudbrightshire). The 'motte' is an outstanding example of the remains of a *motte-and-bailey castle*. Urr is referred to as a *burgh* in 1262.

Urry (or **Hurry), Sir John** (d. 1650). Born *Pitfichie*, Aberdeenshire; leader of one of the *Covenant*ing armies defeated by *Montrose*, but served with Montrose at *Carbisdale*; was captured and beheaded.
Usher Hall (*Edinburgh*). Andrew Usher, a member of the brewing family, gave £100,000 to the city of Edinburgh for the erection of a concert hall; foundation stone laid 1911; opened 1914.
Uthrogle Hospital (Fife). Dedicated to St John Baptist; first mentioned 1380; granted, evidently with an associated chapel, to *Trinity College, Edinburgh*, 1462.

V

Vacomagi. Tribe located in east-central Highlands in Roman times.
Valentia. Roman province organised in late 4th century by Theodosius, general under Emperor Valentinian, in territory recovered from invading tribes; possibly in south-west Scotland, possibly in North Wales.
Valladolid, Scots College at. A college in *Madrid* was transferred to Valladolid 1772 when *Bishop Geddes* brought a dozen students to take possession; driven to Corunna under French occupation, 1808-16, and driven out of Spain again 1937 but returned 1950.
Vallance, William Fleming (1827-1904). At first painted portraits and genre works, then Irish life and character, and finally specialised in sea and shipping scenes.
Valleyfield (Fife). *Burgh of barony* for Preston of Valleyfield 1663.
Valliscaulian Order. See Ardchattan, Beauly, Pluscarden.
Vans (or **Vaus**), **Sir Patrick,** of Barnbarroch (d. 1597). *Parson* of *Wigtown* 1568; ambassador to Denmark 1587; *Lord of Session* (Barnbarroch).
Vassal. See Superior.
Vaus (or **Vascus**), **John** (c. 1490-1538). Born *Aberdeen*; studied in Paris; professor of Latin at Aberdeen 1516; wrote Latin Grammar (1522).
Vaux, de, Family. Acquired barony of *Dirleton* under *William I*.
Veere. See Staple.
Veitch, William (1640-1722). Ordained 1664; outlawed as *Covenanter* 1667 and fled to England; imprisoned on *Bass Rock* after *Bothwell Brig*; found safety in Holland 1683.
Vennel. Narrow passage, lane or wynd, usually between houses in a *burgh*.
Verneuil, Battle of, 17 August 1424. French and Scots, under *John, Earl of Buchan*, and *Archibald, Earl of Douglas*, defeated by English under Duke of Bedford.
Vetch, Samuel (1688-1732). Son of *William Veitch*; educated at Utrecht; commissioned in Dutch army; accompanied *William of Orange* to England 1688; officer in *Cameronian Regiment* at *Dunkeld* 1689; fought in Low Countries; took part in *Darien* expedition; settled in Albany, New York.
Veterinary Colleges. See Dick Veterinary College. College founded in *Glasgow* by James McCall in 1863 was absorbed in *University* 1959.
Veto Act (1833-4). Act permitting majority of male heads of families in a congregation to reject a presentation by a patron, brought up in *General Assembly* 1833 and passed 1834.
Vicar. Incumbent of a parish from which the bulk of revenues had been *appropriated*.
Vienne, John de. Admiral of France; landed in Scotland in May 1385 with force of knights and men at arms to stimulate Scots into invading England; left again November 1385.
Viking Club. Founded 1892 as *Orkney*, Shetland and Northern Society, to deal with northern history, literature, language etc.
Vitrified Forts. Structures of the early centuries of this era, in which the stones have been fused together by the burning of timber core or interlacing.
'Vitruvius Britannicus'. See Campbell, Colin.
Votadini. See Gododdin.
Volusenus. See Wilson, Florence.

W

W.S. See Writers to the Signet.
Waddell, Peter Hately (1817-91). *Minister* of *Girvan* 1844-61 and *Glasgow* 1862-88; edited Poems of *Burns* and *Scott*'s Waverley Novels.
Wade, Field-Marshal George (1673-1748). Served in various theatres of war before becoming Commander-in-Chief in Scotland in 1724 with the task of demilitarising the Highlands; in addition to regulars, he had six Highland companies, which in 1739, increased to ten, formed the *Black Watch Regiment*; between 1725 and 1738 carried out most of his road-making, mainly along the Great Glen, from *Dunkeld* to *Inverness* and from *Crieff* to

Fort Augustus, in all extending to about 250 miles and necessitating 42 bridges; many military roads of later date are wrongly ascribed to him; Commander-in-Chief in England 1745 and operated against *Jacobite* army.

Wade Roads. See preceding entry.

Wadset. Conveyance of land in reversion, that is in 'wad' or pledge for money borrowed; the lender, who acquired possession of the land, was the 'wadsetter'.

Wagering Club. Founded in *Edinburgh* 1775 by Bain Whyt, *W.S.*, and still meeting annually in January; the bets, mostly relating to current affairs, have been recorded in books still extant, and the proceeds go to charity.

Wagonways. Wooden or iron rails were laid for the use of wagons drawn by horses, before steam locomotion; early examples were *Tranent-Cockenzie* 1722, *Fordell* c. 1752 and *Alloa* 1768. See Railways.

Waid, Alexander (1736-1803). Born *Anstruther*; Lieutenant R.N; left money for foundation of an academy for orphan boys and seamen's sons in indigent circumstances; Waid Academy ultimately opened 1886 in conjunction with School Board.

Walker, Helen (d. 1791). Her exploit in walking to London to petition for the life of her sister, condemned to death for infanticide, provided the model for *Sir Walter Scott's Jeannie Deans.* Scott erected a memorial to her in the churchyard of Kirkpatrick-Irongray, Kirkcudbrightshire.

Walker, James (c. 1770-1841). Born *Fraserburgh*; *minister* of St Peter's Episcopalian Chapel, *Edinburgh*; first Pantonian professor of theology; *Bishop of Edinburgh* 1830; *Primus* 1837.

Walker, Robert (1755-1808). Born Monkton, Ayrshire, son of *minister* of Scots Church at Rotterdam; minister of *Canongate*, Edinburgh, 1784.

Walkinshaw, Clementina (c. 1726-1802). Daughter of Walkinshaw of Baronfield; met Prince *Charles Edward* in January 1746; in 1752 he called her to join him on the continent and she became his mistress.

Wall, Maggie (d. 1657). Witch whose execution near Duncrub, on the *Dunning-Auchterarder* road, is commemorated by a cairn.

Wallace Family. The name is associated with the Welsh border, meaning 'Welshman', and it is believed that the first Wallace in Scotland, in the 12th century, had come from Shropshire, but it could have originated on the fringe of the old Welsh or British realm of *Strathclyde*. A contemporary of *William Wallace* was Sir Henry Wallace, Lord Mayor of London.

Wallace, Alexander (fl. 1679). Earliest recorded Pipe-Major, in *Dumbarton's Regiment* 1679.

Wallace, James (d. 1688). *Minister* of Lady Kirk, *Orkney*, and later of *Kirkwall*; wrote 'Description of Orkney'.

Wallace, James (d. c. 1724). Son of preceding; republished his father's book and wrote 'History of Scotland'.

Wallace, John (d. 1723). Born *Closeburn*, Dumfriesshire; a successful *Glasgow* merchant, he left £1400 sterling to found a school (Wallace Hall Academy) in his native town.

Wallace Monuments. (1) Colossal statue near *Dryburgh*, erected by 11th *Earl of Buchan* in 1814; (2) Tower on *Abbey Craig*, completed 1869.

Wallace, Robert (1697-1771). Born Kincardine, Perthshire; *minister* of *Moffat*, *Greyfriars*, *Edinburgh* and New North, Edinburgh; published dissertations on social questions and on population and shares the credit for '*Webster's Census*'.

Wallace, Sir William (c. 1270-1305). Second son of Sir Malcolm W. of Elderslie, Renfrewshire; a leader of resistance to English 1297; in association with *Andrew Moray* was victorious at *Stirling Bridge*; knighted, and a *Guardian* in name of *John Balliol* 1298; defeated at *Falkirk*; gave up Guardianship and lapsed into obscurity; captured by English 1305 and executed in London (23 August).

Wallace's Beef-Tower. The great donjon in *Bothwell Castle*.

Wallace's Cairn. Commemorates skirmish by *William Wallace* at Loudoun Hill, Ayrshire.

Wallace's Larder. Dungeon in Craigs Castle, *Ardrossan*, where *William Wallace* is said to have thrown the bodies of the defenders after he captured the castle.

Wallace's Trench. Name given to tumulus 63 feet in circumference, near Blair Drummond Lodge, Kincardine, *Menteith*.

Walls, William (1860-1942). Born *Dunfermline*; trained in *Edinburgh* and Antwerp; especially interested in painting animals, and helped in formation of Edinburgh Zoo.

Waltheof (d. 1159). Son of Simon de St Liz and Maud, daughter of Waltheof, Earl of Northumberland, and consequently stepson of *David I*; Abbot of *Melrose* 1148.

Walton, Edward Arthur (1860-1922). Born Renfrewshire; studied art with W.Y. MacGregor and painted with *Sir James Guthrie* and

Joseph Crawhall; associated with *Glasgow School*; painted landscape and, later, portraits; after ten years in London, returned to *Edinburgh* 1904.

Wappinschaws. Periodical days of muster, when men had to turn out with their weapons and perform military exercises.

War of Independence. Could apply to Anglo-Scottish Wars from 1296 to the 1540s, but usually means the campaigns between 1296 and 1328; sometimes the renewed war in *David II*'s reign is called the Second War of Independence. See Robert I and Wallace, Sir William.

Warbeck, Perkin (d. 1499). Claimed to be younger of the two Princes murdered in the Tower of London; came to Scotland 1495 and married Katharine Gordon, daughter of 2nd Earl of *Huntly;* left Scotland 1497.

Ward. (1) Feudal *casualty* whereby the *superior* of lands enjoyed them during the minority of the vassal's heir. (2) The duty of garrisoning a castle (= castle-ward) or of doing sentry duty on town walls (= watch and ward).

Wardens of the Marches. Officials responsible for the defence and administration of the Border country, on both sides of the frontier. There were three Scottish wardenries, the East, Middle and West, but two or three could be held by one man.

Wardlaw, Henry (c. 1370-1440). Nephew of *Walter Wardlaw*; *Bishop of St Andrews* 1403; instrumental in establishing *St Andrews University*, of which he was first chancellor.

Wardlaw Manuscript. Genealogy of the *Frasers*, compiled by James Fraser, *minister* of Wardlaw. Now in *National Library*.

Wardlaw, Walter (c. 1317-90). Canon of *Glasgow* 1342; Rector of Paris University 1345; *archdeacon* of *Dunkeld* 1349 and of *Lothian* 1359; secretary to *David II* c. 1363; Bishop of Glasgow 1368; created Cardinal by Avignon Pope 1381.

Wardrop, John, and Co. Banking business in *Edinburgh* c. 1802-10.

Warrender, Sir George John Scott (1860-1917). 7th Baronet; entered navy 1873; took part in naval operations at Boxer Rising; commanded 2nd Battle Squadron of Grand Fleet 1914.

Watch and Ward. See Ward.

Watson, George (d. 1723). Merchant in *Edinburgh* and first accountant of *Bank of Scotland*; left money for foundation of hospital for maintenance and education of sons and grandsons of 'decayed' Edinburgh merchants; in 1870 the institution was reorganised as a day school for boys, and a girls' school was opened 1871.

Watson, James (d. 1722). Printer in *Edinburgh* 1695; published 'Edinburgh Gazette' and 'Edinburgh Courant'; his widow carried on his business.

Watson, James and Robert. Private bankers in *Glasgow*, in business by 1793 in succession to firm set up by David Watson in 1763; failed 1832.

Watson, John. See John Watson's School.

Watson, John MacLaren (1850-1907). See MacLaren, Ian.

Watson, William (1865-1948). Rector of *Inverness Academy* and of Royal *High School, Edinburgh* (1909-14); professor of Celtic at Edinburgh, 1914-38; wrote 'Celtic Place-Names of Scotland' (1926).

Watson-Watt, Sir Robert Alexander (1892-1973). Born *Brechin*, son of joiner; assistant to Professor Peddie of chair of natural history in University College, Dundee (see Dundee University); joined Department of Scientific and Industrial Research 1921 and later became Director of Communications Development; his work developed use of radar.

Watt, George Fiddes (1873-1930). Born *Aberdeen*; successful portrait painter, whose works included many notables of his day.

Watt Institution. See Heriot-Watt.

Watt, James (1736-1819). Born *Greenock*; worked in London, then in *Glasgow*, as instrument-maker; devised separate condenser for steam engine, the flywheel and the governor; entered partnership with Matthew Boulton at Birmingham (Soho works) for manufacture of engines. See also Murdock, William.

Watt, Robert (1774-1819). Born *Stewarton*; schoolmaster at *Symington*; qualified in medicine and practised in *Paisley* and *Glasgow*; published medical papers and catalogue of medical books, then 'Bibliotheca Britannica', a general catalogue of authors with an index of subjects.

Wauchope, Major-General Andrew Gilbert (1846-99). Born Niddrie-Marischal; cadet in navy, but changed to *Black Watch*; served in various colonial wars and at Omdurman; commanded Highland Brigade in South African War; killed at Magersfontein.

Wauchope, Robert (d. 1551). A theologian who, though blind, attained fame on the continent; *James V* refused to have him as *Commendator* of *Dryburgh*, and in 1543 the *Governor Arran* refused to have him as *Bishop of Dunkeld*, though he received a pension from that see; he taught in Paris and was associated with the abbey of St James at *Ratisbon*; appointed Archbishop of Armagh 1539, he attended the Council of Trent.

Waverley, Viscount. See Anderson, Sir John.

Webster, Alexander (1707-84). Son of *minister* of Tolbooth parish, *Edinburgh*, and, after serving at *Culross* (1733-7), was himself appointed to Tolbooth; popular preacher and leading '*Evangelical*', but also a convivial member of intellectual society of Edinburgh; his work in connection with annuities for ministers' widows proved his statistical ability and led him on to compile, through the parish ministers, an unofficial 'census' which gave the population of Scotland in 1755 as 1,265,000; much of the credit for the work belongs to *Robert Wallace*.

Webster's Census. See preceding entry.

Wedderburn, Alexander (1733-1805). Born East Lothian; *advocate* 1752; barrister in London 1753; counsel for Lord Clive and in *Douglas Cause*; M.P. for *Inveraray* burghs; *Solicitor General*, Attorney General and Lord Chancellor (1793-1801); created Lord Loughborough 1780 and Earl of *Rosslyn* 1801.

Wedderburn, David (1580-1646). Master of *Aberdeen Grammar School* 1602-40; professor at *Marischal College*, *Aberdeen* 1614-24; wrote a Latin grammar.

Wedderburn, James (c. 1495-1553). Merchant at Dieppe and Rouen; wrote various verse works, including anti-papal ballads.

Wedderburn, James (1585-1639). Held charges in England; professor of divinity at *St Andrews* 1617; *Bishop of Dunblane* 1636; had an important share in the preparation of the *Prayer Book* of 1637; deposed 1638.

Wedderburn, John (c. 1500-1556). Brother of *James W.* and associated with him in composing anti-papal verses.

Wedderburn, Sir Peter (c. 1616-79). *Advocate*; Clerk of *Privy Council* 1661-8; *Lord of Session* (Gosford) 1668.

Wedderburn, Robert (c. 1515-1557). Brother of *James W.* and associated with him in composing anti-papal ballads.

'Wee Frees'. The minority of the *Free Church* which declined to enter into union with the *United Presbyterian Church* in 1900 and continued as the Free Church.

Weir, Major Thomas, of Kirktown (c. 1600-1670). Born Lanarkshire; lieutenant in army sent by *Covenanters* to protect Ulster colonists 1641; later a major in Lanark's regiment; appointed to command *City Guard* of *Edinburgh*; a *Remonstrant* 1650; outwardly religious, but secretly addicted to various crimes; confessed his guilt at age of 70 and was burned with his sister.

Welch, John (1568-1622). *Minister* of *Selkirk* 1589 and of *Ayr* 1604; married a daughter of *John Knox*; imprisoned and later banished for his adherence to *presbyterianism*; went to France 1606; allowed to return to England 1622 and died in London.

Well of Seven Heads. On road by Loch Oich; when two sons of a 17th century chief of the *Keppoch* MacDonalds were murdered, the seven murderers were captured and killed and their heads cut off and washed in the well before being presented to Keppoch.

Wells, William (1872-1923). Born *Glasgow*; in 1885 went with parents to Australia; returned to study in London and Paris, then lived in Isle of *Man* and Devon; his painting mainly of landscapes.

Welsh, David (1793-1845). Born *Moffat*; *minister* of Crossmichael and *Glasgow*; professor of church history in *Edinburgh*; wrote 'Life of Dr Thomas Brown' and 'Elements of Church History'.

Welsh, Jane (1801-66). Born *Haddington*; descended from *John Welch*; daughter of Dr John W; married *Thomas Carlyle*.

Welwood, William (d. 1622). Professor of law and of mathematics at *St Andrews*; discovered principle of siphon 1577; wrote on 'Sea Law'.

Wemyss (Fife). Named from the coastal caves (*Gaelic* 'uaimh'). Wemyss Castle dates in part from 13th century, but was much altered and enlarged in 16th. West Wemyss became a *burgh of barony* for Wemyss of that *ilk* 1511.

Wemyss, Earldom. Created 1633 for Sir John Wemyss. 4th Earl was a Commissioner for *Union*. David, Lord Elcho (1721-87), was attainted for his part in the '*Forty-Five*, but the title was restored in 1826 to his brother, who built Gosford House in East Lothian and who had succeeded to the Earldom of March; the Wemyss estates in Fife were settled on the 3rd son of the 5th Earl.

Wemyss Family. Sir David Wemyss was one of the ambassadors sent to Norway in 1290 to fetch the *Maid of Norway* and Sir Michael was a little later a supporter of *John Balliol*.

Wemyss Ware. Produced in Fife Pottery, Kirkcaldy, 1883-1930.

West Highland Museum. In Cameron Square, *Fort William*.

West Kerse (Stirlingshire). *Burgh of barony* for Hope of Kerse 1643.

West Register House. See Register House.
Wester Duddingston (Midlothian). *Burgh of barony* for *Duke of Lauderdale* 1673.
Western Bank of Scotland. Founded 1832; failed 1857.
Westminster Assembly. A gathering of English *Presbyterian* divines, at which six Scots were present as 'assistants', which met in 1643 in fulfilment of the *Solemn League and Covenant*; it framed a Confession of Faith, Larger and Shorter Catechisms, a Directory of Public Worship and a Form of Church Government, all of which were accepted by the *Church of Scotland* but found little support in England.
Westminster Confession. See Westminster Assembly.
Westminster-Ardtornish, Treaty of, February-March 1462. John, *Lord of the Isles* and *Earl of Ross*, and the 9th *Earl of Douglas*, became pensioners of the English king, Edward IV, on the understanding that if England conquered Scotland the territories north of the Forth would be divided between them as English *vassals*.
De Wet, James (fl. 1684). Dutch artist who in 1684 was commissioned by *Charles II*, then reconstructing *Holyrood*, to paint over 100 portraits of 'Scottish kings', for which he received £120 a year for two years.
Wet Review. Review of Volunteers by Queen Victoria in *Holyrood* Park, *Edinburgh*, 25 August 1881.
Wheatley Report. Royal Commission under Lord Wheatley recommended reorganisation of local government into regions and districts, 1969; its recommendations, with not inconsiderable modifications, became law 1975.
Wheel Hospital (Roxburghshire). Chapel mentioned 1347 and hospital 1348; attached to *Jedburgh Abbey*; described as 'waste' in 1600.
Whiggamore Raid. After the battle of *Preston* the extreme *Covenanters* of the south-west marched on *Edinburgh* and set up a radical government in alliance with Cromwell.
Whigs. Initially the extreme *Covenanters* of the south-west in the middle and late 17th century; the supporters of the Hanoverian establishment in the 18th; the supporters of reform in late 18th and early 19th; superseded by 'Liberals'..
Whigs' Vault. Apartment in *Dunnottar Castle* where *Covenanters* were confined in 1685.
Whim House (near Lamancha, Peeblesshire). Built by *3rd Duke of Argyll* and sold in 1761 to *James Montgomery*, baron of the *Exchequer*; later occupied by John Maitland Thomson, the record scholar.
Whipmen. The term obviously meant men whose occupation involved handling horses, and there were various organisations of them, with certain associated festivities. In West Linton a Whipman Play was held annually in September; in *Kelso* the Whipman's Ride was an outing annually for ploughmen, grooms and others; in *Ayr* the Whipmen—carriers, coachmen, saddlers and others—formed a benevolent society in 1765 and in 1808 purchased the Whip Inn, which they owned until 1948.
Whistle-Gibbon. Jester to *James IV*.
Whitburn (West Lothian). *Police burgh* under 1862 act.
Whitby, Synod of. In 663 or 664 King Oswiu of Northumbria decided to adopt the Roman ruling on the date of Easter and the form of the tonsure, and the Celtic monks in his kingdom withdrew.
White Cockade. Rosette worn on the hat as a *Jacobite* badge.
White Fish Authority. Established 1951.
White Star Line. Shipping Company formed in 1825 at *Aberdeen*, by George Thompson, initially to convey emigrants to Canada.
Whitekirk (East Lothian). Place of pilgrimage in middle ages, visited by *Aeneas Sylvius Piccolomini* (later Pope Pius II). The existing church is largely 15th century, but was much restored in 1885 and again after being burned by suffragettes in 1913.
Whitford, Walter (c. 1581-1647). *Minister* of *Kilmarnock* 1608, *Moffat* 1610 and Failford 1619 (cf. *Fail*); *Bishop of Brechin* 1635; deposed 1638 and died in England.
Whithorn (Wigtownshire). *Burgh* granted by *Robert I* to *Whithorn Priory*; *royal burgh* 1511.
Whithorn Cathedral and Priory. St *Ninian* is said to have built a stone church at Whithorn c. 400; there were bishops in the 8th century, but no proof of continuity until better evidence begins in early 12th; a romanesque cathedral was begun at that time, and some of its stonework is incorporated in nave walls still standing and largely of 17th century date. There may have been a house of another order by 1161 and before *Premonstratensians* were introduced in 1177; priory property annexed to *bishopric of Galloway* 1605. The original dedication was to St Martin of Tours.
Whitsunday. One of the main *term days*, which continued to be movable, with the Church's Kalendar, until 1693, when it was fixed at 15

May. While the Latin term was 'Pentecostes', 'Whitsunday' was always used in the vernacular.

Whittinghame (East Lothian). An L-shaped tower dating from early 15th century, and still well preserved, belonged successively to *Earls of March*, *Douglases*, *Setons* and *Hays*; it was the scene of a conference in 1567 when the *Earl of Morton* is supposed to have discussed plans for the murder of *Darnley* with *William Maitland of Lethington* and the *4th Earl of Bothwell*. In 1817 the estate was bought by James Balfour of Balbirnie, who built a new mansion nearby.

Whyte, Alexander (1836-1921). Born *Kirriemuir*; *minister* of St George's *Free Church*, *Edinburgh*, 1870-1916; principal of *New College*, Edinburgh, 1909-18.

Wick (*Caithness*). A castle, now dismantled and ruinous, is said to have belonged at the beginning of the 14th century to Sir Reginald le *Cheyne*, and passed to *Oliphants*, *Earls of Caithness*, Dunbars and *Lord Duffus*. Wick was apparently a *burgh of barony* under *Robert II* and became a *royal burgh* 1589.

Wig Club. Founded in *Edinburgh* 1775 for social ends; ceased activities after about 1815.

Wigtown. *Royal burgh* by 1292, probably by 1263; alienated to *Douglases* 1341, recovered by crown 1455. Castle existed by 1291; captured by English 1296, recovered by *Robert I*; only a mound remains. *Dominican* friary founded by *Devorguilla* c. 1267. Burgh school recorded as existing 1513. 'Cripple house' and hospital mentioned 1557-99.

Wigtown, Earldom. Created for Sir Malcolm *Fleming* of Fulwood and *Cumbernauld* 1341; sold to Archibald Douglas, Lord of *Galloway*, 1372; title renewed 1606 for John, 6th Lord Fleming (1567-1619); extinct on death of 7th Earl 1747.

Wigtown Martyrs. Margaret Lauchleson or MacLachlan (c. 1620-?85) and Margaret Wilson (1667-?85) were sentenced to be drowned by the incoming tide for refusing to renounce the *Cameronian* repudiation of the King; there has been much debate as to whether they were in fact drowned, and the verdict must be '*not proven*'.

Wilkie, Sir David (1785-1841). Son of *minister* of Cults, Fife; showed early talent and after some training at the *Trustees' Academy* painted 'Pitlessie Fair' (1804); went to London and worked as portraitist and in depicting social gatherings; among his famous works were 'The Penny Wedding' (1818), 'The Reading of the Waterloo Gazette' (1821), 'The Entrance of George IV to *Holyrood*' and '*John Knox* preaching before the *Lords of the Congregation*' (1832); *King's Limner* in Scotland 1823 and Painter-in-Ordinary in England 1830; found further inspiration on visits to the Continent and Near East.

William I (1143-1214). Known without satisfactory evidence as 'The Lion'; 2nd son of Earl *Henry*, son of *David I*; succeeded *Malcolm IV* 1165; on an invasion of England in 1174 was captured at Alnwick and forced to agree to the *Treaty of Falaise*; married *Ermengarde* de Beaumont 1186; recovered Scotland from feudal overlordship by Quitclaim of *Canterbury*; founded *Arbroath Abbey*; had to deal with rebellions in *Galloway* 1174, Ross 1179 and 1211-2, and in the end established his rule to the Pentland Firth; had one son—*Alexander II*—and three daughters, all of whom married English barons.

William II (1650-1702). Correct Scottish style of William of Orange, William III of England.

William and Mary College (Virginia, U.S.A.). Founded 1693 by *James Blair*.

William Fitzduncan (c. 1090-1151). Son of *Duncan II* and his wife Octreda, daughter of Earl *Cospatric*; married Alice de Rumilly; his sons were William, 'the Boy of Egremont', drowned near Bolton c. 1156, and *Donald* MacWilliam.

William of Orange. See William II.

William, St (d. c. 1201). Born *Perth* and became a baker; on a pilgrimage to Canterbury he was murdered by a boy companion and buried in Rochester Cathedral; canonised 1226.

Williamson, Peter (1730-99). Born Hinley, Aberdeenshire; as a boy was kidnapped and transported to America, where he had many adventures; on his return settled in *Edinburgh*, where he opened a bookshop and started a *penny post*; issued first Edinburgh Directory.

Willock, John (d. 1585). *Dominican* friar at *Ayr*; went to England and to continent because of his religious views and was at Emden; returned to Scotland 1558; for a time *minister* at *Edinburgh*, then *superintendent* of the west; held English rectory of Loughborough and finally retired there.

Wilson, Alexander (1766-1813). Born *Paisley*; as a weaver, his satirical verses, like 'The Shark, or Lang Mills detected', directed against a mill-owner, and his association with radical reformers, brought him into trouble; emigrated to America 1794; schoolmaster near

Philadelphia; turned to ornithology and produced seven volumes on 'American Ornithology'.

Wilson, Andrew (1780-1848). Pupil of *Alexander Nasmyth* and then studied abroad; master of *Trustees' Academy*, Edinburgh, 1818-26; teacher of drawing in Military Academy, Sandhurst; then lived largely in Rome, Florence and Venice.

Wilson, Charles Thomson Rees (1869-1959). Born Glencorse, near *Edinburgh*; worked mainly in Cambridge; inspired by early morning cloud effects observed from *Ben Nevis Observatory*, invented cloud chamber, a tool of particle physics.

Wilson, Sir Daniel (1816-92). Born *Edinburgh*; professor of history and English literature in Toronto 1853 and president 1881; published 'Archaeology and Prehistoric Annals of Scotland' (1851).

Wilson (or Volusenus), **Florence** (c. 1504-post-1551). Born *Elgin*; studied and taught in Paris and Carpentras; wrote philosophical works.

Wilson, Hugh (1833-77). Born in Ross; apprentice engineer on *Clyde* but after an accident entered newspaper business; edited 'Nairnshire Telegraph', 'Fife Herald', '*Elgin* Courant' and other Scottish local papers; started 'Hexham Herald' 1866; editor of 'Manchester Evening News' 1868; started '*Edinburgh* Evening News' 1873.

Wilson, James (1742-1798). Born *Ceres*, Fife; at *St Andrews University* 1757-60; emigrated to America 1765; taught in College of Philadelphia; signed American Declaration of Independence and took part in working out the American constitution.

Wilson, John (1785-1854), 'Christopher North'. Born *Paisley*; professor of moral philosophy, *Edinburgh*, 1820; produced many verses and articles, often describing scenery he had enjoyed; wrote 'Noctes Ambrosianae'; on editorial staff of *Blackwood's Magazine*; bought an estate in Cumberland and spent much time there.

Wilson, John (1804-75). Born *Lauder*, son of a councillor and church *elder*; after attending *Edinburgh University* became missionary with Scottish Missionary Society; went to Bombay 1829; founded 'Oriental Christian Spectator'; already a proficient linguist, he extended his study to Indian languages; founded English School in Bombay 1832 and it developed into Wilson High School and Wilson College.

Wilson, Robert (1803-82). Born *Dunbar;* associated with invention of screw propellor for ships and improvements in steam hammer; engineer in Yorkshire.

Wilson, William (1690-1741). *Minister* of West Church, *Perth,* 1716; joined *Original Secession.*

Wilson, William (1801-60). Born *Crieff;* after editing *Dundee* 'Literary Olio' emigrated to America 1833 and started bookselling and publishing business.

Winchester, John (d. 1458). Came to Scotland with *James I;* canon of *Dunkeld, provost* of *Lincluden, Clerk Register* (1436); *Bishop of Moray* 1437.

Wine Act, 1703. Importation of foreign wines was permitted, although England and Scotland were then at war with France.

Wingate, Sir James Lawton (1846-1923). Born Kelvinhaugh; started in business but turned to art at age of twenty; mainly a landscape painter. Died in *Edinburgh.*

Winram, John (c. 1492-1582). Subprior of *St Andrews Priory* by 1536; sometimes thought to have been author of Archbishop *John Hamilton's* 'Catechism'; had joined reformers by December 1560; *superintendent* of Fife 1561.

Winston Barracks (*Lanark*). Formerly regimental depot of *Cameronian Regiment;* now headquarters of 52nd Lowland Division.

Winter Queen. Elizabeth, daughter of *James VI* (1596-1662), who married Frederick, Elector Palatine, who was briefly King of Bohemia 1619-20; also known as 'The Queen of Hearts'; mother of Princess Sophia and grandmother of George I.

Winter's Academy (*Edinburgh*). Founded by Richard Cooper, who had been treasurer of the *School of St Luke;* did much for education of artists and engravers.

Winton Castle (East Lothian). An earlier castle on site is said to have been built c. 1480 by 1st *Lord Seton;* later castle built 1619 by George, 8th Lord Seton and 3rd Earl of Winton, to designs by William Wallace, King's master mason; estate passed 1779 to Mrs Hamilton Nisbet and in 1885 was acquired by *Ogilvy* family.

Winton, Earldom. Created 1600 for Robert, 6th *Lord Seton; forfeited* by George, 5th Earl, 1716; sentenced to death after his capture at *Preston,* he escaped, and died at Rome in 1749.

Wintour, John Crawford (1825-82). Born *Edinburgh;* specialised in painting miniatures, making medical and anatomical diagrams and (later) landscapes.

Winzet, Ninian (c. 1518-92). Master in *Gram-*

mar School of *Linlithgow* c. 1551; deprived by reformers 1561; criticised reforming policies in 'Certane Tractatis for Reformatioun of Doctryne and Maneris' (1562); fled to Antwerp; published 'Buik of Four Scoir Thre Questiouns'; after visiting Paris, England, Scotland and *Douai,* settled at *Ratisbon,* where he became abbot; also wrote 'Flagellum Sectariorum' (1581) and 'Velitatio in Georgium Buchananum' (cf. Buchanan, George) (1582).

Wishart, George (c. 1513-46). Born in *Angus;* probably taught in *Grammar School* at *Montrose;* charged with heresy and went to Germany and Switzerland, then Cambridge; returned to Scotland 1543 and preached widely; possibly involved in plots against Cardinal *David Beaton,* by whose orders he was arrested; burned at *St Andrews.* See 'Heretics'.

Wishart, George (1599-1671). *Minister* at *Monifieth* 1625, *St Andrews* 1626; on abolition of episcopacy fled to England; taken prisoner by *Covenanters* and imprisoned in Edinburgh; chaplain to *Montrose* 1644; *Bishop of Edinburgh* 1662; wrote an account of Montrose's campaigns.

Wishart, Sir John, of Pittarro (c. 1576). Joined insurgents 1559; Collector General of *Thirds* 1562; joined *Confederate Lords* against Queen *Mary* 1567.

Wishart, Robert (d. 1316). *Archdeacon* of *Lothian; Bishop of Glasgow* 1273; a *Guardian* on death of *Alexander III;* active in resistance to England; captured and imprisoned 1297-1300; took part in *Bruce*'s coronation 1306; captured again, became blind during imprisonment and allowed to return to Scotland after *Bannockburn.*

Witchcraft. First statute against, imposing death penalty, 1563; very active in 1590s; phases of prosecution in 17th century; last recorded execution 1727; laws against it repealed 1736.

Witherspoon, John (1723-94). Born *Gifford; minister* of Beith and then *Paisley;* president of Princeton College, New Jersey, 1768; helped to frame American Declaration of Independence.

Witte, James de. See (De) Wet.

Wizard of the North. See Scott, Sir Walter.

Wizard of Yester. Sir Hugo de Gifford, supposed to have used the Goblin Ha' at *Yester* as a workroom.

Wodrow, Robert (1679-1734). Born *Glasgow;* University Librarian at Glasgow 1697-1701; *minister* of Eastwood 1703; collected material on *Covenanting* history and published 'The Sufferings of the Church of Scotland' (2 vols., 1721-2); left copious manuscript collections, some of which have since been published.

Wodrow Society. Founded 1841 for publication of works of Scottish reformers.

Wolf of Badenoch. See Stewart, Alexander.

Wolves. Ample evidence exists of wolves in medieval times, and there are many tales of their final extinction: the last wolf in the north-east said to have been killed at Kirkmichael, Banffshire, 1644, the last one in Perthshire by Sir Ewen Cameron of Lochiel at *Killiecrankie,* 1680, and the last one of all by a certain MacQueen, a stalker to the laird of Mackintosh, 1743.

Wood, Sir Andrew, of *Largo* (c. 1460-1540). Supposed to have been born in Largo, to which he retired; traded from *Leith* with the 'Flower' and 'Yellow Carvel' and served *James III,* who granted him the lands of Largo in 1483 and knighted him; also served *James IV* and defeated English Stephen Bull off Firth of Forth 1489; employed in expeditions to western isles; commanded the great *'Michael'.*

Wood, John Muir (1805-92). Studied music in Paris and Vienna; music-seller in *Edinburgh* and *Glasgow;* published 'Songs of Scotland'.

Wood, John Philip (d. 1838). Though deaf and dumb from infancy, he became an auditor of excise and published an edition of the 'Peerage of Scotland' by Sir Robert Douglas.

Wood's Hospital (*Largo,* Fife). In 1659 John Wood, a native of Largo, who had made a fortune in London, left nearly £70,000 Scots for the erection of a hospital for 13 indigent and infirm persons of the name of Wood.

Woodhouselee (Midlothian). *Burgh of barony* for Purves of that *ilk* 1664.

Worcester, Battle of, 3 September 1651. Defeat of Scots under *Charles II* and *David Leslie* by Oliver Cromwell.

Worthy Club. Met in 18th century at Newhall, near *Penicuik,* as guests of Sir David Forbes.

Wrangous Imprisonment, Act Anent, 1701. Scottish equivalent of Habeas Corpus Act, prohibiting imprisonment without trial.

Wright, John Michael (1625-c. 1700). Said to have been pupil of *George Jamesone;* went to England and Italy; returned to England in 1650s and painted portraits of contemporaries; continued his work after *Restoration;* known for his 'Highland Chieftain' in *Scottish National Portrait Gallery.*

Writers to the Signet. Originally clerks in the office of the *Secretary,* who kept the *signet,* which in time became the seal under which the various writs of *Diligence* were issued; hence by late 16th century they were solicitors operating procedure before Court of *Session;* the records of the Society date from 1594. See also Signet Library.

Wurzburg, Abbey of St James. One of the *Schottenklöster;* served as Scottish abbey 1595-1803.

Wylie, Sir James (1768-1854). Born *Kincardine-on-Forth;* physician and surgeon who went to Russia in 1790 and served under Czar Alexander I.

Wylie, William Howie (1833-91). Editor of '*Ayr* Advertiser', 'Nottingham Journal', 'Liverpool Courier' and '*Falkirk* Herald'.

Wyntoun, Andrew of (c. 1355-1422). Canon of *St Andrews Priory* and Prior of St *Serf*'s, *Lochleven,* 1395-1413; compiled 'Orygynale Cronikil of Scotland' before and after 1400 at request of Sir John *Wemyss,* tracing history from the Creation in verses which are a valuable source for events in and near his own day and even for some earlier Scottish history where he used material now lost.

Y

Yates, James (1789-1871). Unitarian minister and one of the founders of the Scottish Unitarian Association; contributed much to the 'Dictionary of Greek and Roman Antiquities'.

'Yellow Carvel'. Ship of Sir *Andrew Wood.*

Yeomanry Regiments, Scottish. Between 1793 and 1798 there were raised the Ayrshire, Lothian and Borders, Fife and Forfar, Renfrewshire, Glasgow Light Horse, Carse of Gowrie, Dupplin, Gask, Perth, Perthshire Irregular Cavalry and Perthshire Gentlemen; a Fife troop was raised in 1801, Midlothian 1803, Perthshire 1817, Lanarkshire 1819; in the South African War the Lovat Scouts and the Scottish Horse were raised.

Yester (East Lothian). Lands granted to family of Gifford c. 1190 and passed to *Hays* by marriage in early 15th century. Castle built in 13th century, reputedly by Sir Hugo de Gifford; believed not to have been occupied since early 16th century, but Goblin Ha' survives. For *Collegiate Church* see Bothans.

Yetholm (Roxburghshire). *Burgh of barony* for Wauchope of Niddrie 1665.

Yew Tree, Fortingall. See Fortingall.

Yolande (or Joleta). Daughter of Robert IV, Comte de Dreux; married *Alexander III* 14 October 1285.

York Buildings Company. Purchaser of most of the estates forfeited after 'Fifteen. See Forfeited Estates.

York, Cardinal. See Henry Benedict.

York, Treaty of, 1237. *Alexander II* gave up his claims to the English northern counties and received in return certain estates in Northumberland and Cumberland.

Young, Andrew (1807-89). Headmaster of Niddrie Street School, *Edinburgh* 1830-40; wrote a number of hymns, including 'There is a happy land'.

Young, James (1811-83). After producing oil from 'cannel coal' he went on to manufacture oil from shale in West and Mid Lothian from 1865; known as 'Paraffin Young'. In 1870 founded Chair of Technical Chemistry at *Anderson's College.*

Young, Sir Peter (1544-1628). Tutor to *James VI;* an ambassador to Denmark; an *Octavian.*

Young Pretender. See Charles Edward.

Younger, John (1785-1860). Born *Longnewton;* settled at *St Boswell's* 1811; shoemaker who wrote 'River Angling for Salmon and Trout', an autobiography, and poems under the title 'Thoughts as they rise'.

Yule. Scots term for Christmas.

Z

Zetland. The Norse name of *Shetland,* Hjaltland, produced a pronunciation Yetland, which was spelled Zetland; this curious archaism survived in official usage for Zetland County Council (1889-1975) and in the *Earldom and Marquisate.*

Zetland, Earldom and Marquisate. Earldom created for Laurence *Dundas* 1838; marquisate created 1873 for his grandson.

Zuill. Archaic spelling of *Yule.*

LIST OF MAIN EVENTS

c. 80-85	Campaigns of Agricola
c. 140	Antonine Wall
207-11	Campaigns of Severus
c. 400	Ninian
c. 500	Irish 'Scots' arrived
c. 550	Anglian settlement in south-east
597	Death of Columba
685	Battle of Nechtansmere
794	Scandinavian raids first mentioned
c. 843	Union of Picts and Scots in kingdom of Alba
c. 890	Scandinavian earldom of Orkney
c. 960	Edinburgh held by king of Alba
1018	Battle of Carham
1034	Strathclyde part of Scottish kingdom
1072	Malcolm III submitted to William the Conqueror
1098	Expedition of Magnus Barelegs
1120s	First references to burghs and sheriffs
1138	Battle of the Standard
1175	Treaty of Falaise
1189	Quitclaim of Canterbury
1237	Treaty of York
1263	Battle of Largs
1266	Treaty of Perth
1295	Alliance with France
1296	Battle of Dunbar
1297-8	Rising of Moray and Wallace
1314	Battle of Bannockburn
1320	Declaration of Arbroath
1328	Treaty of Edinburgh-Northampton
1346	Battle of Neville's Cross
1357	Treaty of Berwick
1396	Clan Fight at Perth
1411	Battle of Harlaw
1412	University of St Andrews
1451	University of Glasgow
1468-9	Acquisition of Orkney and Shetland
1488	Battle of Sauchieburn
1493	Forfeiture of Lordship of the Isles
1495	King's College, Aberdeen

1496	Education Act
1505-6	Royal College of Surgeons founded
1507	Printing introduced
1513	Battle of Flodden
1532	Endowment of College of Justice
1542	Battle of Solway Moss
1544-5	Hertford's Invasions
1547	Battle of Pinkie
1554	Mary of Guise Regent
1560	'Reformation Parliament'
	First Book of Discipline
1578	Second Book of Discipline
1583	University of Edinburgh
1587	County Franchise Act
1592	Presbyterian government first authorised
1603	James VI King of England
1609	Statutes of Iona
1610	Episcopal government restored
1616	Education Act
1617	Register of Sasines
1618	Five Articles of Perth
1637	Scottish Prayer Book
1638	National Covenant
1643	Solemn League and Covenant
1651	Cromwellian occupation
1672	High Court of Justiciary established
1682	Advocates' Library founded
1689	Revolution against James VII
1690	Presbyterian government restored
1692	Massacre of Glencoe
1695	Bank of Scotland
	Company of Scotland
1696	Education Act
1707	Union with England
1712	Toleration Act
	Patronage restored
1715	Jacobite Rebellion
1727	Board of Manufactures established
1735	First Secession
1736	Porteous Riot
1745	Jacobite Rebellion
1747	Abolition of Heritable Jurisdictions

1760	Carron Iron Works in operation
1761	Second Secession; Relief Church
1779	First Spinning Mills
1790	Forth and Clyde Canal opened
1803	Commissioners for Highland Roads and Bridges
1812	*Comet* steamship
1822	Caledonian Canal opened
1828	Hot Blast invented
1831	Glasgow-Garnkirk Railway
1832	First Reform Act
1843	Disruption
1853	National Association for Vindication of Scottish Rights
1872	Education Act
1885	Secretary for Scotland appointed
1886	Crofters Act
1889	County Councils established
1900	United Free Church formed
1906	First Labour M.P.s
1928	National Party of Scotland formed
1929	Union of Church of Scotland and United Free Church
	Local Government Act
1939	St Andrew's House opened
1947	Coal Mines nationalised
1948	Railways nationalised
1974	Eleven S.N.P. members of parliament
1974-5	Reorganisation of local government (Wheatley Report)

SOVEREIGNS OF SCOTLAND

(From c. 843, when Kenneth mac Alpin, already king of the 'Scots' of Dalriada, became king also of the Picts and formed a kingdom known as 'Alba'. Down to Malcolm II some of the dates are not certain.)

KENNETH I	c. 843-58	GIRIC / EOCHAID	878-89
DONALD I	858-62		
CONSTANTINE I	862-77	DONALD II	889-900
AED	877- 8	CONSTANTINE II	900-943

MALCOLM I	943-54	MARGARET	1286-90
INDULF	954-62	Interregnum	1290-92
DUBH	962-66	JOHN	1292-96
CULEN	966-71	Interregnum	1296-1306
KENNETH II	971-95	ROBERT I	1306-29
CONSTANTINE III	995-97	DAVID II	1329-71
{KENNETH III / GIRIC?)}	?997-1005	ROBERT II	1371-90
		ROBERT III	1390-1406
MALCOLM II	1005-34	JAMES I	1406-37
DUNCAN I	1034-40	JAMES II	1437-60
MACBETH	1040-57	JAMES III	1460-88
LULACH	1057-58	JAMES IV	1488-1513
MALCOLM III	1058-93	JAMES V	1513-42
DONALD III	1093-94	MARY I	1542-67
DUNCAN II	1094	JAMES VI	1567-1625
DONALD III (restored)	1094-97	CHARLES I	1625-49
EDGAR	1097-1107	CHARLES II (exiled 1651-60)	1649-85
ALEXANDER I	1107-24		
DAVID I	1124-53	JAMES VII	1685-89
MALCOLM IV	1153-65	{WILLIAM II	1689-1702}
WILLIAM I	1165-1214	MARY II	1689-94
ALEXANDER II	1214-49	ANNE	1702-07
ALEXANDER III	1249-86		

(On 1 May 1707 the kingdom of Scotland and the kingdom of England alike came to an end, to be united in a single kingdom of Great Britain.)